Nutshell Series
Hornbook Series
and
Black Letter Series
of
WEST PUBLISHING COMPANY

P.O. Box 64526
St. Paul, Minnesota 55164–0526

Accounting

FARIS' ACCOUNTING AND LAW IN A NUTSHELL, 377 pages, 1984. Softcover. (Text)

Administrative Law

AMAN AND MAYTON'S HORNBOOK ON ADMINISTRATIVE LAW, Approximately 750 pages, 1993. (Text)

GELLHORN AND LEVIN'S ADMINISTRATIVE LAW AND PROCESS IN A NUTSHELL, Third Edition, 479 pages, 1990. Softcover. (Text)

Admiralty

MARAIST'S ADMIRALTY IN A NUTSHELL, Second Edition, 379 pages, 1988. Softcover. (Text)

SCHOENBAUM'S HORNBOOK ON ADMIRALTY AND MARITIME LAW, Student Edition, 692 pages, 1987 with 1992 pocket part. (Text)

Agency—Partnership

REUSCHLEIN AND GREGORY'S HORNBOOK ON THE LAW OF AGENCY AND PARTNERSHIP, Second Edition, 683 pages, 1990. (Text)

STEFFEN'S AGENCY-PARTNERSHIP IN A NUTSHELL, 364 pages, 1977. Softcover. (Text)

NOLAN–HALEY'S ALTERNATIVE DISPUTE RESOLUTION IN A NUTSHELL, 298 pages, 1992. Softcover. (Text)

RISKIN'S DISPUTE RESOLUTION FOR LAWYERS VIDEO TAPES, 1992. (Available for purchase by schools and libraries.)

List current as of January, 1993

American Indian Law

CANBY'S AMERICAN INDIAN LAW IN A NUTSHELL, Second Edition, 336 pages, 1988. Softcover. (Text)

Antitrust—see also Regulated Industries, Trade Regulation

GELLHORN'S ANTITRUST LAW AND ECONOMICS IN A NUTSHELL, Third Edition, 472 pages, 1986. Softcover. (Text)

HOVENKAMP'S BLACK LETTER ON ANTITRUST, Second Edition approximately 325 pages, April 1993 Pub. Softcover. (Review)

HOVENKAMP'S HORNBOOK ON ECONOMICS AND FEDERAL ANTITRUST LAW, Student Edition, 414 pages, 1985. (Text)

SULLIVAN'S HORNBOOK OF THE LAW OF ANTITRUST, 886 pages, 1977. (Text)

Appellate Advocacy—see Trial and Appellate Advocacy

Art Law

DUBOFF'S ART LAW IN A NUTSHELL, Second Edition, approximately 325 pages, 1993. Softcover. (Text)

Banking Law

LOVETT'S BANKING AND FINANCIAL INSTITUTIONS LAW IN A NUTSHELL, Third Edition, 470 pages, 1992. Softcover. (Text)

Civil Procedure—see also Federal Jurisdiction and Procedure

CLERMONT'S BLACK LETTER ON CIVIL PROCEDURE, Third Edition, approximately 350 pages, May, 1993 Pub. Softcover. (Review)

FRIEDENTHAL, KANE AND MILLER'S HORNBOOK ON CIVIL PROCEDURE, Second Edition, approximately 1000 pages, May 1993 Pub. (Text)

KANE'S CIVIL PROCEDURE IN A NUTSHELL, Third Edition, 303 pages, 1991. Softcover. (Text)

KOFFLER AND REPPY'S HORNBOOK ON COMMON LAW PLEADING, 663 pages, 1969. (Text)

SIEGEL'S HORNBOOK ON NEW YORK PRACTICE, Second Edition, Student Edition, 1068 pages, 1991. Softcover. (Text) 1992 Supplemental Pamphlet.

SLOMANSON AND WINGATE'S CALIFORNIA CIVIL PROCEDURE IN A NUTSHELL, 230 pages, 1992. Softcover. (Text)

Commercial Law

BAILEY AND HAGEDORN'S SECURED TRANSACTIONS IN A NUTSHELL, Third Edition, 390 pages, 1988. Softcover. (Text)

HENSON'S HORNBOOK ON SECURED TRANSACTIONS UNDER THE U.C.C., Second Edition, 504

Commercial Law—Continued

pages, 1979, with 1979 pocket part. (Text)

MEYER AND SPEIDEL'S BLACK LETTER ON SALES AND LEASES OF GOODS, Approximately 300 pages, 1993. Softcover. (Review)

NICKLES' BLACK LETTER ON COMMERCIAL PAPER, 450 pages, 1988. Softcover. (Review)

STOCKTON AND MILLER'S SALES AND LEASES OF GOODS IN A NUTSHELL, Third Edition, 441 pages, 1992. Softcover. (Text)

STONE'S UNIFORM COMMERCIAL CODE IN A NUTSHELL, Third Edition, 580 pages, 1989. Softcover. (Text)

WEBER AND SPEIDEL'S COMMERCIAL PAPER IN A NUTSHELL, Third Edition, 404 pages, 1982. Softcover. (Text)

WHITE AND SUMMERS' HORNBOOK ON THE UNIFORM COMMERCIAL CODE, Third Edition, Student Edition, 1386 pages, 1988. (Text)

Community Property

MENNELL AND BOYKOFF'S COMMUNITY PROPERTY IN A NUTSHELL, Second Edition, 432 pages, 1988. Softcover. (Text)

Comparative Law

FOLSOM, MINAN AND OTTO'S LAW AND POLITICS IN THE PEOPLE'S REPUBLIC OF CHINA IN A NUTSHELL, 451 pages, 1992. Softcover. (Text)

GLENDON, GORDON AND OSAKWE'S COMPARATIVE LEGAL TRADITIONS IN A NUTSHELL. 402 pages, 1982. Softcover. (Text)

Conflict of Laws

HAY'S BLACK LETTER ON CONFLICT OF LAWS, 330 pages, 1989. Softcover. (Review)

SCOLES AND HAY'S HORNBOOK ON CONFLICT OF LAWS, Student Edition, 1160 pages, 1992. (Text)

SIEGEL'S CONFLICTS IN A NUTSHELL, 470 pages, 1982. Softcover. (Text)

Constitutional Law—Civil Rights

BARRON AND DIENES' BLACK LETTER ON CONSTITUTIONAL LAW, Third Edition, 440 pages, 1991. Softcover. (Review)

BARRON AND DIENES' CONSTITUTIONAL LAW IN A NUTSHELL, Second Edition, 483 pages, 1991. Softcover. (Text)

ENGDAHL'S CONSTITUTIONAL FEDERALISM IN A NUTSHELL, Second Edition, 411 pages, 1987. Softcover. (Text)

MARKS AND COOPER'S STATE CON-

Constitutional Law—Civil Rights—Continued

STITUTIONAL LAW IN A NUTSHELL, 329 pages, 1988. Softcover. (Text)

NOWAK AND ROTUNDA'S HORNBOOK ON CONSTITUTIONAL LAW, Fourth Edition, 1357 pages, 1991. (Text)

VIEIRA'S CONSTITUTIONAL CIVIL RIGHTS IN A NUTSHELL, Second Edition, 322 pages, 1990. Softcover. (Text)

WILLIAMS' CONSTITUTIONAL ANALYSIS IN A NUTSHELL, 388 pages, 1979. Softcover. (Text)

Consumer Law—see also Commercial Law

EPSTEIN AND NICKLES' CONSUMER LAW IN A NUTSHELL, Second Edition, 418 pages, 1981. Softcover. (Text)

Contracts

CALAMARI AND PERILLO'S BLACK LETTER ON CONTRACTS, Second Edition, 462 pages, 1990. Softcover. (Review)

CALAMARI AND PERILLO'S HORNBOOK ON CONTRACTS, Third Edition, 1049 pages, 1987. (Text)

CORBIN'S TEXT ON CONTRACTS, One Volume Student Edition, 1224 pages, 1952. (Text)

FRIEDMAN'S CONTRACT REMEDIES IN A NUTSHELL, 323 pages, 1981. Softcover. (Text)

KEYES' GOVERNMENT CONTRACTS IN A NUTSHELL, Second Edition, 557 pages, 1990. Softcover. (Text)

SCHABER AND ROHWER'S CONTRACTS IN A NUTSHELL, Third Edition, 457 pages, 1990. Softcover. (Text)

Copyright—see Patent and Copyright Law

Corporations

HAMILTON'S BLACK LETTER ON CORPORATIONS, Third Edition, 732 pages, 1992. Softcover. (Review)

HAMILTON'S THE LAW OF CORPORATIONS IN A NUTSHELL, Third Edition, 518 pages, 1991. Softcover. (Text)

HENN AND ALEXANDER'S HORNBOOK ON LAWS OF CORPORATIONS, Third Edition, Student Edition, 1371 pages, 1983, with 1986 pocket part. (Text)

Corrections

KRANTZ' THE LAW OF CORRECTIONS AND PRISONERS' RIGHTS IN A NUTSHELL, Third Edition, 407 pages, 1988. Softcover. (Text)

Creditors' Rights

EPSTEIN'S DEBTOR-CREDITOR LAW IN A NUTSHELL, Fourth Edition,

Creditors' Rights—Continued

401 pages, 1991. Softcover. (Text)

EPSTEIN, NICKLES AND WHITE'S HORNBOOK ON BANKRUPTCY, Approximately 1000 pages, January, 1992 Pub. (Text)

NICKLES AND EPSTEIN'S BLACK LETTER ON CREDITORS' RIGHTS AND BANKRUPTCY, 576 pages, 1989. (Review)

Criminal Law and Criminal Procedure—see also Corrections, Juvenile Justice

ISRAEL AND LAFAVE'S CRIMINAL PROCEDURE—CONSTITUTIONAL LIMITATIONS IN A NUTSHELL, Fourth Edition, 461 pages, 1988. Softcover. (Text)

LAFAVE AND ISRAEL'S HORNBOOK ON CRIMINAL PROCEDURE, Second Edition, 1309 pages, 1992 with 1992 pocket part. (Text)

LAFAVE AND SCOTT'S HORNBOOK ON CRIMINAL LAW, Second Edition, 918 pages, 1986. (Text)

LOEWY'S CRIMINAL LAW IN A NUTSHELL, Second Edition, 321 pages, 1987. Softcover. (Text)

LOW'S BLACK LETTER ON CRIMINAL LAW, Revised First Edition, 443 pages, 1990. Softcover. (Review)

SUBIN, MIRSKY AND WEINSTEIN'S THE CRIMINAL PROCESS: PROSECUTION AND DEFENSE FUNCTIONS, Approximately 450 pages, February, 1993 Pub. Softcover. Teacher's Manual available. (Text)

Domestic Relations

CLARK'S HORNBOOK ON DOMESTIC RELATIONS, Second Edition, Student Edition, 1050 pages, 1988. (Text)

KRAUSE'S BLACK LETTER ON FAMILY LAW, 314 pages, 1988. Softcover. (Review)

KRAUSE'S FAMILY LAW IN A NUTSHELL, Second Edition, 444 pages, 1986. Softcover. (Text)

MALLOY'S LAW AND ECONOMICS: A COMPARATIVE APPROACH TO THEORY AND PRACTICE, 166 pages, 1990. Softcover. (Text)

Education Law

ALEXANDER AND ALEXANDER'S THE LAW OF SCHOOLS, STUDENTS AND TEACHERS IN A NUTSHELL, 409 pages, 1984. Softcover. (Text)

Employment Discrimination—see also Gender Discrimination

PLAYER'S FEDERAL LAW OF EMPLOYMENT DISCRIMINATION IN A NUTSHELL, Third Edition, 338 pages, 1992. Softcover. (Text)

Employment Discrimination—Continued

PLAYER'S HORNBOOK ON EMPLOYMENT DISCRIMINATION LAW, Student Edition, 708 pages, 1988. (Text)

Energy and Natural Resources Law—see also Oil and Gas

LAITOS AND TOMAIN'S ENERGY AND NATURAL RESOURCES LAW IN A NUTSHELL, 554 pages, 1992. Softcover. (Text)

Environmental Law—see also Energy and Natural Resources Law; Sea, Law of

FINDLEY AND FARBER'S ENVIRONMENTAL LAW IN A NUTSHELL, Third Edition, 355 pages, 1992. Softcover. (Text)

RODGERS' HORNBOOK ON ENVIRONMENTAL LAW, 956 pages, 1977, with 1984 pocket part. (Text)

Equity—see Remedies

Estate Planning—see also Trusts and Estates; Taxation—Estate and Gift

LYNN'S INTRODUCTION TO ESTATE PLANNING IN A NUTSHELL, Fourth Edition, 352 pages, 1992. Softcover. (Text)

Evidence

BROUN AND BLAKEY'S BLACK LETTER ON EVIDENCE, 269 pages, 1984. Softcover. (Review)

GRAHAM'S FEDERAL RULES OF EVIDENCE IN A NUTSHELL, Third Edition, 486 pages, 1992. Softcover. (Text)

LILLY'S AN INTRODUCTION TO THE LAW OF EVIDENCE, Second Edition, 585 pages, 1987. (Text)

MCCORMICK'S HORNBOOK ON EVIDENCE, Fourth Edition, Student Edition, 672 pages, 1992. (Text)

ROTHSTEIN'S EVIDENCE IN A NUTSHELL: STATE AND FEDERAL RULES, Second Edition, 514 pages, 1981. Softcover. (Text)

Federal Jurisdiction and Procedure

CURRIE'S FEDERAL JURISDICTION IN A NUTSHELL, Third Edition, 242 pages, 1990. Softcover. (Text)

REDISH'S BLACK LETTER ON FEDERAL JURISDICTION, Second Edition, 234 pages, 1991. Softcover. (Review)

WRIGHT'S HORNBOOK ON FEDERAL COURTS, Fourth Edition, Student Edition, 870 pages, 1983. (Text)

First Amendment

GARVEY AND SCHAUER'S THE FIRST AMENDMENT: A READER, 527 pages, 1992. Softcover.

First Amendment—Continued

(Reader)

Future Interests—see Trusts and Estates

Gender Discrimination—see also Employment Discrimination

THOMAS' SEX DISCRIMINATION IN A NUTSHELL, Second Edition, 395 pages, 1991. Softcover. (Text)

Health Law—see Medicine, Law and

Human Rights—see International Law

Immigration Law

WEISSBRODT'S IMMIGRATION LAW AND PROCEDURE IN A NUTSHELL, Third Edition, 497 pages, 1992. Softcover. (Text)

Indian Law—see American Indian Law

Insurance Law

DOBBYN'S INSURANCE LAW IN A NUTSHELL, Second Edition, 316 pages, 1989. Softcover. (Text)

KEETON AND WIDISS' INSURANCE LAW, Student Edition, 1359 pages, 1988. (Text)

International Law—see also Sea, Law of

BUERGENTHAL'S INTERNATIONAL HUMAN RIGHTS IN A NUTSHELL, 283 pages, 1988. Softcover. (Text)

BUERGENTHAL AND MAIER'S PUBLIC INTERNATIONAL LAW IN A NUTSHELL, Second Edition, 275 pages, 1990. Softcover. (Text)

FOLSOM'S EUROPEAN COMMUNITY LAW IN A NUTSHELL, 423 pages, 1992. Softcover. (Text)

FOLSOM, GORDON AND SPANOGLE'S INTERNATIONAL BUSINESS TRANSACTIONS IN A NUTSHELL, Fourth Edition, 548 pages, 1992. Softcover. (Text)

Interviewing and Counseling

SHAFFER AND ELKINS' LEGAL INTERVIEWING AND COUNSELING IN A NUTSHELL, Second Edition, 487 pages, 1987. Softcover. (Text)

Introduction to Law—see Legal Method and Legal System

Introduction to Law Study

HEGLAND'S INTRODUCTION TO THE STUDY AND PRACTICE OF LAW IN A NUTSHELL, 418 pages, 1983. Softcover. (Text)

KINYON'S INTRODUCTION TO LAW STUDY AND LAW EXAMINATIONS IN A NUTSHELL, 389 pages, 1971. Softcover. (Text)

Judicial Process—see Legal Method and Legal System

SINHA'S JURISPRUDENCE (LEGAL PHILOSOPHY) IN A NUTSHELL.

Judicial Process—Continued

Approximately 350 pages, 1993. Softcover. (Text)

Juvenile Justice

FOX'S JUVENILE COURTS IN A NUTSHELL, Third Edition, 291 pages, 1984. Softcover. (Text)

Labor and Employment Law—see also Employment Discrimination, Workers' Compensation

LESLIE'S LABOR LAW IN A NUTSHELL, Third Edition, 388 pages, 1992. Softcover. (Text)

NOLAN'S LABOR ARBITRATION LAW AND PRACTICE IN A NUTSHELL, 358 pages, 1979. Softcover. (Text)

Land Finance—Property Security—see Real Estate Transactions

Land Use

HAGMAN AND JUERGENSMEYER'S HORNBOOK ON URBAN PLANNING AND LAND DEVELOPMENT CONTROL LAW, Second Edition, Student Edition, 680 pages, 1986. (Text)

WRIGHT AND WRIGHT'S LAND USE IN A NUTSHELL, Second Edition, 356 pages, 1985. Softcover. (Text)

Legal Method and Legal System—see also Legal Research, Legal Writing

KEMPIN'S HISTORICAL INTRODUCTION TO ANGLO-AMERICAN LAW IN A NUTSHELL, Third Edition, 323 pages, 1990. Softcover. (Text)

REYNOLDS' JUDICIAL PROCESS IN A NUTSHELL, Second Edition, 308 pages, 1991. Softcover. (Text)

Legal Research

COHEN AND OLSON'S LEGAL RESEARCH IN A NUTSHELL, Fifth Edition, 370 pages, 1992. Softcover. (Text)

COHEN, BERRING AND OLSON'S HOW TO FIND THE LAW, Ninth Edition, 716 pages, 1989. (Text)

Legal Writing and Drafting

MELLINKOFF'S DICTIONARY OF AMERICAN LEGAL USAGE, 703 pages, 1992. Softcover. (Text)

SQUIRES AND ROMBAUER'S LEGAL WRITING IN A NUTSHELL, 294 pages, 1982. Softcover. (Text)

Legislation—see also Legal Writing and Drafting

DAVIES' LEGISLATIVE LAW AND PROCESS IN A NUTSHELL, Second Edition, 346 pages, 1986. Softcover. (Text)

Local Government

MCCARTHY'S LOCAL GOVERNMENT LAW IN A NUTSHELL, Third Edition, 435 pages, 1990. Softcover. (Text)

REYNOLDS' HORNBOOK ON LOCAL GOVERNMENT LAW, 860 pages, 1982 with 1990 pocket part. (Text)

Mass Communication Law

ZUCKMAN, GAYNES, CARTER AND DEE'S MASS COMMUNICATIONS LAW IN A NUTSHELL, Third Edition, 538 pages, 1988. Softcover. (Text)

Medicine, Law and

HALL AND ELLMAN'S HEALTH CARE LAW AND ETHICS IN A NUTSHELL, 401 pages, 1990. Softcover (Text)

JARVIS, CLOSEN, HERMANN AND LEONARD'S AIDS LAW IN A NUTSHELL, 349 pages, 1991. Softcover. (Text)

KING'S THE LAW OF MEDICAL MALPRACTICE IN A NUTSHELL, Second Edition, 342 pages, 1986. Softcover. (Text)

Military Law

SHANOR AND TERRELL'S MILITARY LAW IN A NUTSHELL, 378 pages, 1980. Softcover. (Text)

Mining Law—see Energy and Natural Resources Law

Mortgages—see Real Estate Transactions

Natural Resources Law—see Energy and Natural Resources Law, Environmental Law

TEPLY'S LEGAL NEGOTIATION IN A NUTSHELL, 282 pages, 1992. Softcover. (Text)

Office Practice—see also Computers and Law, Interviewing and Counseling, Negotiation

HEGLAND'S TRIAL AND PRACTICE SKILLS IN A NUTSHELL, 346 pages, 1978. Softcover (Text)

Oil and Gas—see also Energy and Natural Resources Law

HEMINGWAY'S HORNBOOK ON THE LAW OF OIL AND GAS, Third Edition, Student Edition, 711 pages, 1992. (Text)

LOWE'S OIL AND GAS LAW IN A NUTSHELL, Second Edition, 465 pages, 1988. Softcover. (Text)

Partnership—see Agency—Partnership

Patent and Copyright Law

MILLER AND DAVIS' INTELLECTUAL PROPERTY—PATENTS, TRADEMARKS AND COPYRIGHT IN A NUTSHELL, Second Edition, 437 pages, 1990. Softcover. (Text)

Products Liability

PHILLIPS' PRODUCTS LIABILITY IN

Products Liability—Continued

A NUTSHELL, Third Edition, 307 pages, 1988. Softcover. (Text)

Professional Responsibility

ARONSON AND WECKSTEIN'S PROFESSIONAL RESPONSIBILITY IN A NUTSHELL, Second Edition, 514 pages, 1991. Softcover. (Text)

LESNICK'S BEING A LAWYER: INDIVIDUAL CHOICE AND RESPONSIBILITY IN THE PRACTICE OF LAW, 422 pages, 1992. Softcover. Teacher's Manual available. (Coursebook)

ROTUNDA'S BLACK LETTER ON PROFESSIONAL RESPONSIBILITY, Third Edition, 492 pages, 1992. Softcover. (Review)

WOLFRAM'S HORNBOOK ON MODERN LEGAL ETHICS, Student Edition, 1120 pages, 1986. (Text)

WYDICK AND PERSCHBACHER'S CALIFORNIA LEGAL ETHICS, 439 pages, 1992. Softcover. (Coursebook)

Property—see also Real Estate Transactions, Land Use, Trusts and Estates

BERNHARDT'S BLACK LETTER ON PROPERTY, Second Edition, 388 pages, 1991. Softcover. (Review)

BERNHARDT'S REAL PROPERTY IN A NUTSHELL, Second Edition, 448 pages, 1981. Softcover. (Text)

BOYER, HOVENKAMP AND KURTZ' THE LAW OF PROPERTY, AN INTRODUCTORY SURVEY, Fourth Edition, 696 pages, 1991. (Text)

BURKE'S PERSONAL PROPERTY IN A NUTSHELL, Second Edition, approximately 400 pages, May, 1993 Pub. Softcover. (Text)

CUNNINGHAM, STOEBUCK AND WHITMAN'S HORNBOOK ON THE LAW OF PROPERTY, Second Edition, approximately 900 pages, May, 1993 Pub. (Text)

HILL'S LANDLORD AND TENANT LAW IN A NUTSHELL, Second Edition, 311 pages, 1986. Softcover. (Text)

Real Estate Transactions

BRUCE'S REAL ESTATE FINANCE IN A NUTSHELL, Third Edition, 287 pages, 1991. Softcover. (Text)

NELSON AND WHITMAN'S BLACK LETTER ON LAND TRANSACTIONS AND FINANCE, Second Edition, 466 pages, 1988. Softcover. (Review)

NELSON AND WHITMAN'S HORNBOOK ON REAL ESTATE FINANCE LAW, Second Edition, 941 pages, 1985 with 1989 pocket part. (Text)

Regulated Industries—see also Mass Communication Law, Banking Law

GELLHORN AND PIERCE'S REGULATED INDUSTRIES IN A NUTSHELL, Second Edition, 389 pages, 1987. Softcover. (Text)

Remedies

DOBBS' HORNBOOK ON REMEDIES, Second Edition, approximately 1000 pages, April, 1993 Pub. (Text)

DOBBYN'S INJUNCTIONS IN A NUTSHELL, 264 pages, 1974. Softcover. (Text)

FRIEDMAN'S CONTRACT REMEDIES IN A NUTSHELL, 323 pages, 1981. Softcover. (Text)

O'CONNELL'S REMEDIES IN A NUTSHELL, Second Edition, 320 pages, 1985. Softcover. (Text)

Sea, Law of

SOHN AND GUSTAFSON'S THE LAW OF THE SEA IN A NUTSHELL, 264 pages, 1984. Softcover. (Text)

Securities Regulation

HAZEN'S HORNBOOK ON THE LAW OF SECURITIES REGULATION, Second Edition, Student Edition, 1082 pages, 1990. (Text)

RATNER'S SECURITIES REGULATION IN A NUTSHELL, Fourth Edition, 320 pages, 1992. Softcover. (Text)

Sports Law

CHAMPION'S SPORTS LAW IN A NUTSHELL,. Approximately 300 pages, January, 1993 Pub. Softcover. (Text)

SCHUBERT, SMITH AND TRENTADUE'S SPORTS LAW, 395 pages, 1986. (Text)

Tax Practice and Procedure

MORGAN'S TAX PROCEDURE AND TAX FRAUD IN A NUTSHELL, 400 pages, 1990. Softcover. (Text)

Taxation—Corporate

SCHWARZ AND LATHROPE'S BLACK LETTER ON CORPORATE AND PARTNERSHIP TAXATION, 537 pages, 1991. Softcover. (Review)

WEIDENBRUCH AND BURKE'S FEDERAL INCOME TAXATION OF CORPORATIONS AND STOCKHOLDERS IN A NUTSHELL, Third Edition, 309 pages, 1989. Softcover. (Text)

Taxation—Estate & Gift—see also Estate Planning, Trusts and Estates

MCNULTY'S FEDERAL ESTATE AND GIFT TAXATION IN A NUTSHELL, Fourth Edition, 496 pages, 1989. Softcover. (Text)

PEAT AND WILLBANKS' FEDERAL ESTATE AND GIFT TAXATION: AN ANALYSIS AND CRITIQUE, 265 pages, 1991. Softcover. (Text)

Taxation—Individual

DODGE'S THE LOGIC OF TAX, 343 pages, 1989. Softcover. (Text)

HUDSON AND LIND'S BLACK LETTER ON FEDERAL INCOME TAXATION, Fourth Edition, 410 pages, 1992. Softcover. (Review)

MCNULTY'S FEDERAL INCOME TAXATION OF INDIVIDUALS IN A NUTSHELL, Fourth Edition, 503 pages, 1988. Softcover. (Text)

POSIN'S FEDERAL INCOME TAXATION, Second Edition, approximately 650 pages, May, 1993 Pub. Softcover. (Text)

ROSE AND CHOMMIE'S HORNBOOK ON FEDERAL INCOME TAXATION, Third Edition, 923 pages, 1988, with 1991 pocket part. (Text)

Taxation—International

DOERNBERG'S INTERNATIONAL TAXATION IN A NUTSHELL, 325 pages, 1989. Softcover. (Text)

BISHOP AND BROOKS' FEDERAL PARTNERSHIP TAXATION: A GUIDE TO THE LEADING CASES, STATUTES, AND REGULATIONS, 545 pages, 1990. Softcover. (Text)

BURKE'S FEDERAL INCOME TAXATION OF PARTNERSHIPS IN A NUTSHELL, 356 pages, 1992. Softcover. (Text)

SCHWARZ AND LATHROPE'S BLACK LETTER ON CORPORATE AND PARTNERSHIP TAXATION, 537 pages, 1991. Softcover. (Review)

Taxation—State & Local

GELFAND AND SALSICH'S STATE AND LOCAL TAXATION AND FINANCE IN A NUTSHELL, 309 pages, 1986. Softcover. (Text)

Torts—see also Products Liability

KIONKA'S BLACK LETTER ON TORTS, 339 pages, 1988. Softcover. (Review)

KIONKA'S TORTS IN A NUTSHELL, Second Edition, 449 pages, 1992. Softcover. (Text)

PROSSER AND KEETON'S HORNBOOK ON TORTS, Fifth Edition, Student Edition, 1286 pages, 1984 with 1988 pocket part. (Text)

Trade Regulation—see also Antitrust, Regulated Industries

MCMANIS' UNFAIR TRADE PRACTICES IN A NUTSHELL, Third Edition, approximately 450 pages, 1993. Softcover. (Text)

SCHECHTER'S BLACK LETTER ON UNFAIR TRADE PRACTICES, 272 pages, 1986. Softcover. (Review)

Trial and Appellate Advocacy—see also Civil Procedure

BERGMAN'S TRIAL ADVOCACY IN A

Trial and Appellate Advocacy—Continued

NUTSHELL, Second Edition, 354 pages, 1989. Softcover. (Text)

CLARY'S PRIMER ON THE ANALYSIS AND PRESENTATION OF LEGAL ARGUMENT, 106 pages, 1992. Softcover. (Text)

DESSEM'S PRETRIAL LITIGATION IN A NUTSHELL, 382 pages, 1992. Softcover. (Text)

GOLDBERG'S THE FIRST TRIAL (WHERE DO I SIT? WHAT DO I SAY?) IN A NUTSHELL, 396 pages, 1982. Softcover. (Text)

HEGLAND'S TRIAL AND PRACTICE SKILLS IN A NUTSHELL, 346 pages, 1978. Softcover. (Text)

HORNSTEIN'S APPELLATE ADVOCACY IN A NUTSHELL, 325 pages, 1984. Softcover. (Text)

JEANS' HANDBOOK ON TRIAL ADVOCACY, Student Edition, 473 pages, 1975. Softcover. (Text)

Trusts and Estates

ATKINSON'S HORNBOOK ON WILLS, Second Edition, 975 pages, 1953. (Text)

AVERILL'S UNIFORM PROBATE CODE IN A NUTSHELL, Second Edition, 454 pages, 1987. Softcover. (Text)

BOGERT'S HORNBOOK ON TRUSTS, Sixth Edition, Student Edition, 794 pages, 1987. (Text)

MCGOVERN, KURTZ AND REIN'S HORNBOOK ON WILLS, TRUSTS AND ESTATES–INCLUDING TAXATION AND FUTURE INTERESTS, 996 pages, 1988. (Text)

MENNELL'S WILLS AND TRUSTS IN A NUTSHELL, 392 pages, 1979. Softcover. (Text)

SIMES' HORNBOOK ON FUTURE INTERESTS, Second Edition, 355 pages, 1966. (Text)

TURANO AND RADIGAN'S HORNBOOK ON NEW YORK ESTATE ADMINISTRATION, 676 pages, 1986 with 1991 pocket part. (Text)

WAGGONER'S FUTURE INTERESTS IN A NUTSHELL, 361 pages, 1981. Softcover. (Text)

Water Law—see also Environmental Law

GETCHES' WATER LAW IN A NUTSHELL, Second Edition, 459 pages, 1990. Softcover. (Text)

Wills—see Trusts and Estates

Workers' Compensation

HOOD, HARDY AND LEWIS' WORKERS' COMPENSATION AND EMPLOYEE PROTECTION LAWS IN A NUTSHELL, Second Edition, 361 pages, 1990. Softcover. (Text)

Advisory Board

PROFESSIONAL RESPONSIBILITY

IN A NUTSHELL

SECOND EDITION

By

ROBERT H. ARONSON
Associate Dean and Professor of Law
University of Washington

DONALD T. WECKSTEIN
Professor of Law
University of San Diego

ST. PAUL, MINN.
WEST PUBLISHING CO.
1991

610 Opperman Drive
P.O. Box 64526
St. Paul, MN 55164-0526

Printed in the United States of America

Library of Congress Cataloging-in-Publication Data

Aronson, Robert H.
Professional responsibility in a nutshell / by Robert H. Aronson and Donald T. Weckstein. — 2nd ed.
p. cm. — (Nutshell series)
Includes index.
ISBN 0-314-83121-5
1. Legal ethics—United States. 2. Attorney and client—United States. 3. Practice of law—United States. I. Weckstein, Donald T. II. Title. III. Series.
KF306.Z9A76 1991
174'.3'0973—dc20 90-28679
CIP

ISBN 0-314-83121-5

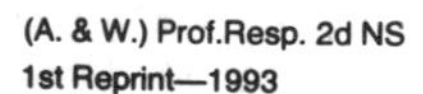

To my father, the late Herman B. J. Weckstein, whose guiding ethical principle for more than fifty years of active law practice was "What can I do for, rather than get from, my clients."

and

To my parents, Bernard and Helene Aronson—both professionals, both responsible, and neither an attorney—for instilling in me a concern about ethics and for providing the educational opportunities that have enabled me to communicate my views to others.

*

PREFACE

To many judges, lawyers and law students, Professional Responsibility is a subject which is neither fit for teaching nor a learned text. This conclusion rests upon two erroneous assumptions: (1) transgressions of the profession's ethical precepts can be avoided simply by acting in a personally moral manner; (2) other issues and problems of professional responsibility cannot be authoritatively resolved and discussion of them will result in little more than a statement of personal preferences.

Most rules of legal ethics, however, are rules of *professional*—not moral—conduct. They reflect a consensus of the legal profession as to how the legal system should operate and the roles that lawyers should play in that system. The rules may require an attorney to act in a manner that is inconsistent with, or irrelevant to, his or her personal moral views. As in other regulatory systems, although there may be disagreement as to the desirability of the rules, they can be stated and adhered to with certainty. As such, the rules can also be learned, explained, and understood. The numbers of lawyers who face disbarment or other disciplinary proceedings and students who fail law school and bar examination questions on professional responsibility provide recurring evidence of the inability of too many persons to learn or adhere to these professional standards.

The successful functioning of the legal system, however, cannot depend solely on erratic disciplinary proceedings or imperfect examinations. As with the law in general, voluntary adherence must be the rule. This can only be achieved if all lawyers and law students become familiar with the standards of professional practice and understand the reasons for them. This cannot be accomplished by any *a priori* reasoning from a personal moral code or from abstract platitudes. Determining the appropriate professional role of the lawyer requires resolving conflicting interests and expectations of self, clients, courts and other decision-making and regulatory bodies, as well as of adversaries, collaborators, the organized profession and the public. A primary aim of this book is to identify and explicate the standards of professional conduct which have emerged from this amalgamation process.

As in all areas of the law, on the other hand, there are unresolved issues of legal conduct and claimed principles about which there remains substantial disagreement among courts and legal commentators. While it is impossible to state "the law" in these areas, the authors have attempted to analyze the differing viewpoints, set forth the relevant considerations, and suggest appropriate resolutions. The authors themselves, however, have not always agreed on the content or application of these unsettled principles of professional responsibility. Therefore, while the authors accept joint responsibility for the statement of rules as they exist in the Code of Professional Responsibility, Rules of Professional Conduct, Code of Judicial Conduct, and statutory and decisional law, criticism and suggested reform of the standards or the system is the sole responsibility of the author of a particular chapter. Professor Weckstein wrote Chapters 1, 2, 3, 4, 5, 7, 14, 16, 21 and 25; Dean Aronson wrote Chapters 6, 8, 9, 10, 11, 12, 13, 15, 17, 18, 19, 20, 22, 23 and 24.

Since the first edition of the Nutshell in 1980, there has been a virtual explosion of materials dealing with issues of professional responsibility. The ABA has replaced the Code of Professional Responsibility (CPR) with the Rules of Professional Conduct (RPC), which have since been adopted in over two-thirds of the states. In 1990, the ABA also adopted a new Code of Judicial Conduct (CJC). The number of state and federal judicial decisions resolving issues of legal ethics also has increased dramatically during the past ten years, with the United States Supreme Court deciding a dozen or so cases each year.

The quantity and quality of scholarship relating to professional responsibility has improved as well. The decade has seen the emergence of a major hornbook (C. Wolfram, Modern Legal Ethics (West 1986)), several comprehensive texts and looseleaf services, and law journals devoted entirely to legal professionalism and ethics. At the same time, there has been a growing recognition that many issues not traditionally considered part of "legal ethics" are nonetheless important to an understanding of "professional responsibility." These issues include: racism, sexism, and other forms of discrimination in the practice of law and in the legal system; changes in the structure of law firms; increasing stress on lawyers resulting in higher incidences of alcoholism, substance abuse, and withdrawal from the profession altogether; concern with balancing the demands of practice against family obligations and outside interests; and efforts to curb overzealous practices such as discovery abuse, harassment of parties, witnesses and opposing counsel, and similar conduct that disrupts the system and makes the practice of law distasteful.

The growing interest in and proliferation of issues of professional responsibility have made it extremely difficult to keep the Nutshell to a manageable size. In an effort to achieve a proper balance, the authors have attempted to raise as many issues relevant to the professional responsibility of lawyers and judges as possible, while focusing primarily on those issues the profession has indicated to be most important by addressing them in the CPR, RPC and CJC.

ROBERT H. ARONSON
DONALD T. WECKSTEIN

April, 1991

The efforts of many people were essential to the completion of this book. As a teacher, I have profited greatly from interaction with my colleagues and students. Although I am indebted to all of them, several merit separate acknowledgment. Jim Brewer, Lois Dightman, Doug Hojem, Catherine Smith and Carol Warner were all research assistants at some time during the researching and drafting of the book. In addition to editing and research assistance, they made many helpful substantive suggestions.

Joni H. Ostergaard deserves special recognition. Her commitment, ability, and attention to detail were invaluable; her skill and professionalism are reflected throughout the book. The quality of her insights into problems of professional responsibility is indicated by her own excellent Comment, *The Failure of Situation–Oriented Professional Rules to Guide Conduct: Conflicting Responsibilities of the Criminal Defense Attorney Whose Client Commits or Intends to Commit Perjury*, 55 Wash.L.Rev. 211 (1979).

In addition to those research assistants who helped with the first edition, the efforts of Lisa Brownlee, Gail Stone and, in particular Kevin Swan, were essential to the completion of the second edition. Also since the first edition, Tom Andrews joined the University of Washington Law School faculty. His enthusiasm for and knowledge of issues in professional responsibility have increased my own knowledge and enthusiasm.

ROBERT H. ARONSON
Seattle, Washington

I would like to thank Dean Walter E. Oberer who, as a teacher at the University of Texas, introduced me to the jurisprudential and other significant and exciting issues of what I and other law students wrongly anticipated would be a dry course in legal ethics. I am also indebted to many other teachers and students of Professional Responsibility who are too numerous to separately identify but have afforded me the opportunity to learn new insights and discuss various aspects of the subject matter. One person among these must be singled out, and he is the late Robert E. Mathews, whose life and teachings have been an inspiration to me and scores of other students of Professional Responsibility. My thanks also to Martha McGill and Patricia Quinn for aid in typing the manuscript as well as for occasional editorial suggestions.

Research and editing of the manuscript of the second edition has been significantly aided by Jamie M.C. Leong and Deborah Schowalter, now of the California Bar.

DONALD T. WECKSTEIN
San Diego, California

*

OUTLINE

	Page
PREFACE	V
TABLE OF CASES	XXVII
TABLE OF STATUTES	XXXVII
TABLE OF RULES	XLI
TABLE OF OTHER AUTHORITIES	LXVII
TABLE OF AUTHORITIES	LXIX

PART I. THE STRUCTURE, SCOPE AND SUPERVISION OF THE LEGAL PROFESSION

Chapter 1. Introduction to Professional Responsibility	1
I. The Meaning of Professional Responsibility	1
II. Professionalism	7
Chapter 2. The Public Image of Lawyers	12
Chapter 3. Standards of Professional Responsibility	19
Chapter 4. The Role of the Organized Bar	27
I. Development of the Organized Bar	27
II. State Bar Associations; Mandatory Membership	32
III. Committees on Professional Ethics	37
Chapter 5. Maintenance of Professional Standards: Admission and Disciplinary Standards and Procedures	39
I. Regulation of the Legal Profession	40

	Page
II. Nature of Professional Standards	42
A. Competence Qualifications	42
1. Education and Apprenticeships	42
2. Professional Examinations	45
B. Citizenship, Residence and Age Requirements	47
C. Character Requirements	50
1. Admission to Practice	50
2. Constitutional Defenses to Moral Character Inquiries	54
3. Disciplinary Proceedings	55
III. Procedural Standards	61
A. Admission Process	62
B. Disciplinary Process	64
Chapter 6. The Duty to Ensure Competence: Professional Discipline, Malpractice Actions, Ineffective Assistance of Counsel Claims, Continuing Legal Education, and Specialization	**72**
I. Introduction	72
II. The Code of Professional Responsibility and the Model Rules of Professional Conduct	74
A. Duty to Maintain One's Own Competence	74
B. Duty to Assist the Profession in Maintaining Competence	77
III. Professional Discipline	78
IV. Malpractice Liability	81
A. Causes of Malpractice Explosion	82
B. Frequently Recurring Malpractice Complaints	83
1. "Customer Relations"	84
2. Legal Negligence and Neglect	85

Page

IV. Malpractice Liability—Continued
C. Liability to Third Parties 88
D. Limiting Liability 89
V. Ineffective Assistance of Counsel 90
A. Evolution of the Right to Effective Assistance 92
B. Standards for Determining the Effectiveness of Counsel 94
C. Procedural Limitations on Claims of Ineffective Assistance 96
VI. Rule 11 Sanctions 98
VII. Continuing Legal Education 100
A. Voluntary Continuing Legal Education 101
B. Mandatory Continuing Legal Education 101
C. Criticisms of Continuing Legal Education 102
VIII. Recertification Examinations 103
IX. Specialization 103
A. Advantages and Disadvantages of Specialization 105
B. Types of Specialization Plans 107
1. Certification 107
2. Identification or Self–Designation 108
3. Designation 108
4. The ABA Model Plan ("Recognition") 109
X. Conclusion 110

Chapter 7. The Unauthorized Practice of Law 111
I. Goals of Unauthorized Practice Laws 113
II. The Law of Unauthorized Practice 115
A. What Is the Practice of Law? 115
B. Incidental Legal Services 118
C. The Public Interest Test 120
D. Waivers 121
E. Legal Clerks and Assistants 121

Page
III. Judicial Control of Unauthorized Practice ... 122
IV. Professional Independence and Unauthorized Practice ... 124
V. Practice Before Administrative and Arbitral Tribunals ... 127
VI. Non–Admitted Attorneys ... 130
VII. Self–Representation; Corporations ... 134
VIII. The Unmet Need for Counsel ... 137
IX. Enforcement of Unauthorized Practice Laws ... 139
X. Anti-trust and Constitutional Restraints on Enforcement of Unauthorized Practice Laws ... 141

PART II. THE DUTY TO MAKE LEGAL SERVICES AVAILABLE

Chapter 8. The Duty to Represent Indigent and Unpopular Clients ... 145
I. The Duty to Represent the Poor ... 145
A. The Duty to Defend the Indigent Accused ... 146
1. The Argument Against the Duty to Defend ... 147
2. The Argument for the Duty to Defend ... 147
3. Appointment by the Courts; Recommendation by the Bar ... 148
B. The Duty to Represent the Indigent in Civil Matters ... 149
1. The Argument for the Duty to Represent 149
2. The Argument Against the Duty to Represent ... 149
II. The Duty to Represent the Unpopular ... 150
A. The Duty to Defend the Unpopular Accused 151
1. The Argument for the Duty to Defend ... 151

Page

II. The Duty to Represent the Unpopular—Continued
2. The Argument Against the Duty to Defend 151
3. "Personal Feelings" and "Community Attitudes" 152
B. The Duty to Represent the Unpopular in Civil Matters 153
C. Appointment by the Courts; Recommendation by the Bar 154

Chapter 9. Implementing the Duty to Make Legal Services Available: Group and Prepaid Legal Services, Legal Aid, Judicare, Legal Clinics, Lawyer Referral, and Public Interest Litigation 156

I. Introduction 156
II. Legal Aid and Public Defender Services 157
A. O.E.O. Legal Services Program 159
B. Legal Services Corporation 159
C. IOLTA Funds 161
D. Ethical Problems of Legal Aid and Public Defender Representation 162
III. Judicare 163
IV. Group Prepaid Legal Services 165
A. Ethical Problems in Group and Prepaid Legal Services Plans 167
B. Additional Problems Affecting Group Legal Services Plans 169
V. Legal Clinics 170
VI. Public Interest Law 172
VII. Lawyer Referral 173

Page

VIII. Additional Resources 174
A. Law Students 174
B. "Jail-House Lawyers" 176
C. Non-Lawyer Resources 176

Chapter 10. Solicitation and Advertising **178**
I. Introduction 178
II. Advertising 179
A. The Sherman Act 179
B. Commercial Speech and the First Amendment 180
C. The Requirement of "Substantial Interest" 182
1. *In re R.M.J.* 182
2. The Response to *In re R.M.J.* 183
III. Solicitation 187
A. Solicitation Involving Political Issues 188
B. Solicitation for Financial Gain 189
1. In-Person Solicitation 189
2. "Targeted" Mail and Newspaper Advertisements 191
IV. Unresolved Issues 193

PART III. THE ATTORNEY-CLIENT RELATIONSHIP

Chapter 11. Confidentiality **195**
I. Introduction 195
II. The General Rule of Confidential Communications 197
A. The CPR: Confidences and Secrets 198
B. The RPC: Information Relating to Representation 199
C. Corporate Communications 200

Page

III. Procedural Aspects 201
IV. Exceptions to Confidentiality 202
A. Consent 202
B. Identity, Occupation, and Address of Client; Fact of Retainer 203
C. Nonlegal Advice or Nonprofessional Capacity 206
D. Necessary to Establish or Collect Fee 207
E. Necessary to Defend Self or Employees 207
F. Disclosures to, or Obtained From, Third Persons 209
G. Jointly Retained Attorney 210
H. Criminal Evidence 211
I. Future Crime 214
1. Future Crime and the CPR 215
2. The RPC and Recent Developments 215
J. Fraud 217
1. The CPR and "Rectifiable Fraud" 217
2. The RPC 218
3. Client Fraud Before a Court—Perjury 219

Chapter 12. Conflict of Interest 222
I. Policies Underlying Conflict of Interest Rules ... 223
A. Loyalty 223
B. Confidentiality 224
II. General Rules: Potential Versus Actual Conflicts 224
A. Determining Whether Representation Is Likely to Be "Materially Limited" or "Directly Adverse" 224
B. The "Appearance of Impropriety" Standard 226
III. Recurring Conflict of Interest Situations 228
A. Conflicts Resulting From Lawyer's Personal Interest 228

Page

III. Recurring Conflict of Interest Situations—Continued
B. Conflicts Resulting From Representation of Adverse Interests of Current Clients 233
1. Insurer–Insured 233
2. Buyer–Seller; Borrower–Lender; Husband–Wife; Etc. 235
3. Representing Multiple Plaintiffs 236
4. Representing Multiple Criminal Defendants 237
C. Conflicts Resulting From Representation of Interests Adverse to a Former Client 239
D. Attorneys Employed by the Government 241
1. General Considerations 241
2. Alternative Approaches 242
a. ABA Formal Opinion 342 (1975) 242
b. RPC 1.11 243
E. Representing Corporations, Labor Unions, Tenant Associations, and Other Entities 245
1. Corporate Wrongdoing 247
F. Imputed Disqualification 248
1. The CPR 248
2. The RPC 250
a. "Screening" 251
IV. Conclusion 252

Chapter 13. Fiduciary Responsibilities: Commingling and Misappropriation 254
I. Introduction 254
II. Record–Keeping and Accounting 255
III. Commingling 255
A. IOLTA Funds 257
IV. Misappropriation 258

Page

V. Clients' Security Funds 259
VI. Preventive Measures 260
VII. Conclusion 261

Chapter 14. Attorneys' Fees 262
I. Introduction 262
II. Types of Legal Fee Arrangements 263
III. Determining the Reasonableness of a Fee 265
IV. Contingent Fees 271
A. Justification 271
B. Legal and Ethical Limits on Contingent Fees 274
C. Payment of Expenses 276
V. Desirability of Written Fee Agreements 277
VI. Division of Fees 278
A. Dividing Fees With Other Lawyers 278
B. Sharing Fees With Non–Lawyers is Generally Prohibited 280
VII. Advertising of Legal Fees 283
VIII. Collection of Fees 284
IX. Attorneys' Liens 287
X. Termination of Employment 289

Chapter 15. Terminating the Relationship: Voluntary and Mandatory Withdrawal 293
I. Introduction 293
II. Applicable Rules 294
A. Accepting Employment 294
B. Withdrawing From Employment 295
1. Mandatory Withdrawal 296
2. Permissive Withdrawal 298
3. Good Cause 299
C. Consequences of Improper Withdrawal 301

Page

II. Applicable Rules—Continued
D. Procedure for Withdrawal 301
1. Court Permission 301
2. Protecting the Client's Interests 302
III. Conclusion 303

PART IV. THE LAWYER IN THE LEGAL SYSTEM: FUNCTIONS AND RESPONSIBILITIES

Chapter 16. The Lawyer as an Advocate: The Adversary System 304
I. Justice and the Adversary System 304
II. Lawyers' Roles in the Adversary System 309
III. Specific Obligations of the Advocate 312
A. Preparation for Trial 314
1. Preparing a Witness for Trial 315
2. Communication With Adverse Witnesses 317
B. Acceptance of "Questionable Cases"; the "Guilty" Client 320
C. Delay 325
D. The Lying Client or Witness 326
1. The Problem 326
2. The Alternatives 327
a. Refuse to Call the Intended Perjurer as a Witness 327
b. Withdraw From Representation 328
c. ABA Standards Relating to the Administration of Criminal Justice: The Defense Function 330
d. The Model Rules 332
e. Nix v. Whiteside 335
f. Pleading ignorance 338
g. The Best Alternative? 339

Page

III. Specific Obligations of the Advocate—Continued
E. Conduct at Trial 343
1. Disclosure of Misleading and Adverse Evidence 343
2. Disclosure of Adverse Legal Authority 347
3. Impeaching the Truthful Witness 349
4. The Rules of Evidence as Ethical Guidelines 351
5. Appeals to Emotion 352
6. Trial Disruption; Offensive Advocacy 354
F. Compensating Witnesses 358
G. Criminal v. Civil Advocacy 360

Chapter 17. The Lawyer and the Fair Trial/Free Press Conflict 362
I. Introduction 362
II. Improper Effect of Unlimited Publicity on the Administration of Justice 363
III. Efforts to Limit Unduly Prejudicial Publicity 368
A. Restrictions on the Press 368
1. Generally 368
2. Pretrial Proceedings 370
3. Discovery 371
B. Restrictions on Lawyers 372
1. Professional Rules 372
2. Court–Imposed Restrictions on Lawyers' Out-of-Court Statements 373
IV. Television in the Courtroom 373
V. Conclusion 376

Chapter 18. The Lawyer as Prosecuting Attorney 377
I. The Role of the Prosecutor in an Adversary System 377

Page

II. Discretion to Charge 379
III. Plea Bargaining 381
IV. Conflicts of Interest 383
V. Responsibility for Ensuring Fair Trials 384
A. Expression of Personal Opinion 386
B. Comment on the Defendant's Silence 387
C. Presenting False, Misleading, or Inadmissible Evidence 388
D. Failure to Disclose Exculpatory Evidence 389
VI. Supervising the Police 390
VII. Interference With Client–Attorney Relationship 391
VIII. Discipline 392

Chapter 19. The Lawyer as Advisor and Negotiator **395**
I. The Lawyer as Advisor 395
II. The Lawyer as Negotiator 399
III. Conclusion 404

Chapter 20. The Lawyer as Corporate or Governmental Employee **406**
I. The Ethical Responsibilities of the Corporate Lawyer 406
A. Advocating the Corporate Client's Interests—The Issues 406
1. Who Is the Client? 406
2. What Are the Client's Interests? 408
B. Competing Interests—Responsible Corporate Representation 408
1. Acts That May Injure the Organization 409
2. The Organization's Social Interests—Lawyer as Advisor 412

Page

I. The Ethical Responsibilities of the Corporate Lawyer—Continued
C. Representing the Organization and a Constituent 414
II. The Ethical Responsibilities of the Government Lawyer 415
A. Who Is the Client? 415
B. Obligations to the Agency and the Public 416
1. Standards of Conduct for Government Lawyers 416
2. The Duty to Disclose Wrongdoing 416
3. The Duty to Resign 417

Chapter 21. The Lawyer as a Neutral: Ethics in Alternative Dispute Resolution 419
I. Sources of Guidance 420
II. Ethical Concerns of the Private Lawyer Serving as a Neutral 422
A. Competence 422
B. Consultation 424
C. Impartiality 429
D. Appearance of Impropriety 433
E. Conflicts of Interests 435
F. Confidentiality 437
G. Fees 443
H. Unauthorized Practice of Law 445
I. Advertising and Solicitation 448
J. Pro Bono Activities 450
III. Related Duties of Lawyers as Client Representatives 451
A. Obligation to Consider Use of ADR Processes 451
B. The Lawyer as an Evaluator 454

Page

Chapter 22. The Lawyer as Judge: Judicial Ethics and Selection 457
I. Introduction 457
II. Disqualification 459
A. Basic Principles and Rules 459
B. 28 U.S.C. § 144 460
C. 28 U.S.C. § 455 460
D. Disqualification in Particular Types of Cases 464
III. Appearance of Impropriety 467
IV. Adjudicative and Administrative Responsibilities 468
A. Adjudicative Responsibilities 468
B. Administrative Responsibilities 471
V. Quasi–Judicial Activities 472
VI. Extra–Judicial Activities 473
VII. Judicial Selection 473

Chapter 23. The Lawyer as Public Leader and Law Reformer 478
I. Introduction 478
II. Duty to Improve the Legal System 479
III. Training for Policy–Making 482
IV. Conclusion 483

Chapter 24. The Lawyer and the Legislature 484
I. Lawyer as Legislator 484
A. Honesty 485
B. Conflict of Interest 486
C. Advertising 488
D. Limitations on the Lawyer–Legislator's Firm 490
E. Limitations After Leaving Legislative Office 491
II. Lawyer as Staff Counsel to the Legislature 492
III. Lawyer as Lobbyist 493

Page

Chapter 25. Professional vs. Personal Responsibilities: Can a Good Lawyer Be a Good Person? **495**

INDEX 505

*

TABLE OF CASES

A., In re, 276 Or. 225, 554 P.2d 479 (Or.1976), *218, 297, 344*
Aetna Life Ins. Co. v. Lavoie, 475 U.S. 813, 106 S.Ct. 1580, 89 L.Ed.2d 823 (1986), *461*
Alcorta v. State of Texas, 355 U.S. 28, 78 S.Ct. 103, 2 L.Ed.2d 9 (1957), *393*
Allee v. Medrano, 416 U.S. 802, 94 S.Ct. 2191, 40 L.Ed.2d 566 (1974), *380*
American Can Co. v. Citrus Feed Co., 436 F.2d 1125 (5th Cir.1971), *249*
Application of (see name of party)
Argersinger v. Hamlin, 407 U.S. 25, 92 S.Ct. 2006, 32 L.Ed.2d 530 (1972), *92, 146, 158*
Austin v. Erickson, 477 F.2d 620 (8th Cir.1973), *239*
Avery, People v., 129 A.D.2d 852, 513 N.Y.S.2d 883 (N.Y.A.D. 3 Dept.1987), *341*

Bagley, United States v., 473 U.S. 667, 105 S.Ct. 3375, 87 L.Ed.2d 481 (1985), *389*
Baird v. State Bar of Arizona, 401 U.S. 1, 91 S.Ct. 719, 27 L.Ed.2d 639 (1971), *54*
Baltes v. Doe I, *No. CL–88–1145–AD (Fla.Cir.Ct., 15th Jud.Cir. 1988), 206*
Banks v. Randle, 337 Pa.Super. 197, 486 A.2d 974 (Pa.Super.1984), *96*
Banks, United States v., 374 F.Supp. 321 (D.C.S.D.1974), *385*
Barnard v. Thorstenn, 489 U.S. 546, 109 S.Ct. 1294, 103 L.Ed.2d 559 (1989), *48*
Bates v. State Bar of Arizona, 433 U.S. 350, 97 S.Ct. 2691, 53 L.Ed.2d 810 (1977), *141, 178, 179, 180, 181, 187, 189*
Belge, People v., 83 Misc.2d 186, 372 N.Y.S.2d 798, aff'd mem. 50 A.D.2d 1088, 376 N.Y.S.2d 771 (1975), aff'd per curiam 41 N.Y.2d 60, 359 N.E.2d 377, 390 N.Y.S.2d 867 (1977), *211*
Benchimol, United States v., 471 U.S. 453, 105 S.Ct. 2103, 85 L.Ed.2d 462 (1985), *382*
Benjamin, United States v., 328 F.2d 854 (2nd Cir.), cert. denied sub nom. Howard v. United States, 377 U.S. 953 (1964), *413*
Berger v. United States, 295 U.S. 78, 55 S.Ct. 629, 79 L.Ed. 1314 (1935), *377*
Berger v. United States, 255 U.S. 22, 41 S.Ct. 230, 65 L.Ed. 481 (1921), *459, 460*
Bersani v. Bersani, 41 Conn.Supp. 252, 565 A.2d 1368 (Conn.Super.1989), *205*
Betts v. Allstate Ins. Co., 154 Cal.App.3d 688, 201 Cal.Rptr. 528 (Cal.App. 4 Dist.1984), *234*
Bigelow v. Virginia, 421 U.S. 809, 95 S.Ct. 2222, 44 L.Ed.2d 600 (1975), *180*
Black v. State Bar of California, 57 Cal.2d 219, 18 Cal.Rptr. 518, 368 P.2d 118 (Cal.1962), *256*
Blackledge v. Perry, 417 U.S. 21, 94 S.Ct. 2098, 40 L.Ed.2d 628 (1974), *380*

Board of Overseers of the Bar v. Dineen, 481 A.2d 499 (Me.1984), *341*
Bobbitt v. Victorian House, Inc., 532 F.Supp. 734 (D.C.Ill.1982), *414*
Bordenkircher v. Hayes, 434 U.S. 357, 98 S.Ct. 663, 54 L.Ed.2d 604 (1978), *379, 382*
Brady v. State of Maryland, 373 U.S. 83, 83 S.Ct. 1194, 10 L.Ed.2d 215 (1963), *389*
Brotherhood of R. R. Trainmen v. Virginia ex rel. Va. State Bar, 377 U.S. 1, 84 S.Ct. 1113, 12 L.Ed.2d 89 (1964), *187*
Brown v. Allen, 344 U.S. 443, 73 S.Ct. 397, 97 L.Ed. 469 (1953), *96*
Buyers Service Co., Inc., State v., 292 S.C. 426, 357 S.E.2d 15 (S.C.1987), *119*

Caplin & Drysdale, Chartered v. United States, 491 U.S. 617, 109 S.Ct. 2646, 105 L.Ed.2d 528 (1989), *93, 238, 392*
Carroll v. State Bar of California, 166 Cal.App.3d 1193, 213 Cal.Rptr. 305 (Cal.App. 4 Dist.1985), *258*
Carroll v. State Bar of California, 162 Cal.App.3d 1094, 209 Cal.Rptr. 740 (Cal.App. 4 Dist.1984), *162*
Carter, In re, [1979 Transfer Binder] Fed.Sec.L.Rep. (CCH) para. 82,175, p. *411*
Chambers v. Maroney, 399 U.S. 42, 90 S.Ct. 1975, 26 L.Ed.2d 419 (1970), *98*
Chandler v. Florida, 449 U.S. 560, 101 S.Ct. 802, 66 L.Ed.2d 740 (1981), *374, 375*
Charge of Judicial Misconduct, In re, 691 F.2d 923 (9th Cir.1982), *470*
Chicago Council of Lawyers v. Bauer, 522 F.2d 242 (7th Cir.1975), *78, 372, 373, 376*
Chicago Teachers Union, Local No. 1, AFT, AFL–CIO v. Hudson, 475 U.S. 292, 106 S.Ct. 1066, 89 L.Ed.2d 232 (1986), *34, 36*
City & County of San Francisco v. Superior Court In and For City and County of San Francisco, 37 Cal.2d 227, 231 P.2d 26 (Cal.1951), *209*
Clark v. United States, 289 U.S. 1, 53 S.Ct. 465, 77 L.Ed. 993 (1933), *214*
Clements v. Fashing, 457 U.S. 957, 102 S.Ct. 2836, 73 L.Ed.2d 508 (1982), *477*
Coleman v. Alabama, 399 U.S. 1, 90 S.Ct. 1999, 26 L.Ed.2d 387 (1970), *93*
Coleman v. Risley, 845 F.2d 884 (9th Cir.1988), *297*
Commonwealth v. ____ (see opposing party)
Committee on Professional Ethics and Conduct of Iowa State Bar Ass'n v. Crary, 245 N.W.2d 298 (Iowa 1976), *340*
Committee on Professional Ethics and Conduct of Iowa State Bar Ass'n v. Humphrey, 355 N.W.2d 565 (Iowa 1984), *193*
Commonwealth Coatings Corp. v. Continental Cas. Co., 393 U.S. 145, 89 S.Ct. 337, 21 L.Ed.2d 301 (1968), *432*
Cone v. State Bar of Florida, 819 F.2d 1002 (11th Cir.1987), *258*
Consolidated Theatres v. Warner Bros. Circuit Management Corp., 216 F.2d 920 (2nd Cir.1954), *249*
Crane v. State Bar of California, 177 Cal.Rptr. 670, 635 P.2d 163 (Cal.1981), *401*
Cultum v. Heritage House Realtors, Inc., 103 Wash.2d 623, 694 P.2d 630 (Wash.1985), *121*

Cunningham v. Superior Court (Ventura County), 177 Cal.App.3d 336, 222 Cal.Rptr. 854 (Cal.App. 2 Dist.1986), *150*
Cuyler v. Sullivan, 446 U.S. 335, 100 S.Ct. 1708, 64 L.Ed.2d 333 (1980), *95, 238, 472*

Doe v. Federal Grievance Committee, 847 F.2d 57 (2nd Cir.1988), *339*
Dondi Properties Corporation v. Commerce Savings and Loan Assoc., 121 F.R.D. 284 (N.D.Tex.1988), *357*
Douglas v. People of State of California, 372 U.S. 353, 83 S.Ct. 814, 9 L.Ed.2d 811 (1963), *93*
Duncan v. Merrill Lynch, Pierce, Fenner & Smith, Inc., 646 F.2d 1020 (5th Cir.1981), *240*
Dunton v. Suffolk County, State of N.Y., 729 F.2d 903 (2nd Cir.1984), *472*

Edison Electric Light Co. v. United States Electric Lighting Co., 44 F. 294 (C.C.N.Y.1890), *210*
Education Law Center, Inc., Matter of, 86 N.J. 124, 429 A.2d 1051 (N.J.1981), *127*
Escobedo v. State of Illinois, 378 U.S. 478, 84 S.Ct. 1758, 12 L.Ed.2d 977, 32 O.O.2d 31 (1964), *93*
Estes v. Texas, 382 U.S. 875, 86 S.Ct. 18, 15 L.Ed.2d 118 (1965), *363, 364, 374, 375*
Evans v. Artek Systems Corp., 715 F.2d 788 (2nd Cir.1983), *407*
Evitts v. Lucey, 469 U.S. 387, 105 S.Ct. 830, 83 L.Ed.2d 821 (1985), *93, 95, 96*

Fields, In re, [1973 Transfer Binder] Fed.Sec.L.Rep. (CCH) para. 79,407, p. *414*
First Wisconsin Mortg. Trust v. First Wisconsin Corp., 584 F.2d 201 (7th Cir. 1978), *240*
Fisher v. United States, 425 U.S. 391, 96 S.Ct. 1569, 48 L.Ed.2d 39 (1976), *210*
Florida Bar v. Furman, 451 So.2d 808 (Fla.1984), *135*
Florida Bar v. Rubin, 549 So.2d 1000 (Fla.1989), *154, 302*
Frazier v. Heebe, 482 U.S. 641, 107 S.Ct. 2607, 96 L.Ed.2d 557 (1987), *49*
Friedman v. Rogers, 440 U.S. 1, 99 S.Ct. 887, 59 L.Ed.2d 100 (1979), *186*

Gannett Co., Inc. v. DePasquale, 443 U.S. 368, 99 S.Ct. 2898, 61 L.Ed.2d 608 (1979), *370*
Garrity v. State of New Jersey, 385 U.S. 493, 87 S.Ct. 616, 17 L.Ed.2d 562 (1967), *68*
General Motors Corp. v. City of New York, 501 F.2d 639 (2nd Cir.1974), rev'g 60 F.R.D. 393 (S.D.N.Y.1973), *242*
Gibson v. Berryhill, 411 U.S. 564, 93 S.Ct. 1689, 36 L.Ed.2d 488 (1973), *143*
Gideon v. Wainwright, 372 U.S. 335, 83 S.Ct. 792, 9 L.Ed.2d 799, 23 O.O.2d 258 (1963), *92, 146, 158*
Giglio v. United States, 405 U.S. 150, 92 S.Ct. 763, 31 L.Ed.2d 104 (1972), *388*
Glasser v. United States, 315 U.S. 60, 62 S.Ct. 457, 86 L.Ed. 680 (1942), *237*

Globe Newspaper Co. v. Superior Court for Norfolk County, 457 U.S. 596, 102 S.Ct. 2613, 73 L.Ed.2d 248 (1982), *369*
Goldfarb v. Virginia State Bar, 421 U.S. 773, 95 S.Ct. 2004, 44 L.Ed.2d 572 (1975), *141, 142, 169, 179, 267, 268*
Goodwin, Matter of, 279 S.C. 274, 305 S.E.2d 578 (S.C.1983), *330*
Goodwin, United States v., 457 U.S. 368, 102 S.Ct. 2485, 73 L.Ed.2d 74 (1982), *380*
Grand Jury Proceedings, In re (Pavlick), 680 F.2d 1026 (5th Cir.1982), *204*
Grievance Committee of Bar of Fairfield County v. Dacey, 154 Conn. 129, 222 A.2d 339 (Conn.1966), *135*
Griffin v. California, 380 U.S. 960, 85 S.Ct. 1102 (1965), *387*
Griffiths, Application of, 413 U.S. 717, 93 S.Ct. 2851, 37 L.Ed.2d 910 (1973), *47*

Hackin v. Arizona, 389 U.S. 143, 88 S.Ct. 325, 19 L.Ed.2d 347 (1967), *137*
Hall v. Small Business Admin., 695 F.2d 175 (5th Cir.1983), *471*
Hallinan v. Committee of Bar Examiners of State Bar, 65 Cal.2d 447, 55 Cal. Rptr. 228, 421 P.2d 76 (Cal.1966), *51, 58*
Hamilton v. State of Alabama, 368 U.S. 52, 82 S.Ct. 157, 7 L.Ed.2d 114 (1961), *93*
Hawkins v. King County, Dept. of Rehabilitative Services, Division of Involuntary Treatment Services, 24 Wash.App. 338, 602 P.2d 361 (Wash.App. 1979), *216*
Hayslip v. Douglas, 400 So.2d 553 (Fla.App. 4 Dist.1981), *463*
Heyer v. Flaig, 70 Cal.2d 223, 74 Cal.Rptr. 225, 449 P.2d 161 (Cal.1969), *89*
Hill v. Lockhart, 474 U.S. 52, 106 S.Ct. 366, 88 L.Ed.2d 203 (1985), *95*
Himmel, In re, 125 Ill.2d 531, 127 Ill.Dec. 708, 533 N.E.2d 790 (Ill.1988), *80, 90*
Hiss, In re, 368 Mass. 447, 333 N.E.2d 429 (Mass.1975), *70*
Holloway v. Arkansas, 435 U.S. 475, 98 S.Ct. 1173, 55 L.Ed.2d 426 (1978), *95, 237*
Hoover v. Ronwin, 466 U.S. 558, 104 S.Ct. 1989, 80 L.Ed.2d 590 (1984), *46*
Hulland v. State Bar, 105 Cal.Rptr. 152, 503 P.2d 608 (Cal.1972), *285*

Imbler v. Pachtman, 424 U.S. 409, 96 S.Ct. 984, 47 L.Ed.2d 128 (1976), *390*
In re (see name of party)

Jacoby v. State Bar, 138 Cal.Rptr. 77, 562 P.2d 1326 (Cal.1977), *171*
Jedwabny v. Philadelphia Transp. Co., 390 Pa. 231, 135 A.2d 252 (Pa.1957), *236*
Johnson v. Avery, 393 U.S. 483, 89 S.Ct. 747, 21 L.Ed.2d 718 (1969), *138*
Johnson v. Zerbst, 304 U.S. 458, 58 S.Ct. 1019, 82 L.Ed. 1461 (1938), *92*
Jorgenson v. Volusia County, 846 F.2d 1350 (11th Cir.1988), *349*

Kavanaugh, State v., 52 N.J. 7, 243 A.2d 225, cert. denied sub nom. Matzner v. New Jersey, 393 U.S. 924 (N.J.1968), *132*
Keller v. State Bar of California, ___ U.S. ____, 110 S.Ct. 2228, 110 L.Ed.2d 1 (1990), *36*
Kimmelman v. Morrison, 477 U.S. 365, 106 S.Ct. 2574, 91 L.Ed.2d 305 (1986), *97*
King Resources Co., Matter of, 20 B.R. 191 (D.C.Colo.1982), *408*
Klemm v. Superior Court of Fresno County, 75 Cal.App.3d 893, 142 Cal.Rptr. 509 (Cal.App. 5 Dist.1977), *226*
Klubock, United States v., 832 F.2d 664 (1st Cir.1987), *204*
Konigsberg v. State Bar of California, 366 U.S. 36, 81 S.Ct. 997, 6 L.Ed.2d 105 (1961), *54*
Konigsberg v. State Bar of California, 353 U.S. 252, 77 S.Ct. 722, 1 L.Ed.2d 810 (1957), *54*

Laird v. Tatum, 408 U.S. 1, 92 S.Ct. 2318, 33 L.Ed.2d 154 (1972), *462*
Lake Utopia Paper Ltd. v. Connelly Containers, Inc., 608 F.2d 928 (2nd Cir. 1979), *438*
Lathrop v. Donohue, 367 U.S. 820, 81 S.Ct. 1826, 6 L.Ed.2d 1191 (1961), *33, 36*
Law Students Civil Rights Research Council, Inc. v. Wadmond, 401 U.S. 154, 91 S.Ct. 720, 27 L.Ed.2d 749 (1971), *54, 55*
Leis v. Flynt, 439 U.S. 438, 99 S.Ct. 698, 58 L.Ed.2d 717, 11 O.O.3d 302 (1979), *131*
Levine v. United States Dist. Court for Cent. Dist. of California, 764 F.2d 590 (9th Cir.1985), *373*
Liljeberg v. Health Services Acquisition Corp., 486 U.S. 847, 108 S.Ct. 2194, 100 L.Ed.2d 855 (1988), *463*
Lovett and Linder, Ltd. v. Carter, 523 F.Supp. 903 (D.C.R.I.1981), *185*
Lowery v. Cardwell, 575 F.2d 727 (9th Cir.1978), *297, 329, 332*
Lyon v. Alabama State Bar, 451 So.2d 1367 (Ala.1984), *185*
Lysick v. Walcom, 258 Cal.App.2d 136, 65 Cal.Rptr. 406 (Cal.App. 1 Dist. 1968), *234*

Mallard v. United States Dist. Court for Southern Dist. of Iowa, 490 U.S. 296, 109 S.Ct. 1814, 104 L.Ed.2d 318 (1989), *146, 155*
Malloy, Matter of, 248 N.W.2d 43 (N.D.1976), *341*
Matter of (see name of party)
Maxwell v. Superior Court of Los Angeles County, 30 Cal.3d 606, 18 Cal.Rptr. 177, 639 P.2d 248 (Cal.1982), *265*
McGlothlen, Matter of, 99 Wash.2d 515, 663 P.2d 1330 (Wash.1983), *229*
McLaughlin v. Superior Court for San Mateo County, 140 Cal.App.3d 473, 189 Cal.Rptr. 479 (Cal.App. 1 Dist.1983), *441*
McMann v. Richardson, 397 U.S. 759, 90 S.Ct. 1441, 25 L.Ed.2d 763 (1970), *94*
McQueen v. State, 475 S.W.2d 111 (Mo.1971), *96*
Meredith, People v., 175 Cal.Rptr. 612, 631 P.2d 46 (Cal.1981), *213*
Meyerhofer v. Empire Fire & Marine Ins. Co., 497 F.2d 1190 (2nd Cir.), cert. denied 419 U.S. 998 (1974), *208*

Miller v. Pate, 386 U.S. 1, 87 S.Ct. 785, 17 L.Ed.2d 690 (1967), *393*
Morrell v. State, 575 P.2d 1200 (Alaska 1978), *209, 213*
Murchison, In re, 349 U.S. 133, 75 S.Ct. 623, 99 L.Ed. 942 (1955), *457*

Nackson, Matter of, 114 N.J. 527, 555 A.2d 1101 (N.J.1989), *205*
Napue v. People of the State of Illinois, 360 U.S. 264, 79 S.Ct. 1173, 3 L.Ed.2d 1217 (1959), *388*
National Ass'n for Advancement of Colored People v. Button, 371 U.S. 415, 83 S.Ct. 328, 9 L.Ed.2d 405 (1963), *170, 173, 187, 188*
National Revenue Corp. v. Violet, 807 F.2d 285 (1st Cir.1986), *142*
Nebraska Press Ass'n v. Stuart, 427 U.S. 539, 96 S.Ct. 2791, 49 L.Ed.2d 683 (1976), *368, 372, 376*
Nemours Foundation v. Gilbane, Aetna, Federal Ins. Co., 632 F.Supp. 418 (D.Del.1986), *251*
New York County Lawyers' Ass'n v. Dacey, 54 Misc.2d 564, 282 N.Y.S.2d 985 (N.Y.Sup.1967), *135*
Nix v. Whiteside, 475 U.S. 157, 106 S.Ct. 988, 89 L.Ed.2d 123 (1986), *220, 297, 335, 336, 338, 340, 342*
North Carolina v. Alford, 400 U.S. 25, 91 S.Ct. 160, 27 L.Ed.2d 162, 56 O.O.2d 85 (1970), *381*

Ohntrup v. Firearms Center, Inc., 802 F.2d 676 (3rd Cir.1986), *301*
Ohralik v. Ohio State Bar Ass'n, 436 U.S. 447, 98 S.Ct. 1912, 56 L.Ed.2d 444 (1978), *188, 190, 191, 192*
Oldtowne Legal Clinic, P.A., Matter of, 285 Md. 132, 400 A.2d 1111 (Md. 1979), *185, 186*
Olwell, State ex rel. Sowers v., 64 Wash.2d 828, 394 P.2d 681 (Wash.1964), *213*
Oring v. State Bar of California, 488 U.S. 590, 109 S.Ct. 858, 102 L.Ed.2d 951 (1989), *194*
Oyler v. Boles, 368 U.S. 448, 82 S.Ct. 501, 7 L.Ed.2d 446 (1962), *379*

Parker v. Brown, 317 U.S. 341, 63 S.Ct. 307, 87 L.Ed. 315 (1943), *179*
Patterson v. Illinois, 487 U.S. 285, 108 S.Ct. 2389, 101 L.Ed.2d 261 (1988), *382*
Pavelic & LeFlore v. Marvel Entertainment Group, ___ U.S. ___, 110 S.Ct. 456, 107 L.Ed.2d 438 (1989), *100*
Peel v. Illinois, ___ U.S. ___, 110 S.Ct. 2281, ___ L.Ed.2d ___ (1990), *185*
Pennington, In re, 73 Wash.2d 601, 440 P.2d 175 (Wash.1968), *254*
People v. ___ (see opposing party)
Perez, People v., 153 Cal.Rptr. 40, 591 P.2d 63 (Cal.1979), *122, 174*
Pike, People v., 58 Cal.2d 70, 22 Cal.Rptr. 664, 372 P.2d 656 (Cal.1962), cert. denied 371 U.S. 941 (1963), *341*
Powell v. State of Alabama, 287 U.S. 45, 53 S.Ct. 55, 77 L.Ed. 158 (1932), *90, 93*
Press-Enterprise Co. v. Superior Court of California for Riverside County, 478 U.S. 1, 106 S.Ct. 2735, 92 L.Ed.2d 1 (1986), *370*
Primus, In re, 436 U.S. 412, 98 S.Ct. 1893, 56 L.Ed.2d 417 (1978), *173, 188*

Professional Adjusters, Inc. v. Tandon, 433 N.E.2d 779 (Ind.1982), *123*
Public Citizen v. United States Dept. of Justice, 491 U.S. 440, 109 S.Ct. 2558, 105 L.Ed.2d 377 (1989), *475*

Richmond Newspapers, Inc. v. Virginia, 448 U.S. 555, 100 S.Ct. 2814, 65 L.Ed.2d 973 (1980), *369, 375*
R.M.J., In re, 455 U.S. 191, 102 S.Ct. 929, 71 L.Ed.2d 64 (1982), *182, 183, 184, 185, 192*
Roberts v. Ball, Hunt, Hart, Brown and Baerwitz, 57 Cal.App.3d 104, 128 Cal.Rptr. 901 (Cal.App. 2 Dist.1976), *456*
Robinson, State v., 290 N.C. 56, 224 S.E.2d 174 (N.C.1976), *331*
Ross v. Moffitt, 417 U.S. 600, 94 S.Ct. 2437, 41 L.Ed.2d 341 (1974), *93*
Rubin v. State, 490 So.2d 1001 (Fla.App. 3 Dist.1986), *154, 302*
Rubin v. State, 467 So.2d 1017 (Fla.App. 5 Dist.1985), *294*
Ruffalo, In re, 390 U.S. 544, 88 S.Ct. 1222, 20 L.Ed.2d 117, 43 O.O.2d 459 (1968), *67, 78, 79*
Ryder, In re, 381 F.2d 713 (4th Cir.), aff'g 263 F.Supp. 360 (E.D.Va.1967), *212*

Sanders v. Russell, 401 F.2d 241 (5th Cir.1968), *132*
Santobello v. New York, 404 U.S. 257, 92 S.Ct. 495, 30 L.Ed.2d 427 (1971), *382*
Schaefer v. State Bar of California, 26 Cal.2d 739, 160 P.2d 825 (Cal.1945), *348*
Schartner, United States v., 426 F.2d 470 (3rd Cir.1970), *386*
Scheps, Commonwealth v., 361 Pa.Super. 566, 523 A.2d 363 (Pa.Super.1987), *302*
Schware v. Board of Bar Exam. of State of N.M., 353 U.S. 232, 77 S.Ct. 752, 1 L.Ed.2d 796 (1957), *42, 50, 51*
Seattle Times Co. v. Rhinehart, 467 U.S. 20, 104 S.Ct. 2199, 81 L.Ed.2d 17 (1984), *371*
Shapero v. Kentucky Bar Ass'n, 486 U.S. 466, 108 S.Ct. 1916, 100 L.Ed.2d 475 (1988), *168, 192, 193*
Sheppard v. Maxwell, 384 U.S. 333, 86 S.Ct. 1507, 16 L.Ed.2d 600, 35 O.O.2d 431 (1966), *363, 364*, 7–8 (dissent)
Shockley v. State, 565 A.2d 1373 (Del.Supr.1989), *338, 339*
Silver Chrysler Plymouth, Inc. v. Chrysler Motors Corp., 370 F.Supp. 581 (D.C.N.Y.1973), aff'd 518 F.2d 751 (2d Cir. 1975), *249*
Skjonsby, State v., 417 N.W.2d 818 (N.D.1987), *341*
Smith v. Phillips, 455 U.S. 209, 102 S.Ct. 940, 71 L.Ed.2d 78 (1982), *385*
Sobol v. Perez, 289 F.Supp. 392 (D.C.La.1968), *132*
Sowers, State ex rel. v. Olwell, 64 Wash.2d 828, 394 P.2d 681 (Wash.1964), *213*
Sperry v. State of Florida ex rel. Florida Bar, 373 U.S. 379, 83 S.Ct. 1322, 10 L.Ed.2d 428 (1963), *129*
Spevack v. Klein, 385 U.S. 511, 87 S.Ct. 625, 17 L.Ed.2d 574 (1967), *55, 68*
Standard Oil Co, United States v., 136 F.Supp. 345 (D.C.N.Y.1955), *241*
Stangland v. Brock, 109 Wash.2d 675, 747 P.2d 464 (Wash.1987), *89*

State v. ____ (see opposing party)
State Bar of Ariz. v. Arizona Land Title & Trust Co., 90 Ariz. 76, 366 P.2d 1 (Ariz.1961), aff'd on rehearing 91 Ariz. 293, 371 P.2d 1020 (1962), *111*
State Bar v. Keller, 21 Wis.2d 100, 123 N.W.2d 905 (Wis.1963), cert. denied 377 U.S. 964 (1964), *129*
State ex rel. v. ____ (see opposing party and relator)
Stolar, Application of, 401 U.S. 23, 91 S.Ct. 713, 27 L.Ed.2d 657, 57 O.O.2d 26 (1971), *54*
Stone v. Powell, 428 U.S. 465, 96 S.Ct. 3037, 49 L.Ed.2d 1067 (1976), *97*
Strickland v. Washington, 466 U.S. 668, 104 S.Ct. 2052, 80 L.Ed.2d 674 (1984), *94, 95, 96, 98*
Summers, In re, 325 U.S. 561, 65 S.Ct. 1307, 89 L.Ed. 1795 (1945), *53*
Summers v. Thompson, 444 F.Supp. 312 (D.C.Tenn.1977), *303*
Supreme Court of New Hampshire v. Piper, 470 U.S. 274, 105 S.Ct. 1272, 84 L.Ed.2d 205 (1985), *48*

Tank v. State Farm Fire & Cas. Co., 105 Wash.2d 381, 715 P.2d 1133 (Wash. 1986), *235*
Tarasoff v. Regents of University of California, 131 Cal.Rptr. 14, 551 P.2d 334 (Cal.1976), *216*
Taylor v. Hayes, 418 U.S. 488, 94 S.Ct. 2697, 41 L.Ed.2d 897 (1974), *466*
Thomas v. Capital Sec. Services, Inc., 836 F.2d 866 (5th Cir.1988), *357*
Tillotson v. Boughner, 350 F.2d 663 (7th Cir.1965), *203*
Twomey, United States ex rel. Williams v., 510 F.2d 634 (7th Cir.1975), *94*

United Mine Workers of America, Dist. 12 v. Illinois State Bar Ass'n, 389 U.S. 217, 88 S.Ct. 353, 19 L.Ed.2d 426, 42 O.O.2d 394 (1967), *187*
United States v. ____ (see opposing party)
United States ex rel. v. ____ (see opposing party and relator)
United States for Use and Benefit of Lord Elec. Co., Inc. v. Titan Pacific Const. Corp., 637 F.Supp. 1556 (W.D.Wash.1986), *252*
United Transp. Union v. State Bar of Michigan, 401 U.S. 576, 91 S.Ct. 1076, 28 L.Ed.2d 339 (1971), *167, 188, 189*
Upjohn Co. v. United States, 449 U.S. 383, 101 S.Ct. 677, 66 L.Ed.2d 584 (1981), *200, 201, 318, 414*

Virginia v. Friedman, 487 U.S. 59, 108 S.Ct. 2260, 101 L.Ed.2d 56 (1988), *49*
Virginia State Bd. of Pharmacy v. Virginia Citizens Consumer Council, Inc., 425 U.S. 748, 96 S.Ct. 1817, 48 L.Ed.2d 346 (1976), *180*

Wade, United States v., 388 U.S. 218, 87 S.Ct. 1926, 18 L.Ed.2d 1149 (1967), *92, 350, LZJ 119*
Wainwright v. Sykes, 433 U.S. 72, 97 S.Ct. 2497, 53 L.Ed.2d 594 (1977), *97*
Walker, Application of, 112 Ariz. 134, 539 P.2d 891 (Ariz.1975), *53*
Walker, People v., 28 Mich.App. 650, 184 N.W.2d 742 (Mich.App.1970), *465*
Waller v. Georgia, 467 U.S. 39, 104 S.Ct. 2210, 81 L.Ed.2d 31 (1984), *371*
Washington v. State, 441 N.E.2d 1355 (Ind.1982), *209*

Wayte v. United States, 470 U.S. 598, 105 S.Ct. 1524, 84 L.Ed.2d 547 (1985), *379*
Wenger v. Commission of Judicial Performance, 175 Cal.Rptr. 420, 630 P.2d 954 (Cal.1981), *469*
Wheat v. United States, 486 U.S. 153, 108 S.Ct. 1692, 100 L.Ed.2d 140 (1988), *93, 95, 238, 472*
Williams v. Missouri Bd. of Probation and Parole, 661 F.2d 697 (8th Cir. 1981), *93*
Williams, United States ex rel. v. Twomey, 510 F.2d 634 (7th Cir.1975), *94*
Willner v. Committee on Character and Fitness, 373 U.S. 96, 83 S.Ct. 1175, 10 L.Ed.2d 224 (1963), *63*
Wood v. Georgia, 450 U.S. 261, 101 S.Ct. 1097, 67 L.Ed.2d 220 (1981), *238*
Woods v. Covington County Bank, 537 F.2d 804 (5th Cir.1976), *244*
Wright by Wright v. Group Health Hosp., 103 Wash.2d 192, 691 P.2d 564 (Wash.1984), *403*
Wunschel Law Firm, P.C. v. Clabaugh, 291 N.W.2d 331 (Iowa 1980), *275*

Yablonski v. United Mine Workers of America, 454 F.2d 1036, 147 U.S.App. D.C. 193 (D.C.Cir.1971), *246*

Zauderer v. Office of Disciplinary Counsel of Supreme Court of Ohio, 471 U.S. 626, 105 S.Ct. 2265, 85 L.Ed.2d 652 (1985), *67, 68, 168, 183, 190, 191, 192, 194, 284*
Zolin, United States v., 491 U.S. 554, 109 S.Ct. 2619, 105 L.Ed.2d 469 (1989), *214*

*

TABLE OF STATUTES

UNITED STATES

UNITED STATES CONSTITUTION

Art.	This Work Page
II, § 8, ¶ 3, Commerce Cl.	142
IV, § 2, Privileges & Immunities Cl.	133
Amend.	
1	42
	54
	55
	135
	138
	141
	142
	143
	179
	180
	183
	187
	188
	189
	283
	362
	371
	372
4	97
	307
5	55
	68
6	90
	93
	122
13	150
14	42
	54
	93
	187

UNITED STATES CODE ANNOTATED

5 U.S.C.A.—Government Organization and Employees

Sec.	This Work Page
500	128

18 U.S.C.A.—Crimes and Criminal Procedure

Sec.	This Work Page
203—205	487

26 U.S.C.A.—Internal Revenue Code

Sec.	This Work Page
6050I	203
	391

28 U.S.C.A.—Judiciary and Judicial Procedure

Sec.	This Work Page
21	459
144	460
	461
455	460
	461
	462
	463
	464
	466
1915(d)	155

WEST'S ANNOTATED CALIFORNIA BUSINESS AND PROFESSIONS CODE

Sec.	This Work Page
6147—6148	278

WEST'S ANNOTATED CALIFORNIA EVIDENCE CODE

Sec.	This Work Page
915(a)	215

POPULAR NAME ACTS

AGENCY PRACTICE ACT

Sec.	This Work Page
500	128

CIVIL RIGHTS ACT OF 1964

Tit.	This Work Page
VII	41

FEDERAL CONFLICT OF INTEREST ACT

Sec.	This Work Page
203—205	487

INTERNAL REVENUE CODE

Sec.	This Work Page
6050I	203
	391

JUDICIARY CODE

Sec.	This Work Page
21	459
144	460
	461
455	460
	461
	462
	463
	464
	466
1915(d)	155

*

TABLE OF RULES

FEDERAL RULES OF CIVIL PROCEDURE

Rule	This Work Page
11	71
	98
	99
	100
26(b)	441

FEDERAL RULES OF EVIDENCE

Rule	This Work Page
104(a)	214
408	400
	440
410	400

AMERICAN BAR ASSOCIATION MODEL RULES OF PROFESSIONAL CONDUCT (1983)

Rule	This Work Page
1.1	59
	74
	76
	100
	101
	184
	295
	400
	423
1.1, Comment	76
	400
1.2	85
	395
	455
	494
	500

AMERICAN BAR ASSOCIATION MODEL RULES OF PROFESSIONAL CONDUCT (1983)

Rule	This Work Page
1.2(a)	85
	285
	313
	328
	396
	397
	402
	453
1.2(b)	13
	322
	323
	499
1.2(c)	322
1.2(d)	214
	296
	325
	336
	398
1.2(e)	214
1.2, Comment	320
	395
	396
	397
1.3	59
	76
	184
	293
	295
	326
1.3, Comment	457
1.4	59
	85
	424
	500
1.4(a)	396
1.4(b)	396
1.4, Comment	397
1.5	184
1.5(a)	265
	266
	267

AMERICAN BAR ASSOCIATION MODEL RULES OF PROFESSIONAL CONDUCT (1983)

Rule	This Work Page
1.5(a) (Cont'd)	274
1.5(a)(3)	268
1.5(b)	277
	443
1.5(c)	278
1.5(d)(1)	275
1.5(d)(2)	274
1.5(e)	170
	279
	444
1.5, Comment	285
1.6	162
	163
	169
	196
	216
	219
	224
	239
	251
	335
	340
	345
	409
	410
	455
1.6(a)	163
	199
	200
	202
1.6(a), Comment	209
1.6(b)(1)	215
	329
1.6(b)(2)	207
	286
1.6, Comment	197
	200
	214
	216
1.7	163
	226

AMERICAN BAR ASSOCIATION MODEL RULES OF PROFESSIONAL CONDUCT (1983)

Rule	This Work Page
1.7 (Cont'd)	227
	232
	233
	234
	250
	383
	402
	415
	435
	436
	455
1.7—1.13	383
1.7(a)	225
	226
1.7(a)(1)	225
1.7(b)	225
	226
1.7, Comment	223
1.8	228
	229
	383
1.8 to 1.13	227
1.8(a)	228
	250
1.8(b)	210
	239
	281
1.8(b)(2)	229
1.8(c)	229
1.8(d)	229
	264
1.8(e)	230
	276
1.8(e)(2)	230
1.8(f)	162
	163
	231
	234
1.8(g)	402
1.8(h)	89
1.8(i)	250

AMERICAN BAR ASSOCIATION MODEL RULES OF PROFESSIONAL CONDUCT (1983)

Rule	This Work Page
1.8(j)(1)	230
1.9	227
	232
	239
	250
	402
1.9(a)	435
1.9(b)	210
	250
1.9(b), Comment	251
1.9(c)	250
	251
1.9(c)(1)	239
1.9, Comment	59
1.10	227
	250
	436
1.10(a)	490
1.10(b)	250
	251
1.10, Comment	227
	251
1.11	59
	227
	241
	243
	488
	491
1.11(a)	251
	383
	384
	491
1.11(c)	486
1.11(c)(2)	244
1.11(d)(1)	243
1.11(e)	244
1.12	59
	227
	421
1.12(a)	437
1.12(b)	437

AMERICAN BAR ASSOCIATION MODEL RULES OF PROFESSIONAL CONDUCT (1983)

Rule	This Work Page
1.12(c)	437
1.12(d)	421
1.13	227
	240
	244
	248
	406
	409
	410
	411
1.13(a)	247
	407
1.13(b)	248
	409
1.13(c)	410
1.13(d)	414
1.13(e)	248
	415
1.13, Comment	245
	414
	416
1.15	59
	254
	255
	261
	265
1.15(a)	255
	256
1.15(b)	255
1.15(c)	257
1.15, Comment	260
1.16	77
	294
	295
	302
	303
	410
1.16(a)	296
1.16(a)(1)	147
	200
	328

AMERICAN BAR ASSOCIATION MODEL RULES OF PROFESSIONAL CONDUCT (1983)

Rule	This Work Page
1.16(a)(1) (Cont'd)	398
1.16(a)(2)	77
1.16(b)	299
1.16(b)(1)	219
	328
	398
1.16(b)(3)	153
	247
	397
1.16(b)(5)	299
1.16(b)(6)	298
1.16(c)	154
	297
	301
	302
1.16(d)	288
	289
	302
1.16, Comment	295
	296
1.17	24
	198
	280
2.1	395
	397
	413
	453
	499
	501
2.1, Comment	395
	396
	413
	453
2.2	236
	402
	420
	421
	424
	434
	435
	436

AMERICAN BAR ASSOCIATION MODEL RULES OF PROFESSIONAL CONDUCT (1983)

Rule	This Work Page
2.2 (Cont'd)	438
	439
2.2(a)	429
2.2(a)(1)	424
	438
2.2(b)	424
2.2(c)	435
2.2, Comment	420
2.3	454
2.3(b)	455
2.3, Comment	455
3.1	293
	296
	322
	324
	344
	398
3.1(a)	325
3.2	326
3.3	239
	298
	332
	333
	334
	335
	338
	494
3.3(a)	339
	340
	345
	494
3.3(a)(1)	344
	388
	494
3.3(a)(2)	211
	219
	332
	334
	345
	494
3.3(a)(3)	347

AMERICAN BAR ASSOCIATION MODEL RULES OF PROFESSIONAL CONDUCT (1983)

Rule	This Work Page
3.3(a)(4)	211
	219
	328
	332
	334
	336
	494
3.3(b)	219
	332
	494
3.3(c)	332
3.3(d)	345
3.3, Comment	220
3.4(a)	346
3.4(b)	317
	325
	344
	359
	360
	494
3.4(c)	356
3.4(d)	315
	326
3.4(e)	323
	351
	385
	386
	388
	389
3.4(f)	319
	346
3.4b	344
3.5(a)	488
3.5(c)	356
3.6	365
	366
	373
	376
3.6(b)(5)	366
3.6(b)(6)	366
3.7	250

AMERICAN BAR ASSOCIATION MODEL RULES OF PROFESSIONAL CONDUCT (1983)

Rule	This Work Page
3.7(a)	231
	232
3.7(b)	232
3.7, Comment	231
3.8	377
3.8(a)	380
	381
3.8(b)	382
3.8(d)	389
	390
3.8(e)	366
	390
3.8(f)	24
	204
	205
	392
3.9	494
4.1	345
	381
	455
	494
4.1(a)	401
4.1(b)	219
	401
4.2	317
	318
	381
	403
4.2, Comment	318
	403
4.3	320
	404
4.3, Comment	319
	404
4.4	326
	350
	351
	380
	398
	402

AMERICAN BAR ASSOCIATION MODEL RULES OF PROFESSIONAL CONDUCT (1983)

Rule	This Work Page
5.1	67
	74
	78
5.2	67
5.3	67
	124
	200
5.4	125
	169
	280
	447
5.4(a)	124
	140
	169
	282
5.4(b)	124
	140
	282
5.4(c)	125
	126
	162
	163
	234
	281
5.4(d)	125
	126
	127
	282
5.5	447
5.5(a)	130
5.5(b)	116
	140
5.5, Comment	124
	137
6.1	146
	150
	156
	158
	162
	294
	450

AMERICAN BAR ASSOCIATION MODEL RULES OF PROFESSIONAL CONDUCT (1983)

Rule	This Work Page
6.1, Comment	146
	158
	174
	294
6.2	151
	152
	154
	295
	300
	323
6.2(a)	147
6.2(b)	148
	287
6.2(c)	153
	295
6.2, Comment	295
6.3	499
6.4	479
	499
7.1	183
	184
	186
	283
	489
	492
7.1 to 7.5	448
7.1(b)	186
7.1(c)	184
	186
7.2	184
	489
7.2(a)	157
	184
7.2(c)	157
	169
	173
	188
	281
	444
	449

AMERICAN BAR ASSOCIATION MODEL RULES OF PROFESSIONAL CONDUCT (1983)

Rule	This Work Page
7.2, Comment	157
	193
	481
7.3	157
	168
	193
	489
7.3 (former)	192
7.3(b)	190
7.3(d)	169
	173
	188
7.4	105
	184
	449
	490
7.4(a)	105
7.4(b)	105
7.4(c)	105
7.5	185
	186
	490
7.5(a)	449
7.5(c)	489
	490
8.1	56
	74
	78
8.2(b)	476
8.3	67
	74
	77
	79
8.4	59
	259
	485
	494
8.4(a)	56
	403
8.4(b)	57
	402

AMERICAN BAR ASSOCIATION MODEL RULES OF PROFESSIONAL CONDUCT (1983)

Rule	This Work Page
8.4(c)	57
	401
	494
8.4(d)	57
	379
8.4(e)	488
	491
	492
	494
8.4, Comment	486

AMERICAN BAR ASSOCIATION MODEL CODE OF PROFESSIONAL RESPONSIBILITY (1969)

Canon

Canon	This Work Page
1	74
	77
	79
2	146
	157
	167
	178
	263
	489
4	162
	224
5	162
	163
	223
	383
6	74
7	293
	312
	412
8	415
	479
	481
9	59
	226

AMERICAN BAR ASSOCIATION MODEL CODE OF PROFESSIONAL RESPONSIBILITY (1969)

Canon

Canon	This Work Page
9 (Cont'd)	227
	254
	256
	434
	491

Ethical Considerations

	This Work Page
1–1	77
1–2	77
	100
1–5	58
1–6	77
2–1	156
	294
2–2	157
2–3	157
2–12	489
2–14	105
2–15	157
2–16	263
2–17	263
	266
	274
2–20	229
	273
	274
2–23	262
2–24	270
2–25	146
	174
	270
2–25 to 2–30	323
2–26	151
	295
	322
2–27	13
	151

Ethical Considerations

	This Work Page
2–27 (Cont'd)	295
2–28	151
	152
	295
2–29	148
	154
	300
	322
2–30	77
	147
	152
	153
	295
	322
2–31	295
2–32	295
	302
3–2	124
	395
3–3	124
3–5	116
3–6	124
4–1	196
4–2	163
	198
	199
	202
4–3	197
	199
4–4	201
	414
4–5	198
4–6	198
5–2	225
5–3	225
5–7	229
	230
5–15	402
5–16	236
	414
5–18	240
	245

Ethical Considerations

	This Work Page
5–18 (Cont'd)	406
5–20	402
	420
5–24	127
6–1	74
	75
6–3	75
6–4	75
	100
6–5	74
6–6	89
7–1	311
7–3	395
	501
7–4	293
7–5	215
	395
	397
	501
7–6	396
7–7	85
	313
	396
	402
7–8	85
	396
	397
	453
	499
	501
7–9	500
7–13	377
7–16	494
7–19	306
7–21	320
	401
7–25	351
7–26	338
7–27	211
8–1	479
8–2	479
8–4	494

Ethical Considerations

	This Work Page
8–5	494
8–8	486
9–3	491
9–5	254

Disciplinary Rules

	This Work Page
1–101(A)	56
1–101(B)	56
1–102(A)(1)	56
	77
1–102(A)(2)	56
	403
1–102(A)(3)	57
	485
1–102(A)(4)	57
	259
	401
	485
	494
1–102(A)(5)	57
	379
1–102(A)(6)	57
1–103	66
	77
1–105(A)	224
2–101	173
	178
	182
2–101(1)	444
2–101(B)	173
	184
2–101(B)(6)	489
2–101(B)(18)	283
2–101(B)(20–25)	283
2–101(B)(23–25)	283
2–101(E)	283
2–101(G)	283
2–101(H)(1)	489
2–102	178
2–102(A)	183

Disciplinary Rules

	This Work Page
2–102(A)(2)	489
	491
2–102(A)(3)	345
2–102(B)	185
	449
	488
	489
2–103	178
	186
	188
2–103(A)	173
	189
2–103(B)	281
	444
	449
2–103(C)	139
2–103(D)	139
	162
	168
	281
	449
2–103(D)(4)(e)	168
2–104	178
	186
2–104(A)	189
2–104(A)(5)	193
2–105(A)	105
2–105(A)(1)	105
2–105(A)(3)	105
2–105(A)(4)	105
2–106(A)	266
	274
2–106(B)	266
	267
2–106(B)(3)	268
2–106(C)	274
2–107	170
	278
2–107(A)	444
2–109(A)(1)	324
2–109(A)(2)	324

Disciplinary Rules

	This Work Page
2–110	294
	303
2–110(A)	302
2–110(A)(1)	301
2–110(A)(2)	288
2–110(A)(3)	289
2–110(B)	296
2–110(B)(1)	398
2–110(B)(2)	297
	302
	328
	330
2–110(B)(4)	301
2–110(C)	298
2–110(C)(1)	298
2–110(C)(1)(b)	215
	328
	398
2–110(C)(1)(d)	298
2–110(C)(1)(e)	397
2–110(C)(2)—(C)(5)	298
2–110(C)(6)	298
	299
3–101	447
3–101(A)	116
	124
	140
3–101(B)	130
3–102	140
	447
3–102(A)	124
	280
	282
3–103	124
	140
	282
	447
4–101	218
4–101(A)	198
4–101(B)	163
4–101(B)(1)	218
	409

Disciplinary Rules

	This Work Page
4–101(B)(2)	198
4–101(B)(3)	198
4–101(C)(1)	202
4–101(C)(2)	211
	214
4–101(C)(3)	215
	329
	409
4–101(C)(4)	207
	286
4–101(D)	199
5–101	234
5–101(A)	153
	228
	383
5–101(B)	231
	232
5–102	231
5–102(B)	232
5–103(A)(2)	229
5–103(B)	230
5–104(B)	264
5–105	233
	234
	402
5–105(B)	415
5–105(C)	226
	415
	437
5–105(D)	242
	243
	248
	383
	490
5–106	402
5–107	231
	234
5–107(A)	281
5–107(B)	126
	163
	281

Disciplinary Rules

	This Work Page
5–107(C)	126
	127
	282
6–101	59
6–101(A)(1)	75
	295
6–101(A)(1)—(A)(3)	77
6–101(A)(2)	75
	400
6–101(A)(3)	75
6–102(A)	89
7–101	457
7–101(A)(1)	313
7–101(B)(2)	398
7–102(A)	296
	302
	330
7–102(A)(1)	324
	344
7–102(A)(2)	324
7–102(A)(4)	297
	328
	331
	388
7–102(A)(5)	344
	388
	401
7–102(A)(6)	317
	325
	344
7–102(A)(7)	214
	398
7–102(B)	218
	219
	325
7–102(B)(1)	217
	218
	333
	340
7–102(B)(2)	339
7–103	377
7–103(A)	380

Disciplinary Rules

	This Work Page
7–103(B)	381
	389
	390
7–104	318
7–104(A)(1)	317
	381
	403
7–104(A)(2)	319
	404
7–105	320
7–106(A)	356
7–106(B)(1)	347
7–106(C)(1)	351
	388
	389
7–106(C)(2)	350
	351
7–106(C)(4)	323
	385
	386
7–106(C)(6)	356
7–106(C)(7)	351
7–107	365
	366
	372
	377
7–107(B)	365
	366
7–109(A)	211
	345
7–109(B)	319
	346
7–109(C)	359
8–101(A)	486
8–101(A)(1)	488
8–101(A)(3)	488
8–103(A)	476
9–101(A)	437
9–101(B)	241
	242
	243
	383

Disciplinary Rules

	This Work Page
9–101(B) (Cont'd)	491
9–101(C)	491
	492
	494
9–102	255
	261
	265
9–102(A)	255
	256
9–102(A)(2)	257
9–102(B)	255

AMERICAN BAR ASSOCIATION
CANONS OF PROFESSIONAL ETHICS (1908)

Canon	This Work Page
12	262
	270
22	348
35	126

AMERICAN BAR ASSOCIATION CODE OF JUDICIAL CONDUCT (1990)

Canon

Canon	This Work Page
2	467
	468
2(C)	467
2A	467
2B	467
	468
3	468
3(A)(7) (former)	375
3A	468
	470
3A(1)	468
3A(2)	469
3A(3)	469
3A(4)	469

AMERICAN BAR ASSOCIATION CODE OF JUDICIAL CONDUCT (1990)

Canon

Canon	This Work Page
3A(5)	470
3A(6)	470
3A(7)	470
	471
3B	468
3B(1)	471
3B(2)	468
	471
3B(3)	469
	471
	472
3B(4)	469
3B(5)	467
3B(6)	467
3B(7)	469
3B(7)(b)	470
3B(8)	470
3B(9)	470
3C	462
	463
3C(1)	462
	463
	470
	471
3C(2)	471
3D(1)	471
	472
3D(2)	471
	472
3E(1)	470
4	472
	473
4(B)	473
4C(1)	473
5	473
5A(2)	477
5A(3)(d)(i)	476
5C(2)	476
7A(3)	477
7B(1)(c)	476

AMERICAN BAR ASSOCIATION CODE OF JUDICIAL CONDUCT (1990)

Canon

Canon	This Work Page
7B(2)	476

AMERICAN LAWYER'S CODE OF CONDUCT

Sec.	This Work Page
5.2	278
5.4	279

ARIZONA RULES OF PROFESSIONAL CONDUCT

Rule	This Work Page
1.6	216

CALIFORNIA RULES OF PROFESSIONAL CONDUCT

Rule	This Work Page
1–400(b)	319
2–100(B)	318
2–100(C)(2)	319
2–200	279
2–300	198
4–200(A)	266
5–100	401
5–200	348
5–210(C)	232

CONNECTICUT RULES OF PROFESSIONAL CONDUCT

Rule	This Work Page
1.6	216

WASHINGTON RULES OF PROFESSIONAL CONDUCT

Rule	This Work Page
1.6	216

TABLE OF OTHER AUTHORITIES

AMERICAN BAR ASSOCIATION OPINIONS ON PROFESSIONAL ETHICS

FORMAL OPINION

Sec.	This Work Page
37	244
184	492
192	486
287	333
296	491
	494
301	489
	491
306	491
	494
318	489
336	485
341	218
	333
342	242
	243
353	298
	333
	334
	335
	338
355	125
	168
	169
	281

INFORMAL OPINION

Sec.	This Work Page
1182	488
	491
1273	75

INFORMAL OPINION

Sec.	This Work Page
1314	297
	334
1318	297
1521	274

TABLE OF AUTHORITIES

Abel, American Lawyers 134 (1989), 161, 172, 481
Administration Off. of U.S. Cts., Jud. Workload Statistics (1983), 399
Amendment to Rules Regulating the Florida Bar (Fla.1987), 136
American Bar Association–American Arbitration Association Code of Ethics for Arbitrators in Commercial Disputes (1977) [Commercial Arbitrators Code], 421, 428, 431, 432, 433, 437, 443, 445, 450
American Bar Association Committee on Evaluation of Disciplinary Enforcement, Ch., Clark, Tom (1970), 65
American Bar Association, In the Spirit of Public Service, A Blueprint for the Rekindling of Lawyer Professionalism (1986), 9
American Bar Association, Minimum Standards for Criminal Justice, Freedom of the Press and Fair Trial (1967) (Medina Report), 367
American Bar Association Standards for Lawyer Discipline and Disability Proceedings (1979), 60, 65, 78
American Bar Association Standards of Practice for Lawyer Mediators in Family Disputes (1984) [ABA Family Mediation Standards], 421, 424, 427, 428, 444
American Bar Association Standards Relating to the Administration of Criminal Justice (1979)
Prosecution Function
1.1(e), p. 377
3.1(b), p. 390
3.9(a), p. 380
3.9(b), p. 380
4.1(b), p. 381
4.1(c), p. 381
4.3(a), p. 382
4.3(c), p. 382
5.2, p. 356
5.6, p. 388
5.6(b), p. 389
5.7(b), p. 350
5.8, p. 388
5.8(b), p. 386
5.9(c), p. 386
5.9(d), p. 386

Defense Function
5.2, p. 396
7.1, p. 356
7.6(b), p. 350
7.7, pp. 331, 332, 336
American Bar Association, Standards Relating to Fair Trial and Free Press (Approved Draft, 1968) (Reardon Report), 365
American Bar Association Statement of Policy Regarding Lawyers' Responses to Auditors Requests for Information (1975), 456
American College of Trial Lawyers, Principles as to Disruption of the Judicial Process (1970), 354
Aronson, Professional Responsibility: Education and Enforcement, 51 Wash.L.Rev. 273 (1976), 78, 145
Auerbach, C., What are Law Clerks For?—Comments on *Nix v. Whiteside*, 23 San Diego L.Rev. 979 (1986), 338
Auerbach, J., Unequal Justice (1976), 481
Bacon, Francis, Essays, 1598, p. 72
Bazelon, The Defective Assistance of Counsel, 42 Cin.L.Rev. 1 (1973), 91
Boston Bar Assoc. Ethics Op. 78–1 (1978), 427
Brakel, J., Judicare (1974), 164
Brennan, W., "The Responsibilities of The Legal Profession" (1968), 478–79
Brickman and Cunningham, Nonrefundable Retainers: Impermissible Under Fiduciary, Statutory and Contract Law, Fordham L.Rev. Vol. 57, p. 149 (1988), 290
Burger, Our Vicious Legal Spiral, 16 Judges J. at p. 22, 49 (1977), 452
Burger, The Special Skills of Advocacy: Are Specialized Training and Certification of Advocates Essential to Our System of Justice?, 42 Fordham L.Rev. 227 (1973), 72
Christensen, Unauthorized Practice of Law: Do Good Fences Really Make Good Neighbors—or Even Good Sense?, 1980 Amer.Bar Res.J. 159, pp. 112, 115
Code of Professional Responsibility for Arbitrators of Labor–Management Disputes, adopted by the National Academy of Arbitrators, American Arbitration Association, and Federal Mediation and Conciliation Service (1974, as amended through 1985) [Labor Arbitrators CPR], 421, 424, 428, 431, 432, 433, 437, 442, 450, 451
Connecticut Bar Assoc. Ethics Op. 35 (1982), 427, 436
Connecticut St. Bar Inf. Op. 1988, p. 186
Cramton, Crisis in Legal Services for the Poor, 26 Vill.L.Rev. 521, 529 (1981), 161

Devine, Letting the Market Control Advertising by Lawyers: A Suggested Remedy for the Misled Client, 31 Buffalo L.Rev. 351 (1982), 185

Ethical Standards of Professional Responsibility for the Society of Professionals in Dispute Resolution (1986) [SPIDR Standards], 421, 424, 428, 429, 443, 448, 450

Florida State Bar Assoc. Ethics Opin. 86–8 (1986), 426, 427, 429, 444

Freedman, M., Client Confidences and Client Perjury: Some Unanswered Questions, 136 Pa.L.Rev. 1939 (1988), 337

Freedman, M., Lawyers' Ethics in an Adversary System (1975), 317, 327

Freedman, M., Professional Responsibility of the Criminal Defense Lawyer: The Three Hardest Questions, 64 Mich.L. Rev. 1469 (1966), 317

Freedman, M., Understanding Lawyers' Ethics (1990), 317, 327

Fried, C., The Lawyer as Friend: The Moral Foundations of the Lawyer–Client Relation, 85 Yale L.J. 1060 (1976), 496

Friedman, L., A History of American Law, 1985, p. 18

Gates and Zilly, "Legal Malpractice," in Professional Responsibility: A Guide for Attorneys (1978), 85

Gellhorn, W., Individual Freedom and Government Restraints 128 (1956), 58

Gillen, Legal Malpractice, 12 Washburn L.J. 281 (1973), 86

Hays, Labor Arbitration—A Dissenting View, Yale Univ.Press at p. 113 (1966), 433

Hazard & Hodes, The Law of Lawyering 310, 312–13 (1985), 420, 439

Holy Bible, The New Testament Luke 11:46, p. 12

Hurst, The Professions in American Life in A.A.L.S. Selected Readings on the Legal Profession 67, 70–71 (West 1962), 10

Joint Conference on Professional Responsibility, Statement of the American Bar Association and Association of American Law Schools, 1, 306, 312, 419, 457, 480

Kaplan, Some Ruminations on the Role of Counsel for a Corporation, 56 Notre Dame Law. 873 (1981), 412

Kennedy, Legal Education as Training for Hierarchy, in The Politics of Law: A Progressive Critique 40–61 (Kairys ed. 1982), 482

Kentucky Bar Assoc. Ethics Op. 335 (1989), 449

Kurland, A., Our State Bar Associations: The Connecticut Bar Association, 50 A.B.A.J. 955 (1964), 29

Kutak, Whom Does the Corporate Counsel Represent?, 2 Corp. Director 1 (1981), 247

Lasswell and McDougal, Legal Education and Public Policy: Professional Training in the Public Interest, 52 Yale L.J. 203 (1943), 482
Luban, The Adversary Excuse, in The Good Lawyer, 1983, p. 360
Maine Bar Assoc. Op. 71 (1986), 449
Mallen and Smith, Legal Malpractice (3rd ed. 1989), 85, 86
Malone, The Lawyer and His Professional Responsibilities, 17 Wash. & Lee L.Rev. 191 (1960), 488
Mann, K., Defending White Collar Crime (Yale, 1986), 398
Maryland State Bar Assoc. Comm. on Ethics Opin. 80–55A (1980), 426
Massachusetts Bar Assoc. Ethics Opinion 85–3 (1985), 425
Mathew 6:24 (King James), 222
Mathews, Negotiation: A Pedagogical Challenge, 6 J.Legal Educ. 94 (1953), 399
Menkel–Meadow, Feminist Legal Theory, Critical Legal Studies, and Legal Education or "The Fem–Crits Go to Law School", 38 J.Leg.Educ. 61 (1988), 482
Michigan Bar Assoc., Mich.Opin. CI–1164 (1987), 345
Mikva, Interest Representation in Congress: The Social Responsibilities of the Washington Lawyer, 38 Geo.Wash.L.Rev. 651 (1970), 493
Mosten and Wasserstrom, The Option of Private Family Law Mediation 22 Beverly Hills B.J. at p. 118 (1988), 453
Nassau County Bar Association [Opinion 82–8] (1982), 449
National Academy of Arbitrators Comm. on Prof. Respon. Opin. No. 3 (1972), 450
National Law Journal, What America Reallty Thinks about Lawyers (Aug. 18, 1986), 14
New Hampshire Bar Assoc. Ethics Op. 1983–4/4 (1983), 426
New York City Bar Assoc. Ethics Opin. 80–23 (1981), 426, 427
Oakes, Lawyer and Judge: The Ethical Duty of Competency, in Annual Chief Justice Earl Warren Conference on Advocacy in the United States: Ethics and Advocacy at 57 (Fin. Report 1978), 79, 98
Oregon State Bar Assoc. Legal Ethics Opin. 488 (1983), 426
Patterson, L. & E. Cheatham, The Profession of Law (1971), 241, 399, 478
Pepper, S., The Lawyer's Amoral Ethical Role: A Defense, A Problem, and Some Possibilities, 1986 Amer.Bar Found.Res. J. 613, p. 497
Post, On the Popular Image of the Lawyer: Reflections in a Dark Glass, 75 Calif.L.Rev. 379 (1987), 15
Report of the Committee on the Operation of the Jury System on the "Free Press—Fair Trial" Issue, 45 F.R.D. 391 (1968) (Kaufman Report), 367

Report of the President's Commission on the Assassination of President Kennedy (Assoc.Press Ed.1964) (The Warren Report), 365
Rhode, Moral Character as a Professional Credential, 94 Yale L.J. 491 (1985), 53
Rhode, Policing the Professional Monopoly: A Constitutional and Empirical Analysis of Unauthorized Practice Prohibitions, Stanford L.Rev. (1981), Vol. 34, p. 1, pp. 115, 141, 144
Rosenberg & Sovern, Delay and the Dynamics of Personal Injury Litigation, 59 Colum.L.Rev. 1115 (1959), 399
Rosenthal, D., Lawyer and Client: Who's in Charge (1974), 396
Saltzman, Private Bar Delivery of Civil Legal Services to the Poor, 34 Hast.L.J. 1165 (1983), 164
Sandburg, Carl, The Lawyers Know too Much, 1920, p. 12
Schaefer, Federalism and State Criminal Procedure, 70 Harv.L. Rev. 1 (1956), 91
Schwartz, The Professionalism and Accountability of Lawyers, 66 Calif.L.Rev. 669 (1978), 503
Schwartz, The Zeal of the Civil Advocate, 1983 Amer.Bar Found.Research J. at p. 543, pp. 360, 503
Shakespeare, King Henry VI, 1590, p. 12
Standards of Practice for Family and Divorce Mediation of the Academy of Family Mediators [AFM Standards], 421, 424, 429, 442, 444, 448, 451
Thibout & Walker, A Theory of Procedure, 66 Calif.L.Rev. 541 (1978), 306
Thode, Canons 6 and 7: The Lawyer–Client Relationship, 48 Texas L.Rev. 367 (1970), 87
Thode, The Duty of Lawyers and Judges to Report Other Lawyers' Breaches of the Standards of the Legal Profession, 1976 Utah L.Rev. 95, p. 80
Virginia State Bar Assoc. Legal Ethics Opin. 511 (1983), 426
Watson, Canons as Guides to Action: Trustworthy or Treacherous, 33 Tenn.L.Rev. 162 (1966), 73
Weckstein, Limitations on the Right to Counsel: The Unauthorized Practice of Law, 1978 Utah L.Rev. 649, pp. 111, 121
Weckstein, Maintaining the Integrity and Competence of the Legal Profession, 48 Texas L.Rev. 267 (1970), 58, 74
8 Wigmore, Evidence 528 (McNaughton rev. 1961), p. 440
§ 2285, p. 195
§ 2291, p. 196
§ 2292, p. 197
Williams, Legal Negotiation and Settlement (1983), 400
Wisconsin Bar Assoc. Ethics Op. E–79–2 (1980), 426
Wolfram, Modern Legal Ethics (1986), 204, 398, 402, 439

*

PROFESSIONAL REPONSIBILITY

IN A NUTSHELL

SECOND EDITION

*

PART I

THE STRUCTURE, SCOPE AND SUPERVISION OF THE LEGAL PROFESSION

CHAPTER 1

INTRODUCTION TO PROFESSIONAL RESPONSIBILITY

I. THE MEANING OF PROFESSIONAL RESPONSIBILITY

Lawyers' professional responsibilities include concepts of morality, ethics, etiquette, and professional values and attitudes. When appropriately conceived, these responsibilities are necessary or desirable incidents of the functions of lawyers in society.

As recognized by a highly regarded Joint Statement of the American Bar Association and Association of American Law Schools, "[t]he grounds for the lawyer's peculiar obligations are to be found in the nature of his calling." When we understand the special services the legal profession "renders to society and the services it might render if its full capacities were realized . . . [we can] then discern what restraints are necessary to keep that office wholesome and effective." Joint Conference (1958).

Thus, lawyers' professional responsibilities are determined by their function, and include all those things that lawyers, individually and collectively, should do to best effectuate their role in society. To determine the specific responsibilities of lawyers, therefore, we must first identify what useful roles lawyers could perform and have fulfilled.

If the main goal of lawyers is to make law work, then the lawyering role is inevitably tied to the function of law itself. History teaches that law and lawyers, whether in primitive or sophisticated form, whether labeled as such or not, are essential elements of all organized societies.

Some purportedly classless—but, in fact, totalitarian—societies, as in the Soviet Union, China, and Cuba, early tried to do away with or minimize the role of lawyers, but have come to recognize the essentiality of a lawyering function if only to help implement government policies and aid in resolving inevitable conflicts among private parties. More recently, as elements of democracy and concern for fairness and due process in governmental administration emerge in eastern Europe, law and lawyers play more prominent roles.

In the United States, law always has played a particularly important role. As De Tocqueville recognized, the high regard and respect for the rule of law, and the key role of lawyers, characterized our early government and society to a greater degree than that of almost any other nation. Woodrow Wilson's comment, that in America almost every question of public policy seemed eventually to become a legal issue, has proved to be not only accurate history, but prophecy. The law has led the way to, or expressed an American moral consensus on, desegregation of the races and recognition of other civil rights, allocation of political power among the people and as between the states vis-a-vis each other and the federal government, and the most basic issues of the creation of life and its termination, as illustrated in cases dealing with birth control, abortion, organ transplants, the right to die, and capital punishment. To the astonishment of many other nations of the world, we reacted to the lawlessness of the Watergate scandal by letting the law take its course against the highest government officials, including the Attorney General and the President.

The willingness of the people to accept this major role of law in our society is not based upon necessary agreement with the results reached, nor, hardly, on admiration for the lawyers and judges involved, but basically on respect for the due process of the law. In other words, it is a preference for settling disputes by use of legal procedures and for attempting to accommodate each individual's freedom, needs, and desires through an ordered process rather than by governmental fiat or an anarcharistic "each man for himself" approach. This concern with adherence to process, even to correct defects in the legal process itself, is embedded in our Constitution and national fiber and constitutes the essence of the rule of law in the United States.

Lawyers have played key roles in establishing this process, operating it, defending and preserving it, and in reforming it. Implicit in the process is the rejection of an "end justifies the means" philosophy. Rules such as those against self-incrimination and unreasonable search and seizure instead reflect a philosophy, based on history and concern for human dignity, that a person shall not be deprived of life, liberty, or property without compliance with those safeguards of fair treatment and deliberation which we know as the due processes of law. A short-circuiting of these processes to more expeditiously punish persons supposed to be dangerous to the social order is, in the words of the late Thurman Arnold, "always a sign of psychological instability of a people." Our society relies upon lawyers, as prosecutors with a responsibility to seek conviction of the guilty but not the innocent, as defense counsel with responsibility to safeguard the rights and interests of an accused person, and as judges, at trial and on appeal, with responsibility to assure compliance with the due processes of the law.

Thus, a lawyer's duty of advocacy, in both criminal and civil cases, to represent a client with loyalty and zeal, comes not from a monetary retainer or game-like competitiveness but arises from the lawyer's role in the administration of justice. As such, the means used to foster the interests of the client are not unlimited but are inherently bound to be executed within the framework of the law. See Chapter 16, The Lawyer as an Advocate.

In addition to serving as "guardians of the due process of law", lawyers also articulate, respond to, and interpret individual and societal needs and demands which manifest themselves as legal claims. Of great importance to a law-abiding society is the role that lawyers play in individualizing the essential generality of the law. The conduct of clients is far more often influenced by their lawyers' interpretation of a statute, regulation or decision as applied to the client's particular circumstances than by any official involvement of a court or other governmental agency in the client's affairs.

Accordingly, lawyers are instrumental in accomplishing the purposes of law: the establishment and operation of governmental processes; the protection of individuals from overreaching by government; the accommodation of individual freedom with essential societal peace and order; the assertion and balanced response to, often conflicting, human wants and desires; the settling and prevention of disputes; the application of general rules and policies to individuals; the invocation and design of other means of ordering human conduct in accordance with the perceived goals of society; and, in general, the administration of justice.

These general societal roles of lawyers are effectuated through particular tasks, such as giving advice, negotiating, planning, advocating, drafting, investigating, researching, lobbying, mediating, adjudicating, teaching, writing, and, on occasion, brokering, securing financing, providing public relations, lending emotional support, and serving as a scapegoat. Clearly, not all of these tasks have the same social utility, relevancy to legal training, and implied professional responsibilities. But, in general, a lawyer's functions can be made more efficacious by the possession and exercise of a number of recurring traits, attitudes and responsibilities. These include: knowledge of law, legal processes, political theory, economics, social organization and human behavior; communication and advocacy skills; loyalty, zealousness, confidentiality, honesty, fairness, attentiveness, sensitivity and discretion; dedication to the ends of the law and adherence to its means; and—in a system dependent on lawyer participation—making legal services available to all who may need them.

Once we recognize these traits as being important for lawyers to possess, there is no assurance that they will find easy application in practice. Competency and basic integrity are essential in every case, yet disbarment and malpractice statistics belie their uniform possession by lawyers. Other responsibilities must be learned, comprehended, adhered to, and adapted. In numerous situations, a lawyer may face conflicting duties, and the application of professional standards may be far from apparent. Can a lawyer disclose confidential damaging information about a client in furtherance of the duty of candor to a court or others? How does a lawyer exercise zeal on behalf of a client who is contemptuous of and seeks to disrupt the legal system which the lawyer is bound to respect? Can a lawyer represent, often at their request, two defendants accused of participating in the same crime, or two plaintiffs in a tort action arising from the same automobile accident, or two persons seeking to create a business partnership, or a husband and wife seeking to dissolve their marital partnership? How does a lawyer for a corporation resolve conflicts between the demands of corporate officers and what the lawyer perceives as the best interests of the corporation? How can a lawyer accommodate the need to earn a living with the profession's duty to provide legal services for all who may need them regardless of their ability to pay?

This book attempts to shed light on the analysis and resolution of problems of this nature by identifying issues and relevant professional standards, and by imparting information on the reasons that lie back of specific restraints from which, according to the ABA–AALS Joint Statement, a true sense of professional responsibility must derive.

Unfortunately, for too many years, the subject of legal ethics, legal profession, or professional responsibility (as it has been variously known) did not enjoy a prominent place either in the law school curriculum or in the concerns of most lawyers. While "Watergate" focused considerable attention on the subject, too many courses, at one extreme, continued to preach pious platitudes or, at the other, present cynical roadmaps on how far one could go without risking disbarment. Although this book has its share of "shoulds", as well as "musts", its main purposes are to provide understanding and guidance for lawyers and law students by exploring underlying concepts in a variety of problematical situations common to the practice of law, to sensitize the reader to the issues involved, and to suggest the rules or other factors, including supporting rationale, that are relevant to their resolution.

Adherence to professional standards by individual lawyers is a product of a variety of sources. Fear of being caught and disciplined for one's dereliction of duties is an inadequate and, at best, partial motivation for doing the right thing. A person's basic integrity (inner disposition) and pressures in particular circumstances (situational controls) undoubtedly influence professional behavior. Many lawyers are guided by service to external concepts, including those of a religious and professional nature. An understanding and belief in the importance of the legal professions' functions in society may motivate lawyers and law students to learn, adhere to, and improve professional responsibility standards.

Contrary to common assumptions, the subject of professional responsibility is immensely practical. It involves the law of lawyering; an area all lawyers must be familiar with regardless of their field of practice. Lawyers' law deals with structure, means, and limitations upon how lawyers earn their living. In a broader and more philosophical sense, it involves an examination of the utility of the roles that lawyers have served and potentially could serve in society. Despite its many detractors, the legal profession is a useful and worthy societal institution. As such, it merits the devotion of its members who should strive to adopt and exercise those responsibilities which will make the profession, the law, and society work best. Knowledge and understanding of those responsibilities—the primary concerns of this Nutshell—are important steps to that objective.

II. PROFESSIONALISM

The problem with the practice of law today, say many practitioners, as well as non-lawyer critics, is that it has become a business rather than a profession. While the two categories are not necessarily mutually exclusive, these observers point to, among other things, Supreme Court decisions permitting commercial advertising, liberalizing rules against solicitation and denying a "learned professional" exemption from the anti-trust laws; the large increase in numbers of lawyers, including many from social and economic classes who have little in common with more genteel lawyers who had dominated the profession; more aggressive competition for clients; "Rambo" style representation of clients' interests at the cost of a decrease in civility to adversaries; an increased willingness of lawyers to sue and testify against one another; less willingness to perform pro bono services; unprecedented high salaries paid to beginning lawyers at prestigious firms; and greater concern with fees, their collection, and the "bottom line".

Some of these changes are for the better, and have eliminated practices which prompted public critics to regard professionalism as an elitist concept which prevented accountability to the public. Yet there is no doubt that there has been an increasing commercialization of the practice of law. In a recent dissenting opinion to a decision affording Constitutional protection to direct written solicitation of legal business, Justice O'Connor lamented this trend and called for a reconsideration of the lawyer advertising cases. Her criticism was grounded in the perceived decrease in lawyer professionalism:

> "One distinguishing feature of any profession . . . is that membership entails an ethical obligation to temper one's selfish pursuit of economic success by adhering to standards of conduct that could not be enforced either by legal fiat or through the discipline of the market. . . . Both the special privileges incident to membership in the profession and the advantages those privileges give in the necessary task of earning a living are

> means to a goal that transcends the accumulation of wealth. That goal is public service. . . . This view of the legal profession need not be rooted in romanticism or self-serving sanctimony, though of course it can be. Rather, special ethical standards for lawyers are properly understood as an appropriate means of restraining lawyers in the exercise of the unique power that they inevitably wield in a political system like ours. Shapero v. Kentucky Bar Association (U.S.1988) (dissenting opinion).

Justice O'Connor went on to identify other characteristics of a profession which distinguish the practice of law from other occupations: Operating a reasonably efficient and fair legal system under modern social conditions requires a trained and specialized body of experts, whose knowledge, by its nature, "cannot be made generally available and it therefore confers the power and the temptation to manipulate the system of justice for one's own ends." This may lead to abuses of the system, as in overly zealous representation of clients' interests, or abuse of the client for the lawyer's benefit. "Precisely because lawyers must be provided with expertise that is both esoteric and extremely powerful, it would be unrealistic to demand that clients bargain for their services in the same arms-length manner that may be appropriate when buying an automobile or choosing a dry cleaner."

Thus, the guiding principle for the offering of professional services is not *caveat emptor* but *credat emptor.* Since acquisition of specialized knowledge and skill is characteristic of a professional, less informed persons must place a great deal of trust in professional certification. Because lawyers typically function in circumstances which offer temptations to serve themselves at the expense of their clients, often without the client being able to detect an act of disloyalty until it is too late, professional codes require that service to the client be given primacy over profit to the practitioner. To implement these inherent professional concepts of service and learning, the legal profession has developed ethical standards and a system of internal controls, including requirements for admission to and maintenance of status in the profession. To this end, membership in the profession is limited to those who successfully complete the requisite training and education, and who have demonstrated an ability and willingness to abide by ethical standards of conduct. Restricting professional status to such individuals is not elitism but an attempt to safeguard the liberty, property and other interests of clients who must put their trust in the character and competence of professionals with whom they deal.

Admission and disciplinary controls [to be discussed in Chapter 5], however, only provide minimum standards of acceptability. The inspiration of professionalism can go further to protect the interests of clients and society. Concern with the deterioration of professional practices, and the public's unflattering perception of lawyers, led the American Bar Association to institute a Commission on Professionalism which issued its report in 1986: ". . . . In the Spirit of Public Service", modestly sub-titled: "A Blueprint for the Rekindling of Lawyer Professionalism." The report contains recommendations pertaining to law schools, practicing lawyers, bar associations, and judges, and a list of general principles which include a need for lawyers to preserve and develop professional integrity, competence, fairness, independence, courage, and a devotion to the public interest. While some of the recommendations detail and expand existing rules of ethics, the Commission recommends that all members of the Bar should resolve to abide by higher standards of conduct than the minimum required by the Model Rules of Professional Conduct and should resist the temptation to make acquisition of wealth a principal goal of law practice.

To a similar end, various ABA Sections and state bar associations have developed creeds and pledges of professionalism, and other statements of professional practice and courtesy. These documents supplement—rather than supercede or amend—existing ethical rules or disciplinary codes, and, while not binding, underscore the importance to practitioners of many professional concepts and practices. These include the need to: subordinate business concerns to professional ones; encourage respect for the law and the legal system; obey the spirit as well as the letter of rules of ethics and aid enforcement of disciplinary standards; be loyal to clients while maintaining objectivity, civility and courtesy, including being respectful of adversaries and judicial officers; encourage settlement of disputes and explore alternatives to litigation; perform pro bono services; and improve the administration of justice.

While these are worthwhile sentiments, they are often easier to state than practice. Unlike earlier times when legal services were rendered by priests to fulfill a religious or public duty, or by squires carrying out feudal or social obligations, lawyers, today, depend on earnings from professional services for their livelihood. This self-interest of practitioners—or the business of practicing law—cannot realistically be denied. Likewise, loyalty and commitment to a client's cause and confidences may sometimes run counter to consideration for the interests of others, including adversaries and tribunals. A good deal of legal ethics, and the concepts explored in this book, balance these conflicting interests of self, clients, others, and the efficient and fair administration of justice.

In general terms, the purpose of professional practice is service to others, placed before the self-interest of the practitioner, but subordinate to the social ends of the body of special learning on which the practice rests. (Hurst, 1962). For lawyers, their societal role is usually accomplished by applying their specialized talents to furthering the interests of their clients, while also earning a living for themselves from this process. But as professionals, lawyers must serve their clients within the bounds of legal and ethical limits, and, to fulfill their social duty of providing legal services to all who need them, lawyers also must be available to others who cannot afford to purchase their services.

In sum, lawyers, as professionals, are learned and skilled persons who serve others before themselves, but for the overall good of society. The essence of a profession is that the measure of success is not the gains amassed for the practitioner, but the service and social function performed.

These sentiments do not, of course, accurately describe all lawyers. The value of the concept of professionalism is not its descriptive nature but its ability to inspire practitioners to strive for a goal of service as a social good. Professional stature for lawyers will be conferred not from self-assertion, ambition, or romanticism of history, but from the fulfillment of function. Achieving the characteristics of a profession make it more likely that its members will act in the interests of the public, and lawyers' understanding of, and compliance with, ethical responsibilities that are formulated for that purpose, will help us fulfill our societal role.

CHAPTER 2

THE PUBLIC IMAGE OF LAWYERS

If professionally responsible lawyers perform useful and important functions in society, why are they so unpopular? While crude anti-lawyer jokes may be primarily a post-Watergate phenomenon, anti-lawyer attitudes certainly are not. The New Testament warns: "Woe unto you also, ye lawyers! for ye lade men with burdens grievous to be borne. . . ." Luke 11:46. Dickens ridiculed lawyers' avarice and delays, and Shakespeare has a revolutionary proclaim as a first priority, "let's kill all the lawyers." KING HENRY VI, 1590. Despite the fact that lawyers were instrumental in the American Revolution, the post-Colonial period saw the reputation of American lawyers at one of its lowest ebbs as they went about collecting debts in accordance with the inherited common-law of England, and often on behalf of English creditors. Carl Sandburg, laudatory biographer of lawyer Abraham Lincoln, also speculated: "Why is there always a secret singing When a lawyer cashes in? Why does a hearse horse snicker Hauling a lawyer away?" THE LAWYERS KNOW TOO MUCH, 1920.

More scientific opinion surveys reveal significant public scepticism regarding lawyers' honesty and ethics, and rate the legal profession below many other occupations and little better than politicians and used car salesmen.

While some of these criticisms may be merited, and others inevitable from the nature of lawyers' functions, closer analysis of these surveys and literary slights suggest that distrust of lawyers may be exaggerated and that the public itself must share much of the responsibility for lawyers' poor image.

The reputation of lawyers comes both from the actions of individual lawyers and from lawyers as a group. As individuals, lawyers represent clients. Some of those clients are not very nice. They may be accused murderer, rapists, child molesters, or drug dealers. They may be greedy business owners, heartless landlords, or polluting corporations. Yet each of those clients is entitled to legal representation, both as a matter of due process of law and because of their human dignity or corporate autonomy. (See Chapters 8 and 16). Although a lawyer's representation "does not constitute an endorsement of the client's political, economic, social, or moral views or activities" [Model Rule 1.2(b)], the public tends to blame the messenger, the lawyer, for the message, the client's cause. Many lawyers are no more fond of their clients than are their adversaries, but to give meaning to the right to representation of all those who need legal services, regardless of personal feelings, "a lawyer should not decline representation because a client or a cause is unpopular. . . ." CPR EC 2–27. Indeed, the nature of our Constitution, particularly, the Bill of Rights, mandates protection of minority rights. Freedom of speech, press, and religion would be empty platitudes without lawyers to safeguard them against suppression. The majority can protect itself through the legislative process and public pressure, but minorities, almost by definition "unpopular", require the assistance of lawyers, whom the public tends to condemn along with their clients.

The revolutionaries in Shakespeare's Henry VI, Dick the Butcher and John Cade, themselves dishonorable scoundrels, were wise in wanting to "kill all the lawyers" so that their rebellion might succeed in accomplishing their other tyrannical reforms such as outlawing literacy, killing all the scholars, courtiers and gentlemen, along with the lawyers, and burning all the laws and records of the realm, for, says Cade, "My mouth shall be the parliament of England." Yes, lawyers might get in the way of such a popular revolution. For lawyers, at least since the Magna Carta, have sought to protect individuals from oppressive governments. That has not always been a popular undertaking, but, it is, nevertheless, a desirable one.

At the same time, lawyers have been instrumental in creating the structure of governments and in operating its processes. Lawyers are, thus, also held accountable for the negative aspects of government. Big Brother needs big lawyers to effectuate the prohibitions of the criminal law, to enforce zoning laws, to collect taxes, and to regulate industrial and personal behavior. Ironically, the same legal profession which protects individuals from the excesses of government may be blamed for such excesses. The Watergate scandal is instructive on this point. Approximately half of the individuals indicted or convicted for Watergate-related crimes were lawyers, and this count does not include the lawyer President who resigned in its wake. Yet, many of the heroes who helped salvage our democratic government and respect for law were also lawyers, such as special prosecutors Cox and Jaworski, Judge Sirica, Senator Ervin, and Justice Department officials Richardson and Ruckleshaus.

Among the legal processes that we lawyers have created is the adversary system. Its rationale and criticisms will be examined in Chapter 16, but at this point it is relevant to note that it creates winners and losers, maximizes loyalties to clients as well as hostilities between parties, and often involves considerable cost and delay. The losing party is unlikely to be happy with the result, and likely to blame the legal system and the other party's lawyer, if not his own, as well. (This is often true in domestic relations matters, where there is usually no winner).

This situation gives rise to an interesting phenomenon. Public opinion surveys indicate that persons who have used the services of a lawyer frequently tend to be very critical of lawyers in general but favorably inclined toward their own lawyer. This suggests both a cause and a partial cure for lawyer unpopularity. A 1986 poll by the National Law Journal sought to identify those things that people liked least and most about lawyers. Aside from criticising lawyers for being too interested in money (an understandable and only partially refutable negative aspect of lawyers), prominent in the first category were that lawyers filed too many unnecessary lawsuits and that they manipulated the legal system without concern for right or wrong. The primary positive characteristics of lawyers were to some extent a mirror image of these criticisms: lawyers give first priority to their clients, and they are able to cut through bureaucractic red tape. Thus, lawyers are both condemned and praised for aggressively and loyally representing their clients' interests, and which it is usually depends upon whether the commentator is or is not the client so served.

To some extent, the best public relations tool available to lawyers is for each lawyer to explain to each client what is being done for that client and why, and why their adversaries' lawyers are obligated to represent their clients with equal fidelity. Yet, many clients do not want to hear such explanations (particularly while their lawyer's meter is running), and prefer a legal counsel who serves only their cause and shares their biases, economic motivations, and hostilities or suspicions toward their adversaries. The client wants a lawyer who will maximize his objectives, even if these are greedy and mean-spirited. As Professor Robert Post observed: "We hate [lawyers] . . . because they are our own dark reflection." Post, 1987.

One aspect of a lawyer's allegiance to clients that the public particularly has difficulty in understanding is the duty of confidentiality. Many fair-minded citizens were outraged when lawyers for a criminal defendant refused to reveal his confession to having murdered two other missing women, even though the lawyers had viewed their bodies, and the girls' parents pleaded in vain for information on their whereabouts. The public outrage was further fueled when the lawyers were cleared of any ethical or criminal improprieties based on their non-disclosure of client confidences. It does little good to ask members of the public whether if they were in the place of the client, they would want such confidences respected. Most people could never imagine themselves as a murderer, and believe they would merit little sympathy or respect if ever they were. In less dramatic situations, lawyers have declined to reveal their clients' fraudulent acts, or even their perjured testimony. The ethics of such protective measures on behalf of a client varies with the jurisdiction and the particular professional responsibility standards that it has adopted. But the legal profession earned little glory from the public when the American Bar Association voted to delete prospective client fraud from the Model Rules of Professional Conduct exceptions to confidentiality (while continuing provisions permitting lawyers to breach client confidentiality when necessary to defend themselves in malpractice or fee disputes). The justification for many lawyering activities of which the public may disapprove requires careful examination of relevant factors. This Nutshell introduces such inquiries, and examines whether particular practices are consistent with professionally responsible behavior and the public interest. If a practice fails to find support of this nature, it should be discarded; if it is a justifiable professional practice, then there is a need for better education of the public regarding it. For example, we need to both reform and eliminate abuses and excesses of the adversary system (including greater reliance on alternatives to litigation) while also better educating the public—and the bar—as to its merits.

Another aspect of the primacy of service to a client's interests, which is basic to the concept of professionalism, meets with both public and lawyer reproachment. That is role-differentiated behavior which requires a lawyer to act on behalf of a client in a different, often less moral, manner than the lawyer would act on her own behalf, or would prefer to act on behalf of another. Lawyers are often uncomfortable when faced with this situation, and some public and professional critics regard such role-playing as amoral behavior which permits lawyers to avoid accountability for the consequences of actions taken for a client. There is much validity in these concerns, but they are more fruitfully explored after we have examined the lawyer's role and ethical obligations more closely in other chapters. The subject will be revisited in Chapter 25.

Although the concept of professionalism draws its strength from the usefulness of the profession's functions to society, it also has tendencies which can run counter to the public interest. By its nature, professional practice must be limited to those who have acquired knowledge and skills not shared by non-professionals. When members of the profession are given a legal monopoly to perform services, and entry to the profession is limited by standards set and enforced by the profession, the potential for abuse is considerable. Thus, the legal profession has been subject to public criticism for excluding non-lawyers from performing most legal services, for unnecessarily limiting admission to practice—even to lawyers from another jurisdiction—and for using this economic monopoly to maintain high fees, perform unnecessary tasks, and engage in other delaying tactics to the benefit of lawyers' income but to the detriment of clients and the public. As more fully explained in Chapter 5, on Admission and Disciplinary Standards and Procedures, and Chapter 7, on the Unauthorized Practice of Law, such entry and competitive restrictions should be narrowly drawn to accomplish legitimate protection of the public, and not used to foster self-serving economic protectionism. In this manner, the public's interest will be served, whether or not the profession's image is improved.

Public criticism of lawyer disciplinary procedures as too little, too slow, and too selective has much merit. Several states, and the American Bar Association, are seeking reforms to bring about greater efficiency in this process, but public distrust on issues of this nature may never be completely dissipated so long as the legal profession controls its own admission and disciplinary process.

Many members of the public also have been critical of the recent leeway allowed for advertising by lawyers, and of the substantial increase in the number of persons admitted to practice law. Although both of these developments would tend to foster competition within the profession, and should appeal to our free-market oriented critics, others find the advertising offensive and "unprofessional" and the growth in the bar as not justified by a public need and conducive of too much emphasis on economic "bottom-line" considerations by lawyers. It is often noted that there are twenty times the number of lawyers per capita in the United States than in Japan, and that this may explain why we have become a debtor nation while Japan has become one of our principal creditors. In fact, however, this compares all American lawyers with only Japanese litigators, or barristers. Many more Japanese law school graduates perform lawyering, or solicitor-type functions, but because of an extraordinary low passage rate on the Japanese national bar exam, very few are admitted to practice in their courts. Whether because of the scarcity of people admitted to the bar, or for other cultural reasons, delays in adjudication in Japan are even more lengthy than those in the United States. Would our public really prefer that system? The real problem is not too many lawyers, but too many chasing too few paying clients. Former President Jimmy Carter was correct when he stated that we were overlawyered and underrepresented. We need to develop better ways of matching the need for legal services (usually by those who lack adequate means to pay for them) with lawyers able to serve those needs, and to devise methods of compensating such lawyers. Interestingly, granting more freedom for lawyers to advertise and market legal services may be a partial means to this end.

In sum, many factors contribute to the lawyer's poor public image, and many measures may be necessary to improve it. Among these are better articulation, practice and enforcement of the standards of professional responsibility which are discussed in this book. A more accurate understanding of the lawyer's role and the reasons for the ethical obligations is also needed by both lawyers and the public. Education to serve those objectives must take place in universities and secondary schools as well as law schools and through the efforts of individual lawyers as well as the organized bar.

For most lawyers, however, our satisfaction must come from knowledge that we are performing an important social function in a responsible manner, and not from public adoration. Professor Lawrence Friedman aptly characterized the history, and likely future, of the American lawyer as one who has "played a useful role, sometimes admired, but rarely loved." L. Friedman, A History of American Law, 1985.

CHAPTER 3

STANDARDS OF PROFESSIONAL RESPONSIBILITY

One common characteristic of a profession, as noted in Chapter 1, is the development of a code of ethics. These codes are designed to reinforce the basic premise of professionalism that service to clients and the public has priority over the self-interest of the practitioner. Because of the vulnerability of clients to the superior knowledge and skills of lawyers, the codes prescribe conduct, or prohibit misconduct, in situations where a lawyer might be tempted to serve herself at the expense of the client. Other standards protect the interests of tribunals and third-parties by constricting lawyer behavior—even for the benefit of clients—involving dishonesty, misrepresentation, or disruption to the administration of justice.

The adoption of a professional code, however, does not necessarily carry with it a means of enforcement. While a "spirit of public service" and influences of peer pressure may induce voluntary compliance by a substantial proportion of professionals, some disciplinary enforcement mechanism usually will be found necessary. In the United States, the enforcement of lawyers' professional codes is a responsibility of individual states and other admitting jurisdictions. (See Chapter 5). These authorities also exercise the legal power, through courts or legislatures, to adopt ethical standards which bind lawyers within their jurisdiction.

Nevertheless, the organized bar, particularly the American Bar Association, has played a major role in the articulation of ethical standards for the legal profession. Initially these standards provided non-binding guides for lawyer conduct, which may have been looked to, and occasionally incorporated, by courts having disciplinary authority. More recently, state and federal jurisdictions—at the urging of the bar—have specifically adopted, sometimes in amended form, the prescriptive rules recommended by the American Bar Association (ABA).

The first codification of standards of ethics in the United States was accomplished by the Alabama State Bar Association in 1887. The Alabama Canons of Ethics incorporated many of the principles proposed in the famous George Sharswood legal ethics lectures to students at the University of Pennsylvania and first published in 1854. Drawing on these and other sources, the American Bar Association, in 1908, adopted the Canons of Professional Ethics, containing 32 canons of professional behavior. These were subsequently amended, in part, and supplemented by an additional 15 canons. The Canons had the advantage of brevity, but they combined general statements of high principles, specifically enumerated duties, appeals to conscience, and particularized prohibitions, without any clear guide as to which statement fell within which category.

In 1964, the then ABA President, later Justice, Lewis F. Powell, appointed a special committee to examine the Canons and make recommendations for changes. The Committee concluded that the Canons needed revision in four principal particulars: "(1) There are important areas involving the conduct of lawyers that are either only partially covered in or totally omitted from the Canons; (2) Many Canons that are sound in substance are in need of editorial revision; (3) Most of the Canons do not lend themselves to practical sanctions for violation; and (4) Changed and changing conditions in our legal system and urbanized society require new statements of professional principles."

Consequently, the Committee proposed, and the ABA House of Delegates adopted in 1969, a new "Code of Professional Responsibility". In form, at least, the Code was a drastic departure from the Canons, but it incorporated most of their substance and many of the interpretative decisions which had been rendered by the ABA's advisory committees on professional ethics.

The Code is much longer and more detailed than the Canons, and is divided into three separate but interrelated parts. There are nine Canons, stated to be "statements of axiomatic norms," which express in general terms the standards of professional conduct expected of lawyers. Each Canon then is implemented by a series of Ethical Considerations (EC) and Disciplinary Rules (DR). The Ethical Considerations were "aspirational in character and represent the objectives toward which every member of the profession should strive," and also were intended to "constitute a body of principles upon which the lawyer can rely for guidance in many specific situations." The Disciplinary Rules are mandatory statements of "the minimum level of conduct below which no lawyer can fall without being subject to disciplinary action". CPR Preamble. The Code also contained rather lengthy footnotes which were intended to relate its provisions to the earlier Canons and interpretative opinions, and were not intended to be annotations of the views of the drafting committee.

The Code of Professional Responsibility was adopted, with minor modifications and omissions, in almost every state and the District of Columbia, and the federal courts regarded it as a source of authoritative guidance. California maintained its own rules format but incorporated many provisions of the Code. A few states incorporated all or selected Ethical Considerations as obligatory, while in some others the adoption was limited to the Disciplinary Rules, although the Ethical Considerations were available for consultation as interpretative aids.

John F. Sutton, the reporter for the Special Committee which drafted the Code, had expressed his hope that the Code would improve upon the old Canons by separating the guiding principles from the prohibitory rules. The latter should be penal in nature and spelled out with particularity, while the former should be affirmative, clear, candid explanations calculated to appeal to the lawyer's intelligence, and should convey the reasons supporting the specific restraints as well as the profession's ideals and aspirations. While, in general, the Disciplinary Rules have fulfilled this standard, the Ethical Considerations are a hodge podge of inspirational guides, reasons for Disciplinary Rules, specific prohibitions, or admonitions that were apparently considered too demanding, or out of accord with common practice, to qualify as Disciplinary Rules. Some of the specific standards probably should be regarded as binding, although they are not also contained in the Disciplinary Rules, while others repeat Disciplinary Rules, but not always in the same language, giving rise to interesting problems of interpretation as to their mandatory character.

Oddly enough, the Code of Professional Responsibility appears to suffer from many of the same defects which the Committee found in the Canons of Professional Ethics. To some extent, changing conditions in our legal system and society, as well as constitutional decisions, have mandated amendments to the Code in almost every year since its adoption. This has been particularly true of Canon Two, which stated that: "A Lawyer Should Assist the Legal Profession in Fulfilling Its Duty to Make Legal Counsel Available," but was followed by a number of Ethical Considerations and Disciplinary Rules which presented formidable obstacles to any lawyer attempting to carry out this objective. Some of these rules regarding advertising, group legal services, and prepaid legal services have since been amended in response to Supreme Court decisions and Justice Department threats.

In its major concern with the courtroom advocacy role of the lawyer, the Code failed to adequately provide for the pluralistic nature of the legal profession which includes practice in administrative proceedings and other specialized areas of law, in legal clinics and other groups, as employees of government and corporate entities, and as subordinates in law firms or supervisors of other lawyers, paralegals, and related employees.

Despite its wide adoption and numerous advances, there was considerable dissatisfaction with the CPR, and less than ten years after its promulgation, the ABA, in 1977, appointed a new "Commission on the Evaluation of Ethical Standards". Known as the Kutak Commission, after its first chairman, the late Robert J. Kutak, and guided by its Reporter, Professor Geoffrey C. Hazard, Jr. of Yale Law School, this body produced a series of drafts of proposed "Model Rules of Professional Conduct". Beginning with the first published discussion draft in January 1980, the

Commission revised and refined its proposed rules in response to criticism and comments of members of the bar, government, and public. After considerable debate, some compromise, and a few close votes, the ABA House of Delegates (the organization's main policy-making agency) adopted The Model Rules of Professional Conduct in August 1983.

The Model Rules reject the somewhat confusing dichotomy between aspirational and binding principles of the Code, and adopt a Restatement format of "black-letter" rules followed by explanatory Comments. Only the Rules, however, were adopted as authoritative, and the Comments were intended as guides to interpretation which explain and illustrate the meaning and purpose of the Rule. Model Rules, Scope. Most publications of the Model Rules also contain comparisons to the CPR provisions for each Rule, and the first "Proposed Final Draft" of May 30, 1981, contained research notes on Legal Background for each Rule, but those notes were not adopted and, while useful for background research, "are not intended to affect the application or interpretation of the Rules or Comments." RPC Scope.

While state adoptions of the Model Rules came more slowly than had been the case with the Code, approximately two-thirds of the states, as of 1990, have adopted the substance of the Rules' provisions. In light of the debate concerning the ABA adoption of some of the more controversial provisions in the Model Rules, it is not surprising that several states have modified some of these provisions. The principal modifications have concerned the scope of confidentiality of information relating to representation of a client, advertising and solicitation, and, in fewer cases, fees, conflicts of interest, and public service obligations. While the details of these provisions will be discussed in the chapters specifically devoted to those topics, it may be noted that the state modifications usually were influenced by existing rules and traditional practices in the adopting jurisdiction, proposals of the Kutak Commission or of other proponents—which were rejected by the ABA House of Delegates—or intervening decisions of the United States Supreme Court announcing constitutional limitations on state regulation of lawyer conduct. For example, on matters of confidentiality, a few jurisdictions opted for greater disclosure obligations (similar to the Kutak Commission proposal), including mandatory disclosures to try to prevent the most serious crimes of violence, while other states narrowed the occasions on which a lawyer could "blow the whistle" on a client.

Some states have rejected the Rules format, preferring to incorporate the substance of changes into their existing Code of Professional Responsibility structure. Even states which have not adopted the Model Rules, such as California, have studied them and revised their own rules, substantially or piece-meal, to reflect new and improved concepts in the Rules. While adopting the format of the Model Rules, effective January 1, 1991, the District of Columbia has enacted substantial modifications and additions to the Rules, including a highly controversial rule permitting non-lawyers who assist in rendering legal services to be partners in law-firms.

The Model Rules themselves have been amended several times since their adoption in 1983. Some of these amendments respond to Supreme Court decisions expanding constitutional protections of advertising and solicitation, others, such as modifications to the conflict of interest rules, attempt to clarify the Rules without altering their substance, and, in February 1990, the House of Delegates approved two new provisions. In response to recent Department of Justice attempts to elicit information about suspected drug offenders by questioning their attorneys, Rule 3.8(f) places ethical restrictions on prosecutorial subpoenas of defense counsel, while new Rule 1.17 is the result of a successful effort by the California bar to persuade the ABA to adopt its rule permitting the sale of a law practice, including goodwill, to another lawyer or law firm. Understandably, most states have not had, or taken, the opportunity to amend their versions of the Model Rules to conform to the ABA modifications.

Despite the many, mostly minor, variations, among the states, the Model Rules now constitute the governing ethical standards in a majority of American jurisdictions. Nevertheless, the pre-existing Code of Professional Responsibility continues to be viable, in whole or in part, in a number of states, and lawyers practicing in such jurisdictions, as well as serious students of professional responsibility, must continue to take account of the Code's provisions.

This "Balkanization" of ethical norms in the United States is regrettable. There are fears—probably unfounded, but possible in the area of disclosure of client confidences—that a lawyer, perhaps admitted to practice in two states, may be required to do in one state what he is forbidden from doing in another. While one would hope for greater uniformity among the states regarding ethical expectations of lawyer behavior, the present diversity reflects the independence of each state as an admitting and disciplinary jurisdiction, and reinforces the fact that professional responsibility does not constitute a simplistic application of common morality but involves multi-source concepts about which reasonable minds can differ.

Although the Model Rules, and especially the Commentary, lack the inspirational language of the Canons, and some of the more general guiding principles of the Code, there is no doubt that the Rules provide more realistic and detailed boundaries for lawyer conduct. With one controversial exception for pro bono service, the Rules eschew non-mandatory "shoulds" or the discretion of "may" in favor of the obligation of "shall" or "shall not" as prescriptions for lawyer behavior.

As an educational tool, in law school or continuing education programs, the Model Rules also constitute an improvement over the earlier ABA standards. Of particular value is the functional organization of the Model Rules which gives more explicit (but still limited) recognition to lawyers acting as advisers, intermediaries, evaluators, and negotiators, and to those representing entities or employed by government.

As had been the case with the Canons and Code, the Model Rules (in a reversal of the original Kutak Commission language) disclaim any intention to affect civil liability. Some courts, however, have relied upon the ethical standards in malpractice, fee, and other civil and criminal disputes. (See Chapter 6). "The Rules are designed to provide guidance to lawyers and to provide a structure for regulating conduct through disciplinary agencies." RPC Scope. However, the Model Rules, like the Code and Canons, do not prescribe disciplinary procedures or a measure of sanctions, which are within the authority of disciplinary jurisdictions and are the subject of other recommended standards adopted by the American Bar Association.

The creeds and recommendations for lawyer professionalism endorsed by the ABA and various state bars deal with ethical practices by lawyers but are not intended to be binding nor to alter the Model Rules or disciplinary codes of the states. Other statements of standards for professional responsibility, most notably the American Lawyer's Code of Coduct, proposed by the American Trial Lawyers Foundation as an alternative draft to the ABA Model Rules and CPR, have influenced the adoption of specific rules in some states.

CHAPTER 4

THE ROLE OF THE ORGANIZED BAR

Organized bar groups, especially the American Bar Association, have played a key role in the articulation of ethical standards for lawyers. (Chapter 3). Bar associations at the state, local and national levels also perform important functions in the interpretation and application of these standards, and many states rely upon the organized bar to initiate and screen disciplinary matters enforcing ethical rules. Moreover, several of lawyers' professional responsibilities can be more effectively performed by concerted action of bar groups than by reliance upon individual initiative. These include the obligation to make legal services available to all who may need them, the establishment and maintenance of legal educational standards, policing of the unauthorized practice of law, providing last resort redress for clients defrauded by lawyers, aiding law reform, and improving the selection of judges and judicial administration.

Many of these responsibilities have been undertaken by professional organizations of lawyers which may have been originally formed to pursue and protect their members' economic and social interests. Thus, bar organizations from their inception to date have sought to serve the sometimes conflicting dual objectives of trade associations and of institutional partners in the administration of justice.

I. DEVELOPMENT OF THE ORGANIZED BAR

Despite the strong influence of English law and customs in the United States, American lawyers have not seen fit to organize themselves strictly on the basis of function. In England, and some commonwealth countries, only barristers are authorized to appear in the courts, with the exception of some lower and local tribunals, while solicitors perform most of the tasks of office lawyers. Barristers are admitted to practice through the Inns of Court, which furnish office space, meals, fellowship, a limited legal education, and, with some governmental surveillance, exercise disciplinary control over the Bar. Solicitors are subject to regulation by the Law Society, presided over by a Council and Master of the Rolls. While membership in the Law Society is voluntary, it has legislative authority to exercise jurisdiction over all practicing solicitors.

The first efforts at organization in America took place on a local level in the middle and late eighteenth century. Lawyers joined these local bar associations for social interaction, joint library facilities, or to control admission and discipline of practitioners. Some of these latter efforts tended to so limit competition that the public counter-reacted and denied licensing powers to the organized bar for years to come. Indeed, the general public aversion to lawyers was so strong after the American Revolution and during the height of Jacksonian Democracy that some states abolished all standards for admission to practice law and sought to suppress or eliminate the legal profession in its entirety.

The modern movement for American bar organization began after the Civil War. In 1870, the Association of the Bar of the City of New York was organized by a number of prestigious lawyers to fight political corruption in that city, and has continued to be involved in law reform efforts. The Association has had a somewhat restrictive membership policy designed to encourage high moral character and public service, but, in its earlier years, selectivity was sometimes difficult to distinguish from discrimination.

The first state-wide bar association was organized in Connecticut in 1875. Similar to local bar associations which preceded it and state and national bar associations which came later, the purposes of the State Bar Association of Connecticut were stated to be: "to uphold and improve the standard of professional qualifications, to maintain the honor and dignity of the profession of the law, to aid all proper measures for the improvement of the jurisprudence of the state, the organization of courts and mode of practice and to promote social intercourse among its members." A. Kurland (1964).

A few years later, in 1878, the American Bar Association was formed by a group of distinguished and generally affluent eastern and southern lawyers who met annually at the vacation resort of Saratoga Springs, New York. Again, the organizing motivation was a mixture of concern with improving legal education and standards for admission to the bar and an opportunity for pleasant socializing with one's peers. Around the turn of the century, the ABA became more of a national organization, attracting a larger membership and leaders who were strong advocates, trial lawyers, and speakers. In the next few years, however, business lawyers and public servants took over leadership of the bar and it retained a conservative outlook and image. National organization caught on and expanded in the 1920's when the ABA enthusiastically embraced the movement to improve standards of legal education and admission to the bar. ABA efforts during this period resulted in the first requirements of a minimum period of formal legal education, implementation of canons of legal and judicial ethics, organization of the American Law Institute and the Conference of Commissioners on Uniform State Laws, and initiation of the *American Bar Association Journal.* The Association also engaged in political action, generally of a conservative nature, but carried on in the name of improving the administration of justice, and began to seek relationships and input from organizations of lawyers in other countries as well as those of the states.

The American Bar Association has a Board of Governors, which functions as an executive body, and a House of Delegates which, since 1936, has been the principal policy-making segment of the Association. Represented in the House of Delegates are members from the various states, larger local bar associations, ABA subject-matter oriented sections, conferences of judges, divisions of law students, young lawyers, and senior lawyers, certain affiliated organizations, and a few at-large members. ABA membership is open to any person of good moral character who is in good standing in a Bar of a state, territory or possession of the United States. Law students can substantially participate in the activities of the Association by membership in the Law Student Division. Approximately half of the lawyers in the United States now belong to the ABA, and the public and national government often regard the Association as speaking on behalf of the American legal profession.

The ABA's current range of activities is massive. There are standing committees dealing with perennial topics such as professional ethics and responsibility, continuing legal education, judicial selection, tenure and compensation, lawyer referral services, legal aid, and professional discipline, and with more contemporary concerns of alternative dispute resolution, environmental law, national security, lawyer competence and professional liability, law practice in the military, legal assistants, professional utilization and career development, public education, and specialization. In addition, there are a number of forum committees in specialized areas, conferences with other professions, and special committees and commissions on subjects ranging from delivery of legal services to the tort liability insurance system, and to special concerns of the elderly, mentally disabled, and women, minority, and government lawyers. Much of the educational and informational work of the ABA is carried on through its sections and divisions which are largely organized by practice or judicial functions but also include economics of law practice, individual rights and responsibilities, legal education and admission to the bar, and separate divisions of judges, senior lawyers, young lawyers and law students.

The ABA supports activities of affiliated organizations such as the American Bar Foundation, which conducts and supports social science research on the legal profession, and the American Bar Endowment which, among other things, provides group insurance for ABA members. Liaison is maintained with related organizations representing the judiciary, government lawyers, bar executives, counsel and examiners, law schools, law reformers, and women and minority lawyers.

Because of earlier restrictive ABA membership requirements, or incompatibility of interests and objectives, a number of special-interest bar associations have been organized. The National Bar Association was formed by Black lawyers in 1925, and, while its members are now welcome into the ABA, the National Bar Association continues to represent the interests of Black persons and lawyers. There is an active Black American Law Students Association, and Hispanic and Asian lawyers and law students have organized national and local bar associations.

The National Association of Women Lawyers was organized around the turn of the century and has been growing in membership, along with a number of state and local bar associations primarily concerned with women's issues.

Other associations of lawyers are organized around special areas of law practice, such as the American Patent Law Association, the Federal Bar Association, National Colleges for District Attorneys and for Criminal Defense Attorneys, the National Legal Aid and Defender Association, and the Association of Trial Lawyers of America. Law teachers are involved in the Association of American Law Schools and the Society of American Law Teachers. The American Judicature Society, organized in 1913, has worked, along with the American Bar Association, to improve court organization and structure and to support merit selection of judges.

Since 1936, the National Lawyers Guild has provided a more activist and liberal alternative to the American Bar Association, and has opened its membership to law students, legal secretaries, para-professionals, and other legal workers.

Over the years, the ABA has been involved in a large number of professional and political activities. The Association has been a major force in improving legal education, accreditation of law schools, education in professional responsibility, formulation of ethical practice standards, and selection of federal judges. While its greatest concern has been with issues that directly affect the administration of justice or the economic interests of its members, the ABA's leadership also has been prominently involved in fighting communism, educating youth about law, and any number of political and social issues.

Until approximately the mid–1960s the American Bar Association could be fairly characterized as a conservative force in American politics. Since that time, the ABA has taken an increasingly activist role in extending legal services to the poor and middle classes, protecting civil rights, and seeking constitutional, legislative, and other political reforms. To some extent, this activity has been prompted by external forces, such as Supreme Court decisions, but it also responds to a general social concern of the Bar's leadership as well as the more liberal views of its younger and broader membership. The members of the American Bar Association, however, like lawyers in general, encompass the entire spectrum of political views and represent, in their own outlook and that of their clientele, all elements of American society. Consequently, the ABA is pressured to become more responsive to the social, economic and political issues of the day, but risks alienation of a substantial segment of its membership when it responds to such pressures. For example, a (since repealed) resolution supporting a woman's right to choose to have an abortion, prompted a flurry of indignant member resignations and critical mail. Thus, the Association continues to face the perpetual organizational dilemma of sticking close to its conservative charter purposes of improving the administration of justice, legal education and standards for admission to the bar, and alienating the political and social activists among its members, or taking stands on the controversial issues of the day and disillusioning another portion of its membership.

II. STATE BAR ASSOCIATIONS; MANDATORY MEMBERSHIP

For most lawyers, participation in organized bar activities is through one of the many state and local bar associations. Most every metropolitan area and rural county has a local bar association which attracts the membership of practitioners interested in social interaction, educational programs, public relations, and programs to serve the bar and the public such as lawyer referral services. attorney fee arbitrations, and ethical advisory committees.

Similar activities may be conducted on a state-wide basis along with more direct involvement in regulatory functions such as admission and disciplinary procedures. These functions and other considerations have induced almost two-thirds of the states to require membership in their state bar association as a condition of practicing law. This type of "integration" of the bar was recommended by the American Judicature Society in 1913, and North Dakota was the first state to so integrate its bar, by statute, in 1921. Thirty-two other states and territorial jurisdictions have since embraced "unification" (as it also is known) of their bars by legislation, court order, or court action pursuant to statutory authorization. A few jurisdictions maintain both voluntary and unified bars (which, in some cases, was brought about by—long since abandoned—attempts to avoid racial integration of the voluntary association when the bar was unified).

Mandatory membership in an integrated bar association has been controversial since its inception. All lawyers in a jurisdiction are required to pay bar dues to support the association's activities—which presumably benefit their members or the administration of justice. This requirement eliminates "free-riders" and provides substantial resources for bar association functions and programs. Not all of an association's activities, however, are endorsed by all of its members, particularly as the relationship of the bar program to the practice of law becomes more strained. Consequently, there have been frequent attempts to prevent or dissolve the integration of state bars or to preclude the expenditure or collection of involuntary dues to support questioned programs.

The Supreme Court first considered a challenge to the constitutionality of the unified bar in *Lathrop v. Donohue* in 1961. A Wisconsin lawyer had sued for a refund of his $15 annual dues, paid under protest, because the State Bar, which had been integrated by court order, expended funds to support legislative activity which he opposed. While no one rationale was endorsed by a majority of the Court, seven justices did join in a holding affirming the constitutionality of Wisconsin's integrated bar, but no definitive disposition was made regarding the rights of dissident members to avoid being compelled to contribute to political causes which they opposed.

Analogies, not appreciated by many leaders of the bar, have been made to the compulsory dues of union-shops, whereby employees have to join the union selected to represent them in order to retain their jobs. Supreme Court decisions in compulsory union-dues cases have recognized a First Amendment right of dissident members to a refund or discount of that part of the union fee that is used for non-collective bargaining related activities, or for political or ideological purposes, and to receive an accounting of union fee supported expenditures, a reasonably prompt opportunity to challenge expeditures before an impartial arbitrator, and to have the questioned funds put in escrow pending the arbitrator's decision. E.g., Chicago Teachers Union v. Hudson (U.S.1986).

A number of courts have applied the union precedents to challenges to unified bar expenditures for activities ranging from support for lawyer spouse and social functions, promotion of prepaid legal services (all of which were upheld in Michigan), to opposition to tort reform legislation (partially prohibited in New Hamshire), to advocacy on behalf of the Nicaraguan Sandinistas (decision, and payment of full dues, deferred in Puerto Rico). While the criteria applied in each of these cases may vary with the wording of the purposes of the unified bar expressed in its charter, the closer the relation of the questioned expenditure to fostering the competence and integrity of the legal profession and the efficient administration of the courts, the more likely that a court will approve compulsory dues to support it. In response to challenges of this nature, unified bar associations in Florida and Michigan, among other states, have instituted refund and specified-purpose dues shifting to allow individual members to avoid contributing to causes which they do not support.

Some members of the unified State Bar of California have been uncomfortable with the State Bar's involvement in a number of political and social issues whose relation to the legal profession and justice system was less than apparent. Among other issues, the annual Conference of Delegates had considered proposals for a nuclear weapons freeze, gun control, repeal of draft registration, a holiday in honor of Martin Luther King, Jr., and participation of the United States in the Olympic games. Conservative members were especially unhappy to see their mandatory dues support Bar lobbying for comparable worth and against harsher criminal penalties. The criticisms ripened into open warfare when the State Bar President, in 1982, launched a program to preserve judicial independence and integrity, which was widely construed as a campaign to prevent the recall of then Chief Justice Rose Bird and other liberal justices who needed voter approval to retain their seats on the state supreme court.

A suit was filed, not only to halt this campaign but to enjoin the State Bar from lobbying, filing amicus briefs which take positions opposed by its members, and financing the Conference of Delegates' debates on political and ideological causes. The suit effectively sidelined the State Bar's participation in the 1986 judicial election which removed the Chief Justice and two colleagues from office, but a narrow majority of the newly-constituted state supreme court ruled in 1989 that, while election campaigning was forbidden, the State Bar could use mandatory dues to support other allegedly political activities which were germane to its broad statutory functions. Rejecting the lower court's reliance on analogies to the union-shop cases, the state supreme court found that the State Bar was a governmental agency which may use unrestricted revenues from dues, taxes, or other sources for any purpose within its authority.

In June 1990, the United States Supreme Court unanimously reversed, and held that while the integrated bar and compelled association was justified by the State's interest in regulating the legal profession and improving the quality of legal services, and the Bar may fund activities germane to those goals out of mandatory dues, it may not so fund activities of an ideological nature which fall beyond those areas. In attempting to define the line between permissible and impermissible mandatory funded activities, the Court rejected California's reliance on the State Bar's broad statutory charter to aid in all matters pertaining to the advancement of the science of jurisprudence or the improvement of the administration of justice. Instead, the high Court reiterated its holding in *Lathrop* that the guiding standard must be whether the challenged expenditures are necessarily or reasonably incurred for regulating the legal profession or improving the quality of legal service available to the people of the state. Recognizing that drawing the line will not always be easy, the Court noted that the extreme ends of the spectrum are clear: "Compulsory dues may not be expended to endorse or advance a gun control or nuclear weapons freeze initive; . . . [but] petitioners have no valid constitutional objection to their compulsory dues being spent for activities connected with disciplining members of the bar or proposing ethical codes for the profession." Keller v. State Bar (U.S.1990).

The Court also rejected California's attempt to distinguish the union-shop precedents and stated that the State Bar could meet its obligations to its members by applying the procedures of *Chicago Teachers Union v. Hudson,* supra, or some alternate procedure that would be better judged upon a more fully developed trial record. Finally, and perhaps significantly, the Court declined to determine the petitioners' broader First Amendment claim, which had not been initially considered by the California courts, for an injunction against use of the integrated State Bar of California name to advance political and ideological causes or beliefs beyond those for which mandatory dues is justified—even though they received voluntary financial support.

Not all challenges to state unified bars have been directed at their involvement in political and ideological activities. Institutional efforts to aid the availability of legal services, a professional obligation of lawyers, have been questioned when they have mandated pro bono service by individual lawyers or required that interest on trust funds held for clients be paid to a bar fund used to support legal services for the needy. (See Chapters 8, 9, and 13).

Attacks on the unified bar have not been limited to judicial actions. There are legislative movements to restrict integrated bar functions to administration of the admission and disciplinary processes, for which mandatory dues may be extracted, while leaving other activities to voluntary bar associations which, presumably, would attract the membership of lawyers who supported their trade-association or public service programs. Sunset legislation, which requires state agencies to periodically justify their existence through detailed studies and reports, also has been applied to unified bar associations in some states.

While there is hardly any issue today which will command overwhelming support of as heterogeneous and outspoken a group as lawyers, bar associations, whether integrated or voluntary, whether national, state, or local, still substantially influence public policy issues affecting lawyers and the administration of justice. Consequently, involvement in organized bar activities can provide an excellent opportunity for interested lawyers to enhance the volume and persuasiveness or their professional voice.

III. COMMITTEES ON PROFESSIONAL ETHICS

The American Bar Association and many state and local bar associations have created committees which render opinions on questions of legal ethics for the guidance of inquiring lawyers. These committees apply the applicable rules to fact situations presented by the inquirer. In general, the committees have no jurisdiction to adjudicate grievances or administer discipline, but are concerned with providing guidance for future conduct.

Some committees try to provide quick responses by letter or telephone to aid inquiring lawyers in resolving pending ethical problems. The ABA Ethics Hotline Service provides references to Association standards and opinions, and some state and local committees have similar telephone "hotline" services which try to give non-binding responses to the questions posed by the caller.

When new, recurring, or significant questions are raised, the committee may render a formal opinion, which is more thoroughly researched, discussed and articulated.

The formal opinions are usually published in the association periodical or otherwise made available for the general information of the bar. Opinions of the ABA Committee on Ethics and Professional Responsibility and of the larger state and local bar associations have been periodically compiled and published. Commercial publications on professional responsibility are now available in looseleaf form, including one sponsored by the ABA, which include reprints or summaries of court cases and ABA, state, and local bar committee opinions on ethical issues.

While the opinions of the various ethics committees are not binding, state and federal courts faced with ethical questions arising in discipline, civil, or criminal cases often refer to these opinions in reaching their own decisions. An attorney who relies on an opinion of the ABA or a local ethics committee cannot claim estoppel against any subsequent court action, but can feel fairly secure that good faith compliance with the committee's guidance will preclude imposition of serious professional discipline. Thus, the opinions of the bar association ethics committees, especially those which are formal and published, constitute an important interpretative aid for resolving issues of lawyers' professional responsibilities.

CHAPTER 5

MAINTENANCE OF PROFESSIONAL STANDARDS: ADMISSION AND DISCIPLINARY STANDARDS AND PROCEDURES

The utility of legal services to society is dependent upon their performance by qualified and trustworthy persons. Without legal training, a person is not likely to understand the complexities of the law nor operate effectively within the legal process. Likewise, the lay person often will be unable to accurately appraise the value and faithfulness of a lawyer's services, at least until it is too late to avoid the consequences of lost liberty or property or lost opportunity for an economic advantage or legal redress. Accordingly, the public seeks assurance that those who hold themselves out as lawyers are worthy of trust.

Membership in the legal profession, therefore, is not simply dependent upon the will of the would-be practitioner. Those persons found wanting in the requisite learning, skill, or moral character need to be denied entry to or removed from the profession or otherwise made subject to corrective action. This is necessary not only to prevent potential harm caused by incompetent or unfaithful service to clients and tribunals administering the law, but also to maintain public respect for, and consequent acceptance of, the legal process, which lawyers are largely responsible for operating.

In this manner, the interests of the public are sought to be protected, but an economic monopoly also is created which may tend to maintain the cost of legal services at a higher level than would be likely with free and open competition. Only the public's interests, not those of the Bar, can justify the continuation of the exclusion of non-licensed persons from the practice of law.

Therefore, the standards of admission and discipline must truly safeguard clients and the administration of justice from the incompetent or immoral practitioner.

I. REGULATION OF THE LEGAL PROFESSION

The public is entitled to rely upon the issuance of a license by a competent authority as an indication that the recipient possesses at least the minimum qualifications to practice law. In the United States, each state or territory is recognized as an admitting jurisdiction and has authority to regulate the legal profession within its borders. In addition, each federal court can adopt its own requirements for admission to practice. Thus, admission as a lawyer in one jurisdiction does not entitle a person to practice law in any other jurisdiction. Likewise, disbarment in one state does not automatically disqualify a lawyer in other places of admission.

These concepts of local autonomy run counter to the desires and expectations of our increasingly mobile society. Frustration is encountered by businesses and individuals with frequent interstate activities, by civil rights organizations seeking redress for the underrepresented in some states, and by lawyers who simply want to relocate in an area with a better economic or meteorological climate. These pressures have brought inroads into traditional local control of the practice of law. All states permit occasional court appearances by out-of-state lawyers for a particular case, and over half of the states (notably excepting the Sunshine State of Florida, the Golden State of California, and the Garden State of New Jersey—the latter to prevent harvesting of local clients by New York and Philadelphia lawyers) extend reciprocity for admission purposes to lawyers who have practiced for a minimum period (usually five years) in another state in which they have been admitted. A multi-state bar examination has been developed which almost all states rely upon as a significant portion of their exam, and about half of the states accept scores made on the multistate exam taken in another state. At the disbarment end, the ABA's Disciplinary Data Bank provides instant access to disqualifications of an attorney in one jurisdiction, which can lead to similar action in others.

Congress has mandated that a lawyer admitted in any American jurisdiction be permitted to practice before any federal administrative agency without demonstrating further character or competence qualifications, with the exception that the Patent Office may still test the specialized legal and technical knowledge of applicants to become patent attorneys. Agencies, however, may be authorized to discipline attorneys who practice before them. While this power has not been regularly exercised by most agencies, with the notable exceptions of the Internal Revenue Service and the Securities and Exchange Commission, the American Bar Association has sought to require all agencies to refer disciplinary matters to state authorities except to the extent necessary to maintain order in an administrative hearing.

Federal courts have generally admitted all attorneys who are licensed in the state where a court is located, but some districts, pursuant to recommendations of a study seeking to improve trial advocacy, are now experimenting with requiring specific trial practice experience, education, examinations and/or peer review before a lawyer is fully licensed to practice in such districts. Other federal courts occasionally have employed, and potentially could employ, additional qualifications of their own device. A federal court is not conclusively bound by a disbarment order of a state from which admission to practice in the federal court has been derived, but the state action normally will be followed unless it is found to lack due process or convincing evidence.

Concerns about professional limitations on the availability, marketing, and adequacy of legal services, and regarding state prohibitions on practice by non-lawyers or out-of-state lawyers, have prompted some calls for federal regulation of aspects of the practice of law. The Supreme Court has eased open this door by its holdings that: lawyers may be engaged in business in interstate commerce and their fee setting practices are subject to federal anti-trust laws; law firm decisions concerning eligibility for partnership are subject to scrutiny under Title VII of the federal Civil

Rights Act; federal administrative agency practice rules preempt state unauthorized practice laws under the Supremacy clause of the Constitution; group legal service plans are subject to protection under the First and Fourteenth Amendments; and bar admission practices favoring state residents violate the Privileges and Immunities clause in the Constitution. (See infra and Chapters 7, 9, and 14).

As these cases illustrate, all state regulation of the legal profession is subject to the Constitution, and the Supreme Court has recognized an increasing scope of bar controls to which constitutional standards apply.

II. NATURE OF PROFESSIONAL STANDARDS

A functional approach to testing the constitutionality of professional standards has been adopted by the Supreme Court. In *Schware v. Board of Bar Examiners* (U.S.1957), the Court held that, to satisfy the due process requirements of the Fourteenth Amendment, a qualification for admission to the bar of a state "must have a rational connection with the applicant's fitness or capacity to practice law."

There is no doubt that some types of moral character and competence qualifications for lawyers can be job related. The more difficult question is whether specifically applied character and competence standards have the required rational relation to the practice of law.

A. COMPETENCE QUALIFICATIONS

1. Education and Apprenticeships

The current American Bar Association standards for accreditation of law schools call for applicants to have completed at least three years of college. Historically, the period of required pre-legal education has been shorter or non-existent, and there are several contemporary departures from this norm. Several states still do not specify any pre-legal education requirement. Nevertheless, most ABA accredited law schools, and a fourth of the states, require an undergraduate degree. Some law schools in states not totally incorporating the ABA standards (notably, California) are satisfied with two years' undergraduate preparation or its equivalent. The requirement of any pre-legal college education was rare in the United States until the 1930's, and is still not the accepted practice in most other countries. Thus, it would be difficult to contend that three years of undergraduate education is essential to the proper preparation of a lawyer. This is especially true in light of the free selection of the type of courses, majors, and schools which is permitted to satisfy the pre-legal educational requirement. On the other hand, since lawyers deal with the whole range of human conduct and societal institutions, the requirement of some exposure to a liberal or general non-legal education is rationally related to the capacity to practice law. When constitutionally challenged, the requirement has been sustained, and, in light of the flexibility allowed by the ABA and most states, compliance with this educational pre-requisite to the practice of law has not been unduly burdensome.

Formal legal education as a requirement to practice law is a relatively recent phenomenon. The traditional preparation for law was by apprenticeship, and a few states still permit study in a law office as an alternative to attendance at law school. The values of a clerkship are recognized by the requirements which survive in isolated jurisdictions for a practice internship or skills course in addition to graduation from law school and by the renaissance of clinical education in the law schools. Nevertheless, three years of full-time or four years of part-time legal education has become the norm and the ABA standard in the United States. Ironically, while the body and complexity of the law has grown in recent years, proposals to shorten the formal period of legal education have been heard. The rationale, other than third-year student boredom and financial burdens of extended education, appears to be a recognition of the futility of trying to acquaint the students with all the legal subjects which might be relevant to their future careers and an acceptance of the more modest objective of exposing them to the fundamental skills and concepts needed to begin the practice of law. While the requirement of a law school education has withstood court challenge in a number of states and would clearly seem to be rationally connected to preparing competent lawyers, the period of attendance necessary to qualify a person to practice could well be subject to modification.

Almost all states specify that an applicant for the bar must have attended an accredited law school. To avoid costly and duplicative investigations, accreditation of a school by the ABA is generally accepted as meeting an individual state's requirements, although a number of states reserve—and a few exercise—the right to accredit other schools which meet the state's own standards. Delegation of official accrediting functions to a nonofficial agency such as the ABA has been questioned, and those states which reserve some discretion to their admitting agency are less suceptible to legal challenge. The State of California is exceptional in its leniency in allowing applicants to attend any law school, without regard to accreditation, to meet the educational requirements for admission to its bar, but those attending a non-accredited law school must pass a "baby-bar" examination on first-year subjects before being permitted to continue to qualify for the bar at such a school. Even this distinction reflects the feeling that accredited and unaccredited schools may be rationally treated in a different manner. While Lincoln may have studied in a log cabin, it would not seem to offend the Equal Protection Clause to require would-be lawyers in these legally complex times to have attended a law school that meets reasonable accreditation standards.

In accrediting law schools, the ABA, and analogous state agencies, are primarily concerned with the quality and size of the faculty (especially full-time), student body, library and physical facilities. The curriculum must be sufficiently comprehensive, rigorous, and lengthy to educate students in the fundamentals of legal knowledge and skills, but considerable flexibility is allowed in selection of particular subjects and in a school's discretion to emphasize theory or practice, or national or local law. While a few states insist on specifying particular courses or subjects to be taken before an applicant may be admitted to practice in such states, the ABA has generally resisted such invasions of faculty autonomy—with the exceptions of mandating instruction in professional responsibility and some practice skills.

2. Professional Examinations

Bar examinations, although almost universally required of applicants to practice law in the United States, have come under attack as unjustified impediments to admission which do not adequately test one's ability to be a competent lawyer. Litigation has been initiated on behalf of racial or ethnic minorities who claim the exams have a discriminatory effect in that larger percentages of such minorities fail although they have graduated from the same law schools as non-minority applicants. Suggested remedies include altering examination standards and techniques as well as eliminating the bar examination for those who have graduated from an accredited law school. This "diploma privilege" is available in a very few states for applicants who attended accredit ed law schools within the particular state concerned. No state has been adjudicated to have intentionally discriminated against minority applicants through its examination, and the concept of the bar exam has been found to have a rational connection to the fitness and capacity of an applicant to practice law. Nevertheless, many states have reviewed their examination requirements to avoid unintentional discrimination and to assure their appropriateness as a screening instrument of those persons who desire to perform the functions of lawyers.

With unprecedented increases in law school enrollment, suspicion has arisen that bar examination grading standards were being set to only admit a fixed percentage of applicants in order to forestall competition with existing practitioners. State bar examiners generally deny such intent, and an anti-trust law challenge on this ground was dismissed by the Supreme Court because the examination process was held to be "state action" exempt from the federal anti-trust statutes. Hoover v. Ronwin (U.S.1984).

While passing a bar examination is a formidable task for anyone, giving rise to a thriving industry in bar review courses, the major portion of applicants do pass the exam on the first or second attempt. The likelihood of being successful after a third try at the exam is statistically small. Consequently, a number of states limit applicants to taking the examination no more than two to five times. These restrictions generally have been upheld, especially where an applicant may be given another chance upon showing of good cause.

Although all states try to examine on the fundamentals necessary to practice law, there is no uniform content to bar examinations in the various jurisdictions. Some examine primarily on local law, while others emphasize general concepts and analytical ability. As previously indicated, almost all states now include the one-day multi-state examination which asks multiple-choice questions on general law in fundamental subjects. Traditional essay-hypothetical questions also constitute a part of virtually all bar examinations, and California has instituted a "performance exam" section which seeks to more closely approximate the skills that lawyers are required to exercise in practice. The examinee is provided with documents from which to gather pertinent facts (rather than having them pre-digested as on the essay questions) and a mini-library of applicable cases, statutes, and rules, and is asked to assume an advocate's or neutral's role by preparing a brief, memorandum, opinion, or other working paper. While this type of examination has its critics, it does provide an appropriate emphasis on analytical skills rather than memorization of rules of law.

For many years, a number of state bar examinations have included questions dealing, at least in part, with legal ethics. Since Watergate turned the public spotlight on the greater need for lawyers to maintain high ethical standards, most states have given a separate examination on professional responsibility. The Multi-state Professional Responsibility Exam, using multiple-choice questions based upon ABA standards, is usually taken by law students during their second or third year, and all but one of the over thirty states which administer it require its passage independent of the general bar examination.

The emphasis placed by bar admission authorities on courses and examinations in professional responsibility is a belated, but welcome, recognition that the subject is both important and teachable. While such efforts do not guarantee adherence to legal ethical standards, they do give some assurance that an applicant to practice law is at least familiar with the substance of those standards.

B. CITIZENSHIP, RESIDENCE AND AGE REQUIREMENTS

While not directly related to competence or character, many states had required that an applicant to the bar be a citizen of the United States, be a resident of the state for a minimum period, and have reached a specified age of majority. The age requirement (lowered to 18 in many states) presents no particular problem in view of the extended educational prerequisites, but both the citizenship and residence qualifications have been successfully constitutionally challenged.

The Supreme Court has held that it is a violation of equal protection for a state to require that a lawyer be a citizen of the United States, at least as applied to resident aliens. This "suspect classification" was not justified by any relevance to the functions of an attorney, the protection of the interests of clients or of the Nation, or by the status of attorneys as "officers of the court" (which is intended to connote the importance of lawyers' responsibilities to the administration of justice but does not constitute them officials of the government). Aliens can be required, however, to take an oath in good faith to support the Constitution of the United States and of the state of admission. Application of Griffiths (U.S.1973).

After several lower courts had struck down one-year residence requirements as not sufficiently related to a legitimate state interest, the Supreme Court held that a New Hampshire court rule requiring that a person be a resident of that state in order to be admitted to practice law violated the Privileges and Immunities Clause, Article IV, Section 2, of the Constitution. Supreme Court of New Hampshire v. Piper (U.S.1985). That clause prohibits less favorable treatment, at least in matters of business or economics, of a non-resident citizen than of a state resident except to the extent that the discriminatory treatment of non-residents is supported by substantial reasons and is narrowly tailored to effectuate such reasons. New Hampshire had contended that state residents would be more available, on short notice, for court proceedings and pro bono activities, would be more likely to keep up on local rules and procedures, and would be subject to better ethical control. The Court found that these reasons were either inapplicable to the applicant, could be served by means other than a residency requirement, or, as applied, failed to meet the constitutional test of substantiality. The facts of the case were particularly supportive of this holding. The applicant lived in Vermont, 400 yards from the New Hampshire border, had been found to be of good moral character and passed the New Hampshire bar examination (which she had been permitted to take upon stating an intent to establish a residence in that state), and intended to practice with an office in New Hampshire.

A similar result was reached by a majority of the Court in striking down a one-year residency requirement for admission to practice in the Virgin Islands despite that territory's geographic isolation and distance from the mainland of the United States and its relatively unique legal practice. The Court exercised its supervisory power over territorial courts and found that the Privileges and Immunities Clause was made applicable to the Virgin Islands by federal statute. Barnard v. Thorstenn (U.S.1989).

The *Piper* rationale was subsequently applied to invalidate a Virginia rule which permitted lawyers licensed in other states (which extended similar privileges to Virginia lawyers) to be admitted "on motion", that is without being required to pass a bar examination, if they became permanent residents of Virginia, and intended to practice full-time as a member of the Virginia bar. The applicant, who was then residing with her husband in Maryland, was denied admission on motion and was told she would have to take the Virginia bar exam, even though she had lived in Virginia for ten years until shortly before her application for admission, and was employed in a legal capacity at a corporate office in Virginia. Thus, but for her residency in nearby Maryland, the applicant substantially satisfied the legitimate purposes of the Virginia rule. Accordingly, the Court held that she could not be treated less favorably than a Virginia resident. Virginia v. Friedman (U.S.1988).

As the Court recognized in *Friedman,* neither Virginia nor any other state is obligated to make admission on motion available to any attorney licensed in another state. Thus a state could deny such privilege entirely, and require both residents and non-residents to pass the local bar examination—a change which has since taken place in Illinois and Missouri.

Despite one or two hold-out jurisdictions, as of 1990, residency requirements for admission to practice law are presumptively invalid. Nevertheless, an alternative requirement of demonstrating an intention to practice law or to maintain an office in the state in which admission is sought may pass constitutional muster and has been adopted in a few states. The Supreme Court, however, has struck down, on non-constitutional grounds, a rule of the Eastern District of Louisiana federal court requiring that members of its bar either be residents of or maintain a law office in Louisiana. The applicant was a Mississippi resident, with a law office in that state, but who also was admitted to practice in the state courts of Louisiana. The Supreme Court found that the rule's discrimination against non-residents was unreasonable, irrational, and inconsistent with principles of right and justice which should be applied by federal courts. Frazier v. Heebe (U.S. 1987). The fact that the applicant already was a member of the bar of the state in which the federal court was located could distinguish this case from those involving initial applications to a state bar.

C. CHARACTER REQUIREMENTS

1. Admission to Practice

Typically, to be admitted to the practice of law in any jurisdiction, the applicant must show that he or she is a person of good moral character. To the extent that this standard is applied to exclude those who are dishonest or unworthy of trust, it is clearly rational. The public needs to be protected from lawyers who would steal a client's money, cheat an adversary, or lie to the court. There are, however, questions about the manner of establishing that, if admitted, a lawyer will be a thief, cheater, or liar. Certainly criminal convictions are relevant, but even in such cases, rehabilitation is possible. The real issue is whether past misconduct suggests present character traits that are likely to lead to future conduct inconsistent with the responsibilities of a lawyer. These questions are left to the judgment of the admitting authorities in each jurisdiction subject to procedural and substantive constitutional safeguards. The more difficult or, at least, more frequently litigated, questions concern attempts to base a finding of lack of good moral character on offenses or other alleged misconduct not directly evidencing traits of dishonesty.

In the *Schware* case, the state court had held that Schware lacked the requisite good moral character for admission to the Bar of New Mexico because of his membership in the Communist Party from 1932–1940, arrests for participation in a (then) illegal strike, and use of aliases. The latter events occurred approximately twenty years before his application to the Bar. On appeal, the Supreme Court found that in light of the circumstances and age of the alleged offenses and the strong current evidence of good moral character, there was no rational justification for a finding that Schware was morally unfit to practice law. Concurring in the holding that the New Mexico decision deprived Schware of due process of law, Justice Frankfurter observed that the responsibilities of the legal profession require "those qualities of truth-speaking, of a high sense of honor, of granite discretion, of the strictest observance of fiduciary responsibility, that have, throughout the centuries, been compendiously described as 'moral character.' "

This formula is easier to state, however, than apply. For example, does the commission of offenses arising out of war protests, civil disobedience, sexual activities, or marijuana usage demonstrate a lack of the requisite moral character for admission to the bar? It is not enough simply to inquire whether there has been a criminal conviction, or even a felony conviction. Aside from the possibility of rehabilitation, the *Schware* "rational connection" test requires that the ground for disqualification, i.e., the crime, be logically related to the likely non-performance of a legitimate professional function or responsibility.

In *Hallinan v. Committee of Bar Examiners* (Cal.1966), an applicant was ordered admitted to the Bar even though he had been arrested several times in the course of a voter registration drive for Blacks, had two misdemeanor convictions arising from civil rights picketing and "sit-ins," and had been involved in nine fist fights over a series of years preceding his application to the Bar. The California Supreme Court rejected the Bar Committee's conclusion that this record demonstrated a propensity for lawlessness or for law violation whenever it suited the applicant's purposes. While acknowledging that acts of civil disobedience which involve violations of the law should be punished by criminal prosecution, the court stated that exclusion from the bar serves a different function. It is proper to exclude those whose fraudulent acts would necessarily impair the basic objects of the legal profession, but the exclusion from the bar of all non-violent civil disobedients "would deprive the community of the services of many highly qualified persons of the highest moral courage." While not condoning the applicant's altercations, the court either dismissed them as "youthful indiscretions" which had taken place years ago or found that they involved provocation or other extenuating circumstances; and, in any event, they neither reflected upon the applicant's honesty or veracity nor showed him unfit for the proper discharge of the duties of an attorney.

While the precedents are not entirely consistent, the rational relations test suggests a similar approach in evaluating the effect of the commission of other offenses on an applicant's moral character. For example, conviction for drug-related offenses should not be automatically disqualifying, but the admitting authorities should examine the circumstances in each case. Relevant considerations would include the harmfulness and quantity of the drug involved, the nature and manner of commission of the offense (e.g., peaceful or violent, open or surreptitious, distribution or personal usage), how long ago the offense was committed and the age of the applicant at that time, the motivation of the applicant at the time, and whether the applicant has been punished for the offense or made restitution to anyone harmed by the offense. Thus, sale of heroin, for profit, to minors by an applicant shortly before seeking admission is more likely to be disqualifying than private usage of moderate amounts of marijuana while the applicant was in college. Even where there was no criminal conviction, discipline imposed by a law school or other educational institution for a relatively minor drug-related offense may be favorably considered by bar admission authorities as relevant to the possibility of rehabilitation and as evidence that the applicant had already paid for his offense.

Although certain sexual behaviors, such as adultery, fornication, and sodomy remain as crimes in some states, and have been said to bring bad repute to the bar, their rational connection to fitness to practice law is not apparent, and modern authorities are not likely to find such behavior disqualifying when committed by consenting adults. Accordingly, non-traditional sexual preferences and cohabitation by unmarried adults may be viewed as unorthodox by many people (including some bar examiners) but have not been found by the courts to be grounds for denying an otherwise reputable person admission to the bar.

Many war protestors have faced scrutiny by admission authorities for their acts of civil disobedience as well as methods of avoiding the military draft. Despite the fact that Illinois once denied admission to a highly principled conscientious objector (later to become a respected law teacher and scholar) who declined to take an oath to support the state constitution because it included an obligation to bear arms [In re Summers (U.S.1945)], most courts today would view such moral or religious objections to war as not incompatible with good moral character. Where, however, an applicant knowingly violated the law by failing to register for the draft, and did not disclose such fact upon inquiry in his admission application, he was initially denied admission to the Bar of Arizona. Application of Walker (Ariz.1975).

As indicated by the *Walker* case, a failure to fully disclose matters relevant to the admission process is likely to be more harshly treated, as evidencing a lack of candor, then would be the underlying incident, which, if disclosed, might be disregarded as a youthful indiscretion or otherwise found not to be disqualifying.

Conduct need not be criminal to constitute a basis for questioning an applicant's moral fitness to practice law, and other behavior which has triggered moral character inquiries includes substance abuse; cheating, plagiarism, or other acts of dishonesty as a student; questionable business or financial transactions, including avoiding financial obligations—although the act of declaring bankruptcy cannot itself be a basis for disqualification for the bar; emotional illness or instability; and engaging in the unauthorized practice of law. The fact of inquiry regarding such matters may cause a delay in the admission process but relatively rarely results in a total bar. See Rhode, Moral Character as a Professional Credential (1985). To be constitutionally tenable, the underlying inquiry in each case must be of the logical relation of the offense and the circumstances of its commission to the responsibilities of a practicing lawyer.

2. Constitutional Defenses to Moral Character Inquiries

Another troublesome issue arises when an applicant claims a constitutional privilege in declining to respond to questions of bar admission authorities.

The Supreme Court has held that a refusal to answer questions about membership in the Communist Party, based on the First and Fourteenth Amendments, was not in itself evidence of a lack of good moral character [Konigsberg v. State Bar of California (U.S. 1957)], but could be a basis for exclusion from the bar on the ground that the applicant's failure to cooperate prevented an adequate inquiry into his moral character. Konigsberg v. State Bar of California (U.S.1961). To support an exclusion on the latter basis, however, the inquiries must not seek constitutionally protected information.

The Court subsequently established, by narrow majorities, that bar admission authorities may inquire about "knowing" or "meaningful" membership in an organization seeking the forceful overthrow of the United States or a state government. Thus, a denial of admission would be justified if the applicant declined to state whether he or she was aware of, personally accepted, and specifically intended to further an organization's aim to overthrow a domestic government by force, violence, or other unlawful means. However, an applicant has a right to refuse to answer questions about "mere membership" in the Communist Party or other allegedly subversive organizations, since the First Amendment prohibits excluding a person from a profession because of political associations or beliefs. LSCRRC v. Wadmond; Baird v. Arizona State Bar; In re Stolar (U.S.1971).

The *Wadmond* case also sustained a New York requirement that an applicant believe "in the form of government of the United States and is loyal to such government." While acknowledging doubts as to the validity of some constructions of the language of this rule, a majority of the Court found that in practice it merely required that the applicant be able to take an oath in good faith to "support the constitution of the United States" and of the State.

Also rejected in *Wadmond* was a broad attack on the good moral character standard for admission to the bar and on the entire New York system of character investigation as having a total impact of chilling the exercise of First Amendment rights to engage in political activities and express political viewpoints. The Court held that, in light of the wide-spread and long usage of similar standards, the New York rule that an applicant possess "the character and general fitness requisite for an attorney" was not unconstitutionally vague or overbroad, especially as narrowly construed to require only an absence of "dishonorable conduct relevant to the legal profession."

It has not been settled to what extent an applicant to the bar may rely upon the Fifth Amendment privilege against self-incrimination in refusing to respond to questions concerning activities that might be regarded as criminal. Overruling an earlier precedent, the Supreme Court has held that a lawyer cannot be disbarred for invoking his Fifth Amendment rights in a judicial investigation into "ambulance chasing," which was a crime under state law. Spevack v. Klein (U.S.1967). If such failure to cooperate, based on a constitutional privilege, cannot be used as a basis for disbarment, it is arguable that neither can it be made a basis for denial of admission to practice. One possible distinction is that the state has the burden of proof in a disciplinary proceeding whereas the applicant usually has the burden of proving moral character and other qualifications for admission to the bar. In any event, an invocation of the privilege against self-incrimination is bound to alert the admission authorities to the need for further investigation of the applicant.

3. Disciplinary Proceedings

It has been said that by admission to practice a court endorses an attorney to the public as worthy of trust in professional matters, and if the attorney subsequently becomes unworthy of that trust, it is the duty of the court to withdraw its endorsement. Thus, the requirement of moral character is not a one-time test to be met by a lawyer only upon admission. Acts of misconduct committed at any time may be a cause for professional discipline. Indeed, if an applicant, in the course of seeking admission to the bar, knowingly falsifies a material fact, or fails to disclose a fact necessary to correct a misimpression known to the applicant to have arisen, such misrepresentation, if not discovered until after admission, will subject him to professional discipline. Model Rule 8.1; see DR 1–101(A). Moreover, a lawyer who, by similar misrepresentation or non-disclosure of unprivileged information, aids, other than as counsel, an application of a person known to be unqualified for admission, will also be subject to discipline. Rule 8.1; DR 1–101(B).

The principal purpose of disciplinary sanctions is not to punish the offending lawyer, but to protect the public by removing from the bar, or taking corrective action against, those persons who have proven unworthy of the trust and responsibilities required of lawyers.

Professional disciplinary sanctions typically include private admonition or reprimand, public reprimand or censure, suspension from practice, and disbarment. Some jurisdictions also impose periods of probation, fines, and requirements of restitution, payment of costs, notices to clients and other lawyers, and re-examinations (usually in professional ethics) as a condition of reinstatement to active practice. The ABA has adopted recommended standards for assessing appropriate discipline and procedures for its imposition.

Disciplinary sanctions may be imposed on an attorney for breaching any rule of professional conduct, doing so through the acts of another or knowingly assisting or aiding another person to do so. RPC 8.4(a); see CPR DR 1–102(A)(1), (2).

The most common complaints against lawyers allege neglect of a client's affairs and overcharging. In many of these cases, the lawyer has simply failed to keep the client adequately informed of the reasons for delay or the basis for a fee, and the complaints are adjusted without formal disciplinary proceedings. The situations which most frequently result in disbarment involve misappropriation of a client's funds or property or commission of a felony.

In light of the fundamental need for trust and honesty by lawyers, "conduct involving dishonesty, fraud, deceit or misrepresentation" is clearly subject to discipline. Nor, despite the vagueness of the standards, can there be quarrel with the relevancy of disciplining "conduct that is prejudicial to the administration of justice . . ." or which adversely reflects on a lawyer's fitness to practice. Rule 8.4(b), (c), (d); DR 1–102(A)(4), (5), (6). These standards apply both to misconduct in the course of legal practice and to that committed when a lawyer acts in other capacities. The disbarment and suspension of several attorneys implicated in the Watergate coverup, although their actions were not performed in their role as members of the bar, were clearly justified on this basis. The criminal allegations against them included obstruction of justice, subornation of perjury, destruction of evidence, filing false statements, perjury, interference with a criminal investigation, and misuse of internal revenue laws and information. These offenses were not analogous to a vacationing lawyer having too much to drink.

The Code, unlike the Rules, also proscribed "illegal conduct involving moral turpitude." DR 1–102(A)(3). While it is frequently a ground for disbarment, the "moral turpitude" standard should not be accepted uncritically. Depending upon, inter alia, the circumstances of the particular offense, the purpose for which the standard was applied, and the particular court applying it, moral turpitude has been held to be present or absent in crimes involving the production, sale, or consumption of liquor, tax evasion, consensual sex offenses, involuntary manslaughter, and assault and battery. Commission of acts of "baseness, vileness and depravity," the usual definition of moral turpitude, certainly justifies inquiry into a person's fitness to practice law, but does not also determine the inquiry. Opinion at any particular time and place of the immorality of an act must give way to the underlying purpose for which the classification, "crimes involving moral turpitude," is being applied: whether to determine an alien's right to emigrate to or remain in the United States, whether to allow the use of an offense to impeach a witness, or whether to exclude or expel an individual from the practice of law. See Weckstein, Maintaining the Integrity and Competence of the Legal Profession (1970).

If conduct involving moral turpitude is equated to that which demonstrates a lack of fitness to practice law, as was done by the California court in the *Hallinan* case, previously discussed, the "moral character" standard becomes more meaningful. The *Hallinan* opinion also is noteworthy for equating the moral character standards for admission and disciplinary proceedings. Although procedural variations may exist, the court rejected the "vested right" theory which suggested greater leniency in a disbarment proceeding. The substantive inquiry in each case should be the same: "Is the applicant for admission or the attorney sought to be disciplined a fit and proper person to be permitted to practice law?" According to the court, this is usually to be determined by whether the individual has committed or is likely to continue to commit acts of "moral turpitude."

The Ethical Considerations of the CPR also suggest that: "Because of his position in society, even minor violations of law by a lawyer may tend to lessen public confidence in the legal profession. Obedience to the law exemplifies respect for law." EC 1–5. But is that enough to justify the application of both criminal and professional sanctions in cases involving misconduct not otherwise relevant to the function of lawyers in society? The reported cases seem to reflect an attitude that attorneys guilty of such conduct will be disciplined only when their misbehavior becomes a matter of public notoriety. While the respect for lawyers, and consequently the law, would seem to suffer the most harm in those cases, it is questionable whether the offender is deserving of any greater penalty because of this happenstance. Discipline in these cases "seems more vindictively punitive than it does selectively preventive." W. Gellhorn 1956. A possible justification for subjecting an attorney to professional discipline who has been guilty of one or more crimes not directly relevant to the practice of law is that such conduct tends to show a disposition to violate the rules of society, which might find expression in professional affairs. The psychological basis for this needs further exploration, and its validity probably varies considerably depending upon the nature of the crime, the degree of repetitiveness, and the psychological makeup of the attorney.

The commentary to Model Rule 8.4 recognizes that a pattern of repeated offenses, even minor ones, can indicate indifference to legal obligation, and that characteristic—rather than the separate consideration of individual offenses of, perhaps, personal but not professional morality—may be relevant to the lawyer's fitness to practice law.

The Model Rules, unlike the Code, the earlier Canons, and many court decisions, eschew the "appearance of impropriety" as a basis for disciplinary offenses. See Comment to Rule 1.9. Nevertheless, the Rules continue the specific offenses, as actual improprieties, of conflicts of interest by former government employees and of commingling of client and lawyer funds, which were classified by the CPR as applications of Canon Nine's obligation to "avoid even the appearance of professional impropriety." See RPC 1.11, 1.12, 1.15; Chapters 12, 13.

Both the Model Rules and the CPR recognize incompetent representation of a client as a disciplinary offense, and the Code specifically commands a lawyer not to "neglect a legal matter entrusted to him." DR 6–101; Rules 1.1, 1.3, 1.4. These ethical obligations are independent of potential civil liability for acts of professional malpractice, but are not likely to be cause for discipline in the absence of habitual or recurring neglect or acts of incompetence. See Chapter 6.

Substance abuse has played a frequent role in many recent disciplinary proceedings. Ironically, alcoholism and drug addiction, as well as mental or emotional illness, have been urged both as a cause for discipline and as a defense to it. The public needs to be protected from a lawyer who is not able to control his conduct or manage his affairs, or those of his clients. As recommended by the ABA, many states now provide for voluntary and involuntary transfer of a mentally or physically disabled lawyer to inactive status, or for a non-disciplinary suspension during the period of disability. See Standard 12, ABA Standards for Lawyer Discipline and Disability Proceedings (1979). Lawyers suffering from alcoholism or drug addiction can be benefited by such status, as well as by an increasing number of available professional assistance programs.

Nevertheless, if substance abuse contributes to the commission of independent offenses, the lawyer may still face disciplinary proceedings. Paul Newman's success in the "Verdict", notwithstanding, neglect of a client's affairs, misappropriation of client funds, and failure to meet court appearances and deadlines are common companions of abuse of alcohol or narcotics by lawyers. Where the offenses are serious, to protect the public from such recurring conduct, many courts will disbar or indefinitely suspend the attorney, leaving the possibility of future reinstatement open if the offender can establish proof of rehabilitation. If, however, the lawyer acknowledges his addiction, and, by the time of final hearing, has taken definitive steps toward recovery, a number of courts will mitigate the disciplinary sanction by shortening the time of suspension, or permitting the offender to continue to practice on probation subject to participation in a recovery program, abstaining from the abused substance, and—in some jurisdictions—association with another attorney.

As is the case with pre-admission involvement with drugs, discipline of a practicing attorney for such conduct varies with the particular circumstances. Trafficking in narcotics, or possession of large quantities for sale may warrant disbarment or lengthy suspension, whereas possession of small quantities, of non-hard drugs, such as marijuana, will not likely be held to involve moral turpitude, and may result in only a censure, or dismissal of the charges if they are unrelated to the attorney's fitness to practice law.

III. PROCEDURAL STANDARDS

It is apparent that in applying sound but general standards like "moral character" or "fitness to practice law," the procedures utilized and the personnel responsible for their application take on great importance.

On the theory that the courts have the inherent authority to determine who may practice before them, the admission and discipline of lawyers has been considered a judicial function. Legislative standards and procedures may be accepted by the courts as reasonable regulations, but where a conflict has developed, the courts have usually held that their rules will prevail. Bar associations, particularly in those states with unified bars, are frequently delegated functions in the admission and disciplinary processes.

The relative absence of non-lawyer participation in the screening and discipline of lawyers has been the subject of much criticism. Former Senator John Tunney of California has likened leaving the discipline of lawyers exclusively in the hands of the legal profession to asking John Erlichman to make the definitive investigation of White House involvement in the Watergate coverup. Despite claims that laymen will be unable to construe professional standards or judge compliance with them, an increasing number of states are adding at least a token number of non-lawyers to professional governing boards. Experience with lay juries in malpractice cases suggests that this is a workable process so long as lawyers are available to educate the lay persons on relevant law and practice, and to exercise professional judgment when needed to resolve particular issues. In any event, non-lawyer participation in the disciplinary process, especially, is a salutary reform to help combat the tarnished image of the legal profession.

A. ADMISSION PROCESS

Following a recommended standard of the National Conference of Bar Examiners, the screening process for admission to the bar may start with the filing by a beginning law student of a declaration of intention to seek admission to practice in a particular jurisdiction. Only a few states, however, commence a character investigation at that time. Although the results of such an investigation could provide useful guidance in questionable cases, there is fear that premature judgments may be made and persons with any record of socially deviant behavior will be dissuaded, or even prohibited, from pursuing a legal education. Moreover, most jurisdictions do not have the personnel or resources to conduct adequate character investigations of large numbers of students, including some who will not complete law school or will ultimately change their minds about where, if at all, they want to practice law. Law schools also resist any such investigative role, for lack of appropriate resources and because of its alleged incompatibility with their educational mission. Nevertheless, a few states impose a duty on the law school administration to attest to their graduates' good moral character, or at least to no knowledge of incidents suggesting a lack thereof.

Upon meeting the educational prerequisites for admission to practice, the applicant is required to complete a detailed questionnaire. Typically, it includes questions about prior criminal (and even juvenile offender) records, college, law school or other occupational disciplinary infractions, involvement in bankruptcy or in court proceedings in any capacity, and places of employment, residence, and schooling. Character references, often from lawyers, and sometimes fingerprinting, may be required. In general, the best approach is one of full disclosure. Failure to disclose a material fact may constitute a subsequent cause for disbarment, and the admission authorities are more likely to view favorably the effect of youthful indiscretions, minor offenses, and rehabilitation for more serious offenses, than they are an attempt to conceal a prior record of such offenses.

The implementation of the admissions process usually will be delegated to a court or State Bar appointed board or committee. Local character-screening committees or persons may also be designated. Some states require an interview with the local committee or with a representative of the state-wide board. Short term residents of a jurisdiction are generally required to have a supplementary character investigation (at an additional cost to the applicant) conducted by the National Conference of Bar Examiners.

If any of these preliminary procedures raises significant questions concerning the moral character of an applicant, a hearing will be afforded before the jurisdiction-wide board or representatives thereof. If the applicant is dissatisfied with the decision of the board, judicial review is available with the ultimate (and sometimes the original) determination made by the highest court of the state or other jurisdiction, except that review of federal constitutional questions may be sought in the U.S. Supreme Court.

Although the practice has been criticized, the general rule is that the applicant has the burden of proving good moral character and satisfaction of other requirements for admission. An absence of negative character evidence and a few current good character references usually suffice to carry this burden. In the event the record reveals evidence negating good character, a hearing is required before a person can be denied admission to practice. The applicant is entitled to the protections of procedural due process of law, including the right to counsel, to present evidence, to know the nature of the evidence against him or her, and an adequate opportunity to rebut it. Confrontation and cross-examination of accusers may also be available, at least when denial of admission depends upon information supplied by a person whose reliability or veracity is brought into question. See Willner v. Committee on Character and Fitness (U.S.1963). Where confidentiality has been promised to those who supply moral character information about the applicant, due process may require that a substitute source of information be relied upon, the confidentiality sacrificed, or that the information not be utilized as a basis for an adverse character finding.

B. DISCIPLINARY PROCESS

In most jurisdictions the disciplinary process begins with the filing of a complaint with a court or grievance committee. The grievance committee may be appointed by an appropriate court or may be a committee of the bar association, particularly in those states with integrated bars. This committee, or a representative thereof, or a specially constituted investigative committee will conduct a preliminary investigation. After learning the lawyer's side of the story and further details from the complainant, the investigative body disposes of many complaints at this stage because they do not involve matters within the jurisdiction of the grievance committee or because they resulted from a misunderstanding which has been cleared up. In a few states, a formal investigative hearing is available before further proceedings may be instituted.

Once formal charges are filed against an attorney, a trial-type hearing is held before a disciplinary board, grievance hearing committee, or specially designated trial court or administrative hearing officer. If the charges are sustained, there may be an appeal from a local hearing body to a state-wide appellate board, or to the courts, in many states to the highest state appellate court. Disciplinary boards frequently are delegated the authority to administer private reprimands or public censures, but suspensions from practice and disbarments generally require court approval.

There has been much public criticism voiced concerning the lawyer disciplinary system. This has ranged from difficulties of initiating complaints to secret and inefficient investigations and hearings, and to prolonged appeals. There also is criticism of the practice in some jurisdictions of combining under one agency the functions of investigation, prosecution and initial adjudication of disciplinary matters.

The bottom-line, however, is the very small percentage of lawyers against whom disciplinary charges are formally initiated (less than .50% in most states), and even fewer number of lawyers who are actually disciplined (about 6% of complaints filed). Whether because of "lawyer jokes" or other aspects of the poor public image of the legal profession, many people believe that there must be a greater number of bad apples in the lawyer barrel, and suspect that the bar screening process either intentionally protects its own (at least in the absence of criminal conviction or public notoriety) or is just plain ineffective.

Nor is criticism of the disciplinary system limited to the public. The 1970 Report of the ABA Committee on Evaluation of Disciplinary Enforcement, chaired by retired Justice Tom Clark, found "a scandalous situation that requires the immediate attention of the profession." The ineffectiveness of the disciplinary process in many jurisdictions was attributed in part to lawyer apathy and even hostility. The Committee's recommendations included the establishment of professional staffs to initiate as well as investigate and prosecute professional grievances, the creation of information sharing agencies and procedures, and the provision of more efficient, effective, and responsible procedures. In 1979, the ABA adopted Standards for Lawyer Discipline and Disability Proceedings which incorporate and expand upon the Clark Committee recommendations. Several jurisdictions, inspired by the Clark Committee report and the public reaction to the Watergate situation, revised their disciplinary procedures.

Faced by threats of legislative reform of the disciplinary system in California, including the possibility of substituting an independent agency for the State Bar as the primary disciplinary body, the Bar adopted a comprehensive overhaul of the system recommended by the State Bar Disciplinary Monitor, a position established by the legislature. The reforms included replacing voluntary hearing officers with full-time judges on the State Bar Court, creating an appellate panel of three judges including one non-lawyer, and beefing up the investigative and prosecuting offices with a full-time staff of investigators and lawyers. To pay for these reforms, the State Bar, with legislative approval, nearly doubled its dues to over $400 per year, 78% of which is used to finance the disciplinary system. (Most unified bars spend between 20 and 40% of their dues for discipline). The early returns in California are encouraging. From 1988 to 1989, disciplinary actions increased by 44%, disbarments by 29%, and suspensions by 66%, while the investigative backlog was reduced from 1894 to 566 cases.

Although the number of lawyers has almost tripled since the 1970 Clark Committee Report, it is doubtful that other states have, or will commit, the level of resources that California is now devoting to the disciplinary effort. It may be that progress in improving disciplinary enforcement can be made in a more cost efficient manner. This is one of several issues that will be explored by a new ABA Commission on Evaluation of Disciplinary Enforcement. The Commission will assemble data on existing systems and reforms, conduct hearings, surveys, and original research, and evaluate the state of disciplinary enforcement in light of changes in the legal profession during the twenty years since the Clark report. The Commission is expected to report its recommendations in 1991.

Whatever the system of discipline in a particular jurisdiction, legal and philosophical issues are likely to permeate it. Some of these issues will now be briefly reviewed.

In the absence of a criminal conviction, most disciplinary complaints come from disgruntled clients. But many attorney acts of misconduct are committed on behalf of clients, often with their knowledge and consent. In other cases, the clients may not be aware of, or care about, their lawyer's unethical conduct. One potentially good source of information about lawyer lapses could be other lawyers practicing with, or in the same community as, the offending lawyer. The CPR imposes an obligation on lawyers, who have unprivileged knowledge regarding another lawyer's violation of the standards of professional conduct, to report such information to an appropriate professional authority. DR 1–103. The Rules limit this obligation to information, which is not confidentially protected, and which raises a substantial question as to the other lawyer's "honesty, trustworthiness or fitness as a lawyer". [RPC 8.3]. This type of "honor code" reporting provision encounters serious enforcement problems. Nevertheless, a recent Illinois case (discussed in Chapter 6) imposed a one-year suspension on an attorney for failing to report another lawyer's misconduct, and the publicity of the case generated a flood of complaint reports from others. When a lawyer engaged in misconduct is associated in the same firm as another lawyer who learns of the misconduct, the Model Rules seem to impose a reporting and corrective obligation. See Rules 5.1, 5.2, 5.3, 8.3. Other than counseling, and perhaps confronting, the offending lawyer, the disclosure obligation raises troublesome personnel and client relations problems. In many cases, however, most such information would relate to the representation of a client and therefore would be confidential, and not subject to disclosure. (See Chapter 11).

A lawyer accused of a disciplinary offense is entitled to the protections of due process of law. The accused has a right to written notice of the charges against him and to a trial-type hearing before the grievance committee or the court itself. In one case an attorney had been disbarred in Ohio partially on the basis of a charge that had been added as a result of the testimony of the attorney and another witness in response to other charges. A majority of the Supreme Court agreed that it would violate due process of law for the federal court to disbar the attorney based upon the untimely added charge in the state proceedings. In re Ruffalo (U.S.1968). In *Zauderer v. Office of Disciplinary Counsel* (U.S.1985) (discussed in Chapter 10 regarding its impact on lawyer advertising), however, the Supreme Court declined to hold that due process was violated when the theory on which the disciplinary board held an advertisement was deceptive differed from that originally alleged by the prosecuting counsel, so long as Zauderer had an opportunity to respond to the board's recommendations before the state supreme court which had the responsibility for imposition of the discipline.

While a disciplinary proceeding is considered neither completely civil nor criminal, but a special proceeding to investigate and control the conduct of lawyers, the Supreme Court, as in the *Ruffalo* case, above, has characterized it as an adversary proceeding "of a quasi-criminal nature." The overriding purpose of professional discipline may be to protect the public from erring lawyers, but—like a criminal prosecution—it does so by imposing a sanction on the offender which is intended to have a punitive as well as deterrent effect. Accordingly, the Supreme Court has equated the "penalty" of disbarment with a criminal sanction in holding that a lawyer may not be disbarred for invoking the constitutional privilege against self-incrimination in a state court investigation of the conduct of attorneys. Spevack v. Klein (U.S.1967). In a companion case, the Court reversed the convictions of police officers which rested in part on evidence given under threat of dismissal if they invoked their Fifth Amendment privilege. Garrity v. New Jersey (U.S.1967). Presumably, the same rule would prevent an attorney from being criminally convicted for testimony which had been elicited in violation of Fifth Amendment rights. Could an attorney who was granted immunity from criminal prosecution be disbarred for refusing to respond to pertinent questions? Or, if he did respond, could he be disbarred, but not criminally convicted, based upon the evidence thus elicited? Since the burden of proof in a disbarment proceeding is on the disciplinary agency, refusal to respond—while under immunity from prosecution—to pertinent questions, would not be cause, by itself, for disbarment, but an adverse inference might be drawn from the lawyer's silence since the immunity strips the attorney of Fifth Amendment protection. Lower court interpretations have read *Spevack* narrowly, and have allowed testimony given under immunity from criminal prosecution to be used in disciplinary proceedings.

The *Spevack* "penalty" analogy, has not been extended to require an indictment or jury trial in a disciplinary proceeding. Two of three states, nevertheless, do provide a right to a jury trial. While non-lawyer participation in the disciplinary process is not inappropriate, there is a risk that a jury will be less likely to understand or sympathize with the need for enforcement of some of the relatively unique professional obligations of lawyers, and may be unduly influenced in other cases by the public image of the profession.

There are other perceptible distinctions between criminal and disciplinary proceedings. The burden of proof required to impose a disciplinary sanction is generally clear and convincing evidence (and, in some states, the civil standard of a preponderance of the evidence), rather than the more onerous burden of finding guilt beyond a reasonable doubt. Thus, it is possible for a lawyer acquitted of a crime to nevertheless be disbarred based on evidence of the same offense. A similar result can occur when a criminal charge has been dismissed because the primary evidence is found to have been unconstitutionally seized or obtained in violation of the *Miranda* rule (requiring that a suspect be given notice of a right to an attorney and to remain silent before incriminating statements may be sought). Unless the disciplinary authorities have conspired with the police in these situations, the evidence could be used as a basis for professional discipline. A disciplinary tribunal considers the whole person to determine whether the interests of the administration of justice and the public require protection by imposition of disbarment or some lesser sanction on the offender. Such discipline should be neither foreclosed nor required by the result of the criminal process, which is designed to punish offenses against society through means which maintain respect for the laws of society.

For like reasons, a lawyer who is acquitted of a criminal charge by reason of insanity may still be suspended from the practice of law, because the issue in the disciplinary proceeding is not culpability but protection of the public. The lawyer's mental illness at the time of the offense, however, may serve to mitigate the extent of the discipline, and if the lawyer subsequently recovers his mental stability, reinstatement would not be precluded.

Because of the distinctions between a criminal and a disciplinary proceeding, it is not prohibited double jeopardy to discipline a lawyer for the same offense of which she has been criminally convicted. Likewise, it is not unconstitutional for a reviewing court to increase the disciplinary sanction beyond that approved by a lower court or grievance committee. Thus an attorney appealing a reprimand or suspension risks the possibility of having the higher court hold that a longer suspension or even disbarment will be imposed.

While a suspension generally provides for reinstatement of the attorney after a fixed period of time, a disbarment is indefinite but not necessarily permanent. In almost all states, a disbarred attorney may seek reinstatement upon a claim of rehabilitation. An interesting example was the reinstatement of Alger Hiss to the Massachusetts Bar in light of his then good character and despite his continuing refusal to acknowledge his guilt of perjury, for which he had been convicted twenty-three years before when he denied providing confidential government information to confessed (and subsequently reformed with a passion) Communist Whittaker Chambers. In re Hiss (Mass.1975).

An attorney who has been disbarred or suspended must refrain from all law practice. Although it is tempting for one trained as a lawyer to continue to try to earn a living in some law-related capacity, where a disbarred or suspended lawyer is found to have engaged in the unauthorized practice of law, courts have denied applications for reinstatement and even converted suspensions into disbarments. Another lawyer who employs a disbarred or suspended attorney in a legal capacity may be guilty of aiding the unauthorized practice of law, and also is subject to discipline.

A person seeking reinstatement to the practice of law, like an applicant for original admission, has the burden of demonstrating current good moral character. In those states providing for automatic disbarment upon conviction of a felony, or one involving moral turpitude, this has the effect of shifting the burden of proof from the disciplinary authorities to the convicted attorney. The fairness of this procedure is subject to question.

Courts may impose conditions on reinstatement following a suspension or disbarment. Such conditions have included restitution to clients or others injured by the misconduct of the attorney; completion of parole or other conditions imposed upon conviction of a crime; proof of current competence, moral fitness and freedom from psychiatric or substance abuse problems; practice in association with other lawyers; and passage of the state bar examination, or, as routinely required in California, the professional responsibility exam.

It must be stressed that professional discipline is not the only, nor necessarily the best, method for controlling lawyer misconduct. In recent years, courts have more aggressively imposed santions on lawyers, including significant fines, assessment of costs, and procedural handicaps for filing frivolous lawsuits, motions, objections, and appeals, or for engaging in unjustified delays, impeding discovery, or disregarding prior admonitions of the court. The federal courts have been especially active in this regard under Rule 11 of the Federal Rules of Civil Procedure, as revised in 1983. In addition, malpractice liability, criminal conviction, contempt of court citations, loss of a client's cause or advantage (and ironically reversal of a client's conviction due to ineffective assistance of counsel), denial or forfeiture of legal fees, disqualification as counsel, and summary court orders to turn over funds or property, are all available to help control, correct, and punish unprofessional behavior. (See also Chapters 6, 12, and 14). But in the long run, the most effective deterrents to unethical conduct will be the lawyer's own conscience, the benefits of a good reputation, and the individual lawyer's realization of the social consequences of the failure to fulfill the legal profession's responsibilities.

CHAPTER 6

THE DUTY TO ENSURE COMPETENCE: PROFESSIONAL DISCIPLINE, MALPRACTICE ACTIONS, INEFFECTIVE ASSISTANCE OF COUNSEL CLAIMS, CONTINUING LEGAL EDUCATION, AND SPECIALIZATION

I. INTRODUCTION

"The greatest trust between man and man is the trust of giving Counsell."

Francis Bacon
Essays, 1598

Provoked by Chief Justice Warren Burger's statement "as a working hypothesis that from one-third to one-half of the lawyers who appear in the serious cases are not really qualified to render fully adequate representation," Burger, The Special Skills of Advocacy (1973), the competence of attorneys has undergone intensive examination and discussion in recent years. In addition, attacks on attorney performance in the press and through increased legal malpractice actions, as well as appeals alleging violation of the right to effective assistance of counsel in criminal cases, have focused both public and professional attention on attorney competence.

Surveys of the legal consumer, the bar, and the judiciary have attempted to determine the extent of attorney incompetence. Many consumers believe that "lawyers are not concerned about doing anything about the bad apples in the legal profession." One–third of the federal appellate court judges surveyed believed that inadequate appellate advocacy by lawyers is a serious problem.

This assessed lack of competence was attributed by the judges to lack of specialized trial skills and knowledge, failure of attorneys to prepare adequately, poor proficiency in planning and managing litigation, poor judgment in structuring the examination of witnesses and appellate briefing, and a lack of general legal knowledge. Despite some differences in details, the bar members surveyed generally agreed with the assessment of attorney performance made by the federal judges. As has been observed, the perceptions of the judiciary may underestimate the competence problem, since courtroom performance represents only about 1% of the legal services being delivered: The other 99% of legal services are delivered within the privacy of attorneys' offices and are not subject to professional scrutiny.

However estimated, there is general agreement that the legal profession has failed to establish and maintain high standards for attorney competence. The repercussions of this incompetence, both for the clients served and for the profession itself, are pervasive. First, based as it is on the adversary model (see Ch. 16, The Adversary System), our legal system assumes that both parties in a dispute are represented by counsel of equal and competent ability: A disparity in the competence of counsel could result in one party's prevailing for the "wrong" reasons, rather than on the basis of the merits of the case. Second,

> the complexity of the services rendered makes it impossible for the subjects of this service to judge whether or not it is good, bad or indifferent. The subject must take the professional, literally, on faith. There is no chance for realistic appraisal or examination of what service is being received, until it is too late. It is this characteristic that imposes such a high ethical burden upon the professional to commit himself first, foremost, and always, to the good of his clients.

Watson, Canons as Guides to Action (1966). Supporting this argument, a 1973–74 ABA opinion survey found that 79% of the public believed that people failed to seek legal advice because they had no means by which to assess attorneys' competence. Third, "[o]n the theory that only those possessed of the requisite learning, skill, and character can be trusted to perform legal services, the bar is granted an economic monopoly." Weckstein, Maintaining the Integrity and Competence of the Legal Profession (1970). The continuing efforts of the organized bar to maintain the provision of legal services within its exclusive domain (see, e.g., Ch. 7, Unauthorized Practice) also imply an obligation to provide the best possible legal services.

The methods for assuring lawyer competence and the available sanctions against incompetent performance represent divergent attempts to protect clients from the results of incompetence and to rid the profession of its least competent members.

II. THE CODE OF PROFESSIONAL RESPONSIBILITY AND THE MODEL RULES OF PROFESSIONAL CONDUCT

The CPR has now been replaced or augmented in over 35 states by the Model Rules of Professional Conduct, (RPC), adopted by the ABA in 1983. Both the CPR and the RPC focus on the duties of the individual attorney to maintain her own professional competence (Canon 6; RPC Rule 1.1) and to assist in maintaining the competence of the profession (Canon 1; RPC Rules 5.1, 8.1, 8.3). However, the RPC are more detailed in defining "competence," and in providing recommended means for its maintenance.

A. DUTY TO MAINTAIN ONE'S OWN COMPETENCE

Canon 6 of the Code provides: "A Lawyer Should Represent a Client Competently." Several corresponding ethical considerations enunciate general duties to "become and remain proficient," EC 6–1, and to be motivated to perform competently from professional pride, not from fear of civil liability or disciplinary action, EC 6–5. The RPC Preamble indicates that a lawyer should be guided by personal conscience and the approbation of professional peers. The Scope section of the Preamble recognizes that the RPC depend primarily upon voluntary compliance, and indicates that the RPC do not form a comprehensive list of moral considerations for lawyers, but only "a framework for the ethical practice of law."

The Code is more specific with respect to three particular forms of attorney behavior: competence, preparation, and neglect. DR 6–101(A)(1) provides that "[a] lawyer shall not . . . [h]andle a legal matter which he knows or should know that he is not competent to handle, without associating with him a lawyer who is competent to handle it." The ethical considerations supporting this disciplinary rule suggest that an attorney should accept employment only in matters in which he is or intends to become competent, EC 6–1; that acceptance of employment in an area in which he expects to become qualified may be made only if it is in good faith and will not result in unreasonable delay or expense to the client, EC 6–3; and that an offer of employment in an area in which the attorney is not and does not expect to become qualified should either be declined or, with client consent, accepted only in association with a lawyer who is competent to handle it, EC 6–3.

The second standard is enunciated in DR 6–101(A)(2): "A lawyer shall not . . . [h]andle a legal matter without preparation adequate in the circumstances." See also EC 6–4. Finally, DR 6–101(A)(3) provides that "[a] lawyer shall not . . . [n]eglect a legal matter entrusted to him." As with "competence," however, "adequate preparation" and "neglect" are not otherwise defined by the Code. ABA Informal Opinion 1273 (1973) does offer some minimal guidance by distinguishing between neglect and negligence:

> Neglect involves indifference and a consistent failure to carry out the obligations which the lawyer has assumed to his client or a conscious disregard for the responsibility owed to the client. The concept of ordinary negligence is different. Neglect usually involves more than a single act or omission. Neglect cannot

be found if the acts or omissions complained of were inadvertent or the result of an error of judgment made in good faith.

As thus defined, "neglect" involves a series of acts or omissions and is a relatively gross violation of the lawyer's professional obligations.

The RPC more specifically describe the competence requirement: "Competent representation requires the legal knowledge, skill, thoroughness and preparation reasonably necessary for the representation." RPC 1.1. The ABA Comment to Rule 1.1 provides guidance for interpreting these four elements. Requisite knowledge and skill can be determined by the nature of the matter, the lawyer's level of experience, and whether consultation with another lawyer of established competence is feasible, among other factors.

A lawyer need not have special training to handle all problems with which he is unfamiliar, since some legal skills—such as analysis of precedent and determination of the legal problems involved—are required in all legal problems. However, Rule 1.3 requires reasonable diligence and promptness in representation, so an inexperienced lawyer must not cause unreasonable delay in preparing for an area of law new to him. When confronted by a legal problem which he is not competent to handle, a lawyer has three options: He may (1) decline to accept the client or withdraw from representing the client; (2) make himself competent through study and training, if he can do so without unreasonable delay or expense; (3) associate with counsel experienced in the area, if the client consents. In an emergency a lawyer may give advice reasonably necessary, even if he does not have the skill which would ordinarily be required. ABA Comment.

The CPR and RPC also contain provisions relating to the attorney's duty to decline employment in circumstances that might foster incompetent performance: "Employment should not be accepted by a lawyer when he is unable to render competent service . . . . Likewise, a lawyer should decline employment if the intensity of his personal feelings, as distinguished from a community attitude, may impair his effective representation of a prospective client." EC 2–30. RPC 1.16 states that a lawyer shall not represent a client if representation would constitute a violation of the RPC or other law, which would include the lawyer's lack of the requisite competence or (by implication) if the lawyer could not be thorough or diligent in representing his client due to the lawyer's "personal feelings."

B. DUTY TO ASSIST THE PROFESSION IN MAINTAINING COMPETENCE

Canon 1 of the CPR provides that "A Lawyer Should Assist in Maintaining the Integrity and Competence of the Legal Profession." The corresponding ethical considerations state that this duty is an affirmative one, EC 1–2, placed on every lawyer, EC 1–1, and includes an obligation to prevent an attorney who is unqualified temporarily or permanently by mental or emotional instability from practicing law, EC 1–6. DR 1–103 requires a lawyer possessing unprivileged knowledge of another's incompetence (through DR 1–102(A)(1) and DR 6–101(A)(1)–(3)) to report her knowledge to the appropriate disciplinary authority and to reveal that information on proper request from such authority.

RPC Rule 1.16(a)(2) provides that a lawyer shall not represent a client if the lawyer's physical or mental condition materially impairs his competence. Failure to report another lawyer's incompetence could be seen as a violation of Rule 8.3 if the other lawyer's incompetence *"raises a substantial question* as to that lawyer's honesty, trustworthiness or fitness as a lawyer in other respects. . . ." (Emphasis added.) "Substantial" refers to the seriousness of the possible offense, not the amount of evidence of which the lawyer is aware. Many jurisdictions have established groups of concerned lawyers to counsel and assist lawyers whose use of alcohol or other substances has impaired their ability or effectiveness. In most instances, communications with such a group are deemed confidential, obviating the duty to report the impaired lawyer. However, it may be necessary to transfer the lawyer to inactive status until the problem is overcome. See ABA

Standards for Lawyer Discipline and Disability Proceedings, Standards 12.1–12.6.

It should also be noted that RPC 8.1, prohibiting false statements of material facts regarding disciplinary matters or admission to the bar, and Rule 5.1, placing a special duty upon partners and supervisory lawyers to "make reasonable efforts to ensure that the firm has in effect measures giving reasonable assurance that all lawyers in the firm conform" to the RPC, are intended to assist in promoting competence.

III. PROFESSIONAL DISCIPLINE

The types of complaints filed by clients with bar disciplinary committees are varied, but do represent the forms of incompetence that are the most frequent sources of public comment. A summary of complaints filed in California indicated that greed, deception, "incompetence," and poor management of the attorney-client relationship were the most prevalent complaints. More specifically, those complaints that resulted in attorney discipline were, in order of frequency, mismanagement of client funds, failure to perform services, gross negligence, deceit of clients, acting without authority, and conflict of interest.

Following In re Ruffalo (U.S.1968), which required that enforcement of disciplinary rules against individual attorneys be applied within the limitations of procedural due process, one federal appellate court held that certain CPR provisions relating to extrajudicial comments by attorneys were unconstitutionally vague and overbroad, and consequently could not be used as a basis for disciplinary proceedings, Chicago Council of Lawyers v. Bauer (7th Cir.1975). See Ch. 17 (Fair Trial/Free Press). One of the authors suggested that, if the standard used for evaluating criminal codes was applied to the CPR's disciplinary rules, they would be found "void for vagueness." Aronson, Professional Responsibility (1976). See also Ch. 5 (Maintenance of Professional Standards). Judge Oakes of the Second Circuit stated that, "as Canon 6 now reads, a charge of unethical competency would fail for want of specificity. . . ." Oakes, Lawyer and Judge: The Ethical Duty of Competency (1978). The failure of the Code to define "competence," "inadequate preparation," and "neglect" in terms of specific behavioral criteria resulted in insufficient guidance for either the individual attorney or a disciplinary committee. The RPC, although more specific in their definitions than the CPR, have not resolved the tension between efforts to avoid vagueness on the one hand and undue restrictions on attorney judgment and prerogative on the other.

Courts have also struggled with the standard of proof required in disciplinary proceedings. The Court in *Ruffalo* held that such proceedings are "quasi-criminal" in nature, since they impose punishment, and therefore entail some procedural rights applicable in criminal proceedings. But, although criminal proceedings require that charges be proved beyond a reasonable doubt, state courts have applied all three levels of proof to disciplinary proceedings: beyond a reasonable doubt, clear and convincing proof, and preponderance of the evidence.

The requirement to report the incompetence, inadequate preparation, and neglect of other attorneys (CPR Canon 1, RPC 8.3), both on request from disciplinary authorities and especially on the attorney's own initiative, has been criticized as unrealistic. Some states that have adopted other provisions of the CPR or RPC have not adopted this requirement or have adopted the hortatory "should inform", rather than the mandatory "shall inform" of RPC 8.3. The fraternalism and social contacts among lawyers and the disinclination to "squeal" on a colleague are most frequently cited as factors preventing attorneys' complaints against one another. The available data on the frequency of attorneys' complaints to bar grievance committees regarding the professional conduct of other attorneys support the argument that the reporting requirements of the CPR and RPC are unlikely to be met.

As an example both of the infrequency of attorney complaints against other attorneys and of the weakness of the disciplinary system in monitoring even blatant attorney misconduct, Professor Thode reported that a particularly notorious (and successful) malpractice suit did not result in a single complaint being filed with the appropriate disciplinary committee. He pointed clearly to the distinctive functions of malpractice actions and professional discipline, and to the notable lack of convergence between these functions in practice: "A successful malpractice action against the lawyer probably satisfied the client; no one protected the general public's interest. Apparently, neither the lawyers nor the judges who knew about this misconduct felt an obligation to bring the matter before the appropriate disciplinary body." Thode, The Duty of Lawyers and Judges to Report Other Lawyers' Breaches of the Standards of the Legal Profession (1976).

The infrequency of attorney discipline resulting from complaints to grievance committees has also prevented the profession's disciplinary system from functioning properly. For example, in California in 1984, 8329 complaints to the bar grievance committee resulted in attorney discipline in fewer than 3% of the cases according to an ABA survey. Another study, which collected available data on discipline from several jurisdictions, found that only between one and two percent of all complaints resulted in any formal disciplinary sanctions.

The controversial In re Himmel decision (Ill.1988) indicates that action by the judiciary can have a profound effect on the reporting of attorney misconduct by other attorneys. In *Himmel,* a lawyer who failed to report another lawyer's misconduct was suspended from the practice of law for one year, despite the lawyer's claim that his obligations of loyalty and confidentiality obligated him not to report his knowledge. See Ch. 11 (Confidentiality) for further analysis of *Himmel.* In the first five months following Himmel's suspension, the Illinois Attorney Registration and Discipline Commission received 331 complaints.

The amount allocated to and spent by disciplinary authorities may substantially impact these results. In California, for example, a substantial increase in funding (more than $100 million over 3 years), derived primarily from increased bar dues, reduced an over three-year backlog of pending cases to six months. The number of attorneys disciplined and the percentage of cases in which discipline was imposed also rose substantially. According to a 1990 report to the legislature, increased disciplinary activity between 1988 and 1989 included: a 44% increase in total disciplinary actions by the State Bar Court from 298 to 430, including 89 disbarment and 221 suspension recommendations; disbarments and resignations with charges pending increased 29% and 28% respectively; suspensions increased 66%; and the case investigation backlog of cases pending more than six months decreased from 1,894 to 566. A substance abuse diversion program and procedures enabling a court to assume jurisdiction over law practices to protect lawyers' clients were also implemented by the State Bar.

Proposals seeking to increase the effectiveness of the disciplinary machinery in monitoring attorney competence have been initiated in several jurisdictions. One proposal, participation by nonlawyers in the disciplinary process, works both to avoid the tendency of grievance committees to be lenient with their professional peers and to increase public respect for and trust in the disciplinary system. A second proposal, to increase the visibility of disciplinary proceedings by making them more public, lessens the impression that they are merely a private settlement of public concerns between self-interested colleagues. A third proposal, maintaining a continuous record of complaints filed and disciplinary action taken against each attorney, ensures better monitoring of repeat offenders. Finally, a standardization of disciplinary action for certain forms of attorney misconduct, and an increased range of potential disciplinary sanctions, has rendered the system more effective and more comprehensive in many states.

IV. MALPRACTICE LIABILITY

Legal commentators unanimously agree that the frequency of legal malpractice suits has increased alarmingly in the past few years.

For example, there was a 250% increase in legal malpractice suits from 1978 to 1980. One leading malpractice insurer alone reported an average 20% annual increase in malpractice claims in a three-year period. The insurer estimated that one in every 20 lawyers is sued for malpractice each year, and recent statistics suggest that most attorneys will face an average of three malpractice claims in the course of their careers. Securities, tax, antitrust, family law and trial attorneys (especially plaintiffs' personal injury attorneys) are reported to be particularly vulnerable to malpractice suits. Although 75% of such suits fail, they are very expensive to try. The cost of defending a legal malpractice suit has been estimated at more than six times the cost of defending an automobile accident suit.

A. CAUSES OF MALPRACTICE EXPLOSION

The reasons advanced for this legal malpractice explosion are varied. One factor contributing to the increase in suits may be a changing social attitude, which places more emphasis on consumer awareness (and has been alternatively described as "palpably litigious"). According to some observers, attorneys are particularly suitable targets for malpractice actions because they frequently have "deep pockets" (carry malpractice insurance). Second, some trial attorneys contend that since, in every case, one party loses, that party may well attribute the loss to the attorney. Third, the attitudes of the legal profession itself are changing: Attorneys are becoming less reluctant to represent clients or to testify as experts in malpractice actions. Also, judicial attitudes are becoming more liberal toward acknowledging professional misconduct and incompetence: Expanding time limits for bringing claims, allowing new theories of recovery, and eliminating the requirement of privity for third party actions in some cases, all exemplify this liberalization.

Fourth, poor interpersonal relationships between attorneys and their clients may contribute to increased malpractice suits. For example, surveys of clients have indicated that as many as one-third believed that lawyers failed to discover and respond to their clients' true concerns. The diminished frequency of a "warm, human relationship" between attorney and client engenders a more suspicious client attitude toward attorney performance. Fifth, the current influx of attorneys, often from new, unaccredited law schools, may work to increase malpractice suits. Sixth, the frequency of medical malpractice suits and the resulting publicity has contributed to making the public "malpractice conscious." This public consciousness may simply be transferred to lawyers. Finally, failings by the bar itself contribute to the increase in malpractice actions: Inadequate disciplinary procedures by the legal profession, ineffective efforts to ensure that lawyers maintain high standards of competence once they are licensed, and the poor performance of individual attorneys may all result in increased suits.

The results of increased malpractice actions have included larger recoveries, higher costs of malpractice insurance, and the lessening availability of malpractice insurance for lawyers. Nationally, the costs of judgments and settlements in legal malpractice cases doubled between 1972 and 1975. One recent award in Ohio totalled $2.35 million, and one law firm whose clients engaged in securities violations settled for over $40 million. The average verdict against personal injury lawyers for malpractice from 1976 to 1981 was over $200,000. Only psychiatrists had a higher average malpractice verdict among professional groups surveyed. In response to generally rising insurance rates, Congress and state legislatures have investigated or enacted legislation curtailing lawsuits and placing caps on awards as a means of reducing insurance rates. This flurry of "tort reform" activity is partially a reaction to some government agencies' inability to secure insurance at any price.

B. FREQUENTLY RECURRING MALPRACTICE COMPLAINTS

The most frequent complaints by clients which ultimately result in malpractice actions against their attorneys involve conflicts of interest, inattention to the client's needs and requests, neglect, and general carelessness. In a recent California study, more than half the claims (and the majority of awards and settlements) were prompted by missed deadlines, such as failing to file suit before a statute of limitations expires, or representing likely adverse parties, such as both husband and wife in a divorce case. Other common complaints include errors in title searches and wills, missed court appearances, misfiled papers, and failing to return a client's calls or answer her letters. Also, fraud, commingling of funds, and errors in legal judgment resulting either in financial loss or criminal conviction are frequent causes for bringing suit. Some complaints are more costly than others. Seven percent of claims in the California study were for conflict of interest, but these claims generated the largest share of payouts, approximately $2.6 million.

1. "Customer Relations"

These types of frequent complaints have clear implications for an attorney's behavior with his client. Before accepting employment from a client, the attorney must realistically assess his ability to handle the additional work. At the outset of the attorney-client relationship, the attorney should: advise his client of the risks involved; not promise or predict a specific case outcome or dollar recovery; advise his client of the amount of time and frequent delays involved in litigation; and explain the basis for computing his fees, as well as court costs and other expenses that the client may be expected to bear. An attorney should attempt to establish a good relationship with his client, including being attentive to the client's concerns and maintaining continuing contact with him. For example, the attorney should return telephone calls and answer letters promptly; forward copies of all pleadings, briefs, memoranda, and relevant correspondence to the client; and keep the client informed by periodic status reports, particularly during long periods of delay. The attorney should maintain complete records, including memoranda of conversations with clients, witnesses, opposing counsel, and others. All oral instructions and important conversations with the client should be confirmed by letter. In the event of unforeseen absence, these records also allow another attorney to continue with the client's case.

Serious problems that develop in the case should not be withheld from the client, and she should be informed of alternative strategies and, when possible, allowed to choose between them. See ABA Comments, RPC 1.2, 1.4; ECs 7–7, 7–8. Actions which may be prejudicial to the client should not be taken without her consent (e.g., release of a party, agreement to a judgment, or settlement). RPC 1.2(a). An efficient bookkeeping procedure for managing client funds and payments should be followed, to avoid negligent commingling of funds. Timekeeping on a client's case should be done contemporaneously, and the client billed periodically, to avoid fee disputes. A calendar system, or "tickle file," that is well-organized and used will prevent missed deadlines for filing and appearances. Also, checklists of tasks to be accomplished in a given case (commercially available) will help remind the attorney of otherwise forgettable details. Association of or consultation with another attorney should not be made without client consent (see Ch. 12). An attorney should not reveal to his clients that he carries malpractice insurance, nor should he criticize a prior lawyer's handling of a case without full appraisal of all material facts.

The majority of the above procedures are based on simple courtesy, common sense, and standard office practices. The remainder of this section will deal with the law of malpractice, rather than "customer relations."

2. Legal Negligence and Neglect

An action for legal malpractice can be based on theories of either tort or contract, or both. In tort, the malpractice action is composed of the same elements as any other action for negligence: a duty of care, breach of that duty, proximate cause, and damage to the plaintiff. The standard of care applied to the attorney's performance is typically "that degree of care, skill, diligence, and knowledge commonly possessed and exercised by a reasonably careful and prudent attorney in the practice of law in his jurisdiction or community." Gates and Zilly, "Legal Malpractice" (1978). See Mallen and Smith, Legal Malpractice (3rd ed. 1989).

Alternatively, "[s]ince an attorney usually undertakes to perform duties pursuant to a contract with his client, the attorney's failure to exercise requisite skill and care is a breach of an expressed or implied contract; thus legal malpractice generally constitutes both a tort and a breach of contract." Gillen, Legal Malpractice (1973). See Mallen and Smith, supra. The attorney's contractual obligations to her client are enforceable in the absence of consideration, and an attorney may be found liable for her gratuitous advice. Since most jurisdictions allow pleading in the alternative, an election of theories is usually not necessary.

Generally, attorneys are not found liable for mere errors in judgment, made in good faith and with an honest belief, nor for a mistake in a point of law that is unsettled by the courts and on which reasonable doubt could be entertained by well-informed attorneys. An attorney is generally found liable for ignorance or nonobservance of statutes, court rules, or court decisions that she knows, or should know, apply to her case; she must discover those rules of law which may be found by standardized legal research techniques. Some courts have applied a more stringent standard, however: Reasoning from the premise of the special fiduciary nature of the attorney-client relationship, those courts have found the standard of care to require a conscientious endeavor on the part of the attorney.

The standard of care in particular areas of law may vary. For instance, an attorney who represents himself as a specialist may be held to the standard of care met by other attorneys of his specialty, and this standard may require expanding the "community" comparison to one beyond the geographic area in which he practices. In the area of securities law, for example, the attorney is usually found to have an affirmative duty to investigate and to disclose material information, and the appropriate standard of care becomes more than mere "reasonableness."

The question of whether an attorney has exercised a reasonable degree of care and skill is one of fact. Traditionally, the standard by which an attorney's actions are measured has been based on expert testimony (by other attorneys). As mentioned supra, the unwillingness of attorneys to testify against one another has lessened in recent years, making this element of proof less difficult to achieve. A few states, however, do permit the trier of fact to determine malpractice without the use of expert testimony when the common knowledge or experience of laypersons is sufficiently extensive to recognize or infer negligence from the facts.

Both the CPR and the RPC claim not to define standards for civil liability of lawyers for professional conduct. As Professor Thode noted, however, "any lawyer representing a client in a malpractice action in a jurisdiction adopting this Code who does not contend that the Code in fact sets a standard to be applied in malpractice cases will himself probably be demonstrating a lack of competence." Thode, Canons 6 and 7: The Lawyer–Client Relationship (1970). Thode observed that the use of the CPR as a set of codified standards for lawyer competence in malpractice actions is similar to the use of traffic regulations in setting standards for tort actions. In attorney malpractice actions, courts have not hesitated to apply CPR and RPC provisions as "some evidence" of the standards of required conduct, and several courts have held that violations of mandatory provisions intended to protect clients create a rebuttable presumption of breach of the standard of care.

The defenses applicable to an ordinary negligence action are also applicable to an action for legal malpractice. For example, in litigation, a successful malpractice action requires persuasive evidence that the client would have prevailed if the attorney had properly prosecuted or defended the action. The running of a statute of limitations will also preclude consideration of a claim. The applicable statute of limitations is one for ordinary negligence or breach of contract; recently, the trend has been to substitute a date of discovery for the former date of negligent action rule: Courts have held that the statute begins to run when the client discovers, or should have discovered, all facts material to a cause of action, or when he suffers appreciable harm, or both. The client can be found contributorily negligent, such as when he fails to provide, or provides false, information to his attorney. However, as mentioned supra, the client's failure to pay for legal services does not relieve the attorney of her duties to perform competently and completely.

The rules of agency and vicarious liability apply to legal malpractice as well: An attorney may be found liable for the negligence of her clerical and secretarial employees, associates, and partners, and for others, such as paralegals, acting within the scope of her authority. An attorney is not liable for the negligent acts of someone who has exceeded his authority or acted outside the scope of his employment.

C. LIABILITY TO THIRD PARTIES

Traditionally, attorneys have had a limited immunity from liability to third persons harmed by their actions, unless fraud or other malicious or intentional acts have been committed. Attorneys are usually not liable for wrongful attachment, malicious prosecution, or interference with a contractual relationship if the advice has been honestly given in a professional capacity.

Third parties pursuing legal malpractice liability generally fall into one of three classes: adversaries, intended beneficiaries, and other parties injured by an attorney or his client. Adversaries are universally excluded from recovery, to protect the attorney-client relationship and to avoid conflicts of interest. Third party beneficiaries, such as beneficiaries of wills, have been most successful in recovering damages against lawyers for malpractice. However, it can be difficult for a third party to prove that he is an intended beneficiary of the attorney-client "contract." Even when the attorney and client do intend to benefit the third party, if some other purpose of the "contract" is seen as superior to benefitting the third party, the third party will be denied recovery. However, attorneys have been held liable to persons who have relied on an examination of title, who are damaged by negligent drafting or execution of wills, or who have relied on legal opinions concerning a stock offering.

Until recently, other (non-beneficiary) third parties could not recover unless they were in privity of contract with the attorney and client. This is still the case in the majority of states. Privity has been seen as necessary to protect the fiduciary nature of the attorney-client relationship. However, appellate decisions and insurance company statistics indicate that the number of third-party claimants is dramatically increasing and now constitutes up to 20% of those persons who sue attorneys.

Since excluding third parties who are without privity can produce unfair results, allowing attorneys to escape responsibility for negligent conduct that injures others, several courts have employed a balancing test in determining whether a third party may establish an attorney's liability. These courts have applied five criteria: the extent to which the attorney's action was intended to affect the third person; the forseeability of harm to others; the degree of certainty that the third person suffered injury; the causal relationship between the attorney's conduct and the injury; and the policy of preventing future harm. See, e.g., Stangland v. Brock (Wash.1987); Heyer v. Flaig (Cal.1969). The five criteria are to be balanced by the courts on a case-by-case basis. This approach may improve fairness to third parties, but perhaps at the cost of consistency.

D. LIMITING LIABILITY

The great increase in malpractice claims and damages recovered presents the temptation for an attorney to negotiate an agreement with clients to preclude or place a cap on malpractice liability. DR 6–102(A) provides that "[a] lawyer shall not attempt to exonerate himself from or limit his liability to his client for his personal malpractice." EC 6–6 justifies this disciplinary rule by stating that a lawyer who properly handles his client's affairs does not need to limit his liability, while one who does not perform adequately should not be permitted to limit it. However, an attorney who is a stockholder in or associated with a professional legal corporation may limit his liability for the malpractice of his associates, as permitted by law. RPC 1.8(h) also prohibits limitation of liability, but adds another exception to those found in the CPR—the lawyer may make an agreement prospectively limiting his liability for malpractice if permitted by law and the client is independently represented in making the agreement. The lawyer may settle a malpractice claim with an unrepresented or former client only after first advising him in writing that independent representation is appropriate.

Obviously, an attorney sued for professional malpractice has a great incentive to settle: The publicity occasioned by the suit, even if the decision is in his favor, could be quite harmful to his reputation and his practice. Frequently, the out-of-court settlement of a legal malpractice action includes stipulations to expunge the record of malpractice charges and to close it to the press and public. As indicated by *Himmel* (Ill.1988), supra, however, it may be considered unethical to agree not to inform the disciplinary authority of misconduct by a client's former attorney as a condition of settlement with the former attorney.

V. INEFFECTIVE ASSISTANCE OF COUNSEL

The right to the assistance of counsel is embodied in the Sixth Amendment to the federal constitution, which provides in part: "In all criminal prosecutions, the accused shall enjoy the right . . . to have the Assistance of Counsel for his defence." The importance of this right has been best stated in the often-quoted words of Justice Sutherland in Powell v. Alabama (U.S.1932):

> The right to be heard would be, in many cases, of little avail if it did not comprehend the right to be heard by counsel. Even the intelligent and educated layman has small and sometimes no skill in the science of law. If charged with crime, he is incapable, generally, of determining for himself whether the indictment is good or bad. He is unfamiliar with the rules of evidence. Left without aid of counsel he may be put on trial without a proper charge, and convicted upon incompetent evidence or evidence irrelevant to the issue or otherwise inadmissible. He lacks both the skill and knowledge adequately to prepare his defense, even though he may have a perfect one. He requires the guiding hand of counsel at every step in the

proceedings against him. Without it, though he be not guilty, he faces the danger of conviction because he does not know how to establish his innocence.

The centrality of the right to counsel has been articulated by Justice Schaefer of the Illinois Supreme Court: "Of all the rights that an accused person has, the right to be represented by counsel is by far the most pervasive, for it affects his ability to assert any other rights he may have." Federalism and State Criminal Procedure (1956).

As Chief Judge David Bazelon of the District of Columbia Circuit noted, however, the right to the assistance of counsel is often merely the right to *pro forma* representation. In sharing a colleague's perception of the prevalence of attorneys who are "walking violations of the sixth amendment," Judge Bazelon reported instances where (a) defense counsel was unaware that the court maintained records of prior convictions, (b) defense counsel advised the court that he would take only a few minutes for summation because he had to move his car before five o'clock, and (c) when defense counsel was questioned by the court for more recent precedent than the 1895 decision on which he was relying, counsel replied that he had been unable to locate a Shepard's citator. The Defective Assistance of Counsel (1973).

The reasons for the prevalence of this "ineffectiveness" are varied. Judge Bazelon attributed the occurrence of such ineffectiveness to the low status involved in provision of counsel to accused indigents, the fact that criminal caseloads are reaching crisis proportions, the lack of incentives for the prosecutor to monitor the quality of her adversary, the tendency of judges to prefer "sweetheart lawyers" who make few motions and cause little trouble, and the kinds of lawyers who represent indigent defendants. He characterized these lawyers as being one of three types: (a) "courthouse regulars," mediocre lawyers who frequent the courtroom, hopefully awaiting receipt of appointments, who rely on a high volume of such appointments to make their living; (b) "uptown lawyers," usually from private practice in corporate, labor, securities, or patent law, who "do their public duty" by representing indigent defendants and are otherwise not seen in the vicinity of the courthouse; and (c) "neophytes," recent law school graduates gaining their experience at the expense of their clients. Most of Judge Bazelon's observations are equally true today.

A. EVOLUTION OF THE RIGHT TO EFFECTIVE ASSISTANCE

The development of a constitutional right to counsel, and by extension, of a constitutional right to effective counsel, is of relatively recent origin. Prior to 1938, the Sixth Amendment right to counsel was viewed as affording only a right to retain counsel. In Johnson v. Zerbst (U.S.1938), the United States Supreme Court found the Sixth Amendment to grant the right to appointed counsel in all federal criminal cases. The right to counsel has been greatly expanded, beginning with the landmark case of Gideon v. Wainwright (U.S.1963), where the right was found to be required for all state felony proceedings. The Court characterized the right to counsel as "fundamental" and set the stage for a series of decisions that have granted the right to counsel at various stages of criminal proceedings. Nine years after *Gideon,* in Argersinger v. Hamlin (U.S.1972), the right to counsel was mandated for trials for any offense, "whether classified as petty, misdemeanor, or felony," for which the penalty involved loss of liberty.

In United States v. Wade (U.S.1967), the Court stated:

> It is central to that principle that in addition to counsel's presence at trial, the accused is guaranteed that he need not stand alone against the State at any stage of the prosecution, formal or informal, in court or out, where counsel's absence might derogate from the accused's right to a fair trial.

Subsequent cases developed a "critical stage" analysis to determine the necessity of representation by counsel in criminal proceedings. Under this analysis, the right to counsel now attaches at line-ups if the accused has been charged, United States v. Wade

(U.S.1967), at interrogations, Escobedo v. Illinois (U.S.1964), at preliminary hearings, Coleman v. Alabama (U.S.1970), at arraignments, Hamilton v. Alabama (U.S.1961), and at appeals granted as a matter of right, Evitts v. Lucey (U.S.1985); Douglas v. California (U.S.1963). Presence of counsel, much less effectiveness of counsel, is not mandated at "non-critical" stages, however. See, e.g., Ross v. Moffitt (U.S.1974) ("discretionary" appeals); Williams v. Missouri (8th Cir.1981, cert. denied, 1982) (habeas corpus).

The Supreme Court has held that the right to counsel guaranteed by the Sixth Amendment encompasses a limited right to be represented by one's preferred attorney, i.e., counsel of choice. See, e.g., Wheat v. United States (U.S.1988). However, a defendant may not insist on representation by an attorney he cannot afford or who for other reasons declines to represent him. Likewise, a trial court may refuse to accept a defendant's waiver of his attorney's conflict of interest. *Wheat,* supra. The court may disqualify defense counsel and insist that the defendant be separately represented to avoid a breach of professional ethics and to ensure the integrity of trial process. In Caplin & Drysdale, Chartered v. United States (U.S.1989), the Court held that a defendant "has no Sixth Amendment right to spend another person's money for services rendered by an attorney, even if those funds are the only way that that defendant will be able to retain the attorney of choice." Thus, it is not a violation of the right to counsel of choice for a court to authorize forfeiture to the government of a defendant's assets, or to enter a restraining order freezing assets subject to forfeiture, even if the assets were intended to be (or had been) paid for bona fide legal services. *Caplin & Drysdale,* supra.

The development of case law finding the right to counsel to include the right to *effective* counsel began with Powell v. Alabama (U.S.1932). In *Powell,* the Court held that assignment of counsel at a time and under circumstances precluding effective aid violated the Sixth Amendment, applicable to the states through the due process clause of the Fourteenth Amendment.

In McMann v. Richardson (U.S.1970), the Court said: "It has long been recognized that the right to counsel is the right to the effective assistance of counsel. . . . [I]f the right to counsel guaranteed by the Constitution is to serve its purpose, defendants cannot be left to the mercies of incompetent counsel. . . ." The leading case of Strickland v. Washington (U.S.1984) indicated that the purpose of effective counsel is to ensure fairness by securing a true adversarial testing process in which the defendant is provided ample opportunity to meet the prosecution's case.

B. STANDARDS FOR DETERMINING THE EFFECTIVENESS OF COUNSEL

The traditional standard for evaluating defense counsel's performance for effectiveness was the "farce and mockery of justice" standard. Under that standard, representation was deemed ineffective only when the trial was such a sham that it shocked the conscience of the court.

Most state and all the federal circuit courts had abandoned the "farce and mockery" standard by 1984 in favor of a requirement of "reasonably effective assistance." The United States Supreme Court adopted this standard in the landmark *Strickland* case, supra, as part of a two-prong test for ineffective assistance. First, the defendant must prove that counsel's performance did not provide "reasonably effective assistance," i.e., that it was not within the prevailing professional norms. The defendant must specify particular acts or omissions which allegedly resulted in ineffective assistance.

The Court in *Strickland* was concerned that if the adversarial process were undermined by ineffective defense counsel the basic fairness of the trial would be suspect. This reflected similar concerns expressed by a federal circuit court that "[w]hile a criminal trial is not a game in which the participants are expected to enter the ring with a near match in skills, neither is it a sacrifice of unarmed prisoners to gladiators." United States ex rel. Williams v. Twomey (7th Cir.1975).

However, the Court in *Strickland* also did not want to encourage convicted criminal defendants to attempt to escape liability by hindsight examination of defense strategy. Therefore, the Court stated that defense counsel's judgments are entitled to a high degree of deference. The Court expressed a reluctance to announce specific standards of effective assistance for fear of reducing defense attorneys' freedom to choose the strategy appropriate in their judgment. The defendant, therefore, must overcome a strong presumption that, under the surrounding circumstances at the time, the challenged action might be considered sound trial strategy. Defense counsel's performance must have been so deficient as to deprive the defendant of a fair trial.

Second, the defendant must prove that any alleged errors were prejudicial: There must be a reasonable probability that, but for the alleged errors, a different result would have been reached. A "reasonable probability" is one sufficient to undermine confidence in the outcome.

In dicta, the *Strickland* Court stated that some cases present a presumption of ineffective assistance of counsel so strong that a case-by-case inquiry is not worth the cost, since the fairness and adversarial balance of the trial are inevitably suspect. Complete actual or constructive denial of assistance of counsel is legally presumed to result in prejudice. Also, where the defendant can show that counsel actively represented conflicting interests, and that this conflict affected counsel's legal performance, he may establish ineffective assistance per se. Holloway v. Arkansas (U.S. 1978); Cuyler v. Sullivan (U.S.1980). In fact, the interest in ensuring conflict-free representation of criminal defendants is so strong that the Court has held that a trial judge may disqualify defense counsel with a conflict, despite the defendant's objections and willingness to waive any conflict. Wheat v. United States (U.S.1988).

The *Strickland* test for ineffective assistance of counsel has been extended to first appeals as of right, Evitts v. Lucey (U.S.1985), and to guilty plea challenges, Hill v. Lockhart (U.S.1985). In both of these cases, the Court emphasized its concern for reinforcing the finality of judgments in criminal cases. In *Evitts,* the Court also stated that the right to effective assistance of counsel applies in every criminal prosecution, without regard to whether defense counsel was appointed or retained. The right to effective assistance of counsel has also been extended by at least one state court to the defendant in a civil paternity action. Banks v. Randle (Pa. Super.1984).

C. PROCEDURAL LIMITATIONS ON CLAIMS OF INEFFECTIVE ASSISTANCE

Severe procedural limitations have been imposed on ineffective assistance claims. First, *Strickland* established not merely a presumption but a "strong presumption" of effective assistance. This is a very high standard for a defendant to overcome. Second, as Justice Marshall stated in his dissent to *Strickland,* the "but for" prejudice test established in *Strickland* will be difficult to meet. Defense counsel's own errors may make a determination of prejudice by an appellate court quite difficult. Where defense counsel's incompetence lay in failing to introduce evidence, for example, there will be no record of the evidence's possible impact. The appellate court will thus have to rely on hindsight. Furthermore, forcing a defendant to show prejudicial impact has been criticized as irrational: "To insist that the defendant now . . . show specific prejudice is requiring him to establish by his own efforts the very things for which the law recognized he needed the assistance of counsel in the first place and which he did not receive." McQueen v. State (Mo.1971) (Seiter, J., dissenting).

Third, the methods available for attacking a conviction on the basis of ineffectiveness of counsel pose a procedural obstacle. The two main methods available are direct appeal and collateral attack through federal habeas corpus petition. Since the likelihood of counsel appealing a conviction directly on the basis of his own ineffectiveness is low, the primary method used is the habeas corpus petition. With Brown v. Allen (U.S.1953), habeas corpus jurisdiction was extended to all constitutional errors, at any stage of the proceedings. However, a "serious burden of justification" is required of federal habeas corpus proceedings. Arguments that over-generous allowal of habeas proceedings on ineffectiveness claims will "open the floodgates," interfere with the finality of judgments, and encourage "writ-writing as a sport" in prisons, have been advanced as reasons to limit its availability.

In Stone v. Powell (U.S.1976), the Court held that a Fourth Amendment exclusionary rule claim may not be challenged by federal habeas corpus petition if the state has provided an opportunity for full and fair litigation of the claim. However, if the habeas petition is based primarily upon counsel's *ineffective assistance* in failing to advance an exclusionary rule claim, *Stone* does not restrict the habeas petitions. Federal courts may grant habeas corpus relief in appropriate cases, regardless of the underlying attorney error. Kimmelman v. Morrison (U.S.1986).

Even if judicial policies generally favored granting habeas corpus relief, there are problems which would likely limit its availability in ineffectiveness cases. First, habeas corpus relief is an after-the-fact remedy and, as such, may provide too little relief too late for defendants convicted because of counsel ineffectiveness. Second, numerous commentators have noted that appellate courts frequently "paper over" ineffectiveness of attorneys. "It is accurate to assert that most courts, this one included, traditionally have resisted any realistic inquiry into the competency of trial counsel." Wainwright v. Sykes (U.S.1977) (Brennan, J., dissenting).

Third, ineffectiveness of counsel may be the result of inadequate pretrial preparation and often does not appear on the record; the invisibility of this information (frequently caused by the very ineffectiveness complained of, as mentioned supra) tends to discourage consideration of the claim. Fourth, appellate courts have been unwilling to second-guess the strategy or tactics of defense counsel. This unwillingness is indicated in the Supreme Court's direction to "eliminate the distorting effects of hindsight." *Strickland,* supra. One difficulty with this cautious judicial posture regarding hindsight has been observed by Judge Oakes: ". . . the Court has meanwhile, to a greater extent than at any time in recent decades, subsumed the rights of the criminal defendant into his counsel's control: counsel's action or inaction binds the defendant even without knowledgeable waiver on the latter's part." Lawyer and Judge: The Ethical Duty of Competency (1978).

The practical results of both the procedural limitations on habeas corpus and the judicial caution in exercising hindsight have been that the courts have refused to recognize many extreme cases of counsel ineffectiveness. For example, in Chambers v. Maroney (U.S.1970), a case in which the attorney met his client for the first time on the way to the courtroom on the morning of trial, the Supreme Court decided the case on the basis that the defendant had not shown that he would have prevailed with an earlier appointment of counsel. In one case, defense counsel's sleeping during periods in which co-defendant's counsel was examining a witness was found not to be ineffectiveness since "the testimony during the periods of counsel's somnolence was not central to [the defendant's] case and that, if it had been, [the trial judge] would have awakened him rather than waited for the luncheon recess to warn him." And, in another case, the court found an ineffectiveness claim insufficient despite counsel's intoxication during the whole trial. The defendant's failure to place his objection to his attorney's drunkenness on the record was found to constitute a waiver of his right to the effective assistance of counsel. Although the case might now be decided differently under the first prong of the *Strickland* test, both *Chambers* and the somnolence case would probably have met with the same results under the prejudice prong of *Strickland.*

VI. RULE 11 SANCTIONS

Another method of improving competency (or at least discouraging incompetency) is the increasing use of sanctions under Rule 11 of the Federal Rules of Civil Procedure and its state counterparts. The Rule provides that all lawyers who sign their names to any pleading, motion, brief, or other paper filed in court, must certify that they believe the paper to be well grounded in fact, that it is supported by existing law or a good faith argument for a change in the law, and that it is not interposed for an improper purpose such as harassment or delay. Prior to signing the paper, the lawyer must conduct a "reasonable inquiry" into the facts and law to determine if they support all assertions contained in it. Pursuant to a 1983 amendment an objective, rather than good faith belief, standard is applied. Any violation of the Rule requires the trial court to impose a sanction upon the lawyer, the client, or both. Sanctions include: warnings; fines payable to the court; assessment of attorney's fees and costs incurred by the opposing party in responding to the improper or frivolous filing; and, on rare occasions, payment of all fees and costs or suspension from practice before the court. For more detailed discussion of Rule 11, see Ch. 5 supra (Maintenance of Professional Standards).

The efficacy of Rule 11 as a means of ensuring, or even improving, the competence of lawyers is at best uncertain. Literally thousands of reported decisions have analyzed the propriety, standards and procedure in the courts' application of the Rule in individual cases. An entire "satellite litigation" explosion over application of the Rule has occurred. Sanctions of hundreds of thousands of dollars, even for a single violation, have been imposed with increasing frequency. While it is clear that the initial unwillingness of courts to impose sanctions under Rule 11 no longer exists (23 reported cases between 1938 and 1983; 688 reported cases between 1983 and 1988), it is less clear whether the competency, validity or propriety of attorney filings has improved. And it appears that courts have given insufficient consideration to the exception for good faith arguments to change the law, imposing Rule 11 sanctions disproportionately on civil rights litigants.

In theory, at least, the requirement of "reasonable inquiry" into both the facts and applicable law would encourage better pleading and discovery practices. Some courts have held that a lawyer must continue to reassess the validity of the client's claims after they are filed and to take appropriate action if it becomes evident that a claim is not well-grounded in fact or law. And one court dealt directly with the competence issue by ordering attorneys for both parties to attend a continuing legal education program on federal trial practice. But whereas Rule 11 sanctions, like malpractice liability, serve as an incentive to become and remain competent (including conducting adequate factual and legal investigation), they do not establish competence directly. And, by holding that Rule 11 sanctions can only be imposed on the signing attorney and not his law firm (Pavelic & LeFlore v. Marvel Entertainment Group, U.S.1989), the Supreme Court weakened the incentive to monitor the competence of partners and associates.

VII. CONTINUING LEGAL EDUCATION

Continuing legal education programs have developed as a partial solution to problems of attorney incompetence. Some commentators have proposed mandatory continuing legal education as an appropriate attack on the myth of lawyer "omnicompetence" or "perpetual competence"—the notion, fostered by intensive preadmission professional screening and minimal post-admission guarantees of competence, that an attorney maintains her competence (and her license to practice) for life. Also, a primary characteristic of the law is its rapidly changing nature: In addition to modifications in traditional areas through court decisions, legislation, and government regulations, entirely new areas of law are created in response to change in societal concerns. In order to maintain her competence, an attorney must keep informed of these developments. This professional need can be met, at least in part, by participation in continuing legal education programs.

Both the RPC and the CPR support the obligation of an attorney to maintain professional competence through continuing education. EC 6–4 and ABA comment, RPC 1.1, mentioned supra, suggest that an attorney who has undertaken employment in an area beyond his competence has a duty to undertake the work and study necessary to qualify himself. EC 1–2 advises that the bar has an affirmative obligation to aid the courts to promulgate, enforce, and improve requirements for post-admission legal education. The RPC impose no such obligation on the bar at large, although the Comment to RPC 1.1 does admonish individual lawyers to "engage in continuing study and education."

A. VOLUNTARY CONTINUING LEGAL EDUCATION

Traditionally, continuing legal education has taken the form of either self-directed study (through periodicals, audio- and videotapes) or voluntary attendance at formal professional educational offerings. Post-admission courses proliferate in the profession: They are offered through local, state, and the national bar associations, law schools, and the Practising Law Institute, among others. As might be expected, voluntary (as opposed to mandatory) continuing legal education is preferred by the majority of attorneys as a method for maintaining competency. Unfortunately, those attorneys most likely to benefit from continuing education programs, e.g., those who are least "successful" and most overworked, are probably also least likely to participate because of time and money constraints.

B. MANDATORY CONTINUING LEGAL EDUCATION

Over 30 states have instituted, through their bar associations, mandatory continuing legal education programs. In these states, an attorney must attend authorized courses for a specified number of hours each year, averaging about 15 hours. In some states, a specified proportion of the required hours must consist of education in Professional Responsibility, and many states grant continuing education credit for courses given "in-house" by firms or corporate legal departments. Mandatory continuing legal education has been upheld as constitutional, so long as the requirements are "rational."

C. CRITICISMS OF CONTINUING LEGAL EDUCATION

Both voluntary and mandatory forms of continuing legal education have been heavily criticized. First, continuing legal education programs have been attacked for not being sufficiently rigorous. Second, the programs cannot guarantee that anything is learned: Typically, all that is required is attendance, rather than participation or active involvement, and testing or assessment of learning is generally not attempted. Third, the minimal number of hours required by the mandatory programs has been seen by some as an "empty gesture" toward developing or assuring competence. And, of course, negligence, neglect, inadequate pretrial preparation, and inadequacies listed under "Customer Relations," supra, are unaffected by continuing education in areas of substantive law.

On the other hand, improvements in continuing education programs have resulted in excellent training by groups such as the National Institute for Trial Advocacy (NITA) and the American Inns of Court Foundation. The Inns, presently numbering over 100, are modeled after the English inns of court, which emphasize learning through close contact with those more experienced, resulting in the creation of an ethos of competence, civility, ethics and collegiality. A local inn of court is composed of judges, law professors, law students, and a cross-section of attorneys from the most experienced to those recently admitted to the bar. Monthly meetings stress practice skills, professionalism and ethics through role playing and demonstrations, while mentoring programs give students and newly admitted attorneys the opportunity to interact with judges and senior attorneys in an informal setting. The phenomenal growth of the American Inns of Court movement and the enthusiasm with which lawyers and judges have participated suggest that voluntary continuing legal education can be effective, if provided under the right conditions.

VIII. RECERTIFICATION EXAMINATIONS

The absence of the testing aspect in continuing legal education programs has led some to advocate "recertification examinations" as an alternative. Specifically, the proposed examinations could take the form of (a) a complete bar examination, (b) a re-examination on recent developments in particular substantive fields, (c) an examination on substantive areas matching the attorney's field of practice, or (d) self-administered tests. With the exception of the latter, recertification examinations would present an opportunity to assess the level of ability of an individual attorney. As such, they would represent a knowledge, rather than a time (as in continuing legal education) requirement. Also, recertification by examination would provide the advantages of protecting the public and expressing a legitimate state interest in excluding unqualified attorneys from practice.

However, such examinations also present major drawbacks. Specifically, the reality that many practitioners are not generalists but specialists, the amount of preparation time involved, the potential effect on minority membership in the bar (considering the high failure rates of some minority groups on standardized pre-admission bar examinations), the probability of false negatives (exclusion by testing of those who are in fact qualified or competent), and the notion that an attorney's profession becomes a "vested property right," after a lifetime investment of education, aspirations, money and time, are all factors that contribute to expected bar opposition to such a proposal. No state has instituted requirements for periodic recertification examinations. In a recent ABA poll, 68% of lawyers responding were opposed to such examinations.

IX. SPECIALIZATION

It is generally agreed that the legal profession has engaged in informal, de facto specialization for a number of years. Surveys of attorneys in Chicago and California indicate that approximately two-thirds consider themselves to be specialists. For a long time, however, attempts to institute formal specialization programs have met with resistance. The ABA, for example, has studied the subject intermittently since 1952, but did not adopt a model specialization plan until 1979. Before adoption of the plan, recommendations were frequently deferred due to bar opposition. However, in a recent ABA poll, 73% of lawyers responding favored some program to certify specialists and permit advertising of specialization. Currently, over one-quarter of the states have some form of bar-monitored specialization in operation. Virtually every state that does not have a specialization plan is considering one.

Specialization has not taken a single form. Actual programs vary from certification to self-designation, and are exemplified by the California, Florida, New Mexico, and ABA plans discussed infra. Certification involves the public designation by an accrediting body of particular attorneys as qualified specialists in certain areas of the law; self-designation, at the other extreme in terms of stringency, involves an attorney's representation of himself as qualified by virtue of experience or interest in certain areas of the law. Specialization is defined as an attorney's devotion of a substantial portion of his practice and professional time to one or a few areas of the law. Specialization plans may be based on a field of law, e.g., zoning, or on a legal skill, e.g., litigation, or on a trade or other segment of society, e.g., hospital administration, or on an institution that dominates an area of practice, e.g., the Securities and Exchange Commission.

The ABA Committee on Specialization has identified three major goals of specialization: (1) To improve the quality of legal services (competence), (2) to increase public access to legal assistance (accessibility), and (3) to decrease the unit cost of legal services to the consumer (cost). With respect to the goal of competence, it must be noted that certain forms of specialization (e.g., self-designation) are likely to be less effective at meeting this goal than are other forms (e.g., certification). Also, the significant proportion of grievances filed and malpractice suits brought against attorneys, involving either inattentiveness and neglect or misappropriation from and deceit of clients, are not addressed by specialization plans.

The CPR and the RPC both recognize the necessity and the fact of lawyer specialization. EC 2–14, n. 36; RPC 7.4. However, absent state controls to ensure special competence, an attorney is prohibited from representing herself as a specialist or as having special training or ability, EC 2–14, DR 2–105(A), RPC 7.4, except in the historically permissible fields of admiralty, patent, and trademark law, EC 2–14, DR 2–105(A)(1), RPC 7.4(a) & (b). An attorney may announce her availability to act as a consultant or associate in certain areas to other lawyers, but the form and frequency of such announcements are strictly limited by the CPR and the RPC. DR 2–105(A)(3); ABA Comment, RPC 7.4. In jurisdictions in which specialists are formally certified, an attorney is allowed to represent herself as a specialist in accordance with that jurisdiction's rules. DR 2–105(A)(4); RPC 7.4(c).

As discussed supra, a specialist sued for malpractice may be held to the standard of care met by other attorneys of that specialty. For this purpose, the "community" comparison may necessarily be extended beyond the geographic area in which the specialist practices.

A. ADVANTAGES AND DISADVANTAGES OF SPECIALIZATION

The first goal of specialization is to increase attorney competence. In particular, it is expected that as an attorney narrows the breadth of his focus to one or two areas, his depth in those areas will increase. Opponents of specialization, on the other hand, argue that it is impossible to assess proficiency and competency in a given field, that programs frequently require "substantial involvement" in a specialty rather than true competence, that specialists will become too narrow in their outlook, and that the overall quality of legal services will deteriorate.

The second goal of specialization is to increase public accessibility to legal services. Specifically, proponents anticipate that clients with a particular legal problem will be able to locate more easily an attorney with proficiency in that problem area. Opponents, however, note that many specialization plans include requirements that disclaimers be placed in any advertisement proclaiming a lawyer to be a specialist. These disclaimers essentially indicate that officially recognized specialization should not be relied upon, but that consumers should conduct their own investigations of attorneys they may wish to hire. Depending on the disclaimers required, the impact of the advertisement on consumers could well be the simultaneous assertion and disclaimer of expertise. In any event, opponents argue that clients are not sufficiently knowledgeable to make intelligent choices between types of specialists.

The third major goal of specialization is to lower the cost of legal services. Although proponents of specialization recognize that a specialist may charge more for each hour of service, they argue that elimination of the need to reeducate himself for each case will result in more efficient use of a specialist's time and decreased costs to consumers. Opponents urge that the higher costs for specialized services will discourage consumer use of any legal services, and that clients would need to consult numerous attorneys for the handling of day-to-day legal work.

A variety of other arguments for and against specialization exists. For example, proponents argue that specialization will result in more innovative solutions to legal problems, while opponents argue that it will result in prolonged and complex handling of legal problems. One of the major disputes is the impact that specialization will have on those attorneys who remain generalists. Proponents urge that specialists and generalists will consult with and complement one another, as in the medical profession. Opponents, however, urge that specialization is inherently biased against rural lawyers and against generalists, and that those groups will suffer loss of prestige and client confidence, resulting ultimately in decreased caseloads and income. Other criticisms have included an anticipated divisiveness and fragmentation of the legal profession as a whole, the necessity for and cost of administrative and enforcement structures for specialists, and the lowering of generalized knowledge of the attorney pool from which judges are selected.

B. TYPES OF SPECIALIZATION PLANS

The above anticipated advantages and disadvantages of specialization are best considered by briefly examining those plans that are already in operation. The plans of three particular states, California, New Mexico, and Florida, will be described since they exemplify the range of possible plans. Before detailing their differences, however, it is important to note that the plans all share certain common elements. First, all specialization plans are voluntary. Second, a specialist is not precluded from practice in other areas nor is a non-specialist precluded from practice in specialty areas by any of the plans. Third, all specialist designations are revocable by the authorizing body, following either failure to complete continuing education and time commitments in the specialty or failure to pass a recertification examination. Fourth, referrals by another attorney to a specialist are deemed to be for the limited purpose of consultation on the problem within the specialty area. Finally, financing of the plans comes solely from plan participants.

1. Certification

Attorneys are required to pass a written, and sometimes also an oral, examination before being certified.

California's program for specialty certification was instituted on an experimental basis in 1973. A significantly modified program was permanently adopted in 1983 and approved by the State Supreme Court in 1985. The experimental program allowed specialization in three areas—criminal law, workers compensation, and tax law—and the permanent plan added family law (immigration and nationality, along with probate, estate planning and trusts, have since been added). A nine-member Board of Legal

Specialization administers the California plan. Attorneys are required to pass a written, and sometimes also an oral, examination before being certified, although in some instances (more stringent) alternatives may be substituted for examinations.

California lawyers were not limited in the number of specialization certificates for which they could apply under the initial program. The California plan requires recertification every five years, with revocation of certification if the attorney fails to pass a written examination or fails to comply with board standards for continuing substantial involvement and legal education in the field. By early 1977, approximately 3,000 of California's 40,000 attorneys had been certified as specialists. By the end of 1989, however, fewer than 2,500 of the state's 122,000 lawyers had been certified in the seven fields available, leading to calls for abandoning the program altogether.

2. Identification or Self–Designation

New Mexico adopted its specialization plan in 1973. The plan is basically one of self-designation: No attempt is made to assess the competence of specialists. All that an attorney must do to become a specialist in New Mexico is to assure the state board that he has spent at least 60% of his time in the specialty field during the immediately preceding five years. To maintain his specialty identification, the attorney must continue to spend a minimum of 60% time in that area and so certify; there are no extra continuing education or other requirements. In addition, attorneys who have not "specialized" in New Mexico may advertise that they are limiting their practices to up to three fields. The New Mexico plan designates 62 fields of specialization, including general practice.

3. Designation

The Florida designation plan for specialization falls between the California and New Mexico plans in terms of rigor. The plan is monitored by a board, subject to court approval. Under the Florida two-tiered system, a lawyer may designate himself a specialist in not more than three of more than two dozen specialty areas, and in addition as a general practitioner. To qualify for specialty designation, the attorney must have five years of law practice, must show substantial experience in the specialty area during three of the five years immediately preceding application for certification, and must agree to continuing legal education in the designated areas. The specialization certificate must be renewed every five years, and is contingent on meeting the CLE requirements in each area of specialization during the prior five years. Although a written and/or oral examination is required, Florida's plan provides that certification in a specialty by an approved organization, or an LLM degree in the specialty area awarded by an approved law school within 8 years of application, may be accepted as a substitute for some of the minimum standards, including any examination.

In addition to certification, Florida also has a designation tier enabling any member in good standing of the state bar to obtain permission to designate up to three areas (from a board-approved list) in which she practices if she: has been engaged in the practice of law for at least three years and has substantial experience in the designated area; has accumulated at least 30 hours of approved CLE in each designated area; provides written references from other lawyers. The Florida Bar Association has been directed to publish notices regarding the difference between certification ("met rigorous requirements of experience and education in those areas") and designation ("met minimum experience and educational requirements under the Florida Designation Plan"). Although such notices reflect good intentions, it is unclear whether potential clients are more likely to be confused than aided by these distinctions.

4. The ABA Model Plan ("Recognition")

The ABA plan is similar in many ways to certification, but the ABA plan reflects a concern that the word "certified" may imply a warranty. The ABA plan attempts to convey merely a statement that the applicable standards have been met. Lawyers who meet the standards may hold themselves out as "Board Recognized Specialists." Attorneys must demonstrate substantial involvement in the desired area during the seven years immediately preceding application and continuing legal education of not less than ten hours for each of the three years preceding application. Applicants must also show that they are qualified through peer review, testing or other methods. There is no grandfather provision on the basis of years of practice alone. The recognition period lasts for five years. The ABA plan also provides for non-lawyer input.

The adoption of a testing requirement is left to the local authority, but the ABA plan directs that, if testing is not required, some equivalent measure of knowledge and skill is necessary. Alternatives to testing are to be more stringent, whereas alternatives to any other part of the plan are to be at least as stringent as those in the ABA Model Plan. Several states have adopted specialization plans largely based on the ABA plan.

X. CONCLUSION

The scope of this chapter is a graphic representation of the diversity of attempts to control the professional competence of attorneys once they have been admitted to practice. This diversity of methods—from professional discipline, to malpractice suits, to reversal of criminal convictions on the ground of ineffective assistance of counsel, to continuing legal education, to specialization—is perhaps the most notable characteristic of the effort. By attacking professional incompetence from different perspectives, the procedures discussed address a variety of forms of lawyer incompetence, but the procedural obstacles inherent in and the weaknesses of each method may prevent detection and correction of all but the most extreme cases of professional incompetence.

CHAPTER 7

THE UNAUTHORIZED PRACTICE OF LAW *

One of the least appreciated services that the organized bar performs is the protection of the public from the unauthorized practice of law. Despite frequent admonitions contained in court opinions and bar journals that the purpose of prohibiting the unauthorized practice of law is to protect the public and not to protect the economic monopoly of the bar, the fact remains that efforts to prevent the employment of non-lawyers to perform legal services are generally resented rather than appreciated.

This was dramatically illustrated when the Arizona Supreme Court held that it was the impermissible practice of law for a real estate broker to fill in blanks on a standard-form purchase contract. State Bar v. Arizona Land Title and Trust Co. (1962). Within months, a referendum was passed, by a margin of almost four to one, adopting a constitutional amendment permitting real estate brokers and salesmen to draft or fill out, without charge, any and all instruments incident to a sale, exchange, or lease of property.

Unauthorized practice can only be defined in terms of the authorized practice. Thus, when the public esteem of lawyers degenerated after the American Revolution, and during the period that Jacksonian concepts of equality prevailed, special qualifications to practice law, save, perhaps, moral character, were eliminated. Accordingly, in many states there was no unauthorized law practice since there were no restrictions on anyone performing legal services. In the latter part of the nineteenth century,

* An earlier version of this Chapter has appeared as Weckstein, Limitations on the Right to Counsel: The Unauthorized Practice of Law, 1978 Utah L.Rev. 649.

however, legislatures and courts revived controls on excessive fees, stirring up litigation, and court appearances by unqualified attorneys. As the legal profession became more organized, resistance to law practice by non-lawyers and corporate enterprises increased, and by 1940 all states required some training to be admitted to practice law, and most adopted concomitant prohibitions against non-admitted persons or entities engaging in the practice, which was expanded to include lawyering activities beyond representative appearances in court.

The involvement of the organized bar in policing unauthorized practice is usually traced to 1914 when the New York County Lawyers Association appointed the first standing committee on unlawful practice. Opposition to non-lawyer practice by the American Bar Association began in 1919, but its unauthorized practice of law committee and other activities designed to aggressively fight the practice did not begin until 1930. Not entirely coincidentally, this was a period of economic depression when lawyers, along with almost everyone else, were struggling to protect their livelihood from competition and economic catastrophe, but it also was a time of growth in organization of the bar, and of expansion of the nature of activities performed by lawyers. From that time to the 1960s, the organized bar sought to preserve the independence of the profession—allegedly for the better protection of the public—by enlisting the aid of the courts in enforcement actions against lay competitors. Today, the bar is more likely to be on the defense attempting to preserve its independence, and its monopoly, not only from non-lawyer competition but from consumers, deregulators, and reform-minded lawyers who see the unauthorized practice prohibitions as inhibiting the more efficient and wide-spread marketing and rendering of legal services. See Christensen, Unauthorized Practice of Law, 1980 Amer.Bar Res.J.

The fact that a motivation for the adoption of unauthorized practice laws may have been protection of lawyers' income rather than protection of the public from incompetent or unscrupulous practitioners does not necessarily make the latter purpose inapplicable or unworthy. The real question is not whether lawyers economically benefit from unauthorized practice laws, but whether these laws do in fact provide significant and needed protection for the public so that on balance the overall public interest is served.

I. GOALS OF UNAUTHORIZED PRACTICE LAWS

The most frequently stated purpose of prohibiting non-lawyers from practicing law is to protect the public from incompetent or unethical performance of legal services. This assumes that lawyers will be more competent and more ethical than non-lawyers in rendering legal services. Requirements for admission to practice law, such as a general and legal education and completion of a bar examination, probably assure that at least a minimum level of competence is attained by lawyers. Although the lawyers' public image may suggest otherwise, the evidence of good moral character required for an applicant to the bar, the existence of standards of professional conduct, the control of conduct through disciplinary machinery and the courts, and the tradition of loyal and zealous service to clients, probably result in lawyers as a whole maintaining fairly high ethical standards.

The more difficult question, is, however, whether one who has not met the same requirements for admission to the practice of law should be assumed to lack the competency and ethics to perform legal services. In many areas of the law, a non-lawyer specialist will have greater knowledge of the field than a lawyer in general practice. For example, real estate brokers may know more property law, trust officers more estate law, architects more construction law, and accountants more tax law than lawyers who themselves do not specialize in these areas. Members of these other professions are often subject to state licensing and professional regulation that mandate adherence to a code of ethics, although the nature of the ethical requirements, their enforcement, and the practice traditions may differ somewhat from those of the lawyer. Laypersons who are competent in particular areas of the law, however, may not recognize or know how to handle problems in fields of law outside of their own specialty, even though the issues may be relevant to transactions within that specialty. The concept of the seamless web of the law becomes familiar to the law-trained person whereas non-lawyers may not be as alert to the peripheral legal problems generated by seemingly routine transactions.

The efficiency of the legal system is also dependent upon the competency and integrity of the advocates who appear before legal tribunals. Lawyers are trained to research thoroughly and knowledgeably the law and facts and to marshal and logically present the relevant evidence. In addition, lawyers are expected to be familiar with court procedures and rules and the limits of ethical advocacy. This training and knowledge not only protects the client but is relied upon by judges who otherwise might have to spend considerable time inquiring into the accuracy and completeness of a litigant's case. Although not all lawyers are effective courtroom advocates, lawyers, as a whole, are less likely than laypersons to make a poorly organized, inaccurate, or incomplete courtroom presentation. While some lawyers have been justly criticized for raising time-consuming objections and technicalities, it is often difficult for a non-lawyer to distinguish between a technicality and a constitutional right. For example, rules which have been developed to explicate a person's privilege against self-incrimination and freedom from unreasonable searches and seizures may be technical but they safeguard fundamental rights. Moreover, in administrative and arbitral proceedings where non-lawyers may appear as representatives, lay advocates sometimes ill serve both their clients and the tribunal by inefficiently introducing evidence and making unwarranted and poorly articulated objections to the evidence offered by their adversary. Of course, lawyers unfamiliar with such forums may be less effective than an experienced and knowledgeable lay advocate, but in general adjudicative proceedings operate best when the parties' representatives are schooled in concepts of relevancy, evidentiary foundations, and the persuasiveness of proofs—qualifications that lawyers are more likely than non-lawyers to possess.

Another claimed justification for protecting lawyers from lay competition is that it helps preserve a strong and independent bar, including a large segment of private practitioners. To whatever extent there was merit to this boot-strapping argument, its force has been largely dissipated by recent developments. The protectionism afforded the practice of law as a "learned profession" is now vulnerable to attack under the anti-trust laws; more lawyers are now competing for available paying clients, with many dependent on big government and big business for their livelihood; and economic competition—fostered by constitutional protection given to the marketing of legal services—both within the profession and with other service providers is now the rule.

All of the arguments in support of the bar's monopoly to perform legal services must be weighed against the right of an individual to freely choose between lawyer and non-lawyer representation, particularly when the latter may be less expensive and more readily available. We should not lightly deny this freedom of choice unless we are convinced that the members of the public lack sufficient knowledge on which to make such choice, will be irrevocably harmed by choosing the layperson over the lawyer, and can be adequately served by available lawyers. To date, the bar has been relatively successful in pressing its case with its brethren on the bench, but there is growing consumer, governmental, and competitor pressure, as well as public sentiment and recognition within the legal profession itself, to reexamine the restrictions on the unauthorized practice of law. See Christensen, (1980); Rhode, Policing the Professional Monopoly, Stanford L.Rev. (1981).

II. THE LAW OF UNAUTHORIZED PRACTICE

A. WHAT IS THE PRACTICE OF LAW?

If the bar's monopoly is to be justified on some basis other than protecting lawyers' income, its scope must be functionally related to its justification. State statutes and judicial opinions typically provide that only a lawyer may "practice law." It, therefore, becomes critical to define what is the practice of law. Unfortunately, it has proven extremely difficult to articulate a satisfactory definition. Some statutes and decisions fail to provide any guidance, others explicate specific illustrations of activities included within the practice of law, but are usually careful to include a caveat that they are not all-inclusive. Some definitions are tautological in nature, stating for example, that the practice of law consists of those activities commonly performed by lawyers. The fact is that lawyers perform many activities that do not require legal training or knowledge, and laymen commonly perform many tasks done by lawyers such as negotiating, investigating, researching facts, financial planning, bookkeeping, giving business and practical—as distinct from legal—advice, securing financing, acting as broker, mediator, go-between or spokesperson, and providing public relations and emotional support.

Both the Model Rules and the CPR prohibit a lawyer from aiding a non-lawyer in an activity that constitutes the unauthorized practice of law, but eschew any attempt to specifically define the prohibited territory since it varies from one jurisdiction to another. Rule 5.5(b); DR 3–101(A). Ethical Consideration 3–5 of the Code, however, does helpfully provide that: "Functionally, the practice of law relates to the rendition of services for others that call for the professional judgment of a lawyer." The essence of this judgment, according to the Code, is the lawyer's "educated ability to relate the general body and philosophy of law to a specific legal problem of a client." Implicit in this definition is the recognition that there are many acts, including the exercise of business or other types of judgment, performed by lawyers that do not constitute the practice of law for purposes of excluding their performance by non-lawyers. Judicial applications of the law of unauthorized practice confirm this limited definition. An analysis of these cases suggests that whether or not a particular activity will be considered off limits to laypersons will depend upon (1) the nature of the activity, (2) any relevant qualifications of the challenged non-lawyer to perform the activity, and (3) the circumstances under which it is performed.

Activities included within the practice of law which potentially are reserved for lawyers include representative appearances before legal tribunals, preparation of pleadings and other documents in connection therewith, drafting of other instruments effecting legal rights and obligations, and giving legal advice.

As a generalization, courtroom advocacy on behalf of another is deemed to be the heart of the lawyer's functions and is most likely to be prohibited to non-lawyers. Since it occurs before a court, it also is easy to detect and police. The other enumerated activities, even though logically within the practice of law, may be permitted when they are performed by laypersons who have at least a limited knowledge of law, are done under supervision of or in conjunction with a lawyer, or are incidental to some other legitimate activity of the non-lawyer.

It has been suggested that the traditional barrister's monopoly should prevail for courtroom representation, but that lay competition should be allowed in the preparation of legal documents and giving of legal advice. While it is true that a qualified legal advocate protects the rights of clients as well as the efficiency and accuracy of the adjudication process, legal training is also important to the solicitor's role. The quality of legal advice and drafting depends not only on legal knowledge, analysis and expression skills, possessed more generally by lawyers than others, but also on the ability to recognize relevant legal issues. As in the practice of medicine, the original diagnosis of a problem is a most critical element. More legal rights may be lost through ignorance of their existence than through sloppy advocacy to achieve their enforcement.

Nevertheless, a few states have gone so far as to statutorily define the "practice of law" as representation of another before a tribunal authorized to make legal decisions, while designating the preparation of legal documents and giving of legal advice as the "business of law." These states usually prohibit non-lawyers from the "practice of law" whether or not done for compensation, while the "business of law" is unauthorized only if the client pays for the services. A dichotomy based upon the presence or absence of compensation misconceives the purposes of unauthorized practice regulation. The intent is not to protect a prospective client *from paying compensation* for incompetent or unethical legal services, but to protect that client *from such services.* It would be of small comfort to a client that he or she did not have to pay for the drawing of a legal document or the giving of legal advice by a non-lawyer whose incompetence resulted in the loss of title to property, an ineffective will, or criminal liability for violation of complex security laws. On the other hand, if one is to be free to choose a non-lawyer to perform certain types of legal services, that freedom should not be denied simply because the layman insists upon being compensated for his services.

B. INCIDENTAL LEGAL SERVICES

There are situations, however, where the payment or absence of compensation may be relevant to the establishment of the unauthorized practice of law. For example, a common exception to the prohibition of law practice by laypersons involves legal services which are incidental to other legitimate functions of the non-lawyer as long as no separate fee is charged for the legal aspects of the transaction. Thus, in most states, a real estate broker may fill in the blanks of a purchase and sale agreement, provided her compensation is for the bringing together of a buyer and seller of the real estate and not for the incidental preparation of the legal document. Some jurisdictions also regard the preparation of deeds granting title, mortgages, and related documents as incidental to the real estate dealer's business function. Similarly, financial institutions and title companies have been permitted to prepare legal documents incidental to the granting of a mortgage or insuring of legal title, and bank trust departments, accountants, and other business representatives, may be allowed to give advice with legal implications or fill in standardized legal documents incidental to their legitimate business services. A few states limit the incident to business exception to filling in of standard forms previously prepared by lawyers, or to giving of legal advice that is simple rather than complex in nature.

Not all jurisdictions have embraced the incidental services approach, or have very narrowly construed it. For example, even at this time when the validity of basic concepts of unauthorized practice are being reexamined, a few courts continue to hold that title companies may not prepare deeds, notes, mortgage loan documents, title search abstracts, nor draft escrow instructions, conduct real estate closings, or give instructions regarding the recording of real estate transaction documents. Decisions in these cases tend to apply syllogistic analysis: if the questioned act constitutes the practice of law, it is unauthorized, and little or no consideration is given to the incidental nature of the legal service, the competency of the provider, the containment of client costs, or the industry practices. See e.g., State v. Buyers Service (S.C. 1987).

The extent to which laypersons may perform legal services incidental to another occupation has been influenced not only by statutes in a jurisdiction but by custom and tradition in the locality. In California, for example, lawyers are infrequently involved in the purchase and sale of residential real estate. Real estate brokers, lending institutions, title insurance companies, and escrow agents handle all details from the initial agreement to closing. Custom is to the contrary in other states, particularly in the east and south, where licensed attorneys may be required to select and prepare real estate transaction documents (which may be filled in by brokers), search and abstract titles, draft escrow instructions and supervise closings. Industry customs also can shield activities from unauthorized law practice restrictions. In the construction industry, it is common for architects to draft contracts and specifications, interpret them, settle disputes which may arise under them, and generally act as advocates and representatives of property owners or developers.

Compensation to the non-lawyer also may be relevant in determining whether a holding out to practice law has taken place. In some jurisdictions, a "holding out" is a necessary element of a finding of unauthorized practice and can be established by evidence that a fee was charged or more than one legal service transaction occurred. Nevertheless, an absence of compensation or the rendering of legal services on just a single occasion does not necessarily preclude a finding of unauthorized practice. A bank employee who draws a will for a customer, without compensation, probably has violated the proscription, whereas a person who proffers advice to a friend that he ought to sue another person who has injured him is not likely to have done so.

C. THE PUBLIC INTEREST TEST

As the preceding discussion has demonstrated, the boundaries of what is and what is not the unauthorized practice of law are not discernible by a simple application of logic to any acceptable definition of the practice of law. Despite efforts by the organized bar, the proposition that only a lawyer can engage in those activities which constitute the practice of law is subject to so many exceptions that it is hardly tenable as a guideline, let alone a rule of law. Consequently, an increasing number of courts and scholars have proposed employment of a test based on the "public interest." Whether or not the questioned activity logically can be classified as the practice of law, the critical issue becomes will the public good be better served by permitting only lawyers to perform that activity or by also allowing other individuals or members of certain occupational groups to perform it under specified circumstances. In one sense, this approach merely restates the basic problem, but recognition of the public interest as paramount at least focuses judicial analysis on the competing relevant policies rather than on syllogistic applications of vague definitions of the "practice of law."

While there is a need for more specific guidelines for the bar, its competitors, and the courts, it is helpful to identify legitimate and pertinent public interests. Among these are competent, if not high, quality legal services, reasonable cost, maximum availability, convenience, and freedom of choice. Pertinent, but not legitimate, is maintaining the legal—or any other—profession's "fair share" of the economic pie.

Those cases applying the public interest approach have combined it with more traditional tests and other safeguards to minimize the risks while maintaining some freedom of choice. Thus, in permitting a licensed real estate salesperson to complete an earnest money form (securing an offer to sell property at a stated price subject to a contingency), the Supreme Court of Washington required that the form be a simple-standard one, approved by a lawyer, be used incidentally to a real estate transaction, which was the main business of the salesperson or broker, that no extra charge be made for the "legal" service, and that the real estate professional be held to the standard of care governing attorneys. In this manner, the client or customer receives more convenient, full-service in the transaction. Cultum v. Heritage House Realtors, Inc. (Wash.1985).

D. WAIVERS

While the concept has yet to receive professional acceptance, an individual might receive even more complete legal-type services, and the greater public interest served, by permitting a "client" to voluntarily agree, in writing, to a knowledgeable waiver of the protection of unauthorized practice laws after disclosure of the principal risks and under conditions that minimize adverse consequences of such a waiver. For example, waivers could be more freely allowed for non-courtroom representation, when legal services are incidental to another legitimate business activity, when no separate legal fee is charged, and when a licensed lawyer is not readily available, or the lawyer's cost would be out of proportion to the service required. For examples of possible waivers, see Weckstein, 1978 Utah L.Rev. at 676–679.

E. LEGAL CLERKS AND ASSISTANTS

When acting under the supervision of a lawyer who takes responsibility for the work product, a law student or paralegal may engage in a wide variety of activities such as legal research, drafting of legal documents, interviewing witnesses, and drafting interrogatories. Under student practice rules adopted in many states, law students who are supervised by lawyers and certified as having completed a minimum level of education are permitted to make court appearances and engage in some or all aspects of the trial of a case. In California, an intermediate appellate court had reversed a felony conviction of a defendant represented pursuant to the State Bar student practice rules on the grounds that such representation by a non-lawyer constituted the unauthorized practice of law and denied the defendant effective assistance of counsel under the Sixth Amendment. The California Supreme Court reversed the lower court's holdings, and separately, upon petition of the State Bar, expressly approved revised student practice rules. People v. Perez (1979).

Attempts by para-professionals to independently provide low-cost legal services, without the supervision of a licensed attorney, have been rebuffed by the courts. As discussed below, relatively-simple legal advice and aid to persons seeking to represent themselves in marital dissolution or bankruptcy proceedings, has been held to be the unauthorized practice of law. Consideration is being given by some states, however, to legislation allowing certified or licensed paralegals, who meet prescribed standards of competence and integrity, to perform limited legal practice without direct supervision of an attorney.

III. JUDICIAL CONTROL OF UNAUTHORIZED PRACTICE

Courts in most states have held that the control of the practice of law is a judicial function. Accordingly, legislation such as that proposed to authorize paralegals to perform limited legal services may not survive a judicial challenge. While courts in many jurisdictions have deferred to reasonable legislation regulating the practice of law, in other cases, courts have struck down—as infringing on inherent judicial power—legislative or administrative rules which were found to violate the courts' concepts of minimum standards for the practice of law. In Indiana, for example, a statute authorizing public adjusters (as distinct from insurance company employees or agents) to negotiate settlements between insurance companies and insureds was found unconstitutional because it permitted the practice of law by persons not admitted to the bar and not subject to the disciplinary rules of the court. Professional Adjusters, Inc. v. Tandon (1982).

With or without legislative authorization, non-lawyer mediators have run into resistance in some states if they offer legal advice, particularly in marriage-dissolution mediations. Moreover, a lawyer who works with a mental health professional in such mediations may face charges of aiding the unauthorized practice of law or unethical sharing of fees with a non-lawyer. (See Chapters 14, Fees; 21, Lawyers as Neutrals).

Judicial control over who may appear in court, and draw related pleadings and motions, may reasonably be justified by the court's need to protect itself from inefficient and incompetent advocates and to safeguard its standards of justice by protecting litigants from inadequate representation. It is less clear that the concept of the lawyer as an "officer of the court" necessitates that the courts control who is entitled to draft legal documents or render legal advice unconnected with any pending or contemplated litigation.

While courts have often declined to be bound by legislation extending the right to practice law, the power to make unauthorized practice a crime is a legislative one. Consequently, if a statute decriminalized particular legal practice activities, a court would not likely sustain a criminal conviction for such activities but might still enjoin or apply other remedies against them.

The extent of judicial control of the practice of law is, of course, dependent on a particular state's constitutional allocation of powers. Public dissatisfaction with a court's interpretation of unauthorized practice may be met, as in the Arizona real estate brokers' case, referred to above, with a rectifying state constitutional amendment.

IV. PROFESSIONAL INDEPENDENCE AND UNAUTHORIZED PRACTICE

Canon 3 of the Code of Professional Responsibility admonished lawyers to assist in preventing the unauthorized practice of law because the public interest is best served in legal matters by a regulated profession committed to high standards of ethical conduct and legal competence. EC 3–3. To effectuate this objective, it was deemed essential to preserve the personal nature of the relationship of client and lawyer [EC 3–2], and to prohibit a lawyer from aiding the unauthorized practice of law [DR 3–101(A)], sharing fees with a non-lawyer (subject to narrow exceptions) [DR 3–102(A)], or forming a partnership with a non-lawyer if any of its activities involved the practice of law [DR 3–103]. These Disciplinary Rules are incorporated in the Model Rules, but the latter two are classified as in furtherance of the goal of preserving the professional independence of a lawyer. RPC 5.4(a), (b). These rules are not intended to prevent lawyers from employing clerks, para-professionals, lay investigators, and secretaries and delegating tasks to them, as long as the lawyer supervises and retains responsibility for their work. EC 3–6, RPC 5.5 Comment. Nor do such rules interfere with a lawyer employing or contracting with accountants, economists, financial and technical advisers or other specialized personnel to assist in the rendering of services to a client. Model Rule 5.3 requires lawyers to make reasonable efforts to supervise and adopt measures to see that such non-lawyers' conduct conforms to the lawyer's professional obligations, and makes supervising attorneys responsible for breaches of professional conduct rules which the lawyer ratified or could have avoided, mitigated or remedied.

Law firms have long employed non-lawyers of varying qualifications in order to offer more efficient and economic services to their clients. Larger firms have employed non-lawyers, with experience in business and management, to serve as office and business managers. These arrangements, however, had to avoid compensating the non-lawyers by a percentage of legal fees received (except to the extent they participated—as may be required by tax laws—in a profit-sharing compensation or retirement plan), and a non-lawyer could not control the professional judgment of lawyers nor hold an ownership interest in a law firm (except, temporarily, a fiduciary representative of a deceased lawyer). Model Rule 5.4(c), (d). (See Chapters 12, Conflicts of Interest; 14, Fees). In adopting Model Rule 5.4, the ABA rejected proposals of the Kutak Commission which would have tailored the limits on lay involvement in legal services, management, and compensation to the specific evils against which the rule is directed: protection against interference with independent professional judgment and client confidentiality, conflicts of interest, unethical solicitation or improper fee arrangements.

Recent developments, however, may lead to the undermining of the more traditional approach reflected in the adopted rules. In 1987, the ABA Committee on Ethics and Professional Responsibility adopted an advisory opinion endorsing, with specific safeguards, for-profit pre-paid legal service plans, and specifically permitted a plan-sponsor to retain a portion of subscriber payments to cover both administrative costs and a *profit.* The Rule prohibiting fee sharing with a non-lawyer was avoided by restricting its scope to the evils it was meant to prevent: interference with a lawyer's independent professional judgment and avoiding unreasonably high fees (which pre-paid plans are designed to counter). ABA Formal Opinion 355. The result is probably a sound one, although the Committee, purporting to rely on legislative history, seemed to ignore the House of Delegates rejection of the similar approach of the Kutak draft. (See also Chapter 9, Implementing the Duty to Make Legal Services Available).

Some law firms also have been forging alliances with non-law professionals to provide a complete package of legal and related services to their clients. In several major firms, this has taken the form of organizing subsidiaries offering, inter alia, financial, real estate, economic, political and environmental services. Effective in 1991, the District of Columbia Court of Appeals has adopted a modification of the ABA Model Rules which includes a provision expressly allowing a law firm to give an ownership or financial interest in the firm to non-lawyers who assist in providing legal services to clients. Although the rule seeks to prohibit violations of professional ethics by non-lawyer law firm participants, and makes the lawyer members responsible for their conduct, the ABA has been asked to oppose such attempts to permit non-lawyers to become partners in law firms or otherwise allow them to hold an equity interest or share in legal fees. Opponents of the District of Columbia rule fear that it will lead to unauthorized practice of law, insufficient protections of professional judgment, disclosure of client confidences, improper solicitation, and the destruction of the independence of the legal profession, its traditional self-regulation, professional values of public service and the priority given to clients over economic profits.

This reaction is somewhat reminiscent of the traditional opposition to allowing a corporation to practice law or to hire lawyers to practice for it. The theory had been that only a natural person could be tested for requisite skills, take an oath to uphold the Constitution and laws, meet educational qualifications, and exercise the confidential fidelity required of lawyers. The old Canons also regarded the corporate entity as an impermissible lay intermediary between its lawyer employees and the clients, [Canon 35]. The CPR and Model Rules have dropped the forbidden "intermediary" language but continue to prohibit lay exploitation or control of legal services. DR 5–107(B), (C); RPC 5.4(c), (d). In addition to the possible representation of conflicting interests faced by lawyer employees who render legal services to third parties on behalf of a corporation, there was thought to be a risk of violation of ethical proscriptions against sharing legal fees with a non-lawyer entity, disclosure of client's confidential communications, solicitation of business, and commercialization of the profession.

Given an appropriate economic incentive, the legal profession recognized that its prohibition against corporations practicing law had placed form over substance. Accordingly, in order to gain significant tax advantages available to corporate employees, organizations of lawyers and doctors successfully lobbied the various state legislatures to authorize the practice of law, medicine, and other professions through professional associations or corporations. These entities were designed to have sufficient corporate characteristics to qualify as corporations for tax purposes but, in order to safeguard traditional professional standards, ownership and control were limited to members of the relevant profession, and some other corporate attributes, such as limited liability, were adopted in attenuated form. In most every state, the professional corporation is now accepted as a normal business structure for the practice of law, and is expressly recognized by ABA ethical standards. DR 5–107(C), EC 5–24; RPC 5.4(d).

It is permissible in some jurisdictions for non-lawyers to be members of boards of directors of non-profit, legal service corporations or associations, and federal government supported programs have required community or lay participation in policy making of legal service providers. While the lay directors and managers may play a role in the adoption of general policies regarding the type of cases to accept or clients to serve, the application of those policies is left to lawyer staff members who have a direct relationship with the client, and there can be no lay control of, or interference with, that relationship or with the exercise of independent judgment by the staff lawyers. See Matter of Education Law Center, Inc. (N.J.1981); (See also Chapter 9, Implementing the Duty to Make Legal Services Available).

V. PRACTICE BEFORE ADMINISTRATIVE AND ARBITRAL TRIBUNALS

Although the practice of law clearly includes appearances on behalf of another before a tribunal with authority to decide legal controversies, the proscription against such practice by non-lawyers does not always apply to appearances before administrative agencies. At one extreme are decisions by state courts striking down legislation or administrative rules permitting non-lawyers to serve as advocates in quasi-judicial proceedings before public utility commissions, workers compensation boards, or other state agencies, on the theory that only the court may authorize one to practice law. Thus, while a layperson may attempt to negotiate another worker's compensation claim or fill out an application for such benefits, only a lawyer is permitted to appear in a representative capacity before the boards in some jurisdictions. Other states and the federal courts take a more permissive approach and defer to legislative or administrative rules regulating who may appear before administrative adjudicative bodies. The federal practice runs the gambit from requiring that only lawyers may appear as advocates before boards such as the FCC to permitting any person, or any one of good moral character, to appear in a representative capacity before boards such as the NLRB. In between these extremes are agencies that restrict representative appearances to persons, in addition to lawyers, who exhibit requisite professional qualifications. For example, the Internal Revenue Service admits to practice certified public accountants, and "enrolled agents" who pass tests of competency or experience, and the Interstate Commerce Commission authorizes appearances by "class B" practitioners who successfully complete an examination on transportation law and practice.

As a result of the Agency Practice Act of 1965 [5 U.S.C.A. § 500 (1976)], any lawyer licensed by the highest court of a state is entitled to practice before all federal administrative agencies (other than the Patent Office, which individually certifies lawyer and non-lawyer patent attorneys based upon their demonstrated competency in this technical field). Several federal agencies, however, do retain the right to disbar from practice before them individual lawyers who commit unethical acts or engage in contemptuous behavior. (See Chapter 5, Maintenance of Professional Standards).

Unless the parties agree otherwise, in most states there is no restriction on who may appear as an advocate before arbitration tribunals even though arbitrators (who need not be lawyers) render decisions on legal and factual questions that are subject to only limited judicial review. In many labor, commercial, and construction arbitrations, familarity with the subject matter of the dispute, and some experience in adjudicative hearings, is more important to the parties than legal knowledge and experience.

Many administrative and arbitral tribunals are designed to adjudicate controversies in an informal, inexpensive, and expeditious manner, and it is feared that these objectives might be frustrated if only lawyers, with their relative high costs and legal proficiency, were allowed to represent the parties. Nevertheless, parties often opt to use lawyers in matters involving significant legal issues, or substantial principles or financial exposure, as in administrative adjudication of valuable operating licenses.

Lawyers often are not required or even prohibited from appearing as advocates in small claims courts. The low monetary jurisdiction of these courts is said to justify this departure from the policy that lawyers are needed to protect litigants, and a safety valve is provided by allowing a losing defendant to take an appeal *de novo* to a higher court, complete with lawyer and other procedural safeguards.

The doctrine of federal supremacy limits a state's authority to require that only lawyers may practice administrative law within its jurisdiction. In *Sperry v. Florida* (U.S.1963), the Supreme Court held that Florida lacked the power to preclude a non-lawyer patent agent from activities involving representation of clients before the U.S. Patent Office, even though those activities might constitute the practice of law. Wisconsin has interpreted the *Sperry* doctrine as allowing it to exclude a non-lawyer transportation practitioner from representing clients before the State Public Service Commission but not from activities within the state, often for the same clients, as a Class B practitioner before the ICC. State Bar v. Keller (Wis.1963).

The full dimensions of this supremacy doctrine have not yet been defined. It is probable that accountants and enrolled agents are free from state regulation of their federal tax practice to the extent that it is permitted by the IRS. It also is possible that lawyers who are licensed in one state may be beyond the regulatory authority of another state when they confine their activities in the latter state to the practice of federal law, but, in the absence of regular or *pro hac vice* admission to practice in a particular court, appearances by out-of-state lawyers in such court generally have not been authorized—even in cases substantially or totally involving questions of federal law.

VI. NON-ADMITTED ATTORNEYS

In the United States, each state and federal jurisdiction is entitled to regulate the admission to practice law within its own jurisdiction. Thus, a lawyer admitted to practice in California has no right to practice law in Nevada. While federal courts maintain their own roster of admitted attorneys, admission to the bar of the state in which the federal court is located is usually sufficient to enable a lawyer to practice in the federal forum. The restrictive approach to multi-jurisdiction practice has been based on the assumptions that the laws and procedural rules vary from state to state, and passing a bar examination or practicing law in one state is insufficient to demonstrate competency to practice under the laws of another state. In addition, each state has been traditionally free to make its own determination of the moral character of applicants to its bar. Both the Code and the Model Rules prohibit a lawyer from practicing in a jurisdiction where doing so would violate that jurisdiction's regulation of the legal profession. DR 3–101(B); RPC 5.5(a).

Many of the litigated cases involve attempts of clients served by out-of-state attorneys to avoid payment of fees for such services. If the services constitute the unauthorized practice of law, holding that the fee contract is unenforceable is a recognized means of effectuating that public policy even though it may give a windfall to the client (who may have benefited by the services but is not required to pay for them). While this factor may be taken into account, courts have denied fees to attorneys particularly where the services concerned matters of traditional local regulation, such as domestic relations or property law, and were performed within a state in which the lawyer was neither admitted nor associated with local counsel. The geographic jurisdiction in which the services were performed would not seem to be significant, unless the non-admitted attorney was holding himself out as a lawyer in such state, but the nature of those services, whether dealing primarily with federal or interstate law, on one hand, or local law, on the other, should be influential. Other relevent factors include whether the out-of-state lawyer disclosed the jurisdictional limits of his right to practice, the client's informed consent, and the extent to which the services included applications of the law of the non-admitted state.

If the legal services to be rendered contemplate appearance in a local court, to which the out-of-state lawyer had not been admitted, it is quite common for such attorney to be admitted in that court *pro hac vice,* or "for this case only". Most jurisdictions limit this privilege to occasional appearances by lawyers not resident in the state concerned. In addition, it is common to require that a local attorney also be associated on the case to ensure that the non-resident attorney will be made aware of local procedures and laws and that the court can maintain disciplinary control over counsel in the case. In a controversial decision, the Supreme Court held that there was no constitutional right to admission *pro hac vice* and, consequently, the State of Ohio could deny such appearances without a hearing to the non-locally-admitted lawyers selected by the publisher of Hustler magazine to defend him on obscenity charges. Leis v. Flynt (U.S.1979). The dissenting opinion of Justice Stevens (joined by Brennan and Marshall) argued, among other grounds, that this was the type of case, involving an unpopular defendant, in which the client should be entitled to out-of-state counsel of his choice. While the Supreme Court has not directly ruled on the right of a criminal defendant to retain a non-locally admitted lawyer (as distinct from the lack of a constitutional right of the lawyer to appear), unless an interlocutory appeal is granted to the defendant, it may be difficult to directly raise the issue on appeal from a conviction since the question will then become whether the defendant was denied effective assistance of counsel in being forced to use a local, and presumably competent, attorney. (See Chapter 6, The Duty to Ensure Competence).

Once a jurisdiction permits a lawyer to appear *pro hac vice,* it probably cannot withdraw that permission without good cause, and a hearing, if demanded. Good cause would include unethical conduct in the matter in question. See State v. Kavanaugh (N.J. 1968) where F. Lee Bailey was denied permission to continue as *pro hac vice* counsel after wide distribution of a letter in which he claimed that his client could not get justice in the New Jersey courts.

During the active days of the civil rights movement in the South, a federal district court adopted regulations requiring that an attorney be admitted to the bar for at least five years, make no more than one *pro hac vice* appearance during any one year, and be associated with local counsel. This effectively denied the right of counsel to litigants seeking civil rights remedies or defending, on constitutional grounds, actions brought against them. Local counsel were generally not available to serve and many of the out-of-state lawyers who volunteered to represent these litigants were relatively recent admittees to the bar. Ultimately, these regulations were struck down as schemes to prevent enforcement of civil rights legislation and because they imposed unreasonable restrictions that went beyond any legitimate qualifications for *pro hac vice* appearances. Sanders v. Russell (5th Cir.1968); Sobol v. Perez (E.D.La.1968).

In some states it is possible for a lawyer who has been practicing in one state to be admitted "on motion," that is, without having to take another bar examination. Generally, admission on motion is limited to those lawyers who have practiced for a minimum period of time, usually five years, in a state which would grant reciprocal opportunities for admission on motion. Thus, admission to practice on motion seems to depend more upon economic and political considerations than on concern with ensuring that lawyers admitted elsewhere are competent, ethical, and knowledgeable about local laws. Standards for admission to or exclusion from the bar of a state must be consistent with federal constitutional principles.

Due Process precludes a state from denying admission to an applicant without procedural fairness or on grounds not rationally related to the functions of lawyers. Requirements that an out-of-state lawyer have practiced a reasonable number of years for admission on motion, or that others pass an examination, are not irrational. But it does seem constitutionally suspect for a state to admit experienced attorneys on motion from one state but not from another because of lack of reciprocity (even though the latter state's standards for admission to the bar are no lower than that of the state in which admission is sought or than that of other states from which reciprocal admission would be granted).

As previously noted, the doctrine of federal supremacy may allow an out-of-state attorney, who has been admitted to practice in the federal courts, to handle matters that deal exclusively with federal laws or administrative practice.

As discussed in Chapter 5, regarding standards for admission to practice, the Supreme Court has found that residency requirements for admission to a state bar, whether on motion or by examination, unconstitutionally discriminate against non-residents in violation of the Privileges and Immunities clause. While an applicant may still be required to express a good faith intention to practice in the state in which admission is sought, or maintain an office there (but not likely be required to practice full-time in such state), these developments do realistically permit lawyers to carry on an active practice in more than one jurisdiction.

The advent of the Multi-state Bar Examination has lessened the burdens of being admitted to practice in more than one state. This examination represents an explicit recognition of a common core of law among the various states, and several states now accept an applicant's score on a Multi-state Bar Examination taken in another state.

While the recognition of state sovereignty may have been appropriate in the early days of the American Republic, several factors in the late Twentieth Century suggest the need for greater ease in permitting the interstate practice of law. Among these are increased mobility of the population; interstate and international activities of business clients; the predominance of similarities rather than differences among laws of the various states as evidenced and, in turn, influenced by, the adoption of Uniform State Laws; legal education emphasizing nationally oriented teaching materials; American Bar Association accreditation of law schools which affords graduates the right to take a bar examination in any state; the broad range of federal laws and impact of constitutional restrictions on state laws; and the leadership of the Federal Rules of Procedure and Federal Rules of Evidence as models for state courts. In addition, many lawyers tend to specialize in their practice by legal subject matter rather than by geographical location. Thus, a business or corporation lawyer in any state needs to have extensive knowledge of federal securities law and even a lawyer who concentrates in estate and probate work, which may have peculiar local variations, cannot adequately counsel clients unless she is thoroughly conversant with federal tax laws. Other fields such as labor law, antitrust law, tax law, or transportation law, are so federalized that the specialist probably spends ninety percent of her time applying federal law and the other ten percent applying state laws whose development has been greatly influenced by the federal laws.

Factors such as these have led many law firms to establish branch offices in several states and the District of Columbia. This has brought about the advent of national, and even international, law firms, similar to existing accounting firms, which facilitate service to clients with multi-state interests.

VII. SELF-REPRESENTATION; CORPORATIONS

While it may be true that one who represents himself has a fool for a client, a long-standing exception to unauthorized practice rules is that an individual is free to appear before a court on his own behalf or to otherwise perform legal services for himself.

Some individuals—preferring to save a buck and sacrifice a lawyer—have attempted to represent themselves with the aid of published forms, guide books, "do-it-yourself" kits, and non-lawyer advisors. The bar, with mixed success, has generally resisted these encroachments on their traditional terrain. The publication of books and kits which contain standard forms for wills, trusts, marital dissolutions, or bankruptcies, along with instructions for their use, have been held, in most cases, to be permissible activities, either not constituting the practice of law or protected by the First Amendment. Where, however, the distribution of such aids is accompanied by legal advice pertaining to particular individuals, the courts generally hold that the line between aiding persons to represent themselves and engaging in the unauthorized practice of law has been crossed. For example, Norman Dacey's book on "How to Avoid Probate" (and lawyers) was held to be protected, but his offering of estate planning counseling to individual potential mutual fund customers was condemned as unauthorized practice. New York County Lawyers' Ass'n v. Dacey (N.Y.1967); Grievance Comm. v. Dacey (Conn.1966). A fine line also is drawn between a non-lawyer acting as a scrivener for someone performing his own legal services, which is permissible, and drafting legal instruments for him, which generally constitutes unauthorized practice. In many cases, individuals who purchase do-it-yourself divorce, bankruptcy, or other legal forms ask for assistance in filling out the forms, defining terms contained in them, or instructions on where and how to file them. These forms are sometimes sold by experienced paralegals or legal secretaries who also provide typing services, but they risk violation of state unauthorized practice laws if they respond to such inquiries. This is particularly true if the respondent has advertised the availability of services assisting individuals who seek to represent themselves in legal matters. The State of Florida, which has been quite aggressive in seeking to combat the unauthorized practice of law, has retreated from total condemnation of non-lawyers giving any legally related advice to assist self-representation [see e.g., Florida Bar v. Furman (Fla.

1984)], to adoption of a court rule expressly permitting nonlawyers "to engage in oral communications to assist individuals in the completion of legal forms [approved by the court] . . . [which are] reasonably necessary to elicit factual information to complete the form(s) and inform the individual how to file such forms." Amendment to Rules Regulating the Florida Bar (Fla. 1987). Moreover, in the Comment accompanying Model Rule 5.5, prohibiting a lawyer from assisting a person to engage in the unauthorized practice of law, it is stated that "a lawyer may counsel nonlawyers who wish to proceed pro se" (represent themselves in court).

Complications arise when the "person" seeking self-representation is a corporation. Of necessity, a corporation must act through natural persons. The question then arises as to whether non-lawyer employees, officers or directors who act for the corporation may perform legal services for it. As a general rule, a corporation may not appear in court *in propria persona,* or by nonlawyer corporate employees. Court appearances on behalf of a corporation may be made only by lawyers who are licensed to practice in the forum jurisdiction or have received permission to appear *pro hac vice.* On the other hand, non-lawyer or out-of-state lawyer employees commonly are permitted to prepare legal documents, give legal advice, or render other internal legal services for the corporation. National or multi-national corporations frequently employ lawyers who are officed in states where they are not admitted to practice. Attempts to preclude such lawyers from performing non-litigative legal services for the corporation would be unrealistic and unnecessarily restrictive. Since these corporations do not lack sophistication regarding the need for qualified legal counsel, the policy of protecting the public from their own ignorance in this regard would seem inapposite. Nevertheless, there is justification for requiring that court appearances on behalf of the corporation be made by, or in association with, a locally licensed lawyer who is presumably familiar with local law, procedures, and court rules, and will be subject to the disciplinary authority of the local courts.

It is not unethical aiding of the unauthorized practice of law for a lawyer to provide professional advice and instruction to non-lawyers whose employment (presumably not including legal services for third parties) requires knowledge of the law, such as claims adjusters, accountants, social workers, and government personnel. Model Rule 5.5, Comment. While a corporation or other business may use lawyer employees to conduct its own legal affairs, it may not use them to perform legal services for others. Interesting situations develop with collection agencies that file suit to collect claims referred to them. If the agency receives a good faith assignment of the claim from the original creditor, the agency then becomes the real party in interest and may bring suit through an attorney of its choice. If, however, the creditor has employed the agency to collect the claim on its behalf, or has assigned the claim only for purposes of collection, then it would be the unauthorized practice of law for the agency to retain a lawyer to bring suit on the claim on behalf of the creditor, unless the creditor has also authorized the agency to select a lawyer who would have a direct attorney-client relationship with the creditor and would not share legal fees with the collection agency.

VIII. THE UNMET NEED FOR COUNSEL

It may be laudable to require that for one's own benefit, he or she must seek legal services only from qualified counsel, but it is untenable to insist upon such a requirement when qualified legal counsel is not available. This "catch 22" aspect of the unauthorized practice laws has been recognized in a few cases.

While his views did not prevail, Justice Douglas questioned "whether a State, under guise of protecting its citizens from legal quacks and charlatans, can make criminals of those who, in good faith and for no personal profit, assist the indigent to assert their constitutional rights." Hackin v. Arizona (U.S.1967). In that case the court dismissed an appeal, for want of a substantial federal question, of a non-lawyer who had been convicted of unauthorized practice for representing an indigent prisoner in his attempt to fight extradition to another state on a murder conviction.

Subsequently, the Supreme Court ruled that a "jailhouse lawyer" could not be disciplined for aiding another prisoner in preparing a writ of habeas corpus, at least in the absence of an available alternative means of assistance. The state's interests in preserving prison discipline and limiting the practice of law to licensed attorneys were found insufficient to justify this restriction on the right of prisoners to petition for habeas corpus. The Court noted that: "The power of the States to control the practice of law cannot be exercised so as to abrogate federally protected rights." Johnson v. Avery (U.S.1969). All members of the Court had doubts as to whether lawyers should have the exclusive right to aid others in the preparation of such writs, and Justice Douglas would have extended a right to laymen—in and out of prison—"to act as 'next friend' to any person in the preparation of any paper or document or claim, so long as he does not hold himself out as practicing law."

These decisions, however, have not been construed as extending to an inmate seeking, for example, habeas corpus relief (for which a state usually does not assign counsel) a right to be represented by a non-lawyer in the court proceeding itself.

In a series of group legal service cases, the United States Supreme Court has established that "collective activity undertaken to obtain meaningful access to the courts is a fundamental right within the protection of the First Amendment" and efforts to frustrate that right through the application of unauthorized practice laws and ethical proscriptions against solicitation were unconstitutional. (See Chapter 9). Thus, union or other association members were constitutionally entitled to band together and delegate authority to their officers to channel cases to selected attorneys to seek better protection of the members' legal rights to desegregated education or redress, under state or federal law, for personal injuries. Some dissenting judges questioned whether the public interest in accessible, competent, and economical legal services justified the Court's interference on constitutional grounds with the traditional state regulation of the legal profession, but these cases did provide the impetus for eventual acceptance of group legal services by the ABA. DR 2–103(C), (D).

These decisions, as well as those lower court cases striking down unreasonable restrictions on *pro hac vice* appearances where qualified local counsel was not available, suggest that an individual's right to counsel—including counsel without a local license to practice law—may sometimes outweigh a state's interest in regulating the practice of law. This is especially true when local legal counsel is not available because of the limited financial means of the client, the specialized or unpopular nature of the case, and the lack of governmental obligation in the particular type of case to furnish a qualified lawyer. It is a strange logic that justifies the freedom of an individual to choose to represent himself, no matter how incompetently, but denies him the right to receive aid of another, more competent person, but who is not a lawyer. Rather than totally prohibit such aid, the law should guard against non-lawyers who misrepresent their status or seek to exploit people in need of legal assistance.

IX. ENFORCEMENT OF UNAUTHORIZED PRACTICE LAWS

Efforts to deter the unauthorized practice of law have included education, negotiation, and prohibition. The bar has attempted to educate the public to the dangers of bringing their legal problems to non-lawyer personnel, and to educate would-be non-lawyer practitioners of activities which are forbidden to them. Bar associations have negotiated conference agreements with organizations representing other professions and occupations whose activities are closely related to the law, such as accountants, architects, bank and trust companies, collection agencies, insurance agencies, title insurance companies, and real estate brokers. These agreements have served both an educational function and as a basis for voluntary compliance by the non-lawyer parties. However, such treaties dividing economic markets among competitors may run afoul of antitrust laws. For this reason, the ABA and state bars have abrogated many of their conference agreements, or no longer seek compliance with them.

Prohibitory enforcement of unauthorized practice laws include: criminal penalties; contempt of court citations and sanctions for violations thereof; and injunction proceedings, brought upon application of an interested party, which is often a bar association committee or public prosecutor. In some states *quo warranto* proceedings may be brought against a corporation which exceeds its powers by practicing law or against individuals who, without authority, seek to exercise the functions of the "office" of attorney. The issuance of this writ may result both in forbidding the performance of certain activities in the future and in the imposition of a fine for past offenses. Forfeiture of fees also has been imposed on individuals, including non-resident lawyers, whose performance of legal services is found to constitute unauthorized practice.

Deterrence also is accomplished by the threat of disciplinary sanctions against lawyers who assist others in activities that constitute unauthorized practice, share legal fees with laypersons (subject to limited exceptions for law firm employees or representatives of deceased firm members), or form partnerships with non-lawyers when any of its activities consist of the practice of law. CPR DR 3–101(A), 3–102, 3–103; RPC 5.4(a), (b), 5.5(b). To advise lawyers and others on what type of activities to avoid, bar associations committees have promulgated opinions defining the scope of unauthorized practice. Since many businesses that render law-related services employ or consult lawyers, these ethical restraints on cooperation by such members of the bar effectively supplement direct action against non-lawyers engaged in unauthorized practice.

In an extensive study, published in 1981, Professor Deborah Rhode reported that the bar in all but seven states is actively engaged in unauthorized practice enforcement, mostly centered on lay form preparation and related advice. In 1979, 80% of the matters were informally resolved, 10% resulted in formal complaints, and judicial findings of unauthorized practice were made in only 5% of the total matters in which the bar had taken action. Although the bar insists it acts to prevent harm to the public, specific allegations of harm were made in only 11% of the reported cases in the prior decade, and only 2% of the inquiries, investigations or complaints in 1979 arose from injured consumer complaints. Professor Rhode concludes that: "At every level of enforcement, the consumer's need for protection has been proclaimed rather than proven. . . ." Rhode, 34 Stan.L.Rev. (1981).

X. ANTI-TRUST AND CONSTITUTIONAL RESTRAINTS ON ENFORCEMENT OF UNAUTHORIZED PRACTICE LAWS

Does a system that excludes non-lawyers from practicing law, as enforced by bar associations and defined by lawyers who serve as judges, violate the federal Constitution or anti-trust laws? Competition is certainly restrained, as it is with the giving of any exclusive franchise, but the restraint may be justified if the qualifications for the exclusive license to practice law are not unreasonable. Education, examination, and moral character requirements have been sustained as constitutional because of their rational relation to the practice of law, although the total exclusion of non-lawyers from performing many legal functions has not been directly tested under the Due Process clause or federal antitrust laws. Nevertheless, there may be serious problems in allowing the bar to define the scope of its own economic monopoly.

The Supreme Court has held that activities of the legal profession can be subject to the federal anti-trust laws, and struck down a state bar association minimum fee schedule as illegal price fixing. Goldfarb v. Virginia State Bar (U.S.1975). Subsequently, however, the Court held that an ethics rule prohibiting lawyer advertising which was adopted by a state supreme court was "state action" and exempt from attack as anti-competitive under federal anti-trust statutes. Bates v. Arizona State Bar (U.S.1977) (striking down the advertising rule as violative of the First Amendment). The

Goldfarb case was distinguished on the ground that the Virginia State Court had not *required* the anti-competitive activities.

Bar committees, even of unified state bar associations, that issue advisory opinions which attempt to delineate activities that constitute the unauthorized practice of law, and inhibit lawyers from cooperating with such ventures, have been alleged to violate anti-trust laws. Consequently, a number of bar associations have either ceased such activities or, in an attempt to protect the opinions from anti-trust attack, have reformed the opinion process to involve participation of the public and review by a state official or judicial body.

The current system of unauthorized practice of law enforcement also may be vulnerable on constitutional grounds.

It has been held that state laws which restrict otherwise legal interstate business activity pursuant to their unauthorized practice of law regulations may violate the Commerce Clause of the Constitution. Thus, a Rhode Island statute which defined debt collection as the practice of law was found to unconstitutionally burden interstate commerce as applied to an Ohio corporation which engaged in nation-wide debt collecting on behalf of its creditor customers. Even though the statute prohibited debt collection by non-lawyer Rhode Island, as well as out-of-state, agencies, it was found to be discriminatory because it limited the business of debt collecting to members of the Rhode Island bar. Thus, the state effectively barred "out-of-staters from offering a commercial service within its borders and confers the right to provide that service—and to reap the associated economic benefit—upon a class largely composed of Rhode Island citizens." National Revenue Corporation v. Violet (1st Cir.1986).

The group legal services cases (discussed in Chapter 9) involved charges, among others, that the union and NAACP plans violated state proscriptions against the unauthorized practice of law. The Supreme Court held that those general claims, lacking specific proof of harm, must give way to the First Amendment protections of free speech and association. As these cases suggest, constitutional rights of speech and petition may be violated by unauthorized practice laws which tend to limit expression and access to the court system. The requirement that a would-be client employ a licensed lawyer in order to obtain needed legal assistance imposes significant costs and burdens on consumers, and inhibits the free speech of potential lay practitioners. Regulations of this nature must be justified by more than bare assertions of the organized bar that the restrictions are for the public's own good.

Other First Amendment protections also may be implicated by unauthorized practice laws and their enforcement. The vagueness and broadness of definitions of the practice of law, unless limited by custom, practice, or interpretative decisions would seem to invite challenge, although there is, as yet, little evidence of the success of any such efforts.

When the generality of the controlling law is combined with the broad discretion and self-interest of enforcement agencies, due process concerns also become apparent. The Supreme Court has affirmed a holding that due process is violated by a state professional regulatory board adjudicating questions of unauthorized practice when the members of the board stand to benefit economically by restricting the activities of competitors. Gibson v. Berryhill (U.S.1973).

To meet potential First Amendment and due process objections, jurisdictions must demonstrate a compelling need for restricting lay practitioners from rendering legal services and that such regulation is narrowly tailored to serve that need. As Professor Rhode demonstrated, however, there has been little or no showing of a direct relationship between unauthorized practice prohibitions and preventing concrete harm to the public. Indeed, she suggests that the analysis in unauthorized practice cases falls short of constitutional mandates in two important respects: "Courts have not required any factual showing that unqualified restraints on lay practice are necessary—or even closely related—to the states' interest in preventing incompetent assistance. Nor have courts inquired whether that interest could be realized through less restrictive means." For example, "courts have typically inquired only whether challenged activity calls for 'legal' skills, not whether lay practitioners in fact possess them." Rhode, Stan.L. Rev. (1981).

Among the means that are less restrictive than total exclusion of non-lawyers which might adequately protect the public from incompetent or unethical legal services are: (1) legal recognition and acceptance of activities that other professionals have, and competently can, perform based on their training and experience, whether or not those activities are also performed by lawyers; (2) registration, certification, or even licensure, of lay practitioners in various fields to perform specifically identified "legal" services, based upon an expressed minimum standard of training, experience or testing, and subject to revocation for proven incompetence or unethical behavior; (3) adoption of standards of malpractice liability equivalent to those of lawyers performing such services; (4) permitting "clients" to exercise their free choice by voluntary waiver of the protection of unauthorized practice laws.

In an atmosphere of antitrust and constitutional challenges, and consumer activity by groups such as HALT (Help Abolish Legal Tyranny), these and other proposals are now being studied by the legal profession and public policy makers. Segments within the organized bar and the judiciary are reexamining and reforming their approach to the regulation of the unauthorized practice of law. Non-lawyers play an increasing role in the advisory opinion and enforcement processes, and courts are more likely to view the issue as one of maximizing the public interest rather than applying sterile logic. These are steps in the right direction, and, in the opinion of many lawyers, are to be preferred to hostile "reform" resulting from court challenges or legislative overhaul.

PART II

THE DUTY TO MAKE LEGAL SERVICES AVAILABLE

CHAPTER 8

THE DUTY TO REPRESENT INDIGENT AND UNPOPULAR CLIENTS

The bar's—and the individual attorney's—characterizations of the duty to represent the poor and the unpopular reveal much about the perception of the role of law and the legal profession in society. In reviewing the limited, noncoercive duty to represent the poor and the unpopular embodied in the CPR and RPC, it is important to reflect on the heightened duty that would be entailed in application of any rational theory of professional responsibility. Implementation of a true adversary system, for example, might create a positive duty to represent the poor and unpopular regardless of the individual attorney's desire to choose her clients freely. Alternatively, in a truth-oriented system the individual attorney might be required to distinguish between her moral beliefs about her client and the truth to be sought to reach the ultimate goal of justice. As will be seen, however, as it now exists the attorney's duty to represent the poor and unpopular is largely moral (and virtually unenforceable), and does not comport with any systematic model of professional responsibility. See generally Aronson, Professional Responsibility: Education and Enforcement (1976).

I. THE DUTY TO REPRESENT THE POOR

The ethical posture of the attorney should be shaped by a view of the law not merely as a business, but as the primary means of ordering society. Such an "uneconomic" view of the profession raises the possibility of an ethical duty to represent clients who are unable to pay for the lawyer's services. Since "time is money," especially for the private practitioner, it has been argued that forcing a lawyer to represent an indigent client at an economic loss amounts to a taking of property without just compensation. Nevertheless, the CPR states that "[t]he basic responsibility for providing legal services for those unable to pay ultimately rests upon the individual lawyer," and that "[t]he rendition of free legal services to those unable to pay reasonable fees continues to be an obligation of each lawyer. . . ." EC 2–25. See also ABA Comment, RPC 6.1. This principle would appear to be an essential component of professionalism. See also Mallard v. U.S. Dist.Ct. for S.Dist. of Iowa (U.S.1989) ("[I]n a time when the need for legal services among the poor is growing and public funding for such services has not kept pace, lawyers' ethical obligation to volunteer their time and skills *pro bono publico* is manifest."). However, the response of the individual attorney to the moral suasion of Canon 2 and RPC 6.1 remains voluntary in most situations, for no disciplinary rule compels the lawyer to represent the poor. Only when the courts or the local bar are the impetus for representation may special affirmative duties arise. Because the constitutional right to counsel in criminal cases mandates the specific obligation to defend the poor, the obligation to represent the poor in civil and criminal matters will be discussed separately.

A. THE DUTY TO DEFEND THE INDIGENT ACCUSED

The indigent criminal defendant has a right to counsel at no cost whenever conviction could result in incarceration. Gideon v. Wainwright (U.S.1963); Argersinger v. Hamlin (U.S.1972). It is estimated that over 60% of criminal defendants are unable to retain private counsel. Thus, this right to free legal assistance creates an enormous concomitant duty for the legal profession to provide counsel.

1. The Argument Against the Duty to Defend

Some practitioners believe that the duty to defend the poor is solely a societal one, not practically or ethically chargeable to the individual attorney. They argue that characterizing the duty as personal creates an arbitrary distinction between lawyers and other licensed persons, such as doctors or architects, who are not generally thought to be obligated to serve the poor without compensation. The burden is said to be doubly unjust when the attorney is called upon to defend an accused criminal. It is in just such situations, when freedom or life itself may be at stake, that the client most needs expert legal help. Since most private attorneys are not well-versed in criminal law and, additionally, may perform their task grudgingly because of inadequate compensation, the client may not receive the effective legal assistance that he is constitutionally guaranteed. Indeed, the RPC and CPR may require a lawyer to avoid appointment in a criminal case. EC 2–30 provides that the lawyer should not accept employment "when he is unable to render competent service. . . ." RPC 1.16(a)(1) provides that a lawyer must not represent or must withdraw from representing a client "where representation will result in violation of the [RPC] . . .," for example, if the lawyer is not competent to represent that client as required under Rule 1.1. Similarly, Rule 6.2(a) provides that a lawyer may avoid appointment by a tribunal if "representing the client is likely to result in violation of the [RPC]. . . ." Many believe that the combination of inexpertness in criminal law and inadequacy or absence of pay will render competent service highly unlikely.

2. The Argument for the Duty to Defend

Such an attitude, coupled with the expanding right to counsel afforded the indigent criminal defendant, has in fact resulted in greater representation by professional criminal defense "specialists" in public and private defender offices funded by the government. However, when potential conflicts of interest arise, private attorneys will still be retained—for instance, when defendants implicate one another or the number of needy defendants exceeds the agencies' capabilities (see Ch. 12, infra). In addition, in many smaller communities no public defender organization exists; indigents must be defended by persons who volunteer—either spontaneously or at the request of the local bar association—or who are appointed by the court.

Some members of the private bar continue to see the duty to defend the indigent as part of their role as lawyers, much as doctors who work in open-door clinics perceive their role as physicians extending beyond economic considerations. Unless and until criminal defense for the poor, like health care for the poor, is totally government-financed, attorneys who volunteer their time in defense of the poor will be necessary to guarantee this constitutional right.

3. Appointment by the Courts; Recommendation by the Bar

The attorney who "volunteers" under coercion, e.g., who is appointed by the court or requested by a local bar association to take a criminal case, owes a moral duty to defend, not only to society and the defendant, but to the court and bar. Although the attorney is often paid only a small statutory fee, which usually does not cover the actual costs of defense, insufficient monetary compensation is not a legitimate reason for declining or withdrawing from an assigned case: "When a lawyer is appointed by a court or requested by a bar association to undertake representation of a person unable to obtain counsel . . . he should not seek to be excused from undertaking the representation except for compelling reasons." EC 2–29. The unlucrative nature of defense of an indigent is not a "compelling reason;" attorneys appointed by the court have been found in contempt for refusing to defend indigents. However, RPC Rule 6.2(b) states that if representing the client is "likely to result in an unreasonable financial burden" on the lawyer, she may avoid the appointment.

What of the defendant who is too well-off to qualify for free defense (for which the attorney is at least partially recompensed by the government) and yet too poor to afford adequate legal representation? If such a person asks an attorney to defend, no right to counsel has been established in civil cases, and neither the CPR nor the RPC contain disciplinary provisions creating an affirmative duty to represent the poor.

B. THE DUTY TO REPRESENT THE INDIGENT IN CIVIL MATTERS

1. The Argument for the Duty to Represent

It has been noted, however, that the poor's needs for legal services are often greater than those of other citizens. The poor come in contact with the law more often than most. Not only are they more likely to be arrested and charged with a crime, but many of the services that the middle class receive through private means are provided to the poor through governmental conduits. The rigors of obtaining and maintaining food stamps, aid to dependent children, welfare, and social security are replete with procedural devices which are reviewable in the courts to ensure constitutional, legislative and administrative appropriateness. The working poor are more likely to need tenant and consumer protection than are their middle class counterparts. Since the ethical duty to make the legal profession easily accessible to all is not dependent on the civil or criminal nature of the legal problem confronting an indigent member of society, the moral duty to provide free legal services to the poor is arguably just as great in civil matters as is the constitutional duty implicit in the guarantees of counsel to indigent criminal defendants.

2. The Argument Against the Duty to Represent

A more economic view of the profession, however, leads many practitioners to oppose vehemently any suggestion that the rendition of free legal services to the poor be raised to a level any higher than the moral exhortations of the Ethical Considerations

(CPR) or the Preamble and Comments of the RPC. The predecessor to Rule 6.1 of the RPC in the Kutak Commission's Discussion Draft required that all attorney's *must* "render unpaid public interest legal service." The proposal brought numerous and impassioned protests: Some attorneys argued that the program would be an inequitable "tax" on a licensed profession, that it would raise overhead costs, that it constituted involuntary servitude in violation of the 13th Amendment, and that it could only be justified if the state also forced utility companies or beauticians, for example, as members of other regulated industries, to "give away" professional services to those unable to afford them. See, e.g., Cunningham v. Superior Ct. (Cal.1986) ("No one would suggest that the individual grocer or builder should take the responsibility of providing the food and shelter needed by the poor.").

II. THE DUTY TO REPRESENT THE UNPOPULAR

Representation of the unpopular often will not have the immediate economic effect on the lawyer that representation of the poor does, but the impact it may have on the lawyer's practice has played a large part in keeping the duty to represent the unpopular from becoming a positive one enforced by disciplinary rules. The same concerns that underlie representation of the poor—constitutional guarantees of counsel to criminal defendants, access to the judicial system for civil litigants—create strong moral obligations to represent the unpopular. Indeed, in England, the profession's commitment to access to the legal process has led to a rule that a barrister must take any case brought to him (with very limited exceptions) if the client can pay an adequate fee. It should be kept in mind that essentially economic concerns also can motivate the refusal to represent unpopular clients. This economic concern is illustrated by the willingness of many attorneys to represent "unpopular" corporate giants who can ease the financial pinch that might otherwise be imposed on the attorney representing their views. The following sections analyze more closely the obligation of the attorney who professes philosophical or moral distaste for the unpopular potential client.

A. THE DUTY TO DEFEND THE UNPOPULAR ACCUSED

Criminal defense of the unpopular, like that of the poor, supra, now has a constitutional basis. Representation of the unpopular criminal defendant had a long and illustrious tradition, however, before it was constitutionally mandated. John Adams defended the soldiers charged with the Boston Massacre in 1770; Thomas Erskine defended Thomas Paine against charges of seditious libel and treason during the 1790s in England; Clarence Darrow's clients ranged from political timebomb Eugene Debs to social misfits Loeb and Leopold and religious pariah John Scopes.

1. The Argument for the Duty to Defend

Defense of social outcasts—those against whom society turns because of the heinous nature of the crimes they are presumed to have committed, because of their politics or religion, or simply because of their skin color or birthplace—is based on society's obligation to provide every accused with a fair trial. The attorney's ethical responsibility requires "acceptance . . . of his share of tendered employment which may be unattractive both to him and the bar generally," EC 2–26. This requirement is imposed despite "[t]he personal preference of a lawyer to avoid adversary alignment against judges, other lawyers, public officials, or influential members of the community." EC 2–28. "Regardless of his personal feelings, a lawyer should not decline representation because a client or cause is unpopular or community reaction is adverse." EC 2–27. Cf. ABA Comment, RPC 6.2.

2. The Argument Against the Duty to Defend

Although the defense of an unpopular client gives an individual lawyer the satisfaction of knowing that he has preserved a societal ideal, the potential economic and political toll of such defense may underlie the absence of a disciplinary rule to enforce the moral obligation to defend the unpopular. Many attorneys apparently fear economic and political reprisals—loss of clients and the good will of fellow attorneys, denial of political appointments, ostracism by the community in general—if they defend an unpopular accused. Erskine lost his position as Attorney General to the Prince of Wales for his defense of Paine, and many attorneys have been asked to leave partnerships, have lost clients, and have been denied political appointments for defending the unpopular. Frank Armani, for example, although praised by courts and bar ethics committees for defending and maintaining the confidences of Robert Garrow (whose murder of two young women had not yet been discovered), lost most of his clients, faced a number of disciplinary and criminal prosecutions, suffered a heart attack, faced marital problems, and received death threats from an enraged public. Indeed, some attorneys have themselves been jailed for their actions in support of unpopular defendants. Algernon Sidney Sullivan was imprisoned for his demands that the Confederate sailors he defended be given a fair trial and treated as prisoners of war in their New York prosecution for piracy during the Civil War. Fear of such societal disapproval is not considered an adequate reason to decline employment, EC 2–28, RPC 6.2 (unless "likely to result in an unreasonable financial burden on the lawyer").

3. "Personal Feelings" and "Community Attitudes"

The Ethical Considerations of the CPR do permit an attorney to avoid the duty to represent an unpopular defendant if his "personal feeling, as distinguished from a community attitude, may impair his effective representation of a prospective client." EC 2–30. Before deciding that his reaction to the prospective client is severe enough to justify refusal to represent, however, the attorney should examine the source of his beliefs. To the extent that the attorney's "personal feelings" are a reflection of the "community attitude" (or fear of loss of income because of that attitude), the attorney should remember that guilt is a legal definition, not a function of adverse public reaction, that the defendant must be considered innocent until proven guilty, and that every defendant has a right to a fair trial to establish guilt or innocence.

If the attorney truly cannot resolve his difficulties with the defendant's political or moral beliefs or actions, he then should, under EC 2–30, decline to represent the unpopular defendant. The client may prefer no counsel to the degradation of his beliefs or actions which some attorneys have undertaken in their "representation" of unpopular clients. In fact, if counsel is truly adversely affected by his feelings ("personal interests" under DR 5–101(A)), the Code would appear to forbid acceptance of employment. Likewise, RPC 6.2(c) permits the attorney to seek to avoid appointment if the cause is so repugnant as to be "likely to impair the client-lawyer relationship or the lawyer's ability to represent the client." Cf. RPC 1.16(b)(3) permitting withdrawal if the client "insists upon pursuing an objective that the lawyer considers repugnant or imprudent".

B. THE DUTY TO REPRESENT THE UNPOPULAR IN CIVIL MATTERS

Representation of the unpopular in civil matters does not have the same constitutional urgency as does defense of the unpopular accused. However, the representation of unpopular clients often entails defense of unpopular causes and brings into sharp relief issues of free speech and equal protection. The attorney who represents the unpopular civil client fosters important societal commitments to equal access to the judicial system and assurance of constitutionally guaranteed freedoms. These commitments are arguably as important as the right to a fair trial protected by defense of the unpopular criminal accused.

The American Civil Liberties Union, which specializes in representation of unpopular clients, lost much member support and public prestige for its representation of Nazis who wished to march in primarily-Jewish Skokie, Illinois. The ACLU's experience with Skokie provides a valuable lesson concerning the duty to represent an unpopular client. It demonstrates the need, on the part of the public, the profession and the individual attorney, to separate the content of the unpopular client's beliefs and actions from her right to think and act in that, or any, way. The public hostility to representation of the unpopular reflects the necessity for educational efforts by the profession to apprise the public of the need for and function of representation of all parties in the judicial process.

C. APPOINTMENT BY THE COURTS; RECOMMENDATION BY THE BAR

If, despite the moral obligation to defend the indigent and unpopular, a person cannot obtain legal representation, the court may appoint counsel or ask the local bar association to find an attorney. In such an instance, the attorney may be excused from undertaking the representation only for "good cause," RPC 6.2, or "compelling reasons," EC 2–29. "Compelling reasons" do not include such factors as "the repugnance of the subject matter of the proceeding, [or] the identity or position of a person involved in the case. . . ." Also, Rule 1.16(c) provides that, if "ordered to do so by a tribunal, a lawyer shall continue representation notwithstanding good cause for terminating the representation." Thus, attorney Ellis Rubin was held in contempt for refusing to continue representing a murder defendant who insisted on testifying falsely at trial. Rubin v. State (Fla.App.1986). Subsequently, Rubin was publicly reprimanded by the Florida Supreme Court for his conduct in refusing to proceed despite the court order. Florida Bar v. Rubin (Fla.1989).

Although attorneys may be required by courts to represent indigent and unpopular clients, it is less clear whether courts may require that attorneys do so *without compensation.* A number of state courts have struck down or significantly limited court appointment of attorneys where adequate compensation was not provided, while others have held that the privilege of practicing law entails a duty to assist the court. Such decisions are likely to help attorneys seeking some (or better) funding for representation of indigent clients. However, to the extent that they rely upon the increasingly held view that the law is no more than a service-oriented business, and that lawyers have no additional obligations as "officers of the court", they are unfortunate.

In Mallard v. United States Dist.Ct. for S.Dist. of Iowa (U.S. 1989), the Court overturned the trial court's holding that the federal appointment statute granted power to *compel* an unwilling attorney to represent an indigent litigant in a civil case. However, the Court's ruling was based on a reading of the statutory authority in question (28 U.S.C.A. § 1915(d)). The Court reserved ruling on whether federal courts have *inherent* power to compel representation by unwilling attorneys, but reaffirmed "lawyers' ethical obligation to assist those who are too poor to afford counsel." It would appear that the four dissenters, when joined by Justice Kennedy (who concurred only with respect to the statutory construction of § 1915(d)), constitute a majority for finding inherent authority by courts to compel attorneys, as "officers of the court", to represent the indigent. Such authority could potentially be invoked by individual trial courts, or pursuant to the authority of the states' highest courts to promulgate ethical codes for regulating attorneys. Whether state courts will exercise that authority is an issue currently in flux.

CHAPTER 9

IMPLEMENTING THE DUTY TO MAKE LEGAL SERVICES AVAILABLE: GROUP AND PREPAID LEGAL SERVICES, LEGAL AID, JUDICARE, LEGAL CLINICS, LAWYER REFERRAL, AND PUBLIC INTEREST LITIGATION

I. INTRODUCTION

"The need of members of the public for legal services is met only if they recognize their legal problems, appreciate the importance of seeking assistance, and are able to obtain the services of acceptable legal counsel. Hence, important functions of the legal profession are to educate laypersons to recognize their problems, to facilitate the process of intelligent selection of lawyers, and to assist in making legal services fully available." EC 2–1. See also ABA Comment, RPC 6.1.

Both the RPC and CPR contain provisions designed to make legal services equally accessible to all potential consumers. The principles underlying these provisions spring from the recognition that the comparatively minimal use of legal services by low and middle income persons has been due more to the inaccessibility of those services than to lack of legal problems. The inability to identify legal problems or to make an informed selection of a particular attorney is only part of the problem, however. For many Americans, a major obstacle to use of legal services is cost, or the belief that a lawyer usually charges more than his time is worth. In addition, physical inaccessibility hinders the seeking of legal services by groups of people without law offices in their area.

The RPC and CPR encourage lawyers to improve the availability of legal services to all, both by individual efforts and by supporting programs designed to serve the legal needs of low and middle income persons. Ethical barriers to supporting programs such as legal aid and prepaid legal services have been diminished or eliminated by recent Canon 2 amendments and provisions of the RPC.

The RPC and the ethical considerations of Canon 2 direct attorneys to assist laypersons to recognize legal problems through advertisements and articles, seminars, lectures, and civic programs, EC 2–2; RPC 7.2(a) and Comment, as well as through proper in-person advice, RPC 7.3; EC 2–3. Lawyer referral systems and "other ethical plans which aid in the selection of qualified counsel" are also encouraged. EC 2–15; RPC 7.2(c) and Comment.

Basic to Canon 2 and corresponding RPC provisions is the principle that persons unable to pay all or part of reasonablc fees should still be able to obtain legal services. To this end, lawyers are encouraged to support legal aid offices, prepaid plans, and other programs designed to make legal services more accessible. These directives recognize that while the rendition of services to those unable to pay reasonable fees is the responsibility of each individual attorney, group programs can be the most equitable and effective means of meeting the need. Chapter 8 suggests the *duty* of the bar and individual attorneys to provide legal services; this chapter details some of the *means* to implement that duty, either voluntarily or through government action.

II. LEGAL AID AND PUBLIC DEFENDER SERVICES

Although private legal aid societies have operated in the United States for over a century, support from government and the organized bar for free and low cost services to low income persons is fairly recent. The ABA has traditionally emphasized the pro bono obligation of individual attorneys, but attempts by the organized bar to mandate pro bono work have met with an unenthusiastic response. See Chapter 8, supra. The current Canon 2 position in support of legal aid programs, echoed in RPC

6.1 and Comments, represents the realization that pro bono work by all attorneys has been impossible to mandate and that, as a voluntary system, is unlikely to reach most persons in need of legal services.

Until the 1960s, existing legal aid was provided by private legal aid societies and, for capital offenses, by court appointed attorneys. The inadequacies of this system were clear by 1963 when, in Gideon v. Wainwright, the United States Supreme Court declared that every person accused of a felony has the right to assistance of counsel and, therefore, every indigent so accused has the right to have counsel provided at public expense. In an attempt to meet the increased demand for provision of free criminal defense to accused felons who could not afford to retain private counsel, public defender offices were developed throughout the country following *Gideon.* The Criminal Justice Act of 1964 and similar state legislation required the courts to establish procedures for appointment and compensation of counsel for indigent defendants.

The need for competent criminal defense attorneys was expanded by Argersinger v. Hamlin (U.S.1972), when the Supreme Court declared that "absent a knowing and intelligent waiver, no person may be imprisoned for any offense, whether classified as petty, misdemeanor, or felony, unless he was represented by counsel at his trial." Since about 65% of all felonies and 47% of all misdemeanors in the U.S. are committed by indigents, the public defender system, other legal aid programs, and court appointed counsel provide the defense for about one-half of all criminal cases annually.

Public defender organizations stress the importance of providing attorneys who are trained in criminal defense. However, court appointed attorneys are still a major source of legal aid to indigent criminal defendants, and are often the only source in areas not served by a public defender's office or in matters in which the public defender would experience a conflict of interest.

A. O.E.O. LEGAL SERVICES PROGRAM

Although court appointed attorneys and public defender offices provided *criminal* defense to the indigent, private legal aid societies and individual pro bono work were the only sources of *civil* legal aid until 1965: In that year, the first federally funded legal aid program was created under the Office of Economic Opportunity. Federal funds were provided to locally controlled programs if their design and purpose were consistent with O.E.O. guidelines. The goal of this original Legal Services Program was "to further the cause of justice among persons living in poverty by mobilizing the assistance of lawyers and legal institutions and by providing legal advice, legal representation, legal counseling, education in legal matters, and other appropriate legal services." "Other appropriate legal services" initially included: attempting law reform through test cases and legislation to protect the interests of low income persons; taking a community advocacy role at city council meetings, utility rate hearings, and press debates; training lay advocates; educating community groups for confrontation with community officials; and helping communities to develop their own political and economic resources, such as tenants' unions and welfare recipient councils.

Such political activities were unpopular with local agencies that were a direct or indirect source of the originally required 20% local funding. Vice President Agnew characterized the program's spending of public funds to oppose administration policies as "tax funded social activism that transfers great power in community affairs from elected officials to self-appointed ones."

B. LEGAL SERVICES CORPORATION

In 1974 the Legal Services Program was transferred to the independently organized Legal Services Corporation, created by Congress in response to the imminent termination of the O.E.O. and to urging by the ABA that legal services be freed from the political pressures surrounding a government agency. Although the program remains committed to enhancing the responsiveness of the legal system to impoverished communities as a whole, as well as to serving the legal needs of individuals, restrictions on the scope of Legal Services Corporation (LSC) activities represent a move to depoliticize Corporation programs. For example, Legal Services attorneys are specifically prohibited from engaging in or encouraging others to participate in political activities such as public demonstrations, picketing, boycotts, strikes, or any civil disturbance. LSC programs may not undertake voter registration drives or even provide voters with transportation to the polls. Further, attorney participation in and program funding of lobbying activities are prohibited, and class action suits may not be undertaken without express approval of a project director. Thus, under the Nixon administration, restrictions on "political" activities by LSC offices included cases involving undocumented workers, draft resisters, abortion or school desegregation. In addition, costs may be awarded to any successful defendant who can show that the Corporation or a plaintiff represented by it commenced or pursued an action for the purpose of harassment or malicious abuse of process. And the Reagan administration attempted to abolish the LSC altogether.

The Corporation's national board of eleven directors is appointed by the President with the advice and consent of the Senate, but the Corporation is committed to a neighborhood orientation. Legal Services offices are located for maximum access to the population served. Local boards comprised of community representatives and local attorneys draft the goals and guidelines for each office with the special needs and resources of the community in mind.

Annual Congressional funding is supplemented by state and local government appropriations and by contributions from charitable organizations. In areas of conflict of interest and specialization, as well as in the training of program personnel, pro bono work by local attorneys has been particularly important.

Although the LSC was established to provide equality of access to the legal system, it has never had sufficient resources to reach more than a relative handful of the country's low income population. During the period it was best funded and most in favor, the LSC was estimated to be handling only one-eighth of the needs of the poor. Cramton, Crisis in Legal Services for the Poor, 26 Vill. L.Rev. 521, 529 (1981); and, although quality service depends on well-trained and experienced personnel, the Corporation has not been able to offer the salaries or other incentives necessary to attract the top law graduates or to keep experienced attorneys. Further, the Reagan administration required the LSC to devote 10% of its budget to encouraging and supporting representation by private attorneys. See Abel, American Lawyers 134 (1989) (citing a study which found that private practitioners were incompetent to practice poverty law (because they lacked expertise) or uninterested in doing so (because they derived greater rewards from their paying clients)). It is unlikely that the Corporation will meet its goal of providing quality legal services to the entire indigent population as long as legal services programs remain low priority items to members of Congress and state legislatures.

C. IOLTA FUNDS

However, the progressive curtailment of funding of the LSC helped to fuel the financial success of IOLTA (Interest On Lawyers' Trust Accounts) plans. Under these plans, client funds are kept in an interest bearing account. See Ch. 13 (Fiduciary Responsibilities). The interest on the account is not returned to the client, but is instead transferred to some non-profit organization responsible for funding law oriented projects such as: legal services programs; loans for law students; programs designed to improve the administration of justice; and other programs intended to provide legal services to the indigent or to educate the public concerning their legal rights. Typically, such plans require that only those *short term, nominal* client funds that cannot be utilized to provide a positive return to individual clients (i.e., where the cost of administering the account is greater than the interest to be earned over the period the funds are expected to be deposited) may be placed in the pooled IOLTA account. Because the cost of administering the account for an individual client would result in no positive return, mandatory IOLTA plans have been upheld against takings clause challenge by clients. See, e.g., Carroll v. State Bar of California (Cal.1984, cert. denied, 1985). Most states have made use of this source of funds to significantly improve the financing of representation for those who could not otherwise afford it.

D. ETHICAL PROBLEMS OF LEGAL AID AND PUBLIC DEFENDER REPRESENTATION

DR 2–103(D) authorizes lawyer cooperation and employment with legal aid or public defender offices that are operated or sponsored by duly accredited law schools, bona fide nonprofit community organizations, government agencies, or approved bar associations. The RPC contain no specific requirements for "acceptable" legal aid or public defender offices; support of "all proper efforts to meet [the] need for legal services" is encouraged by the ABA Comment to RPC 6.1, with legal aid offices being specifically mentioned. However, certain more specific ethical principles in the CPR, of particular significance to any attorney with legal services affiliations, are mirrored by RPC provisions. For example, lay intermediaries such as legal services program directors or program sponsoring groups must not be allowed to interfere with an attorney's duty under Canon 4 and RPC 1.6 to preserve the confidences and secrets of her client, and under Canon 5 and RPC 1.8(f) and 5.4(c) to exercise independent professional judgment on her client's behalf. There is a danger that, in an attempt to further the organization's goal of making institutions responsive to the poverty community as a whole, a legal services attorney may lose sight of the immediate needs of her client. A client's interest in quick settlement, for example, may conflict with the program's interest in pressing a test case. The CPR and RPC clearly indicate that in all instances of conflicting interests, those of the individual client must take precedence. See Ch. 12, infra.

RPC 5.4(c) and 1.8(f), as well as DR 5–107(B), protect the independence of an attorney's professional judgment by prohibiting any regulation or direction by persons recommending, employing, or paying an attorney to provide legal services to a third person. The ABA Ethics Committee has interpreted DR 5–107(B) to allow the National Board to establish broad eligibility criteria and local boards to set specific standards and decide what services will be provided in light of community needs. This interpretation would almost certainly apply to RPC 5.4(c). Once the client has been accepted and assigned to an individual staff attorney, that attorney makes the decisions on how best to handle the case. The only exception permits supervision of the staff attorney by another office attorney, since the office professional staff is the equivalent of a firm and the attorney-client relationship may be expanded to a firm-client relationship. See EC 4–2; ABA Comment, RPC 1.6. Canon 5 and RPC 1.7 also prevent attorneys with Legal Services affiliations from representing any individual who may have a conflict of interest with another person being represented by staff attorneys, unless the consent of both parties is obtained upon full disclosure. Thus, alternative counsel normally must be found for either the husband or wife in divorce actions and for one of the parties whenever opposing litigants are indigent.

RPC 1.6(a) and DR 4–101(B), requiring the preservation of client confidences, limit the disclosures that staff attorneys may make to governing boards. DR 4–101(B) has been construed by the ABA Ethics Committee to allow reasonable disclosure to directors for study and research and for supervision of services. Staff lawyers are prohibited, however, from disclosing files containing client confidences and secrets to inspectors from outside the agency without the client's consent.

III. JUDICARE

Another method of delivering legal services to lower income persons that has been operating successfully in some areas is the Judicare system. Not to be confused with Medicare, Judicare eligibility is based on income level rather than age. The program provides state or federally funded legal services delivered by private practitioners.

Under OEO–funded programs, persons eligible for Judicare services learned of the program and applied for their Judicare cards at county welfare offices, hospitals, and community centers. Referral by community agencies was an important element of the program since there were no neighborhood Judicare offices. Following referral, an eligible Judicare client presented her card to the private attorney of her choice, who was free to accept the client or not. Upon acceptance of a client, the attorney submitted a notice of retainer to the central administrative office; that office checked the client's eligibility to ascertain that the service was covered by the program. Judicare covered mostly civil matters. Attorneys were compensated for each case completed at set flat or hourly rates.

Judicare proponents emphasize the advantages of utilizing private attorneys. About one-third of all low income persons do not have access to a legal aid office. Judicare gives indigents the same freedom to choose their own attorneys afforded to clients able to pay for legal services. There is some evidence that Judicare clients may be more satisfied with their attorneys than are Legal Services clients with staff attorneys. J. Brakel, Judicare (1974). Cf. Saltzman, Private Bar Delivery of Civil Legal Services to the Poor, 34 Hast.L.J. 1165 (1983) (proposing combined staffed-office, private practitioner approach).

The major drawback of the Judicare system is that it does not provide the community education and training programs or commitment to law reform and community advocacy emphasized by Legal Services Corporation programs. Private attorneys selected by the Judicare client may be understandably less eager to press test cases, especially when compensation is limited. Although it has been estimated that delivery of legal services by private practitioners costs the taxpayer substantially more than legal aid office services, Judicare proponents claim that the cost is about equal. After originally opposing Judicare programs, in 1983 the

LSC (with a Reagan-appointed board) reversed itself and required that over 10% of grant funds be used to involve private practitioners in providing indigent legal services. In 1984 the ABA strongly backed increased use of Judicare programs by the LSC. Many state and local bar associations have initiated programs in which volunteer attorneys are assisted and coordinated by a central staff.

IV. GROUP PREPAID LEGAL SERVICES

In the view of the ABA, the major objective of the American legal system is preventive law—avoidance of legal problems before they occur. Until recently, only businesses and a small number of wealthy individuals have used the legal system in this way. For most Americans, the apparently high cost of legal services has discouraged regular use. Ironically, the 70% of Americans who rarely use a lawyer's services are the group least able to bear the burden of major legal expense that may result from neglect of legal needs.

Legal aid programs have begun to serve the preventive needs of the poor, but there is a huge gap in coverage between those eligible for free legal services and those able or willing to buy services at the private bar's market prices. While maximum income levels for free legal service programs approximate welfare and public assistance eligibility levels, group and prepaid programs are aimed at both middle income persons and the "working poor." The inability to recognize legal problems, a lack of understanding of what a lawyer does, and unfamiliarity with lawyers or a means of selecting a lawyer add to the reluctance of low and middle income persons to make use of the legal system. Group and prepaid legal services plans are designed to provide preventive services by acquainting the consumer with his legal needs, connecting the client with competent counsel, and providing the needed services at a price the consumer can afford.

Group legal services plans have been developed by unions, trade associations, professional organizations, consumer cooperatives, automobile clubs, credit unions and other organizations whose members are likely to share similar legal needs. Increasingly, such plans are being marketed by private lawyers and firms. The volume of legal work and the efficiency made possible by the common interests of group members allow groups to provide affordable services through in-house counsel or to contract with private attorneys to provide services to members at reduced rates. The group selects or recommends the attorneys for its members and may offer consumer education on group-related legal problems. Over 10 million Americans are now covered by some form of group legal services plan.

Many group plans are for *prepaid* legal services; they provide members with specific services, such as a certain amount of consultation, for a set prepaid amount, or utilize a risk-spreading concept to offer legal insurance coverage to members. Prepaid plans have the advantage of encouraging consumers to use legal services preventively, since the initial sum has been paid. Insurance companies and non-profit corporations also offer prepaid plans to individuals. Bar associations have helped organize both group and individual plans.

Prepaid plans vary widely in coverage and organization. Plans are "open" or "closed" depending on who provides the legal services. Like the Blue Cross and Blue Shield medical plans, open panel plans allow the consumer to select any attorney. Some partially open panel plans limit selection to attorneys who voluntarily register to serve plan members. Closed plans give more responsibility for attorney selection to the sponsoring group, much like the HMO medical plans. Groups may hire in-house attorneys, retain a private firm to meet members' needs, or allow members to choose an attorney from a carefully selected closed panel.

Members of a group may receive plan coverage automatically as a benefit of membership, or they may be given the opportunity to join the plan voluntarily. Automatic plans tend to offer more comprehensive coverage because they have a broader base over which to spread operation costs. This is because their members make less use of plan services than do the members of voluntary plans, who usually join because they have or anticipate having legal needs. Some plans serve the needs of the individual only; others cover families and dependents of members.

The functions of the sponsoring group vary with the type of plan offered. The organization determines policy matters such as coverage, cost to members, settlement, and fees, and handles the administrative duties of collecting prepayments, maintaining eligibility records and processing claims. Plans based on the insurance concept require larger monetary reserves than do plans offering negotiated reduced rates.

A. ETHICAL PROBLEMS IN GROUP AND PREPAID LEGAL SERVICES PLANS

A number of ethical barriers to group and prepaid legal services plans have been overcome by the line of United States Supreme Court decisions culminating in United Transportation Union v. State Bar of Michigan (U.S.1971), which declared "collective activity undertaken to obtain meaningful access to the courts" to be a "fundamental right within the protection of the First Amendment. . . . [T]he right would be a hollow promise if courts could deny associations of workers or others the means of enabling their members to meet the costs of legal representation." See Ch. 10, infra. Support for any prepaid or group program was long in coming from the organized bar because of the ethical problems inherent in an attorney being employed or supervised by a party other than her client. Initial ABA approval of prepaid programs (in response to both the *United Transportation Union* series of decisions and the demand from various groups for such means of gaining access to affordable services) was limited to open panel plans, because open plans preserve the client's right to choose any attorney and are less susceptible to lay intermediary interference or control over the attorney-client relationship. Although some of the rules based on the ABA's preference for open over closed plans have been carefully deleted from CPR Canon 2, the risk of third-party control and conflict of interest have influenced many groups to select open plans.

DR 2–103(D) now allows attorneys to cooperate with any bona fide organization that recommends, furnishes or pays for legal services for its members or beneficiaries, providing certain ethical safeguards are observed: The plan should be sponsored by a non-profit organization; if organized for profit, the organization must not employ, direct, select, or supervise participating attorneys. Thus profit-making organizations must have open plans, except if the organization bears ultimate financial responsibility for the member (e.g., casualty insurance companies). Even then, the interests of the client—not the organization—must dictate the course of the representation. Lawyers may have no affiliation with plans that they know to be in violation of any laws or with clients whom they know seek services as a result of conduct prohibited by the disciplinary rules.

DR 2–103(D)(4)(e) safeguards the plan members' right to choose attorneys not affiliated with the legal services plan. The program must provide outside counsel when it would be unethical, improper, or inadequate for attorneys affiliated with the plan to represent a member in a particular matter—for example, when a plan member sues his spouse, another plan beneficiary, or the plan's governing board. Many closed plans have provided members with the option of selecting outside attorneys and being compensated at plan rates.

Although the original draft of the RPC contained language specifically supportive of group legal services, this language was dropped from the final draft, leaving the RPC largely silent on this issue. Following *Zauderer and Shapero* (see Ch. 10, infra), however, RPC 7.3 was amended, and subsection (d) now provides that a lawyer may participate with a prepaid or group legal service plan which "uses in-person or telephone contact to solicit memberships or subscriptions for the plan from persons who are not known to need legal services in a particular matter covered by the plan." According to ABA Formal Opinion 87–355 (1987), participation in a for-profit legal service plan is subject to compliance with specific RPC guidelines applicable to all lawyers and firms. Under RPC 5.4, for example, neither the plan nor the participating lawyer may permit the sponsoring organization to interfere with the lawyer's exercise of independent professional judgment on behalf of the client. The plan member becomes a client of the lawyer, and the plan sponsor should have no dealings on legal issues with plan subscribers once their matters have been referred to the lawyer. Improper interference with the lawyer's judgment could also occur if the plan sets limits on the amount of time the lawyer may spend on each client's case or requires that the lawyer agree not to represent the client beyond the scope of the agreement in the plan.

In addition, the plan must contain no requirement that would interfere with the lawyer's duty of confidentiality under RPC 1.6 or the lawyer's compliance with conflicts of interest provisions. Therefore, quality control mechanisms are improper if they lead to disclosure by the lawyer of information relating to the representation of the client without her consent. Although it might be argued that the lawyer's participation in a prepaid legal services plan violates RPC 5.4(a) (improper fee-sharing with a non-lawyer) or RPC 7.2(c) (giving anything of value to another to recommend the lawyer's services), Opinion 87–355 and RPC 7.3(d) clearly indicate that a lawyer may ethically participate in a for-profit prepaid legal service plan.

B. ADDITIONAL PROBLEMS AFFECTING GROUP LEGAL SERVICES PLANS

Designers of group and prepaid legal services plans must also consider the effect of antitrust law, insurance regulation, the internal revenue code, and federal pre-emption of state regulation of employee benefit plans under the Employee Retirement Income Security Act.

In Goldfarb v. Virginia State Bar (U.S.1975), the Supreme Court held that a minimum fee schedule, drafted by a county bar association, (that would have affected all attorneys practicing in the area) constituted price fixing in restraint of trade and a violation of the Sherman Act. Since legal services affect out of state parties, the Court held that they are a part of interstate commerce. With respect to group legal services plans, then, members must be free to negotiate lower fees for services from area attorneys, an impossibility if all area attorneys serve an open plan with set fees.

Member control of fee schedule development has been suggested as a possible solution. Fees set by the state in its regulatory capacity would also be exempt from antitrust law as sovereign action under the Parker v. Brown exception to the Sherman Act. State bar association proposals to establish prepaid legal services corporations with fee schedules have been disapproved by the Justice Department, however; and a proposed fee schedule governing a multi-state plan was found by the ABA Ethics Committee to be in violation of DR 2–107, which requires that division of fees by attorneys be in proportion to services performed and responsibility assumed. Under RPC 1.5(e), however, division of fees between attorneys is permitted if, pursuant to written agreement with the client, "each lawyer assumes joint responsibility for the representation."

The effect of insurance regulations on group and prepaid plans differs from state to state. Some states prohibit insurance company plans as an unauthorized form of insurance. Although state insurance boards have the advantage of being pre-existing agencies familiar with the necessary regulation, the propriety of the Insurance Commissioner interfering with attorney activity is questionable.

V. LEGAL CLINICS

Another approach to providing affordable legal services to low and middle income persons is the legal clinic. Like medical clinics, legal clinics cut costs by increasing efficiency through systemization, mechanization, increased volume and specialization. Whether privately organized or sponsored by bar associations or law schools, successful legal clinics implement certain procedures designed to make legal services more accessible as well as less costly.

A key factor in cost cutting is use of paralegal personnel to do much of the work traditionally done by attorneys. With the help of systemized forms developed to cover routine legal matters, paralegals can handle initial client interviews and can brief the attorney, resulting in shorter yet more effective attorney-client consultation. Paralegals assigned to each case can screen client calls and answer most inquiries on the current state of the case; but they should not make decisions or engage in conduct reserved by the RPC or CPR for licensed attorneys. See Ch. 7, supra.

Clinics do increase the accessibility of legal services by going to the people to be served: Storefront offices make it easier for clients to drop in, and clinics with several offices make optimum use of attorneys by circulating specialists to different locations on different days. Accessibility is increased by keeping evening and weekend hours and by taking credit cards and time-deferred payments.

The time saved by systemization, specialization, and the use of paralegals allows the clinic lawyer to devote more time to developing a close attorney-client relationship. Clinic lawyers practice preventive law both through this personal interaction with clients and by various activities designed to disseminate legal information to area consumers. Although legal clinics are usually funded by law schools or state and federal grants, the legal clinic concept could be profitable due to the economies of scale and other advantages indicated above. In Jacoby v. State Bar of California (Cal.1977), the California Supreme Court found "trivial" allegations that the use of the name "Legal Clinic" by private attorneys was misleading. In fact, the ABA itself funded an $80,000 "experimental, innovative legal clinic program for the delivery of legal services." The generally routine nature of clinic legal business also makes the legal clinic attractive to young attorneys just starting to practice law.

The legal clinic concept has been very successful in the past 15 years. In just ten years (between 1974 and 1984), the number of such legal clinics grew from eight to more than a thousand. Abel, American Lawyers 138 (1989). In 1985, Hyatt Legal Services had grown to 674 lawyers (second largest firm in the country) in 192 law offices and was seeing 300,000 clients a year. Jacoby & Meyers had 297 lawyers (thirty-first place) and 175,000 clients, although both firms had fallen back somewhat by 1987. Id.

VI. PUBLIC INTEREST LAW

Public interest groups or law firms are another source of legal assistance for those whose needs fit within the context of a particular group's specialized advocacy. Organizations like the Project on Corporate Responsibility, the Center for Auto Safety, the Environmental Defense Fund, the Sierra Club, the Consumers Union, the Medical Committee for Human Rights, and the American Civil Liberties Union, among many others, help persons whose legal problems fall into specified areas. The use of law students, either paid or pro bono, has greatly increased the amount of legal work these public interest groups can perform. In addition to providing free or very low cost legal assistance, employment of students by public interest groups helps to develop the students' recognition of their law reform and public leadership obligations and their ability to engage in public interest litigation effectively.

Public interest law is based on the premise that government by itself cannot represent the public interest in dealings with the public or in the regulation of industry. Within their areas of interest—the environment, civil liberties, consumer safety, etc.—the groups aim for direct participation in the decisionmaking processes of government agencies and private corporations. They have worked for judicial recognition of the private citizen's role in agency deliberation and encouraged broad consumer standing in the courts to enforce the law as "private attorneys general."

Advertising is important to public interest law both as a method of educating consumers on the issues and of increasing the likelihood that individuals with potential test cases will find their way to the group concerned. DR 2–103(A) prohibits private practitioners from soliciting cases except as allowed under the publication and broadcast guidelines of DR 2–101(B). However, when a political issue is involved, an attorney will be disciplined for in-person solicitation only if there is actual harm to the client. Public interest groups are free to recruit test cases at public meetings and to advertise their services and the nature of their operation. See NAACP v. Button, In re Primus, and Ch. 10, infra.

VII. LAWYER REFERRAL

Even where group and prepaid legal services, legal aid clinics, and public interest group advocacy are available, under-utilization of these services can be a problem if those in need do not know how to locate legal assistance. Lawyer referral programs are designed to improve consumer access to legal aid by coordinating the delivery of an area's legal services. Often sponsored by state or local bar associations, the typical program invites area attorneys to join an open panel from which individuals are selected to serve the consumers who write or phone for referrals. Most programs provide a certain amount of consultation at no cost or for reduced rates to encourage consumer use. Some also provide necessary additional work at reduced rates.

The effectiveness of a referral system varies with the goals and resources of the individual program. It is vital that the public be made aware that referral is available. Although DR 2–101 and RPC 7.2(c) and 7.3(d) permit the necessary advertising, they do not guarantee that program coordinators will actively promote their service.

VIII. ADDITIONAL RESOURCES

The existence of publicly created programs to improve the accessibility of legal services does not relieve the private bar of its concurrent obligation. The individual attorney bears the ultimate responsibility for meeting the population's legal needs. EC 2–25; ABA Comment, RPC 6.1. Pro bono work is vital to public interest and legal aid programs. Some private firms have created pro bono departments supported by the firm as a whole. There are, however, means of extending legal aid that supplement the services of licensed attorneys. Among these are programs utilizing law students, "jail-house lawyers," and consumers themselves.

A. LAW STUDENTS

Law students deliver legal services by serving as clerks and interns with agencies and private firms and by participating in law school clinical programs. Clinical education may be offered through classes or through extra-curricular programs: In either case, a program has the advantages of the physical plant, library, secretarial, and other services available at a law school.

Sensitively directed programs can be a means of creating involvement and relevance in legal education; but it is important that participants be given careful supervision. Clinical programs can be merely band-aid efforts to serve a small group in need of legal services, or they can provide training in attorneys' ethical duties to their clients and make participants aware of the rewards of serving a particular segment of the population.

Most states have provisions to certify law students for limited practice under the supervision of a licensed attorney. This enables students in clinical programs, under supervision, to give advice, negotiate settlements, and argue before the courts, and to serve as investigators, researchers, and drafters of legal documents.

A potential threat to the efficacy of California's clinical programs was removed by that state's supreme court. In People v.

Perez (Cal.1979), the California Supreme Court held that participation in a criminal defense by a certified law student under supervision of a public defender and pursuant to a program designed by the State Bar to assure the competency of representation, did not per se impair the defendant's constitutional guarantee of effective assistance of counsel.

The court noted that a defendant represented under a clinical program can challenge the effectiveness of the representation by the supervising attorney and the certified student, but that the challenge must be reviewed under the same standards as those governing cases that do not involve certified students. In a closing note, the court described the benefits conferred by clinical programs: "The student, under the supervision of an experienced trial lawyer, gains exposure and training in actual trial techniques instead of mere sterile description or observation of them; the litigant obtains the participation of an enthusiastic young law student, who in all likelihood will devote more time and energy to the case than the harassed and overworked public defender."

Recent efforts to foster student concern for public interest work, while providing assistance to attorneys and agencies engaged in such work, have included instituting mandatory pro bono commitments in law schools, establishing loan forgiveness programs for students entering into public service work following graduation, and seeking matching funds from law firms for contributions by law student public service projects. Tulane Law School was the first ABA-approved law school to require all of its students to perform community service (20 hours) prior to graduation. This precedent was given a boost by the decision of the University of Pennsylvania Law School in 1989 to require all students to perform 70 hours of unpaid professional service before they can graduate. In addition to providing an expected 15,000 hours of free legal service each year, the program is intended to instill a spirit of public service in young lawyers, whether or not they may choose to pursue public interest law.

In addition, an increasing number of law schools have instituted loan forgiveness programs whereby students are required to pay back a decreasing amount of student loans for each year they engage in public service work after graduation. Under most such programs, after a stated period of time, the entire loan is forgiven. At least three law schools (CUNY at Queens, Antioch and Northeastern) have developed nontraditional curricula, seeking specifically to prepare public interest lawyers. This increased emphasis on public service commitment, along with exposure to public interest practice during law school, is likely to produce lawyers who are willing and qualified to provide the necessary effort and resources to ensure legal representation to all who need it.

B. "JAIL–HOUSE LAWYERS"

A source of legal aid for prisoners has long been the "jail-house lawyer," a prisoner who gains legal knowledge by working on his own case and assists fellow prisoners with legal problems. Although some institutions have discouraged such activity and others have allowed it to flourish, several prisons have undertaken programs to encourage and supervise prisoner self-help. Prisoners may be given paralegal training as part of the regular work program. Supervision by administrators can both ensure that all inmates have equal access to available legal aid and discourage formation of a black market in legal services.

C. NON–LAWYER RESOURCES

Several non-lawyer resources routinely assist consumers in meeting legal needs. Such problems as property acquisition, estate planning, wage garnishment, personal injury, and property damage are often handled by real estate brokers, financial institutions, title companies, insurance companies, labor unions, employers, notaries, and justices of the peace. Since the extent to which consumers utilize such non-lawyer resources depends largely on local law, it is helpful for bar associations to make available information concerning which services may be obtained from lay sources and which legal problems should always be entrusted to an attorney. See Ch. 7, supra. The public also should be warned of areas in which non-legal counselors may have a conflict of interest with the consumers they advise.

The creation of systems (such as mandatory or voluntary arbitration) in which consumers can help solve their own legal problems is another means of extending access to legal services. Self-representation is common before administrative agencies and in small claims courts. Legislative simplification of the law can make self-help a viable alternative in certain matters (e.g., uncontested divorce and disposition of property without a will).

CHAPTER 10

SOLICITATION AND ADVERTISING

I. INTRODUCTION

Lawyer advertising and solicitation are among the most frequently debated professional responsibility and ethical issues. Canon 2 provides that "a lawyer should assist the legal profession in fulfilling its duty to make legal counsel available." The accompanying ethical considerations emphasize the importance of the legal profession's educating laypersons to recognize their problems, thus facilitating the process of intelligent selection of lawyers and assisting to make legal services fully available.

However, the disciplinary rules, prior to post-*Bates* amendments and adoption of the RPC, prohibited almost all forms of media advertising and direct solicitation. Specifically, DR 2–101 severely restricted the forms of publicity a lawyer might receive through the media; DR 2–102 listed the limited conditions under which a lawyer or law firm might use professional cards or directory listings; DR 2–103 prohibited a lawyer (with specific exceptions) from recommending the employment of associates; and DR 2–104 forbade a lawyer who had given unsolicited advice from accepting employment, except under specific conditions.

Historically, the rule on advertising and solicitation was clear: Neither was allowed in any case. However, much criticism was leveled at those blanket restrictions. Commentators have suggested that the rules were developed to protect the established bar from competition by ethnic minorities at the turn of the century. Enforcement could harm neither small town practitioners nor large urban law firms, since both could rely on word of mouth recommendations from their own communities or constituencies. The CPR perpetuated the discriminatory distribution of legal services by allowing "advertising" in professional directories and "solicitation" of a lawyer's friends, relatives and former clients.

Rather than furthering the goal of making legal services available, the Code resulted in a "country club" approach that encouraged unsolicited offers of information only to acquaintances and former clients. As a result, those who most needed assistance and information concerning legal rights and remedies—often those in low or middle income groups—were the ones from whom this information was withheld. Further, in obtaining clients, the rules gave a tremendous advantage to established attorneys to the detriment of others, particularly those newly admitted to the bar. This problem was compounded by large increases in the number of new attorneys without an accompanying growth in legal jobs.

Gradually, the courts have recognized that the legal profession's obligation to make legal services available, and the First Amendment rights of lawyers to express (and the public to receive) information about legal services, cannot be reconciled with broad prohibition of advertising.

II. ADVERTISING

A. THE SHERMAN ACT

Many observers had argued, following the Supreme Court decision in Goldfarb v. Virginia State Bar (U.S.1975), that advertising restrictions violated the Sherman Act antitrust provisions. In *Goldfarb,* the Court struck down a minimum fee schedule that had been approved by the Virginia State Bar, on the ground that the practice of law was a form of commerce and thus within the scope of the Sherman Act. However, in Bates v. State Bar of Arizona (U.S.1977), the Court distinguished *Goldfarb* based on the state-action exemption to the Sherman Act, established in Parker v. Brown (U.S.1943). This state-action exemption was not applied in *Goldfarb* because the fee schedule was established and enforced by the Virginia State Bar rather than mandated by the Virginia State Supreme Court. In *Bates,* however, the advertising restriction was the "affirmative command" of the Arizona Supreme Court, the "ultimate body in wielding the State's power over the practice of law." Since active state regulation of professionals was recognized by the Court to be central to the state's power to protect the public, disciplinary rules containing advertising restrictions that clearly reflect that state policy will not be overturned as violative of the Sherman Act.

B. COMMERCIAL SPEECH AND THE FIRST AMENDMENT

Prior to *Bates*, the Supreme Court had recognized First Amendment protection for certain forms of commercial speech. The extension of First Amendment protection to commercial speech was justified principally on the basis of the value to consumers of the information supplied by such speech. In Bigelow v. Virginia (U.S.1975), the Court recognized First Amendment protection for an advertisement of out-of-state abortion information and services. Public interest was served because the advertisement was directed at a diverse audience and conveyed information to those with an interest in keeping informed concerning developments in the law. Later, in Virginia Pharmacy Board v. Virginia Consumer Council (U.S.1976), the Court found that price advertising of standardized, prepackaged drugs was protected under the First Amendment, and again stressed the importance of maintaining a free flow of commercial information to better educate the public.

Bates involved two attorneys who were prosecuted for having published a listing of their services, offered at "reasonable rates," in a newspaper. The Court found that the Arizona restriction on lawyer advertising did not violate the Sherman Antitrust Act. However, the Court did find that the disciplinary rule violated the First Amendment "in that it prevented publication in a newspaper of a truthful advertisement concerning the availability and terms of 'routine legal services.'" While the Court found First Amendment protection for the "commercial speech" in *Bates,* the focus of the opinion and of legal commentators has been on the interests of the *public* in receiving information concerning the availability and nature of legal services.

In *Bates,* opponents of lawyer advertising advanced many objections to allowing advertising. They argued that advertising would have an adverse effect on professionalism by undermining the dignity of the profession and clients' confidence in attorneys, and on the administration of justice by "stirring up" litigation, particularly of unwarranted claims. Opponents also argued that advertising would raise the cost of legal services, while lowering the quality of the services provided. The Court rejected these arguments, finding them insufficient to overcome the First Amendment interests of truthful commercial free speech of lawyers and their clients.

The Court recognized, however, that advertising for professional services is especially susceptible to abuse through false, deceptive, or misleading advertisements: "[B]ecause the public lacks sophistication concerning legal services, misstatements that might be overlooked or deemed unimportant in other advertising may be found quite inappropriate in legal advertising." Therefore, prohibition of "false, deceptive, or misleading" lawyer advertising is permissible. Where the particular advertising is inherently likely to deceive, or where the record indicates that a particular form of advertising has in fact been deceptive, states may impose appropriate restrictions. However, the Court's "preferred remedy is more disclosure, rather than less."

Bates is properly regarded as a landmark decision, but the scope of the holding is actually quite narrow. A blanket prohibition of lawyer advertising was prohibited, and accurate, nonmisleading price advertising for "routine" services was specifically protected. The definition of "routine" was left largely to the states. The definition of "false, deceptive, or misleading" was also left to the states.

The bar's narrow reading of the *Bates* holding, attempting to conform only to the minimum relaxation of advertising regulation required under *Bates,* necessitated a series of Supreme Court decisions invalidating new attempts to limit advertising. The ABA formulated but did not adopt as an amendment to the CPR a simple prohibition (almost certainly valid) against false, misleading or deceptive advertising (a "directive" rule). Instead, the ABA adopted, as the new DR 2–101, a provision which added to such a prohibition a list of permitted statements, (a "regulatory" rule). Under this "laundry-list" approach, only very specific items were permitted in an advertisement. Slight deviations from the "list" constituted grounds for discipline.

C. THE REQUIREMENT OF "SUBSTANTIAL INTEREST"

1. *In re R.M.J.*

The Missouri bar adopted rules even stricter than the ABA. If a lawyer wanted to advertise fields of practice in which she worked, Missouri provided not only an exclusive list of fields, but required use of the precise language authorized, (e.g., "tort law," not "personal injury"). In addition, verbatim use of a disclaimer—that listing areas of practice did not "indicate any certification or expertise therein"—was required. The rules also prohibited listing that the attorney was licensed in a state other than Missouri. After an attorney was disciplined for not using the precise language called for, the restrictions (and by implication, the "laundry-list" approach) were struck down in In re R.M.J. (U.S.1982) as too restrictive on lawyers' commercial speech.

In re R.M.J. expanded the guidelines for regulating lawyer advertising. First, if the information is inherently misleading, ("false, deceptive, or misleading information," *Bates*), it may be banned outright. Second, to restrict other (not-inherently-misleading) information the state must assert a substantial interest in regulating the speech. Third, any such interference with speech must be in proportion to the interest served. Fourth, any restrictions must be narrowly drawn, so that the restrictions are no more extensive than is necessary to serve the state interest.

Because the Missouri Supreme Court could not justify its restrictions on the listing of fields of practice or the jurisdictions in which the attorney was licensed (neither of which are inherently misleading), the United States Supreme Court struck down the restrictions. The Court found that, although listing fields of practice was potentially misleading, advertising such information could not be prohibited if it could also be presented in a non-deceptive fashion. Thus, "a warning or disclaimer might be appropriately required . . . in order to dissipate the possibility of consumer confusion or deception," but the listings could not be prohibited altogether. The Court held that "although the states may regulate commercial speech, the First and Fourteenth Amendments require that they do so with care and in a manner no more extensive than reasonably necessary to further substantial interests."

2. The Response to *In re R.M.J.*

In an attempt to meet the requirements of *In re R.M.J.*, the ABA adopted in the RPC the "directive" scheme for restrictions on advertising that had been rejected for amendments to the CPR. The RPC provide a two-step analysis: First, if any of the information is "false or misleading," it is prohibited outright. Rule 7.1. Information is "false or misleading" if, for example, it "contains a material misrepresentation of fact or law, or omits a fact necessary to make the statement considered as a whole not materially misleading", or it "is likely to create an unjustified expectation about results the lawyer can achieve."

The requirement under DR 2–102(A) that communications about legal services be "dignified" is not included under RPC 7.1. Such a requirement may not pass the criteria of *In re R.M.J.*, since it is rather subjective and serves no definable state interest. In fact, the Court cast doubt on dignity requirements in Zauderer v. Office of Disciplinary Counsel of Supreme Court of Ohio (U.S. 1985). The Court stated that

> although the State undoubtedly has a substantial interest in ensuring that attorneys maintain their dignity and decorum in the courtroom, we are unsure that the State's desire that attorneys maintain their dignity in their communications with the public is an interest substantial enough to justify the abridgment of their First Amendment rights.

Rule 7.1(c) prohibits comparison with other lawyers' services, unless the comparison can be factually substantiated. (If comparison cannot be independently verified, it can be misleading.) However, statements that a lawyer's fees are reasonable or that "services are rendered competently and promptly" can be verified by reference to objective standards, independently established by the profession. See Rules 1.1, 1.3, and 1.5.

In addition to the general ban in RPC 7.1 against false or misleading advertising, Rules 7.2 through 7.5 treat specific advertising and solicitation issues. Thus, Rule 7.2 imposes housekeeping requirements. Copies or recordings of the advertisements must be kept for two years after their last dissemination, to permit review and to allow for the possibility that the improper character of an advertisement may not appear until after it is used. Also, the name of at least one lawyer who is responsible for the advertisement must be included in every communication. Such time-place-manner restrictions, if neutral as to content, would appear to be proper. They inform the reader of the identity of the advertiser, facilitate determination of the truthful character of the ad, and go no further than is necessary to accomplish these ends.

Another time-place-manner restriction pertains to the type of media used to advertise. Among the various media, newspapers are the least and television the most controversial. Several courts have sustained prohibition of the use of billboards for legal advertising, but these decisions were handed down before *In re R.M.J.,* and probably are no longer viable. Also, while some argue that broadcast media are inherently more susceptible to fraudulent or deceptive messages, both the CPR and RPC specifically allow use of television and radio ads, as long as the ads satisfy the other applicable rules. DR 2–101(B); RPC Rule 7.2(a).

Under Rule 7.4, an attorney may list fields of practice, but claims of expertise are prohibited unless the attorney has satisfied state specialization requirements, engages in admiralty practice, or has been admitted to practice before the U.S. patent and trademark office. The ABA Comment to Rule 7.4 suggests that a lawyer may not use the phrases "is limited to" or "concentrated in," since these convey a secondary meaning implying formal recognition as a specialist. See discussion of specialization, Chapter 6, supra. No specific designations of fields of practice are required, however. It has been suggested that if a lawyer advertises, listing fields of practice, and she is sued for malpractice related to one of those fields, she should be held to a specialist's higher degree of care, since the purpose or effect of listing such fields is to imply a greater degree of experience or expertise in that area. Devine, Letting the Market Control Advertising by Lawyers: A Suggested Remedy for the Misled Client, (1982). See Chapter 6, supra.

One effort to better inform the consumer is to require a disclaimer of expertise with respect to listed fields of practice. This requirement was not contested in *In re R.M.J.,* although the Court noted in dicta that such a disclaimer "might appropriately be required." Such a disclaimer has been upheld against a constitutional challenge by at least one state court, on the ground that the bar had a substantial interest in preventing the public from being misled through the listing of fields of practice. Lyon v. Alabama State Bar (Ala.1984, *cert. denied,* 1984). However, disclaimers have also been criticized as hypocritical. "[T]he disclaimer type of ad is even more pernicious in that it deliberately states an untruth, i.e., lack of expertise in areas in which the lawyer believes that he or she is a qualified expert." Lovett and Linder, Ltd. v. Carter (D.R.I.1981). The difference between the lawyer's own beliefs as to his expertise and the truth of the matter may render such criticisms less valid.

In Peel v. Attorney Reg. & Disciplinary Com'n (U.S. 1990), the Court held that discipline imposed on an attorney for advertising his certification as a trial specialist by the National Board of Trial Advocacy (NBTA) violated his First Amendment rights. According to the plurality opinion, the attorney's statement of certification as a trial specialist was true and verifiable; rather than a "claim" as to "quality," the statement included objective facts supportive of an inference of quality. Even if the NBTA standards were not well known, there was no evidence that the representation would be associated with governmental action or that consumers would be misled if they did not inform themselves of the precise standards for certification. However, the State's interest in avoiding the potential for misleading consumers might justify screening certifying organizations or requiring a disclaimer about the certifying organization or the standards of a specialty.

Justice Marshall, in a concurring opinion, joined the plurality in finding that the statement of NBTA certification was not actually or inherently misleading, and thus could not be prohibited. But he believed that it was *potentially* misleading in causing individuals to believe that the NBTA is a federal government agency, is somehow sanctioned by the states in which the attorney indicated he is licensed to practice, or that the attorney is a better trial lawyer than attorneys without the certification. Since facts, as well as opinions, may be misleading without adequate information, Justice Marshall would permit a state to require: (1) a disclaimer that the NBTA is a private organization not affiliated with or sanctioned by the State or Federal government; (2) additional information to minimize the potential for misleading consumers; or (3) information about NBTA's certification requirements so that consumers could draw their own inferences concerning the attorney's qualifications and expertise.

RPC 7.5 and CPR DR 2–102(B) both deal with firm names. The CPR prohibits the use of trade names. However, the name "Shannon & Johnson Hollywood Law Center" was held not to be misleading or a "trade name" as that phrase is used in DR 2–102(B). Rather, "trade name" was defined as "a word or phrase other than lawyers' names which tends to mislead the public as to the identity or services of a law firm." In re Conduct of Shannon (Ore.1982). But see Matter of Oldtowne Legal Clinic, P.A. (Md. 1979) (complete prohibition of such trade names defended as protection against potentially misleading commercial speech with no informational value concerning the legal services provided). The Supreme Court has approved a ban on the use of trade names in professional advertising, on essentially the same grounds as *Oldtowne Legal Clinic.* Friedman v. Rogers (U.S.1979) (ban on optometrists' use of trade names permissible).

The use of a trade name is permitted by RPC 7.5, unless the trade name would be misleading under Rule 7.1. However, if the name implies a connection with a government agency or a public or charitable legal services organization, it is prohibited. "If a private firm uses a trade name that includes a geographical name such as 'Springfield Legal Clinic,' an express disclaimer that it is a public legal aid agency may be required to avoid a misleading implication." ABA Comment to Rule 7.5.

Other examples of misleading advertising include: "statements likely to create an unjustified expectation about results the lawyer can achieve," RPC 7.1(b) (e.g., "My last three clients each received a recovery of over $500,000"); an ad that "compares the lawyer's services with other lawyers' services, unless the comparison can be factually substantiated," RPC 7.1(c) (e.g., "One of five best criminal defense lawyers in the state"); an ad that appears to be a newspaper article entitled "Biker Awarded $250,000 for Accident," because it misleadingly appears to be written by a neutral source (Conn.Bar Inf.Op.1988).

III. SOLICITATION

Both in its disciplinary rules and ethical considerations, the CPR prohibits an attorney from volunteering advice to a layperson with the aim of obtaining employment for himself or his associates. Under DR 2–103, an attorney may not recommend his own or his associates' employment to a layperson who has not sought such advice and may not reward others who recommend him. DR 2–104 prohibits the acceptance of employment resulting from in-person unsolicited advice given to a layperson. However, employment by a close friend, relative, or former client, and employment resulting from activity designed to educate the public to recognize legal problems, are excepted. The former exception continues the ABA's approval of "country club" solicitation, while the latter incorporates a recognition of the First Amendment protections extended by NAACP v. Button (U.S.1963) and its progeny (discussed infra) into the Code.

The traditional justifications for solicitation prohibitions parallel those supporting advertising restrictions. Prohibitions on direct solicitation are believed to be necessary to prevent fraud and misrepresentation, to eliminate the incentive to stir up fraudulent or merely needless litigation, and to maintain the dignity of the legal profession. The additional dangers of overreaching and high pressure "sell" tactics are present with solicitation; for, unlike most advertising, solicitation often involves direct, face-to-face contact with potential clients.

A. SOLICITATION INVOLVING POLITICAL ISSUES

Despite the dangers inherent in solicitation, the Supreme Court (even before *Bates*) had recognized First Amendment protection in certain limited situations. These cases involved organizations that sought to provide their members or beneficiaries with legal information and assistance. The group legal services cases began with NAACP v. Button (U.S.1963), where the Court held that NAACP recruitment, at public meetings, of plaintiffs for school desegregation suits was a mode of expression and association protected by the First and Fourteenth Amendments. This decision was followed, in Brotherhood of Railroad Trainmen v. Virginia ex rel. Va. State Bar (U.S.1964), by extension of First Amendment protection to a union legal services plan that channeled all members' personal injury claims to selected lawyers. Later, in United Mine Workers v. Illinois State Bar Ass'n (U.S. 1967), the Court recognized First Amendment protection for solicitation, even though it was not political in nature as had been the speech in *Button;* in *United Mine Workers,* the union had hired attorneys to press members' worker's compensation claims. Finally, in United Transportation Union v. State Bar of Michigan (U.S. 1971), the Court reversed a state injunction attempting to prohibit "ambulance chasing," and approved the union's payment of investigators to actively solicit injured members to employ certain attorneys under contingent fee arrangements. In the latter case, the Court emphasized that "collective activity undertaken to obtain meaningful access to the courts is a fundamental right within the protection of the First Amendment." The results of these cases are reflected in changes incorporated into DR 2–103. See RPC 7.2(c); 7.3(d) (group legal services). See Chapter 9, supra.

When political issues are at stake in solicitation, the Court has insisted that states regulate with precision and impose discipline only after a finding of actual harm. In In re Primus (U.S.1978), the Court reversed discipline imposed on an attorney who had solicited a woman for an ACLU-sponsored class action suit; the suit sought damages for welfare mothers who had been sterilized, allegedly as a condition of receiving Medicaid payments. Since the suit involved a substantial civil liberties question, the solicitation received greater First Amendment protection than had it been commercially-motivated.

In finding First Amendment protection for the solicitation, the Court noted that litigation by the ACLU is a form of political expression and association, like that involved in NAACP v. Button, supra, rather than a technique for settling private disputes. Its primary purpose is to define the scope of constitutional protections rather than to profit from the recovery of counsel fees. These characteristics served to establish the ACLU's solicitation of potential litigants as non-commercial. The solicitation thus merited greater protection under the First and Fourteenth Amendments than the proposal of a business transaction proscribed in *Ohralik,* infra. The relatively nonintrusive nature of a written offer of legal assistance and the absence of potential financial gain to the attorney diminished, in the Court's view, the risks of undue influence, overreaching, and invasion of privacy. Since preventive regulation was therefore unjustified, broad prohibition of solicitation unduly burdened the fundamentally political speech and associated conduct of the attorney. States are therefore constrained to regulate political speech with greater precision than commercial speech and may impose sanctions only after determining that solicitation has in fact resulted in harm to the client.

B. SOLICITATION FOR FINANCIAL GAIN

1. In-Person Solicitation

In Ohralik v. Ohio State Bar Ass'n (U.S.1978), discipline of an attorney for in-person solicitation for financial gain under circumstances likely to result in harm to the client was held to be constitutionally permissible. The attorney had sought out two young women injured in an automobile accident, while one was still in traction in the hospital and the other had only been released the prior day, and obtained agreement from each to employ him as her attorney. He used a concealed tape recorder in conversations with them and their parents, refused to withdraw from the case when so requested, and sued each for breach of contract; he eventually received a third of one woman's recovery despite her employment of another attorney to pursue the accident claim. The Ohio Supreme Court imposed indefinite suspension after affirming findings that he had violated Disciplinary Rules 2–103(A) and 2–104(A) prohibiting recommendation or acceptance of personal employment after offering unsolicited advice to a layperson.

The United States Supreme Court affirmed the discipiine despite the attorney's claim that his conduct was an exercise of free speech which could not be infringed without a showing of actual harm to his clients. Although it acknowledged First Amendment protection of commercial speech, the Court distinguished in-person solicitation from the informative advertising permitted in *Bates,* supra. "[I]nformed and reliable decision-making" about legal services by non-lawyers was seen as unlikely to be furthered by direct solicitation for financial gain. Recognizing that rules banning solicitation may have originated from mere conventions of etiquette, the Court nonetheless identified important state interests legitimately served by the ban. These include the dangers of harm to the clients involved as well as harm to society in general, such as the assertion of fraudulent claims and the generation of unnecessary litigation (historically referred to as "barratry"). Further, when in-person solicitation for financial gain is directed at persons who are more vulnerable to persuasion as a result of injury or unsophistication, as were the two young accident victims in the case before the Court, there is an important state interest in preventing potential harms such as undue influence or overreaching by the attorney. The preventive nature of state regulation under circumstances where harm is likely to occur convinced the Court that proof of actual harm to the client in such cases is immaterial.

Since the facts of *Ohralik* presented the Supreme Court with a typical "ambulance chasing" situation, the Court was not required to define other circumstances presenting inherently sufficient danger of harm to justify regulation. However, other courts have described factual situations which create heightened susceptibility (and where a ban on communications with "potential" clients was therefore held permissible): the scene of an accident, in a funeral parlor, outside a courtroom, and during the time the victim is still suffering from injuries. And RPC 7.3(b) now prohibits solicitation *in any form* if: "(1) the prospective client has made known to the lawyer a desire not to be solicited by the lawyer; or (2) the solicitation involves coercion, duress or harassment."

2. "Targeted" Mail and Newspaper Advertisements

Ohralik appeared to create a small window of opportunity for bar associations wishing to ban certain kinds of advertising, i.e., defining such advertising as "solicitation for financial gain." Thus, in *Zauderer,* supra, an attorney was disciplined for placing a newspaper ad directed towards women who had used the Dalkon Shield intrauterine device. The ad stated that many lawsuits had been prosecuted against the maker of the Dalkon Shield, that women who had used the device should not assume that possible lawsuits by them were foreclosed due to the passage of time, and that the attorney was currently handling such lawsuits and was willing to represent other women asserting similar claims. The Disciplinary Counsel stipulated that the ad was not misleading, but claimed that such an offer of specific legal advice constituted solicitation. Coupled with the solicitous nature of advertising specific legal advice to those known to need legal services of the kind provided by the lawyer, Disciplinary Counsel argued that a ban should be applied, if only to stop other lawyers who might place deceptive solicitous ads.

The United States Supreme Court rejected these arguments, stating that the concerns it identified with respect to in-person solicitation in *Ohralik* did not necessarily apply to advertising specific legal advice in a newspaper: newspaper ads do not invade the reader's privacy, have much less risk of overreaching or exerting undue influence, lack the coercive force of the personal presence of a trained advocate, and are not likely to involve pressure for an immediate decision on the offer of representation.

Such ads are more conducive to reflection and the exercise of choice on the consumer's part. The Court noted that the state's interest in preventing deception was indeed substantial, but cited prior holdings that rules restricting non-misleading commercial speech must be narrowly crafted. Since newspaper ads offering specific legal advice were not as potentially misleading as in-person solicitation, regulation less severe than prohibition was required.

Disciplinary Counsel also argued that permitting "newspaper solicitation" would "stir up litigation." The Court found that the state had an insubstantial interest in preventing litigation, which is not evil in itself. "The State is not entitled to interfere with . . . access [to civil courts] by denying its citizens accurate information about their legal rights." *Zauderer,* supra. Therefore, even if a truthful and non-misleading advertisement had a tendency to (or did in fact) encourage the filing of suits, there was insufficient justification for allowing imposition of discipline upon a lawyer for placing such an ad.

Undeterred by the language, if not the holding, of *Zauderer,* a number of state bar disciplinary committees sought to impose discipline on attorneys who had sent letters "targeted" at persons believed to need "legal services of the kind provided by the lawyer in a particular matter," in violation of former RPC 7.3. Again, such "targeted" letters were defined as solicitation, rather than advertising. However, in Shapero v. Kentucky Bar Ass'n (U.S.1988), the Supreme Court held that the distinction in former RPC 7.3 between "targeted" mail and advertising "distributed generally to persons not known to need [the particular] legal services . . ., but who are so situated that they might in general find such services useful," was not justified by any of the Court's previous decisions. Therefore, the court reversed Kentucky's refusal to approve an attorney's letter he proposed to send "to potential clients who have had a foreclosure suit filed against them," which advised that "you may be about to lose your home," that "[f]ederal law may allow you to . . . ORDE[R] your creditor to STOP," that "you may call my office . . . for

FREE information," and that "[i]t may surprise you what I may be able to do for you."

The Kentucky court did not find the proposed letter false or misleading, but instead relied on *Ohralik* in holding that targeted, direct-mail "solicitation" by a trained lawyer to a potential client "overwhelmed" by his legal troubles creates a serious potential for undue influence. In reversing, the Supreme Court stated that the two factors underlying *Ohralik*—the strong possibility of improper lawyer conduct and the improbability of effective regulation—are much less a risk in the targeted mail context than with respect to in-person solicitation. Like the newspaper ads in *Zauderer,* letters do not entail the coercive presence of a trained advocate or the pressure for an immediate yes-or-no response, but can simply be set aside to be considered later, ignored, or discarded. Further, although a personalized letter presents an increased risk of isolated abuses or mistakes, as stated in *In re R.M.J.,* the mere potential for abuse does not justify blanket prohibition. Rather, the lawyer could be required to file the letter with a supervisory agency and to prove or verify factual statements, actual abuses could be penalized, or the state could require that the letter be labeled as an advertisement.

Subsequent to *Shapero,* RPC 7.3 was amended to prohibit only solicitation, in-person or by "live telephone contact," of persons "with whom the lawyer has no family or prior professional relationship when a significant motive for the lawyer's doing so is the lawyer's pecuniary gain." All written or recorded communications "soliciting professional employment from a prospective client known to be in need of legal services in a particular matter" must include the words "Advertising Material", on the outside of the envelope for written communications and at the beginning and ending of any recorded communication.

IV. UNRESOLVED ISSUES

Despite the substantial attention the Court has paid to advertising and solicitation, a number of issues have not yet been resolved:

(1) Is solicitation of potential class action plaintiffs in an employment discrimination case, motivated both by "political" and remunerative considerations, constitutionally subject to discipline without a showing of actual harm? DR 2-104(A)(5) directs that a lawyer may accept but may not seek other class members. RPC 7.3 prohibits solicitation when pecuniary gain is a "significant motive," and the Comment to RPC 7.2 states that neither Rule 7.2 nor 7.3 "prohibits . . . *notice* to members of a class in class action litigation." (Emphasis added.)

(2) Will special restrictions be permitted with respect to television advertising, e.g., the use of actors, action scenes or visual effects? In Committee on Professional Ethics v. Humphrey (Iowa 1984), the court upheld its rule prohibiting the use of television ads containing background sound, visual displays, more than a single, non dramatic voice or self-laudatory statements. The rule was applied to ads using actors to portray persons recommending that one who has been injured "through the negligence of others" should talk to a lawyer, and to portray a receptionist in a law office who tells the viewer to call a particular law firm. After the Supreme Court vacated the judgment and remanded for reconsideration in light of *Zauderer,* the Iowa Supreme Court reaffirmed its injunction, and the U.S. Supreme Court dismissed the appeal from that decision (U.S.1986).

(3) May a state ban legal advertising containing client testimonials as presumptively misleading? In 1989, the Supreme Court accepted certiorari, heard oral argument, and then dismissed on technical procedural grounds an appeal by an attorney who had been disciplined for running radio ads that featured an account by a former client named Sharon S. of her satisfaction with the outcome of an insurance dispute the attorney's firm had handled on her behalf. Oring v. California State Bar. The client added that if she had "any legal problem, car accident or anything, I would definitely go back to Grey & Oring."

PART III

THE ATTORNEY-CLIENT RELATIONSHIP

CHAPTER 11

CONFIDENTIALITY

I. INTRODUCTION

The confidentiality that attaches to the communications of a client to his lawyer is of ancient origin. It is one of a limited number of exceptions to the general rule that the public has a right to every person's evidence. As such, the privilege is narrowly construed.

Wigmore has outlined four conditions necessary for the existence of *any* privileged communication:

(1) The communications must originate in a *confidence* that they will not be disclosed.

(2) This element of *confidentiality must be essential* to the full and satisfactory maintenance of the relation between the parties.

(3) The *relation* must be one which in the opinion of the community ought to be sedulously *fostered.*

(4) The *injury* that would inure to the relation by the disclosure of the communications must be *greater than the benefit* thereby gained for the correct disposal of litigation.

8 Wigmore, Evidence § 2285 (McNaughton rev. 1961) (emphasis in original).

Wigmore suggested that the fourth condition is the only one open to dispute under a claim of the attorney-client privilege; but the attorney-client privilege, although resulting in the exclusion of otherwise valid testimony and permitting the withholding of certain evidence from the court, has been justified on numerous grounds. Historically, the privilege was granted in consideration for the oath and honor of the attorney. The privilege is also tied indirectly to the notion of self-incrimination, since the attorney is identified with his client and would otherwise be able to use the client's own words against him. The fiduciary nature of the relationship between attorney and client, approaching a "sacred trust," has been offered as a justification for the privilege. The privilege has also been advanced as a necessary element in the "interest and administration of justice."

Less abstractly, the existence of the privilege has been attributed to the necessity of freedom of consultation between attorney and client, ABA Comment, RPC 1.6; EC 4–1, and to insuring the client's subjective freedom of mind that his confidences will be held inviolate. Such freedom of consultation allows the fullest exposition of facts necessary for adequate representation, encourages the early seeking of legal assistance, and ensures the proper functioning of the adversary system. Also, it has been suggested that client confidences must be maintained in order to avoid "greater mischiefs," such as the possibility that an opposing party might prevail in a lawsuit merely by calling the client's attorney to testify against him, or the conviction of an innocent person because she failed to disclose embarrassing or potentially incriminating information to her attorney. The application of the privilege may result in shielding the guilt of a client, although that is not its purpose. Wigmore has aptly summarized the competing policy considerations:

> . . . [T]he privilege remains an exception to the general duty to disclose. Its benefits are all indirect and speculative; its obstruction is plain and concrete. . . . It is worth preserving for the sake of a general policy, but is nonetheless an obstacle to the investigation of the truth. It ought to be strictly construed within the narrowest possible limits, consistent with the logic of its principle.

8 Wigmore, Evidence § 2291 (McNaughton rev. 1961).

In addition to confidentiality based on privilege, the rules of agency also contribute to the protection of confidential client information. In the law of agency, originally a creature of private arrangement, the rule of confidentiality is an expression of the agent's duty to protect the principal's interests, and it is understood to apply without regard to the source of the information or the public or private status of the person to whom unauthorized disclosure might be made. While most of the case law on attorney confidentiality deals with privilege, and while the two concepts overlap to a great extent, it has always been clear that the agent's duty is broader than the privilege. See, e.g., RPC 1.6 (Comment); CPR EC 4-3.

II. THE GENERAL RULE OF CONFIDENTIAL COMMUNICATIONS

The classic definition of the attorney-client privilege has been stated as follows:

> (1) Where legal advice of any kind is sought (2) from a professional legal adviser in his capacity as such, (3) the communications relating to that purpose, (4) made in confidence (5) by the client, (6) are at his instance permanently protected (7) from disclosure by himself or by the legal adviser, (8) except the protection be waived.

8 Wigmore, Evidence § 2292 (McNaughton rev. 1961). It must be remembered, however, that the attorney-client privilege is justified on the basis of policy considerations and may sometimes give way under the challenge of competing policy considerations.

The tension between the policies of confidentiality and attorney candor has found expression in debates over attorneys' professional rules of ethics. Many attorneys criticized the CPR as allowing definitions of "confidences" which were too narrow to further the policy goals of the ethical duty of confidentiality. At the same time, others found too many exceptions to the rule of confidentiality in the CPR. As a result, when the RPC were adopted in

1983, they contained a broader privilege and generally narrower exceptions.

A. THE CPR: CONFIDENCES AND SECRETS

Canon 4 of the CPR provides that "[a] lawyer should preserve the confidences and secrets of a client." A confidence is defined as "information protected by the attorney-client privilege under applicable law," and a secret is defined as "other information gained in the professional relationship that the client has requested be held inviolate or the disclosure of which would be embarrassing or would be likely to be detrimental to the client." DR 4-101(A). The privilege of confidential communications is personal to the client and cannot be waived by the attorney. The privilege may apply to documents as well as to oral communications between attorney and client.

For the attorney-client privilege to exist, it is not necessary that a fee have been paid to the attorney, nor that the attorney accept employment for the client, nor that litigation be pending. The duty of the attorney to maintain the confidence outlasts her employment by the client, EC 4–6, and extends to an obligation to refuse employment that might cause her to reveal confidences received from previous clients, EC 4–5. See Ch. 12 (Conflict of Interest). Thus, the sale of an active law practice has been prohibited because it would involve unauthorized disclosure of client confidences. EC 4–6. But cf. RPC 1.17 (adopted in February, 1990) and Calif. RPC 2–300, altering the traditional rule to permit the sale or purchase of a law practice under narrowly defined conditions. For the same reason, the CPR suggests that an attorney should provide for the protection of his clients' confidences and secrets following the termination of his practice by death, disability, or retirement. EC 4–6.

Confidences and secrets may not be used to the disadvantage of the client, DR 4–101(B)(2); EC 4–5, nor may they be used to the advantage of the attorney or a third person, unless the client consents, DR 4–101(B)(3); EC 4–5. EC 4–2 warns that "[a] lawyer must always be sensitive to the rights and wishes of his client and act scrupulously in the making of decisions which may involve the disclosure of information obtained in his professional relationship."

The duty of an attorney to preserve a client's confidences and secrets does not preclude her disclosure of information to her colleagues: The CPR anticipates the practical necessity of disclosure to the attorney's clerical employees, and finds an obligation that the attorney exercise care in the selection and supervision of such employees so that client confidences and secrets will be maintained. DR 4–101(D); EC 4–2. An attorney may also disclose the confidences of a client to her partners or associates, unless the client instructs her to the contrary. EC 4–2.

Absent client consent, a lawyer should not associate another attorney in the handling of a legal matter. EC 4–2. However, "[u]nless the client otherwise directs, it is not improper for a lawyer to give limited information from his files to an outside agency necessary for statistical, bookkeeping, accounting, data processing, banking, printing, or other legitimate purposes, provided he exercises due care in the selection of the agency and warns the agency that the information must be kept confidential." EC 4–3.

B. THE RPC: INFORMATION RELATING TO REPRESENTATION

The RPC rule on confidentiality is broader than that in the CPR. Rule 1.6(a) states that "[a] lawyer shall not reveal information relating to representation of a client unless the client consents after consultation. . . ." Thus, the RPC provision includes all "related" information, regardless of whether the lawyer learned the information before, during or after representation, and regardless of its source. ABA Comment.

Under the RPC, "secrets" (no longer so termed)—information not directly covered by the attorney-client privilege—are more broadly protected than under the CPR. If the information relates to the representation, it is not to be disclosed absent the client's informed consent. The lawyer need not speculate whether or not disclosure would be detrimental or embarrassing to the client, and the client is not required to request confidentiality. The RPC Comments, like the CPR, note that the professional duty regarding confidentiality is broader than the attorney-client privilege, and that a lawyer should not accept employment if it will result in a violation of the rule on confidentiality. See Rule 1.16(a)(1).

Along with specific exceptions to the rule, see infra, Rule 1.6(a) allows disclosures "impliedly authorized in order to carry out the representation." In litigation, for example, some information may be revealed during negotiations to "facilitate a satisfactory conclusion." Comment to Rule 1.6. Also, the Comment specifically allows disclosure of information to other lawyers in the firm "in the course of the firm's practice," unless the client has given contrary instructions regarding that particular information. A lawyer has "implied authorization" to make necessary disclosures of her client's information to her nonlawyer staff, but she must "make reasonable efforts to ensure that the [nonlawyer assistants'] conduct is compatible with [her] professional obligations. . . ." RPC 5.3.

C. CORPORATE COMMUNICATIONS

The attorney-client privilege applies to corporate clients as well as to individuals. Prior to the case of Upjohn Co. v. United States (U.S.1981), the privilege had been held to protect only the communications of those corporate officers who fell into a "control group." The rationale behind this limitation was that only those corporate "officers and agents . . . responsible for directing [the company's] actions in response to legal advice" possessed the information needed by the corporation's lawyers. (*Upjohn,* supra, citing the lower court's definition.) Only senior management, it was stated, could be said to possess an identity analogous to the whole corporate "person" to which the privilege should extend.

The Court in *Upjohn* rejected the "control group" test as contrary to the purposes of the privilege. One such purpose is facilitating the free flow of information from client to lawyer. For example, the lawyer will often only get the information she needs from individuals beyond the defined "control group." If these individuals are not protected by the privilege, the Court noted, the communication of relevant information would be frustrated. Under *Upjohn,* then, where the client is a corporation or other organizational entity, the privilege applies to (1) communications, (2) made by the organization's employees, (3) concerning matters within the scope of their duties, (4) to the organization's counsel acting as such, (5) at the direction of organizational superiors, (6) in order to secure legal advice. Information voluntarily disclosed by an employee concerning misconduct he had observed outside the scope of his employment responsibilities would not be privileged, even if made to the organization's attorney.

III. PROCEDURAL ASPECTS

The existence of the attorney-client privilege with respect to a given communication is a matter of law, not ethics, and is for judicial determination, based on a weighing of competing policy considerations. Since once it is waived it cannot be redeemed, the privilege must be claimed at the threshold, and the burden of proof regarding the existence of the privilege is generally found to be on the one claiming it. Contrary to the *waiver* of the attorney-client privilege, which must be made by the client himself, the *claim* of privilege may be asserted by the attorney on behalf of his client. Indeed, the attorney has a professional duty to assert the privilege, EC 4–4. The ABA has advised that, when an attorney is uncertain of the applicability of the attorney-client privilege, he should resolve that doubt in favor of maintaining client confidences. The specific showing that must be made by one seeking to destroy the attorney-client privilege on the ground that the client sought the attorney's aid in the commission of a crime or fraud will be discussed infra.

IV. EXCEPTIONS TO CONFIDENTIALITY

As in many other areas, the law of attorney-client privilege is as much defined by its exceptions as by its affirmative duties. Many of the exceptions to the privilege are based on the notion of client waiver, either actual or constructive. The justifications for them are as varied as the exceptions themselves, and will be discussed respectively.

A. CONSENT

DR 4–101(C)(1) and RPC 1.6(a) both allow disclosure with client consent, although the CPR provision requires "full disclosure" before consent, while the RPC require "consultation." A client can waive her privilege by disclosure of the confidential communication itself; consent need not be written, but can be by word or act or by omission to speak or act. Several courts have suggested that waiver can be effectuated by any conduct by the client which indicates that she did not expect or intend that her statements to the attorney would be kept confidential. An obvious example is where the communication is made to the attorney in a crowded elevator (i.e., in the presence of third persons). There exists some case law, however, indicating that the client's conduct must show "explicit and convincing evidence" of an intent to waive her privilege.

The privilege being personal to the client, the attorney cannot waive it. Several cases have suggested in dicta, however, that the revelation of a confidence by an attorney in the presence of his non-objecting client can effect a waiver. In the event that the attorney maintains confidential information that is shared by two or more clients (e.g., business partners, family members), he must obtain the consent of all before revealing it. EC 4–2; RPC 1.6(a). Additionally, after the death of a client, the client's heirs or personal representatives can claim the privilege (except against each other) and may consent to the disclosure of a confidential communication.

B. IDENTITY, OCCUPATION, AND ADDRESS OF CLIENT; FACT OF RETAINER

The weight of common law authority is that the identity of the client and the fact of retainer do not fall within the scope of the attorney-client privilege. This exception has been justified primarily on two grounds: First, the attorney must name an actual client in order to prove the existence of the relationship under which the privilege is claimed and, second, the identity of the client who retains an attorney to represent her in litigation should not, in fairness to the opposing party, be shrouded in mystery. Some courts have justified the exception on the basis that the retention of an attorney is merely a part of the creation of the attorney-client relationship; other courts have justified the exception on the basis that the establishment of the attorney-client relationship is not usually intended to be a "confidential communication" and therefore does not fall within the privilege. Thus, in those "exceptional circumstances" where the nature of the attorney-client transaction has been previously disclosed and it is the identity which is intended to be confidential, the identity of the client has been held to be privileged, since such revelation would otherwise result in disclosure of the entire transaction. Anonymous taxpayers have been the primary beneficiaries of this rule, since "[t]he disclosure of the identity of the client . . . would lead ultimately to disclosure of the taxpayer's motive for seeking legal advice." Tillotson v. Boughner (7th Cir.1965).

An issue which has been of great concern to criminal defense lawyers and has caused substantial disagreement among courts and bar disciplinary committees involves an attorney's duty under 26 U.S.C.A. § 6050I to report receipt of $10,000 or more in cash from a client, along with the client's identity, to the IRS. This cash-reporting obligation appears to conflict with the attorney's obligation not to reveal confidential information without the client's consent, particularly if discovery of the client might lead to the initiation of a criminal investigation. However, the courts have almost uniformly rejected claims of confidentiality. Similarly, courts have generally rejected lawyers' assertions of privilege regarding the name of the person paying their fee, e.g., a third party who paid attorney's fees and bond money for drug runners (In re Grand Jury Proceeding (Pavlick) (5th Cir.1982)). Courts have held that the lawyer can be compelled to reveal "whether a particular person retained the lawyer, the details of the retainer, the amount of the fee, who paid the fee, and a client's whereabouts." Wolfram, Modern Legal Ethics 259–60 (1986).

Ethics opinions have suggested that the attorney warn the client (or third party) at the outset of the duty to report certain information and, if the client insists that, for example, the attorney accept over $10,000 in cash and not report it, the attorney should decline or withdraw from representation. Other committees have suggested that the attorney include a notice on the required reporting form that the identity of the payor has been withheld because of a claim of client confidence. Although viable in theory, this approach has been unavailing in several jurisdictions where U.S. attorneys have sent letters to lawyers threatening prosecution for failure to supply the payors' names. A number of courts have noted that, regardless of the privileged nature of client information, subpoenaing the attorney or other compelled disclosure can often be unnecessarily detrimental to the attorney-client relationship. Therefore, prosecutors should not seek such subpoenas without exhausting other means of obtaining the information. In order to protect the attorney-client relationship from such governmental intrusion, a number of states adopted ethical rules requiring prosecutors to obtain judicial approval before they subpoena a lawyer to testify or provide other evidence against a client. In United States v. Klubock (1st Cir.1987) (en banc), the application of the Massachusetts rule to federal prosecutors practicing in the state was upheld.

The increased use of Justice Department subpoenas to defense counsel (over 640 in 1989) in an effort to fight the "war on crime" prompted the ABA in 1990 to add Rule 3.8(f) to the

Model Rules. RPC 3.8(f) prohibits prosecutors from subpoenaing a lawyer in a criminal proceeding unless:

(1) the prosecutor reasonably believes:

(a) the information sought is not protected from disclosure by any applicable privilege;

(b) the evidence sought is essential to the successful completion of an ongoing investigation or prosecution;

(c) there is no other feasible alternative to obtain the information; and

(2) the prosecutor obtains prior judicial approval after an opportunity for an adversarial proceeding.

The occupation of a client is also generally held not to be privileged information, for reasons similar to those justifying the non-privileged nature of his identity, whereas the courts are split as to whether the client's whereabouts are privileged. A court's ruling may depend upon the extent to which it is clear that the client intended such information to be confidential and, normally, his address would seem to fit logically within the same rule as identity and occupation (i.e., presumed not to be privileged, absent "exceptional circumstances").

Although the location of a fugitive client is privileged, several early ABA advisory opinions indicated that the whereabouts of a client who jumped bail, or violated probation by leaving the jurisdiction, were not privileged, because the behavior of the client represented a "continuing wrong" and therefore fell within the future crime exception to the privilege, infra. Compare In re Nackson (N.J.1989) (under the circumstances, attorney not required to reveal location of client who jumped bail and was a fugitive) with Bersani v. Bersani (Conn.Super.1989) (attorney required to reveal whereabouts of client who left jurisdiction with her children in violation of dissolution court's order). In the case of bail jumping, the ABA Committee advised that if the client refused to surrender himself to the authorities following the attorney's recommendation, the attorney should withdraw from the case. In the case of probation violation, the Committee recommended that the attorney advise the proper authorities if the client continued to persist in his violation.

In a celebrated case in Florida, the police were seeking a hit-and-run driver who allegedly ran down a pedestrian in a crosswalk. A person consulted a lawyer and stated that "my name is 'so and so' and I think I may have been involved in the accident described in the paper." The client asked the lawyer to communicate with the authorities in an effort to negotiate a plea, but not to reveal his identity. The court held that the attorney-client privilege protected information that would lead to identifying the client, and that the crime or fraud exception (see infra) did not apply because the substantive violation occurred only when the driver was at the scene of the accident and ended when he left the scene. Baltes v. Doe I (Fla.Cir.Ct.1988).

With respect to each of the above communications, it is the intent of the client that the information be kept confidential which must determine its privileged or non-privileged nature. The rules regarding specific categories, such as identity or residence address, should be seen only as placing the burden of proof on one or the other of the parties based on the likelihood of confidential intent. Any burden so assigned should be rebuttable.

C. NONLEGAL ADVICE OR NONPROFESSIONAL CAPACITY

In order to be protected as within the attorney-client privilege, a communication must be concerned primarily with legal matters. Thus, courts have excluded communications from the protection of the privilege when they were concerned primarily with business advice, and the privilege has been particularly susceptible to destruction when an attorney also served as an adviser in a second professional role, e.g., as an accountant, a realtor, or an F.B.I. investigator. However, the inclusion of some nonlegal considerations in a communication does not, of itself, destroy the privilege.

D. NECESSARY TO ESTABLISH OR COLLECT FEE

RPC 1.6(b)(2) and Comment and DR 4–101(C)(4) provide that an attorney may reveal confidences or secrets when necessary to establish or collect fees. The exception has been justified on the grounds that, as between attorney and client, the intention is to disclose rather than to withhold such information and, second, that the client is deemed to have waived the privilege by receiving legal consultation from the attorney. The rule has been criticized by legal commentators, who see it as another instance of promoting the financial well-being of the attorney over the sanctity of the professional relationship. On the other hand, the client should not be able to refuse to pay an earned and agreed upon fee by shielding the fee agreement from disclosure.

E. NECESSARY TO DEFEND SELF OR EMPLOYEES

DR 4–101(C)(4) also provides that a lawyer may reveal confidences or secrets when necessary to ". . . defend himself or his employees or associates against an accusation of wrongful conduct." RPC 1.6(b)(2) applies this exception to controversies between the lawyer and client and to criminal charges or civil claims against the lawyer "based upon conduct in which the client was involved, or to respond to allegations in any proceeding concerning the lawyer's representation of the client." However, the disclosure "should be no greater than the lawyer reasonably believes necessary to vindicate innocence, the disclosure should be made in a manner which limits access to the information to the tribunal or other persons having a need to know it, and appropriate protective orders or other arrangements should be sought by the lawyer to the fullest extent practicable." ABA Comment. As written, both the RPC and CPR expand the common law attorney-client privilege. Historically, the privilege allowed an attorney to reveal confidences only when an accusation of wrongdoing was made *by his client.* Under the RPC, CPR and applicable case law, however, an accusation of attorney wrongdoing *from any source* may permit the attorney to reveal the confidences of his client. See Meyerhofer v. Empire Fire & Marine Ins. Co. (2d Cir.1974).

In *Meyerhofer,* an attorney who had worked on the registration of securities for his firm's client and who had disagreed with his superiors over their nondisclosure of certain facts in the registration statement, resigned from the firm. He then filed an affidavit with the Securities and Exchange Commission, detailing his efforts to convince his firm to rectify the nondisclosure and reporting their contemplated nondisclosure in another securities registration. Subsequently the attorney was named, along with the law firm, the client and other firm members, as a defendant in a stockholder's suit for violations of the securities law and for negligence, fraud and deceit. In exchange for having his name dropped as a defendant, the attorney presented a copy of his earlier affidavit to the plaintiff's attorneys. The trial court order, dismissing the plaintiff's cause of action on the ground that the attorney and the plaintiff's attorneys had violated the CPR prohibitions against disclosure of confidential communications and the appearance of impropriety, was reversed on appeal. The federal appellate court found that the attorney had not violated Canon 4, since he "had the right to make an appropriate disclosure with respect to his role in the public offering," and since information obtained from the client was incidental, rather than central, to the disclosure that he made.

Self-protective disclosure has been sharply criticized as contrary to the policy behind the privilege, since it may serve to discourage client disclosures, and since it allows the attorney to reveal confidences without his client's actual or constructive consent. Additionally, through these RPC and CPR provisions, there is the possibility that an adverse party may strip the attorney-client relationship of its privileged nature simply by naming the attorney as a co-defendant, for example, in alleged drug or RICO conspiracies. However, some protection from abuse is afforded by the requirement, as with other challenges to the privilege, of a preliminary showing of some foundation to the accusation before the privilege will give way.

F. DISCLOSURES TO, OR OBTAINED FROM, THIRD PERSONS

Information that would otherwise fall within the attorney-client privilege is not protected if it has been disclosed, even inadvertently, to a third person. The justifications given for this exception are that the attorney and client have parted with their exclusive confidence if another person obtains knowledge of it, and that the attorney-client privilege does not apply to one who is a "stranger" to the relationship. If the client reveals the confidence, waiver applies. However, if the attorney reveals confidential information without the client's consent, the confidence should still be protected to the extent possible. An attorney who subsequently becomes privy to such information has an ethical duty to protect against further improper revelation.

Under the CPR, information or objects acquired *by* an attorney must have been communicated or delivered to him by the client in order to be privileged; information obtained from a third person or source by an attorney acting for his client is not privileged (although it may constitute a "secret"), unless the third person served as an intermediary, necessary to interpret or explain the client's condition. Thus, in a California case, information communicated to a doctor, solely for purposes of litigation, who then communicated it to the client's attorney, was held to be privileged under the attorney-client rather than the doctor-patient privilege. City and County of San Francisco v. Superior Court (Cal.1951). See Morrell v. State (Alaska 1978). According to the ABA Comment to RPC 1.6(a), information relating to the representation is protected "whatever its source."

Several courts have held that information obtainable from any public source is not within the protection of the privilege. See, e.g., Washington v. State (Ind.1982) (defendant's former lawyer properly testified in sentence enhancement proceeding about existence, nature, and date of prior convictions). And it is at least questionable whether, under the CPR, disclosure of information already public would be considered "embarrassing." If not, such information might be outside the scope of protection granted to "secrets." RPC 1.8(b), however, provides that a lawyer "shall not use information relating to the representation of a [current] client to the disadvantage of the client . . ." This prohibition would seem to apply even to public information. Rule 1.9(b) prohibits similar use of information regarding a former client, but provides an express exception for information that "has become generally known."

Although information communicated to a lawyer in confidence is privileged, "[i]f documents are not privileged while in the hands of a party, he does not make them privileged by merely handing them to his counsel." Edison Electric Light Co. v. United States Electric Lighting Co. (C.C.S.D.N.Y.1890). In Fisher v. United States (U.S.1976), taxpayers who were being investigated by the Internal Revenue Service obtained from their accountants and passed to their attorneys certain documents relating to their returns. On subpoena by the government, the attorneys refused to produce the documents. Against claims under the Fifth Amendment and, implicitly, the attorney-client privilege, the Court ruled that the documents were not privileged either in the hands of the lawyers or their clients. The Court based its holding on the fact that the subpoenas did not involve "compelled testimonial self-incrimination," since the papers had been prepared voluntarily and the subpoenas did not involve personal compulsion of the clients.

G. JOINTLY RETAINED ATTORNEY

When an attorney acts for two or more clients sharing a common interest, neither party may exercise the attorney-client privilege in a subsequent controversy with the other. This exception to the attorney-client privilege can apply to partners, joint trustors, makers of mutual wills, and persons having no formalized business relation between themselves (e.g., husband and wife).

However, the presumption of shared confidences can be overcome by agreement of the attorney and clients. Communications between clients and a jointly retained attorney *are* privileged as against non-clients.

H. CRIMINAL EVIDENCE

DR 7-109(A) provides that "[a] lawyer shall not suppress any evidence that he or his client has a legal obligation to reveal or produce." Accord, EC 7-27; RPC 3.3(a)(2) and (a)(4). DR 4-101(C)(2) allows an attorney to reveal client confidences or secrets when permitted under disciplinary rules or required by law or court order. Taken together, these rules provide that an attorney's ethical obligation to maintain confidences and secrets is overcome when she or the client is required by law to reveal or produce evidence.

The common law that addresses this issue is notable for its lack of clarity. In one cause celebré, People v. Belge (N.Y.1975), during a discussion between attorney and client regarding a potential insanity defense to pending charges of murder, the client revealed his commission of other murders and the location of the bodies. The attorney, who discovered one of the bodies pursuant to the client's confidential communication and who did not disclose this information prior to trial, was indicted for violation of statutes requiring decent burial and the reporting of death without medical assistance. The dismissal of the indictment against the attorney was affirmed, on the ground that the attorney-client privilege attached insofar as the communications were to advance the client's interests. Subsequently, the New York State Bar Committee on Ethics found that the lawyer's failure to disclose his knowledge of the two unrelated homicides was not improper and that such disclosure would have, in fact, violated his ethical obligations under the CPR.

The result is less clear when the incriminating evidence is not communicated but *presented* to the attorney. Those courts which have addressed the issue have held that an attorney may not take or retain possession of the "fruits or instrumentalities" of a crime. One attorney, who took possession of a sawed-off shotgun and money, purportedly to prevent his client from disposing of them (and also to prevent the police from discovering them), was suspended from the practice of law for 18 months, despite the fact that he had consulted two judges and an attorney for the state before acting. In re Ryder (4th Cir.1967). The trial court ruled that the attorney's conduct was more than the mere exercise of the attorney-client privilege. The appellate court, in affirming the suspension, stated:

> It is an abuse of a lawyer's professional responsibility knowingly to take possession of and secrete the fruits and instrumentalities of a crime. Ryder's acts bear no reasonable relation to the privilege and duty to refuse to divulge a client's confidential communication. Ryder made himself an active participant in a criminal act, ostensibly wearing the mantle of the loyal advocate, but in reality serving as accessory after the fact.

In another case, an appeal from a conviction of contempt by an attorney who had refused to obey a subpoena duces tecum for the production of physical evidence received from his client, the court ruled that the knife held by the attorney and assumed to have come into his possession through a confidential communication from his client, was within the attorney-client privilege. The court went on to say:

> We do not, however, by so holding, mean to imply that evidence can be permanently withheld by the attorney under the claim of the attorney-client privilege. . . . The attorney should not be a depository for criminal evidence (such as a knife, other weapons, stolen property, etc.), which in itself has little, if any, material value for the purposes of aiding counsel in the preparation of the defense of his client's case. Such evidence . . . could clearly be withheld for a reasonable period of time. It follows that the attorney, after a reasonable period, should, as an officer of the court, on his own motion turn the same over to the prosecution.

State ex rel. Sowers v. Olwell (Wash.1964). The court continued by suggesting that, even following the attorney's surrender of evidence that was potentially incriminating to the client, the attorney-client privilege could and should be "maintained" by making certain that the source of the evidence was not disclosed in the presence of the jury.

It would seem that *Olwell* begs the question: Are the policies supporting the attorney-client privilege and its limitations best served by compelled disclosure of physical evidence presented to the attorney by his client? *Olwell* would require that the evidence is not privileged but may be ethically withheld for a "reasonable period of time." If the foundation for the privilege includes the attorney's fiduciary relationship and the need for complete candor and trust on the part of the client, that trust is violated *whenever* the lawyer turns over the evidence to the prosecution. The feeling of betrayal could only be exacerbated by the fact that only the defendant (and not the jury) will be aware of how the prosecution obtained the evidence. See People v. Meredith (Cal. 1981), where an attorney's investigator, based on information disclosed by the client, found the murder victim's partially burned wallet in a barrel behind the client's house. The court held that the confidentiality privilege extends "not only to the initial communication between client and attorney but also to any information which the attorney or his investigator may subsequently acquire as a direct result of that communication." However, if the attorney moves, removes, or alters the evidence in any way, the original location and condition of the evidence lose the protection of the privilege; only the source of the information (i.e., the attorney) should not be revealed to the trier of fact. Accord, Morrell v. State (Alaska 1978) (lawyer required to turn over to prosecutor "kidnapping plan" drawn by client and found by client's friend). A safe rule of thumb for counsel, then, is: "You can look but you better not touch." See "Poison Ivy," by the Coasters.

In addition, it has been suggested that because the attorney is not responsible for the uncounseled acts of his client, he could explain to his client the importance of the evidence and the impropriety of a lawyer retaining the fruits or instrumentalities of a crime, and then allow the client to decide what to do. It is the authors' opinion that rather than this "Anatomy of a Murder" approach, the attorney-client privilege, as well as the criminal justice system, would be better served by the attorney's preservation of the evidence, subject to valid subpoena, accompanied by sufficient documentation to support his actions.

Again through DR 4–101(C)(2) and RPC 1.6 (Comment), a similar constructive waiver of the attorney-client privilege may occur when an attorney advises his client to destroy criminal evidence. DR 7–102(A)(7) provides that an attorney shall not, in his representation of a client, "[c]ounsel or assist his client in conduct that the lawyer knows to be illegal or fraudulent." Accord, RPC 1.2(d).

I. FUTURE CRIME

It is a generally recognized rule that the attorney-client privilege is destroyed when the client reveals the intention to commit a crime and the attorney is unable to dissuade him from his plan. Requests for advice to assist a client's criminal conduct are not protected.

> There is a privilege protecting communications between attorney and client. The privilege takes flight if the relation is abused. A client who consults an attorney for advice that will serve him in the commission of a fraud will have no help from the law. He must let the truth be told.

Clark v. United States (U.S.1933). See RPC 1.2(d) & (e). In United States v. Zolin (U.S.1989), the Court interpreted Federal Rule of Evidence 104(a) to permit a federal trial court to hold an *in camera* hearing to determine whether the future crime or fraud exception applies. Once the party seeking to establish the crime-fraud exception has demonstrated a "factual basis adequate to support a good faith belief by a reasonable person . . . that *in camera* review of the materials may reveal evidence to establish the claim", the judge may engage in such *in camera* review to determine the applicability of the privilege. In making the showing, the party opposing the privilege may use any relevant evidence, even if not independent of the alleged confidential communication, that was lawfully obtained and has not been adjudicated to be privileged. Id. But cf. Cal.Evid.Code § 915(a) (West 1966 & Supp.1989) ("the presiding officer may not require disclosure of information *claimed to be privileged* under this division in order to rule on the claim of privilege") (emphasis added).

1. Future Crime and the CPR

DR 4–101(C)(3), which provides that a lawyer may reveal "[t]he intention of his client to commit a crime and the information necessary to prevent the crime," reflects the common law. See also EC 7–5. An ABA ethical advisory opinion has stated that an attorney *must* disclose when the facts in his knowledge indicate beyond a reasonable doubt that a crime will be committed. The CPR provides for permissive withdrawal as well when a client "[p]ersonally seeks to pursue an illegal course of conduct." DR 2–110(C)(1)(b).

Before the attorney-client privilege will be found to be waived under the exception, there must be a prima facie showing or colorable claim of intent to commit a crime. A mere assertion of an intended crime or fraud is not sufficient to destroy the privilege. The extent to which the intent of the client to perjure himself destroys the privilege is discussed infra and in Ch. 16.

2. The RPC and Recent Developments

RPC 1.6(b)(1) allows an attorney to disclose client confidences in order "to prevent the client from committing a criminal act that the lawyer believes is *likely to result in imminent death or substantial bodily harm* . . ." (emphasis added). In those cases where the intended criminal act is likely to result in death or substantial bodily harm, the same analysis as applied under the CPR has generally been employed. However, the limitation to crimes involving substantial bodily injury permits less disclosure than in the originally proposed draft, and much less than the CPR, leading Senator Arlen Specter (R–Pa.) to propose a "Lawyer's Duty of Disclosure Act of 1983." This Act would have subjected an attorney to a maximum $5,000 fine and one year imprisonment if she failed to make a timely disclosure to federal officials of crimes or fraudulent acts intended to be committed by clients. Senator Specter claimed that the RPC "would allow, though not require, a disclosure to prevent a threat to one's life, but not to one's life savings . . . [,] creating a safe haven for white-collar crime." Although the Bill was not enacted, most states that adopted the RPC retained the broader exception for *any* future crime. See, e.g., Md., N.J., N.H., Wis., Wash. Rule 1.6.

Criticism has also been leveled at the permissive nature of the Rule 1.6 exception providing that failure to disclose is not a violation of the Rule, even when disclosure might prevent a murder. Instead, the Comment to Rule 1.6 advises the lawyer to consider various factors in deciding whether or not to disclose, and urges the lawyer to "seek to persuade the client to take suitable action." Again, a number of states that adopted RPC 1.6 made disclosure *mandatory* in death-threatening situations. See, e.g., Ariz. and Conn. Rule 1.6 (mandatory disclosure of information reasonably necessary to prevent client from committing crime likely to result in death or substantial bodily harm; permissive disclosure of client's intent to commit any crime and information necessary to prevent it). Further, whereas the ethical provision of the RPC is only permissive, the lawyer could be compelled to reveal the information in a judicial proceeding under the "future crime or fraud" exception to the attorney-client privilege. See also Tarasoff v. Regents of University of California (Cal.1976) (psychiatrist subject to liability for failure to warn foreseeable victim of threat by patient, since disclosure permissible under applicable code of ethics when patient threatens substantial bodily injury); Hawkins v. King County (Wash.App.1979) (*Tarasoff* applicable to lawyers, but only where "it appears beyond a reasonable doubt that the client has formed a firm intention to inflict serious personal injuries on an unknowing third person").

J. FRAUD

There is a heated dispute in the legal literature over the advisability of requiring an attorney to reveal her client's fraud if the client himself refuses to do so. See Ch. 16 infra. Some authors have argued that the confidential nature of the attorney-client relationship encourages the client's disclosure of all information, including admission of fraudulent representations, that full disclosure by the client is essential to adequate assistance of counsel, and that turning the client's confidences against him is a subversion of the policies behind both the attorney-client privilege and the adversary process. Others, elevating the search for truth as the primary goal of the adversary system, have argued that the attorney's function should be to participate in wise and informed decisions and that the privilege should give way when it obstructs that goal. This policy conflict is greatest when the fraud is perpetrated upon the courts, such as when the client contemplates or commits perjury. The CPR and RPC address the problem of client fraud differently, and the criticisms of each reflect the competing policies in this area.

1. The CPR and "Rectifiable Fraud"

DR 7–102(B)(1) provides that an attorney who receives information clearly establishing that "[h]is client has, in the course of the representation, perpetrated a fraud upon a person or tribunal shall promptly call upon his client to rectify the same, and if his client refuses or is unable to do so, he shall reveal the fraud to the affected person or tribunal, except when the information is protected as a privileged communication." In spite of its apparently strong wording, which suggests mandatory revelation, the disciplinary rule leaves much room for attorney discretion: The fraud must be "clearly establish[ed]," must occur in the "course of representation," and cannot be revealed "when the information is protected as a privileged communication." The advisory opinion interpreting the rule states that "[t]he tradition . . . that permits a lawyer to assure a client that information given to him will not be revealed to third parties is so important that it should take precedence, in all but the most serious cases, over the duty imposed by DR 7–102(B)." ABA Op. 341 (1975).

Prior to the 1974 amendment to the CPR that added the clause, "except when the information is protected as a privileged communication," the attorney was faced with contradictory duties to maintain the client's confidence (DR 4–101) and to reveal it (DR 7–102(B)). A number of states did not adopt the 1974 amendment, leaving attorneys in a difficult position. The Oregon Supreme Court, in reviewing disciplinary action charging an attorney with misleading the trial court, was confronted with the contradictory demands of DR 4–101(B)(1) and DR 7–102(B)(1). In In re A. (Or.1976), an attorney had unsuccessfully attempted to persuade his client to correct a misleading, but not actually false, statement to the court; following the court's apparent reliance on the client's statement, the attorney did not himself undertake to correct the court's misapprehension and did not withdraw from the case. Two members of the State Bar's Review Committee believed that the attorney's conduct constituted participation in the client's intentional misleading of the court; two members believed that the attorney had acted properly; the deciding member of the Committee, while agreeing with the dissenters that the duty of confidentiality took precedence over the duty to reveal fraud, voted to impose discipline because the attorney had improperly failed to withdraw. The court, quoting with approval from the dissenting disciplinary committee opinion that the attorney "would have been criticized by someone regardless of what he did" in this situation, dismissed the complaint against him. However, the court did adopt prospectively the Oregon state bar's ensuing advisory opinion, which requires withdrawal when the client refuses to rectify his fraudulent statements to a court.

2. The RPC

The failure to resolve this conflict between the duties of candor and confidentiality, coupled with the failure of a number of jurisdictions to adopt the 1974 amendments to the CPR, left attorneys in an untenable position. Adoption of the RPC provided one response to this situation.

The RPC eliminated the CPR fraud exception to the nondisclosure duty (DR 7–102(B)). There is no requirement (or even permission) in the RPC to reveal a client's fraud, unless the failure to do so would constitute "assisting" the client's criminal or fraudulent act; and even then, information protected under RPC 1.6 (including all *past* conduct and even *future* crimes not involving death or substantial bodily injury) may not be disclosed. RPC 4.1(b). Under Rule 1.16(b)(1), the lawyer may *withdraw* if the client "persists in a course of action involving the lawyer's services that the lawyer reasonably believes is criminal or fraudulent."

Some legal commentators have found fault with the RPC for not including the fraud exception, and many states have adopted a version of Rule 1.6 that includes a fraud exception. Some jurisdictions have instituted mandatory disclosure to prevent a client's fraudulent act, while others have adopted permissive disclosure. At least two states also require the lawyer to rectify criminal or fraudulent acts in the furtherance of which the lawyer's services had been used.

3. Client Fraud Before a Court—Perjury

The Model Rules come down more heavily on the side of candor when the client has committed or intends to commit a fraud upon the court. Under Rule 3.3(a)(2), a lawyer may not knowingly "[f]ail to disclose a material fact to a tribunal when disclosure is necessary to avoid assisting a criminal or fraudulent act by the client." Under Rule 3.3(a)(4), "[i]f a lawyer has offered material evidence and comes to know of its falsity, the lawyer shall take reasonable remedial measures." And under Rule 3.3(b), these duties of disclosure "apply even if compliance requires disclosure of information otherwise protected by rule 1.6." Respect for the client's confidences dictates that the lawyer "seek to pesuade the client that the evidence should not be offered or, if it has been offered, that its false character should immediately be disclosed." If the client refuses, however, the rule is clear that the attorney must inform the court or the other party of the deception.

The courts have not been clear about what standard of confidentiality they expect a lawyer to maintain when a client apparently intends to commit perjury. Attorneys are almost universally prohibited from putting on a perjurious non-client *witness.* However, the standard for a *client's* intended perjury is far less clear. There would appear to be no impediment, in the RPC or otherwise, to revealing a *civil* client's perjury (assuming refusal to rectify the situation). On the other hand, revelation of a criminal defendant's confidences implicates the privilege against self-incrimination, and the rights to counsel, to testify in his own behalf, and to due process. As stated in the ABA Comment to RPC 3.3:

> The most difficult situation, therefore, arises in a criminal case where the accused insists on testifying when the lawyer knows that the testimony is perjurious. The lawyer's efforts to rectify the situation can increase the likelihood of the client's being convicted as well as opening the possibility of prosecution for perjury. On the other hand, if the lawyer does not exercise control over the proof, the lawyer participates, although in a merely passive way, in deception of the court.

The Comment concludes that if the client refuses to rectify the situation and withdrawal is not permitted or will not remedy the problem, then the attorney should make disclosure to the court, unless the jurisdiction has interpreted the due process and right to counsel constitutional provisions as requiring that counsel present an accused as a witness if the accused wishes to testify, even if counsel knows the testimony will be false.

In Nix v. Whiteside (U.S.1986), a criminal defendant sought habeas corpus relief for ineffective assistance of counsel because his attorney induced him not to testify falsely by threatening to withdraw and inform the trial court if the client testified falsely. The Court held unanimously that defense counsel's successful threat did not constitute ineffective assistance of counsel. However, in concurring opinions, four justices clearly indicated that the decision should not be read to establish a required—or even uniformly proper—attorney response to a criminal defendant's intended perjury. Rather, as stated by Justice Brennan:

> This Court has no constitutional authority to establish rules of ethical conduct for lawyers practicing in the state courts. Nor does the Court enjoy any statutory grants of jurisdiction over legal ethics.
>
> * * *
>
> . . . Lawyers, judges, bar associations, students and others should understand that the problem has not now been "decided."

The effort to resolve the tension between the attorney's obligations of candor and confidentiality is discussed more fully in Ch. 16 (The Lawyer as an Advocate: The Adversary System).

CHAPTER 12

CONFLICT OF INTEREST

> No man can serve two masters: for either he will hate the one, and love the other; or else he will hold to the one, and despise the other. Ye cannot serve God and mammon.
>
> Matthew 6:24 (King James)

"Conflict of interest" is a concept that traverses all areas of the law and affects every lawyer regardless of the nature of his or her practice. A conflict of interest exists whenever the attorney, or any person represented by the attorney, has interests adverse in any way to the advice or course of action which should be available to the present client. A conflict is present whenever this tension exists—even if the attorney eventually takes the course of action most beneficial to the present client. An impermissible conflict between clients may exist if there is substantial discrepancy in the parties' testimony, incompatibility of positions in relation to an opposing party, or substantially different possibilities of settlement of claims or liability.

When a conflict or potential conflict of interest arises, a conscientious attorney usually faces three possible courses of action: (1) inform all interested parties of the present or potential conflict, inform them of all possible and probable consequences of the conflict should the attorney continue to represent both parties, and continue dual representation with their express, informed consent; (2) after informing the interested parties of the conflict, withdraw from the representation of one of the parties; (3) withdraw from the representation of both parties.

If, despite a potential conflict of interest, the attorney continues to represent the interested parties, the burden will be upon that attorney to demonstrate that: (1) no conflict existed; (2) the voluntary, informed consent of all affected parties was obtained;

or (3) any action in which the attorney had a personal interest was fair *and* the client gave her informed consent. Under some circumstances, the client must also be advised to obtain independent legal advice before consenting to a conflict. Sanctions available for improper representation of conflicting interests include disqualification from or injunction against appearing in the matter, disciplinary proceedings against the attorney, loss of fee, or potential personal liability for injury to either client. Lawsuits alleging conflict of interest constitute one of the fastest growing areas of litigation in the United States. The RPC contain at least *seven* specific sections dealing directly with conflict of interest, a rather clear expression of the profession's concern with problems in this area.

I. POLICIES UNDERLYING CONFLICT OF INTEREST RULES

A. LOYALTY

Loyalty is one of the most important aspects of a lawyer's relationship with his client. Comment, RPC 1.7; CPR Canon 5. In an adversary system, the client depends upon the attorney's undiluted loyalty to his client's interests. The potential variety of interests which might dilute a lawyer's loyalty to his clients includes the attorney's personal interests (e.g., financial security, prestige, and self-esteem) and the interests of third persons (family, friends, business associates, employer, the legal profession, and society as a whole).

The representation of more than one party to a transaction often results in the dilution of loyalty to one or both: buyer and seller, borrower and lender, insurer and insured, consenting mother and adopting parents, seller and issuer of securities, husband and wife, multiple personal injury plaintiffs, or multiple criminal defendants. An attorney's loyalty to a client may also be adversely influenced by loyalty to a former client, whether the present representation is related or unrelated to the former representation.

B. CONFIDENTIALITY

RPC 1.6 and Canon 4 of the CPR are premised on the belief that preserving a client's secrets and confidences is often as important to the client as winning his lawsuit or avoiding embarrassment or undue expense. Whereas loyalty relates to zeal or diligence, confidentiality relates to information which the client has entrusted to her lawyer.

This emphasis on preserving a client's confidences also extends beyond the particular attorney involved. The possibility of even an unintended leak of such confidences is in large part responsible for the imputed disqualification of law partners, spouse-attorneys, and even attorneys sharing office space but not otherwise associated.

II. GENERAL RULES: POTENTIAL VERSUS ACTUAL CONFLICTS

A. DETERMINING WHETHER REPRESENTATION IS LIKELY TO BE "MATERIALLY LIMITED" OR "DIRECTLY ADVERSE"

The CPR mandates that a lawyer decline or withdraw from employment when his independent professional judgment on behalf of his client will be, or is likely to be, adversely affected. DR 5–105(A). Thus, if loyalty to a present or former client, the intensity of the lawyer's personal feelings, or a perceived duty to the public or profession might impair the effective representation of a prospective or current client, the lawyer should decline employment at the outset. Although defined somewhat differently, both the CPR and RPC distinguish between potential and actual conflicts.

The CPR describes a range of situations—from mere possibility to reasonable probability—that will produce an impermissible conflict. For example, a lawyer should not own property in which her client also has an interest, because this "may interfere with the exercise of free judgment on behalf of her client." EC 5–3. Also, a lawyer is advised not to accept employment if there is a "reasonable probability that [her personal interests] will affect adversely the advice to be given or services to be rendered to the prospective client." EC 5–2. If the property interests of a lawyer do not currently conflict with the independent exercise of her professional judgment, but "the likelihood of interference can reasonably be foreseen" by the attorney, she should "decline employment or seek to withdraw unless the client consents after full disclosure." Id.

The RPC focus on the impact of conflicts and potential conflicts on the lawyer's representation of his client. Thus, a lawyer generally may not represent a client with interests *"directly adverse"* to those of another client. RPC Rule 1.7(a). This prohibition ordinarily extends to acting as an advocate against a client the lawyer represents in some other matter, even if the matters are unrelated. However, if the interests of two clients are merely generally adverse, such as the economic interests between competitors, the lawyer may undertake representation of one client if he "reasonably believes the representation will not adversely affect the relationship with the other client." Rule 1.7(a)(1).

There is a *potential* conflict when the lawyer's choices for his client may be restrained at some point—i.e., in furtherance of some contrary interest, the lawyer may not consider or be willing to adopt alternatives available to his client. A potential conflict exists under RPC 1.7(b) when the representation of a client "may be materially limited by the lawyer's responsibilities to another client or to a third person, or by the lawyer's own interests." Although representation is not precluded in such instances, a lawyer may not undertake representation in the face of a potential conflict unless the lawyer: (1) reasonably believes the representation will not be adversely affected; and (2) the client consents after "consultation." The lawyer must consider what the likelihood of a conflict is, and if it occurs, whether it will materially affect his professional judgment.

The "consultation" required for effective client consent under RPC 1.7(a) & (b), like the "full disclosure" required under CPR DR 5–105(C), has received substantial interpretation by courts and bar disciplinary committees. Thus, in Klemm v. Superior Court of Fresno County (Cal.App.1977), the court held that attorneys who undertake to represent parties with divergent interests owe the highest duty to each to make full disclosure of all facts and circumstances necessary to enable the parties to make an informed decision. This "full disclosure" should include areas of potential conflict, the desirability of seeking independent legal advice, the fact that information from either of the parties will not be confidential with respect to the other party, and the course of action the attorney will take if an actual conflict arises. "Consultation" or "full disclosure" implies communicating "all of the facts and implications" of an attorney's representation of multiple clients and any circumstances which might cause a client to question the undivided loyalty of the lawyer. A number of courts have held that the attorney must also advise the client of the desirability of consulting independent legal counsel, and the Comment to RPC 1.7 suggests that even if the client chooses not to seek independent legal advice:

> when a disinterested lawyer would conclude that the client should not agree to the representation under the circumstances, the lawyer involved cannot properly ask for such agreement or provide representation on the basis of the client's consent.

B. THE "APPEARANCE OF IMPROPRIETY" STANDARD

Prior to adoption of the RPC, many of the decisions regarding conflict of interest relied upon the notion of avoiding "even the appearance of professional impropriety." See CPR Canon 9. Lawyers were told to judge conflict situations by their appearances, and to avoid those which might appear improper, even if in fact they were not. Of course—regardless of any official standard—to promote public confidence in lawyers and the legal system it is best to avoid appearances of impropriety. Fostering public confidence requires more of a lawyer than avoiding the overt influence of interests other than those of his client.

Criticism of the appearances standard has been widespread. One problem with the standard has been how to use it in disciplinary matters. Canon 9 is not a mandatory rule. Attorneys must therefore guess as to when it will be applied or interpreted as part of other specific rules. Some courts have used the appearance of impropriety as a strict disqualifier; any hint of impropriety disqualified the lawyer from the representation. Another approach has been to take the appearance of impropriety into account as one of many factors in deciding whether there has been an impermissible conflict of interest. The mixed approaches taken by courts and bar disciplinary commissions led to confused and contradictory standards, leaving lawyer and client alike unsure of how to proceed in some situations. Further, in determining the appearance of impropriety or lack thereof, the trier of fact must speculate about what would appear improper and to whom, (e.g., the public, the bar, all reasonable people, etc.). Therefore, courts have increasingly refused to employ an appearance of impropriety analysis in conflicts situations.

The RPC do not include the appearances standard. In fact, the standard is specifically rejected in favor of a "functional approach," concentrating on preserving confidentiality and avoiding positions actually adverse to the client. ABA Comment, RPC 1.10. The RPC deal with actual conflicts and guidelines for use in recurring conflict of interest situations. After establishing a general rule in Rule 1.7, Rules 1.8 to 1.13 deal with common conflict of interest problem areas: Rule 1.8 outlines prohibited transactions; Rule 1.9 establishes guidelines for former client conflicts; Rule 1.10 lays out a general rule for imputed disqualification; Rule 1.11 addresses successive government and private employment; Rule 1.12 relates to the former judge or arbitrator; and Rule 1.13 provides guidance for the lawyer representing a corporation or other organizational entity. In providing such specific, detailed rules the RPC attempt to take a much more utilitarian approach to conflicts problems, in an attempt to avoid the vagaries of the appearances standard.

III. RECURRING CONFLICT OF INTEREST SITUATIONS

A. CONFLICTS RESULTING FROM LAWYER'S PERSONAL INTEREST

There is a great temptation for the lawyer to temper his loyalty to his client where his own financial interest is involved. For this reason, all personal financial interests, particularly business dealings between attorney and client from which the attorney benefits, are very closely scrutinized for any unfairness on the attorney's part. When an attorney is called into question for entering into a transaction with his client, the attorney must by affirmative evidence defeat the presumption of overreaching, undue influence, or fraud arising out of the fiduciary relationship, or the transaction will be set aside.

Disciplinary Rule 5–101(A) provides: "Except with the consent of his client after full disclosure, a lawyer shall not accept employment if the exercise of his professional judgment on behalf of his client will be or reasonably may be affected by his own financial, business, property, or personal interests." RPC 1.8 is much more specific than DR 5–101(A). Thus, a lawyer may not "enter into a business transaction with a client or knowingly acquire ownership, possessory, security or other pecuniary interest adverse to a client unless:" (1) the transaction is fair and reasonable; (2) the client is informed in writing of the terms of the agreement in a manner that the client can understand; (3) the client is given a reasonable opportunity to seek the advice of independent counsel; and (4) the client consents in writing. RPC 1.8(a). See DR 5–104(A).

Attorney business dealings can include buying or selling a business or property, giving or receiving a loan, taking shares of stock or some other "piece of the action" in the client's business in lieu of a fee, or engaging in a joint business or real estate venture with a client. In attempting to rebut the presumption of fraud or undue influence in business dealings with his client, the attorney has the burden of showing: "(1) there was no undue influence; (2) he . . . gave the client exactly the same information or advice as would have been given by a disinterested attorney; and (3) the client would have received no greater benefit had he or she dealt with a stranger." In re McGlothlen (Wash.1983). Lawyers who, while serving as counsel to the general or managing partner of a real estate venture, receive a financial interest in addition to (or in lieu of) payment of their legal fees, are particularly vulnerable to suits for damages if the venture fails. Although not precluded under the RPC if all of the conditions of Rule 1.8 are met, practically speaking these lawyers become virtual guarantors of the success of the venture.

Certain business transactions are believed so inherently likely to affect the attorney-client relationship that they are prohibited altogether. For example, a lawyer may not prepare an instrument giving the lawyer or her close relatives any substantial gift, by will or other method, unless the lawyer is related to the donee.

RPC 1.8(c). Likewise, a lawyer is prohibited from negotiating for literary or media rights to a "portrayal or account based in substantial part on information relating to the representation" of a client. RPC 1.8(d). There is simply too great a temptation to allow the value of the case for movie or book purposes to influence the conduct of the litigation. The conflict inherent in such literary or media rights agreements is not only ethically improper, but can result in reversal of a criminal defendant's conviction on the basis of ineffective assistance of counsel.

Generally, improper financial involvement with clients also occurs when, in connection with contemplated or pending litigation, a lawyer acquires a financial interest in the outcome of that litigation. Despite this prohibition, a reasonable contingent fee is permissible in civil litigation, because it may be the only means by which the indigent or near indigent can obtain legal counsel. RPC 1.8(b)(2); DR 5–103(A)(2); EC 5–7, 2–20. Furthermore, a lawyer may properly secure collection of fees for services rendered by use of liens against the client's present and future income which may include a pending judgment. RPC 1.8(j)(1); EC 5–7. The extent to which such liens, including liens on the client's property, are permissible is dependent primarily on state law. See Ch. 14 (Fees and Liens).

There are also several other, narrowly circumscribed exceptions to the general proscription against acquiring a financial interest in the outcome of litigation. Disciplinary Rule 5–103(B) provides:

> While representing a client in connection with contemplated or pending litigation, a lawyer shall not advance or guarantee financial assistance to his client, except that a lawyer may advance or guarantee the expenses of litigation, including court costs, expenses of investigation, expenses of medical examination, and costs of obtaining and presenting evidence, provided the client remains ultimately liable for such expenses.

DR 5–103(B) is premised on the belief that although a lawyer may have advanced or guaranteed financial help to her client with the purest of motives—a desire to assist a client in serious financial need—such well-intentioned actions create serious ethical problems. A lawyer's financial interest or obligation in her client's cause limits the exercise of her independent and professional judgment—for example, when a settlement is offered which might satisfy her own interest in the verdict but does not advance the interest of her client to the maximum degree.

Like the CPR, the RPC prohibit a lawyer from advancing a client's living costs while permitting an advance of "court costs and expenses of litigation." RPC 1.8(e). However, the RPC are more permissive in providing that repayment may be contingent on the outcome of the case. In practice, the distinction between the CPR and RPC is not significant because courts and bar associations interpreted DR 5–103(B) to permit a lawyer to advance litigation expenses to indigent clients and in other circumstances where repayment was a virtual impossibility unless there was a recovery. See also RPC 1.8(e)(2) ("a lawyer representing an indigent client may pay court costs and expenses of litigation on behalf of the client" regardless of any recovery). Several states have recognized the financial straits that some clients may find themselves, particularly in personal injury or medical malpractice cases involving substantial medical expenses. Often, these plaintiffs can be induced to accept a reduced settlement if defendants can prolong discovery and litigation. In such circumstances, advancement of living or medical expenses by the lawyer may be seen as essential to providing the client's opportunity for a fair recovery.

An attorney's personal financial interest in the outcome of the litigation may be removed when a third party finances the suit; but that arrangement often creates a conflict of interest regarding loyalty to the client and the third party. In some instances, the potential for or appearance of dilution of loyalty to the client is so great that a third-party arrangement is proscribed altogether. For example, an attorney may not obtain trust business for his trust company employer by drafting documents free of charge naming the trust company as executor or trustee. Even when payment by someone on behalf of the client is permitted, the attorney must: (1) obtain the client's informed consent; (2) prevent interference with the attorney's independence of judgment; and (3) protect the client's confidential information from disclosure, including disclosure to the person paying the fee. RPC 1.8(f); DR 5–107. See, e.g., discussion of insurer-insured infra.

Finally, a lawyer ordinarily may not act as advocate at trial when she is likely to be a "necessary" witness. RPC 3.7(a); DR 5–101(B), 5–102 (if she knows or it is "obvious" that she "ought to be called as a witness"). As stated in the Comment to RPC 3.7:

> Combining the roles of advocate and witness can prejudice the opposing party and can involve a conflict of interest between the lawyer and client.
>
> The opposing party has proper objection where the combination of roles may prejudice that party's rights in the litigation. A witness is required to testify on the basis of personal knowledge, while an advocate is expected to explain and comment on

evidence given by others. It may not be clear whether a statement by an advocate-witness should be taken as proof or as an analysis of the proof.

Further, to the extent that the attorney's interest in the case diminishes her credibility, the client's case may be harmed by the attorney's dual roles. Decisions under the CPR held that the attorney's testimony must be genuinely *needed* and not just *helpful,* and most courts have deferred to counsel's and her client's best judgment as to whether the client's interests would be better served by having the attorney not testify or not serve as counsel. However, if there is a question as to whether the attorney will be called as a witness, all doubts should be resolved in favor of withdrawing from the case.

Exceptions to the rule of disqualification include instances where "the testimony relates to an uncontested issue" or "the nature and value of legal services rendered in the case." RPC 3.7(a). See DR 5–101(B). In a proceeding concerning an uncontested will, for example, a lawyer may testify as to the testamentary capacity of the decedent. Likewise, the lawyer may testify to the value of services rendered to the client when the client's suit against another includes a legitimate cause of action for attorney's fees. Another exception is permitted where the lawyer has been called by the *opposing party,* unless the testimony would be adverse to the client and thus a violation of RPC 1.7 or 1.9. RPC 3.7(b); DR 5–102(B) (the testimony "is or may be prejudicial to his client"). A final exception applies where "disqualification of the lawyer would work substantial hardship on the client" due to the distinctive value of the lawyer or his firm, the additional expense to the client of retaining new counsel, or the imminency of trial at the time it is discovered that counsel's testimony may be necessary. A number of courts and Calif. RPC 5–210(C) permit the lawyer to serve as an advocate and witness, regardless of any other exceptions, if the lawyer has the client's informed, written consent.

B. CONFLICTS RESULTING FROM REPRESENTATION OF ADVERSE INTERESTS OF CURRENT CLIENTS

As indicated above, a lawyer may not represent clients whose interests are directly adverse or where the representation of one might be materially limited by the representation or interests of another, unless the affected clients consent after consultation and the lawyer reasonably believes that the representation will not be adversely affected. RPC 1.7. See DR 5–105 (in addition to obtaining consent after "full disclosure," it must be "obvious that he can adequately represent the interest of each"). The test is an objective one: Since the attorney's belief must be *reasonable* (or, under the CPR, it must be "obvious") that his judgment will not be affected by the conflict, his judgment is subject to hindsight review, which may include knowledge of damage that has in fact occurred. Certain situations have arisen with sufficient frequency to have engendered specific rules regarding the propriety of dual representation. Awareness of the rules applicable to such commonly recurring problem areas can help to avoid mistakenly accepting or continuing representation in such cases.

1. Insurer–Insured

Liability insurance policies usually contain the following provisions: (1) that the insurer will hold the insured harmless within the monetary limits of the policy; (2) that the insurer will provide a lawyer to represent the insured with respect to any claim or action covered under the policy; and (3) that the insured will cooperate with the insurer in the defense against such claims or actions. Interests of the insurer and the insured arising out of the insurance contract will be virtually identical when an action is brought by a third party against the insured for damages within the policy limits.

Despite this initial unity of interest, however, events occurring at various stages of the litigation often cause the interests of the insurer and the insured to differ, if not actually conflict. It is then that the attorney selected and paid by the insurer but expected to maintain "an undeviating and single allegiance" to his client (the insured) is most susceptible to acting unethically. In addition to the general requirements of RPC 1.7 and DR 5–101 & 5–105, the lawyer must ensure that payment of her fee by the insurance company does not interfere with her independence of judgment or induce her to disclose confidential information obtained from the client. RPC 1.8(f); RPC 5.4(c) (prohibiting a lawyer from allowing person paying for legal services to direct or regulate lawyer's professional judgment on behalf of client); DR 5–107. In effect, the courts have treated only the insured as the client, or the insurer and insured as dual clients of the attorney.

A common conflict arises when a claimant offers to settle for a sum within the limits of a liability policy. For example, in one case, the insurer rejected the plaintiff's offer to settle for $5,000—well within the $10,000 policy limit. The attorney appointed by the insurer to defend the action did not include the insured in the settlement negotiations and did not fully advise him of settlement offers. The trial resulted in a $45,000 verdict for the plaintiff. The insurer was later held liable to the insured for the amount of the judgment. Hamilton v. State Farm Ins. Co. (Wash.1974). An attorney was held to have committed malpractice as a matter of law for rejecting a $10,000 settlement offer (on insurer's instructions), when the jury returned a verdict in the amount of $225,000. Lysick v. Walcom (Cal.1968). See Betts v. Allstate Ins. Co. (Cal.App.1984).

In such cases, it is the lawyer's responsibility to inform the insurer of its duty to the insured and the likelihood of legal liability should it fail to fulfill that duty. If the desires of the insurer and insured cannot be reconciled, the lawyer should withdraw with proper notice.

Conflict of interest also exists when the policy covers negligently inflicted harm but not intentionally inflicted harm, and the insured is sued on a claim alleging both; when the policy covers those driving the insured's car with his consent and the attorney defends a claimant's suit against the insured on the ground that the driver did not have the insured's consent; when counsel impeaches the insured on the witness stand for the benefit of the insurer who is not a party to the suit; or in any reservation of rights representation. See Tank v. State Farm Fire & Cas. Co. (Wash.1986).

2. Buyer–Seller; Borrower–Lender; Husband–Wife; Etc.

An obvious conflict exists when an attorney attempts to represent both buyer and seller, particularly if he has had a long-standing relationship with one of them. In such cases, the attorney must not represent both. However, if the parties have already agreed on the basic terms of the agreement and the attorney acts primarily as a "scrivener," he may normally represent both parties after obtaining their consent. The lawyer should disclose in advance the full significance of the representation of conflicting interests, including the pitfalls that may arise in the course of the transaction which might mandate or make it desirable that one or both parties obtain independent counsel. In fact, a number of courts have held that the "consultation" or "full disclosure" necessary to make consent effective includes advice to seek independent legal advice at the outset. Both parties must consent to the attorney's possible withdrawal from representation of one but not both parties. The decision as to whom the attorney will represent in such an event should be made at the outset, as well.

It is not sufficient that the attorney believes himself able adequately to represent potentially differing interests, or even that all parties have consented. The possibility of subconsciously favoring the interests of either party, the appearance of impropriety that may arise from even the slightest dissatisfaction, the likelihood of receiving confidential information from one party that is damaging or helpful to the other, and the possibility that a court will subsequently disagree with the attorney's decision that he was able adequately to represent both interests—all dictate extreme caution in these situations.

The temptation to represent potentially conflicting interests is particularly difficult to resist in family disputes. Often the attorney is the "family lawyer" and has represented husband, wife, and even the children, on previous occasions. At a minimum, the attorney must ensure that each understands the possible conflicts and their consequences, particularly the potential necessity for him to withdraw from representation of one or both and his inability to use confidences received from any of the parties in a subsequent suit between them. Many of the principles applicable when a lawyer acts as an intermediary with respect to two or more clients have been incorporated into RPC 2.2, permitting such representation only in very limited circumstances. In fact, the inherent conflict in attempting to represent both husband and wife, even in an "amicable" dissolution, led a committee of the American Academy of Matrimonial Lawyers to propose that dual representation be prohibited altogether.

3. Representing Multiple Plaintiffs

Conflicts of interest occasionally arise during the representation of multiple plaintiffs. Because of this potential, each client must have the opportunity at the outset of the representation "to evaluate his need for representation free of any potential conflict and to obtain other counsel if he so desires." EC 5–16. Even where there is consent, if the clients' interests come into actual conflict during the course of representation, the attorney must withdraw from representing at least one of them.

These principles, along with the importance of avoiding both the appearance of impropriety and the possible subconscious effects on an attorney's loyalty to his client, were evident in Jedwabny v. Philadelphia Transportation Co. (Pa.1957). In that case, the court upheld the granting of a new trial because of the trial judge's failure to ascertain whether a plaintiff had full knowledge of his attorney's conflict of interest. Plaintiff driver was one of three plaintiffs represented by the same attorney in a personal injury action. The defendant transportation company joined the plaintiff driver as a defendant; the jury found the driver and the transportation company jointly liable. Because the result was a verdict against the driver in favor of plaintiffs represented by the same attorney, the court held that it was essential that the judge ensure that the driver "had been fully informed and had an intelligent and complete understanding of his then legal status." In dictum, the majority indicated that because the conflict was inherently adversarial, joint representation might never be justified in this type of situation. Even assuming full disclosure and consent to be represented by a single attorney, when the transportation company joined the driver as co-defendant, it was no longer feasible for a single lawyer to represent the differing interests adequately.

4. Representing Multiple Criminal Defendants

The sixth amendment to the United States Constitution provides that "[i]n all criminal prosecutions, the accused shall enjoy the right . . . to have the Assistance of Counsel for his defense." In Glasser v. United States (U.S.1942), violation of conflict of interest principles when representing multiple criminal defendants reached constitutional dimensions. In that case, Glasser and a co-defendant were convicted of conspiracy to defraud the United States. When the co-defendant discharged his attorney during the trial, the judge asked Glasser's attorney to act as counsel for both defendants. Although the co-defendant was amenable, both Glasser and his lawyer expressed reservations before acceding to the appointment. The Supreme Court held that Glasser had been denied his sixth amendment right to effective assistance of counsel. The Court stated that the sixth amendment right "contemplates that such assistance be untrammeled and unimpaired by a court order requiring that one lawyer shall simultaneously represent conflicting interests. If the right to the assistance of counsel means less than this, a valued constitutional safeguard is substantially impaired."

More recently, in Holloway v. Arkansas (U.S.1978), the Supreme Court relied heavily on *Glasser* in reversing the convictions of three men because the trial judge had refused to order separate counsel for them. The public defender had requested several times during trial that separate counsel be appointed because he faced the risk of conflicting interests. The judge's refusal to appoint separate counsel and failure to ascertain whether there was an actual danger of prejudice required an automatic reversal, according to the Court.

As discussed supra, Ch. 6, the Court has severely restricted the ability of criminal defendants to obtain reversal of convictions on the basis of ineffective assistance of counsel. A particularly difficult requirement is that the defendant demonstrate "prejudice", i.e., a "reasonable probability" that the lawyer's incompetence caused a difference in the outcome of the trial. With respect to ineffectiveness claims based on conflicts of interest, however, the Court presumes prejudice subject to rebuttal. Although the defendant must show that an actual conflict adversely affected her attorney's performance, Cuyler v. Sullivan (U.S.1980), the ineffectiveness claim is not waived by the defendant's failure to object to the joint representation at trial. Wood v. Georgia (U.S.1981). In fact, despite a defendant's limited Sixth Amendment right to counsel of choice (see Caplin & Drysdale, Chartered v. United States (U.S.1989), the Court has held that a trial court's interest in the rendering of just verdicts justifies the disqualification of defense counsel, over the defendant's objections, when the court determines that an actual conflict exists. Wheat v. United States (U.S.1988).

Although representation of co-defendants by a single attorney is not per se violative of effective assistance of counsel guarantees, the possibility of a conflict must at least be considered. In many cases in which the co-defendants' interests and defenses at trial are identical, the individual treatment accorded them at sentencing might create a desire on the part of defense counsel to argue that one is less culpable, more contrite, a better rehabilitative risk, or has a more compelling family situation. In such cases, the attorney has a conflict of interest, because any such argument necessarily suggests that the other defendant deserves a harsher sentence; both defendants cannot be less culpable.

Defense counsel is faced with an obvious conflict when her clients have inconsistent defenses. For example, the defendant was denied effective assistance of counsel when her attorney did not assert a lack of responsibility defense warranted by the evidence because of possible harm to the co-defendant's case. Austin v. Erickson (8th Cir.1973). The possibility (particularly the appearance) of diluted loyalty is heightened if counsel is paid by only one co-defendant, or if the co-defendants are husband and wife.

The multiple criminal defendant cases above indicate that the need for counsel to disclose fully all potentially conflicting interests to his clients is greatest in this area.

C. CONFLICTS RESULTING FROM REPRESENTATION OF INTERESTS ADVERSE TO A FORMER CLIENT

After the professional relationship with a client has terminated, the lawyer's duty to avoid conflicts of interest is still applicable with respect to future clients. Under RPC 1.9, a lawyer who has represented a client in a matter may not thereafter represent a second client in the *same or a substantially related matter* in which that person's interests are materially adverse to the interests of the former client, unless the former client consents after consultation and a full disclosure of the material facts. Nor may the attorney use confidential information relating to the representation to the disadvantage of the former client, even in an unrelated representation. RPC 1.9(c)(1) (except when permitted or required under RPC 1.6 or 3.3, or "when the information has become generally known"); RPC 1.8(b). Although there is no specific former client provision in the CPR, decisions interpreting the CPR conflict of interest rules applied the "substantial relationship" test.

The scope of a "matter" in relation to this rule depends on the particular situation or transaction. If the lawyer has been directly involved in a matter or specific transaction, subsequent representation of clients whose positions are adverse to the former client is prohibited. On the other hand, if the lawyer has formerly represented a client in one matter and a subsequent matter arises in which the lawyer is representing a new client in a new matter, the position of which is adverse to the former client, but the transaction is not "substantially related" to the former representation, then the lawyer may represent the new client. See, e.g., Duncan v. Merrill Lynch, Pierce, Fenner & Smith (5th Cir.1981) (absent specific description of the prior matters, broker did not meet its burden of proving that a "substantial relationship" existed between the present and prior matters), cert. denied (U.S.1981).

Because the attorney's duty of loyalty is to the corporation as an entity and not its officers and directors, RPC 1.13; EC 5–18 (and see discussion infra), change of control within the corporation will not necessarily remove the bar against subsequently representing conflicting interests, even if there is no evidence that the attorney received confidential information while acting for the corporation.

A different problem arises when substitute counsel seeks access to the predisqualification work product of prior counsel. In a case of first impression, a panel of the Seventh Circuit held that access should be refused because use of that work product would be equivalent to continuing representation by the disqualified counsel. The court believed that an attorney's work product necessarily involves his own impressions, opinions, conclusions, and legal theories concerning the case; physical withdrawal by the attorney alone may not be sufficient to cure the appearance of impropriety.

Following rehearing *en banc,* however, the Seventh Circuit reversed, holding that, instead of per se disqualification of the work product, the question of access must be answered on a case-by-case analysis, with access denied only when that analysis demonstrates any "taint of confidentiality or other improper advantage gained from the dual representation." First Wisconsin Mortgage Trust v. First Wisconsin Corp. (7th Cir.1978).

D. ATTORNEYS EMPLOYED BY THE GOVERNMENT

1. General Considerations

> Unlike the private lawyer, who can identify his duty of loyalty to an individual client, the government lawyer works for an abstraction, the identity of which is so diffused that the duty of loyalty is not only hard to identify, the harm to the government of obtaining a personal benefit is often difficult to perceive. (Patterson & Cheatham 199.)

Although the CPR provides only that "[a] lawyer shall not accept private employment in a matter in which he had substantial responsibility while he was a public employee" (DR 9–101(B)), RPC 1.11 and the Federal Conflict of Interests Act are more specific. Under the Act, a lawyer is permanently disqualified with respect to matters in which he personally and substantially participated, and is disqualified for one year with respect to any matter which was "under his official responsibility . . . at any time within a period of one year prior to the termination of such responsibility."

In United States v. Standard Oil Co. (S.D.N.Y.1955), decided prior to passage of the statute, the court referred to the general principles of the Code to determine what constitutes substantial participation. In denying a government motion to disqualify a former government lawyer and his firm, the court stated:

> [W]here an attorney has worked for a vast agency of the United States government, as in the instant case, it is hardly reasonable to hold that an appearance of evil can be found in his undertaking a case against the government where there is not some closer factual relationship between his former job and the case at hand than that the same vast agency is involved.

Similarly, the Second Circuit has emphasized actual knowledge acquired while working on a particular suit rather than the attorney's supervision of the office in which it was pursued. The test for whether the "matters" in the present and former suits were "the same" was "not whether the two actions rely for their foundation upon the same section of the law, but whether the facts necessary to support the two claims are sufficiently similar." General Motors Corp. v. City of New York (2d Cir.1974).

2. Alternative Approaches

a. ABA Formal Opinion 342 (1975)

Opinion 342 interprets DR 5–105(D), which was amended in 1974 to extend disqualification of an attorney under any disciplinary rule to all partners in the firm. Prior to the amendment, this vicarious disqualification rule had not been applied to disqualifications under DR 9–101(B), which provides: "A lawyer shall not accept private employment in a matter in which he had substantial responsibility while he was a public employee."

Opinion 342 outlines policy considerations supporting restrictions on former government employees, including "the treachery of switching sides," the "safeguarding of confidential governmental information from future use against the government," the "need to discourage government lawyers from handling particular assignments in such a way as to encourage their own future employment in regard to those particular matters after leaving government service," and "the professional benefit derived from avoiding the appearance of evil." The rationale for extending disqualification to the firm of a former public employee, according to the ABA, is primarily to prevent circumvention of the disciplinary rules by the disqualified lawyer.

On balance, the Opinion holds that the ability of the government to recruit and the right of litigants to have trained counsel outweigh prevention of the "appearance of switching sides" and related policies with respect to vicarious disqualification. The committee also took the position that strict application of DR 5–105(D)—disqualification of the firm—to former public employees disqualified by DR 9–101(B) would frustrate the policy considerations underlying DR 9–101(B).

The Opinion concludes that disqualification under DR 5–105(D) can be avoided if precautions outlined in a two-part process are taken. First, the firm must develop screening measures to isolate the disqualified lawyer from the matter in question and from any fees to be received in connection with that matter. Then the government agency must review the proposed screening measures. If the agency is satisfied that the individual will be screened effectively from participation and from fees, and that there is no appearance of significant impropriety, the government may waive disqualification of the firm.

b. RPC 1.11

Under RPC 1.11, a lawyer may not represent a private client in connection with a matter in which he participated "personally and substantially" as a public officer or employee, unless the appropriate government agency consents after consultation. If the lawyer is or becomes associated with a firm representing a private client, no lawyer in the firm may represent the client unless the disqualified lawyer does not participate in the matter (i.e., is "screened") and receives no fees therefrom, and written notice is promptly given to the appropriate agency "to enable it to ascertain compliance with the provisions" of Rule 1.11. It is evident that the policies identified in ABA Opinion 342 for limiting the cases in which a former government attorney should be disqualified underlie the requirement of personal and substantial participation and the definition of "matter" in RPC 1.11(d)(1):

> Any judicial or other proceeding, application, request for a ruling or other determination, contract, claim, controversy, investigation, charge, accusation, arrest or other particular matter involving a specific party or parties; . . . .

Although defined somewhat differently than Rule 1.11, the Opinion 342 interpretation of "matter" in DR 9–101(B) is consistent with judicial treatment of Rule 1.11:

> [T]he term seems to contemplate a discrete and isolatable transaction or set of transactions between identifiable parties. . . . The same lawsuit or litigation is the same matter.

> By contrast, work as a government employee in drafting, enforcing or interpreting government or agency procedures, regulations, or laws, or in briefing abstract principles of law, does not disqualify the lawyer . . . from subsequent private employment involving the same regulations, procedures, or points of law; the same "matter" is not involved because there is lacking the discrete, identifiable transactions or conduct involving a particular situation and specific parties.

In addition to disqualification from representing a subsequent client in the same matter, a lawyer may not, in the representation of a client, use any confidential government information gained about a person while employed by a government agency, when the client's position is adverse to that person. As employed in the Rule, the term "confidential governmental information" includes information obtained under governmental authority which "the government is prohibited by law from disclosing to the public or has a legal privilege not to disclose, and which is not otherwise available to the public." RPC 1.11(e). Otherwise, the private client could obtain an unfair advantage due to his attorney's access to governmental information about an adversary.

Finally, RPC 1.11(c)(2) prohibits a government lawyer from negotiating for private employment with a party or its attorney in any matter in which the lawyer is participating personally and substantially. The principle underlying this subsection is avoidance of "the manifest possibility that a former government lawyer's action as a public official might be influenced (or open to the charge that it had been influenced) by the hope of later being employed privately to uphold or upset what he had done." Woods v. Covington County Bank (5th Cir.1976) (quoting ABA Opinion No. 37 (1931)). See also discussion of RPC 1.13 infra.

E. REPRESENTING CORPORATIONS, LABOR UNIONS, TENANT ASSOCIATIONS, AND OTHER ENTITIES

The ethical responsibilities of attorneys who represent organizational entities have long been the source of confusion, uncertainty, stress and, more recently, malpractice litigation. One of the primary difficulties for an attorney representing an organizational entity, particularly with respect to potential conflicts of interest, is in determining who is the "client."

CPR Ethical Consideration 5–18 provides:

> A lawyer employed or retained by a corporation or similar entity owes his allegiance to the entity and not to a stockholder, director, officer, employee, representative, or other person connected with the entity. In advising the entity, a lawyer should keep paramount its interests and his professional judgment should not be influenced by the personal desires of any person or organization.

When various members of a particular entity come into conflict, it is often difficult to determine which of the competing interests should be deemed those of *the* entity for purposes of legal representation. This problem of identifying the institutional interest involved arises most often in derivative suits against corporations and unions wherein the officers are charged with misconduct in the management of the organization. According to the ABA Comment to RPC 1.13, "[m]ost derivative actions are a normal incident of an organization's affairs, to be defended by the organization's lawyer like any other suit. However, if the claim involves serious charges of wrongdoing by those in control of the organization, a conflict may arise between the lawyer's duty to the organization and the lawyer's relationship with the board." Also, the interests of the organization in the outcome of the litigation may be adverse to those of the defendant-officers; the attorney's familiarity with the facts involved in the litigation might unfairly tip the scales against plaintiffs from the outset; familiarity with the organization's affairs might make the attorney a very likely witness if the proceedings go to trial. In such cases, it would be inappropriate for an attorney to represent both the organization and its individual officers.

In some instances, the attorney will be disqualified from representing *either* the organization or its individual officers. For instance, in Yablonski v. United Mine Workers (D.C.Cir.1971), union members brought an action under the Labor–Management Reporting and Disclosure Act against the UMWA and three named officers for an accounting of funds dispersed and for restitution of funds misappropriated and misspent. Regular UMWA counsel represented the union and the individual defendants at the initial stages. When plaintiffs moved to disqualify UMWA counsel for conflict of interest, the firm withdrew as counsel for the individual defendants in the instant case, although it continued to represent the union officers in other cases. The firm resisted withdrawal as counsel for UMWA, contending that its withdrawal from representation of the officers removed any possible conflict of interest. However, the union's need for objective counsel, the possibility of future conflicts of interest, and the appearance of conflict of interest were primary concerns of the court in requiring the firm's withdrawal.

Although problems in determining the "institutional interest" of an entity most commonly arise in the context of corporate or union derivative suits, such problems are not limited to any particular type of entity or litigation. For example, a legal aid society which has agreed to represent a local tenants' association must represent the association's interests and not those of the officers alone. Similar problems confront the lawyer for a large state university. Does the lawyer represent the president, the board of regents, the student body, or the state taxpayers? If conflicts develop among these groups, is there an automatic duty to represent a particular segment, or may the lawyer choose those whom he believes to be acting in the best interests of the university as an entity?

In a partnership or similar organization, conflicts between the partners or other individuals of equal status should be treated as conflicts between clients, as analyzed supra. However, where an organization, such as a corporation or university, has an internal hierarchical structure of authority and responsibility, the CPR provides little guidance concerning to whom the attorney should communicate and from whom the attorney should take direction. RPC 1.13(a) is intended to provide better guidance: "A lawyer employed or retained by an organization represents the organization *acting through its duly authorized constituents.*" (Emphasis added.) In most circumstances, then, the organization will have determined its "duly authorized constituents" through statutes, bylaws, or similar regulations. These rules, along with the law defining the authority of agents, will determine the boundaries of decisionmaking power with respect to specific employees within an organization.

1. Corporate Wrongdoing

Normally, a lawyer may rely on the judgment of "authorized constituents" concerning whether policy and business decisions are in the best interest of the organization. Thus, decisions regarding contract provisions, manufacturing processes, product design and environmental impact that may involve serious adverse consequences to the organization, including the risk of liability, are properly within the scope of the constituent's authority. Therefore, once the lawyer advises the responsible person or persons within the organization, he may accept the decision, even if it is contrary to his advice. See Kutak, Whom Does the Corporate Counsel Represent?, 2 Corp. Director 1, 5 (1981). If the lawyer finds the conduct, although lawful, to be "repugnant or imprudent," he may withdraw from representation. RPC 1.16(b)(3).

If the conduct is not only imprudent, but is a "violation of a legal obligation to the organization, or a violation of law which reasonably might be imputed to the organization, and is likely to result in substantial injury to the organization," the lawyer *must* take further action. RPC 1.13(b). Whereas the framework for determining the appropriate action, including who within (or outside) the corporation the attorney should consult, is provided in RPC 1.13 and discussed in greater detail in Ch. 20 infra, the corporate attorney should be mindful of the potential conflicts inherent in these situations, and that the conflicts rules were not intended to be superseded by RPC 1.13. See, e.g., RPC 1.13(e) ("A lawyer representing an organization may also represent any of its directors, officers, employees, members, shareholders or other constituents, *subject to the provisions of rule 1.7.*") (emphasis added).

F. IMPUTED DISQUALIFICATION

All of the rationales underlying more general conflict of interest problems are relevant in this area also. A member of a firm who represents interests adverse to those of the clients of other firm members could be influenced by a desire not to antagonize the other members or harm the firm financially. In addition, and of primary importance in this area, is the possible use of confidential information obtained through the firm's relationship. Although the potential for abuse is greatest in a law partnership, where all members of the firm are responsible to the client, imputed disqualification can extend beyond partners.

1. The CPR

Disciplinary Rule 5–105(D) provides: "If a lawyer is required to decline employment or to withdraw from employment under a Disciplinary Rule, no partner, or associate, or any other lawyer affiliated with him or his firm, may accept or continue such employment."

By its terms, DR 5–105(D) is not limited to situations where either the loyalty to the client or the duty of confidentiality are likely to be compromised by representation of a disqualified attorney's partners or associates; nor is the DR limited to conflict of interest situations. Under the DR, lawyers who shared office space and a former law clerk have been disqualified, and the proscription against serving as both attorney and witness in the same cause disqualifies all of the testifying attorney's partners and associates as well. Further, the Rule has been held to prevent an attorney from accepting litigation against his partner's past client, even though he was not a partner at the time of the prior litigation. The disqualification attaches to any firm which the attorney subsequently joins. Thus, in Consolidated Theatres v. Warner Bros. Circuit Management Corp. (2d Cir.1954), a partnership was disqualified from appearing against clients of the former law firm of one of its partners, despite the lack of any direct evidence of access to information which could be used against the company in the present suit. However, in Silver Chrysler Plymouth, Inc. v. Chrysler Motors Corp. (E.D.N.Y. 1973), the court denied a motion to disqualify plaintiff's attorney who had formerly been a young associate in the 80–member law firm which represented the defendant auto manufacturer. The court considered the attorney's possible personal exposure to the defendant's confidential information while in the firm, any reasonable imputation of knowledge, and the appearance of impropriety, and held that the attorney would not be irrebuttably presumed to have knowledge of the confidences of every attorney in the firm.

Countervailing policy considerations, in addition to those enunciated in *Silver Chrysler Plymouth,* include the unavailability of alternative counsel due to the rural nature of the area or the limited number of attorneys with expertise in the field, the value to the client of the knowledge and expertise gained from a long-standing relationship of attorney and client, and the interests in permitting clients to retain attorneys of their own choosing and in not unduly restricting the mobility of attorneys between private firms and government service or from one firm to another.

In *Silver Chrysler Plymouth,* the court cited the accelerated tendency toward specialization in the bar, and the resulting limitation on the number of firms with the necessary expertise in highly complex areas of the law, as creating a need for flexibility in decisions concerning vicarious disqualification for conflicts of interest.

2. The RPC

The harsh results under the CPR, sometimes unsupported by the rationales underlying disqualification, and the tendency of courts to find exceptions to disqualification due to the changing nature of legal practice, created the impetus for a less inclusive disqualification rule in the RPC. RPC 1.10 provides:

> (a) While lawyers are associated in a firm, none of them shall knowingly represent a client when any one of them practicing alone would be prohibited from doing so by rules 1.7, 1.8(c), 1.9, or 2.2.
>
> * * *
>
> (c) A disqualification prescribed by this rule may be waived by the affected client under the conditions stated in rule 1.7.

Thus, imputed disqualification under the RPC is limited to specific conflict of interest situations. Unless representation by an attorney's partners or associates would violate the general conflict of interest tests under RPC 1.7 and 1.9, the individual attorney's disqualification under RPC 1.8(a) (business transaction with a client), 1.8(i) (family relationship to a lawyer representing adverse client), or 3.7 (acting as attorney and witness in the same trial), is not imputed to the attorney's law firm.

In addition to specifying situations in which neither the loyalty nor confidentiality principles for imputed disqualification apply, the RPC specifically recognize the substantial changes in the size and multi-jurisdictional nature of law firm practice, the interest in not precluding other persons from having reasonable choice of legal counsel, and the increased mobility of attorneys between firms. Instead of the irrebuttable presumptions and prophylactic rules applied under the CPR, RPC 1.9(b) & (c) and 1.10(b) provide for imputed disqualification only, when the attorney sought to be disqualified had *actual* (rather than *presumed*) access to confidential information, or when the subject matter of the prior and present representation is the "same or substantially related." "Thus, if a lawyer while with one firm acquired no knowledge or information relating to a particular client of the firm, and that lawyer later joined another firm, neither the lawyer individually nor the second firm is disqualified from representing another client in the same or a related matter even though the interests of the two clients conflict." ABA Comment, RPC 1.9(b).

Likewise, once a lawyer leaves a firm, the firm may represent a client with interests materially adverse to those of a client represented by the formerly associated lawyer, regardless of when the formerly associated lawyer represented the client, unless: "(1) the matter is the same or substantially related to that in which the formerly associated lawyer represented the client; and (2) any lawyer remaining in the firm has information protected by Rules 1.6 and 1.9(c) that is material to the matter." RPC 1.10(b) and Comment.

a. "Screening"

The emphasis on avoiding use of confidential information to the detriment of a client or former client, as opposed to irrebuttable presumptions and avoiding even the appearance of impropriety, has led some courts to permit a law firm or attorney to rebut the presumption of access to confidences through *"screening."* Occasionally referred to as erecting a "Chinese Wall" between a disqualified attorney and her partners or associates, cf. Nemours Foundation v. Gilbane (D.Del.1986) ("cone of silence" a more apt description), screening involves isolating the disqualified lawyer from other lawyers in a firm to rebut the presumption of shared confidences. Screening is specifically permitted in the RPC only with respect to former government attorneys. Under RPC 1.11(a), if a former government lawyer is disqualified, the lawyer's firm may undertake or continue representation of a client if the appropriate government agency is provided written notice and "the disqualified lawyer is screened from any participation in the matter and is apportioned no part of the fee therefrom."

Some courts still adhere to the rule that if an attorney who moves to a firm possesses confidential information relating to a client, then his new firm is *presumed* to have knowledge of the information as well. However, a trend has been developing to permit the new firm to rebut the presumption of access to such confidential information by screening the new attorney. These courts generally require that "specific institutional mechanisms" must be established by the firm when the tainted lawyer joins the firm. In addition to requiring that the screened attorney not share in any fees, those courts that permit screening to avoid disqualification of a law firm have imposed some combination of the following requirements: (1) attorneys at the firm must be instructed to have no discussions regarding the matter with the screened attorney; (2) the screened attorney must not discuss the present or former matter with any attorney in the new firm; (3) no memoranda or other documents may be shown to the screened attorney; (4) the client files with respect to the matter should be kept in a secure place, off-limits to the screened attorney (with a prominent notice to that effect).

At least one court has required that the screened attorney and the firm submit sworn affidavits that these "specific institutional mechanisms" have been established. Lord Electric Co. v. Titan Construction Corp. (W.D.Wash.1986). If screening measures have been established as required, a fair balance is achieved with respect to the former client's right to preserve confidences, and the new client's right to employ counsel of its own choosing and the attorney's ability to move from one firm to another without necessarily "tainting" the entire firm.

IV. CONCLUSION

Attorneys generate numerous complaints resulting in litigation or grievance committee action because they knowingly or unknowingly undertake representation of conflicting interests. Most of these complaints can be avoided if attorneys consider and comprehend the various rationales behind the rules *before* commencing representation of a potential client, and withdraw or at least seek guidance if a conflict arises.

The potential number and manifestations of conflict of interest situations are limitless. For example, if an attorney's representation of two clients in unrelated matters requires that he argue for a change in the law that would be beneficial to one but detrimental to the other, what is his ethical duty? There is little if any potential for misuse of confidential information, but would the tension created cause him to give less than undivided loyalty to one or the other? Would the voluntary and informed consent of both obviate the need to withdraw?

What about the government attorney who learns about confidential or semi-confidential *procedures* not relevant to any one case, but applicable to all? May the attorney entering private practice make use of such knowledge to the detriment of his former employer?

Clearly, an attorney for two defendants cannot properly agree to trade the guilty plea of one in an exchange for a lesser charge for the other. Is it equally improper for an attorney working in a legal aid or defender organization and constantly dealing with the same prosecutor to plea bargain when steadfast refusal to do so would be beneficial to one client but detrimental to numerous other present and future clients, especially if the present client has himself benefited from his attorney's past willingness to bargain in connection with other clients?

Entirely satisfactory answers to these and many other questions may not exist. However, awareness of these subtle (as well as the obvious) influences should at least result in efforts to adopt procedures that minimize the possibility of conflicts, and to determine carefully the most ethical alternative should a conflict unavoidably arise.

CHAPTER 13

FIDUCIARY RESPONSIBILITIES: COMMINGLING AND MISAPPROPRIATION

I. INTRODUCTION

Attorneys are frequently entrusted with clients' funds to pay for taxes, court costs, fines, attorney expenses, and the like, or funds collected on behalf of clients as a result of settlements or judgments. Canon 9 of the CPR and RPC 1.15 provide rules and guidelines for the proper handling and separation of client funds from those of the lawyer or law firm. Misappropriation and commingling of clients' funds with those of the attorney account for a large share of the disciplinary actions brought against attorneys. "[T]here are few Canons of Professional Ethics more fundamental, more clearly defined, more easily followed, more necessary to promote public trust and confidence in the legal profession, and yet more frequently breached than Canon 11 [now Canon 9 of the Code of Professional Responsibility]." In re Pennington (Wash.1968). With regard to clients' funds, EC 9–5 states that "[s]eparation of the funds of a client from those of his lawyer not only serves to protect the client but also avoids even the appearance of impropriety, and therefore commingling of such funds should be avoided."

Because of the fiduciary nature of the client-lawyer relationship, a lawyer must separate from his own properties, and endeavor to keep safe, those funds and other properties belonging to the client. This is not merely an aspirational goal; any violation of the rules governing use of a client's property will subject a lawyer to substantial discipline, even if no actual loss has occurred. In addition, in the event of any loss of such funds, the lawyer is subject to personal liability whether or not he profited personally in any respect.

II. RECORD-KEEPING AND ACCOUNTING

RPC 1.15 and DR 9–102 offer more specific guidelines for preserving the identity of funds and property of a client. For example, a lawyer must give prompt notice to the client of receipt of the client's funds or other properties, identify and label them properly and place them in a safe place (e.g., a safe deposit box), maintain complete records and render appropriate accounts ("full accounting" if so requested) to the client about them, and pay promptly or deliver upon request the funds or other properties. RPC 1.15(a) & (b); DR 9–102(A) & (B). This latter obligation also applies to requests by the client to make payments to third parties out of client funds.

Many jurisdictions have established audit and reporting requirements to assure implementation of adequate accounting procedures by state attorneys. Typically, these regulations provide for auditing of attorney trust account and other records upon complaint or reason to suspect non-compliance, or randomly at any time and for any reason. Lawyers may also be required to execute an annual written declaration or questionnaire affirming compliance with the applicable regulations, and failure to comply with the audit or declaration requirements constitutes grounds for immediate suspension from practice. If "adequate safeguards" are employed to ensure that clients' privacy rights are not unduly infringed by disclosure or audit of attorneys' trust records, mandatory audits do not impermissibly infringe on the clients' rights.

III. COMMINGLING

Commingling occurs when an attorney fails to keep her clients' funds separate from her own. "[C]ommingling is committed when a client's money is intermingled with that of his attorney and its separate identity lost so that it may be used for the attorney's personal expenses or subjected to claims of his creditors." Black v. State Bar (Cal.1962). Often, commingling occurs as a result of poor office management and inadequate bookkeeping, and precludes a lawyer from determining whether she is spending her or her client's money. Although the attorney may be guilty of no moral turpitude, the client's monies can still be put in jeopardy and made unavailable to him in the event of attachment of the account by the lawyer's creditors or bank failure. The failure to keep accurate records may also prevent the attorney from being able to account for and properly disburse a client's funds when requested. In addition, careless and unintentional "borrowing" from client funds is especially easy when they are commingled with those of the lawyer or law firm. Canon 9 of the CPR was "adopted to provide against the probability in some cases, the possibility in many cases, and the danger in all cases that such commingling will result in the loss of clients' money." Black v. State Bar (Cal.1962).

As a basic protection, all funds belonging in whole or in part to the client must be deposited in a separate account, and the only funds belonging to the lawyer or firm which may be deposited there are funds sufficient to pay bank charges. Unless the client consents, the account must be maintained in the state where the lawyer's office is situated. RPC 1.15(a). See DR 9–102(A) (no exception for client consent). Until 1980, when check-writing demand accounts were permitted to bear interest, client funds had been kept primarily in non-interest-bearing trust accounts. Although the ABA has concluded that the disciplinary rules do not obligate or prohibit attorneys' placing funds of the client in an interest-bearing account, agency law may obligate the attorney to use an interest-bearing account when money is to be kept for an extended period of time. Any interest earned is of course money which belongs to the client.

When an attorney receives funds which only partly belong to the client (e.g., estate funds, funds relating to a client's real estate transactions, insurance proceeds from a client's injury, and advance expense payments or fee deposits which are unearned at the time of receipt), he must deposit such funds in the client's trust account, rather than the attorney's office account. Funds may be withdrawn, with adequate notice to the client, from the trust account when needed to pay expenses or as the fees are earned. However, if a dispute arises concerning whether or how much the attorney is entitled to withdraw, "the portion in dispute shall be kept separate by the lawyer until the dispute is resolved." RPC 1.15(c). Accord, DR 9–102(A)(2).

For example, suppose that pursuant to a written fee agreement, a client pays her attorney $5,000 (which is deposited in the client's trust account) as an advance on the attorney's $100 hourly fee rate. After the attorney expends 25 hours on the client's behalf, the client and the opposing party agree that the party will dismiss the lawsuit in return for client's payment of $20,000. The client, believing that the attorney has not been sufficiently aggressive in dealing with the opposing party, demands that the attorney return the entire $5,000. The attorney should return $2500 (the undisputed amount requested by the client), and retain the remaining $2500 in the trust account until the dispute is settled.

A. IOLTA FUNDS

Occasionally, funds are retained for a client that are nominal in amount or expected to be held for a short period of time so that the interest to be earned over the period the funds are expected to be deposited, less the cost of establishing and administering the account (including the cost of the lawyer's services, preparing any required tax reports, and the capability of the financial institution to calculate and pay interest to individual clients), is unlikely to yield a net positive return to the client. In such cases, the attorney could place the client's funds in a pooled, interest-bearing account, but it would be improper for her to retain the accrued interest. As of December, 1988, all but two states had instituted Interest on Lawyers' Trust Account (IOLTA) programs which permit or require lawyers to deposit such funds in an interest-bearing account. The accrued funds are then paid to an agency specified by the state supreme court or legislature for charitable, law-related purposes (e.g., legal aid, written or audio-visual materials to help the public understand the law and the legal system, law school clinical programs, etc.). Those courts that have considered the issue, have upheld these IOLTA programs against due process and equal protection challenges. See, e.g., Cone v. The Florida Bar (11th Cir.1987), cert. denied (U.S.1987); Carroll v. State Bar of California (Cal.App.1985), cert. denied (U.S.1985).

Increasingly, courts have employed reprimands and public censure to discipline attorneys guilty of commingling, as well as suspension for a specified period of time in more serious cases. The harsher punishments of suspension from practice and disbarment are more commonly reserved for the more serious cases of misappropriation.

IV. MISAPPROPRIATION

Misappropriation of client funds may occur on a variety of levels or develop in stages. Careless and unintentional misappropriation of clients' funds due to commingling or poor recordkeeping may eventually evolve into outright embezzlement; what started as "borrowing" continues and increases in amount. Attorneys in financial difficulties occasionally may even borrow from separate clients' trust accounts, without permission, to cover their own expenses. There are also those attorneys whose misappropriation and misuse of clients' funds amounts to deliberate stealing from the outset.

The response of the legal profession to misappropriation of clients' funds by attorneys has traditionally been suspension for a specified period or disbarment. To be subject to disbarment, the attorney must have exhibited some element of fraud or dishonesty in his behavior. Disbarment is generally not warranted in cases of mere carelessness in recordkeeping or delay in reporting collections. The fact that the attorney intended to repay the money later at the time he appropriated it to his own use has been found to be no defense to disbarment proceedings. Neither does repayment of the amount wrongfully withheld or misappropriated preclude disbarment proceedings. If the misappropriation was made without fraudulent intent and was followed by exemplary behavior and restitution before disciplinary charges were brought, the disciplinary penalty may be reduced accordingly.

Courts have disagreed as to whether the misappropriation of funds received in a capacity other than that of attorney should still result in disciplinary action. Some courts have held that the money withheld from a client must have come to the attorney while acting in her professional capacity. However, others have held that since misconduct justifying disbarment is not limited to acts committed strictly in the lawyer's professional capacity, see, e.g., RPC 8.4; DR 1–102(A)(4), but extends to all misconduct that would prevent admission to the bar, it is immaterial whether the money came into the attorney's hands in a professional or nonprofessional capacity.

In the case of law firms, when one partner misappropriates client funds without the other partners' knowledge, the others are civilly liable for the amount due the client, but are not subject to discipline proceedings like the guilty attorney. If, however, the partners are aware of the misappropriation, they too can be disciplined. The failure of these disciplinary measures to make the injured client whole, however, has led to the institution of clients' security funds.

V. CLIENTS' SECURITY FUNDS

Since 1959, almost every state has established a clients' security fund, through court rules or the action of state bar associations, to reimburse clients who have been injured by the dishonest actions of their lawyers. The funds are typically financed by appropriations from general bar dues or direct assessments of the state's attorneys or bar association members. The funds were created with at least two objectives in mind. First, the legal profession recognizes its moral obligation to rectify the wrong committed against a client who placed trust in a member of a profession priding itself on the honor, learning, and skill of its practitioners.

Since disciplinary action against the defalcating attorney may be totally inadequate to restore lost funds to an injured client, the bar established clients' security funds as a means of satisfying this "debt of honor" owed by the profession. A second objective of such funds is to preserve the legal profession's privilege to regulate itself without outside intervention by demonstrating to the public that it will be accountable for the transgressions of its members. According to the Comment to RPC 1.15: "Where such a fund has been established, a lawyer should participate."

An injured client's claim against a clients' security fund is usually reviewed by a board of trustees who administer the fund, decide which claims merit reimbursement, and set the amount. Clients' security funds restrict their reimbursements to losses due to intentional attorney misconduct, and refuse to reimburse losses arising from attorney negligence. Fearing an avalanche of claims that would deplete their assets, some bar associations do not widely publicize the existence and nature of the funds; however, as a result, many injured clients go unrecompensed for lack of any information about the very existence of the fund. Other bar associations maintain active public relations programs, publicizing the names of clients reimbursed, the name of the defalcating attorney, and the nature of his misconduct.

Clients' security funds as presently operated have been criticized for requirements that the client first exhaust his remedies against the attorney or that the attorney first be disciplined or convicted on criminal charges before claims against the fund can be satisfied. Such requirements, as well as the presence of maximum dollar limitations on reimbursements in many funds, may induce an aggrieved client instead to seek a private settlement.

VI. PREVENTIVE MEASURES

In addition to the punitive and remedial functions that disciplinary action and clients' security funds provide, preventive measures designed to inform attorneys and guide their handling of client funds have been implemented in a number of jurisdictions.

Guidelines for accounting and recordkeeping established in several states provide, in greater detail than RPC 1.15 or DR 9–102, what procedures should be followed by attorneys to safeguard their clients' monies. Wisconsin, for example, requires that a lawyer maintain and preserve complete records pertaining to clients' funds or assets for at least six years. Such records would include trust fund checkbooks and stubs, bank statements, cancelled checks, and account books showing dates, amounts, and ownership of all deposits and withdrawals. Records kept in accordance with such guidelines are easier to audit if investigation of the attorney is necessary due to client complaints. And as indicated supra, some states require attorneys to file annual reports or answer questionnaires concerning the status of their records and client trust accounts.

VII. CONCLUSION

The traditional disciplinary sanctions imposed by courts and the Bar on attorneys who commingle or misappropriate their clients' funds, combined with the growing importance of clients' security funds, recordkeeping requirements, and compliance checks, act as both a guide and a warning to lawyers of the need for proper handling of monies entrusted to their care.

CHAPTER 14

ATTORNEYS' FEES

I. INTRODUCTION

Canon 12 of the 1908 Canons of Professional Ethics stated that "It should never be forgotten that the legal profession is a branch of the administration of justice and not a mere money-getting trade." While this sentiment remains true today, the contemporary problems of lawyers' fees differ significantly from their historical antecedents. In early European times, legal services were often performed without direct compensation by priests, knights, and others as part of their service to the church, state, lord, or some other higher authority. In many countries, and at times in a few of the United States, the payment of fees for legal services has been forbidden. Even today, a British barrister technically receives an honorarium rather than a fee for his or her services. As a consequence, barristers have been unable to maintain a suit for nonpayment of legal fees and, until a recent case, were considered immune from malpractice suits because of the lack of a contractual relationship with the client.

Times have changed from when fees for legal services were prohibited, then declined, then accepted, then expected, and now are demanded, at least in most cases. Regardless of our proud professional history, the fact is that the lawyers of today, unlike their brethren of the past who performed legal services as an avocation rather than a vocation, are dependent upon the fees they earn from law practice for their livelihood. Without charging and collecting fees, today's lawyers could not eat, pay their rent, support their families, give donations to their law schools, or engage in other necessary and worthy, but costly, activities. Nevertheless, it is still regarded as unseemly in many quarters for lawyers to haggle over fees, and EC 2–23 of the Code admonishes lawyers to avoid controversies over fees and to not sue for a fee unless necessary to prevent fraud or a gross imposition by the client.

On the other hand, EC 2–16 suggests that the legal profession cannot remain a viable force in fulfilling its role in society unless its members receive adequate compensation for services rendered and the Code and Model Rules provide that reasonable fees should be charged clients with the ability to pay them. More pointedly, EC 2–17 suggests that adequate compensation is necessary to enable the lawyer to serve clients effectively and to preserve the integrity and independence of the Bar. Could these provisions be suggesting that lawyers have an ethical obligation not only to serve their clients well, but to serve themselves well, as well? There is some merit to the theory that a lawyer who enjoys a decent standard of living is less likely to be tempted to ignore or bend ethical rules, or more likely to be willing to accept a share of unpopular clients, stand up to government overreaching, or otherwise exercise professional integrity and independence. The need, however, in these days of escalating legal fees and concern for the consumer, is to control the cost of legal services.

Since the availability of legal services to all those who need them is inexorably connected with the cost of those services, the CPR appropriately includes the subject of fees for legal services as an implementing provision under Canon 2, which proclaims that a lawyer should assist the legal profession in fulfilling its duty to make legal counsel available. It is hoped that progress in this regard can be accomplished through efficiency in the rendering and marketing of these services rather than by unduly reducing the net income of lawyers. (See Chapter 9, Implementing the Duty to Make Legal Services Available).

II. TYPES OF LEGAL FEE ARRANGEMENTS

Every type of fee agreement involves a risk of conflicts arising between lawyer and client. At the most basic level, a client wants as much legal service as possible for the least cost, whereas a lawyer gains by investing as little time and effort as is necessary to earn a fee. This conflict, however, is inherent in any sale of services, and safeguards are found in the lawyer's professional obligation to give priority to a client's interests over self-interest, and to charge no more than a reasonable fee.

In common representational arrangements, the method of structuring the fee significantly influences the degree to which a lawyer's and client's interests may diverge.

Legal fees are of three basic types: A fixed charge, such as $500 for drafting a will or $1000 for forming a corporation; an hourly charge, which nowadays usually ranges from $75 an hour to $500 per hour; or a contingent fee, whereby the attorney receives a fixed percentage of monies recovered or saved for the client and receives no fee if there is no recovery or saving.

Recently, lawyers and clients have been negotiating creative fee agreements which may combine various elements of these basic types. For example, a "kicker" might be added to an hourly or fixed fee for a favorable result, a minimum fee might be provided under an otherwise contingency fee arrangement, or there might be a joint evaluation of the value of the services rendered which could augment or reduce an otherwise time-based fee.

It can be easily seen that, regardless of the best interests of the client, a lawyer receiving a flat or contingent fee benefits by quickly disposing of a matter whereas an attorney paid by the hour may benefit by dragging the case on. Safeguards, in addition to professional attitude, may thus be desirable in the form of law, ethics, or contract.

One method of lawyer compensation which is expressly prohibited by both the Model Rules and Code because of the conflicts of interest created is an agreement, made or negotiated prior to the conclusion of representation, giving the lawyer literary or media rights to a portrayal or account based in substantial part on information relating to the representation of the client. RPC 1.8(d); DR 5–104(B). California, however, has allowed a criminal defendant in a newsworthy case to sign a voluntary and knowing waiver of the potential conflicts—which were spelled out in detail—pursuant to the client's desire to select his own counsel rather than accept a court appointed lawyer. Maxwell, (Cal.1982).

Fixed or hourly fees may be paid in advance, as the services are rendered, or upon their completion, or by some combination of these payment arrangements. Fees not yet earned should be maintained in a separate client trust account and not commingled with general funds belonging to the lawyer. See RPC 1.15; CPR DR 9–102; (Chapter 13, Fiduciary Responsibilities). An attorney also may be paid a retainer whereby the client contracts to have the lawyer available, that is on call, to perform general or specific legal services during an agreed upon time period. Because of the security of the arrangement for the attorney, the fee is usually less than would be earned on a straight-time basis, and is considered earned whether the actual services rendered fall short of expectations or exceed them. Pre-paid legal service plans are a variation of such retainer agreements. There is often a further understanding that services beyond those encompassed by the retainer, such as litigation, will require separate compensation. Occasional difficulty is encountered, however, in determining the entitlement of the lawyer to receive the full retainer amount if the lawyer's services are terminated prematurely. (See Termination of Employment, infra).

III. DETERMINING THE REASONABLENESS OF A FEE

The Model Rules mandate that a lawyer's fee "shall be reasonable." RPC 1.5(a). Despite the fact that clients frequently complain about the amount of legal fees they are charged, few lawyers are disciplined for charging more than a reasonable fee. In part, this is because many of the complaints involve misunderstandings which are due more to undercommunication than overcharging. When discipline is imposed, the attorney's conduct is usually aggravated by a failure to perform promised services, by deception or disloyalty directed toward the client, and by inadequate or improper accounting for the lawyer's time or the client's funds. In addition, fee disputes are more likely to be resolved by fee arbitration or mediation, or litigation than by disciplinary proceedings.

Moreover, there is considerable disagreement concerning what is a reasonable fee and whether an attorney should be subject to discipline for charging fees which have been freely contracted for unless the client has been overreached or the fees are clearly disproportionate to the services rendered. In California, for example, a disciplinary offense is only committed when a legal fee is "illegal or unconscionable." CA RPC 4-200(A).

The ABA Code states that "A lawyer should not charge more than a reasonable fee" [EC 2-17], but a disciplinary offense is only committed when a lawyer charges a "clearly excessive fee": That is, one which a lawyer of ordinary prudence has a definite and firm conviction that it is in excess of a reasonable fee. DR 2-106(A), (B). These provisions recognize that it is very difficult to judge the reasonableness of a fee and that a fair deal of leeway must be extended to the individual practitioner.

Both the Code and the Rules provide guidelines for determining the reasonableness of a fee, but they are probably more helpful in rationalizing fees already charged than in aiding the discretion of an attorney attempting to determine what fee should be charged. DR 2-106(B); RPC 1.5(a).

These or similar factors are relied upon by courts in fixing or approving the amount of fees awardable under various "fee shifting" statutes. The normal American rule is that each party, win or lose, pays its own legal fees. By contrast, in England, it is common for the losing litigant to be compelled to reimburse the prevailing party's legal fees and costs. An increasing number of federal and state statutes, for example, redressing violations of civil rights, authorize the court to award reasonable fees to the prevailing party. While thc extensive statutory provisions and judicial interpretations of these fee shifting statutes are beyond the scope of this Nutshell, it is noteworthy that, among other things, the Supreme Court has allowed enforcement of a fee agreement in addition to the amount awarded by the court, approved of legal fee awards that exceed the amount recovered by the plaintiff on the merits, affirmed fee awards based upon favorable settlements, and allowed settlements which involve a waiver of attorneys' fees. This last situation, unfortunately, creates a conflict in the interests of clients and their lawyers, and some jurisdictions have attempted to ethically condemn offers of settlement conditioned on a waiver of fees.

In each case, the establishment of a fixed fee, hourly charge, percentage amount or other fee arrangement should be influenced by the factors enumerated in Rule 1.5(a) and DR 2–106(B). In practice, the key considerations appear to be the fee customarily charged in the locality, the experience, reputation and ability of the lawyer or law firm, the time required to properly perform the services, the ability of the client to pay, and whether the legal services involve novel or difficult questions or require special skills for proper performance.

In the past, an important guide to fees charged by attorneys was the minimum fee schedules in their particular localities. These schedules contained recommended hourly fees, per diem for court appearances, and fixed fees for common legal transactions. While they were officially labeled recommended minimum fees, in practice they were more likely to be the average fees, or, as one critical commentator put it, the minimum fee charged by the highest priced lawyer in the community.

Although it would be difficult to find any case disciplining a lawyer for charging less than the fee suggested in applicable minimum fee schedules, most lawyers did, in fact, conform their charges to those schedules, whether out of fear of discipline, ease of calculation, or as a form of convenient justification to the client. However in 1975 the United States Supreme Court held that minimum fee schedules constitute a form of price-fixing in violation of the federal antitrust laws. In this landmark case, *Goldfarb v. Virginia State Bar* (U.S.1975), the court found that the rendering of legal services could constitute business in interstate commerce and that there was no basis for a so-called "learned profession" exemption from the antitrust laws. In other words, it was recognized that the practice of law was a business as well as a profession, and this finding has been used to justify further challenges to restrictive lawyer trade practices.

In response to the *Goldfarb* decision, most all minimum fee schedules have been abolished. The Supreme Court, however, continues to recognize a state-action exemption from the federal anti-trust laws for regulation of the legal profession. Accordingly, several state legislatures and courts have validly imposed fee schedules on lawyers practicing in those jurisdictions particularly regarding contingent fees in medical malpractice and some other cases. These fee schedules are more likely to be aimed at avoiding overreaching by attorneys than at protecting their income.

While the ABA has deleted any direct reference to the use of recommended fee schedules, it retains as a guideline for determining the reasonablenes of a fee that which is "customarily charged in the locality for similar legal services." RPC 1.5(a)(3); DR 2–106(B)(3). Certainly, fees charged by other lawyers in a locality are relevant to determining the reasonableness of a fee which is challenged as being excessive. In establishing fees—absent a conspiracy or other joint effort to impose particular fees, it is likely that lawyers, as other business persons, will want to be aware of what their competitors are charging although now they must rely upon sporadic hearsay information and occasionally available surveys instead of an officially promulgated fee schedule.

It is quite common that a higher fixed or hourly fee will be charged by those lawyers who are experienced, specialized in the area in which they are consulted, or enjoy a reputation for being particularly able. Although the hourly charge may exceed that of less experienced colleagues, a more experienced lawyer may be expected to perform tasks within an area of specialization more quickly and efficiently, thus keeping the total fee reasonable.

The gross fee charged by a lawyer must also take into account the cost of maintaining the law office. Some out-of-pocket costs attributable to a particular case, such as transcripts of depositions, out-of-town travel, and fees paid to witnesses, normally will be charged directly to a client in addition to the agreed upon fee. Most fees, however, must contribute to the substantial overhead cost involved in office rent, employees' salaries and benefits, maintenance of the law library, purchase or rental of computers, typewriters, duplicating machines, and other office equipment, and purchase of office supplies. It is not unusual for these costs to constitute one-third to one-half of the amount of an hourly fee.

In some cases, fees have been calculated by determining in advance a desired net income, adding that to the office overhead cost, and then dividing by the number of anticipated billable hours for each attorney. While it is commonplace for a lawyer to spend upwards of 50 to 60 hours a week at the office or working at home, many of these hours are devoted to administrative tasks, conferences with other attorneys and visitors, public service activities, and other tasks for which a client may not be billed. Consequently, billable hours are more likely to run around 35–40 per week.

It is important for an attorney to keep careful records of how time is spent. Studies have determined that those lawyers who do keep time cards earn more than those who do not. Not only does this provide a more accurate basis for billing and aid in the efficient use of time, but such records can be extremely helpful in explaining to a client the basis for the amount billed. Although many attorneys may choose not to charge for brief telephone calls and reviewing routine correspondence, that decision is best made in light of the nature of the case, amount involved, and relationship with the client after records of all such items are kept and the total time devoted to a client is calculated.

One problem with charging on the basis of hours worked is that the lawyer has little incentive to limit the number of hours devoted to a client's cause. It is a cost-plus method of charging whereby the lawyer increases his income with each additional hour worked. This practice has been particularly criticized in the taking of depositions. The amount involved in the litigation and the client's ability to pay may either temper this indulgence or encourage it. By contrast a lawyer receiving a flat or contingent fee may be motivated to limit the amount of hours devoted to a case, and seek settlement at an earlier date—sometimes without adequate discovery to determine the true value of the client's cause.

While surveys and anecdotal information indicate that lawyers frequently consider a client's ability to pay in setting fees, the standard factors do not include any such guideline. Lawyers have been appropriately urged to charge a reduced or no fee to those who cannot pay the customary price, [see EC 2–24, 25; CPE, Canon 12], but there is no corresponding reference allowing lawyers to charge more to their wealthier clients, whether as a form of subsidizing services to the poor or otherwise. Nevertheless, the amount involved in a transaction is expressly recognized as a relevant factor, presumably on the basis that it increases the responsibility of the lawyer and potential malpractice liability, and in some cases may involve more complex transactions than would otherwise be the case. It cannot be ignored that the existence of a large *res* from which a fee may be recovered is likely to justify the devotion of more hours of a lawyer's time and to provide an obvious temptation for sharing the wealth. It is common practice, often with the sanction of a supervising court, for an attorney to be compensated on the basis of a percentage of the assets involved in estate administration or property transfer. Yet it still seems appropriate for a lawyer to be guided by the language of the old Canons of Professional Ethics that: "A client's ability to pay cannot justify a charge in excess of the value of the service, though his poverty may require a less charge, or even none at all." Canon 12.

Understandably, lawyers charge more for a complex or difficult transaction than a routine one. It costs less to draft a simple will than one with complex trusts and other provisions or one involving a testator who is a resident of a foreign country. Routine matters can be handled by junior associates or paraprofessionals, and by computerized forms, and billed at a lower rate, while a client can expect to pay more for legal services requiring special skills, knowledge or experience.

In addition to these factors which attorneys typically take into account in establishing their fees, others that are relevant to judging the reasonableness of a fee include: whether acceptance of an instant matter will preclude other employment by the lawyer, for example on the basis of a conflict of interest, if this is apparent to or explained to the client; the imposition of special time limits on performance of the legal services; the nature and length of professional relationship with the client; and the results obtained by the lawyer, including the agreement upon a contingent fee or some combination of a fixed and contingent fee.

IV. CONTINGENT FEES

A. JUSTIFICATION

Since a client normally is interested in maximizing recovery, the results that a lawyer obtains for a client are relevant to the amount of fee the client is willing to pay. Making the amount of the fee contingent on the recovery also provides an incentive for greater effort by the lawyer, and a basis for calculating the fee which is relatively easy for the client to understand. While "winning" is clearly relevant to the setting and collection of legal fees, the question remains whether, in the words of philosopher-coach Vince Lombardi, "It is the only thing." To a large extent, charging on the basis of a contingent fee makes it so.

In England and many other countries, the contingent fee is prohibited as a form of champerty because it permits a client to carry on litigation in exchange for a promise to the lawyer of a share in the recovery. Although most states in the United States prohibit a lawyer from accepting an assignment of a percentage of the client's cause of action as a legal fee, they do not similarly condemn, as champertous, contingent fees whereby the lawyer receives a percentage of the recovery as a fee and no fee at all if there is no recovery. Such contingent fee arrangements are the accepted and common practice in plaintiff's personal injury litigation, debt or account collection, and eminent domain proceedings. All American jurisdictions, with the forsaking of the common law on this question by Maine and Massachusetts, now regard such contingent fees as legal.

There is fear, however, that a contingent fee arrangement makes the lawyer an interested party and destroys the objectivity usually deemed of importance to the function of independent advisor or effective advocate. There also has been concern that the use of the contingent fee permits a lawyer to speculate in litigation and may encourage the bringing of vexacious and unfounded suits. There is no empirical data to support the latter allegation, and indeed, one would suspect that since lawyers collect nothing on suits that they lose for their clients, they would be quite circumspect in accepting cases which they thought lacked merit. Of course, speculation could be encouraged by increasing the lawyer's percentage of the recovery inversely to the likelihood of recovery. Indeed, in some jurisdictions, there has been justifiable concern regarding the high percentage contingent fees charged by some lawyers. This has led courts in New York and New Jersey, for example, to impose a maximum 50% for a contingent fee to a lawyer and to provide for decreasing percentages as the dollar amount of recovery increases, and other states, like California, have regulated the amount of contingent fees in medical malpractice cases to discourage the institution of frivolous or nuisance suits. While it has been claimed that such fee schedules impair freedom of contract and equal protection of law, these claims have thus far been dismissed by the courts in light of their power to impose reasonable regulations upon attorneys and prevent abuses of fee charging. Moreover, as state imposed fee schedules, they do not run afoul of federal antitrust laws.

Concern also has been expressed that lawyers working under a contingent fee arrangement might prove too willing to settle cases for inadequate sums since a high volume of quick settlements could provide a good income without investing too much time or effort in each of the cases. This would be especially true if the lawyer received the same percentage, for example, one-third of any recovery, whether obtained by settlement or litigation. On the other hand, an escalating percentage to the lawyer if recovery is obtained through litigation, or an even higher percentage if a successful appeal is taken, could be said to encourage the lawyer to litigate rather than settle.

Despite these possible abuses, contingent fees have been accepted on the grounds that (1) they permit people who would not otherwise be able to afford legal services to pursue recovery of their legitimate claims, (2) successful prosecution of the claim produces a fund from which a legal fee can be paid, and (3) such fees give the lawyer a strong incentive to work in the client's interest and to seek prompt resolution of pending disputes. In fact, it even has been suggested that the contingent fee is preferable to the hourly charge in almost all cases because of its tendency to encourage the lawyer to reduce costs and perform promptly. This benefit, carried to an extreme, can also have the undesirable result of cutting costs by cutting services. The reduced recovery which such cut-rate service would bring to both client and lawyer, however, may discourage the lawyer from not fully protecting the client's interests.

The Ethical Considerations of the CPR caution that "a lawyer generally should decline to accept employment on a contingent fee basis by one who is able to pay a reasonable fixed fee," but cautiously add that "it is not necessarily improper for a lawyer, where justified by the particular circumstances of a case, to enter into a contingent fee contract in a civil case with any client who, after being fully informed of all relevant factors, desires that arrangement." EC 2–20. The practice that is encouraged is to give those clients who can afford it the option of paying on a fixed or hourly basis but not to deny to any client a contingent fee arrangement when that is the client's informed preference. Thus, a 1986 Informal Opinion of the ABA Ethics Committee advises that a "client with a meritorious claim . . . should not be required to relinquish a share of the claim to get representation if he has the money to pay a reasonable fixed fee and is willing to assume the contingency risk." Informal Opin. 86-1521.

While, at least in the United States, there is no longer any question as to the ethics or legality of contingent legal fees in general, there are specific and public policy limitations on such fees in particular cases.

B. LEGAL AND ETHICAL LIMITS ON CONTINGENT FEES

Contingent fee agreements, like all legal fees, must be reasonable. RPC 1.5(a); see CPR EC 2-17; DR 2-106(A). Lawyers have been disciplined for charging clearly excessive contingent fees, and many state and federal courts claim inherent jurisdiction to review the reasonableness of contingent fees as part of their regulation of the practice of law because of the intimate relationship of such fees and a client's ability to obtain adequate legal remedies.

Contingent fee arrangements have been held to be illegal or against public policy in specific types of cases. One cannot represent a defendant in a criminal case on a contingent basis both because such cases do not produce a *res* from which to pay the fee and because such fees may induce, or give the appearance of inducing, resort to unethical or illegal means in order to achieve an acquittal. RPC 1.5(d)(2); CPR EC 2-20; DR 2-106(C). It seems equally reprehensible, and cases have so held, to employ a part-time prosecutor on a contingent fee basis since the overriding obligation of the prosecutor is to do justice not simply obtain convictions.

Although the Code merely advised that "contingent fee arrangements in domestic relations cases are rarely justified" [EC 2-20], the Model Rules, by amendment of the House of Delegates to the Kutak proposal, prohibit a lawyer from entering into, charging, or collecting any fee in a domestic relations matter "which is contingent upon the securing of a divorce or upon the amount of alimony or support, or property settlement in lieu thereof. . . ." RPC 1.5(d)(1).

Most jurisdictions have prohibited contingent fees in divorce cases because of their tendency to discourage reconciliations and divert monies to the attorney that might be deemed essential for the support of the former spouse or children. Some cases, however, have shown flexibility in allowing a lawyer to collect a percentage of a property settlement in actions independent of the dissolution proceeding itself or where the contingent nature of the fee is not likely to have any influence upon the fact of dissolution or the minimum support required for children of the marriage.

Certain federal and state legislation and administrative regulations also prohibit contingent fees when an attorney is employed as a lobbyist (for other than recovery of a private claim) or procurer of government contracts. Since such government action affects the legal rights of persons beyond the immediate represented parties, attorneys should not be encouraged through contingent fee arrangements to reflect only the interest of their private clients at the expense of the general public.

Various jurisdictions limit contingent fee contracts in other respects as to permissible percentage, requirements of writing, required period of voidability at option of client, specification of terms, and subject matter. An Iowa case declared a contingent fee for defense of an unliquidated tort claim (to be based on the difference between the damages sued for and the amount awarded) against public policy as likely to result in unreasonable fees. Wunschel Law Firm v. Clabaugh (1980). While there is a need to control excessive fees, this case seems too inflexible and counter to the current interest among both lawyers and clients for evolving more creative ways in which to structure reasonable fee agreements which encourage incentives while minimizing conflicts.

Where an attorney enters into a contingent fee arrangement which is found to be contrary to public policy, the courts are split on the question of whether the attorney should, nevertheless, be permitted to recover the value of his or her services on a *quantum meruit* basis.

C. PAYMENT OF EXPENSES

One distinction which until recently had been maintained in theory between a contingent fee and a champertous assignment of a percentage of the cause of action to the attorney was that the client must remain liable for any expenses of litigation which the lawyer may have advanced or guaranteed. A lawyer may advance on behalf of the client, or guarantee to the supplier, payment of court or deposition costs and the expenses of investigations, medical examination, and other costs of obtaining and presenting evidence, but the client ordinarily remains ultimately responsible for the payment or reimbursement of these expenses whether or not a favorable recovery is obtained. In practice, however, it is speculated that few attorneys actually pursued collection of these expenses when there was no recovery on behalf of an impoverished client. In recognition of this reality, the Model Rules now provide that the payment of such litigation expenses may be contingent on the outcome of the matter, and that a lawyer may pay the court costs and expenses of litigation on behalf of an indigent client. RPC 1.8(e). (See Chapter 12, Conflict of Interest).

In other cases, many attorneys follow the practice of asking in advance for an estimated amount of money to cover these expenses or of billing the client for them as they occur. Other expenses that a lawyer may incur on behalf of a client, such as for telephone calls and local travel, may be absorbed by the lawyer, regardless of the outcome of the litigation.

In most jurisdictions it is considered improper for an attorney to advance or guarantee general financial assistance to a client even though the client is unable to work, perhaps because of an injury which is the subject of the pending legal matter, and has no other means of adequate support. This type of "maintenance" contract is prohibited even where the client in need of funds may be pressured to accept a less than satisfactory offer of settlement. In other jurisdictions, a lawyer may be permitted to loan funds to the client or guarantee a loan from others to cover living expenses once the attorney-client relationship has been established but not as a means of inducing or soliciting representation of the client. The client remains legally liable for repayment of such loans regardless of whether the lawyer is successful in obtaining a recovery for the client.

In calculating the amount of the recovery, a percentage of which an attorney becomes entitled to as a contingent fee, it is especially important to have an understanding as to whether litigation costs and other expenses that the attorney incurred on behalf of the client will be deducted before the attorney's share is determined. Failure to disclose and discuss accounting for costs and expenses can lead to misrepresentations on the part of the lawyer or misunderstandings on the part of the client, and strongly support the requirement that a contingent fee agreement be in writing.

V. DESIRABILITY OF WRITTEN FEE AGREEMENTS

Experience has demonstrated that misunderstandings and disputes concerning legal fees often occur when there is no writing evidencing the fee contract. Accordingly, the Kutak Commission had proposed that the basis of a lawyer's fee shall be communicated to the client in writing before the lawyer renders substantial services except in an emergency or where a continuing agreement is implied from previous services paid for by the client. The Model Rule, as adopted, however, was watered down from a required to a recommended practice: "When the lawyer has not regularly represented the client, the basis or rate of the fee shall be communicated to the client, preferably in writing, before or within a reasonable time after commencing the representation." RPC 1.5(b). While compliance with this provision should avoid many misunderstandings, attorneys are well advised to make written fee agreements part of their standard operating procedure.

Accord, Amer. Lawyer's Code Conduct, Rule 5.2. Indeed, some states have gone further and required written fee agreements when the lawyer has not regularly represented the client (New Jersey), or for most fee contracts with non-corporate clients exceeding a minimum amount ($1000 for fees and expenses in California). California's Business and Professional Code also specifies that lawyers shall render itemized bills to their clients, that contingent fee agreements shall be in writing, and that failure to comply with the writing requirement in either case renders the fee contract voidable at the option of the client but still entitles the lawyer to a reasonable fee. B & P Code Sections 6147–48.

The Model Rules, as well as some states independently, also require that contingent fee agreements be in writing. RPC 1.5(c). As previously indicated, such agreements are often prone to misunderstanding and susceptible to abuse, and it is especially important to spell out in writing the method for determining the fee, any variation in percentages to which the lawyer is entitled in the event of settlement, trial or appeal, and how expenses are to be treated in calculating the amount due the attorney. The Model Rule also requires that the client be provided with a written statement after conclusion of the matter showing, in the event of a recovery, the remittance to the client and how it was determined.

VI. DIVISION OF FEES

A. DIVIDING FEES WITH OTHER LAWYERS

Traditionally, and by the terms of the CPR, legal fees may be shared among lawyers who are partners or associates in a law firm which renders services to the client or by other lawyers when the fee is divided in proportion to the services performed and responsibility assumed by each lawyer. The Code further provides that any fee-sharing arrangement, other than among lawyers in the same firm, must be fully disclosed to the client, the client's consent to it must be obtained, and the total fee must not clearly exceed reasonable compensation for all the legal services rendered by all the lawyers to the client DR 2–107.

In many areas of the country, however, it is quite common for a lawyer to send a forwarding fee to another lawyer who has recommended a client to him. This fee, usually based upon a percentage of the total fee paid by the client, has been of questionable propriety. According to the ABA Committee on Professional Ethics, the selection of one attorney by another does not involve the performance of legal services or assumption of responsibility and, if nothing more was done by the first attorney, it would be unethical for the attorney who performs the actual legal services to share the fee paid by the client with the forwarding attorney.

This rule has been criticized because it is contrary to common practice and because it may discourage lawyers who are initially contacted by clients from referring the case to more qualified or specialized practitioners. The rule also is somewhat inconsistent with the sharing of fees by partners and associates in a firm in accordance with their partnership interest or salaries and without regard to the proportion of services actually performed by a particular firm member for the client. These considerations have led to a slight but important change in the Model Rules provision from that in the CPR. Lawyers may share fees either by sharing the services performed, *or* if "by agreement with the client, each lawyer assumes joint responsibility for the representation. . . ." RPC 1.5(e). In addition, the total fee must be reasonable, and the client, after being advised of the fee sharing arrangement, must not object to the additional lawyers' participation. The Rule essentially allows partnership-type responsibility to be assumed by the forwarding attorney. California goes even further and permits fee sharing among lawyers engaged in a referral so long as the client consents after a full, written disclosure of the arrangement, and the total fee paid is not unconscionable and does not exceed that which would be charged by the servicing lawyer alone. CAL RPC 2–200. The ATLA Code of Conduct also allows fee sharing with client consent. ALEC Rule 5.4.

The evil of the referral fee occurs when an attorney becomes a broker of legal services, one who solicits business which is then referred to another attorney for a percentage of the fee earned by the latter. The forwarding attorney thus does not engage in the practice of law but earns a livelihood by feeding business to other practitioners. A different ethical response may be justified, however, where a lawyer normally engages in law practice but refers an occasional client to an attorney in another state or to one who practices another field of law to better serve that client's needs. Permitting the referring lawyer to share in the ultimate legal fee may not be undesirable, particularly where he has performed some legal services or assumed continuing responsibility, and the client is not required to pay a higher or unreasonable fee because of the sharing arrangement.

A lawyer who retires or otherwise leaves a law firm may continue to receive reasonable payments from the firm on the basis of having previously contributed to the earnings used to fund the retirement plan or separation agreement.

In 1989, the ABA adopted an amendment to the Model Rules, patterned after a similar California rule, allowing a lawyer or law firm to sell or purchase a law practice, including goodwill. Compliance with specified conditions regarding notice to clients, option to retain other counsel, and limitation on increases in fees is required. RPC 1.17. The purchasing and selling lawyers, thus, will be able to share fees as part of the consideration for the price paid for the practice.

B. SHARING FEES WITH NON-LAWYERS IS GENERALLY PROHIBITED

For a lawyer to share a legal fee with a non-lawyer is generally condemned as an aid to the unauthorized practice of law [DR 3-102(A); RPC 5.4], or as a form of compensation for soliciting legal business. Thus, if a client is in need of accounting, insurance, banking, or other services in addition to those rendered by the lawyer, these non-lawyer specialists should be compensated directly by the client or by the lawyer employing them in a fixed amount without regard to the fee paid to the lawyer. Likewise, where a lay person performs investigative services or a collection agency makes preliminary but unsuccessful attempts to collect a debt owed to the client, the client or subsequently employed lawyer may pay such individuals for their services but may not base the payment on a percentage of the lawyer's fee or the amount collected.

It is also unethical and illegal solicitation for a so-called investigator to be compensated by the lawyer for the act of referring the case to him, but reasonable and usual membership fees may be paid to bona fide legal service organizations. DR 2-103(B); RPC 7.2(c).

A business, such as a bank, which employs lawyers may not collect fees for legal services or otherwise share in fees generated by the rendition of legal services. A lawyer, however, who renders other than legal services for a client may share in a fee paid to a lay person or agency. For example, with full disclosure and the client's consent, a lawyer may share in a commission for aiding the brokerage of real estate, provided such commission sharing is consistent with state real estate sales laws.

For a lawyer to accept compensation for legal or other services from one other than a client might create a conflict of interest, and the lawyer may accept such payments only if the client has consented after full disclosure and the third party does not attempt to direct, regulate, or otherwise interfere with the professional judgment of the lawyer in rendering legal services to the client. DR 2-103(D), DR 5-107(A), (B); RPC 1.8(b), 5.4(c). These are important safeguards to maintain in group legal service plans.

An early ethics opinion had advised that rental charges for an office may not be based upon a percentage of the fees earned by a lawyer. Adherence to this prohibition could inhibit the development of store-front legal clinics in shopping centers where the normal leasing agreement bases the rental payment to the landlord upon a percentage of the income received by the tenant. The rationale of the earlier opinion also is inconsistent with ABA Formal Opinion 355 (1987) which approved of for-profit, prepaid legal service plans retaining a share of subscriber fees to cover both administrative expenses and a profit. (See Chapter 7, Unauthorized Practice of Law).

Lawyers may not form partnerships with non-lawyers if any of the business activities include the practice of law. DR 3–103; RPC 5.4(b). Likewise, a non-lawyer may not own an interest or be a director or officer of a professional corporation or association formed to practice law for a profit, except that an executor or administrator of the estate of a lawyer member may hold the latter's stock or interest for a reasonable time during administration of the estate. DR 5–107(C); RPC 5.4(d). A recent, controversial innovation in the rules adopted in the District of Columbia, however, expressly authorizes the holding of an ownership or financial interest in a law firm by non-lawyers who assist the firm in rendering legal services. (See Chapter 7, Unauthorized Practice of Law).

It is now recognized that non-lawyer employees of a law firm may participate in a retirement or profit-sharing plan of the firm, even though the benefit is based on a percentage of legal fees earned. In addition, when a lawyer dies, his former firm, or a successor lawyer who completes pending legal matters, may make a reasonable payment to his estate or beneficiaries. DR 3–102(A); RPC 5.4(a). While there is no requirement of an exact allocation, such payments may be regarded as delayed compensation for services previously rendered by the now-deceased attorney. A similar theory supports the propriety of payments made to a former law partner or associate pursuant to a separation or retirement agreement, whether the non-practicing attorney is considered as a lay person or a lawyer at the time such payments are received.

When a client requires the services of lawyers in different states, neither lawyer is considered a layperson for the purpose of dividing legal fees and both may share in the fee paid so long as they share services and/or responsibilities.

VII. ADVERTISING OF LEGAL FEES

One of the benefits claimed for permitting lawyers to advertise is that the competition brought about by advertising may reduce the cost of legal services. The ability to advertise fees is a key ingredient in bringing about competitive pricing. However, unlike the sale of undifferentiated products, such as liquor and prescription drugs where price advertising has resulted in reductions to the consumers, legal services are highly individualized both to the lawyer and the client being served. Consequently, it is very difficult to accurately advertise a standard price for a legal transaction. Nevertheless, many lawyers and law firms do have standard hourly charges and rate schedules for common legal transactions that can be communicated to the public with the caveat that complexities or variations in the services required may alter the amount of the fee. A growing number of legal clinics and law firms are in fact advertising or otherwise providing standard fee schedules to potential clients.

In light of these developments and the Supreme Court decision holding that the advertising of standard legal services and fees are protected speech under the First Amendment, (see Chapter 10), the ABA amended the Code of Professional Responsibility to expressly permit fee advertising subject to certain restrictions. DR 2–101(B)(18), (20)–(25), (E), (F), (G). The Code specifically provides that lawyers may advertise fees for initial consultation, availability of a written schedule of fees, contingent fee rates (provided that the statement discloses whether the percentages are computed before or after deduction of costs), and whether credit cards or other credit arrangements are accepted. In addition, a lawyer may advertise an hourly rate, range of fees, or fixed fees for specific services, provided that the advertisement discloses that charges will vary depending upon the particular matter to be handled. DR 2–101(B)(23–25).

The Model Rules do not specifically address advertising of legal fees but would allow it within the general restriction that the advertising not be false or misleading. RPC 7.1. The Supreme

Court's decision in the *Zauderer* case (U.S.1985), while striking down several of Ohio's restrictions on lawyer advertising, affirmed the state court's holding that Zauderer's failure to include in his contingent fee advertising that clients might be liable for significant litigation costs was deceptive. [See Chapter 10, Solicitation and Advertising].

VIII. COLLECTION OF FEES

While a lawyer should attempt to avoid controversies over fees with clients, there is no prohibition against suing a client for a fee especially when necessary to prevent fraud or a gross imposition by the client. However, when a client questions the amount of the fee, in most jurisdictions the attorney has the burden of establishing that the fee charged or agreed to is fair and equitable. This is especially true when the amount or basis of the fee was not determined until after the creation of the attorney-client relationship. In such cases, there may be a presumption of undue influence by the attorney over the client which the attorney must seek to rebut by showing good faith, the reasonableness of the amount of the fee, a lack of pressure upon the client to agree to the fee, and the opportunity for or actual receipt by the client of advice concerning the fee agreement from another lawyer or disinterested person. The maturity, intelligence, and degree of sophistication and experience of the client also have been considered relevant factors in such cases. (See Chapter 12, Conflict of Interest).

Many embarrassing fee disputes could probably be avoided if attorneys would take the initiative to bring up the question of fees during the first conference with the client, and preferably before the relationship of attorney and client has been established. In addition, written fee agreements, careful record keeping, and frequent communications to the client will help to avoid subsequent challenges by the client and help the attorney to justify the fees charged.

A lawyer should carefully consider both the consequences and alternatives to filing a law suit to collect a legal fee. A substantial number of malpractice actions are filed as counter-claims to lawyers' suits for legal fees from clients who have become dissatisfied with the legal services rendered or fees charged therefor. A Comment to Model Rule 1.5 recommends that a lawyer should conscientiously consider submitting to an established fee arbitration or mediation procedure, and some states or bar associations require an attorney to offer the option of fee arbitration to a client who disputes the amount or basis of the lawyer's fee demand. Many state and local bar associations have established procedures for binding or non-binding arbitration of fee disputes and increasingly are including lay representation on the arbitration panels.

To avoid controversies over the collection of fees, some attorneys employ various financial security devices. Except in a very few states, it would be champertous for an attorney to secure the payment of a fee by contracting to receive an assignment of a part of a client's cause of action. Likewise, in many jurisdictions an attorney cannot prevent a settlement of a client's cause of action by insisting upon approving any settlement between the client and a third party. See RPC 1.2(a).

If a client's financial situation does not permit payment of a legal fee in a lump sum, the attorney may, and in appropriate cases should, accept installment payments as the work progresses, or even after it has been completed.

A lawyer should not resort to overly zealous actions to obtain payment of fees. As the California Supreme Court has stated, an attorney violates the duty of fidelity to a client when, "in his zeal to insure collection of his fee, he assumes a position inimical to the interests of his client." Hulland v. State Bar (Cal.1972). Thus, even though fees may have been properly due from a client, it has been held to be unethical for a lawyer to expose the client to liability to a third party, threaten to withhold services, particularly at a critical time, unless the fee is paid (or, even worse, attempt to increase the agreed upon fee under such circumstances), threaten legal action against the client under circumstances involving oppression, or disclose or threaten to disclose a client's confidences to others. A lawyer, however, may reveal a client's confidences or secrets to the extent they are necessary to establish the lawyer's right to a fee or to otherwise defend himself or his associates from a client's accusation of wrong doing. DR 4–101(C)(4); RPC 1.6(b)(2).

A fee agreement may be secured by having the client sign a promissory note to the attorney but such note should not include a provision for confession of judgment nor, according to the ABA Professional Ethics Committee, a discount for early payment. In most jurisdictions an attorney may charge interest on delinquent fee accounts but normally only with the client's consent in a written fee agreement or otherwise. In addition, the attorney must be careful to comply with any applicable disclosure and other requirements of federal or state consumer protection laws.

To avoid conflicts between the role of a lawyer as attorney for and creditor of a client, it is preferable that a client unable to timely pay an agreed upon retainer make arrangements to borrow funds from some other source. An attorney may assist a client in obtaining a loan and may accept bank credit cards, such as Visa or Master Card whereby the client's financial institution pays the lawyer's fees and extends an equivalent credit to the client. The debtor-creditor relationship is then between the client and the bank, although if the lawyer failed to perform in accord with professional or contract standards, the client could assert defenses against the creditor bank to the extent authorized by recent federal and state consumer protection legislation. Direct loans from a lawyer to a client must meet the strict fiduciary standards of a lawyer doing business with a client. (See Chapter 12, Conflict of Interest).

The advent of pre-paid legal service plans permits attorneys to be compensated, at least in part, before services are actually rendered, by clients enrolled in the plan or by an association which provides the plan for its members. Legal services are often offered at reduced fees through such plans, and this type of financing provides both a secure source of clientele and of payment to the participating attorneys.

In the absence of a court appointment or other compelling circumstances, an attorney is not obligated to perform legal services for those unable or unwilling to pay a reasonable fee, and may even decline a court appointment that would likely result in an unreasonable financial burden. RPC 6.2(b). Once an attorney agrees to represent the client, however, he should not withhold services necessary to protect the client's interest in an attempt to coerce payment from the client. While a client's deliberate disregard of an obligation to pay legal fees justifies the attorney's withdrawal from representation, before withdrawing the lawyer must take reasonable steps to avoid foreseeable prejudice to the rights of the client. In addition to receiving permission from any tribunal before which the client's case is pending, the lawyer should give adequate notice to the client of the intention to withdraw, allow time for the client to employ other counsel, refund all pre-paid fees not already earned, and return any papers or property to the client unless the lawyer is entitled to retain them as security for the payment of his fees. (See Chapter 15, Termination of the Relationship).

IX. ATTORNEYS' LIENS

In most jurisdictions, a lawyer may enforce payment of legal fees by use of a retaining or a charging lien.

Retaining liens have been recognized at common law and resemble mechanics' liens which permit a person to retain property worked on until payment has been made for the work. Thus, the attorney's retaining lien is possessory and passive. It attaches to all papers, funds, or property of the client which come into the attorney's hands through their professional relationship. It does not, however, apply to documents, funds or property which the attorney holds as a trustee, for safe-keeping, or as security for an indebtedness other than the payment of legal fees.

The retaining lien may be used to secure the payment of all legal fees due whether or not the unpaid fee relates to the matter in which the attorney acquired possession of the property. In other words, if more than one legal matter was handled by an attorney for the same client, the attorney may retain properties received in connection with any of such matters until the legal fees owing from services in all of them have been paid. If the attorney files papers in his possession with a court or otherwise releases a client's property, the lien on such papers or property is lost. An attorney may also voluntarily abandon the lien.

Several states now regulate attorneys' retaining liens by statute and may alter the common law scope, such as by requiring notice to the client to perfect the lien.

When a lawyer is discharged and the client employs a successor attorney, if the first lawyer's fees remain unpaid, the need to turn over the client's papers to the new attorney will depend upon several factors, including whether retention would not merely inconvenience the client but cause substantial prejudice to continued representation of the client's interests, whether the lawyer withdrew from representation without cause, and whether there is a legitimate dispute concerning the fee which is due. When the original lawyer is required to relinquish client files otherwise covered by a retaining lien, she may retain other property or funds in her possession sufficient to secure payment of legal fees and, in some jurisdictions, demand that the client substitute other security for their payment. The ethical standards merely incorporate the law of the applicable jurisdiction by providing that, upon withdrawal, a lawyer may retain a client's papers "to the extent permitted by other law." RPC 1.16(d); see DR 2–110(A)(2).

An attorney's charging lien also has derivations in the common law but is created and regulated by statute in most jurisdictions. It may be asserted on any judgment or settlement of a cause of action prosecuted by the attorney on behalf of the client. It is more limited than the retaining lien in that it applies only to funds or property received in the case for which legal fees are due. In addition, it is an active lien, which means it must be asserted in order to become effective. It is generally asserted by the attorney giving notice of the claim for fees to the judgment or settlement debtor, or by filing notice in accordance with statutory provisions in the jurisdiction. Once such notice has been given, the debtor remains liable for the attorney's fees even if he has paid the entire sum awarded or agreed upon to the attorney's client.

A charging lien applies only to causes of action asserted by the attorney on behalf of the client and not to other legal matters for which fees may be due, such as the drafting of wills and other non-litigative documents and the giving of legal advice.

When an attorney receives the proceeds of a settlement or judgment from a third party or its insurance company, the attorney is entitled to a lien on such payment to the extent that legal fees are due. Because attorneys are prohibited from commingling their clients' funds with their own, the attorney should deposit any check received for such payment in a client's trust account and then withdraw that portion of the funds due for legal fees. If the amount of the legal fees is disputed, a lawyer may not withdraw the disputed portion until such dispute is resolved. (See Chapter 13, Fiduciary Responsibilities).

In the few states which do not recognize common law or statutory attorneys' liens, such as California, at least the charging lien may be created by express or implied contract with the client.

X. TERMINATION OF EMPLOYMENT

Many occasions arise when an agreement to render legal services for a client is not completed either upon the initiative of the lawyer, the client or for causes beyond the control of both. In the event that the lawyer has received a fee in advance, he must refund to the client any portion of that fee which has not been earned at the time of termination of his employment. RPC 1.16(d); DR 2–110(A)(3). In this situation, as well as where services have been rendered for which a fee has not been paid, the lawyer's right to compensation will vary depending upon the reason for termination and the valid terms of the fee agreement.

Particular difficulty may be encountered with so-called non-refundable retainers. These retainer fees are stated to be earned upon the agreement of the lawyer to become available to serve the client. But what if the client determines to discharge the lawyer, or the purpose of the retainer is frustrated, before any substantial legal services are performed, for example, if disputing spouses reconcile or a criminal charge against the client is dropped without any intervention on the part of the just-retained defense counsel? Some compensation may properly be due the lawyer because of her disqualification from representing any conflicting interests with those of the client, and for the period during which the lawyer was available to serve the client. But to permit the lawyer to keep the entire retainer, especially of a large amount, would appear to violate the proscription against charging unreasonable, clearly excessive, or unconscionable fees (depending on the jurisdiction). It also has been persuasively contended that enforcement of the contracted-for retainer price, regardless of the extent of services performed, is inconsistent with the accepted concept that a client should be able to discharge an attorney without cause and without economic penalty; with trust and fiduciary principles applicable to attorney-client relations; and with the normal contract law standards which would strike down excessive liquidated damage contracts as unenforceable penalties. See Brickman, Fordham L.Rev. (1988).

In these and other lawyer termination cases the issue usually is whether the lawyer is entitled to be paid (1) the contracted fee, including anticipatory profits, (2) compensation based upon *quantum meruit* for the value of services rendered, or (3) no fee at all.

Because of the close, confidential relationship which is expected to exist between attorneys and clients, a client is free to discharge his attorney for any cause or no cause at all if the client no longer feels comfortable with that attorney. In an ordinary personal service contract, if there is a discharge without cause that violates the contract, the innocent party would be entitled to the value of the contract including lost and anticipated compensation and profits. Although some jurisdictions apply this rule to legal service contracts, it imposes a substantial economic burden on the client to pay both the full contract price of a discharged lawyer and that of a newly retained one, and, thus, substantially restricts the client's freedom to choose an attorney or discharge one at will. For this reason, an increasing number of jurisdictions hold that an attorney is only entitled to recover the value of services up until the time of discharge. The same result usually is reached when the attorney justifiably withdraws from the employment or when the contract is terminated because of the death of either of the parties before the services have been completed.

In determining the reasonable value of the services rendered, the contract between the parties may be taken into account. Where the contract was for a contingent fee, and the contingency of judgment or settlement had not occurred prior to the attorney's termination, the value of the services will normally be held not to exceed the fee which would have been earned based upon the client's ultimate recovery. This puts the first attorney at the mercy of the abilities and success of a second lawyer, but the alternatives of requiring the client to pay one-third of the recovery, for example, to both of the attorneys or to have the two attorneys share a single one-third contingent fee would appear to be unjust and unduly harsh on the client or the attorneys. If no recovery is ultimately obtained, the first lawyer will either receive no fee, or at best, a *quantum meruit* recovery.

In the event a client discharges an attorney with cause, or the attorney withdraws without justification from the employment, the attorney may forfeit any right to compensation, although some jurisdictions have indicated that a *quantum meruit* recovery may still be possible. Similarly, when an attorney and a client enter into a contract which is unenforceable because of public policy, for example, a contingent fee agreement in a divorce case, the attorney may still be entitled to recover in *quantum meruit,* unless the services to be performed by the attorney are illegal in themselves or the particular jurisdiction views its public policy against the type of fee contract to be stronger than the possible injustice of denying the attorney recovery for the value of services rendered. The good faith of the parties and whether they were in *pari-delicto* in entering into their transaction are relevant in determining whether the attorney will be entitled to any compensation.

A lawyer who violates ethical precepts against, for example, solicitation, representation of conflicting interests, fee splitting, or aiding the unauthorized practice law, has been held in many jurisdictions to forfeit any right to compensation even though valuable services may have been rendered to the client.

CHAPTER 15

TERMINATING THE RELATIONSHIP: VOLUNTARY AND MANDATORY WITHDRAWAL

I. INTRODUCTION

An attorney may become dissatisfied with the progress of a particular case or with the nature of the relationship he has with a particular client for a variety of reasons. Likewise, the client may become dissatisfied for any number of reasons. In such circumstances, withdrawal may be appropriate. Since this chapter deals with withdrawal as an *option,* the termination of the attorney-client relationship by operation of law, such as when an attorney accepts a judicial appointment, will not be discussed herein. Neither will termination of the relationship upon motion for disqualification by opposing counsel be discussed.

An attorney may face contradictory duties as a result of his role as advocate for the client on the one hand, and as officer of the court on the other. See, e.g., Chapter 11 (Confidentiality); Chapter 16 (Adversary System). The potential for conflict also exists when an attorney considers withdrawing from a case. For example, when a client insists on filing an appeal that his attorney considers frivolous, the attorney has the obligation, as an officer of the court, not to waste the court's time, RPC 3.1; EC 7–4, and the obligation, as an advocate, to represent her client zealously, CPR Canon 7, or with reasonable diligence, RPC 1.3. Similarly, when an attorney thinks that her client may have perjured himself, the attorney's duty to the court is to avoid being a party to fraud upon the tribunal, but withdrawal may bring hardship to the client who is entitled to a full hearing on all the issues supporting his cause. See Chapter 16 (Adversary System); Chapter 11 (Confidentiality).

Although the existence of conflicting obligations may be clear, the proper course of action concerning withdrawal under any given circumstances is not always apparent. Indeed, there is no universal rule as to what facts and conditions justify, or even require, an attorney's withdrawal. Disciplinary Rule 2–110, several Ethical Considerations, and RPC 1.16 offer some guidelines; however, inconsistent approaches to the same issue between jurisdictions, and the absence of decisions on certain issues in others, provide an attorney with the means for, at best, an informed guess as to whether withdrawal is appropriate under the circumstances. An incorrect decision could result in a contempt citation. See, e.g., Rubin v. State (Fla.App.1986), cert. denied (U.S.1987) (contempt citation upheld with respect to lawyer's refusal to proceed to trial because of client's intent to testify untruthfully).

The rules regarding the right of an attorney to withdraw from a case are intended to protect the client when withdrawal would leave him without adequate protection of his legal rights, to protect the attorney from unfair treatment by the client, to preserve the integrity of the judicial system by preventing the attorney from becoming a party to illegal or unethical conduct instigated by his client, and to assure that litigation will not be interrupted by unnecessary or improvident withdrawal. Although withdrawal may occasionally be the right of an attorney, it must be exercised cautiously and never as an excuse to gain leverage on a client or to avoid unremunerative or otherwise distasteful representation.

II. APPLICABLE RULES

A. ACCEPTING EMPLOYMENT

An attorney is not required to accept employment from every person seeking his representation. However, a stated objective of the legal profession is to provide legal services to all those in need of them. RPC 6.1 and Comment; EC 2–1. In accordance with this goal, an attorney should not lightly decline employment: It is the duty of each individual practitioner to accept his share of generally unpopular or unattractive legal representation. RPC 6.2 and Comment; EC 2–26. Likewise, an attorney should not reject tendered employment because of the community's attitude toward the client or cause, Comment, RPC 6.2; EC 2–27, nor should the identity or position of the person against whom the client may be aligned be a reason for declining employment, EC 2–28. Conversely, an attorney should avoid employment when the intensity of his personal feelings toward the case would interfere with effective representation, RPC 6.2(c); EC 2–30, or when he is not competent to deal with the issues in the case, RPC 1.1, 1.16 (Comment); DR 6–101(A)(1), EC 2–30. Also, he should not accept employment when he knows the client has retained other counsel in the matter, unless the other counsel has given her approval, withdrawn, or been discharged. EC 2–30.

The acceptance of employment implies that the attorney will conduct the action to its conclusion. This should normally include, for example, continuing representation of a convicted defendant through appeal, EC 2–31, although an attorney may contract to represent a client only at trial. See also RPC 1.3, Comment (diligent representation until conclusion of all matters undertaken for client includes at least advising client of possibility of appeal). Since a lawyer is not required to accept every case, and since withdrawal following acceptance is difficult to accomplish, careful consideration of potential ethical problems before commencing representation is the best way to avoid difficult withdrawal problems.

B. WITHDRAWING FROM EMPLOYMENT

Although an attorney may generally accept or decline employment at his discretion, he must have a justifiable cause for withdrawal once the client's case has been accepted. Ethical Consideration 2–32 states that an attorney should not withdraw from a case absent compelling circumstances and not before carefully considering the possible adverse effects on his client. RPC 1.16, on the other hand, does not contain similar language, but delineates specific bases for withdrawal, including a catch-all ("other good cause for withdrawal exists"). What constitutes "good cause" or "compelling circumstances" can be extremely varied and necessarily depends upon the facts of any particular case.

1. Mandatory Withdrawal

In some circumstances, attorneys are required to seek to withdraw under RPC 1.16(a) and DR 2–110(B). There are three situations in which withdrawal from a case is mandatory:

(1) When it is obvious that the attorney's employment will result in the violation of a DR or RPC. For example, when it is obvious that the client is bringing the action merely for the purpose of harassment (refusal of an offered settlement which is perfectly reasonable, recommended by his attorney, and includes all requested damages), the conduct would violate DR 7–102(A)(1) (if the action "would serve merely to harass"). See Comment, RPC 3.1 (if the action is "taken primarily for the purpose of harassing"). In most cases, vindictiveness or harassment will not be the sole purpose for bringing the suit. At some point, the attorney may wish to consider permissive withdrawal as an alternative to aiding the client in conduct that is at least partly (if not "merely" or "primarily") undertaken to harass another. Likewise, when continued representation would constitute a conflict of interest, withdrawal is required. See Chapter 12 (Conflict of Interest). However, if a client merely *suggests* a course of action that would result in a violation of professional rules, the lawyer is not obliged to withdraw, but may discuss the legal consequences of such a course of action. RPC 1.2(d); 1.16, Comment.

(2) When the attorney's mental or physical health renders unreasonably difficult (CPR) or materially impairs (RPC) her ability to represent the client. Withdrawal is then mandated as part of the lawyer's responsibility to ensure effective assistance. See Chapter 6 (Competence).

(3) When the attorney is discharged by the client. The client's right to discharge the attorney is largely unlimited and ends the lawyer-client relationship. At least one jurisdiction (Colorado),

however, has held that an indigent defendant may not discharge court-appointed counsel without leave of court. If the court insists that a lawyer continue representation notwithstanding such a client's purported discharge, the lawyer is obliged to follow the court's direction. RPC 1.16(c).

Some jurisdictions, pursuant to DR 2–110(B)(2) supra, also require withdrawal when a client has perjured himself and refuses to permit disclosure. See Ch. 11 (Confidences) and Ch. 16 (The Adversary System). In those jurisdictions the general rule is that the attorney is bound by the attorney-client privilege and thus may not disclose the nature of the client's conduct; but, the attorney is also bound by DR 7–102(A)(4) not to use perjured testimony, and is therefore required to withdraw from further representation. The ABA adopted this approach in opinions interpreting the CPR. See ABA Op. 1314; ABA Op. 1318. See also In re A. (Or. 1976) (withdrawal mandatory when client refuses to permit disclosure of fraud perpetrated on tribunal).

In Nix v. Whiteside (U.S.1986), the Court held that a criminal defense attorney's threat to withdraw (and inform the court) if the client testified falsely did not constitute ineffective assistance of counsel. In dicta, the Court suggested that withdrawal was appropriate, but stopped short of indicating that it was mandatory because withdrawal "when this situation arises at trial gives rise to many difficult questions including possible mistrial and claims of double jeopardy." In addition, if a motion to withdraw would betray the perjury to the trier of fact in a criminal case—i.e., in a bench trial to the judge—the lawyer may be required to remain in the case, but not pursue actively or use the perjured testimony. Coleman v. Risley (9th Cir.1988), *interpreting* Lowery v. Cardwell (9th Cir.1978) (cessation of questioning of defendant, request for immediate recess, and request to withdraw without stating reasons together served to alert judge, *who was also the fact-finder,* that accused had perjured herself, depriving her of her right to a fair trial). See Ch. 16 (The Adversary System).

Any objections to withdrawal in criminal cases would not apply to intended perjury in civil cases. However the RPC do not favor—and in some cases prohibit—withdrawal when a client has already perjured himself. Under RPC 3.3, the lawyer must first attempt to convince the client to rectify his perjury. See ABA Op. 87–353. If the client does not respond to the lawyer's admonition, the lawyer should seek to withdraw, but only if withdrawal will remedy the situation and is possible under the circumstances. Rule 3.3, Comment. Otherwise, the lawyer must inform the tribunal of the client's fraud or perjury.

2. Permissive Withdrawal

Both the CPR and RPC list specific circumstances which can justify withdrawal; arguably both also allow discretion beyond those specifics. However, the requirements of the CPR and RPC are not identical. Under either set of rules, an attorney may withdraw for "other good cause." DR 2–110(C)(6); RPC 1.16(b)(6). The CPR, though, requires that the attorney believe in good faith that the appropriate tribunal will find other good cause, whereas the RPC merely require that such good cause exist.

The CPR's requirements are set forth in DR 2–110(C), which contains what appears to be an exclusive list of circumstances in which the CPR will allow withdrawal. Most of these grounds deal with a client's refusal to follow her counsel's considered legal advice. DR 2–110(C)(1). For example, if the client insists that the lawyer file a frivolous action, or pursues or insists on an illegal course of action or one contrary to the attorney's judgment or to the CPR, the attorney may withdraw. Withdrawal is also permitted if the client deliberately disregards an agreement with the attorney as to fees and expenses. An attorney may also request withdrawal when: (1) her continued employment is likely to result in the violation of a Disciplinary Rule; (2) she finds it difficult to work with co-counsel, to the detriment of the client; (3) her mental or physical condition makes it difficult for her to complete the services; or (4) her client knowingly and freely assents to the severing of the relationship. DR 2–110(C)(2)–(5).

This apparently exclusive list does provide some discretion. For example, DR 2–110(C)(1)(d) states that an attorney may properly request withdrawal when "other conduct [of the client] renders it unreasonably difficult for the lawyer to carry out his employment effectively." As noted supra, an attorney may also request withdrawal when she believes "in good faith, in a proceeding before a tribunal, that the tribunal will find the existence of other good cause." DR 2–110(C)(6).

The RPC appear to permit withdrawal more freely, dividing permissive withdrawal into two classes. Generally, a lawyer may withdraw for any reason if it can be done without "material adverse effect on the interests of the client." RPC Rule 1.16(b). The lawyer may withdraw, even if there is material adverse effect on the client's interests, when the circumstances fall within one of the subsections listed in the Rule. These circumstances focus on the client's behavior: (1) the lawyer reasonably believes that the client's persistent course of action involving the lawyer's services is criminal or fraudulent; (2) the client has used the lawyer's services to commit a crime or fraud; or (3) the client has rendered the representation unreasonably difficult.

In addition, the RPC permit withdrawal due to financial problems between the client and lawyer. If the client fails to fulfill an obligation regarding the lawyer's services, the lawyer must give reasonable notice that she will withdraw if this failure continues, and may then withdraw. Also, if the representation will create an "unreasonable financial burden" for the lawyer, Rule 1.16(b)(5) permits withdrawal. Finally, an attorney may request withdrawal if "other good cause" exists.

3. Good Cause

Because there is no simple rule defining good cause, the most that can be offered for guidance is a summary of what several courts have stated concerning the issue. Courts have variously held that good cause exists when: there are irreconcilable differences between attorney and client with respect to the conduct of the case; there has been a total breakdown of the attorney-client relationship and the client refuses to cooperate with the attorney; the client engages in conduct tending to degrade or humiliate the attorney or surreptitiously involves him in improper conduct such as subornation of perjury; the client insists upon a frivolous appeal; the attorney is unable to locate the client; and the client insists upon engaging associate counsel against whom the attorney has strong personal or professional objections.

On the other hand, grounds stated to be insufficient for withdrawal have included the client's refusal to consent to an increase in fee or to pay a fee arising from other, unrelated proceedings. In addition, EC 2–29 provides that when an attorney is appointed by the court, the "repugnance of the subject matter of the proceeding, the identity of a person involved in the case, the belief of the lawyer that the defendant in a criminal proceeding is guilty, or the belief of the lawyer regarding the merits of the civil case" do not constitute sufficient cause for withdrawal. Also, an attorney may not use the excuse that he does not customarily handle criminal cases in order to withdraw from a criminal case to which he has been appointed. RPC 6.2, on the other hand, permits the attorney to seek to avoid appointment if the client's objective is so repugnant to the lawyer as to impair the client-lawyer relationship or his ability to represent the client.

On some issues there appears to be a split of authority regarding good cause. While the majority of cases holds that refusal to settle (contrary to the attorney's advice) can never in itself be a sufficient basis to withdraw, at least one federal jurisdiction would allow such a course of action. When refusal to settle is an indication that the attorney-client relationship has totally broken down, however, withdrawal would usually be permitted.

Two primary factors are considered, at least by some courts, when a motion to withdraw is filed. The first is whether or not any conflict between client and attorney would be likely to recur with new counsel. If the problem is likely to be repeated, then it is questionable whether the attorney may properly withdraw, leaving the problem on another's doorstep. For example, if a client is merely obnoxious or argumentative, cooperation between the client and *any* attorney might be difficult. He still deserves his day in court, however, and an endless series of substituted counsel would serve no legitimate purpose. The second factor is whether the attorney is representing a client in a civil, criminal or court-appointed case: The attorney's ability to withdraw decreases respectively.

C. CONSEQUENCES OF IMPROPER WITHDRAWAL

An attorney who improperly withdraws from a case exposes herself to liability for the resulting neglect of the case and may lose the right to compensation for her services. Likewise, an attorney who does not withdraw from a case when she is required to do so by a DR, RPC, or the law of a given jurisdiction, is subject to disciplinary action.

D. PROCEDURE FOR WITHDRAWAL

1. Court Permission

Most jurisdictions require court permission for withdrawal, even in civil cases, if the court has jurisdiction over the case. DR 2–110(A)(1); cf. RPC Rule 1.16(c) (lawyer must continue representation when ordered to do so by tribunal). Therefore, a lawyer may not be allowed to withdraw even if professional rules seem to indicate his withdrawal is mandatory. "Mandatory" withdrawal means only that the lawyer must seek to withdraw, while "permissive" withdrawal means that the lawyer may seek to withdraw, but is not required to do so. Neither term indicates that the lawyer necessarily will be permitted to do so by the court. (Presumably, if withdrawal is neither mandatory nor permissive, the lawyer may not even seek to withdraw.)

For example, DR 2–110(B)(4) requires withdrawal after a client has discharged her lawyer. However, the court in Ohntrup v. Firearms Center, Inc. (3d Cir.1986) held that, because the trial court had not granted its permission, and such permission was required for withdrawal, the lawyer was required to remain in the case. The court rejected the argument that the lawyer would be forced into the unethical position of representing a client after discharge. But see Commonwealth v. Scheps (Pa.Super.1987) (court must grant motion for mandatory withdrawal after discharge).

Even when a lawyer is required to seek withdrawal due to his client's perjury, the court may deny his motion and force him to maintain representation. In Rubin v. State (Fla.App.1986), rev. denied (Fla.1986), cert. denied, (1987), attorney Ellis Rubin discovered that his client intended to lie on the stand. Rubin therefore moved to withdraw, as required by the CPR. See DR 2–110(B)(2) (mandatory withdrawal when representation will result in violation of Disciplinary Rule); DR 7–102(A) (lawyer must not present perjured testimony). The trial court denied his motion, stating that Rubin could meet his ethical responsibilities by adopting the passive approach suggested in *Lowery,* supra. After the court of appeals affirmed this ruling, Rubin still refused to continue in the case. The trial court cited him for contempt, and the court of appeals affirmed Rubin's jail sentence. Subsequently, Rubin was publicly reprimanded by the Florida Supreme Court for his "deliberate defiance of judicial authority," despite the court's disagreement with the passive procedure outlined by the trial court. Florida Bar v. Rubin (1989).

2. Protecting the Client's Interests

Not only must an attorney have good cause before she may withdraw, but she must also take certain steps to insure that the client is not prejudiced by the withdrawal. RPC 1.16(c) and (d) and DR 2–110(A) require that reasonable notice be given to the client, allowing ample time to employ substitute counsel; that the attorney deliver to the client all papers and property to which the client is entitled; that she refund to the client all fees paid in advance that have not been earned; and that if the particular tribunal requires leave of court (which is the general rule), it must first be obtained. Ethical Consideration 2–32 adds that an attorney should suggest substitute counsel and cooperate with counsel subsequently employed. RPC 1.16 requires only that the lawyer take reasonably practical steps necessary to protect the client's interests, including "allowing time for employment of other counsel."

An attorney's withdrawal that prejudiced the client has been held to constitute reversible error. For example, in Summers v. Thompson (M.D.Tenn.1977), it was held that an attorney's failure to give proper notice of his withdrawal to the accused in a criminal proceeding deprived the defendant of his constitutional right to effective assistance of counsel. It has also been held that, in order to prevent prejudice, an attorney intending to withdraw after trial but before appeal must first file a notice of appeal in order to preserve the client's rights.

III. CONCLUSION

The above discussion indicates that an attorney is clearly justified in withdrawing from certain cases. Such instances include those specifically delineated in RPC 1.16 or DR 2–110, or those mandated or approved in a particular jurisdiction. In other situations, such as that of the perjuring client, further judicial development is necessary before an attorney can conclusively determine whether withdrawal is either justified or required, i.e., whether circumstances constituting "other good cause" exist.

PART IV

THE LAWYER IN THE LEGAL SYSTEM: FUNCTIONS AND RESPONSIBILITIES

CHAPTER 16

THE LAWYER AS AN ADVOCATE: THE ADVERSARY SYSTEM

I. JUSTICE AND THE ADVERSARY SYSTEM

To appreciate the lawyer's responsibilities as an advocate, one must first understand the nature of the system in which the lawyer operates. The adversary system is probably the most criticized and least understood institution of the law.

The primary purpose of the adversary system is to resolve disputes in accordance with justice. Each element, dispute settlement and justice, is essential to its purpose and provides the basis for the involvement of lawyers.

Disputes can be settled by flipping a coin or by other arbitrary means but these lack justice—and do not require law trained personnel. Numerous agencies, governmental, religious, charitable, and others, may conceive of their functions as including the dispensing of justice, while judicial tribunals attempt to do so only incidentally to deciding real controversies, and lawyers play key roles in this process.

The adversary system of adjudication evolved from more primitive systems of settling disputes, such as trial by battle and ordeal and oath-swearing, which presumed to invoke the power of the Almighty on behalf of the litigant whose cause was just. Our present system of trial by jury or judge assumes that a process which is just will yield a just result. In other words, at least in the long run, adherence to good means will produce good ends. This assumption, and the resultant paramount concern with process, provide the key to the understanding of the adversary system and the lawyers' role therein.

What, then, are elements of a just process, i.e., a process likely to settle disputes in accordance with justice? Of central, but not total, concern is that the process should be calculated to determine the truth. Accuracy should be sought in findings of fact and conclusions of law.

In the adversary system this is accomplished by having each side, with the aid of persons skilled in the law, develop and present its interpretations and contentions concerning the relevant facts and law to an impartial decision-maker. We know that two half-truths do not necessarily equal the whole truth, yet, while this system of judging partisan advocacy may (as Churchill suggested of democracy) be itself defective, it seems better than all other known methods of adjudication.

Not everyone, of course, agrees with this conclusion, and critics abound who would modify the system by mitigating the degree of partisan advocacy and placing a greater emphasis on "truth" seeking, or abolish it entirely in favor of a "scientific inquiry into the truth." But can there really be any such thing when we are trying to reconstruct past events and determine their legal impact by rules of policy for settling the instant and, perhaps, future disputes? Unlike the physical scientist who seeks to test hypotheses by laboratory control of influencing factors, the "legal scientist" cannot experimentally replicate prior facts or test the impact of future application of rules of law. These are questions of judgment. Indeed, it has been observed that scientific inquiries seek to resolve "cognitive" conflicts where resolution based on a neutral, verifiable standard serves the interest of all concerned parties, and thus, "truth" is the appropriate and often obtainable objective. Where, however, the conflict is a distributive one, in that any outcome which will serve the interests of one party will adversely affect those of the other party—as in the typical legal dispute—there can be no objectively correct solution, and the end sought must be "justice". Resolution of subsidiary cognitive conflicts in accord with the truth may contribute to the achievement of justice but cannot substitute for, nor dictate, the exercise of judgment in reaching the result. See Thibaut & Walker (1978).

Moreover, if a judge were to be responsible for searching out the law and facts, marshaling them by weight and relevance, as well as determining their ultimate accuracy and significance, it is likely that he could not perform the first and second of these tasks as well as a partisan advocate, and the judge's neutral performance of the third would no doubt be compromised by his involvement in the earlier functions. The controversy surrounding the Warren Commission's report on the shooting of President Kennedy may have been prompted in part by the lack of adversary proceedings, despite the acknowledged integrity of its members and the extent of their investigation.

In the adversary system, differing functions are identified and delegated to different personnel. Thus, legal research and factual investigation are performed by partisans with the incentive for thoroughness. The fruits of their search are presented as persuasively as possible to a neutral arbiter who can critically evaluate each presentation and argument with the aid of a counter-presentation and argument. The advocates also anticipate that their contentions may be rejected, and they are prepared to absorb that possible disappointment. Whereas an "impartial investigator" without the aid of adversary proceedings may find it difficult to fairly weigh testimony and theories contrary to a preliminary hypothesis developed upon incomplete evidence. "An adversary presentation counters the natural human tendency to judge too swiftly in terms of the familiar that which is not yet fully known . . . ." CPR EC 7–19.

It is for these reasons that the highly regarded Joint Statement on Professional Responsibility concludes that the adversary system is not a regrettable necessity or "concession to the frailties of human nature, but an expression of human insight in the design of a social framework within which man's capacity for impartial judgment can attain its fullest realization."

It should be noted, however, that occasional departures from and limitations upon the adversary nature of our system of adjudication have been made. Since the ultimate goal is a just decision, experience may demonstrate that the process can be improved by some legal limits on partisanship and selected requirements of cooperation rather than competition.

It is important to recognize that while determination of the truth is a basic element of justice, it is possible to have a just process for settling a dispute without having learned the precise and complete truth. A post-event inquiry can rarely, if ever, reconstruct the whole truth and nothing but the truth. There are inevitable distortions in the perceptions, memories, and communications of witnesses and advocates, as well as in the ability of judges and juries to accurately hear, understand and recall what has been presented in court. More importantly, a just process for settling disputes serves purposes in addition to ascertainment of the truth.

In the United States, our Constitution and our tradition of respecting the dignity of individuals and their important relationships have sometimes resulted in the exclusion of evidence that would clearly aid the accuracy of judicial inquiry. We extend an absolute right to a defendant in a criminal case to refuse to testify or give a pre-trial statement even though he or she may have more knowledge about the case than any other person. Likewise, we exclude evidence seized in violation of the Fourth Amendment and incriminating statements made in the absence of *Miranda* warnings, regardless of the accuracy and reliability of such evidence. And in civil as well as criminal cases, confidential communications with attorneys, spouses, and sometimes others are lawfully kept from the judge and jury even though they could further the finding of the facts. Sensitivity to human dignity, freedom, autonomy, and relationships, as embodied in our Constitution and other laws, is thus an element of a just process.

Parenthetically, it should be noted that the adjudication systems of other countries which exhibit less respect for the individual may subordinate the finding of the truth to other values such as the primacy of the state or the indoctrination of its subjects. Thus, in the Soviet Union, China and Cuba, lawyers' functions and responsibilities have differed significantly from those of advocates in the United States.

Closely related to our concern for the individual is the concept that our process of adjudication should be calculated to satisfy potential litigants. If those persons who may be called before a court or seek redress therein, and that potentially includes everyone, anticipate that they will receive a fair trial, litigants will be more likely to willingly submit themselves to the process and to accept the result of it. The public acceptance of court decisions and orders is essential to the survival of the rule of law. Our legal system would soon collapse if the National Guard or federal troops had to be called out to enforce all, or even a sizeable number of, court judgments.

We cannot expect that every litigant will express satisfaction with the result in each case (philosophical losers are probably the exception), but they should be able to acknowledge that the process of decision was fair, and that it justifies the confidence of potential litigants in general.

One principal way in which this is done is to provide for the participation of the parties in the process. All parties have an opportunity, personally or through a qualified legal representative, to present their case, hear and challenge that of the other party, and in a criminal case, confront their accusers.

A further sense of vicarious participation is provided by the availability of a right to a jury of the party's peers, although practical considerations limit the extent to which a jury can be truly representative.

Another element of justice found in the adversary system is that the decision-maker, whether judge or jury, be impartial. No system of adjudication can be expected to find the truth, satisfy the parties, or otherwise fairly operate if the decision-maker is subject to bias, prejudice, improper influence, or bribes.

There is also a requirement that decisions be made in accordance with general rules. These rules, procedural and substantive, need to be available to potential litigants. If not pre-existing, they can be molded or created in conformance with known general principles to apply to the instant case and others like it. In this way, some degree of consistency and predictability can be achieved and equals treated equally.

Decisions must also be reasoned and not arbitrary or the product of an emotional reaction. To warrant the parties' acceptance, a decision ought to be responsive to their presentations.

It should be emphasized that we are not dealing with justice in the abstract but in the context of settling real disputes between real people. As illustrated by the legal doctrine of *res adjudicata,* it is sometimes more important that a matter be settled than that it be settled right. Chief Justice Warren popularized the slogan that "Justice delayed is justice denied." Thus, efficiency in decision-making is a goal of our system, although other values are often given precedence so long as at some reasonable point there is a final determination of the dispute.

There are undoubtedly other elements of justice, perhaps found in the adversary system of adjudication, perhaps not. Philosophers have written much on the concept of justice without achieving a uniform definition. The modest purpose of these introductory observations has been to identify certain elements of a just process of decision-making which provide the foundation for particular responsibilities of those persons operating within the system.

II. LAWYERS' ROLES IN THE ADVERSARY SYSTEM

In most cases, justice in decision-making becomes meaningful only when each party has the aid of a person knowledgeable in law, familiar with court procedures, and articulate and loyal in advocacy. In short, a lawyer. Litigants are not equal. Parties who come before a court vary in resources, education, ability to communicate, and experience and familiarity with decision-making procedures and personnel.

Of course, lawyers also differ in knowledge and talent, but if the licensing system is sound, a client ought to be assured of an advocate who at least meets minimum standards of competence and is able to function within the system more effectively than the client could do alone. While persons of wealth, large corporations, and governments may employ more able counsel than the poor and uneducated, the adversary system will function properly only if each party is represented by a person who is familiar with the substantive and procedural law, skillful in communication, and loyal and zealous on behalf of the client. Because of its importance to the accomplishment of justice, the effective assistance of legal counsel is recognized as a constitutional right of most criminal defendants and of accused persons in some quasi-criminal situations. While civil litigants also are entitled to be served by retained counsel of their choice, those unable to afford the legal fees may have to depend upon legal aid services or the benevolence and professional attitude of individual lawyers.

The elements of justice—approximation of the truth, respect for human dignity, satisfaction of potential litigants, and party participation in the process of decision-making—can be effectuated only if each litigant is able to call upon a loyal and knowledgeable legal representative to zealously discover the facts, research the law, convincingly present the case to an impartial decision-maker, stand ready to rebut the presentation of adversaries, and safeguard the constitutional and other legal rights of the client. These rights include protection against a biased or prejudiced decision-maker or against a decision which is arbitrary, the product of undue emotion rather than reason, or not in accordance with general rules equally applied. This is not merely a negative responsibility; the lawyer is expected to make positive contributions to a reasoned decision in accordance with valid general principles and good public policy through accurate and complete research and effective advocacy.

Thus viewed, partisan, competent, and lawful representation not only aids the client but, by promoting wise and informed decisions, aids the court and the development of the law.

A first and continuing obligation of a lawyer, then, is to be competent. External evaluation of compliance with standards has been extensive prior to admission to practice but is only beginning to be recognized as a post-admission requirement. (See Chapter 6).

Of equal importance in our adversary system is that counsel be loyal to the client. "The duty of a lawyer, both to his client and to the legal system is to represent his client zealously within the bounds of the law . . ." CPR EC 7–1. Note that this partisanship does not arise from any retainer paid by the client to the lawyer, but is imposed upon the lawyer by the legal system, regardless of the presence or absence of financial remuneration. There is no basic conflict between the duty of a lawyer to the client and to the court. In the adversary system, loyalty and zealousness in representation of the client is the primary duty of the lawyer as an officer of the court.

Since our process seeks accurate as well as full discovery of the facts and law, it is necessary that an advocate's loyalty and zeal be qualified by an obligation of honesty and avoidance of fraudulent or obstructive conduct. The law may also modify the partisan role of the advocate where experience indicates that justice can be achieved better by a departure from a strictly adversarial process. For example, a prosecuting attorney has a duty to protect the innocent as well as to seek conviction of the guilty, and all counsel may have to comply with specific pre-trial discovery and disclosure requirements.

The possession by lawyers of minimum standards of competence and integrity is vital for the protection of the interests of the court as well as those of the clients. In order to dispatch its business efficiently and fairly, the court must rely on legal counsel to make accurate, thorough and orderly presentations. To the extent an advocate distorts, misleads, confuses, disrupts or unduly delays the court, the process of decision-making and, ultimately, justice is frustrated, and the lawyer has failed to fulfill his professional responsibilities within the adversary system.

The elements of just decision-making may also be characterized as aspects of "due process," that constitutional guarantee of fundamental fairness and rationality in the application of the law. Lawyers—as members of the constitutional conventions and legislative bodies, as judges, and as advocates—have played a major role in fashioning the due process of law, are largely responsible for operating it, and are its primary guardians. The responsibilities of the lawyer in the adversary system do not begin and end with serving clients. They include an obligation to safeguard and improve the institutions of the law and its processes.

In the words of the Joint Statement on Professional Responsibility, the "lawyer's highest loyalty . . . runs, not to persons, but to procedures and institutions. . . . It is chiefly for the lawyer that the term 'due process' takes on tangible meaning. . . . For the lawyer the insidious dangers contained in the notion that 'the end justifies the means' is not a matter of abstract philosophical conviction, but of direct professional experience." The Statement notes that lawyers have a duty to educate the public about the dangers of non-adherence to due process of law, and that their role imposes "a trusteeship for the integrity of those fundamental processes of government and self-government upon which the successful functioning of our society depends."

III. SPECIFIC OBLIGATIONS OF THE ADVOCATE

The general standard for the advocate, according to the Code of Professional Responsibility, is that "a lawyer should represent a client zealously within the bounds of the law" Canon 7. Interestingly, the Model Rules do not contain a black-letter obligation of zealous representation, but in the Comments to the duty to act with reasonable diligence (Rule 3), it is stated that a lawyer "should act with commitment and dedication to the interests of the client and with zeal in advocacy upon the client's behalf." A concept clearly rejected by both the Code and the Rules is that the duty of a lawyer is to do everything that will help the client "win" or for a defense counsel to do anything to "get the client off". As the Comments to Rule 3 recognize, "a lawyer is not bound to press for every advantage that might be realized for a client" but "may take whatever lawful and ethical measures are required to vindicate a client's cause. . . ."

Accordingly, for the adversary system to function properly, and for the lawyer to be worthy of the trust imposed by the system, the advocate must temper zeal with lawfulness. Nevertheless, significant and difficult questions may arise in determining whether or not particular conduct by a lawyer which appears to benefit the client is within or beyond the bounds of the law.

It is recognized that the law governing attorneys' conduct encompasses not only criminal and civil law but rules of court and professional regulations, including the Model Rules and the Disciplinary Rules of the CPR to the extent they are adopted by individual jurisdictions. In some cases, as in pre-trial discovery obligations, these rules and regulations attenuate the adversary role of counsel. In other situations, counsel is given discretion to exercise professional judgment. Clear limits placed upon the partisanship of the advocate must be adhered to, regardless of what may be considered to be the best interests of the client. But in the absence of client consent or specific legal or ethical restrictions, the advocate is obligated to pursue the objectives of the client. In general terms, the merits of a client's cause or ends sought by the client should not be sacrificed by counsel, but there is room for professional discretion regarding the means used to pursue such objectives. RPC 1.2(a); CPR DR 7–101(A)(1), EC 7–7. In each situation, the lawyer should consult with the client, but must abide by the client's decision as to whether to accept an offer of settlement, or, in a criminal case, whether to plead guilty or innocent, waive a jury, or testify.

While the exercise of moral judgment by an attorney is permitted (and, indeed, encouraged) when counseling a client, once a lawyer accepts the role of advocate before a legal tribunal, it has been contended that the lawyer's personal concepts of morality should not be allowed to inhibit the range of services which the client is entitled to under the law. This does not mean that the lawyer should engage in abusive tactics, ignore local customs and professional courtesies, or fail to exercise a personal judgment on matters not affecting the merits of a client's cause. But if the lawyer's own scruples will prejudice the legal rights of the client, the lawyer must forego the former in favor of the latter, or, where permissible, decline to accept or withdraw from the representation of the client. (See Chapters 8 and 15).

While the law is clearly a limit on a lawyer's advocacy, it is not always clear what are the limits of the law. Moreover, there are occasions where lawful obligations of the lawyer conflict.

A. PREPARATION FOR TRIAL

In preparing a matter for trial, as with other functions, a lawyer must exercise reasonable care and competence. Clients and courts depend upon the attorney to thoroughly research the law, investigate the facts, interview witnesses, and timely file all appropriate pleadings. Neglect of a legal matter entrusted to a lawyer is unethical as well as an element of legal malpractice. Trial lawyers are often busy and may underestimate the time necessary to prepare and try a case, which may lead them to accept a heavier caseload than they can adequately handle. An attorney should not make a trial or other commitment unless he intends to keep it or arrange for substitute counsel.

While delay and neglect in the preparation of a matter are problems that have become too common, some attorneys err in the other direction by becoming overly zealous or partisan in preparing a case. Abuse of discovery has become an especially noisome problem, adding to the cost, delay, and unpleasantness of resort to litigation. In addition to sanctions imposed by courts for such tactics, the Model Rules expressly prohibit a lawyer from making a frivolous discovery request or failing to make a reasonably diligent effort to comply with a proper request by an opposing party. RPC 3.4(d). The following materials examine some of the other more common situations raising questions of this nature.

1. Preparing a Witness for Trial

As a general rule of good trial practice, a witness should not be put on the stand unless the attorney has first had an opportunity to interview the individual. Knowledge, memory, sincerity, demeanor, and skills of expression should all be probed and observed beforehand to avoid unpleasant surprises at trial, to minimize testimonial weaknesses, and, if there is a realistic choice, to determine whether or not to use a particular witness. These are legitimate tactics and essential to adequate trial preparation. But it is not proper to prepare a witness by putting words in his mouth or by inducing him to commit perjury.

The line between unethical coaching and proper preparation is not a bright one. Drawing of the line can be especially delicate in preparing a client for the witness stand. To what extent may a lawyer educate the client about the law when the lawyer knows that the client may be tempted to alter his story to gain a legal advantage? In the famous "Anatomy of a Murder" situation, a client confesses to his lawyer that he has killed another person. If the client explains how the homicide occurred, may the lawyer advise him, "If that's really the way it happened, you may be guilty of first degree murder, but if events transpired to cause you to kill in self-defense, or in the heat of passion, you may get off entirely or only be guilty of a lesser crime. Now think about it and let me know how it really happened and whether there are other facts that I should know about." Has the lawyer sought to suborn perjury or only to make the client realize the consequences of what he has said and to be sure his recitation of the facts was accurate and complete? While slight changes in the words used, inflections, tone of voice, and facial expressions could alter the apparent intent of the lawyer's advice, on its face, this situation seems to indicate that the lawyer has unethically participated in the creation of evidence which he knows is false.

This result is less clear when the lawyer lectures the client about the law of homicide and its different degrees and consequences *before* the client has told his story. Similar problems arise in civil cases when, for example, a client has been in an automobile accident and the lawyer summarizes the law of negligence and contributory negligence before the client explains how the accident happened. An asserted justification for such attorney conduct is that the lawyer's function is to remove or reduce any disadvantage that the client may suffer because of his relative lack of knowledge about the law. Thus, if a client could go to a law library and look it up (assuming three years of attending law school classes are largely irrelevant), why can not the lawyer similarly educate the client? This "I am a law book" approach bears too much resemblance to "I am a gun (or mouthpiece) for hire," and ignores any element of professional judgment or social obligation.

Professor Monroe Freedman considered the "Anatomy of a Murder" situation one of the three hardest questions in the practice of criminal defense law. He initially approved of the lawyer's educating the client as to the relevant law and consequences of his recited actions. Influential to Freedman was the then practice of respectable estate planning lawyers who advised clients, desiring to reduce their taxable estates by making gifts in their elderly years, to create evidence of their expectation to live for many years to come. Thus, booking passage for a cruise in three years, writing letters to relatives and friends of an intention to visit in four years, or, perhaps, taking a five-year subscription to Playboy, would tend to negate the conclusion that the gifts were made in contemplation of death. Professor Freedman could see no reason why lawyers should be permitted to advise affluent clients to construct evidence to create a legal advantage while denying a similar opportunity to a less fortunate criminally accused person. Subsequently, Freedman reconsidered his conclusion but not his reasoning. He concluded that it would be unethical for both the estate lawyer and the criminal defense lawyer to suggest that the client create false evidence. M. Freedman (1966), (1975); see (1990).

This latter position is sound, but note that the lawyer's conduct is improper only if the advice or information on the applicable law is given under circumstances that show the lawyer intended or anticipated that the client would create a story or situation which the client knew was contrary to the facts. In other words, it is permissible, and strongly advisable, for the lawyer, in light of the applicable law, to methodically probe the client's memory, make sure important points are not overlooked, help the client to organize, effectively verbalize and tailor his anticipated testimony to relevant facts helpful to his cause, and even rehearse the testimony and probable cross-examination. The ethical line is crossed, however, if the lawyer counsels or assists a witness to testify falsely, or participates in the creation of evidence which the lawyer knows is false. RPC 3.4(b), CPR DR 7–102(A)(6).

2. Communication With Adverse Witnesses

Adequate preparation for trial includes interviewing, whenever possible, the witnesses against your client as well as those in support of your case. This becomes a particularly sensitive matter when a lawyer seeks to interview an adverse party. If that party is represented by counsel, the opposing lawyer may not communicate with the party on the subject matter of the case without the prior consent of the attorney representing the party, or if authorized by law to communicate directly as may be the case with a public official. RPC 4.2; CPR DR 7–104(A)(1). In this manner, each attorney is permitted to represent her client without interference from the opposing attorney. A lawyer may not circumvent this proscription by causing another person, such as the client or an investigator, to engage in unconsented-to communications or to carry offers of settlement undisclosed to the opposing counsel.

Where the adverse party is a corporation it is less clear as to which of its employees may be considered as represented by the corporation's counsel for purposes of requiring that attorney's consent to their interview by opposing counsel. Earlier authorities had held that only high level managerial employees, or the corporate control group, qualified for the protection of the rule. But in 1981, the Supreme Court expanded the privilege of non-disclosure to communications to the corporate attorney from any employee concerning matters within the scope of the employee's duties. *Upjohn Co. v. United States* [See Chapter 11, Confidentiality]. Since that time, a number of jurisdictions have similarly expanded the scope of the corporate party, represented by counsel, to include employees, not within the control group, whose statements regarding the scope of their duties could legally bind their corporate employer. See e.g., RPC 4.2 Comment; California Rules of Professional Conduct 2–100(B). While some jurisdictions continue to adhere to the managerial control group approach, others—in order to provide a bright-line test—preclude an attorney from interviewing, without counsel's consent, any corporate employee concerning a matter in which the corporation or the employee is known to be represented by counsel.

Although the rules do not expressly exempt interviews by prosecutors, or their investigators, of potential criminal defendants known to be legally represented, the current Attorney General of the United States maintains that the Supremacy of federal law entitles U.S. Attorneys to conduct investigations (including undercover ones) of such persons without seeking consent of their counsel. There is some case authority to support the position that compliance with Model Rule 4.2, or its equivalent, would frustrate normal law enforcement investigations, but the ABA maintains that no such exemption from the rule should be recognized.

The rules against a lawyer communicating with a party regarding a matter in which the lawyer knows the party is represented, without consent of such counsel, do not appear to require that the represented party be adverse to the lawyer's client although the CPR Disciplinary Rule is titled "Communicating with One of Adverse Interest". DR 7–104. Nor are the rules' applications limited to communication initiated by the lawyer. California, however, adds a useful exemption for communications from parties seeking a second opinion or to change lawyers [CAL RPC 2–100(C)(2)], but it also expressly prohibits solicitations for paid professional employment, by any means, to a person known to be represented by another lawyer in the matter. CAL RPC 1–400(b).

In preparing a case for trial, a conscientious attorney will want to interview, or upon proper demand and notice, take the deposition of adverse witnesses, as well as parties. In a deposition, the lawyer for the adverse party will be given notice and an opportunity to be present. To interview an adverse witness, however, an attorney normally is not required to obtain the consent of opposing counsel, but the attorney should identify herself as the lawyer for the other party and inform the witness of the reason for the interview. In the case of sensitive witnesses, such as complainants in criminal cases, treating physicians, and others who may possess privileged information, common courtesy—and advisory ethical opinions in some jurisdictions—require that notice be given to opposing counsel of an intention to interview such witnesses. Upon receipt of such notice, counsel cannot request the witness to refrain from voluntarily giving relevant information to the other party (unless the witness is a relative, employee or agent of the client) [RPC 3.4(f)], nor advise the witness to secrete himself or leave the jurisdiction. CPR DR 7–109(B). But the lawyer for the party for whom the witness is expected to testify will want to consult with the witness to safeguard against possible abusive questions. Without protective consultation, an unrestricted interview of a treating physician, for example, could result in disclosure of privileged information, which had not been authorized by the patient, who is the person with authority to waive the privilege.

When a client's adversary is not represented by counsel, it usually will be necessary for the lawyer to communicate directly with the adverse party. In this situation, the lawyer should not offer any advice, other than the advisability of securing legal representation [CPR DR 7–104(A)(2); RPC 4.3 Comment], and the lawyer should not state or imply that she is disinterested. If the unrepresented person appears to misunderstand the lawyer's role, she should make reasonable efforts to correct the misunderstanding. RPC 4.3.

In their zeal to serve their clients, lawyers sometimes threaten to institute criminal charges against another party solely to obtain an advantage in a civil matter. Under the Code, this is considered unethical because the criminal process, which is designed to protect the interests of society as a whole, is abused when attorneys seek to use it to coerce settlement of a dispute between private parties. DR 7-105; EC 7-21. This proscription was not carried over into the Model Rules, although it has been retained by a number of states which have adopted other aspects of the Model Rules. (See Chapter 19, Lawyer As Advisor and Negotiator).

B. ACCEPTANCE OF "QUESTIONABLE CASES"; THE "GUILTY" CLIENT

While a lawyer has considerable latitude in determining whether or not to accept offered employment, there are limits upon his or her discretion. The employment must be for a lawful purpose. Thus, the ABA Committee has ruled that it would be improper to accept a retainer from individuals engaged in illegal conduct to defend them in the event they were caught. More clearly, the lawyer may not aid them in their illegal activities or in their attempts to avoid discovery. See Comments to Model Rule 1.2, which also state that the use of a lawyer's advice in a client's course of action that is criminal or fraudulent does not, by itself, make the lawyer a party to such action, but the lawyer may not knowingly assist a client in criminal or fraudulent conduct. If a lawyer learns that a client is engaged in illegal conduct, the lawyer cannot further such conduct, and may have to withdraw, but "[t]here is a critical distinction between presenting an analysis of legal aspects of questionable conduct and recommending the means by which a crime or fraud might be committed with impunity." Nevertheless, once a crime has been committed, the lawyer may accept the case even though the client admits his guilt or the lawyer learns of it from other sources.

The permissible representation of a "guilty" client has been justified on several grounds. There are many instances in which a person appears to be guilty but is later found to be innocent. In a few cases, unfortunately, the freedom from guilt has not been discovered until after conviction or even execution of the accused person. Such cases, rare as they may be, are used to support arguments against the death penalty and in favor of extensive appellate and collateral review of criminal convictions, and they help give rise to an assortment of procedural safeguards at the trial level. Our values are thus embodied in the characterization of our legal system as permitting a hundred guilty men to go free rather than to convict one who is innocent.

Even voluntary confessions are not totally reliable. Due to psychological problems, desire for publicity, protection of others, or even mistake, people have been known to confess to crimes which they did not commit. False confessions are not uncommon after the discovery of a spectacular crime. Moreover, a person may have in fact committed what he or she believes to be a criminal act but be unaware of an existing legal defense or mitigation. Thus, a homicide may be classified as first degree murder, manslaughter, or justifiable, depending upon the circumstances of its commission.

While these are practical reasons for affording an apparently guilty person legal counsel, the underlying justification is broader and safeguards the rights of even those persons who are in fact guilty. As our legal system has developed, a high value has been placed on respecting the dignity of individuals and maintaining the integrity of the state and the procedures by which society condemns its erring members. Consequently, no person is deemed legally guilty of a crime unless he or she has been so found by a judge or jury in accordance with the due processes of law, which include the right of an accused person to remain silent and be presumed innocent, subject to the ability of the prosecution to prove guilt beyond a reasonable doubt. The right to counsel is not only among the safeguards afforded a criminal defendant but is often a prerequisite to the utility of other rights. Therefore, the constitutional presumption of innocence, the right of all persons to a fair trial, and the concept of due process in general, would be rendered meaningless if lawyers were not permitted to accept representation of apparently guilty persons.

Nor is there any ethical impropriety in pleading such a client "not guilty." This plea does not assert the fact of innocence but simply allocates the burden of proof. It invokes the defendant's right to have the state attempt to prove his guilt beyond any reasonable doubt of the judge or jury. As stated in Model Rule 3.1, even though a lawyer may not bring or defend a proceeding on a frivolous basis, a criminal defense counsel "may nevertheless so defend . . . as to require that every element of the case be established."

For many lawyers, the motivation to protect the innocent is not the primary reason for their defense of the apparently guilty or unpopular client. Rather, their overriding concern is with the system itself, with maintaining due process of law and the right to a fair trial for all. For other lawyers, this safeguarding of means is not enough, and they want to believe in the cause of their clients. While this is not a requirement for acceptance of cases, neither is it prohibited as a basis for rejecting them. Subject to limitations regarding appointments to represent indigents, a lawyer may refuse to accept as clients those whose causes he does not endorse. See CPR EC 2–26, 2–29, 2–30; RPC 1.2(b); (Chapter 8, The Duty to Represent Indigent and Unpopular Clients). Nevertheless, if a lawyer has a policy against representing clients whom he believes are guilty, he must make that policy known to potential clients. See RPC 1.2(c).

As discussed more fully elsewhere (see Chapter 8), attorneys who are appointed by a court to represent indigent defendants have less discretion in determining whether to accept or maintain the appointment. Permission of the court would be required to reject or withdraw from employment, and the closer the trial date, the greater must be the stated cause for withdrawal. Lawyers are admonished by the Ethical Considerations of the CPR that, in the absence of compelling reasons, they should not decline court or bar association requests to represent a person unable to employ counsel. Compelling reasons do not include repugnance of the subject matter, or of the identity or position of a person involved in the case, or the belief of the lawyer regarding the guilt of a criminal defendant or the merits of a civil case. Unpopularity of a client or cause should not deter the lawyer, but employment should be declined if the intensity of the lawyer's personal feeling, as distinguished from a community attitude, may impair effective representation of the client. Obviously, the line is not easy to draw and would be even harder to police. Appointment or employment of those lawyers who could not render competent or effective service should not be made, but this should not provide a rationalization for avoidance of the profession's obligation to provide counsel for the indigent and unpopular. See EC 2–25 to 2–30. The Model Rules incorporate the duty to not decline appointments by a tribunal, except for good cause, such as that the representation is likely to result in violation of the Rules or other law, but expand the concept of good cause to include that representation of the client is likely to cause an unreasonable financial burden to the lawyer. RPC 6.2. As the Model Rules now make clear, a lawyer's representation of a client, by appointment or retainer, "does not constitute an endorsement of the client's political, economic, social or moral views or activities. RPC 1.2(b).

Once an attorney has accepted representation of a client, he should employ all lawful and reasonable means to seek the client's objectives. However, he may not state in court his belief in the innocence or in the cause of the client, nor may an attorney state a personal opinion of guilt or lack of merit in the opponent's cause. CPR DR 7–106(C)(4); RPC 3.4(e). The attorneys' opinions are irrelevant. Their function is to present the best case for their clients. Should an attorney be permitted to state his personal belief in the innocence of a client or justness of his cause, an inference to the contrary would arise whenever an attorney failed to make such an assertion on behalf of a client, and the right to a fair trial would be imperiled.

While an attorney need not personally believe in a client's case, his evaluation of it is not irrelevant. A lawyer may not present a claim or defense in litigation that is unwarranted under existing law unless a modification, reversal, or extension of that law can be supported by good faith argument. CPR DR 2–109(A)(2), 7–102(A)(2); RPC 3.1. Thus, an attorney need not be deterred by a statute if he can make a good faith argument for its unconstitutionality, nor by a judicial precedent if its bounds are unclear or its holding subject to possible reconsideration in light of more recent decisions, trends elsewhere, or even respectable academic or popular sentiment in favor of its overthrow.

Where the law is not an obstacle but the client's case is weak on the facts, the lawyer may still pursue it unless the purpose is merely to harass or maliciously injure another person. If that is the client's motivation, the attorney may not file a suit, assert a position, conduct a defense, or delay a trial to effect such a purpose. CPR DR 2–109(A)(1), 7–102(A)(1); RPC 3.1. This constraint should make unethical "nuisance claims", sometimes made in malpractice and personal injury cases, without good faith belief in the merits, and filed to harass an insurance company or other party into buying peace through a settlement which may be smaller than the costs of defending.

In those states which retain the fault concept for divorce, an attorney will sometimes file an action on grounds such as extreme cruelty when factual support for the general allegation is weak, at best. Nevertheless, both the husband and wife may favor the divorce, and there is unlikely to be any contest or rebuttal facts. While it is not the lawyer's function to judge his client's cause, in some states it may be considered unethical for a lawyer to file a divorce action when he is convinced that no reasonable argument could be made that the statutory grounds for divorce, as construed by the courts of the state, can be satisfied by the facts of his client's case. Equivocation is necessary on this issue because the practice has become common in many states to simply not inquire into the factual basis of uncontested divorce actions. It is almost like the common counts of ejectment when all parties, including the court, were aware that the established pleadings bore no real relationship to the facts. But such a judicial fiction or professional understanding, in effect, amends the statutory grounds for divorce without compliance with the legislative process.

It is clear that an attorney may not manufacture evidence to support an action or otherwise take part in a fraud upon the court. CPR DR 7–102(A)(6), (B); RPC 1.2(d), 3.1(a), 3.4(b).

In those states with restrictive divorce laws, it is not unusual for the consulted attorney to suggest that the client seek a likely uncontested divorce in another jurisdiction. This is not improper *per se,* but the courts have indicated that the original attorney should not become a party to a fraudulent proceeding elsewhere such as when a knowingly false allegation of residency is made. The Alabama State Bar curtailed a growing divorce mill in that state, a few years ago, by declaring unethical the representation of a divorce client when the Alabama attorney knew or had reasonable cause to believe that neither party was a *bona fide* resident of the State.

C. DELAY

The often lengthy delays in resolving matters through litigation have been the target of public criticism from at least the time of Dickens to the present. Many parties would rather accept an inadequate settlement than endure the uncertainties and hardships of prolonged pre-trial and court proceedings. Since lawyers know this, they and their clients have used delay as a pressure tactic. It has been alleged, for example, that in order to induce the acceptance of a lower settlement than probably could be obtained by continued negotiations or at trial, some insurance companies have delayed settling claims of persons in desperate need of funds. The Code does not expressly condemn the making of a claim or defense for the purpose of delaying the effect of an acknowledged legal right of another, unless it is intended to harass or maliciously injure that person. The Model Rules take a more direct approach to the problem of delay by requiring a lawyer to act with reasonable diligence and promptness in representing a client (Rule 1.3), to make reasonable efforts to expedite litigation consistent with the client's interests (Rule 3.2), to not make frivolous discovery requests and to comply diligently with lawful discovery requests of an opposing party (Rule 3.4(d)), and to not use means that have no substantial purpose other than to embarrass, delay or burden a third person (Rule 4.4). Even more effective are federal and several state court rules of civil procedure which require an attorney to sign pleadings and provide that such signature constitutes a certification that to the best of the attorney's knowledge and belief there is good ground to support the pleading and that it is not interposed for delay. Willful violations of the rule are not only grounds for discipliary action, but are likely to result in significant sanctions against the attorney or her client. (See Chapters 5 and 6).

D. THE LYING CLIENT OR WITNESS

1. The Problem

Another of Monroe Freedman's three hardest questions for the criminal defense attorney is presented when a client tells the attorney that he plans to testify to matters which the attorney knows are untrue. Freedman hypothesizes the following situation. A defendant is falsely accused of a crime, but there is substantial circumstantial evidence indicating his guilt, including testimony by a witness placing the defendant near the scene of the crime at the time it was committed. Although the defendant admits to his attorney that he was in fact at that place at that time, he insists on taking the stand both to falsely contradict that damaging testimony and to truthfully deny his guilt. May the attorney permit him to so testify? Freedman concludes that the attorney should advise the defendant that the false testimony would be unlawful and attempt to persuade him not to testify untruthfully, but if he persists in so testifying, the attorney should proceed in the normal fashion to present the testimony and argue the case to the jury. Freedman's opinion would be the same even if the client admitted his guilt to the attorney, and insisted on testifying to a false alibi. The right to counsel, according to Freedman, can be effective only if the lawyer can learn all that the client knows about the relevant facts without having to reveal the client's confidences. Freedman reaches the uncomfortable conclusion that the attorney should allow the perjured testimony because he finds all other alternatives less satisfactory. M. Freedman (1975), (1990).

2. The Alternatives

The obligations of an attorney faced with the desire of a client to use false testimony, and the ethical alternatives available, may vary somewhat depending upon whether the testimony is to be given by the client, and whether the trial is criminal or civil. The authorities are in agreement that a lawyer should not knowingly offer false evidence, and should seek to dissuade a client from doing so. There is less agreement, however, on how a lawyer should deal with a client, who is a defendant in a criminal case, and who rejects the lawyer's admonition and persists in his desire to testify falsely even after the lawyer informs him that such perjury is unlawful. No alternative course of action in this situation is without legal and practical problems, but, as the following summary exploration indicates, we are moving closer to a professional consensus.

a. Refuse to Call the Intended Perjurer as a Witness

An attorney probably can refuse to call any witness in a civil case and a witness other than the accused in a criminal matter. Tactical considerations, however, militate in favor of having parties testify in most cases. The parties generally have the most first-hand knowledge about the facts of a contested matter, and juries and judges place great weight on their testimony and demeanor. In a criminal trial, despite a defendant's constitutional privilege to remain silent and refuse to take the witness stand, it is suspected that unfavorable inferences may consciously or unconsciously be drawn from a failure of an accused to deny, under oath, evidence of his guilt. In any event, whatever the tactical advantages or disadvantages, the decision as to whether a criminal defendant will testify is ethically for the client to make, after consultation with his lawyer RPC 1.2(a). Moreover, the client probably has a constitutional right to testify despite the objections of his lawyer. The attorney may attempt to limit the client's testimony to matters on which perjury is unlikely, but the criminal defendant-client may refuse to agree to so confine his testimony, or may unexpectedly volunteer perjured testimony on direct or cross-examination, or the judge or jury may find the restricted testimony unconvincing.

b. Withdraw From Representation

Where a client insists on seeking to testify falsely, an attempt to withdraw from the representation is called for. An attorney *may* withdraw if a client seeks to pursue an illegal course of conduct [DR 2–110(C)(1)(b); see RPC 1.16(b)(1)] (and perjury is illegal) and *must* withdraw if continued employment will result in violation of a Disciplinary Rule [DR 2–110(B)(2)] or Rule of Professional Conduct [RPC 1.16(a)(1)]. Since the rules forbid the knowing use of perjury or false evidence, [DR 7–102(A)(4); RPC 3.3(a)(4)] withdrawal is mandatory unless permission is denied by the tribunal before which the case is pending. But this approach creates other difficulties. The court may not permit withdrawal, especially if the trial has started or its commencement is imminent. Even if withdrawal were permitted, it simply would transfer the problem to another attorney from whom the client might withhold important but incriminating information or, conversely, reveal it and cause the same dilemma for the new attorney. If the judge presses the attorney for a reason for the withdrawal request, may the attorney reveal the prospective perjury? Does such a disclosure, even *in camera,* violate the client's confidence and prejudice his right to a fair trial?

The authorities are not consistent on whether an attorney, in attempting to justify a request for withdrawal, may disclose the defendant's intent to commit perjury, particularly when learned through a confidential communication. Such disclosure would not appear to violate the attorney-client privilege because a long-recognized exception to that privilege allows an attorney to reveal a client's announced intention to commit a crime, and perjury is a crime. But the ethical duty of confidentiality is broader. Although the CPR parallels the legal privilege in this regard [DR 4-101(C)(3)], the Model Rules limit the discretion of an attorney to disclose a client's future criminal acts to those "likely to result in imminent death or substantial bodily harm"—a category not including the announced intention of a client to commit perjury. RPC 1.6(b)(1).

Once a trial has commenced, the difficulties of attempts to withdraw by counsel are exacerbated. In a non-jury murder trial, on direct examination, the defendant denied that she shot the victim. Defense counsel then requested a recess, and, in the judges chambers, made a motion to withdraw but said he could not state the reason. The motion was denied, and when the trial resumed, counsel did not ask any further questions of the defendant and made no reference to her questionable testimony in closing argument. The Ninth Circuit held that the defendant's constitutional rights were violated by counsel's request for withdrawal to the judge, who was also the trier of fact, when it was made apparent that the attorney believed his client was testifying falsely. Lowery v. Cardwell (9th Cir.1978).

In jury trial cases, the judicial response has ranged from: permitting defense counsel seeking to withdraw to inform the court, out of the presence of the jury, of the client's intention to commit perjury; to encouraging counsel to just state she has irreconcilable conflicts with her client (which could relate to matters other than client perjury); to holding that disclosures which revealed the client's intended perjury directly or by citation to rules against use of such testimony violated the client's rights. In some cases, it has been suggested that the motion to withdraw be heard by a judge or panel other than the trial judge. Even when a withdrawal motion, unsupported by disclosure of client confidences, is denied by the trial judge, it is desirable to attempt to make a confidential record before another judge in order to protect the attorney in the event subsequent litigation ensues or disciplinary charges are brought against her.

In Matter of Goodwin (S.C.1983), an appointed defense counsel learned during the course of trial that the defendant intended to take the stand and present perjured testimony. When the defendant refused to waive the privilege of confidentiality as to this information, in an *in camera* hearing, counsel supported her motion to withdraw by citation to CPR provision DR 2–110(B)(2), mandating withdrawal when the lawyer's continued employment will result in violation of a Disciplinary Rule and DR 7–102(A), which prohibits, among other things, a lawyer's knowing use of perjured testimony. The trial court denied the motion, and when counsel still refused to go forward with the trial, held her in contempt of court. The State supreme court affirmed, (including the decision not to impose sanctions because of the good faith of counsel and novelty of the issue in South Carolina) and stated: "While an attorney has an ethical duty not to perpetrate a fraud upon the court by knowingly presenting perjured testimony, the defendant has a constitutional right to representation by counsel. . . . Had the trial judge allowed the withdrawal, any new attorney he appointed would, if faced with the same conflict, have moved to withdraw, potentially resulting in a perpetual cycle of eleventh-hour motions to withdraw. Worse, new counsel might fail to recognize the problem and unwittingly present false evidence. . . ." Instead, the court suggested that the counsel should employ the procedure then recommended in the ABA Standards For Criminal Justice Relating to the Defense Function.

c. *ABA Standards Relating to the Administration of Criminal Justice: The Defense Function*

When counsel is required to remain in a criminal case, without resolution of the issue of the client's desire to testify, the attorney may attempt to invoke the narrative testimony procedure of the ABA Defense Function Standards. Based upon the provision of the Code in DR 7–102(A)(4) that: "In his representation of a client, a lawyer shall not . . . knowingly use perjured testimony or false evidence", a compromise was suggested by the original edition of the ABA Standards for Defense Attorneys § 7.7 which allowed the attorney to introduce the defendant to tell his story, but the attorney could not ask other questions to develop it nor make reference to any false testimony in final argument. In this manner, the defendant's right to testify would not be abridged, but neither would his lawyer "use" false testimony. This solution may not be practical, however, because the prosecutor could successfully object to the defendant's narrative testimony, and, even if permitted, the judge or jury might receive the prejudicial impression that the attorney does not support the client's testimony.

The attorney in this situation must tread a thin line in avoiding both "use" of the alleged false testimony and prejudicing the defendant's rights by conveying to the trier of fact her belief that the testimony is false. A variation of the procedure was held to violate due process in a criminal trial when an attorney introduced a witness but fell silent while the defendant took over the questioning to elicit what the attorney believed was false testimony. The court stated that the defendant could represent himself and accept the consequences of his defense, but it was error to allow appointed counsel to continue in the case with only partial control of it. The right of a criminal defendant to counsel did not, according to the court, include a "right to insist that counsel assist him by presenting in evidence testimony which counsel knows, or reasonably believes, constitutes perjury." State v. Robinson (N.C.1976).

The use of the procedure previously recommended in the ABA Defense Function Standards, while generally endorsed by the Court, proved ineffective when invoked by defense counsel in a *non-jury* trial, after normal questioning of the defendant was underway and counsel was surprised by what he believed to be false testimony. Lowery v. Cardwell, supra.

When the ABA revised the Criminal Justice Standards in 1979, it did not include proposed standard 4–7.7 providing for narrative testimony by a criminal defendant believed by defense counsel to be perjurious. Instead, it deferred the question of appropriate defense counsel conduct until the ABA House of Delegates acted upon the Model Rules then being formulated by the Kutak Commission. In 1983, the ABA adopted Model Rule 3.3 which, as indicated in the next section, appears to be inconsistent with the original Defense Function Standard.

Despite good faith efforts by counsel, as in a number of the cases described above, false evidence may nevertheless be introduced at trial. The attorney's obligations when confronted with this situation raise additional considerations which both influence, and are influenced by, the attorney's duty to avoid knowingly introducing such false evidence. The provisions of the ABA Model Rules reflect this interaction.

d. *The Model Rules*

Rule 3.3 provides that a lawyer shall not knowingly offer evidence that the lawyer knows is false and may refuse to offer evidence that she reasonably believes is false. RPC 3.3(a)(4), (c). In addition, the Rule states that if a lawyer comes to know of the falsity of material evidence which she previously offered, "the lawyer shall take reasonable remedial measures" [RPC 3.3(a)(4)], and the lawyer shall not knowingly "fail to disclose a material fact to a tribunal when disclosure is necessary to avoid assisting a criminal or fraudulent act by the client". RPC 3.3(a)(2). The Rule provides that these "duties continue to the conclusion of the proceeding, and apply even if compliance requires disclosure of information otherwise protected by rule 1.6"—the rule providing for the confidentiality of matters relating to the representation of a client. RPC 3.3(b). While not a part of the rule, the comments state that, subject to possible overriding constitutional requirements of criminal defense counsel, an attorney's first response to learning that false evidence has been offered is to confidentially remonstrate with the client, and if that fails, the advocate should seek to withdraw. "If withdrawal will not remedy the situation or is impossible, the advocate should make disclosure to the court."

The ABA Committee on Professional Ethics in Formal Opinion 353 (1987) considered the impact of Model Rule 3.3 on earlier ABA opinions dealing with the introduction of perjured testimony. Opinion 287 (1953) had held that where a client refused to correct prior false statements, whether in a civil or criminal case, the duty of an attorney to keep communications from his client confidential should take precedence over the attorney's obligation of candor to the court or of disclosing a fraud or deception practiced on the court. Opinion 287 had interpreted the old Canons of Professional Ethics, and appeared to be inconsistent with the CPR until DR 7–102(B)(1) was amended in 1974 to provide that a lawyer's duty to reveal an unrectified fraud to the affected person or tribunal does not apply when the information is protected as a privileged communication. DR 7–102(B)(1). A subsequent opinion extended the exception to the disclosure requirement to "secrets" of the client, that is, information, from whatever source, that the client requests to be held inviolate or the disclosure of which would be embarrassing or detrimental to the client. ABA Opinion 341 (1975). As a consequence of this opinion, a lawyer would almost never have to reveal a client's subsequently discovered perjury, but many states, which had adopted the CPR, declined to incorporate the 1974 amendment giving priority to confidentiality over rectifying a fraud on the court.

As Opinion 353 concludes, Model Rule 3.3 reverses that priority and overrules Opinion 287 to the extent it did not require the attorney to correct evidence learned to be false before the conclusion of the proceeding. Thus, on the facts hypothesized in Opinion 287, a lawyer would not have a duty to correct false testimony in a divorce proceeding learned of three months after entry of a final decree, but would have to correct a statement given by a criminal defendant, upon a judge's inquiry relating to sentencing, known by counsel to be false at the time it was made.

ABA Opinion 353 endorsed the comment to Rule 3.3 that disclosure to the court is the only reasonable remedial measure, under 3.3(a)(4), available to an attorney if the client is unwilling to correct the perjury, since "withdrawal can rarely serve as a remedy for the client's perjury." [fn. 7]. Moreover, the Opinion reaches the same conclusion under RPC 3.3(a)(2), requiring disclosure to a tribunal of material facts when necessary to avoid "assisting" a client's criminal or fraudulent act. The Committee notes that perjury is a crime and a fraud, and assistance by an attorney is not limited to the criminal law concepts of aiding, abetting or subornation of perjury, but "is intended to guide the conduct of the lawyer as an officer of the court as a prophylactic measure to protect against client perjury contaminating the judicial process."

Interestingly, the ABA Committee extended its construction of Rule 3.3 to reconsider another controversial Committee opinion. Informal Opinion 1314 (1975) had stated that if a client ignored his lawyer's advice and insisted on giving false testimony, the lawyer should further advise the client that she must either withdraw prior to his false testimony, or report the perjury, if committed, to the tribunal. Opinion 353 endorsed this result—although not the earlier opinion's reasoning—but, on authority of Model Rule 3.3(a)(2) and (4), rejected Opinion 1314's distinction that a lawyer may not disclose a client's perjury, the false nature of which the lawyer did not know in advance but only learned of subsequently due to the client's confidential communication. Opinion 353 concluded that under the Model Rules, a lawyer can not disclose a client's stated intention to commit perjury, but must disclose the perjury—once committed—so long as the lawyer learns of its falsity prior to the conclusion of the proceeding.

Note that, contrary to the CPR's provisions, the ABA Committee now construes the Model Rules to give less protection to a committed crime, perjury, under RPC 3.3, learned of by a subsequent confidential communication of the client, than it does, under Rule 1.6 to an announced intention to commit the same crime learned of when disclosure could still prevent the commission of the crime. This reversal of the usual approach of giving greater confidential protection to a lawyer's knowledge of completed crimes than of future crimes may have come about for two reasons. First, the political processes of the ABA House of Delegates resulted in approval of the Model Rules with less consistency in its provisions than had been contained in the drafts proposed by the Kutak Commission, and, second, the ABA chose to accord greater weight to rectifying frauds on the court than to preventing frauds from being committed against third parties in general.

The Model Rules also can be used to prevent clients, including criminal defendants, from committing frauds on the court by an approach to dissuading client perjury endorsed in Opinion 353, and approved by a majority of the Supreme Court in the important case of Nix v. Whiteside (U.S.1986), which (not coincidentally) adopted arguments made in the amicus brief of the ABA.

e. *Nix v. Whiteside*

In order to support a claim of self-defense to a murder charge the defendant told his appointed defense counsel that he wanted to testify that he saw a gun or "something metallic" in the victim's hand. This was inconsistent with some prior statements of the defendant and other witnesses, and with the physical evidence known to defense counsel. Consequently, counsel told the defendant that such testimony would be perjury to which counsel, as an officer of the court, could not allow him to testify. Moreover, counsel warned the defendant that if he insisted on giving such false testimony, counsel would seek to withdraw, would have a duty to advise the court of the perjury, and would probably be allowed to impeach that testimony. The defendant agreed to go along with his counsel, and testified at the trial but did not mention having seen a gun or something metallic. His conviction for second degree murder was affirmed on appeal, and defendant sought habeas corpus relief in the federal courts on the grounds that he was denied effective assistance of counsel and of his right to present a defense because of his appointed defense counsel's refusal to allow him to testify as he had proposed. Reversing a decision of the Eighth Circuit, the Supreme Court held that the defendant failed to meet the requirements for setting aside a conviction based on ineffective assistance of counsel. Nix v. Whiteside (U.S.1986).

To obtain such relief, the Court has required that the petitioner establish both that his attorney committed a professional practice error, and that the defendant was prejudiced by such error. (See Chapter 6, The Duty to Ensure Competence). The Court unaminously agreed that petitioner had not met his burden in this regard, and that, as a matter of law, he could not be prejudiced by being denied the opportunity to commit perjury since any right to testify in his own defense does not include the right to testify falsely.

Chief Justice Burger, speaking for the Court, went on to discuss "the range of 'reasonable professional' responses to a criminal defendant client who informs counsel that he will perjure himself on the stand." Justice Burger specifically approved of the tactics of defense counsel in this matter, "whether seen as a successful attempt to dissuade his client from committing perjury" or as a threat to withdraw from representation and disclose the illegal scheme. Although Iowa, where the conviction occurred, had adopted a version of the Code of Professional Responsibility, the Chief Justice cited with approval Model Rules 1.2(d), prohibiting a lawyer from counseling a client to engage, or assisting a client, in conduct known to be criminal or fraudulent, and 3.3(a)(4), including the comments thereto that if material false evidence has been offered, its false character should be disclosed. Moreover, Justice Burger commented that the compromise in ABA Standards for Criminal Justice 4.7–7, was inconsistent with the Model Rules which reject "any participation or passive role whatever by counsel in allowing perjury to be presented without challenge." [fn. 6].

According to Justice Brennan, this "essay regarding what constitutes the correct response to a criminal client's suggestion that he will perjure himself is pure discourse without force of law." Thus while Brennan and three other justices concurred in the constitutional ruling that defendant Whiteside was not entitled to have his conviction set aside on the grounds of denial of effective assistance of counsel, they dissented from the Court's attempt to share its vision of ethical conduct on the thorny issue of how a defense attorney ought to act when faced with a client who intends to commit perjury. Brennan notes that lawyers, judges, bar associations, students and others should understand that the problem has not now been "decided".

Justice Brennan's observation finds support in a number of developments and commentaries which indicate that several aspects of the client perjury problem remain to be resolved or may be revisited in more appropriate cases.

Professor Monroe Freedman suggests that defense counsel failed to adequately address issues of the implications of disclosure of client confidences on Fifth Amendment rights of the defendant, of possible distinctions in prohibitions on perjury and witness tampering or bribery of the judge or jury (which the Court equated), and of how certain a lawyer must be that the client will commit perjury before other actions are required. Freedman, Univ. of Penn.L.Rev. (1988).

Freedman and others also fault some of the legal conclusions drawn by Justice Burger especially that virtually all of the sources of authority speak with one voice in approving defense counsel Whiteside's professional behavior in this matter. Professor Carl Auerbach, for example, questions the Court's mis-lumping of the CPR and the Model Rules on whether counsel may or must disclose client perjury (the latter clearly tends more toward disclosure than the former) and the failure of the deciding courts (and their clerks) to carefully examine the Code and case law in Iowa (where the trial took place) which did not support a disclosure obligation in this matter. Auerbach, San Diego L.Rev. (1986).

Indeed, as recognised in ABA Opinion 353, the Whiteside decision may have removed the constitutional qualification in the comments to Rule 3.3 regarding permitted disclosure of perjury by a criminal defendant, but each state is free to reject that (or any other) provision of the Model Rules and impose its own ethical limitations on such disclosures. Moreover, a state also can continue to use the ABA Criminal Defense Standards narrative approach, subject to constitutional limitations against prejudicing a defendant's right to a fair trial. Delaware, which had adopted Model Rule 3.3, nevertheless preserved narrative testimony by a criminal defendant who his counsel thought would commit perjury (and a refusal to make closing argument based thereon) as an ethical option which—at least in a jury trial—does not violate the defendant's right to effective assistance of counsel. Shockley v. State (Del.1989).

f. Pleading ignorance

In discussing these situations, it has been assumed that the attorney "knows" that the client's proposed testimony will be false. The issue of how certain counsel needs to be that his client's testimony will be false was raised in Justices Stevens and Blackmun's concurring and dissenting opinions in Nix v. Whiteside. Many experienced lawyers will argue that an attorney can never be absolutely certain of such matters and, therefore, should give the client the benefit of the doubt. Unfortunately, this is more often a rationalization than a reason. While in theory it may be only for God to "know" and the court to "declare", in fact, attorneys as well as others must frequently accept the law's assignment of responsibility for acts based upon "reasonable proof of knowledge", and even for acts that should have been, but may not have been actually, known to be unlawful. Thus, the Code's Ethical Considerations state that a lawyer should not present evidence which "he knows, or from facts within his knowledge should know, . . . is false, fraudulent, or perjured." EC 7-26.

But before Model Rule 3.3's provisions are invoked, the lawyer must *know* that the client's testimony will be or was false. According to the Rules Terminology section, this denotes "actual knowledge of the fact in question" but a person's knowledge "may be inferred from circumstances." A federal appeals court has agreed that actual knowledge, rather than mere suspicion, that a witness had testified falsely in a deposition was required to trigger the duty under the Code provision, DR 7–102(B)(2), requiring a lawyer to promptly reveal a fraud to a tribunal when the lawyer "receives information clearly establishing that . . . a person other than his client has perpetrated a fraud" on such tribunal. The court stated, however, that this does not require proof beyond a moral certainty. Doe v. Federal Grievance Comm. (2d Cir.1988). There also is authority requiring that defense counsel should have knowledge beyond a reasonable doubt that the client is going to commit, or has committed, perjury before invoking the pre-emptive and disclosure remedies of Model Rule 3.3(a). See Shockley v. State, (Del.1989).

By general definition, perjury is committed when a witness testifies to matters which he or she believes to be false. Thus, if a client tells his lawyer that he intends to testify falsely, absent a reasonable basis to question the client's assertions or his mental soundness, the lawyer must be presumed to "know" that such testimony will be perjurious. Such knowledge may also come from other sources which the attorney cannot ignore unless they are known to be unreliable. An attorney should give his client the benefit of a sincere doubt, but that does not include using evidence which he reasonably believes is false. Good trial preparation, as well as good ethics, require that the attorney investigate questionable aspects of proposed testimony, although a lawyer is not obligated to pursue extraordinary measures in an attempt to cast doubt upon his client's case.

g. *The Best Alternative?*

As we have seen, no one alternative to handling the situation of the apparently perjurious client is without its difficulties. Nevertheless, there is agreement on some fundamental steps that a lawyer must take. The Model Rules clearly proscribe a lawyer from knowingly offering false evidence. To avoid this situation, all authorities agree that the lawyer must try to persuade the client not to testify falsely. If the client insists on doing so, in a civil case, the lawyer may decline to call the client as a witness or seek to withdraw from representation. In a criminal case, withdrawal also is a possibility but usually not a very viable option. Thus, greater persuasive efforts may be in order. Nix v. Whiteside finds no constitutional infirmity in threatening the criminal-defendant client with withdrawal, and possible impeachment and disclosure of any committed perjury. But whether this approach is ethically permissible may vary with the jurisdiction of the trial. Likewise, whether the lawyer may actually disclose the perjury—as distinct from threatening to do so—will depend upon whether the jurisdiction has adopted RPC 3.3(a), and the ABA's interpretation thereof. For example, the State of Washington precludes disclosure of information protected by Rule 1.6 on confidentiality, and several states, including New York, adhere to the amended version of DR 7–102(B)(1) of the Code which similarly gives priority to client confidentiality over candor to the court.

The courts, while hardly uniform, have been more inclined to require, particularly in civil cases, that lawyers reveal uncorrected false evidence from which their clients may have benefited. An Iowa attorney, who was also the witness' paramour, was disbarred for knowingly permitting his client to lie in response to questions by the opposing attorney at a deposition in her divorce case. The attorney was criticized for not attempting to stop the testimony, seek to correct it, withdraw from the case, or reveal the truth to anyone (although the examining attorney, through his own investigation, was aware of the false nature of the testimony). In dicta, the court stated that perjury by the client falls outside of the attorney-client relationship (and here the lawyer's knowledge was obtained through a non-professional relationship with the client) and that the attorney had a duty to disclose the perjury. Committee v. Crary (Iowa 1976).

By contrast, a North Dakota lawyer, who was surprised by his client's false testimony at a pre-trial deposition in a civil action, was told he should have urged the client to disclose the true facts, and, if the client refused, to have nothing further to do with him, but the attorney "need not disclose the fraud to the court." In re Malloy (N.D.1976).

The judicial response to intended or accomplished client perjury may be influenced not only by whether the issue arises in pre-trial or trial proceedings and the civil or criminal nature of the proceeding but by the way the issue is raised, for example, in direct appeal, collateral attack on a criminal conviction, or in disciplinary proceedings against the attorney. Defense counsel could be held to have violated professional standards without a conclusion that there was prejudice to the fact-finding process, which would be necessary for a court finding of ineffective assistance of counsel. Claims have been made, unsuccessfully so far, in a reverse Whiteside situation, that effective assistance of counsel has been denied by the attorney's presentation of perjured testimony. See State v. Skjonsby (N.D.1987); People v. Avery (N.Y.App.Div.1987).

Yet, a Maine court upheld disbarment of a defense counsel in a criminal case who examined the defendant in a normal manner and took no action when the defendant falsely denied his whereabouts at the time of the crime. The judge hearing the disbarment action found that the defense counsel knew the defendant would testify falsely, and knew the testimony was false at the time it was given. The appellate court stated: "While the lawyer has a duty to act zealously on his client's behalf, that duty is subject to ethical limitations which the lawyer may ignore at his peril. Among these is the 'affirmative obligation to inform the court of the falsity of a client's assertions.' . . . There is no more egregious violation of a lawyer's duty as an officer of the court, and no clearer ethical breach. . . ." Board of Overseers of the Bar v. Dineen (Me.1984).

While this language may appear extreme, it does reflect the attitude of many judges, and members of the public—and perhaps a considerable number of lawyers.

Despite the inadequacies of the suggested alternatives, it is difficult to accept the conclusion that to allow a client to commit perjury is the least of the evils.

As the Supreme Court of California has stated, "it is manifestly incorrect, indeed, repugnant . . . to infer . . . that counsel may knowingly allow a witness to testify falsely, whether he be a criminal defendant or otherwise." People v. Pike (Cal.1962). Nix v. Whiteside makes it clear that the procedural safeguards to which a criminal defendant is entitled do not include the right to lie. The assumption of the adversary system is that justice will result from a contest between strong presentations of the best case for each side, but this does not contemplate the presentation of a manufactured or nonexistent case. An apparently "guilty" client is entitled to his day in court, including the right to a loyal and zealous counsel and the right to make the prosecution prove its case beyond a reasonable doubt, but his rights do not include the opportunity to create reasonable doubts through the use of knowingly perjured testimony.

In Canada, the applicable standards seek to avoid the lying client dilemma by clearly forbidding the presentation of perjured testimony and requiring the attorney to notify the client in advance of that prohibition. The Model Rules provisions and Nix v. Whiteside provide the basis for a similar practice in the United States. While this may cause the devious client to withhold pertinent and incriminating information in some cases, that seems a lesser sacrifice than allowing an attorney to knowingly use perjured testimony. Moreover, in most cases, the client will be better served if he reveals the full facts to the attorney and permits the attorney intelligently to plan the best strategy for the case, than if the client goes on the stand, commits perjury, and risks a probing cross-examination by the prosecutor or the contradictory testimony of other witnesses which reveal the deceptions in the defendant's story.

E. CONDUCT AT TRIAL

Some of the most difficult ethical problems occur during the course of a trial. They are difficult both because they may arise in an emotionally charged atmosphere, with little or no time for study and reflection, and because they often involve seeming conflicts between loyalties to the client and those to the court or the administration of justice. Many of these situations, however, like that of the lying witness, can be anticipated when preparing for trial, thus providing an opportunity to consider alternative strategies and resolutions. A few of the other more common and controversial situations will now be examined.

1. Disclosure of Misleading and Adverse Evidence

In his autobiography, the late distinguished Professor Samuel Williston related an incident which occurred while he was representing a defendant in a financial matter. At the close of the trial, the judge stated as one reason for his decision a supposed fact which Williston, on the basis of a letter in his client's file, knew was unfounded. Since the plaintiff had not asked that the letter or file be produced, Williston did not volunteer to correct the judge's error. Although he felt uncomfortable at the time, he had no doubt of the propriety of his keeping silent.

Williston's judgment is in accord with existing authorities. It has been suggested, however, that the duty of an attorney for a party who has the burden of proof may be different. If the attorney for that party presented purported facts which were contrary to reliable evidence in his possession, and sought the court's aid in obtaining affirmative relief, there are more elements of a positive misrepresentation. In the Williston case, the perpetuation of the error in fact finding was not due to any misrepresentation on his part, and he was entitled to sit back and let the plaintiff try to prove his case.

If an attorney possesses information which destroys the basis for a client's legal relief, a claim or counterclaim which nevertheless seeks such relief could be condemned as false, frivolous, or fraudulent or as an action intended to harass or maliciously injure another. CPR DR 7–102(A)(1); RPC 3.1. Likewise, a lawyer may not make a false statement of fact or participate in the creation of evidence which he knows is false. CPR DR 7–102(A)(5), (6); RPC 3.3(a)(1), 3.4(6). Thus, it would be improper to assert in court that the fact was X when the lawyer knew from evidence in his possession that the fact was Y. Where, however, the lawyer's investigation has produced reliable evidence of both X and Y as the fact, it probably would not be unethical to introduce only the evidence supporting X, which favored the client's position.

The line between permissible advocacy and misrepresentation, however, is not always a bright one. Courts are sometimes faced with the question of whether a lawyer is required to seek rectification of not only false testimony but misleading evidence. Where a party in a divorce proceeding gave incomplete responses to questions by the court and opposing counsel, including that his mother was in Salem—without volunteering the material fact that she was dead and buried there, the Oregon Supreme Court held that his attorney did not have to disclose the deception, since his knowledge of it was based on confidential communications. The lawyer was required, however, to try to persuade the client to reveal the deception, and, if the client refused, to withdraw from further representation of him. The lawyer was not disciplined in this particular instance because, at the time of the case, the requirement of mandatory withdrawal was not yet clear and the lawyer had tried to figure out what behavior was proper on this difficult issue. In re A. (Or.1976).

A Michigan ethics committee has given its approval of non-disclosure of truthful, but misleading evidence, by advising that it would not be unethical for a criminal defense attorney to call alibi witnesses to truthfully testify that the defendant was with them at the time the crime was alleged to have been committed—even though the attorney had been told by the defendant that he committed the crime and that the victim was mistaken as to the time of its commission. To treat truthful evidence differently based upon what the client had told his counsel would violate the client's confidentiality. Mich.Opin. CI–1164 (1987).

By contrast, the New Jersey Supreme Court has come down strongly in favor of disclosure of the misleading nature of offered evidence. In its adoption of the Model Rules, the court added to Rule 3.3—over considerable opposition of its bar—a provision that a lawyer shall not knowingly "fail to disclose to the tribunal a material fact with knowledge that the tribunal may tend to be misled by such failure."

This requirement is probably inconsistent with the ethical standards in most jurisdictions. Model Rule 3.3(a)(2) prohibits a lawyer from knowingly failing to disclose a material fact to a tribunal "when such disclosure is necessary to avoid assisting a criminal or fraudulent act by the client. . . ." Rule 4.1 is similar as regards the obligations of disclosure to third persons in general, but specifically adds "unless disclosure is prohibited by Rule 1.6" (on confidentiality). The disclosure obligations to tribunals, however, in RPC 3.3(a), are given priority over the protections of Rule 1.6. The limited disclosure duty under these rules is indicated by the Terminology section of the Model Rules which states that "fraud" or "fraudulent" denotes conduct having a purpose to deceive and not merely negligent misrepresentation or "failure to apprise another of relevant information."

The Rules do helpfully provide, however, that in an ex parte proceeding (when the other party does not have a right to notice and rebuttal) a lawyer must inform the tribunal of all material facts known to the lawyer "which will enable the tribunal to make an informed decision, whether or not the facts are adverse." RPC 3.3(d).

The Code is even less demanding in only requiring counsel not to "conceal or knowingly fail to disclose that which he is required to reveal"—presumably by other provisions of law, ethics, or court order. DR 2–102(A)(3). Likewise, the Code provides that "a lawyer shall not suppress any evidence that he or his client has a *legal obligation* to reveal or produce." DR 7–109(A). [Emphasis added]. Model Rule 3.4(a) similarly prohibits a lawyer from "unlawfully" altering, destroying, or concealing material having potential evidentiary value, or unlawfully obstructing another party's access to evidence, or counseling or assisting another person to do so.

These provisions merely incorporate existing state or federal law, but these include requirements of discovery practice in most jurisdictions (which also provide for sanctions for unlawful non-compliance). Procedures for depositions, interrogatories, and other discovery reduce the likelihood that adverse evidence, at least when not confidentially privileged, will remain undiscovered by the careful attorney.

Similarly, a lawyer may not secrete a witness, advise her to leave the jurisdiction [CPR DR 7–109(B)], or request a person other than a client (or client's relative, agent or employee) to refrain from giving voluntary information to another party except to protect that person's interests from being adversely affected. RPC 3.4(f). An early New York County Bar Association opinion held that it was not improper for an attorney for a defendant to fail to disclose the existence of an eyewitness, apparently unknown to the minor plaintiff, even though the plaintiff's tort action was dismissed for insufficient evidence. Once again, it would have been unethical for the defendant's attorney to attempt to hide the existence of that witness or book passage for him on a slow boat to China.

It may be concluded that in most jurisdictions silence—even when it may give rise to a false inference—is less likely to constitute an unethical misrepresentation if: the other party has the burden of proof on the issue, especially if the silent lawyer represents a criminal defendant; the "silent" attorney has introduced only evidence thought to be truthful, or no evidence at all on the issue; the attorney knows of the possible misleading implication only because of confidential information she has received; the attorney has not personally misrepresented or secreted any material facts and has not induced another person to do so; and the proceeding is an adversary one where each attorney will have an opportunity to prepare, engage in pre-trial discovery, and cross-examine witnesses to probe for omitted adverse evidence.

2. Disclosure of Adverse Legal Authority

In the course of your opponent's argument to the court, it becomes apparent that he is unaware of a significant recent case favorable to his contentions. If the judge does not indicate familiarity with the case, do you have any obligation to bring it to the court's attention? The advocate's instinctive reaction is in the negative. After all, why should one lawyer do the other's home-work? Nevertheless, the CPR and the Rules require a lawyer to disclose legal authority "in the controlling jurisdiction" known to be "directly adverse" to the position of the client and which is not disclosed by opposing counsel. DR 7–106(B)(1); RPC 3.3(a)(3). This codifies, but restricts, earlier ABA Committee opinions which required disclosure of decisions—from any jurisdiction—which a judge should clearly consider in deciding the instant case. The current duty is less onerous for the attorney but ironically requires the disclosure only of those authorities with the greatest potential to damage the client's cause.

What is the justification for this departure from a strictly adversary presentation, and why should a lawyer have a greater obligation to disclose adverse legal authorities than adverse facts?

Silence of an advocate in the situation of a possibly erroneous finding of fact is generally justified by the lawyer having acquired knowledge of the contrary facts through a client's confidential communication or secret. Unlike information about adverse law, such adverse factual information is privileged from disclosure. On the other hand, it could be argued that the applicable law is equally available to both sides, whereas the relevant facts may not be. Modern discovery practices, however, should minimize the difference in availability of facts from law.

It has been settled that a lawyer has an obligation to avoid knowingly making a false statement of law, including relying upon a statute which has been repealed or a case which has been overruled. Thus, to assert that a particular proposition is the law in the controlling jurisdiction, when that proposition appears to have been completely or partially undermined by a recent case, is a misrepresentation of the state of the law, tantamount to making a false statement of law, and is different only in degree, not kind, from citing an overruled case.

Of course, if the recent adverse case is distinguishable, not from the highest court in the jurisdiction, or otherwise construable as not controlling, these points can and should be raised. Indeed, better advocacy probably results when an attorney cites and distinguishes or challenges the soundness of an adverse precedent, thus diffusing its impact, than when he leaves it to be belatedly discovered, and dramatically presented by his opponent. In practice, it is likely that the opponent or the court will ultimately discover the directly adverse case and that any error of law will be corrected, even if only on appeal. Thus, failure to disclose the case may either result in a waste of limited judicial time or, if not ultimately discovered, in the perpetuation of a possible error of law. In this regard, an error of law caused by the failure of the court to be fully informed may also influence the disposition of other cases, and is therefore more harmful than an error of fact which affects only the parties to the instant controversy.

Even in California, which has not adopted a rule requiring the disclosure of adverse law (and still employs language similar to old Canon 22 in its RPC 5–200), the court, in declining to discipline a lawyer for failing to cite a state appeals case which had rejected a contention made by him, stated that the lawyer "should in all fairness have directed the trial court's attention to the decision and argued to the court the contentions which he makes here that the case was not controlling." Shaeffer v. State Bar (Cal.1945).

Particularly with the availability of computerized legal research, and good advocacy discovering, disclosing, and—if necessary—distinguishing applicable legal precedents from the controlling jurisdiction, discipline for violation of the obligation to reveal adverse law should be rare. But because of the imposition on the legal system, such violations have been the subject of sanctions by the federal courts. Jorgenson v. County of Volusia (11th Cir. 1988).

3. Impeaching the Truthful Witness

The last of the three situations which Monroe Freedman characterized as the hardest for the defense counsel raises the question of whether it is ethical to impeach a witness who you know is telling the truth. This dilemma is not, of course, encountered only by criminal defense counsel but may occur in any type of litigation. The problem may be illustrated as follows: A witness for the prosecution testifies that shortly before the time when an alleged robbery was committed he saw your client in a bar near the scene of the crime. Your client verifies this fact, but you learn that the witness has poor eyesight, was slightly drunk at the time, and has a criminal record. May you use these matters in an attempt to cast doubt upon the accuracy or credibility of the witness? Most writers and authorities would respond affirmatively. Cross-examination and use of admissible impeachment evidence are among the common tactics that lawyers employ to present their cases in the best light and to diminish the persuasiveness of the opponent's case. They are legitimate aspects of the adversary system, and more often aid rather than obstruct the search for truth and justice. A counsel has a right to place a witness in his or her true perspective. Thus, if a witness is irritable, unduly hostile, or overly cautious, those factors distract from persuasiveness and may be brought out—even played upon—by opposing counsel. If the truthfulness of the witness's testimony is known only because of a confidential communication from a client, it is arguable that a failure to impeach the witness on otherwise legitimate grounds would be inconsistent with the policy of confidentiality because it would prejudice the client's interests based upon privileged information. Moreover, it is not the advocate's role to judge a witness's credibility. To limit a lawyer to impeaching only witnesses she believes are not telling the truth would place the lawyer in the position of assessing each witness's credibility, and if she fails to use a known basis for impeachment, the inference may arise that no such basis exists.

An oft quoted dictum of Justice White recognizes that while a prosecutor has a duty to ascertain the true facts, "defense counsel has no comparable obligation. . . . If he can confuse a witness, even a truthful one, or make him appear at a disadvantage, unsure or indecisive, that will be his normal course. Our interest in not convicting the innocent permits counsel to put the State to its proof . . . Undoubtedly, there are some limits which defense counsel must observe but more often than not, defense counsel will cross-examine a prosecution witness, and impeach him if he can, even if he thinks the witness is telling the truth, just as he will attempt to destroy a witness who he thinks is lying." United States v. Wade (U.S.1967) (Concurring and dissenting opinion).

The ABA Standards for Criminal Justice, as amended in 1979, draw a subtle but significant distinction in the prosecutorial and defense functions. A prosecutor's *belief* that a witness is telling the truth does not preclude cross-examination, but the prosecutor should not discredit or undermine a witness she *knows* is testifying truthfully. Standard 3–5.7(b). A defense lawyer's "belief or knowledge that the witness is telling the truth", however, "does not preclude cross-examination, but should, if possible, be taken into consideration by counsel in conducting the cross-examination." Standard 4–7.6(b).

It would be appropriate to ban a *misuse* of impeachment of a known truthful witness by, for example, going beyond the introduction of accurately based impeachment evidence and directly suggesting that the witness was not telling the truth. And any witness is entitled to be protected from credibility attacks based on inadmissible evidence designed to unduly harass or embarrass him, or from suggested grounds for impeachment which the cross-examiner knows are without foundation. Accordingly, while neither the Code nor the Model Rules proscribe an advocate from impeaching a witness known to be testifying truthfully, DR 7–106(C)(2) does prohibit a lawyer from asking a question that is intended to degrade a witness. (See also RPC 4.4).

4. The Rules of Evidence as Ethical Guidelines

The zealous representation which a lawyer owes to his client must be performed within the bounds of the law. Does that mean that an intentional departure from the rules of evidence would be unethical? Provisions of the CPR could be so construed. The Ethical Considerations state that a lawyer is not justified in "consciously violating" rules of evidence and procedure [EC 7–25], and the Disciplinary Rules forbid a lawyer from "intentionally or habitually" violating any established rules of procedure or of evidence. DR 7–106(C)(7). If these precepts are read to preclude malicious or premeditated evasions of the rules of evidence in order to bring before a tribunal matters that it may not properly consider, they are sensible and justified. On the other hand, if they are meant to label as unethical questions that call for a hearsay answer or attempts to short-cut proof by asking leading questions or departing from the best evidence rule, they are neither practical nor sound.

Objections to evidence are frequently waived by nonassertion, and it would not seem unethical for a lawyer to test the waters, or the alertness and knowledge of opposing counsel, by failing to adhere to the sometimes complex and technical rules of evidence. The primary distinction which should be drawn is between violations of evidentiary rules concerned with the form of the question or response, and those concerned with the substance of the material sought to be introduced. Only intentional violations of the latter type should be condemned, unless the violation of form is combined with an attempt to unduly harass or degrade the witness.

These considerations are directly addressed by more specific provisions of the CPR and of the Model Rules. Thus, a lawyer should not "allude to any matter that he has no reasonable basis to believe is relevant to the case or that will not be supported by admissible evidence" [DR 7–106(C)(1); RPC 3.4(e)] or "ask any question that he has no reasonable basis to believe is relevant to the case and that is intended to degrade a witness or other person." DR 7–106(C)(2); see RPC 4.4. Accordingly, any knowing attempt by an attorney to introduce irrelevant evidence which may prejudice the outcome of the case is properly condemned. Some examples of irrelevant and improperly alluded to evidence are specifically addressed in the Code and Rules, and are discussed elsewhere in this chapter. These include introduction of false evidence; personal opinions of counsel (as distinct from argument based on admissible evidence) as to the justness of a cause, credibility of a witness, culpability of a civil litigant, or guilt or innocence of an accused; or evidence intended to disrupt a proceeding.

In light of the complexity of the law of evidence and the trial judge's broad discretion in applying it, a lawyer should not be censured for departures from evidentiary rules unless they are intentional and clearly established. The possibility of reversal of a favorable judgment because of errors in the admission of evidence also provides some sanction against intentional violations.

5. Appeals to Emotion

Attorneys are sometimes condemned for arousing passion and prejudice during the trial of a case, but it is not improper *per se* to make an emotional appeal or to engage in actions which prejudice an opponent's cause. Indeed a basic function of an advocate is to induce the judge or jury to act favorably toward his client and against the interests of opposing parties. In this sense a lawyer's actions are frequently and properly calculated to prejudice an adversary's case. It is only when prejudice or emotion is unrelated to the legal and factual merits of the case, or the emotional impact will likely outweigh its probative value, that the attorney's conduct becomes questionable. Emotional pleas to arouse sympathy for a maimed plaintiff or hostility for a cold-blooded killer are relevant to the issues of damages and punishment, respectively. Emotions which naturally flow from the consequences of the facts of a case may be referred to, and played upon, within the bounds of legal relevancy. An occasional case has suggested that an attorney may even shed tears on behalf of his client when the crying is sincere and merited by the circumstances. (A Florida trial court, however, recently set aside a million dollar personal injury verdict because plaintiff's lawyer, "as was his frequent practice", improperly appealed to jurors sympathies by shedding tears.)

The vice in improper emotional or prejudicial appeals is in their irrelevancy or lack of rational relation to the merits of the case. Thus, appeals to racial, religious, national, or regional prejudice have been held to be unethical and reversible error (at least when substantially prejudicial and not remedied by trial court instructions). Whether a party is represented by a "big-city Yankee lawyer" should have no bearing on the outcome of a case tried in a small southern community, but the fact that the plaintiff was left unconscious and bleeding after being struck by a later apprehended hit-and-run driver is a relevant, although highly emotional, fact of an action for damages.

In making a closing argument, attorneys have a wide latitude to discuss and interpret the law and facts and to draw inferences and conclusions therefrom, but such argument may not refer to irrelevant factors or inadmissible evidence. One may seek sympathy for a hapless victim of poverty who stole bread to feed his family, but not try to inflame a bible-belt jury against a defendant because he is an atheist. As previously indicated, it is also unethical for an attorney to assert his personal belief in the justness of a cause or guilt or innocence of an accused, or conversely, to suggest that the opposing lawyer does not believe in his own client's case. Personal *knowledge,* subject to limitations of confidential privilege and conflicts of function, may be introduced as evidence. An advocate's private *beliefs* are irrelevant and their disclosure in court would tend to unfairly prejudice a party whose attorney, for whatever reason, chose to remain silent in regard to his personal feelings about a client's case.

Inflammatory language or references which go beyond admissible facts, especially when reiterated after a sustained objection or warning to cease such behavior, may be condemned as unethical conduct and prejudicial error which impair the opportunity for a fair trial. Such behavior may constitute trial disruption and frequently merits sanctions for contempt of court as well as professional discipline if engaged in on a repeated basis.

6. Trial Disruption; Offensive Advocacy

On occasion, especially in connection with so-called "political trials," an attorney engages in, or encourages or condones his client's engaging in, extensive inflammatory or obstructive behavior with the intent, or at least the consequence, of disrupting the trial proceedings. Since we have progressed from trial by battle to more civilized forms of verbal combat, the courts have insisted that trial proceedings be conducted with dignity and decorum.

> "Unless order is maintained in the courtroom and disruption prevented, reason cannot prevail and constitutional rights to liberty, freedom and equality under law cannot be protected. The dignity, decorum and courtesy which have traditionally characterized the courts of civilized nations are not empty formalities. They are essential to an atmosphere in which justice can be done." Principles as to Disruption of the Judicial Process, American College of Trial Lawyers (1970).

The lawyer has an obligation within these Principles "to represent every client courageously, vigorously, diligently and with all the skill and knowledge he possesses;" but also "to conduct himself in such a way as to avoid disorder or disruption in the courtroom" and "to advise any client appearing in a courtroom of the kind of behavior expected and required of him there, and to prevent him, so far as lies within the lawyer's power, from creating disorder or disruption in the courtroom."

The tactics and antics of the defendants and their counsel in the "Chicago Seven" trial, exacerbated by the presiding judge's insensitivity, dramatized the confrontation between the need for decorum and overly zealous advocacy. Leonard Weinglass, one of the defense counsel, stated that: "Under ordinary circumstances, the actions of the defendants would be considered disrespectful. But these were not ordinary circumstances." Nevertheless, the Principles of the American College of Trial Lawyers note that a lawyer is not relieved of the obligations to avoid courtroom disorder or disruption "by any shortcomings on the part of the judge," nor by "the legal, moral, political, social or ideological merits of the cause of any client." To conclude otherwise would allow the dignity of judicial proceedings to be dependent on the *dramatis personae* of each trial and run counter to notions of equal justice under general laws. Respect for a judge is based upon the office held and not the individual temporarily occupying it. Abuse of that office, however, may be cause for reversal in a particular case.

In a "political trial" the charges which are formally brought and adjudicated may not be the real reason for the prosecution. Rather it may be an attempt by the political party in power to silence or injure a dissident movement by alleging general conspiracy-type, instead of—easier to defend against—conduct-type, offenses. When this political motivation of the prosecution is combined with a purpose of the defendants to undermine the existing political structure by, *inter alia,* generating disrespect for the legal system and its officers, the constitutional system of adjudication is put to a severe test. But the rule of law cannot react in emotion. The passion of the litigants should be met by even-handed insistence on maintaining essential decorum while perhaps overlooking those excesses of zeal which manifest them selves in breaches of etiquette rather than order. Disruptions or obstructions to a fair trial, such as persistence in pursuing inadmissible lines of inquiry or the making of disrespective and provocative comments and interruptions, despite prior warnings, may be punished as contemptuous conduct and as unethical behavior when engaged in by attorney advocates.

The ABA Standards Relating to both the Prosecution and the Defense Functions admonish a lawyer to manifest professional respect toward the judge, opposing counsel, witnesses and jurors, to not engage in tactics intended to irritate the court or opposing counsel, and to comply promptly with orders and directives of the court; but a lawyer has a right to make respectful requests for reconsideration of adverse rulings and a duty to have the record reflect such rulings or judicial conduct which the lawyer considers prejudicial to the client's legitimate interests. Standards 3–5.2, 4–7.1.

More generally, the CPR states that "a lawyer shall not . . . engage in undignified or discourteous conduct which is degrading to a tribunal." DR 7–106(C)(6). But what is undignified, discourteous, or degrading to one judge or lawyer may not be to another. Should it be considered unethical or contemptuous for a woman lawyer to wear slacks in court, for a male lawyer to wear his long hair in a ponytail, for a lawyer to refuse to stand when a judge enters the courtroom, or for a lawyer to address the judge as "Joe" or "Julie" rather than "Your Honor"? The former two examples would seem to be matters of personal taste and not ethics, while the latter may be discourteous but not fairly construed as so lacking in decorum as to impede the administration of justice.

The Model Rules are more focused but cryptic. RPC 3.5(c) simply provides that a lawyer shall not "engage in conduct intended to disrupt a tribunal." The Rules also provide, as does the Code in substance, that a lawyer shall not "knowingly disobey an obligation under the rules of a tribunal except for an open refusal based on an assertion that no valid obligation exists". RPC 3.4(c); see CPR DR 7–106(A).

To render the questioned action unethical, these rules require an evil state of mind or intention of the advocate. The underlying purpose of particular forensic tactics is relevant in determining their culpability. In general, a lawyer may: (1) engage in, perhaps, overzealous advocacy intended to aid her client in the litigated matter; or (2) intend to serve a cause of the client not directly implicated in legal issues framed in the instant proceeding; or (3) simply want to disrupt the proceedings for political or other reasons. All three tactics may result in trial disruption, and may overlap in intention, but they merit independent analysis.

Examples of the first category have already been extensively considered and range from unethical introduction of false evidence to undue emotional appeals. Another, more recently troublesome phenomenon has been hardball litigation and pre-trial tactics alternately described as "Rambo," "scorched earth," and "take no prisoners" advocacy. Characteristics of such advocacy generally include discourtesy, harassment, rudeness, and uncooperativeness. Since some firms proudly proclaim their commitment to this type of practice, it may be designed not only to achieve immediate objectives for a particular client but to attract other clients who value obsequious devotion to their cause more than independent professional judgment.

Faced with a rash of Rambo-like advocacy, the federal district judges for the Northern District of Texas, sitting en banc, adopted standards of litigation conduct applicable to civil actions. Incorporating provisions from the Dallas Bar Association's Guidelines of Professional Courtesy and Lawyer's Creed, the court requires, *inter alia,* that lawyers treat each other, opposing parties, the court, and court staff with courtesy and civility, adverse witnesses and suitors with fairness and due consideration, and cooperate with opposing counsel. The standards state that no client has a right to demand that counsel abuse the opposite party or indulge in offensive conduct, and that effective advocacy does not require antagonistic or obnoxious behavior. Because breaches of such standards interfere with the administration of justice, consume valuable judicial and attorney time to resolve, and increase costs, delay and animosity of litigation, the court made them subject to sanctions which include "a warm friendly discussion on the record, a hard-nosed reprimand in open court, compulsory legal education, monetary sanctions, or other measures appropriate to the circumstances." Dondi Properties Corp. v. Commerce Savings and Loan Ass'n (N.D. Tex.1988) quoting Thomas v. Capital Security Services (5th Cir.1988).

The Dondi Standards, as they have become known, were adopted, according to the court, because: "Our system of justice can ill-afford to devote scarce resources to supervising matters that do not advance the resolution of the merits of a case; nor can justice long remain available to deserving litigants if the costs of litigation are fueled unnecessarily to the point of being prohibitive."

These considerations are even more persuasive in attempting to control "disruptive" behavior in the second two categories where no adversary advantage is sought for the client on the merits of the immediate case but the tactics are directed at some more general political or other objective. Recent trials around the country, for example, of protestors against abortion who were accused of trespass, obstruction, and similar offenses on the premises of family planning or medical clinics have involved attempts by the defendants and their counsel to continue their abortion protest in court rather than specifically respond to the offenses with which they have been charged. Once a judge has ruled that evidence concerning their underlying "pro-life" cause is inadmissible, continued attempts to invoke it fall under the second category of introducing facts and argument found irrelevant to the instant proceeding in order to serve a broader cause of the client. Lawyers who persist in such efforts, after warnings from the bench, are subject to sanctions and contempt citations.

Such trials, as with other politically or cause-motivated defenses, often involve disruptive behavior in the third category which is not intended to influence the court (and usually just irritates the judge) but to advance the client's underlying cause by seeking publicity for it. Thus, vocal demonstrations and name-calling in the courtroom, if organized, encouraged, or participated in by counsel may become a basis for professional discipline as well as contempt citation. Civil disobedience may be an effective tactic for just causes, but if it interferes with the orderly administration of justice or a fair trial in the court room, its participants must expect to pay the consequences.

F. COMPENSATING WITNESSES

It is, of course, improper to bribe a witness. But not all compensation to a witness is forbidden. Appearing as a witness in a trial may be very time consuming and cause the witness to suffer a loss of income from his or her occupation. Therefore, it is not improper to advance, guarantee, or acquiesce in the payment of reasonable compensation for loss of work time and expenses to a witness for attending and testifying at a trial or other hearing. DR 7–109(C). Such payments are often necessary and customary for expert witnesses who also are entitled to receive a reasonable fee for their time and professional services rendered in connection with a legal matter.

Neither experts nor other witnesses, however, may be offered or receive an inducement that is prohibited by law. RPC 3.4(b). Accordingly, the ABA Code, reflecting common law policy, declares that it is improper to make compensation of a witness "contingent upon the content of his testimony or the outcome of the case." DR 7–109(C). The former proscription is clearly desirable, but the latter may give rise to problems for an indigent litigant who has no means by which to compensate an expert witness except out of a money judgment sought in the pending litigation. While the Disciplinary Rule has withstood constitutional challenge on the basis of its alleged irrationality and denial of equal access to the courts, legitimate questions have been raised regarding the total prohibition on contingent witness fees. For example, when necessary or clearly desirable expert testimony may not be obtainable by an indigent plaintiff in a personal injury, malpractice, or antitrust suit except upon obtaining a favorable recovery, an arrangement for such a conditional fee might be permitted if the amount was fixed (not contingent as to amount on the testimony given or on amount of the judgment), reasonable, disclosed to and approved by the court. Any temptation to commit perjury will be minimized by such factors as well as by the concern of most experts for their reputation within their field and their desire to avoid potentially embarrassing cross-examination.

In some jurisdictions, law enforcement agencies compensate informers and offer witness protection programs to encourage former criminal conspirators to break their code of silence and testify against hard-to-convict organized crime figures. Prosecutors who initiate or approve of such arrangements, or who engage in the common practice of negotiating favorable plea bargains for accused persons willing to turn against their former fellows in crime, clearly offer inducements for favorable testimony, but, according to the RPC, they are only unethical if "prohibited by law". Rule 3.4(b). Cross-examination, however, is available to expose this "interest" of the witness, and allow his credibility to be judged accordingly.

G. CRIMINAL v. CIVIL ADVOCACY

Murray Schwartz, David Luban, and a number of other scholars, have begun to question whether the legal profession has been too willing to accept extremes of zealous advocacy in all contexts which may only be justified in defense of criminally accused persons. Schwartz, The Zeal of the Civil Advocate, 1983 Amer. Bar Found. Research J.; Luban, The Adversary Excuse, in The Good Lawyer, 1983. The hard ethical questions which Monroe Freedman posed for the criminal defense lawyer involving client perjury, legal lectures to new clients, and cross-examination of truthful witnesses might be easier for civil advocates and prosecutors to answer.

The defense of criminal cases involve special circumstances including: constitutional protections not generally applicable to civil litigation—e.g. the presumption of innocence and right to effective assistance of counsel; a more exacting burden of persuasion and disclosure on the prosecutor; frequent inequality in time and resources favoring the prosecution's ability to prepare and present the case against the defendant; the severity of potential sanctions from imprisonment to the death penalty; and our society's historical concern to avoid conviction of an innocently accused person. These circumstances allow a lawyer for a criminal defendant to plead him innocent (although he has told the lawyer he is guilty), to offer no affirmative testimony, and to raise reasonable doubts by cross-examining truthful witnesses and by other means short of knowing use of false evidence, bribery or other forms of corruption. Civil litigants, however, may not merit or need such indulgences, and it is arguable that a greater priority should be given to the disclosure of the truth, and less to confidentiality, and to more exacting lawyer moral-accountability in civil trials.

Neither the Code nor the Rules (with the exception of pleading a known-guilty client innocent and possible limitations on disclosure of client perjury) differentiate between the ethical conduct required of civil and criminal defense advocates. Examples of permissible adversary zeal are often taken from criminal defense practice and may or may not have equal validity outside of that context. If criminal defense counsel is ethically forbidden to engage in specified conduct, there is an *a fortiori* argument that it should also be forbidden to civil advocates. But the reverse need not follow. The standards could distinguish the ethical obligations of the civil advocate and criminal defense counsel, just as they do the latter from lawyers with prosecutorial functions. Other functions of lawyers—advisor, negotiator, mediator, and legislative advocate are now recognized as requiring more than a simple application of courtroom adversary ethics in another location. These role-differentiated ethical responsibilities are discussed elsewhere in this Nutshell, and, perhaps, future editions will merit separate treatment for criminal and civil advocates. (See Chapter 25).

CHAPTER 17

THE LAWYER AND THE FAIR TRIAL/ FREE PRESS CONFLICT

I. INTRODUCTION

The Sixth Amendment guarantees that "the accused shall enjoy the right to a . . . public trial, by an impartial jury." On the other hand, the First Amendment provides that "Congress shall make no law . . . abridging the freedom of speech, or of the press." Simply stated, the occasional conflict between these two rights represents the fair trial/free press issue: While it is the right of the accused to be tried by an impartial jury, it is also the right of an individual to comment on and the press to print events pertinent to the indictment or trial of the accused. The clash between these two rights occurs when public comment prevents the jury from basing its verdict solely on the evidence as presented during the trial. The concern is that inflammatory pretrial publicity may cloud the minds of prospective jurors, or that public comments during the trial may bring notoriety to the case that may influence the judgment of those actually sitting in the jury box.

In the balancing of the right to a fair trial and the freedoms of speech and of the press, the free and responsible expression of ideas must be weighed for at least two reasons: First, opening the legal process for discussion promotes intelligent reform through public education and encourages constructive criticism of system weaknesses; it can promote the exposure of misconduct and corruption and thereby facilitate their prevention. Second, when the legal process is observable by the public, defendants are protected from "Star Chambers"; further, open and responsible discussion may prevent a particular defendant from being "railroaded" on insubstantial evidence in order to satisfy an emotional community's need for retribution.

This chapter discusses the fair trial/free press dilemma, focusing first upon the effect of unlimited publicity on the right to a fair trial, then upon efforts to limit its improper effect, and finally upon an issue of fairly recent re-emergence—television in the courtroom and its effect on the administration of justice.

II. IMPROPER EFFECT OF UNLIMITED PUBLICITY ON THE ADMINISTRATION OF JUSTICE

In the early cases that squarely presented it with instances of extrajudicial publicity affecting the fairness of a defendant's trial, the United States Supreme Court's response was merely to reverse the conviction and remand for a new trial. In 1965, however, with the sensational trial of Billie Sol Estes, the Court began to take a more aggressive stance against certain sources of prejudicial publicity. Estes v. Texas (U.S.1965).

Estes was charged with swindling. Massive publicity surrounded the trial, including the televising of a pretrial hearing and parts of the trial itself. In a 5–4 decision, the Court held that such televising constituted a denial of due process. Four of the justices took the position that any televising of any part of a defendant's trial constituted a denial of due process; the fifth vote for reversal—a concurrence by Justice Harlan—was narrower, suggesting that the televising of a *notorious* case resulted in a violation of due process.

Thus, for the first time, the Court in *Estes* went beyond mere reversal of a conviction and imposed restrictions on certain activities of the media in order to limit prejudicial publicity.

One year later, in Sheppard v. Maxwell (U.S.1966), the Court went further and gave specific direction to trial judges to take steps to limit the effects of prejudicial publicity. In that case Dr. Sam Sheppard was charged with the murder of his wife. Pretrial publicity included rumors, accusations, inaccurate information, inadmissible evidence, and inflammatory editorials. During the trial, the activities of the innumerable newspersons covering the case led Justice Clark to write for the Court: "The fact is that bedlam reigned at the courthouse during the trial and newsmen took over practically the entire courtroom, hounding most of the participants in the trial, especially Sheppard." The Court held that the "circus like" atmosphere denied Dr. Sheppard his right to a fair trial.

More important than the reversal itself is the fact that the Court outlined specific steps the trial court could have taken to limit the effect of prejudicial information on the jury. Specifically, change of venue, continuance, and sequestration of the jury were suggested. In order to prevent the influx of prejudicial information, the Court suggested detailed procedures that would limit it at its inception:

> [T]he trial court might well have proscribed extrajudicial statements by any lawyer, party, witness, or court official which divulged prejudicial matters, such as the refusal of Sheppard to submit to interrogation or take any lie detector tests; the identity of prospective witnesses or their probable testimony; any belief in guilt or innocence; or like statements concerning the merits of the case.

Although the Court did not suggest direct controls on the press, it did indicate that reporters could be warned about reporting prejudicial information that included inadmissible evidence. Without elaboration the Court added: "Given the pervasiveness of modern communications and the difficulty of effacing prejudicial publicity from the minds of the jurors, the trial courts must take strong measures to ensure that the balance is never weighed against the accused."

Although the Court directly addressed the fair trial/free press conflict for the first time in *Estes* and *Sheppard,* by both stating that the balance should never be weighed against the accused and at the same time failing to consider the propriety of restraining the press, it left resolution of the conflict to lower courts and legal commentators. Furthermore, the Court's implicit assumption that trial courts could constitutionally limit the speech of attorneys and parties to the action, without discussion of limitations on that power, engendered considerable confusion among those who subsequently attempted to draft workable rules.

Several studies into the fair trial/free press issue followed the *Sheppard* case. The Report of the Warren Commission in 1964 had severely criticized the treatment of the Kennedy assassination by the news media. The Commission suggested that standards of conduct to prevent prejudicial publicity be formulated and adopted. This Warren Commission recommendation is credited with spurring the ABA, through its Advisory Committee on Fair Trial and Free Press, to study the issue. The resulting Reardon Report stopped short of recommending statutory restraints on the press, but it did recommend limited use of the court's contempt power against any person who "disseminates by any means of public communication an extrajudicial statement relating to the defendant or to the issues in the case that goes beyond the public record . . . that is wilfully designed . . . to affect the outcome. . . ." In addition, the report suggested techniques to limit the effect of prejudicial publicity similar to those recommended in *Sheppard:* sequestration of the jury; change of venue; continuance; cautionary instructions to jurors; and exclusion of the public from certain pretrial hearings such as evidentiary hearings.

The recommendations of the Reardon Committee led to the adoption of DR 7–107: Generally, any attorney associated with a proceeding may not make statements that are reasonably likely to interfere with a fair trial. See RPC 3.6 ("substantial likelihood of materially prejudicing an adjudicative proceeding") More specifically, DR 7–107(B) proscribes: statements concerning the character, reputation, credibility, or criminal record of the accused, a party, or a witness; the possibility of plea bargaining; the identity of prospective witnesses; the performance or results of any examinations or the failure of the accused to submit to examinations;

and opinions as to the guilt of an accused, the merits of a defense of a party, or the merits of a case.

The RPC also follow the Reardon Report, but in light of constitutional questions regarding DR 7–107, see infra, RPC 3.6 does not mirror the scheme of regulation set up by the CPR. The RPC's standard modifies the CPR language, making RPC limitations on lawyer commentary far less strict than those of the CPR. Rule 3.6 prohibits public comment only if the lawyer *"knows or reasonably should know"* that her comment will have a "*substantial* likelihood of *materially* prejudicing" an adjudicative proceeding (emphasis added). Rule 3.6 also transforms the specific list of DR 7–107(B) into an inclusive (but not all-inclusive) list of statements that will ordinarily materially prejudice a proceeding. Although the rule's list substantially follows the CPR's list, Rule 3.6 expressly removes the CPR's permission to reveal the identity or nature of physical evidence, since such evidence will often be the object of pretrial suppression hearings that could be circumvented by pretrial publicity. In addition, Rule 3.6(b)(5) lists information which the lawyer knows or reasonably should know is likely to be inadmissible as one of the items whose release by a lawyer would ordinarily materially prejudice a proceeding.

The RPC impose at least one special requirement in this area on prosecutors: Rule 3.8(e) cautions prosecutors to exercise special care to prevent personnel associated with the prosecution (e.g., the police) from making extrajudicial statements prohibited under Rule 3.6. Also, under Rule 3.6(b)(6), no lawyer should publicly state that a defendant has been charged with a crime unless the lawyer also states that the defendant is innocent until proven guilty.

The recommendations of the Reardon Committee and the proscriptions of the CPR and RPC otherwise apply equally to attorneys for the defense and the prosecution. It has been argued that although prosecution statements should be so limited, limiting the speech of defense attorneys is improper, if not unconstitutional. Two factors support this argument: First, the prosecution's view of the case is represented in the indictment, which may contain information (whether accurate or not) that can seriously injure the reputation of an accused. Further, despite the defendant's right to be presumed innocent until proven otherwise, the theoretical presumption of innocence does not always exist in the eyes of the public once the indictment is issued. In fact, it is argued, the opposite is more often the case. Since publicity favorable to the accused may at most negate police statements and promote the presumption of innocence, defense counsel should be able to respond freely to the charges against his client. Merely allowing the accused to respond is not sufficient to counteract the public charges in most instances, it is argued, since most nonlawyers do not have sufficient facility with legal arguments to make an adequate response.

Despite the above arguments, however, the Reardon Committee believed that its restrictions should apply to defense and prosecution alike for four reasons: First, the prosecution is already disfavored because the restrictions apply only to defense counsel and not to the defendant herself. Second, the Committee stated (without elaboration) that the state has the same right to a fair trial as does the accused. Third, the Committee recognized that, practically, "[i]t is hard to see how the prosecution can be expected to remain silent in the face of a defense crusade in the media." Finally, the Committee was concerned that defense attorneys might have a greater interest in their own advertising than in representation of their clients. Another argument, although not explicitly advanced by the Reardon Committee, is that a proscription on extrajudicial comment by all attorneys (thereby removing the incentive to retaliate) is most likely to avoid "trial by the press" instead of trial by the jury.

Two other major studies, the Medina Report and the Kaufman Report questioned the constitutionality of judiciary control over statements of police, lawyers, and the media.

To further complicate matters, studies by social scientists on the effect of prejudicial media coverage tend to undermine the basic assumption underlying the imposition of limits on public comment—that such comment *actually* affects the minds of jurors.

These studies have found that jurors tend to be so seriously committed to following the judge's instructions concerning their obligation to the administration of justice that such commitment overcomes the prejudicial effect of pretrial publicity. These studies have been criticized for the inadequacy of their methodology, but they do tend to question the necessity of restricting the constitutionally protected rights of speech and press and suggest the most sparing use of those restrictions necessitated by extreme cases of undue prejudice such as *Estes* and *Sheppard.* In any event, some control over prejudicial publicity is necessary to ensure the *appearance* as well as the fact of an impartial jury.

III. EFFORTS TO LIMIT UNDULY PREJUDICIAL PUBLICITY

In addition to the various studies and revised disciplinary provisions engendered by *Estes* and *Sheppard,* further litigation was inevitable.

A. RESTRICTIONS ON THE PRESS

1. Generally

In Nebraska Press Ass'n v. Stuart (U.S.1976), a state court order which prohibited petitioners from reporting the existence and nature of confessions made by the defendant and other facts "strongly implicative" of the accused in a sensational murder case was at issue. The trial court order, as modified by the Nebraska Supreme Court, was issued in an attempt to limit prejudicial publicity concerning a case that had already attracted much media attention.

In striking the order, the United States Supreme Court applied the clear and present danger standard (whether "the gravity of the 'evil,' discounted by its improbability, justifies such invasion of free speech as is necessary to avoid the danger"). The Court held that to justify such prior restraint, "the trial judge . . . [must first] determine (a) the nature and extent of pretrial coverage; (b) whether other measures would be likely to mitigate the effects of unrestrained pretrial publicity; and (c) how effectively a restraining order would operate to prevent the threatened danger."

In 1980 the Court established the right of the press and general public to have access to criminal trials. In Richmond Newspapers v. Virginia (U.S.1980), the Court decided (in a plurality opinion) that the right of access of the press and public ensures that the constitutionally protected discussion of governmental affairs will be an informed discussion. The opinion noted that there has been an historical presumption of open trials, and that the right of access plays a significant role in the judicial process and the functioning of government. In the public scrutiny of trials the plurality found protection for the integrity of the fact-finding process of the courts, and a reinforcement of the appearance of fairness.

The right of access is not absolute; rather, the state must meet a heavy burden of justification to bar such access, and the circumstances justifying such a bar are limited. Any order restricting access must meet the three-part test applied in other prior restraint situations: First, access must present a clear and present danger or serious and imminent threat to the defendant's right to a fair trial; second, the order must be narrowly drawn; and third, no less restrictive alternative can be available.

The magnitude of the state's burden in attempting to restrict access was demonstrated in Globe Newspaper Co. v. Superior Court (U.S.1982). In that case, a state statute required that the courtroom be closed whenever a minor victim was to testify in a sexual offense case. The state asserted two justifications for restricting access in such situations: protecting minor victims of sexual offenses from further trauma and embarrassment, and encouraging such victims to come forward. The Court held that these goals were not sufficient to justify a mandatory closure of the courtroom. Courts are still free to fashion closure orders in specific cases, although such orders must meet the three-part test noted above.

2. Pretrial Proceedings

Generally, pretrial proceedings are more subject to access restrictions than are trials. In Gannett Co., Inc. v. DePasquale (U.S.1979), a newsman sought to vacate and enjoin a court order excluding the public and press from a pretrial suppression hearing in a murder prosecution. The issue presented the Court was whether members of the public have an enforceable right to a public trial that can be asserted independently of the parties in the litigation, both of whom agree that it should be closed. The Court held that under the Sixth and Fourteenth Amendments members of the public do not have a constitutional right to attend all portions of criminal trials and that any right of the press to attend a criminal trial under the First and Fourteenth Amendments was not violated by orders closing the *pretrial* suppression hearing and *temporarily* denying access to the transcript of the suppression hearing in order to ensure the defendant's right to a fair trial.

The opinion characterized the pretrial suppression hearing as a screen to filter out unreliable or illegally obtained evidence; publicity about these hearings poses special risks of unfairness because it may influence public opinion against a defendant and inform potential jurors of inculpatory information that is inadmissible at trial. The trial judge has an affirmative constitutional duty to minimize the effects of prejudicial pretrial publicity and must balance the competing values: the constitutional rights of the press and public against the defendant's right to a fair trial. The Supreme Court found that an open pretrial suppression hearing would result in the "reasonable probability of prejudice" to the defendant. The "denial" of access was only temporary (once the danger of prejudice had passed, a transcript of the suppression hearing became available to the press and public).

In Press–Enterprise Co. v. Superior Court (U.S.1986), on the other hand, the *Press–Enterprise* newspaper sought a *transcript* of a pretrial hearing. The California trial court denied the request, but the United States Supreme Court reversed. The Court noted that preliminary hearings as conducted in California have a tradition of accessibility and are sufficiently like a trial to find that public access plays a significant role in their functioning. Therefore, court orders restricting access to such transcripts must meet the same requirements as restrictions with respect to trials. The Court required that a trial court, in order to create a valid order restricting press access to preliminary hearings in California, make specific, on-the-record findings that "closure is essential to preserve higher values and is narrowly tailored to serve that interest." The First Amendment, the Court stated, requires that there be a "substantial probability" that access would deprive the defendant of a fair trial, not merely a "reasonable likelihood" (the former California standard). See also Waller v. Georgia (U.S.1984) (applying similar restrictions with respect to suppression hearings).

3. Discovery

In Seattle Times Co. v. Rhinehart (U.S.1984), the Court held that courts may severely limit the use of information obtained through the discovery process. The *Seattle Times* had printed several stories about a spiritual group lead by Mr. Rhinehart, who, together with the group and others, subsequently sued the *Times.* In a pretrial motion, plaintiffs sought a protective order prohibiting disclosure of membership information the *Times* wished to obtain through discovery. The trial court granted an order barring the *Times* from using the information in any way except where necessary to prepare and try its case.

The protective order was upheld by the Supreme Court as not offensive to the First Amendment for three reasons. First, a party-litigant does not have a First Amendment right to access to information obtained solely through discovery. Therefore, continued court control over the information did not carry the same dangers of government censorship that such control might have in other situations. Second, the information at issue would not have been available but for the discovery process. Since discovery is essential to reduce surprise at trial and pretrial delay, a protective order in appropriate cases both encourages the use of discovery and discourages its abuse. Third, the order would not fall into the classic example of prior restraint because the *Times* was free to use any information it found outside the discovery process. Thus, First Amendment rights were implicated to a far lesser extent by this order than would be the case in a different context.

B. RESTRICTIONS ON LAWYERS

1. Professional Rules

Nebraska Press Ass'n v. Stuart (U.S.1976) established "clear and present danger" to the fairness of a defendant's trial as the proper standard in determining when restrictions *on the press* may be constitutionally imposed. Although the Court did mention in passing restraints imposed *on attorneys,* determination of the legitimacy and scope of restrictions on attorneys was left to the lower courts. The issue was squarely faced, however, in a Seventh Circuit case—Chicago Council of Lawyers v. Bauer (7th Cir. 1975).

In *Bauer,* it was contended that the Code's "no comment" provisions (see DR 7–107), as incorporated in the rules of the District Court of the Northern District of Illinois, unconstitutionally deprived lawyers of their right to free speech. The Seventh Circuit agreed, holding that the standard by which extrajudicial comment was judged under the Code ("reasonable likelihood of interference with a fair trial") was vague and overbroad, and that only "those comments that pose a 'serious and imminent threat' of interference with the fair administration of justice can be constitutionally proscribed."

The court noted the necessity of striking a proper balance between all the various interests: the First Amendment rights of attorneys to comment publicly on pending litigation and to hear and read such public comment by other attorneys; the right of the accused to defend his reputation; the interest of public justice; and the Constitutional mandate of a fair trial for the accused. The court also noted that attorneys are often in the best position to comment on current litigation in order to "act as a check on the government by exposing abuses or urging action." The proper balance, in the opinion of the court, was to adopt the serious and imminent threat standard. Such a standard only narrowly limits the right to speak while it protects the fairness of a defendant's trial.

The *Bauer* court was the first to give serious weight to the First Amendment rights of attorneys with regard to the fair trial/free press issue; however, the adoption of RPC 3.6 indicates the general acceptance of the *Bauer* analysis. See discussion of RPC 3.6 supra.

2. Court–Imposed Restrictions on Lawyers' Out-of-Court Statements

In Levine v. United States District Court (9th Cir.1985), the Ninth Circuit noted that restraints on the speech of trial participants—lawyers and parties—are rarely invalidated where those restraints meet the three-part prior restraint test described above. However, the case also indicated the need for such orders to be precisely crafted in order to avoid overbreadth. *Levine* involved the first trial of an FBI agent for spying, so the case already had attracted widespread publicity that might impede a fair trial. The district court held that the "circus-like" atmosphere created by the attorneys' "performing their arguments outside the courtroom impedes the fair and effective administration of justice." The Ninth Circuit agreed, stating that uncontrolled statements by lawyers in the case constituted a serious and imminent threat to the administration of justice. But, despite the threat noted above, the Ninth Circuit found that the trial court's order was overbroad: many statements that would bear "upon the merits to be resolved by the jury," presented no danger to the administration of justice. The order was therefore overbroad in forbidding all such statements.

IV. TELEVISION IN THE COURTROOM

Permitting television coverage in the courtroom always presents potential problems for maintaining the balance between fair trial and free press. Experiments in allowing television continue in many states and have generally received favorable comment from courts and observers. The issue is not, however, a new one.

At one time, *Estes v. Texas* was thought to have settled the issue of television in the courtroom. As indicated above, *Estes* held that televising portions of a defendant's trial was a critical factor in denying him his right to a fair trial. Among those aspects of television camera use that posed sufficient threat to a fair trial to constitute a denial of due process, the Court included: televising pretrial hearings could lead to prejudice in the minds of prospective jurors; jurors, knowing they are being televised, may be self-conscious and worry more about their "performance" than about what is being said on the stand; non-sequestered jurors may see and be influenced by edited versions of the trial; new trials may be jeopardized when jurors have seen portions of the prior case; witnesses may be so conscious of the cameras that they modify their testimony; the necessarily increased supervisory responsibilities of judges and the potential for "playing to the camera" (particularly if an election is upcoming) may distract them from their obligation to ensure a fair trial; and grandstanding by attorneys may deprive defendants of effective assistance of counsel.

Subsequently, however, the Court approved states' continued experimentation in allowing television coverage and significantly relaxed the severe restrictions on television coverage which had seemed to be imposed by *Estes.* In Chandler v. Florida (U.S. 1981), the Court affirmed a Florida conviction despite the televising of the defendant's trial over his objections. The Court reinterpreted *Estes,* focusing on Harlan's concurrence, and stated that the holding in *Estes* did not establish a constitutional rule that all television coverage of trials was an inherent denial of due process, but established only that the use of television in *that* case denied due process. Rather than a per se rule prohibiting television cameras in the courtroom, the proper course for protecting due process rights in such situations is for the defendant to show that, *in his particular case,* the jury's ability to adjudicate his case fairly was *in fact* compromised by electronic media coverage.

In reaching its decision, the *Chandler* Court relied on several important factors. First, the Court noted that technology had changed greatly since *Estes,* allowing, for example, the use of natural lighting for the newer, less bulky television equipment. Thus, television coverage today would be less distracting than it was at the time *Estes* was decided. Second, no empirical data had been presented regarding the effects of television cameras on the judicial process under all circumstances. In light of the lack of data, state experimentation with television should be allowed to continue. Third, the Court noted that there were safeguards built into the Florida program to prevent the worst problems envisioned in *Estes.* These protective measures have included the use of only one camera "shared" by the networks and the delay of broadcasts until the case has been concluded or the jury has been sequestered. In the much publicized Ronnie Zamora case in Florida, for example, the trial judge denied a request by the jurors to view themselves on television following each day of testimony. *Chandler* did not establish whether broadcast media have the same right of access to public trials as the print media and the public. See *Richmond Newspapers,* supra.

By 1985, forty-three states permitted television coverage either on an experimental or permanent basis. See also Code of Judicial Conduct former Canon 3(A)(7) (judge may authorize coverage "under rules prescribed by a supervising appellate court or other appropriate authority" under conditions which "allow such coverage in a manner that will be unobtrusive, will not distract the trial participants, and will not otherwise interfere with the administration of justice"). The 1990 revision of the CJC removed the entire issue from regulation in the CJC. State regulations address various considerations, including the effect of consent or objection by parties or witnesses, whether the jury should be televised, whether some types of trials should not be broadcast, procedural issues (e.g., whether a pretrial hearing is required to review a decision regarding broadcast), and whether broadcasters have an obligation to provide balanced reporting.

Although commentators will probably continue to argue about when television cameras should or should not be allowed in the courtroom, they generally agree that "sensitive" cases, such as juvenile and rape cases, should be closed to television to protect against undue embarrassment and invasion of privacy.

V. CONCLUSION

The mid–1960s saw the beginning of a more aggressive judicial stance on the fair trial/free press issue. The U.S. Supreme Court indicated that it was the trial judge's responsibility to limit the effect of prejudicial publicity on a defendant's trial, and trial judges acted on its recommendation. The "gag order" imposed on the press in Nebraska Press Ass'n v. Stuart was an example of a trial judge's going too far; the right of freedom of the press mandated that other measures must be attempted first. *Bauer,* along with the adoption of RPC 3.6, indicate that limitations on the freedom of speech of participants in a trial should also be a last resort. More generally, the trend of judicial opinion and the experiments with television in the courtroom illustrate an increasing concern that the doors of the courthouse be opened to the public and that the business of the court be freely discussed. The defendant's right to a fair trial before an impartial jury has not been forgotten, however. Instead, the emphasis has shifted from curtailing public comment whenever potentially prejudicial to permitting such comment unless the threat to a fair trial, whether from the press or the participants, is "serious and imminent," "clear and present." Now if only the Supreme Court will permit the televising of its own arguments. . . .

CHAPTER 18

THE LAWYER AS PROSECUTING ATTORNEY

I. THE ROLE OF THE PROSECUTOR IN AN ADVERSARY SYSTEM

Prosecutors, like all attorneys, are required to conform their conduct to the standards of the RPC and CPR. As advocates of the state, however, they also face special ethical problems that arise from the great powers of their office and the dual role it fulfills. On the one hand, the adversarial model of truth-finding used in our legal system exerts pressure on the prosecutor to secure convictions by presenting the strongest possible case. At the same time, it is clear that "the duty of the prosecutor is to seek justice, not merely to convict." Berger v. United States (U.S. 1935); ABA Standard 1.1(c), The Prosecution Function (1971); Comment, RPC 3.8; EC 7–13. This duty is reflected in RPC 3.8 and DR 7–103, which prohibit the prosecutor from instituting criminal charges that are known to be not supported by probable cause, and which require the disclosure of evidence to the defense that negates guilt or mitigates the offense. Although these rules and DR 7–107 (which deals with the proper limits of pre-trial publicity, discussed in Chapter 17, supra), are the only sections of the RPC and CPR directed specifically to the prosecutorial function, both Codes in their entirety serve as a framework for evaluating prosecutors' ethical obligations.

The ethical dilemmas faced by prosecutors are often similar to those of other attorneys. For example, they equally share obligations to avoid the use of false evidence, the assertion of personal opinions as to credibility, or communication with jurors. However, the prosecutor's situation is complicated by the power of her office and the competing interests it must serve. Unlike other lawyers, the prosecutor's client is never a person, but always the symbolic concept of "the state." Even with an individual client, it may be difficult to determine the course of legal conduct in his best interest; as a result, the client's wishes rather than the attorney's preferences must normally dictate the representation. The prosecutor's determination of what her client, "the People," wants in a given case is even more problematic. At the same time that there may be community sentiment in favor of strict law enforcement, there may also exist an opposing belief in the right of every accused person to due process of law.

The vast majority of local prosecutors in the United States are elected officials, subject to the pressures of the political process. Many are elected according to partisan affiliations. While there is a clear value in maintaining democratic control over an office that wields such tremendous discretionary power in enforcing the law, the temptation for the prosecutor to exercise that power consistent with political popularity may undermine his duty to administer justice impartially. Many political leaders began their careers as prosecutors. The opportunities to become familiar to the public through publicity in major cases and to gain popularity by securing convictions pose a severe threat to the prosecutor's independent professional judgment.

Appointed prosecutors are also subject to political pressures, subtle or flagrant. In 1971, then-Deputy Attorney General Richard Kleindienst urged U.S. Attorneys to do whatever they could to keep the Nixon administration in power. When the political process intrudes into the administration of justice, upholding the public trust may become impossible. Nonetheless, independent professional judgment on behalf of the public interest remains strong among many prosecutors: For example, 65 lawyers in the Civil Rights Division of the Justice Department protested the implementation of Nixon's "Southern strategy," in contravention of what they considered to be a clear legal mandate for school desegregation in Mississippi.

II. DISCRETION TO CHARGE

The decision to charge a person with a crime is the heart of the prosecutorial function. As long as the prosecutor has probable cause to believe that the suspect has committed a crime, he has total discretion in deciding whether to prosecute and, if so, with what charge. Bordenkircher v. Hayes (U.S.1978). He may not make his decision on a discriminatory basis such as race or religion; nor may he make his decision in an attempt to prevent the exercise of a protected statutory or constitutional right. Wayte v. United States (U.S.1985). However, to challenge his decision as discriminatory, a defendant must demonstrate both failure to prosecute other, similarly situated persons and purposeful discrimination. Id.; Oyler v. Boles (U.S.1962). This strong presumption of prosecutorial propriety is coupled with a qualified immunity for misconduct in advocacy, although the immunity has been held not to apply to acts that are not within the prosecutor's jurisdiction.

The inherent discretionary nature of the decision to charge gives tremendous power to the prosecutor and bears significant responsibilities. As court dockets have grown crowded, the prosecutor's limited resources require that many cases be handled rapidly. The prosecutor must make decisions at several levels of the law enforcement process, including who to investigate, detain, charge, and to whom to offer plea bargains. Proper and improper considerations, including public opinion, the need for information in other cases, or even the political views of the suspect, may influence the decisions that are made. Use of an "enemies list" to direct investigation and charging may be regarded as conduct prejudicial to the administration of justice, in violation of RPC 8.4(d) or DR 1-102(A)(5), but bar grievance committees normally abstain from inquiry into political crimes. Although flagrant abuse of discretion may lead at least to outside scrutiny by legislative committees or grand juries, most prosecutors retain unchecked discretion.

At a minimum, a prosecutor is subject to discipline if she charges when she knows that the charges are not supported by probable cause. RPC 3.8(a); DR 7–103(A); Prosecution Standard 3.9(a). The CPR adds an objective test to this subjective standard: the prosecutor also must not bring charges if it is obvious that they are not supported by probable cause. DR 7–103(A). RPC 4.4 prohibits conduct that has "no substantial purpose other than to embarrass, delay, or burden a third person," which would seem to preclude harassing prosecutions. The prosecutor may decline prosecution for a variety of reasons, including personal doubt about the guilt of the accused, weighing of the harm caused by the crime against the severity of possible punishment, or the cooperation of the accused in law enforcement action directed at other suspects. Prosecution Standard 3.9(b). While the Standards formerly rendered it proper to decline prosecution following long non-enforcement of a law with community acquiescence (e.g., Sunday closing laws), the amended Standards exclude this as a proper consideration since it could provide an apparent justification for dereliction of duty, such as the non-enforcement of gambling laws.

To enjoin prosecution on the ground that it is undertaken in bad faith, it must be shown that the prosecutor has "no genuine expectation of conviction," a difficult test to meet. Allee v. Medrano (U.S.1974). As Justice Robert Jackson once suggested, the great number of laws on the books make it likely that anyone who is the subject of sustained scrutiny can with some justification be charged with a crime. The motivation for the prosecutor's decision to investigate and charge thus becomes important if it is to be exercised impartially and justly. In Blackledge v. Perry (U.S.1974), a prosecutor's decision to charge a misdemeanant, who had successfully appealed and obtained a new trial, with a felony was held to violate due process since it was vindictively motivated by the appeal and would inhibit exercise of this legal right. Where a change in the charging decision occurs *before* the original trial, however, the Court has held that there is no reason to presume that the prosecution has become vindictive. United

States v. Goodwin (U.S.1982) (misdemeanor defendant decided not to plead guilty but to seek jury trial; thereafter prosecutor decided to charge defendant instead with felony based on same incident). It has also been held improper to prosecute with the motive of inducing the defendant to drop charges he had filed against the police who mistreated him. Although some standards exist regarding the decision *to charge,* courts have refused to review the decision *not to prosecute* out of deference to separation of powers.

III. PLEA BARGAINING

Limited prosecutorial resources and extreme congestion in criminal courts exert great pressure on the prosecutor to dispose of his caseload by accepting guilty pleas to lesser offenses. It has been estimated that between 65 and 95% of criminal defendants plead guilty; some critics of plea bargaining suggest that this is in large part due to overcharging with crimes for which a conviction could not be obtained. A Department of Justice study found prosecutors in one metropolitan area used this technique as a means of inducing guilty pleas. The probable cause test of RPC 3.8(a) and DR 7–103(B) ostensibly prohibits such overcharging, but there seems to be little likelihood that it would come to the attention of disciplinary committees.

In the past, a defendant was required to admit guilt to plead guilty, but judges may now accept a plea of guilty from a person who claims to be innocent as long as there is an admission that the evidence is strong and seems incontrovertible. North Carolina v. Alford (U.S.1970). For this reason prosecutorial good faith is particularly important; thus, in bargaining with the defendant, the prosecutor is subject to discipline for any false statements or representations to the defendant or defense counsel. See RPC 4.1; Prosecution Standard 4.1(c). It is also unprofessional conduct for a prosecutor to discuss a plea with the accused except in the presence of counsel if the defendant is represented, according to Prosecution Standard 4.1(b), RPC 4.2, and DR 7–104(A)(1). However, the Supreme Court has held that prosecutors may initiate questioning of a criminal defendant who has been indicted but has not yet asked for a lawyer, even though his Sixth Amendment right to counsel has attached. Patterson v. Illinois (U.S.1988). A defendant in such a position should still be protected by the *Miranda* warning requirement and the prosecutor's ethical obligation under RPC 3.8(b) to assure that the accused "has been advised of the right to and the procedure for obtaining, counsel and has been given reasonable opportunity to obtain counsel."

Any promise by a prosecutor concerning the sentence to be imposed is *per se* unprofessional conduct, since it is a promise beyond his power to fulfill. Prosecution Standard 4.3(a). Promising to recommend a lenient sentence if asked may constitute fraud if the court normally asks for no recommendation from the prosecutor. Since promises made in the course of plea bargaining are inducements that affect the voluntary nature of a guilty plea, the prosecutor has a duty to keep them. Santobello v. New York (U.S.1971). But see United States v. Benchimol (U.S.1985) (prosecutor, after agreeing to recommend sentence, not required to explain reasons for recommendation to judge or to make recommendation "enthusiastically"). If the prosecutor is unable to fulfill a commitment that helped to induce a guilty plea, a duty arises to avoid prejudice to the defendant by assisting in withdrawal of the plea; however, according to the language of Prosecution Standard 4.3(c), failure to do so will not subject the prosecutor to disciplinary sanctions.

The proper stance for the prosecutor in plea negotiations is thus one of open and frank presentation of his intentions and powers. A prosecutor who adopts an overly adversarial approach and seeks to force pleas by confusing or coercing the defendant violates the duty to seek justice rather than convictions. However, the Supreme Court has held that a threat to indict a defendant under a habitual criminal statute because he will not plead guilty to the underlying charge is not a violation of due process. Bordenkircher v. Hayes (U.S.1978).

IV. CONFLICTS OF INTEREST

As attorneys and public officials, prosecutors must exercise independent professional judgment in accord with RPC 1.7–1.13 and CPR Canon 5. Their ability to meet these standards may be threatened by conflicts of interest which arise between their public duties and private lives. RPC 1.7 and 1.8 and DR 5–101(A) prohibit employment if the attorney's personal interests may affect his professional judgment, while DR 9–101(B) forbids private employment in a matter in which the lawyer had substantial responsibility as a public official. Accord, RPC 1.11(a). Private attorneys can resolve many potential conflict of interest problems by fully disclosing the facts to a client and obtaining informed consent (see Ch. 12, supra); however, it is generally acknowledged that the public cannot give its consent to a conflict of interest. (Note, however, that RPC 1.11(a) does allow subsequent private representation if the former government employer consents after consultation.) Therefore, most jurisdictions require that the position of prosecutor be full-time and prohibit simultaneous private practice of law, although some jurisdictions with smaller government budgets allow the prosecutor to take private cases. Both the ABA and the National District Attorneys Association recommend full-time positions for prosecutors to improve the professional skills of the prosecutor and to reduce the chance of conflicts of interest.

When the prosecutor turns to private practice to supplement her income, a severe danger of conflicting interests arises. Such a conflict may harm the public's interest in zealous enforcement of the law or the defendant's right to unbiased consideration of his case. For example, a prosecutor who represented an individual in a divorce proceeding when a criminal action was underway against the other spouse was held to have violated the defendant's due process rights.

The partners and associates of a prosecutor are under similar constraints, since they may not take any client that the prosecutor could not. RPC 1.11(a); DR 5–105(D). When an associate of a firm is a part-time assistant attorney general, the firm's representation of a client in a claim against the state has been called unprofessional conduct. Since the prosecutor's public duties may be difficult to delegate to another, the solution to such problems must for the most part rest in limiting private practice by prosecutors or carefully scrutinizing the activities of firms that have associates in the prosecutor's office. Under RPC 1.11(a), "screening" is permitted as a mechanism for allowing *successive* private representation by an otherwise disqualified firm if the "disqualified lawyer is screened from any participation in the matter and is apportioned no part of the fee therefrom [and] written notice is promptly given to the appropriate tribunal to enable it to ascertain compliance with the provisions of this rule."

As noted above, the decision to charge is seldom open to challenge once the prosecutor has probable cause to believe that a crime has been committed. As long as the partisan political process is used to select prosecutors, a strong likelihood will exist that politics will enter into at least some prosecutorial decisions. To the extent that politics are a reflection of society's concerns about which problems most deserve the attention of law enforcement, consideration of these expressed concerns should frankly be recognized as necessary and appropriate. When, however, the political process is more concerned with personalities and continued political success and these concerns direct prosecutorial energy, a clear conflict of interest arises.

V. RESPONSIBILITY FOR ENSURING FAIR TRIALS

Despite the presence of defense counsel as a trained adversary, the prosecutor's role as an advocate demands recognition of special responsibilities toward the court and the defendant during trial. This stems in part from the duty to seek justice rather than convictions and also reflects the protections given to a criminal defendant as part of the presumption of innocence. The judge or jury is obligated to find guilt or innocence solely on the basis of the material presented in court in accordance with the law; the prosecutor must bear a substantial burden of avoiding any conduct that will prejudice this reasoned decisionmaking. Unfortunately, as the record of prosecutorial misconduct preserved in appellate decisions demonstrates, adversarial zeal sometimes leads to improper argument or use of evidence.

As indicated infra, appellate review is an inadequate means of controlling prosecutorial trial misconduct. Even in a case in which the prosecutor violated his duty under DR 7–106(C)(4) (accord, RPC 3.4(e)) to avoid expression of personal belief in guilt and called the defendant "a vicious, murderous pig," the appellate court found sufficiently strong evidence of guilt to justify upholding the conviction and made no recommendation that disciplinary proceedings be brought against the prosecutor. In another case, a prosecutor who made faces to the jury conveying disbelief in the testimony was condemned as unethical; his act was considered even worse than an open statement of disbelief, since it was an attempt to influence the jury in a manner that the defense counsel would fail to observe and to which he would thus be unable to object. Finding no appreciable effect on the verdict, however, the court declined to order reversal or a new trial. The Supreme Court itself has held that "the touchstone of due process analysis in cases of alleged prosecutorial misconduct is the fairness of the trial, not the culpability of the prosecutor." Smith v. Phillips (U.S.1982). Prosecutorial misconduct by itself, the Court held, does not justify a new trial. Understandably, other considerations may outweigh the desire of the courts to deter prosecutors from future misconduct by overturning convictions. It is less understandable that the bar has ignored examples of misconduct recorded in appellate decisions that clearly appear to violate disciplinary rules or standards adopted by the ABA and state jurisdictions.

Occasionally, prosecutorial misconduct will be so severe that the trial judge will squarely confront it. In one extreme example, United States v. Banks (D.S.D.1974), the judge dismissed charges against one of the leaders of the American Indian Movement after he concluded that "incidents of misconduct formed a pattern throughout the course of the trial [which] leads me to the belief that this case was not prosecuted in good faith or in the spirit of justice. The waters of justice have been polluted. . . ." The judge also found that a prosecutor offered testimony directly contradicted by a document in his possession, either through gross negligence or intentional deception.

Such a conclusion and remedy is, however, unusual. More often, the judge relies on the defense to object to improper argument and sometimes is sympathetic to the sentiments expressed by the prosecution. In reviewing a conviction for assault upon a police officer with intent to murder, no impropriety was found in an argument that jurors "may find him guilty or not guilty. . . . You may say to [the officers and the Police Department] we don't mind if you get shot; we don't care, and we are not going to support law enforcement in this county." Although it would seem clearly to be an attempt to appeal to the passions of the jury by injection of an extraneous issue, since it assumes that the defendant is in fact guilty and will be acquitted only if the jurors are opposed to law enforcement, the court considered this argument a "mere plea for law enforcement." Cf. United States v. Schartner (3d Cir.1970) (prosecutor's remark, "if you do not convict, the guilty will escape," deemed to be reversible error). The Prosecution Standards adopted by the ABA do not call for discipline of a prosecutor who appeals to prejudice or distracts the jury from its proper function with irrelevant issues; instead, they weakly recommend that a prosecutor "should" avoid such argument, although failure to do so will not constitute unprofessional conduct. Prosecution Standards 5.9(c), (d).

A. EXPRESSION OF PERSONAL OPINION

Certain forms of unethical courtroom behavior are, however, clearly recognized as justifying discipline: According to RPC 3.4(e), DR 7–106(C)(4) and Prosecution Standard 5.8(b), it is unprofessional conduct to express a personal opinion as to the truth of any testimony or the guilt of a defendant. The prosecutor is allowed to argue for a conclusion on the basis of the evidence, but a fine line separates proper from improper comments. For example, while some courts have found it improper to ask the jury in closing argument "to come to the decision which I think you should come to, based on the evidence, that the defendant is guilty as charged," others have held it proper to say "I believe the evidence has shown the guilt of the defendant." Although a jury would seem likely to understand the statement "I would not ask you to send an innocent man to the penitentiary" to reflect the prosecutor's belief in the defendant's guilt, the Alabama Supreme Court found no impropriety in it. Such comments, or those of the prosecutor who asked the jury in his summation, "Did you see those eyes on that killer?", remove the prosecutor from his appropriate role as an advocate and make him an unsworn witness with the unsavory advantage of appearing to know more about the facts than has been admitted into evidence.

The same rationale explains the ban on personal opinion as to the credibility of witnesses. One court held it to be impermissible comment for the prosecutor to describe a government witness as "one of the best undercover agents we have" and one who "puts his life on the line." The credibility and character of witnesses is to be measured by the finder of fact after the adversarial process has exposed inconsistency or provided corroboration, and the testimonials of the prosecutor have no place in the process. Statements of personal opinion by the prosecutor may be particularly dangerous because of jurors' faith in her resulting from the prestige of her office and the availability of information from police investigations. This greater credibility necessitates recognition of greater responsibility for maintaining a professional attitude and avoiding personal involvement in the case.

B. COMMENT ON THE DEFENDANT'S SILENCE

Since the state has the burden of proof beyond a reasonable doubt in a criminal case, the defendant need not prove anything. The Supreme Court has held that the self-incrimination clause of the Fifth Amendment is violated by prosecutorial comment on the accused's silence. Griffin v. California (U.S.1965). Although a jury might on its own draw an impermissible inference of guilt from the defendant's failure to testify, it is highly improper for the prosecutor to encourage that inference, particularly since it is unlikely that jury instructions can cure the error once the thought has been expressed or suggested.

There is general agreement that it is not improper for the prosecutor to state that certain evidence is "uncontroverted," unless, in the context of the trial, the jury would most likely conclude that the defendant would be the natural source of contradiction. On the other hand, comments on the unwillingness of a defendant to take a lie detector test and on the failure of the defendant to call witnesses have been held to be improper. The latter may be proper, however, if a witness alleged to be able to corroborate the defense theory is particularly accessible to the defendant but not to the prosecution; otherwise, comments on any of these subjects constitute an impermissible attempt to shift the burden of proof to the defendant.

C. PRESENTING FALSE, MISLEADING, OR INADMISSIBLE EVIDENCE

The prosecutor must scrupulously avoid misleading the court or the jury as to the evidence, and may be disciplined for knowingly offering false evidence, failing to withdraw it upon discovering its falsity, intentionally misstating the evidence, or bringing evidence before the court without a good faith belief in its admissibility. These strictures are enumerated in RPC 3.3(a)(1) and DR 7–102(A)(4), (5); RPC 3.4(e) and DR 7–106(C)(1); and Prosecution Standards 5.6 and 5.8. Thus, it has been held to be a violation of due process to falsely deny that a government witness has received immunity in return for testifying, Giglio v. United States (U.S.1972), or to fail to correct a witness' false denial of receiving promises in return for his testimony, Napue v. Illinois (U.S.1959).

Although knowing presentation of false evidence is an infrequent form of prosecutorial misconduct, offers of inadmissible evidence or the making of impermissible comments with the purpose of bringing inadmissible matter before the judge or jury, prohibited by RPC 3.4(e), DR 7–106(C)(1) and Prosecution Standard 5.6(b), appear often in appellate decisions. One point at which errors of this type occur is during the opening argument. The prosecutor at that time outlines the case and the expected proofs that will be made. Care must be taken to avoid allegations that will not be substantiated by facts offered into evidence at trial. It has been held improper, for example, to mention a confession in the opening argument before the court has found it to be voluntary in nature; and, during examination of a witness, it is serious misconduct for a prosecutor to justify a line of questioning by advising the court that she will present supporting witnesses when she knows she is unable to do so.

D. FAILURE TO DISCLOSE EXCULPATORY EVIDENCE

After a request for its production by the defense, the suppression by the prosecutor of evidence that was material to guilt or punishment was held to violate due process in Brady v. Maryland (U.S.1963). The *Brady* rule was further refined in United States v. Bagley (U.S.1985), which held that impeachment as well as exculpatory evidence must be disclosed if "material," but that withheld evidence is "material" such as to require reversal of a conviction only if there is a reasonable probability that, had the evidence been disclosed to the defense, the result of the proceeding would have been different. The command that the prosecution must seek justice rather than convictions dictates that the adversarial model must yield at some point to cooperation by the prosecutor with the defense. The RPC and CPR therefore go beyond the constitutional requirement of disclosure in providing that a prosecutor must make timely disclosure to the defense of evidence that tends to negate guilt, mitigate the degree of the offense, or reduce punishment. DR 7–103(B); RPC 3.8(d) ("except when the prosecutor is relieved of this responsibility by a protective order of the tribunal"). Thus, the RPC and CPR establish an independent duty to disclose without any request.

It is likewise unprofessional conduct for the prosecutor to avoid pursuing evidence because she believes it will damage the prosecution's case or aid the accused. Of course, this does not impose a duty on the prosecution to undertake the role of defense investigator. It merely warns the prosecutor that investigation must not cease merely because there appears some likelihood of uncovering evidence that does not help to secure a conviction. Even after the trial concludes with a conviction, the Supreme Court has noted that the ethics of the office require a prosecutor who acquires information casting doubt on the correctness of a conviction to disclose the evidence to an appropriate authority. Imbler v. Pachtman (U.S.1976). See RPC 3.8(d); DR 7–103(B).

VI. SUPERVISING THE POLICE

The CPR and RPC ignore the issue of relations between prosecutors and police, while the ABA Prosecution Standards suggest only that the prosecutor provide legal advice to police officers and cooperate in training them. There is no hint that the prosecutor has any duty to supervise police activity, other than the prohibition in Standard 3.1(b) of the encouragement or use of illegal means to secure evidence. (See also RPC 3.8(e), requiring prosecutors to exercise reasonable care that police do not make improper extrajudicial statements to the press.) One of the surprising aspects of this prohibition is that there is no proscription against the use of evidence so obtained. In fact, this is inevitably the stage at which the prosecutor has the most control over the investigative process. One commentator has stated that knowing use of illegally obtained confessions and evidence has long been a practice in prosecutors' offices, although it is the police who are actually engaged in the illegal activity. Since police obtain information for the purpose of securing convictions, prosecutors can exert considerable influence over them by clarifying the permissible bounds of procedure and carefully using only properly obtained evidence. In cases considering the use of false testimony, the state has been charged with the knowledge of its agents, including the police. In this manner police misconduct becomes prosecutorial misconduct, and otherwise proper convictions may be lost if the prosecutor has not ensured the proper training of the police.

An even more severe—though hopefully less common—problem is that of criminal activity by individual police, including discriminatory law enforcement, illegal arrests with excessive force, bribery or extortion, and even homicide. The American Civil Liberties Union charged in 1970 that, during a 19 month period, although 107 Los Angeles policemen had committed a total of 117 offenses punishable by state law for which they were disciplined by their department, none was ever prosecuted by the district attorney. Serious incidents, such as the Chicago police riots of 1968 directed against protesters and hapless bystanders alike, or the sadly common cases of police assaults on social and racial minorities, further point to the need for prosecutorial supervision of police, including the instigation of criminal charges when justified.

VII. INTERFERENCE WITH CLIENT-ATTORNEY RELATIONSHIP

In recent years, state and federal prosecutors have increasingly attempted to obtain information about criminal defendants from their lawyers. These efforts have included: threats to charge defense counsel as co-conspirators unless they provide information against their clients in grand jury proceedings; vigorous enforcement of "money laundering" or "cash reporting" provisions such as 26 U.S.C.A. § 6050I (requiring that receipt of $10,000 or more in cash from a client be reported, *along with the client's identity,* to the IRS); and increased use of fee forfeiture provisions prior to trial to enjoin the use of a defendant's funds to retain counsel, or after trial to recoup any attorney's fees paid to defense counsel.

Although these actions, as part of the "war on crime," are all constitutionally *permitted,* despite their negative impact on the client-attorney relationship (see, e.g. Caplin & Drysdale, Chartered v. United States (U.S.1989) and discussion in Ch. 11), there are significant possibilities for abuse by prosecutors. Commentators and some courts have recognized the potential for interfering with—or even preventing—those accused of certain crimes from obtaining effective counsel of their choosing. The Department of Justice issued its own guidelines for regulating when federal prosecutors should issue subpoenas to defense counsel. However, the increased use of Justice Department subpoenas to defense counsel (over 640 in 1989) prompted the ABA in 1990 to add Rule 3.8(f) to the RPC. RPC 3.8(f) prohibits prosecutors from subpoenaing a lawyer in a criminal proceeding unless:

(1) the prosecutor reasonably believes:

(a) the information sought is not protected from disclosure by any applicable privilege;

(b) the evidence sought is essential to the successful completion of an ongoing investigation or prosecution;

(c) there is no other feasible alternative to obtain the information; and

(2) the prosecutor obtains prior judicial approval after an opportunity for an adversarial proceeding.

VIII. DISCIPLINE

The proper limits of prosecutorial conduct are often difficult to define, due in large part to the reluctance of the bar either to set rules of conduct for prosecutors or to take disciplinary action against them for violation of the few clear rules. Although some prosecutors have been disbarred for acts such as bribery or the commission of a felony, review of prosecutorial misconduct by bar grievance committees is rare and discipline, if imposed, is usually mild. Even when discipline is recommended by a grievance committee, court review may mitigate it. After Attorney General

Richard Kleindienst was convicted of lying under oath during his confirmation hearings, the District of Columbia Bar recommended a one year suspension of his license to practice; the D.C. Court of Appeals reduced the suspension to one month.

There are various reasons for the failure of the organized bar to regulate prosecuting attorneys. Both the courts and the bar are more likely to sympathize with conservative community interests than with the individuals, primarily criminal defendants, who may suffer from the misconduct of a prosecutor. The political nature of the prosecutor's office in many jurisdictions and its inherent discretionary power—greater than that of police or judiciary—make it a dangerous opponent. As a result, overzealous prosecutors are more likely to be commended than condemned. An example of this tendency is a decision of the Illinois State Bar: It found no reason to discipline a prosecutor who had introduced into evidence clothing with large stains described as blood, successfully resisted a defense motion to inspect them, and secured a conviction while knowing that the stains were in fact paint. Since some blood was present on the shorts, the bar grievance committee concluded that there had been no unethical conduct. The Supreme Court, however, found that use of the clothing constituted deliberate misrepresentation by the prosecutor and overturned the murder conviction. Miller v. Pate (U.S.1967). And, following a U.S. Supreme Court reversal of a murder conviction based on a prosecutor's misconduct in eliciting inaccurate testimony from a key witness with knowledge of its inaccuracy, Alcorta v. Texas (U.S.1957), the prosecutor was named "Outstanding Texas Prosecutor" by the Texas Law Enforcement Foundation.

One rationale for the refusal of the bar to consider prosecutorial misconduct is the nature of the adversary system. According to this argument, the truth in a case can be determined only when each side forcefully presents its position, and the fact-finder chooses the most credible version. Sometimes this argument results in an appellate court excusing otherwise improper prosecutorial conduct on the ground that it was in response to provocation by defense counsel. This even-handed game theory of the criminal process ignores the differences between prosecution and defense, including the presumption of innocence afforded the defendant and the burden of proof that the prosecution must carry. Prosecutors are not mere civil litigants but represent the state, and as the Joint Conference on Professional Responsibility noted, they cannot take the standard of an attorney appearing on behalf of an individual client as a guide for their conduct.

CHAPTER 19

THE LAWYER AS ADVISOR AND NEGOTIATOR

The roles of advisor and negotiator, when filled by an attorney, present different practical and ethical considerations than those presented by the role of advocate. Consequently, this chapter will consider the special ethical duties imposed on an attorney who is serving as an advisor or negotiator.

I. THE LAWYER AS ADVISOR

The advisory role of an attorney is different than the adversarial role, requiring attention to the future conduct of the client, EC 7–3, and to the client's personal responses to the potential alternatives. See EC 3–2; RPC 2.1, 1.2 and Comments. Since attorneys have been trained to deal with legally relevant facts and within the adversary model, the focus on the personal and emotional aspects of a legal decision are particularly problematic for many attorneys. Although the advisory role is a pervasive one in law practice and is crucial both to the attorney's effectiveness and to the client's satisfaction, many professional rules fail to discriminate between the advisory and adversarial roles assumed by the attorney.

Both the RPC and CPR recognize some differences between the roles of advisor and advocate. While the attorney in an advocate's role is instructed to resolve doubts as to the bounds of the law in favor of his client, an advisor is instructed to "give his professional opinion as to what the ultimate decisions of the courts would likely be as to the applicable law." EC 7–3. Accord, EC 7–5. See Comment, RPC 2.1. When the client's state of mind in electing a course of conduct is relevant to its legality, however, the attorney may resolve reasonable doubts about that state of mind in favor of his client. EC 7–6. Cf. RPC 1.2 (Comment).

Within the advisory context, most commentators endorse a "participatory" role for the client. For example,

> [t]he case law on professional responsibility fails to protect clients against incompetent attorneys by unfairly treating the client as if he were the informed and responsible decision maker . . . while, at the same time, the legal profession denies the client access to the very information which might provide a basis for the assumption of some client responsibility.

D. Rosenthal, Lawyer and Client: Who's in Charge 144 (1974). This criticism of the reduced role of the client in the client-lawyer relationship would appear to be met to some degree by the CPR *aspirational* provisions that "the decision whether to forego legally available objectives or methods because of non-legal factors is ultimately for the client and not for [the lawyer]," EC 7–8, and that all decisions affecting the merits of a cause or substantially prejudicing his rights should be made by the client, EC 7–7. See ABA Defense Function Standard § 5.2 (1971); RPC 1.2(a), RPC 2.1 (Comment). In advising the client, the attorney should assist him by helping to identify the alternative courses of conduct available and by exploring the repercussions—legal, practical, moral, and emotional—inherent in each. EC 7–8.

However, in addition to not being mandatory, neither of these CPR provisions deals with the duty to provide the information necessary for the client to make informed decisions. Under the RPC, the lawyer must keep the client "reasonably informed about the status of a matter," "promptly comply with reasonable requests for information," and "explain a matter to the extent reasonably necessary to permit the client to make informed decisions regarding the representation." RPC 1.4(a) & (b). Thus, "a lawyer negotiating on behalf of a client should provide the client with facts relevant to the matter, inform the client of communications from the other party and take other reasonable steps that permit the client to make a decision regarding a serious offer from another party." Comment, RPC 1.4. All settlement offers or proffered plea bargains *must* be communicated to the client, and the client's ultimate decision whether to accept such offers, after consultation with the lawyer, must be accepted by the lawyer. RPC 1.2(a); 1.4 (Comment).

Rule 1.2(a) provides more generally that the lawyer must abide by the client's decisions concerning the "*objectives*" of representation and must consult with the client concerning the "*means*" by which they are to be pursued. The lawyer may assume ultimate responsibility for "technical and legal tactical issues, but should defer to the client regarding such questions as the expense to be incurred and concern for third persons who might be adversely affected." Comment, RPC 1.2.

The Comment notes that the "client-lawyer relationship partakes of a joint undertaking," and does not resolve the dilemma encountered when the client, after consultation, disagrees with the lawyer concerning the means to be employed. Rule 2.1 indicates that the lawyer may properly advise the client of relevant moral, economic, social and political factors, and "should not be deterred from giving candid advice by the prospect that the advice will be unpalatable to the client." Comment, RPC 2.1. See also EC 7–8; Report of the Joint Conference on Professional Responsibility (1958) (an attorney should "preserve a sufficient detachment from [her] client's interest so that [she] remains capable of sound and objective appraisal of the propriety of what [her] client proposes to do"). According to the CPR, an attorney whose client elects a course of conduct different from that recommended by the attorney may either continue to represent the client, unless the client elects a course of conduct that is illegal or frivolous, EC 7–5, or may withdraw if the client "[i]nsists, in a matter not pending before a tribunal, that the lawyer engage in conduct that is contrary to the judgment and advice of the lawyer, but not prohibited under the Disciplinary Rules," DR 2–110(C)(1)(e); RPC 1.16(b)(3) ("client insists upon pursuing an objective that the lawyer considers repugnant or imprudent").

In advising his client, the attorney may refuse to aid or participate in conduct which he believes to be unlawful, DR 7–101(B)(2), see RPC 1.2(d), and may withdraw if the client "[p]ersonally seeks to pursue an illegal course of conduct," DR 2–110(C)(1)(b), see RPC 1.16(b)(1). An attorney must not counsel or assist the client in conduct known to be illegal or fraudulent, DR 7–102(A)(7), RPC 1.2(d) ("*criminal* or fraudulent," apparently not including illegal conduct that is not criminal), and must withdraw if the client is "having steps taken for him . . . merely for the purpose of harassing or maliciously injuring any person," DR 2–110(B)(1). Cf. RPC 1.16(a)(1) (representation will violate the RPC or other law); 3.1 (improper to frivolously bring or defend an action or assert or controvert an issue); 4.4 (improper to use means with no substantial purpose other than to embarrass, delay or burden a third person).

Rule 1.2(d) provides that although a lawyer may not "counsel" or "assist" in conduct that is criminal or fraudulent, she may "discuss the legal consequences of any proposed course of conduct with a client." The ABA Comment adds that there "is a critical distinction between presenting an analysis of legal aspects of questionable conduct and recommending the means by which a crime or fraud might be committed with impunity." The Rule thus apparently permits a lawyer to "discuss" the means by which the client might engage in criminal or fraudulent conduct as long as she does not recommend them. See Wolfram, Modern Legal Ethics at 694–95 and notes. As noted by Kenneth Mann, however, there is an "extremely narrow line between insufficient preparation and improper influence":

> The attorney has to bring . . . a client to understand how to organize his thoughts and what to emphasize. But it is also true that . . . attorneys . . . improperly influence a client by letting him know, even if only by hinting, what to leave out and what to include and how to shape facts so that an appearance of propriety is created where in fact wrongdoing occurred.

Defending White Collar Crime 137 (Yale, 1986). For further discussion of the difficulties in advising clients when the attorney "knows" or "believes" or "reasonably believes" that the client intends to engage, or use the information to engage, in criminal, illegal or fraudulent conduct, see Chapters 25 (Professional vs. Personal Responsibilities); 11 (Confidentiality); 15 (Terminating the Relationship); and 16 (The Adversary System). For a discussion of the special considerations involved in advising a corporate or governmental client, see Chapter 20.

II. THE LAWYER AS NEGOTIATOR

Negotiation has been defined as "the process of reaching decisions by coordinating mutual but differing interests where there is no superior authority," L. Patterson & E. Cheatham, The Profession of Law 119 (1971), and as "a process of adjustment of existing differences, with a view to the establishment of a mutually more desirable legal relation by means of barter and compromise of legal rights and duties and of economic, psychological, social and other interests . . . accomplished consensually as contrasted with force of law," Mathews, Negotiation: A Pedagogical Challenge, 6 J.Legal Educ. 94 (1953). While negotiation has been institutionalized in domestic relations and labor law in the United States, it is also central to settlement of civil suits, plea bargaining, contract formation and revision, and work with administrative agencies.

A major advantage of negotiated, rather than litigated, settlement of disputes is that it relieves the burdens on an already overburdened court system. One study of personal injury suits in New York City, for example, found less than one in 25 suits to reach trial and less than one in three of those going to trial to reach a verdict. Rosenberg & Sovern, Delay and the Dynamics of Personal Injury Litigation, 59 Colum.L.Rev. 1115 (1959). See Admin.Off. of U.S.Cts., Jud. Workload Statistics at A20 (1983) (94.2% of all federal civil cases in 1982). As well, since successful negotiation requires conciliation and compromise rather than a sharpening of disagreements, it more often results in a satisfactory resolution for the parties involved. The policy of encouraging out-of-court settlement of disputes is reflected in the Federal Rules of Evidence, with respect to both civil and criminal matters. Fed. R.Evid. 408 (offers to compromise are not admissible as proof of liability or validity of a civil claim); Fed.R.Evid. 410 (offers to plead guilty or nolo contendere are not admissible in any action against the person who offers the plea).

The attorney acting as a negotiator is called upon to exercise skills different from those used in advocacy and, consequently, is believed by many commentators to be less effective in this role. First, as in performance of an advisory role, attorneys may not be aware of the principles of human motivation that prompt a specific client to desire certain legal ends and may not have the skill or the inclination to discover those goals desired by their clients. Second, since many lawyers view settlement to be a less time-consuming and perhaps less important task than other legal work, they may not prepare adequately by accumulating the facts necessary to negotiate competently. See RPC 1.1 and Comment; DR 6–101(A)(2). Third, the role of negotiator requires the attorney to act within an accommodative and conciliatory model, as contrasted with an adversarial one, and may be difficult for the attorney to perform. See Williams, Legal Negotiation and Settlement 19 (1983) (lawyers employing "cooperative" style of negotiation significantly more effective than those employing a "competitive" style). Hopefully, the increased emphasis in law schools and continuing legal education programs on negotiation issues and skills will begin to offset the past emphasis on adversarial representation and advocacy.

As with the attorney acting as an advisor, an attorney acting as a negotiator will find few ethical standards related specifically to that role, although in the RPC there is generally increased attention paid to lawyering roles other than litigation advocacy. Major issues that arise for the attorney in negotiation include: honesty, communicating with other parties, threatening suit, and multiple representation. Each of these issues will be discussed in turn.

The attorney acting as a negotiator has the same duty as attorneys acting in other roles to avoid untrue statements. He may not "engage in conduct involving dishonesty, fraud, deceit or misrepresentation," RPC 8.4(c); DR 1–102(A)(4), or knowingly make a false statement of material fact or law, RPC 4.1(a); DR 7–102(A)(5). In addition, RPC 4.1(b) requires that the lawyer "disclose a material fact to a third person when disclosure is necessary to avoid assisting a criminal or fraudulent act by a client, unless disclosure is prohibited by rule 1.6." Since Rule 1.6 permits disclosure only of crimes involving imminent death or substantial bodily injury, however, it would seem that the duty to disclose in Rule 4.1(b) is illusory. This apparent problem is mitigated in those many states that have: made the revelation of *any* crime permissible; included a fraud exception to Rule 1.6 (or made disclosure necessary to prevent a client's fraudulent act *mandatory*); or required the lawyer to rectify criminal or fraudulent acts in the furtherance of which the lawyer's services had been used. See Chapters 11 (Confidentiality) and 16 (The Adversary System).

The duty of candor is supported especially in contract negotiations by the common law doctrine that contracts will not be enforced by the courts if obtained by fraud or deceit, and in labor negotiations by "good faith" bargaining requirements. Under general agency law as well, an attorney cannot use fraud or deceit if the client is not legally permitted to do so.

In negotiating a civil suit, the CPR provides that an attorney "shall not present, participate in presenting, or threaten to present criminal charges solely to obtain an advantage in a civil matter." It is believed that such misuse of the criminal process undermines public confidence in the legal system, may unduly discourage valid law suits, and if successful, will cause crimes not to be reported. See EC 7–21. In fact, the bases for the prohibition appear equally applicable to threats concerning administrative or disciplinary charges, and a number of jurisdictions prohibit such threats. See, e.g., Cal. RPC 5–100. Both direct threats and indirect statements clearly intended to be coercive are proscribed. See, e.g., Crane v. State Bar (Cal.1981) (statement in letter that "the Attorney General's office will be requested to assist us in solution," with a notation that copies were sent to a named attorney general).

The RPC do not contain a specific prohibition of such threats. According to the drafters, a specific rule was unnecessary, since fraudulent or other abusive threats would be covered by more general provisions such as RPC 4.4 ("no substantial purpose other than to embarrass, delay or burden a third person") and 8.4(b) (criminal conduct adversely reflecting on honesty, trustworthiness or fitness). However, the general rules would only appear to prohibit threats that were illegal (e.g., extortion), and would not necessarily include threats that were well-founded with respect to the criminal activity involved. As stated by Professor Wolfram: "The behavior permitted by the Model Rules, if engaged in by a client legally in some states, is sufficiently close to the edge of legality and so unappealing a tactic in general that it would better have been prohibited outright in the Model Rules." Modern Legal Ethics at 718.

The RPC and CPR recognize that there may be many matters not involving litigation in which a lawyer may properly represent multiple clients with potentially differing interests. See, e.g., RPC 1.7, 2.2; DR 5–105; EC 5–15. An aggregate settlement involving two or more of an attorney's clients may not be made, however, unless each client consents after consultation, including disclosure of the "existence and nature of all the claims or pleas involved in the proposed settlement and of the participation of each person in the settlement." RPC 1.8(g); DR 5–106. It must be remembered in this context that the client has the ultimate authority in deciding whether to accept a settlement offer. RPC 1.2(a); EC 7–7. If an attorney attempts to intermediate between two clients, she must strictly comply with the requirements of Rule 2.2; and if she has served as an arbitrator or mediator in matters involving former or present clients, she should not represent subsequently any of the parties involved in the dispute. RPC 2.2, 1.9; EC 5–20. For a general discussion of conflict of interest, see Chapter 12.

In negotiating on behalf of a client, a lawyer may not communicate concerning the subject of the representation with another party known to be represented by counsel without counsel's consent, unless authorized by law. RPC 4.2; DR 7–104(a)(1). The reason for the rule is a simple one:

> . . . The rule is to prohibit lawyers from taking advantage of litigants who are represented by counsel. . . . This is for the protection of the client. A client who has selected counsel is entitled at all times to the advice and guidance of such counsel selected. If lawyers representing adverse interests seek to compromise or settle matters directly with litigants represented by counsel, then they are ignoring the relationship that exists for the protection of the litigants.

In re Atwell (Mo.App.1938). It would thus clearly be improper for an attorney to bypass opposing counsel and negotiate directly with counsel's client.

The Comment to RPC 4.2 provides that where an organization is involved, the Rule "prohibits communications by a lawyer for one party concerning the matter in representation with persons having managerial responsibility on behalf of the organization, and with any other person whose act or omission in connection with that matter may be imputed to the organization for purposes of civil or criminal liability or whose statement may constitute an admission on the part of the organization." But cf. Wright by Wright v. Group Health Hospital (Wash.1984) ("[T]he best interpretation of 'party' in litigation involving corporations is only those employees who have the legal authority to 'bind' the corporation in a legal evidentiary sense, i.e., those employees who have 'speaking authority' for the corporation."). Although parties to a matter may communicate directly with each other, an attorney who "prompts" the client or provides information for purposes of negotiation that would give his client an unfair advantage risks violating RPC 8.4(a) and DR 1–102(A)(2) by violating Rule 4.2 through the acts of another. And it should also be noted that RPC 4.2 "covers *any* person, whether or not a party to a formal proceeding, who is represented by counsel concerning the matter in question." Comment to RPC 4.2 (emphasis added).

In many cases, particularly at the negotiation stage, a lawyer must deal with persons who are unrepresented by counsel. There is a danger that the lawyer might, intentionally or unintentionally, take advantage of the unrepresented person's lack of knowledge concerning his rights. Therefore, DR 7–104(A)(2) provides that the lawyer shall not give advice to an unrepresented person "other than the advice to secure counsel, if the interests of such a person are or have a reasonable possibility of being in conflict with the interests of the client." RPC 4.3, on the other hand, does not appear to prohibit advice to an unrepresented person. Rather, the lawyer must not state or imply that she is disinterested, and when she "knows or reasonably should know that the unrepresented person misunderstands the lawyer's role in the matter, the lawyer shall make reasonable efforts to correct the misunderstanding." Although broader than DR 7–104(A)(2) in not being limited to unrepresented parties with interests adverse to the client, RPC 4.3 would seem to permit the lawyer to give advice to an unrepresented person whose interests *are* adverse, so long as the lawyer declares her bias on behalf of the client. However, the Comment to Rule 4.3 provides that the lawyer "should not give advice to an unrepresented person other than the advice to obtain counsel." And, in addition to any ethical problems, an attorney who gives advice to an unrepresented person risks being held to have "represented" that person for purposes of conflict of interest analysis or malpractice liability.

III. CONCLUSION

While the RPC and CPR contain a few specific rules directed to the attorney who is acting either as an advisor or negotiator, much of the guidance for attorneys acting in these roles depends on extrapolating from more general principles for professional conduct. Considering the frequency with which attorneys serve in these roles, and the importance of the roles for the settlement of disputes, it is perhaps unfortunate that professional rulemakers have not directed more attention to the particular ethical issues engendered by the roles of advisor and negotiator. Hopefully, the lawyer as advisor and negotiator will be treated with greater detail in new codes presently under consideration by the American Academy of Matrimonial Lawyers, the American Trial Lawyers Association, and numerous state and county bar associations. See Chapter 25 (Professional vs. Personal Responsibilities).

CHAPTER 20

THE LAWYER AS CORPORATE OR GOVERNMENTAL EMPLOYEE

Corporate and government attorneys are, of course, governed by the RPC or CPR as are other lawyers. However, the nature of their practices may present special ethical dilemmas. Because the immense power wielded by their employers can cause the consequences of unethical behavior by corporate or government attorneys to be so grave, it is especially important that these lawyers understand the nature of their duty to clients and to society at large. The RPC, in Rule 1.13, recognize the lawyer's special role where the client is an organization. This chapter applies RPC 1.13 and other general ethical considerations presented elsewhere to the practice of the government and corporate lawyer.

I. THE ETHICAL RESPONSIBILITIES OF THE CORPORATE LAWYER

A. ADVOCATING THE CORPORATE CLIENT'S INTERESTS—THE ISSUES

1. Who Is the Client?

The lawyer who acts as counsel—either retained or in-house—for a corporation would appear to have the same ethical dilemmas as any attorney representing a "person." However, while a corporation may enjoy the same legal status as a "real" person, it is obviously quite a different beast. The CPR states that "[a] lawyer employed or retained by a corporation or similar entity owes his allegiance to the entity and not to a stockholder, director, officer, employee, representative, or other person connected with the entity." EC 5–18. Determining the interests of the corporation, which are to be kept paramount by counsel, is often difficult.

For instance, during incorporation, merger, or takeover, who "represents" the corporation? In-house or outside counsel may, perhaps mistakenly, too readily adopt the corporate officers' interests as those of the corporation, for she is hired, paid, and potentially fired under their management.

The RPC take a more functional approach, but one which does not render identification of the "client" much easier. Rule 1.13(a) affirms that a lawyer employed by an organization represents the organization; however, the Rule also recognizes that the organization cannot act except through "duly authorized constituents," defined in the Comments as "[o]fficers, directors, employees and shareholders." The by-laws or other internal regulations may indicate who is "duly authorized" in a given situation, but otherwise the Rule provides little guidance as to who the lawyer's "client" is in ambiguous situations.

Although theoretically a lawyer is hired by the corporation, lawyers are in fact hired by individuals employed by the corporation, so the identity of the client can be very unclear if the hiring individual's motives are unclear. For example, in Evans v. Artek Systems Corp. (2d Cir.1983), the defendant corporation moved that the plaintiff's law firm should be disqualified, because the plaintiff's firm had previously represented the corporation, and therefore had a conflict of interest with its former client. (See Ch. 12, Conflicts of Interest.) Since the president of the corporation had consulted the firm earlier, the district court granted the motion. However, the court of appeals held that the mere fact that the individual consulting the law firm was the president of the corporation did not in itself create an attorney-client relationship between the firm and the corporation. There was some evidence that the president consulted the firm on his own behalf or on behalf of a minority faction within the corporation, but the record was unclear. The capacity in which the firm had been hired would be decisive in the matter of disqualification, so the court remanded the case for a determination of who the client had been.

2. What Are the Client's Interests?

Even if the lawyer clearly represents the corporation, she may have difficulty divining her client's actual interests. Again, her direction as to what those interests are must come from individuals within the corporation. Those individuals may have interests that diverge from the corporation's best interests. Determining where the corporate client's interests lie can thus be a daunting task. One court has held that lawyers cannot rely on the characterizations of a corporate director regarding the corporation's interests. A chief executive officer in In re King Resources Co. (B.R.D.C. Colo.1982) falsely indicated that the corporation favored a takeover effort. The court held that, because the law firm had failed in its obligation to investigate the corporation's wishes fully, it would not receive payment of its legal fees, amounting to over $115,000.

B. COMPETING INTERESTS—RESPONSIBLE CORPORATE REPRESENTATION

In addition to determining what the *"client's"* interests are, it is often difficult to identify what the corporate client's *"best"* interests are. The interests most often represented by the corporate attorney are those that promise short-term economic gains. Under the law of agency, a lawyer's obligation to the corporation is normally fulfilled by providing competent advice to the authorized constituents, and the lawyer may assume that they will act within the scope of their authority. In some cases, though, pursuit of short-term pecuniary goals may subject the corporation to injury, either legal liability or long-term financial damage. For example, the company may risk potential negligence or products liability for failure to modify product design or clean up a toxic dump site. In addition, the corporation may have responsibilities to society; such responsibilities can also be construed as "interests." The lawyer's immediate contacts in the organization may ignore—and may expect the lawyer to ignore—these factors. Most commentators have characterized such decisions as matters of "risk management," within the authority of those responsible for such matters.

Therefore, the lawyer is not believed to be required to challenge the decisions within the organization hierarchy.

The CPR's ethical considerations only vaguely suggest that a lawyer's role as advisor may provide her with an avenue for promoting the corporation's interests in fulfilling its noneconomic obligations. On the other hand, RPC 1.13 provides some guidance for attorneys dealing with *improper or illegal actions* which may injure the corporation.

1. Acts That May Injure the Organization

The interests of an individual "constituent" of an organization may diverge from those of the organization itself. What must the corporate attorney do when she knows that an officer is committing his corporation to a course of action which, though immediately profitable, exposes the corporation to some form of legal liability? One obvious solution might be to reveal the intended action to the stockholders or appropriate outside authority, and thus forestall injury to the organization and to society. RPC 1.6 is quite strict, however, prohibiting the revelation of information related to the representation unless necessary to prevent a crime that is likely to result in imminent death or substantial bodily harm. The CPR also provides little help. Disciplinary Rule 4–101(B)(1) states that a lawyer may not reveal knowledge of a client's past crimes; however, a lawyer may reveal otherwise confidential or secret information in order to prevent a client from committing a future crime. DR 4–101(C)(3). Although this CPR standard might provide a sufficient guideline for the attorney apprised of her client's illegal conduct, (see Ch. 11, supra), its utility is minimal in the white collar world of corporate crime, where past acts often prove and are intertwined with the intent to violate provisions of, for example, the securities laws.

RPC 1.13(b) gives some direction to a lawyer faced with possible injury to the corporate client by the conduct of one of its own employees. The action, intended action, or refusal to act must meet four criteria to bring Rule 1.13(b) into play: The lawyer must know that (1) the actor is an "officer, employee, or other person associated with the organization;" (2) the conduct is being taken in a matter related to the lawyer's representation; (3) the conduct creates a "violation of a legal obligation to the organization, or a violation of law which reasonably might be imputed to the organization;" and (4) the conduct is "likely to result in substantial injury to the organization." Some actions are thus clearly not within Rule 1.13: acts by outsiders, acts unrelated to the lawyer's representation of the organization, merely imprudent acts (not illegal or in violation of legal obligations), and acts which threaten less-than-substantial injury.

If the situation meets these four criteria, then the lawyer must proceed "as is reasonably necessary" to promote the best interests of the organization. The Rule provides three possible alternatives the lawyer may use: she may (1) ask the actor to reconsider; (2) advise that a separate legal opinion be obtained and offered to the "appropriate authority" in the organization; or (3) go over the actor's head. In extreme situations, "if warranted by the seriousness of the matter," she may refer the matter to the highest authority in the organization. In pursuing whatever measures the lawyer chooses, the Rule requires that she consider several factors, including the seriousness of the violation and its repercussions, the scope and nature of the representation, and the actor's corporate responsibilities and possible motivations. The lawyer must also seek to minimize the risk of revealing confidential information to outsiders, and to limit disruption caused by any measures taken.

What if the attorney's efforts are of no avail? Or, what if she goes to the highest authority, who promptly endorses the injurious activity? Rule 1.13(c) provides for a single, not particularly satisfying, response: the lawyer may resign. Thus, while Rule 1.13 provides more specific direction than did the CPR, it seems to come down to little more than an invocation of the rule on permissive withdrawal (RPC 1.16). A previous (and unenacted) draft of Rule 1.13 provided a far more effective final resort for the attorney unable to alter the actor's course: the lawyer could reveal information otherwise protected by Rule 1.6, but only if the highest authority had endorsed the actor's conduct, and if revealing the information would be in the organization's best interests. This option would have provided a far more potent means of acting in the organization's behalf than the series of more mild steps suggested by the enacted version of Rule 1.13.

Regardless of the requirements of the RPC or CPR, lawyers may be required by agencies with licensing power to go beyond simply advising the wrongdoing corporate constituent of the wrongfulness of the conduct. The Securities and Exchange Commission decided in In re Carter (S.E.C.1981) that "there comes a point at which a reasonable lawyer must conclude that his advice is not being followed . . . and that his client is involved in a continuing course of action violating the securities laws. At this critical juncture, the lawyer must take further, more affirmative steps. . . ." In *Carter,* two lawyers advised the corporate president and in-house counsel of the disclosure requirements regarding management's material omissions and misstatements in its representations to the S.E.C., to the stockholders, and to the public. When the corporate officers would not heed their repeated advice, they did not inform anyone about the client's failure to disclose. As a result, an S.E.C. administrative law judge decided that the lawyers had committed professional misconduct, and would no longer be allowed to practice before the commission. For the lawyers, this was a drastic penalty indeed, especially since they had apparently satisfied the ethical requirements of the CPR. (The RPC were as then not yet adopted.)

On appeal to the full Commission, the decision was reversed. The S.E.C. decided that the lawyers had not intended to assist the violations by their silence. "Rather, they seemed to be at a loss for how to deal with a difficult client." The S.E.C. decided that then-current ethical standards (mainly the CPR) were inadequate and that attorneys should be required to take affirmative steps when they know their advice is no longer being heard. The principal suggestions involve seeking other avenues within the corporation to attempt to change the disclosure decision. If the lawyer fails to take "affirmative steps," the Commission implied that it had a responsibility to remove that lawyer from securities practice.

> [I]f a lawyer violates ethical or professional standards, or becomes a conscious participant in violations of the securities laws, *or performs his professional function without regard to the consequences,* it will not do to say that because the lawyer's duty is to his client alone, this Commission must stand helplessly by while the lawyer carries his privilege of appearing and practicing before the Commission on to the next client. . . . [When management is clearly not taking the lawyer's advice anymore], no lawyer may claim that . . . he need do no more than stubbornly continue to suggest disclosure when he knows his suggestions are falling on deaf ears.

(Emphasis added.) It has also been suggested that, under certain circumstances, a lawyer's silence could subject him to liability as an aider in the wrongdoing. See, e.g., Kaplan, Some Ruminations on the Role of Counsel for a Corporation, 56 Notre Dame Law. 873 (1981).

2. The Organization's Social Interests—Lawyer as Advisor

Under the adversarial view of the attorney's role, the client's interests, *as perceived by the client,* are paramount. The attorney has the right—even the obligation—to aid his corporate client in achieving all legal objectives. One study revealed that corporate attorneys seemed unwilling to *counsel,* to play the corporation's "conscience;" instead, they saw themselves as *advocates* only, furthering the necessary legal ramifications of economic views independently developed by management. This approach to representation certainly has its support in the CPR: "A Lawyer Should Represent a Client Zealously Within the Bounds of the Law," Canon 7.

The validity of the "hired gun" view of the attorney's duty is, however, open to serious question—especially when considered in light of the growing belief that corporate responsibility extends beyond the duty to stockholders to turn a profit and includes an obligation to improve (or at least not injure) the society from which it profits. More consistent with this evolving belief is adoption of a truth-oriented perception of ethical responsibilities. Under this view of lawyers' ethics, counsel should encourage the corporate client to reveal questionable past acts and to refrain from "unreportable" activity in the future, in order to protect itself from additional penalties or charges. In this way, the attorney properly advises the client while fulfilling his duty to society as well. See RPC 2.1 (permitting an attorney to refer to "nonlegal" moral, economic, social, or political considerations in advising a client) and the ABA Comment to RPC 2.1 (recognizing that "moral and ethical considerations impinge upon most legal questions;" therefore, an attorney may have a responsibility as an advisor to indicate that "more may be involved than strictly legal considerations"). As one federal appellate court has noted, "[i]n our complex society the accountant's certificate and the lawyer's opinion can be instruments for inflicting pecuniary loss more potent than the chisel or the crowbar." United States v. Benjamin (2d Cir.1964). Although the economic harm inflicted on employees and stockholders by revelation might be raised in support of the lawyer's advocate role, counseling that prevents illegal (and expensive) activity will serve in the long run both those most directly affected by the corporation's economic fortunes and society at large.

The S.E.C. has found, in the advisory nature of corporate securities work, special justification for a higher standard of professional responsibility:

> Very little of a securities lawyer's work is adversary in character. He doesn't work in courtrooms where the pressure of vigilant adversaries and alert judges check him. He works in his office where he prepares prospectuses, proxy statements, opinions of counsel, and other documents that we, our staff, the financial community, and the investing public must take on faith. This is a field where unscrupulous lawyers can inflict irreparable harm on those who rely on the disclosure documents

they produce. Hence we are under a duty to hold our bar to appropriately rigorous standards of professional honor.

In re Fields (S.E.C.1973).

C. REPRESENTING THE ORGANIZATION AND A CONSTITUENT

Individuals within a corporation who deal with the attorney may, over time, come to believe that she is their personal attorney, too. This could lead them to unrealistic expectations of what the attorney will do in a conflict between themselves and the corporation, and it may have implications for confidentiality. Therefore, RPC 1.13(d) requires that, where the organization's interests are adverse to a constituent's interests, the lawyer must explain to the constituent that the organization is the client. Accord, EC 5–16.

Normally, any discussions the lawyer holds with individuals within the organization (in their official capacity) are protected by confidentiality rules. Thus, if the organization asks the lawyer to investigate a matter, interviews with members of the organization are protected. See Upjohn Co. v. United States (U.S.1981), discussed in Ch. 11 (Confidentiality). However, the attorney must be careful not to reveal to such individuals information related to the representation of the organization, except as provided by the confidentiality rules. The individual is not entitled to such information, since he is not the "client." The attorney should also inform the individual that discussions between them may not be privileged where the organization's interests are adverse to those of the individual. RPC 1.13, Comment. Accord, EC 4–4. Indeed, the constituent should understand that anything he says to the corporate counsel is "known by the corporation." The constituent cannot later assert a conflict of interest with respect to the corporation's attorney based on previous conversations with that attorney. See, e.g., Bobbitt v. Victorian House, Inc. (D.Ill.1982).

When the individual's interests are adverse to those of the organization, general conflict of interest rules prohibit the lawyer from representing both. RPC 1.7; DR 5–105(B), (C); see Chapter 12, supra. Otherwise, Rule 1.13(e) specifically allows dual representation of, for example, a corporate officer and the corporation. However, an appropriate official, other than the person whom the attorney wishes to represent, must give the corporation's consent.

II. THE ETHICAL RESPONSIBILITIES OF THE GOVERNMENT LAWYER

The ethical problems of the government lawyer are often similar to those of the corporate attorney—but the government lawyer's client is bigger, more powerful, and ultimately, may be society itself. The federal bar has noted the frequent inadequacies of the CPR in addressing the government attorney's ethical dilemmas; the Federal Ethical Considerations [FEC] were devised to supplement the general guidelines of the Code and will be discussed here. Of course, government lawyers are subject to the CPR or RPC, in addition to any special codes of conduct. The prosecutor's responsibilities have been discussed in Ch. 18, supra; this section examines the duties of other government attorneys in the executive and legislative branches. See also Ch. 24.

A. WHO IS THE CLIENT?

In a government "of the people," it might be thought that the government attorney's client *is* "the people." FEC 8–1, in stating that "paramount consideration is due the public interest," suggests that the government lawyer's duty under CPR Canon 8 to "Assist in Improving the Legal System" is greater than that of the private attorney. However, identifying the obligation to the "public interest" provides the attorney with no means of determining what that interest is. Therefore, some commentators draw the client less broadly, making the government lawyer primarily responsible to the agency for which he works.

B. OBLIGATIONS TO THE AGENCY AND THE PUBLIC

Characterization of the government lawyer's primary client either as "the people" or the agency will determine his duties in a variety of situations. The existence of a "Watergate" or "Iran–Contra" scandal within a governmental agency raises several ethical quandries which, in the recent past, have not been adequately resolved by the attorneys involved. Some of these problems will be briefly discussed here.

1. Standards of Conduct for Government Lawyers

The first problem raised by questionable activities of government officials, particularly attorneys, is the standard of conduct to which they should be held. It has been argued that the public servant owes a special duty to society, and that the government lawyer can therefore be charged with a higher standard of conduct than his private counterpart. Thus, although the private attorney might be able to find justification in the RPC or CPR for the destruction of certain documents, the destruction takes on special significance—and is subject to special strictures—when undertaken by a government lawyer.

2. The Duty to Disclose Wrongdoing

If the government employee is held to a higher standard of conduct, is the government lawyer obligated to disclose wrongdoing at times when other attorneys would not be so obligated? The Comment to RPC 1.13 indicates that the Rule is applicable to government, as well as corporate, attorneys. The Comment goes on to state, however, that "when the client is a governmental organization, a different balance may be appropriate between maintaining confidentiality and assuring that the wrongful official act is prevented or rectified, for the public business is involved. . . . Therefore, defining precisely the identity of the client and prescribing the resulting obligations of such lawyers may be more difficult in the government context. Although in some circumstances the client may be a specific agency, it is generally the government as a whole. For example, if the action or failure to act involves the head of a bureau, either the department of which the bureau is a part or the government as a whole may be the client for purpose of this Rule." Thus, if the attorney believes her primary duty is to the public, and if intra-agency disclosure under FEC Canon 4 has been unproductive, revelation to outside sources of secret papers disclosing employees' illegal activities is ethically defensible.

However, such extra-agency action will surely affect the attorney's ability to function within the agency. FEC 8–3 discusses the difficulties in serving the public interest when the attorney is likely to undermine his position in the agency:

> Lawyers in federal service . . . should conduct themselves so as to encourage utilization of their advice within the agencies, retaining at all times an obligation to exercise independent professional judgment, even though their conclusions may not always be warmly embraced. The failure of lawyers to respect official and proper confidences discourages resort to them.

3. The Duty to Resign

As intimated above, public exposure of governmental activities, although possibly permitted because of the overriding public interest, may require resignation by the involved official. "[W]hen [the lawyer's] conscience compels him publicly to attack a decision which is contrary to his professional, ethical or moral judgment . . . he should be prepared to resign before doing so, and he is not free to abuse professional confidences reposed in him. . . ." FEC 8–2. Such a position creates an economic barrier to public disclosure that will rarely be crossed; if the attorney's duty is ultimately to the public, FEC 8–2 should not be read to require actual resignation before disclosure, but rather a willingness to resign if necessary.

Alternatively, it has been suggested that the government attorney has a duty *not* to resign in some situations. For instance, the attorney who is asked to perform an illegal act can either resign, forcing the government employer to find another official willing to break the law, or justifiably refuse to undertake the task, forcing the government employer to fire him (presumably with the additional burden of giving reasons for the discharge) or to forego the proposed illegal action. No RPC, CPR or FEC provision is directly applicable to such a dilemma, but the notion that the public interest requires the lawyer to remain in his position does have some moral force.

Thus, as is the case for the corporate lawyer, the government attorney faces many ethical dilemmas not fully answered by the RPC or CPR. In addition to previously discussed problems of interpreting the RPC and CPR, corporate and government attorneys must resolve ambiguities concerning their advocacy and counseling functions, identify the nature of their "client," and consider the effect of their actions on the public interest.

CHAPTER 21

THE LAWYER AS A NEUTRAL: ETHICS IN ALTERNATIVE DISPUTE RESOLUTION

> In the duties that the lawyer must now undertake, the inherited traditions of the bar often yield but an indirect guidance. Principles of conduct applicable to appearance in open court do not, for example, resolve the issues confronting the lawyer who must assume the delicate task of mediating among opposing interests.
>
> Report of the Joint Conference on Professional Responsibility, AALS–ABA (1958).

Lawyers have made important contributions to society not only as advocates but, as noted in the Joint Conference Report, as designers of the framework of collaborate effort. A lawyer may represent clients seeking a mutual objective such as forming a corporation or other business association, or draft the charter for a religious or civic organization, or even for a governmental or international undertaking. The skills and knowledge that the lawyer brings to such tasks—in analysis, issue recognition, drafting, law, governmental processes, and the ability to recognize competing contentions—also equip lawyers to serve effectively as adjudicators, mediators, and evaluators.

The next Chapter deals explicitly with the role of the lawyer as a public judge, while this Chapter identifies a number of ethical issues, and provides some guidelines, for private lawyers who act in a neutral capacity.

The various ethical obligations will be discussed both in general and with particular application to the primary alternative dispute resolution roles of (1) adjudicator, who makes a binding or recommended decision for the parties, as an arbitrator, private judge, or fact-finder; and (2) a neutral who helps the parties reach their own agreement, as a mediator, conciliator, intermediator, mini-trial presider, neutral evaluator or advisor, or ombudsman. While in each of these roles the lawyer acts as a third-party neutral, each process has significant characteristics that may vary her ethical obligations. Although non-lawyers also serve in many of these roles, lawyer-neutrals may have ethical responsibilities that go beyond those of non-lawyers.

I. SOURCES OF GUIDANCE

The ABA Code of Professional Responsibility merely provided that a lawyer may serve as an impartial arbitrator or mediator if disclosure is first made of present or former client relationships. EC 5–20.

With the increased popularity of various forms of alternative dispute resolution [ADR] since the 1970's, one might have expected the Model Rules to provide greater guidance to the lawyer involved in these processes. This expectation has been only partially met. Model Rule 2.2 provides that a lawyer may act as an "intermediary between clients" in accordance with the limitations there specified. This Rule is expressly limited to a lawyer jointly representing two or more clients who share a mutual objective but may have conflicting interests that have to be resolved or anticipated. As such, Rule 2.2 is little more than a specific application of other Rules dealing with conflicts of interest, scope of representation, and confidentiality. Its inclusion as an independent rule, however, was a recognition that intermediation is one of the important differing roles that lawyers perform. See Hazard & Hodes, Law of Lawyering 310 (1985). Yet, as a Comment to Rule 2.2 makes clear, the Rule "does not apply to a lawyer acting as an arbitrator or mediator between or among parties who are not clients of the lawyer. . . ." This excludes from coverage of the Model Rules the more common roles that lawyers may perform as neutrals in a non-representative capacity. Nevertheless, the provisions of Rule 2.2 can be a source of useful guidance for lawyers acting as mediators who do not represent any party to the mediation. The ABA Standing Committee on Dispute Resolution is formulating a proposed amendment to the Model Rules expressly authorizing lawyers to serve as mediators subject to specified safeguards similar to those in Rule 2.2.

Model Rule 1.12 applies conflict of interest principles to lawyers who previously acted as judges or arbitrators to restrict their subsequent employment by parties to their adjudications. The Rule expressly excludes, however, arbitrators who served as partisans of the party in a multi-member arbitration panel. RPC 1.12(d). Similarly, this Chapter is concerned with lawyers who serve in a neutral capacity and does not discuss the ethics of lawyers selected as party-representatives in tripartite arbitrations whose role may incorporate that of advocacy as well as adjudication. When arbitrators are not expected to be neutral, they are exempt from most of the ethical obligations regarding impartiality, relationships with the parties, and ex parte communications, but they may be subject to other ethical considerations, according to the ABA–American Arbitration Association Code of Ethics for Commercial Arbitrators.

A Comment to RPC 2.2 appropriately notes that a lawyer serving as an arbitrator or mediator may be subject to other applicable codes of ethics. Among the more prominent ethical standards, to which reference is made in this Chapter, are: ABA Standards of Practice for Lawyer Mediators in Family Disputes (1984) [ABA Family Mediation Standards]; Ethical Standards of Professional Responsibility for the Society of Professionals in Dispute Resolution (1986) applicable to mediators, arbitrators and other neutrals [SPIDR Standards]; ABA–American Arbitration Association Code of Ethics for Arbitrators in Commercial Disputes (1977) [Commercial Arbitrators Code]; Code of Professional Responsibility for Arbitrators of Labor–Management Disputes, adopted by the National Academy of Arbitrators, American Arbitration Association, and Federal Mediation and Conciliation Service (1974, as amended through 1985) [Labor Arbitrators CPR]; Standards of Practice for Family and Divorce Mediation of the Academy of Family Mediators [AFM Standards].

Other organizations also have adopted standards and codes addressed to their areas of concern, and some publish interpretative opinions of their ethics committees.

A number of bar association ethics committees have issued advisory opinions dealing with lawyers serving as mediators, particularly in domestic dissolution disputes. While a strong majority of these opinions approve of the practice under specified safeguards, they are not all in agreement concerning either the acceptability of the practice or the ethical limitations to be placed upon it. Thus, lawyers who serve as family mediators should consult such opinions as well as judicial and legislative authorities in the jurisdiction in which they practice. In addition, the concerned lawyer will want to consult the growing regulation and literature on ADR processes and ethical practices.

II. ETHICAL CONCERNS OF THE PRIVATE LAWYER SERVING AS A NEUTRAL

A. COMPETENCE

While a competent lawyer will want to explore with a client the advisability of using alternative dispute resolution methods in lieu of or in addition to litigation [see infra], not all lawyers may be competent to serve as a neutral in such ADR processes. While many lawyers have experience as arbitrators in court-annexed proceedings or as judges *pro tem,* it is apparent that some lawyers possess a better judicial temperament than others and are better able to conduct and control an adjudicative hearing. Although a lawyer's skills of analysis, issue spotting, articulation, drafting, knowledge of law and process, ability to understand arguments supporting different results and to exercise independent judgment are valuable assets for arbitrators and mediators, serving in a mediative capacity requires some skills and characteristics which many lawyers do not possess or comfortably exercise. Successful mediations often emphasize party communications, effective listening, interpersonal relations, openness, fairness, flexibility, and informality. Lawyers by virtue of their legal training, experience and disposition typically find greater comfort with a more structured rule and rights oriented procedure. The qualities of loyalty, zealous representation, confidentiality, and to some extent control or dominance of the client, however valuable they may be for the advocate, run counter to many desirable characteristics of a mediator. The mediator must stress impartiality, party control of the dispute and its resolution, receptivity and equity, and seeks to foster openness and trust between the parties. Indeed, those state bar ethics opinions that advise against lawyers acting as mediators in domestic dissolutions do so in part because of the intrusions on loyalty and confidentiality that such a non-traditional lawyer role would require.

Nevertheless, a large number of lawyers do possess, or can when called upon exercise, mediative abilities and characteristics, and have served effectively as neutral facilitators. There is evidence that many more law students today than in years past have a stronger "justice" perspective than adversarial one, and with the increased opportunities for training in mediation and other ADR processes in law schools, there should be no current shortage of lawyers who can very competently serve as mediators.

Lawyers, however, must be careful not to assume a role of therapist or some other function which is not within their professional qualifications. Mental health professionals also serve successfully as mediators, and in some situations (subject to unauthorized practice concerns, discussed infra), a lawyer-therapist mediation team can be very effective.

Model Rule 1.1 states that competency requires that a lawyer exercise the legal knowledge, skill, thoroughness and preparation reasonably necessary for a representation. Lawyers serving as neutrals have no less an obligation. They also must have sufficient knowledge regarding the subject matter of the nature of the dispute to be resolved, and of the dispute settlement process to be employed, to be able to comprehend the issues, appreciate a variety of possible resolutions, and otherwise operate effectively as a neutral in the process. Lawyer-neutrals also have a responsibility to keep current with relevant developments, principles and practices, and to maintain and improve their skills. See SPIDR Standards; Labor Arbitrators CPR 1, A, B, C–2; AFM Standards.

Reasonable diligence and promptness in arranging or attending hearings and conferences, and in drafting a settlement agreement or arbitration award also are required of lawyers and others serving as neutrals. Parties in labor arbitrations have frequently complained about the inability or unwillingness of some arbitrators to render their awards within a specified time (usually 30 or 60 days), and when a lawyer's practice commitments prevent timely performance, she should not undertake the additional burden of serving as an arbitrator.

B. CONSULTATION

Model Rule 2.2(a)(1) requires that an intermediary consult with each client concerning the implications of the common representation (including that the lawyer's role is not the normal one of partisan for either client), and explain the advantages and risks involved and the effect on the attorney-client privileges. Then the lawyer must obtain each client's consent to go ahead with the intermediation. As with any representation of potential or actual conflicting interests, written evidence of the consent, while not required, can avoid possible misunderstandings and future problems. (See Chapter 12, Conflict of Interest).

Consultation must continue thoughout the process concerning decisions to be made and the considerations relevant to them. RPC 1.4; 2.2(b); see ABA Family Mediation Standard IV.

State and local ethics opinions which have endorsed lawyers serving as mediators have adopted consultation requirements similar to those of Rule 2.2 except that the mediator must explain that he does not represent any or all of the parties. The Massachusetts Bar Association opinion, however, regards the lawyer-mediator as not representing any of the parties until an agreement is drafted which inevitably involves choices of language that necessitate the mediator taking on a dual-representational role. The mediator must consult with the parties concerning this change in functions. Mass.Opin. 85–3.

Because a mediator typically does not represent any of the parties, the ethics opinions also urge or require lawyer-mediators to explain the advantages of each party employing independent counsel to review the decision to enter mediation, to consult with during the process, and to review—or draft—any settlement agreement that may be reached. To maintain neutrality, the mediator should not recommend specific attorneys to the parties but may suggest the use of available lawyer referral services or provide a list of qualified lawyers in the community.

Among the advantages that mediation is thought to provide over litigation are direct participation of the interested parties and cost savings on attorney's fees. Consequently, many mediators prefer that the parties' lawyers not take an active role in the mediation sessions. In some cases, the party-lawyers may be present at the mediation to consult with their clients as needed. While lawyers, of course, are entitled to bill for this time, there should still be an overall financial savings compared to litigation, especially if an early settlement is achieved. Other benefits of mediation, such as reductions in party animosity and adversarial maneuvering also tend to limit monetary as well as emotional expenditures. There may be occasions when the presence of party-counsel is especially desirable, as, for example, when one of the parties in a marital dissolution is much less informed, articulate and assertive than the other, or when there are complex taxation or other legal issues to be addressed. Whatever the role of independent counsel, the mediator should discuss it with the parties and reach an understanding before proceeding with the mediation sessions.

At the outset the mediator should explain the process, and how, unlike an arbitrator, a mediator has no authority to resolve the dispute and that the parties retain both the power to settle their controversy or to walk away from mediation at any time without reaching a resolution. The mediator, however, will want to ascertain that the parties are entering the mediation in good faith and will honestly attempt to resolve their differences.

In addition, the mediator must be satisfied that the relationship of the parties and their bargaining ability is appropriate for mediation. If the nature of the controversy is complex or the legal issues difficult, a family mediator should not continue participation unless the parties are advised by separate and independent counsel. See Florida Opin. 86–8; New York City Opin. 80–23.

Other ground rules and implications of the mediation should be gone over in the initial meeting, and it is good practice to document these in a writing which is signed by the parties. Matters which may be addressed include whether and when private caucuses will be held with each party, agreements and limitations on confidentiality, an understanding that the lawyer-mediator may not subsequently represent either party concerning the subject matter of the dispute, information on the nature of the costs and fees involved, the extent to which the mediator may or may not actively recommend settlement terms, and whether the mediator will be willing and able to give legal advice during the mediation and to draft a document reflecting any agreement reached by the parties.

One advantage of a lawyer serving as a mediator is the legal knowledge that she brings to the process, but whether a lawyer-mediator should, or ethically may, give legal advice to the parties is a very difficult issue.

Some of the ethics opinions which have addressed the question are concerned that if a lawyer-mediator gives legal advice to either or both parties, she necessarily takes on a representative role and cannot remain totally impartial. See New Hampshire Opin. 1983–4/4; Wisconsin Opin. E–79–2 (1980).

Other opinions have indicated acceptance of a lawyer-mediator giving legal information, but not advice, as an impartial advisory attorney. See Maryland Opin. 80–55A; Oregon Opin. 488 (1983); Virginia Opin. 511 (1983). The distinction incorporates concepts of unauthorized practice of law whereby legal advice applies general principles of law to a party's actual or contemplated transactions while legal information only informs the parties of the relevant provisions of law without applying them to a particular set of facts. ABA Family Mediation Standard IV–C provides: "The mediator may define the legal issues, but shall not direct the decision of the mediation participants based upon the mediator's interpretation of the law as applied to the facts of the situation."

Still other ethics opinions, probably the majority, allow the lawyer-mediator to give legal advice so long as it is given in the presence of all parties and the mediator is satisfied that it can be done without destroying her neutrality. See Florida Opin. 86–8; Boston Opin. 78–1; Conn.Opin. 35 (1982); New York City Opin. 80–23 (1981). Some lawyer-mediators respond to a party's request for information on how a court might resolve an issue by making non-binding predictions which are not to be interpreted as legal advice. There is a question as to whether this distinction is more semantic than real, at least as seen by the parties. Once again, the mediator can best protect herself and the parties by recommending that they employ independent counsel.

The mediator should discuss with the parties both the consequences of reaching a voluntary settlement and of failing to achieve one. When settlement is reached it should be understood whether the parties will enter into a written, binding contract, or something short of that, whether the mediator, the parties, or their independent counsel will draft any written settlement, and that, in any event, the settlement should be reviewed by independent counsel before it is finally executed. If further legal procedures are anticipated, such as seeking court approval of a marital dissolution agreement, the parties should be consulted by the mediator as to who will be responsible for its accomplishment.

Parties to a mediative process sometimes agree that if a voluntary resolution is not achieved, the dispute will be submitted to an arbitrator for binding resolution. If the mediator also is to serve as the arbitrator (known as a med/arb proceeding), the nature of the procedure and its consequences should be discussed at the outset, particularly regarding the use of confidential information revealed in the mediation phase. See SPIDR Standards, Use of Multiple Procedures. Likewise, consultation and agreement will be necessary if the possibility of the mediator serving as an arbitrator occurs for the first time during or after the mediation process.

Occasionally, an arbitrator is asked to help the parties try to settle their dispute. Although arbitration is an adjudicative proceeding, not designed to foster compromise or settlement *per se,* it is permissible for the arbitrator to affirmatively respond to a joint request to serve in a mediative role. An arbitrator, however, should not unilaterally seek to act as a mediator unless both parties are likely to be receptive to the suggestion (without any pressure) or a mediation role was previously authorized and anticipated. See Commercial Arbitrators Code, Canon IV–H, I; Labor Arbitrators CPR 2–F. Consultation must be held concerning any such change in the arbitrator's role, and, unless otherwise agreed or authorized by the initial appointment, he should afford the parties an opportunity to select another arbitrator if the mediation efforts are unsuccessful. [See SPIDR Standards, Multiple Procedures]. Pre-hearing conferences with the arbitrator, or with an agency administering the proceedings, may be held to explain the process, clarify issues, agree upon the admissibility of exhibits, seek stipulations regarding uncontested facts, and resolve other procedural and house-keeping matters.

While an arbitrator should be reluctant to forsake the adjudicative responsibility previously assumed, relations with the parties may justify a suggestion that they negotiate on their own or explore other forms of dispute resolution. A mediator also may conclude, after initiation of the process, that the matter is not presently conducive to mediation among the parties, and he should consult with them concerning the advisability of involving other professionals, including therapists or lawyer-litigators. See ABA Family Mediation Standard V.

C. IMPARTIALITY

A lawyer serving as a third-party neutral is expected to be free of bias and interest concerning the subject matter of the dispute and the parties to the controversy. Consequently, the neutral must disclose any business or personal affiliation with the parties or other information that may reasonably bear upon impartiality.

"Impartiality", according to the SPIDR Standards, means "freedom from favoritism or bias either by word or by action, and a commitment to serve all parties as opposed to a single party." Since there is at least a potential conflict of interest among parties to an intermediation, the neutral must obtain their informed consent before proceeding with the joint representation, and may not accept the role unless the lawyer reasonably believes that she can act impartially and the matter can be resolved on terms compatible with the parties' best interests and without improper effect on other responsibilities the lawyer has to any of the clients. RPC 2.2(a). The rule does not preclude a lawyer who has previously represented a client from accepting an intermediary role involving joint representation of that client after consultation and consent in accordance with the safeguards for representing conflicting interests. (See Conflicts of Interests, infra; Chapter 12, supra).

A number of authorities, however, discourage or prohibit a lawyer serving as a mediator for present or former clients, particularly in divorce mediations. Florida's Opinion [No. 86–8] conditions its approval of divorce mediation, among other requirements, on the lawyer not having previously represented either of the parties and not doing so "in any legal matter" during the mediation. Interestingly, the AFM Standards, while prohibiting mediation by a professional who previously provided legal or counseling services to *one* of the parties, allows the parties to consent to the mediation if such services have been provided to *both* parties and the prior relationship has been discussed and the role of the mediator is made distinct from it. It has been questioned whether restrictions applicable to lawyer advocates for a prior client should equally apply to therapists whose counseling role is quite different. Even where mediation involving one or more present or former clients may be undertaken, the mediator must disclose all prior relationships, consult with the parties concerning their possible impact on the mediation, clarify that she represents neither party in the mediation, and receive their informed consent before proceeding.

While a mediator must not favor one party, she does not forsake neutrality by raising questions of fairness and feasibility for the parties to consider. Commentators differ, however, on the degree to which a mediator should intervene to preclude a voluntary settlement which unduly favors one party or short changes the interests of persons not represented in the mediation, for example, a child in a divorce mediation, or the general public in a labor or environmental mediation. A labor mediator, who traditionally regards his role as facilitating the negotiation process between the parties is less likely to second guess a settlement voluntarily reached by the parties, than a family mediator who is aware that a court must approve the settlement and is concerned about its fairness and impact on a party who is not represented or who suffers from a power or bargaining imbalance. If a mediator is convinced that a proposed resolution will be inequitable or unworkable, particularly if one or both parties are not represented by independent counsel, it may be best to terminate the mediation and withdraw rather than advocate changes and risk a loss of neutrality.

It is not inconsistent with the mediator's neutral role to make suggestions or recommendations to the parties for resolving their disputes, and even to give an honest assessment—usually in a private caucus—of the reasonableness or likely reception of a party's proposals. Mediators vary in their assertiveness concerning such matters, and the key consideration remains that the decision is for the parties to make.

The type of mediative process selected by the parties also influences the appropriate degree of assertiveness of the neutral. A judicial reference to a private settlement judge may be expected to resemble the atmosphere of a public judge's settlement conference complete with authoritative evaluations and verbal arm-twisting. A neutral evaluator is expected to give an "expert" opinion but in a less authoritarian manner, and without actively seeking to persuade the parties to accept it. A mini-trial judge, despite the title, is expected to be relatively passive and generally presides over presentations and discussions by each parties' lawyer-representatives and principal decision-makers. In some usage, especially in the early development of labor relations, a conciliator was more concerned with facilitating communications between the parties whereas a mediator was more assertive in making recommendations to the parties. In most areas, today, the terms are interchangeable and usually subsumed under the mediator label.

Arbitrators and other neutrals who adjudicate disputes must maintain an impartiality analogous to that of judges. State and federal statutes provide for vacating arbitration awards where there was corruption or evident partiality by an arbitrator, and procedural rules and codes of ethics for arbitrators, and, to some extent, judicial codes of conduct provide further ethical guidance.

Unlike public judges, however, arbitrators—especially in commercial and court annexed cases—may have professional and business dealings with parties and lawyers who appear before them in an arbitration. Indeed, the arbitrator's practice or business experience in the field of concern is often an important qualification for his selection as an arbitrator. The safeguards against arbitrator partiality in this regard are provided by extensive disclosure requirements of any financial or personal interest in the outcome of the arbitration, and, to the extent likely to create an appearance of partiality or bias, any existing or past financial, business, professional, family or social relationships with parties, their counsel, or prospective witnesses. Commercial Arbitrators Code, Canon II; see Labor Arbitrators CPR 2–B, D. Once disclosure is made, the parties can agree—without participation of the arbitrator—to waive any basis for disqualification. If either party asks the arbitrator to withdraw, ordinarily he should do so unless the reason for the challenge is not substantial, the arbitrator believes he can act fairly and impartially, and withdrawal would cause unfair delay or expense to another party. When an agency administers the arbitration, it may have procedures for making the disqualification decision, especially if the issue is raised before the hearing; otherwise the challenged arbitrator, or majority of a panel, will decide the question. Even if the parties express a willingness to waive a basis for disqualification, the arbitrator should withdraw if there is a clear conflict of interest.

In *Commonwealth Coatings v. Continental Casualty* (U.S.1968), the Supreme Court set aside a tripartite panel's unanimous award in a construction arbitration because the neutral arbitrator failed to disclose a sporadic, but significant business relationship with one of the parties. Although there was no actual evidence of fraud, bias or improper motives on the part of the arbitrator, the Court majority, citing inter alia, the disclosure requirements of the American Arbitration Association Rules and the Canons of Judicial Ethics, concluded that an arbitration tribunal, like a judicial one, must not only be unbiased but avoid even the appearance of bias.

Unlike a mediator who may hold private caucuses with the parties, or an ombudsman who seeks settlement of a grievance by independent communications with interested parties, an arbitrator, like a judge, should neither initiate nor consider ex parte communications concerning a pending matter. Except for setting a time and place for a hearing, and similar housekeeping matters, an arbitrator should not discuss a case with one party in the absence of the other party or parties. Such communication also can take place with consent of the absent party (as, for example, on a site visit at which each party has an opportunity to be present), and an ex parte hearing may be held if a party with due notice fails to show up. Commercial Arbitrators Code, Canon III–B; Labor Arbitrators CPR 5–C. Written communications to or from the arbitrator must be accompanied or immediately followed by copies to all parties.

Although judges may only consult disinterested experts on the law if both parties are given an opportunity to respond, it is commonly recognized in labor arbitration that a case may be discussed with another arbitrator on a confidential basis so long as the assigned arbiter takes sole responsibility for the decision.

D. APPEARANCE OF IMPROPRIETY

Arbitrators make binding decisions that are subject to very limited judicial review, and they share with judges the need to avoid even an appearance of impropriety. See Commercial Arbitrators Code, Canon III.

To an extent, this standard simply reinforces the requirements to maintain impartiality, disclose any interest or relationship which might create an appearance of partiality or bias, and to avoid unauthorized ex parte communications. Avoiding the appearance of impropriety also could contribute to ethical admonitions to arbitrators to conduct a fair hearing with courtesy and patience, and to not inject themselves into settlement discussions in the absence of joint requests or expectations of the parties (as might be the case with "permanent" umpires in labor arbitration).

Another area in which the appearance of impropriety of arbitrators has been questioned concerns their acceptance of "rigged awards." The late Federal Judge (and former arbitrator) Paul Hays in a wide-ranging attack on the preferred judicial treatment accorded labor arbitration called the rigged award "a shocking distortion of the administration of justice" because it purports to be the decision of the arbitrator when in fact it is based upon agreement of the parties and is uttered by the arbitrator as their "ventriloquist's dummy." Hays, Labor Arbitration—A Dissenting View (1966). Nevertheless, it is considered ethically acceptable for an arbitrator to issue a "consent" or "agreed" award (to use the less loaded terms) if the arbitrator makes sufficient inquiry to be satisfied that it is fair, sound, lawful, and consistent with professional responsibility. Labor Arbitrators CPR 2–I. While Hays believes an agreed award is intended to be misleading (to workers and supervisors affected by it), there may be both political and judicious reasons for parties to agree to accept a solution—if the arbitrator will order it—but not on their own. Their constituents may more likely accept an arbitrator's award than a voluntary agreement for settling a difficult dispute. This is especially true in resolving "interest" disputes over the creation of new contract terms, such as wages, than "rights" or "grievance" disputes over the interpretation and application of existing contracts. In commercial arbitrations, unlike the practice in many labor arbitrations, an arbitrator who is satisfied with the propriety of the terms of an agreed award also should state in the award that it is based upon an agreement of the parties. Commercial Arbitrators Code, Canon V–D.

Since labor arbitrators depend for their selection and compensation on their acceptability to the parties, Judge Hays also questioned the propriety of a system of adjudication in which the judge depends for his livelihood, or a part of it, "on whether he pleases those who hire him." Nevertheless, it is almost impossible for an arbitrator to craft an award settling a controversy that pleases both adversaries. In fact, experienced arbitrators, supported by surveys of union and management representatives, believe that greater party acceptability is accorded to those who make a clean decision for one party or the other (unless the facts clearly call for something less) than to arbitrators who tend to split the difference or try to work out other compromise awards.

While not normally expected of lawyers performing mediative dispute settlement, the avoidance of an appearance of impropriety has been invoked by a few bar association opinions, applying Canon 9 of the CPR, to advise against joint representation of clients seeking a divorce, mediation of a dissolution among present clients, or accepting payments by a non-lawyer mediation service for giving legal advice to divorcing parties. In fact these would constitute actual improprieties, and the Model Rules have not carried forward the duty of a lawyer to avoid the appearance of impropriety. Consequently, whether an attorney is serving as an intermediary, pursuant to Rule 2.2, or as a mediator, her conduct must avoid such violations of specific rules but she need not comport herself as Caesar's wife.

E. CONFLICTS OF INTERESTS

The obligation that a mediator or arbitrator be impartial necessarily includes avoidance of conflicting interests. The existence of such conflicts can be completely disqualifying or waivable upon disclosure, consultation, and informed consent.

Model Rule 2.2 applies general conflict of interest principles to a lawyer functioning as an intermediary. The lawyer must reasonably believe that she can represent each client without adversely affecting the representation of the other, and must obtain both client consents after consultation which includes an explanation of the implications of the common representation and the advantages and risks involved. RPC 1.7. The lawyer also must reasonably believe that the matter can be resolved on terms compatible with the clients' best interests, that there is little risk of material prejudice to those interests if the matter is not successfully resolved, and that the common representation can be undertaken impartially and without improper effect on other responsibilities that the lawyer has to any of the clients. The clients also need to be made aware that the attorney-client privilege and other confidentiality rules generally do not apply among jointly represented clients.

If, at any time during the joint representation either the lawyer or clients conclude that the intermediation cannot effectively continue without adversely affecting the interests of a client, the lawyer shall withdraw. RPC 2.2(c).

Once the intermediation is terminated, the clients become former clients, and are entitled to the protections of Model Rule 1.9 against the lawyer subsequently representing materially adverse interests or using confidential information to the disadvantage of a former client. Contrary to provision in Rule 1.9(a) allowing former clients to consent to later representation of adverse interests, Rule 2.2(c) adopts a complete bar on the lawyer subsequently representing any of the clients in the matter that was the subject of an intermediation. The degree to which the lawyer inevitably learns confidences of the clients in the process, and the likelihood of further conflict following a failed intermediation, preempts the ability of the former client to consent to adverse representation in the matter. Or, viewed from the perspective of the lawyer, the judgment is made by the rules that any reasonable lawyer serving as an intermediary must believe that subsequent representation of any one client relating to the subject matter of the intermediation will inevitably adversely affect the relationship with another former client. See RPC 1.7.

Many of the guiding principles contained in Model Rule 2.2 have found acceptance in mediation. In fact, while a lawyer normally may not represent both a husband and wife in seeking to negotiate a separation agreement or property settlement, even in connection with an uncontested, no-fault divorce, the authorities have been more hospitable to a lawyer-mediator, representing neither of the spouses, helping them to resolve their conflicts. The mediator must make full disclosure of the nature of her role and the process and of the conflicts of interest and risks involved, receive informed consent from parties capable of understanding their options, advise them to seek independent legal counsel, and be satisfied that she can competently and impartially undertake to resolve their differences.

Although there are states which permit a mediation when a former client gives informed consent, most bar opinions limit lawyer-mediators to situations where neither party has been a client of the lawyer.

There is more uniformity in prohibiting the lawyer-mediator from subsequently representing either party in a maritial dissolution or other proceeding relating to the matters mediated. The Connecticut State Bar opinion [No. 35 (1984)] would also disqualify other members of the mediator's law firm. This position is consistent with Model Rule 1.10 which applies imputed disqualification to associates of lawyers precluded from representing a party to an intermediation under Rule 2.2, although the affected client may waive the disqualification after consultation. Where the lawyer serves as an impartial advisor rather than a full-scale mediator, subsequent representation by the lawyer is more likely to be acceptable with informed consent.

After appropriate disclosure of prior relationships with the parties, an arbitrator may serve, despite the presence of a possible disqualification, if both parties consent. The arbitrator should withdraw, however, irrespective of the expressed desires of the parties, if there is a clear conflict of interest. Labor Arbitrators CPR 2–B; see Commercial Arbitrators Code, Canon II.

A lawyer who serves as a neutral arbitrator should not thereafter represent either party in relation to any aspect of the arbitrated matter, nor negotiate for employment with any party or other lawyer involved in the arbitration matter. RPC 1.12(a), (b); CPR DR 9–101(A). The Model Rules do, however, permit a lawyer-arbitrator to subsequently represent a party in connection with the matter which was arbitrated if "all parties to the proceeding consent after consultation." RPC 1.12(a). While the Code does not contain a similar express consent provision for a lawyer who has served in a judicial capacity, it is arguably implied from the general conflict of interest provisions. DR 5–105(C). The Rules also expressly permit screening of a disqualified arbiter to enable others in his law firm to undertake or continue representation of party to a prior arbitration. RPC 1.12(c).

F. CONFIDENTIALITY

Unlike a judicial trial, the parties to an arbitration or mediation avoid airing their problems—and sometimes highly personal or trade secrets—in public. The willingness and ability of the neutral to maintain the parties' confidences are important to both party acceptability of her and of the process. Thus, confidentiality of disclosures at an ADR proceeding is a key concern of the parties and the neutral. The bases for confidentiality, as well as its legal protection, however, may vary with the type of ADR proceeding employed.

Mediations, whether concerned with family, community, labor, professional malpractice, partnership formation or dissolution, business or other disputes, often involve personal information and deep-seated feelings on sensitive issues. To encourage a full and candid consideration of these matters, confidentiality of the process is critical. Parties need to feel secure, absent extraordinary circumstances, that their statements, admissions, and offers of settlement will not be revealed by other parties or the mediator. In the context of an appellate mediation conference, the Second Circuit noted:

> If participants cannot rely on the confidential treatment of everything that transpires during these sessions then counsel of necessity will feel constrained to conduct themselves in a cautious, tight-lipped, non-committal manner more suitable to poker players in a high-stakes game than to adversaries attempting to arrive at a just resolution of a civil dispute. This atmosphere, if allowed to exist, would surely destroy the effectiveness of a program. . . . Lake Utopia Paper Ltd. v. Connelly Containers, Inc. (1979).

Moreover, since a mediator typically has no discovery power (although normal judicial discovery rules would be available prior to mediation of a matter in litigation), the expectation of confidentiality is an important incentive to the voluntary disclosure of information necessary to a full hearing and successful mediation.

Accordingly, the various voluntary standards for mediators encourage confidentiality of the process and discourage the mediator from disclosing information acquired from the mediation. The goal of confidentiality and its legal achievement, however, are not totally in unity.

A lawyer serving as an intermediary, pursuant to Rule 2.2, is instructed to consult with each client concerning the effect of the common representation on the attorney-client privileges. RPC 2.2(a)(1). Since the attorney-client privilege does not apply as between commonly represented clients, if litigation eventuates, an intermediary could be compelled to testify at the instance of one client regarding information revealed during the common representation by another client. Professor Hazard (the Reporter for the Kutak Commission) apparently believes that—in the absence of joint agreement otherwise—"client confidences normally protected under Rule 1.6 will be shared among all the clients . . . [and] is necessary for the representation to be carried out properly. . . . If any one of the parties balks at sharing his confidences, that is proof positive that the mediation is doomed to fail, and therefore should not be attempted." Hazard & Hodes, The Law of Lawyering 312–13 (1985).

Well maybe; but not so in most mediations. In practice, most mediators agree to hold in confidence information which is given to them in a private caucus with a party unless that party authorizes its disclosure to other parties. Of course, understandings concerning the confidentiality of such disclosures should be reached when the mediator consults with the parties regarding the ground rules of the proceedings.

While the practice of a mediator honoring a party's confidentiality within the process is more common in some types of mediation than others, Professor Wolfram observes that even in an intermediation under Rule 2.2, "it should be permissible for the lawyer and all clients to undertake the representation on the explicit understanding that some client's information will not be shared with one or more other clients involved so long as withholding the information does not operate unfairly to disadvantage or mislead any other party to the mediation." Wolfram, Modern Legal Ethics 729 (1986).

Since a mediator, unlike an intermediary under Rule 2.2, does not represent the parties to the mediation, there is no attorney-client privilege attaching to communications made in the course of the process. The mediator should so advise the parties during their initial consultation.

Nevertheless, there are other ways in which confidentiality of what takes place within mediation can be protected from disclosure. These include voluntary agreement, statutory protections, and judicial interpretation of rules of evidence, common law and public policy.

By common practice, and in accordance with recommended standards, most mediators secure agreement from the parties, usually in writing, that the mediation sessions will be confidential, that none of the parties will subpoena or otherwise require the mediator to testify about or disclose matters that transpired in mediation, and that the mediator will not voluntarily disclose information learned in the mediation to any third party. The mediator should also advise the parties regarding any known legal limitations on confidentiality in the jurisdiction concerned, and that he will resist any attempt to compel his testimony, and will notify the parties if subpoened.

While most mediators and parties can be expected to honor such agreements, their legal enforceability is subject to doubt in some jurisdictions. There is a public policy against agreements to suppress evidence, and, as Wigmore expressed the common-law view, "no pledge of privacy . . . can avail against demand for the truth in a court of justice." 8 Wigmore, Evidence 528 (1961). Nevertheless, there are countervailing public policies favoring voluntary dispute settlement, and several courts have recognized the importance of confidentiality to the success of mediation. In quashing attempts to compel mediators to testify, courts have placed a greater value on the openness and candor of the parties and neutrality of the mediator, as necessary to maintain the integrity and effectiveness of the mediation process, than on requiring the disclosure of relevant evidence.

In other cases, however, the courts have declined to uphold the confidentiality of mediation in the absence of statutory authority.

Some protection of statements made during mediation is available under rules of evidence making offers of compromise made in negotiations privileged or not legally relevant. Federal Rule of Evidence 408 embodies and broadens this policy and excludes evidence of conduct or statements made in compromise negotiations, as well as offers of settlement, but only if made in an attempt to compromise a claim which was disputed as to validity or amount. Thus, there is no bar to the use of such evidence to prove bias of a witness, negate a contention of undue delay, or for other purposes. It is at least arguable that other rules of evidence enabling the court to balance the probative value of evidence against its undue prejudice could be invoked to avoid prejudicing the mediation-settlement process.

Information concerning mediation is less likely to be protected from discovery proceedings which encompass not only admissible evidence but information "reasonably calculated to lead to the discovery of admissible evidence." Fed.Rule Civ.Proc. 26(b). In balancing the need for mediator confidentiality against the broad discovery policies, courts may be disinclined to prohibit relevant requests in the absence of a recognized evidentiary privilege or clear statutory policy favoring confidentiality of mediation.

A growing number of jurisdictions are enacting statutes to provide confidentiality to the mediation process and protect mediators from being compelled to testify. While adopting a clear policy recognizing the importance of confidentiality to mediation, the statutes have enacted justified exceptions to the policy. Exceptions which might out-balance the need for mediation confidentiality could include reporting of child abuse or other specified serious crimes, permitting a mediator to defend an action for damages brought against her, or reporting of serious attorney misconduct.

The statutes generally permit all parties to the mediation to consent to waive its confidentiality in specific cases, and, in a few states, the parties must sign a written agreement of confidentiality to invoke the protection of the statute.

Special considerations may apply to court-annexed or compelled mediations. For example, in California, which mandates conciliation of child custody and visitation rights in domestic dissolution disputes, if the mediation does not resolve the issues, the court appointed conciliator may make a recommendation to the family court judge. The recommendation becomes a matter of public record, and it has been held that either party may cross-examine the conciliator regarding the basis of the recommendation. McLaughlin v. Superior Court (Cal.App.1983).

There is considerable research interest in dispute settlement processes, and mediators and arbitrators are often asked to cooperate in such efforts. Family mediators are expected to obtain the consent of the parties before releasing information concerning mediated matters, and should render anonymous all identifying information used for research or training. AFM Standards, Release of Information.

Unless disclosure is required or authorized by law, arbitrators also are expected to respect the confidentiality of the proceedings. It is permissible for a labor arbitrator to discuss aspects of a case in a class or with another arbitrator provided there is no breach of essential confidentiality. An arbitrator may donate arbitration files to a library or educational institution, without express consent of all the parties involved, but should honor any requests of parties to maintain privacy of specified matters, and may ask that recent cases be withheld from public availability for a certain interval.

An arbitrator should not disclose an award prior to its issuance to the parties, and should not make it public without the consent of the parties. Parties sometimes request that names of grievants or witnesses be deleted from awards and opinions that are made public, and such requests should be honored. There are several publication services of labor arbitration awards, but an arbitrator should not submit an award or accompanying opinion to such publications without consent of the parties after they have received the award. Requests for publication prior to the award place the parties in an unfair position in that they may be apprehensive that a negative response could influence the arbitrator's disposition of the matter. The Labor Arbitrators CPR has been recently amended, however, to permit an arbitrator to request permission to submit the award for publication at the hearing, as well as after issuance of the award, so long as the parties are given at least 30 days after the date of the award to revoke or deny permission to publish. Labor CPR 2–C–1(c).

Arbitrators—*a fortiori* lawyer-arbitrators—should not use confidential information acquired in the arbitration for their own advantage, that of a third party, or to affect adversely the interest of another person or entity. Commercial Arbitrators Code, Canon VI–A.

Arbitrators often enjoy immunity from civil liability similar to that of judges for acts taken in an adjudicative capacity, but are not completely free of an obligation to testify concerning aspects of proceedings over which they have presided. Arbitrators might be called to testify, for example, in criminal trials where they had learned of relevant events in the arbitration, or in a breach of fair representation suit by an employee alleging that the union representing him in the arbitration performed perfunctorily or with discrimination toward him.

G. FEES

A lawyer serving as a neutral should abide by both the regulations on fees in the Model Rules or Code and any rules specifically applicable to the dispute settlement service being rendered. Thus, the lawyer may not charge an unreasonable or illegal fee. Divisions of fees with other lawyers, for example, co-mediators, should be in accordance with the services performed or responsibility assumed, the fee sharing should be made known to the clients or parties who should be given an opportunity to object to the arrangement, and the total fee must be reasonable. (See generally, Chapter 14, Attorneys' Fees). Divisions of fees with non-lawyers are strictly regulated and are further discussed in connection with aiding the unauthorized practice of law, infra.

A lawyer-neutral has a duty to explain the bases of fees, costs or other charges at the outset of the process, and preferably should commit the compensation agreement to a writing, signed by and given to the parties. RPC 1.5(b); SPIDR Standards, Disclosure of Fees.

Although there is no express prohibition in the Rules or Code on a lawyer charging a contingent fee for rendering third-party dispute settlement services, any such fee, at least in the United States, would be inappropriate for the judging function of an arbitrator, and a fee based upon the outcome of a mediation is generally prohibited. Florida Bar Opin. 86–8; ABA Family Mediation Standard I–F; AFM Standards, Contingent Fee.

The manner of sharing of fees, and the method of payment, shall be agreed to by the parties and the mediator, and advanced unearned fees should be promptly returned to the parties. Normally, mediation fees will be shared equally, but an employer may pay for a mediation or ombudsman service for its employees and government or non-profit agencies often provide some labor, child custody, and community mediation services free of charge.

The AMF Standards specifically prohibit commissions, rebates or similar forms of remuneration for referring clients for mediation services, which approach is consistent with the ban on referral or forwarding fees for legal services adhered to in most jurisdictions. See RPC 1.5(e), 7.2(c); CPR DR 2–101(I), 103(B), 107(A).

Arbitrators are usually compensated on a per diem basis, although hourly or per case charges, or fixed retainers for "permanent umpires," may alternatively be used. Per diem or hourly charges should be in accordance with actual time devoted to a matter or allocated for a hearing, and the arbitrator's fee schedule should be communicated in advance to the parties by the arbitrator or an agency administering the selection of the arbitrator. The fee schedule should indicate whether and what the arbitrator charges for study and travel time, as well as hearing time, whether a cancellation, postponement or docketing fee is assessed and how much, and what expenses are expected to be reimbursed. A fixed ratio of study days to hearing days is inconsistent with a per diem method of charging, and should not be used unless specifically agreed to by the parties. Expense reimbursement must not exceed actual expenditures (a per mileage charge is common for travel by private automobile) and if related to two or more cases or sets of parties, should be allocated appropriately. Adequate records to support fee and expense charges must be maintained and made available upon request of the parties or an administering agency. An arbitrator may decrease a normal fee due to the financial condition of a party (with knowledge and consent of the other party) or the parties, or when the total normal charges would not be compatible with the case decided.

An arbitrator's fees and expenses are normally shared equally by the parties but some arbitration clauses provide for the arbitrator to allocate all or an appropriate portion of the fees to the losing party. This is not an unethical practice. In other cases, a government agency may pay a fixed or per diem fee to the arbitrator (as in court-annexed and some labor arbitrations) or an employer may agree to pay the entire fee of an arbitration involving its employees.

While labor arbitrators are usually compensated for all hearing and study time, commercial arbitrators often serve without charge in one day or abbreviated arbitrations. Where compensation is to be paid or expenses reimbursed, a clear understanding should be reached—often through an administering agency—and arbitrators "should scrupulously avoid bargaining over the amount of payments or engaging in any communications concerning payments which would create an appearance of coercion or other impropriety." Commercial Arbitrators Code, Canon VI–D.

H. UNAUTHORIZED PRACTICE OF LAW

Non-lawyers have long and effectively served as mediators, arbitrators and in other third-party dispute settlement roles. While a lawyer's skills and knowledge are often useful in these processes, it would not be in the public interest for members of the bar to attempt to preempt these functions for themselves. Accordingly, it is usually not considered the unauthorized practice of law for a non-lawyer, or a lawyer admitted in another jurisdiction, to serve as a third-party neutral dispute resolver. Non-lawyer as well as lawyer-neutrals, however, must have the competency to undertake the particular type of dispute resolution role and should defer where legal issues or technical matters with which they are unfamiliar are likely to predominate.

Even when a non-lawyer neutral feels comfortable in dealing with issues that may arise, there are occasions where he may cross the line into the unauthorized practice of law.

The practice of law is generally defined to include the giving of legal advice and the drafting of instruments affecting legal rights and obligations, whether or not in connection with a matter in litigation. (See Chapter 7, Unauthorized Practice of Law). Consequently, if a non-lawyer neutral, for example, in a divorce mediation, advises either or both parties as to their legal rights, or draws up a property settlement or separation agreement—as other than a scrivener of terms agreed upon by the parties, she may be engaging in the unauthorized practice of law. As discussed above (see Consultation, supra), however, there is a fine line between providing general information about the law and applying legal principles to the specific situation of individual parties. The former may be done by a lay person but the latter requires the exercise of the type of legal judgment that generally requires involvement of a lawyer.

An appealing argument could be made that a non-lawyer mediator's involvement in the practice of law should not be unlawful so long as it is incidental to other legitimate services, no separate fee is charged for the legal aspects of the services, and no complex legal matters are involved. (See Chapter 7, Unauthorized Practice). Moreover, the public interest can be said to favor some leeway for mediators to drift into legal areas so that they may continue to provide valuable dispute resolution assistance to people who otherwise would not have the financial ability to employ lawyers or engage in litigation. Mediation of landlord-tenant disputes and other forms of community dispute resolution often are of this nature even though questions of legal rights (e.g., to refund of security deposits) arise. Even when greater financial stakes are at risk, there is a public interest in encouraging voluntary settlement of disputes.

Unauthorized practice can be avoided when parties are each represented by independent legal counsel who can advise them regarding legal questions that arise during the mediation and can prepare or approve any agreements. Thus, lay as well as lawyer-mediators should encourage consultation with independent legal counsel whenever feasible.

Another solution—which brings forth its own set of problems—is to use a mediation team consisting of a lawyer and a non-lawyer professional who is appropriate for the subject of the mediation. Mental health professionals often mediate domestic relations disputes with lawyers, and resolution of construction disputes, for example, might benefit from involvement of a lawyer-engineer or lawyer-architect mediation team. Each professional brings an occupational competency and aptitude which is valuable to the process and provides a balance not offered by a sole mediator. The lawyer's skills and knowledge are available for clarifying legal issues and drafting agreements, while, for example, a psychologist could deal with the emotional elements that inevitably arise in a family mediation.

The lawyer member of a mediation team, however, must be alert to avoiding the unethical acts of aiding the unauthorized practice of law, sharing fees for legal services with a non-lawyer, and forming a partnership with a lay person to render legal services. See RPC 5.4, 5.5; CPR DR 3–101, 102, 103. Thus, lawyers may not enter into a partnership or corporation with non-lawyers if any part of the services offered constitute the practice of law; a lay-mediator who shares office space with a lawyer may not advertise her location as being in a law office or imply that they are in a business together which involves the practice of law; a lawyer may not give legal advice to the non-lawyer mediator who then renders such advice to the parties; and a lawyer-mediator who is compensated by a lay agency or person must be careful to exercise professional judgment independent of direction or regulation by the payor and must not share fees received for legal services with the non-lawyer entity.

It is permissible, however, for a lawyer to employ or compensate a co-mediator counselor on a fee basis, for an agency to employ lawyers who receive the total compensation for their legal services which are rendered free of agency direction or control, or for the parties to pay a set fee which is shared by the mediators and agency (for overhead and administration) so long as it is not divided among lawyers and non-lawyers on a percentage basis.

A lawyer also may participate with non-lawyers in mediations that do not require the exercise of professional legal judgment or otherwise involve only dispute settlement services which are permissible for lay-persons.

Occasionally, a state attempts to invoke unauthorized practice regulations to prevent non-lawyers from serving as arbitrators of particular types of cases. While a jurisdiction, government agency, or the parties to an arbitration are certainly free to require that their adjudicators be legally (or otherwise professionally) qualified, the use of restrictions on who can practice law seems inappropriate in this context.

I. ADVERTISING AND SOLICITATION

The provisions of the Model Rules (and the CPR to the extent they are constitutional) relating to advertising and solicitation apply to lawyer neutrals if their dispute settlement services involve the practice of law. (See RPC 7.1 to 7.5; Chapter 10, Solicitation and Advertising). The general prohibition against misleading or deceptive communications also applies to offers of dispute resolution services whether or not they may be considered as the practice of law. Thus, advertising must honestly represent the services to be rendered, no claims of specific results or promises which imply favoritism may be made, and neutrals should make only accurate statements about the process, its costs and benefits, and their own qualifications. See SPIDR Standards, Advertising and Solicitation; AFM Standards, Advertising. Rebates, commissions, or similar forms of remuneration for referral of parties for dispute resolution services should neither be given nor received by neutrals. It would not seem unethical, however, for a neutral to pay a legitimate administrative cost for a listing with a dispute resolution center, non-profit referral agency, or bona fide legal services organization. See RPC 7.2(c); CPR DR 2–103(B), (D). But see Kentucky Opin. 335 (1989).

The prohibitions on misleading communications and other provisions of the professional conduct standards have been applied to lawyer mediators even without any representational relationship with the parties. Thus, while a Maine Opinion [No. 71 (1986)] advised that a law firm may offer and advertise a private divorce mediation service, it was considered misleading and improper to advertise that the services are "new and unique", the firm has "41 lawyer years" of experience, or that the firm will work "with both spouses, something your divorce lawyer is not allowed to do." Nassau County Bar Association [Opinion 82–8] found a divorce mediation center's statement that hiring "separate lawyers . . . is costly . . . [and] often only complicates matters" to be "false, deceptive, and blatantly misleading", and the claim that divorce mediation is quicker, less expensive and far less painful than representation by separate counsel was "misleading [and] cannot be measured or verified". While aspects of these opinions seem overly defensive on the part of the practicing bar, they illustrate the care that lawyers must take in making claims on behalf of their dispute settlement services.

Whether a mediation service involving lawyers may operate under a trade name depends on whether the jurisdiction follows the Model Rules, allowing the practice so long as the name is not deceptive [see RPC 7.5(a)] or the provision in the Code prohibiting private practice under a trade name. DR 2–102(B).

A lawyer may be listed as an approved attorney by a mediation center, so long as the list does not violate advertising or speciality disclaimer rules, and a lawyer may advertise that his practice is limited to mediation so long as there is no claim of specialization, unless so authorized in the jurisdiction. See RPC 7.4.

Arbitrators may indicate a general willingness to so serve, and may seek to be listed on recognized, non-profit panels but must be candid and fully responsive regarding their qualifications and availability, and must not seek to influence any administering agency by gifts or other improper means.

It is considered unethical for an arbitrator to solicit specific appointments from parties or administering agencies, and labor arbitrators are prohibited from advertising for or soliciting arbitration assignments. Commercial Arbitrators Code, Canon 1–B; Labor Arbitrators CPR 1–C–3. Despite the Supreme Court's striking down of restrictions on truthful advertising by lawyers and permitting of written solicitations of business, the labor arbitration community, led by the National Academy of Arbitrators [NAA], has maintained its opposition to such practices by arbitrators. For example, the NAA's ethics committee has concluded that an arbitrator's plan to send a letter to parties for whom he had recently heard cases announcing his unavailability for several months, while on an overseas trip, would improperly imply the suggestion that they refer future cases to him upon completion of the trip. The committee would approve, however, of an arbitrator communicating his temporary unavailability to parties who requested his services or with whom he had a continuing relationship. NAA Ethics Opin. No. 3 (1972).

J. PRO BONO ACTIVITIES

A lawyer's pro bono obligations, pursuant to Model Rule 6.1, may be partially fulfilled by volunteering to serve as an neutral dispute resolver. Lawyers are needed on fee arbitration panels and in court-annexed arbitration programs where they usually serve with no or reduced compensation. Community and other mediation programs benefit from the voluntary, no-fee, participation of lawyers as mediators, board members and advisors. Public service activities of this nature are encouraged both because of the lawyer's position in society and the benefits to the public of such non-litigative dispute resolution services.

Professional organizations of dispute resolvers also impose public service obligations. The SPIDR Standards recognize that a neutral should provide pro bono services, as appropriate, engage in efforts to educate the public about the value and use of neutral dispute resolution procedures, and participate in the development of new neutral practitioners. A similar training obligation is recognized for experienced labor arbitrators, and family mediators are admonished to not only participate in their own professional growth and continuing education but to join with other mediators and related professionals to promote mutual professional development. Labor Arbitrators CPR 1–C–2; AFM Standards, Training and Education. Family mediators also are obligated to promote the advancement of mediation by encouraging and participating in research, publishing and other forms of professional and public education.

A mediator is encouraged to provide some mediation services for nominal or no fee, and commercial arbitrators frequently serve without compensation and labor arbitrators are encouraged to reduce or forgo their fees when justified by the financial condition of a party or parties or the nature of the case. [See Fees, supra].

III. RELATED DUTIES OF LAWYERS AS CLIENT REPRESENTATIVES

A. OBLIGATION TO CONSIDER USE OF ADR PROCESSES

While this chapter has focused on the ethical problems that may confront a lawyer who accepts a role as a neutral dispute resolver in ADR processes, we hope that this emphasis has not had the effect of discouraging lawyers from acting in this capacity. There are many benefits to clients, lawyers, and society of utilizing these alternative procedures. So much so that the question legitimately arises as to whether a lawyer has an ethical duty to clients to explore the use of ADR rather than, or prior to, resorting to litigation. Although the concept is only beginning to be articulated, the recognition of such a duty has much merit and is consistent with other professional responsibilities of the lawyer.

Former Chief Justice Burger believed that lawyers would recommend litigation less often if they understood that "people with problems, like people with pains, want relief, and they want it as quickly and inexpensively as possible." Burger, 16 Judges J. (1977). Mediation, arbitration and similar ADR processes resolve controversies more quickly, less expensively, and with less pain than litigation. In addition, the greater degree of client control and autonomy and individualized justice available in these processes is likely to encourage client satisfaction.

Although the vast majority of legal controversies are settled by negotiation, frequently the settlement does not occur until the eve of trial or even during the trial. Use of mediation or court-annexed arbitration is likely to bring about a negotiated settlement at an earlier date—before extensive discovery expenses, legal fees, and hostile emotions have been run up to uncomfortable levels.

Clearly the use of a more expeditious, less costly, and more accommodating dispute resolution process benefits clients, the courts, and the public. But what about the lawyers who stand to lose the legal fees that the client avoids and who give up some degree of client control? As a professional, the lawyer must subordinate his self-interests to those of the client. (See Chapter 1–II, Professionalism). Moreover, lawyers can benefit by more efficiently disposing of their cases, by having fewer hassles over legal fees with clients who are likely to be more satisfied with both the fee and service, and by playing a professional role which is less antagonistic and, for many lawyers, more personally satisfying. (See Chapter 25, Professional vs. Personal Responsibilities). Indeed, as more and more clients recognize the advantages of ADR, they may expect their lawyers to discuss the appropriateness of alternative procedures and use them when in the clients' best interests. The failure of lawyers to do so may find the sophisticated client shopping for a new lawyer.

Another incentive for lawyers to explore the possible use of ADR with their clients is the avoidance of potential malpractice claims. Just as advocates may have an obligation to discuss settlement options with their clients—and pursue them when appropriate, lawyers should also consult with clients about processes, such as mediation, which may enhance the likelihood and fairness of settlement. Clients may be less likely to belatedly second-guess a settlement agreement when a mediator or advisory arbitrator has recommended it. Employment of ADR processes are almost always less costly—in dollars, time and emotions—than litigation, and lawyers who fail to consult with their clients on these alternatives may not be adequately representing the best interests of their clients.

Model Rule 1.2(a) requires a lawyer to consult with a client as to the means by which the client's objectives are to be pursued. The Comments add that "the lawyer . . . should defer to the client regarding such questions as the expense to be incurred and concern for third persons who might be adversely affected." Certainly, exploration of use of ADR procedures as a means of pursuing client objectives impacts on the expense to be incurred and may incorporate concern for third parties, for example, children in a marital dissolution matter.

In advising a client a lawyer is not limited to strictly legal concerns. See RPC 2.1; CPR EC 7–8; Chapter 19, Lawyer as Advisor and Negotiator. "Advice couched in narrowly legal terms may be of little value to a client, especially where practical considerations such as cost or effects on other people, are predominant." RPC 2.1, Comment. Consultation regarding ADR options can effecuate this broader advisory role of the lawyer.

For reasons of this nature, two experienced family lawyers and mediators have taken the position that: "the lawyer's duty to advise a [domestic relations] client about the option of private mediation is a key element of the family lawyer's ethical responsibility, and that the failure to do so could result in malpractice exposure. . . ." Mosten and Wasserstrom, 22 Beverly Hills B.J. (1988).

To the extent this conclusion possesses validity—as may well be increasingly recognized—it also has application to client consultation regarding other forms of alternative dispute resolution and other areas of law.

B. THE LAWYER AS AN EVALUATOR

Evaluations undertaken by a lawyer for a client but for use by third persons are expressly recognized by the Model Rules. RPC 2.3. As with the role of the lawyer as an intermediary, the ethical constraints on this evaluation role are specific applications of other rules.

The evaluation function governed by Rule 2.3 needs to be distinguished from several somewhat similar roles. Unlike a mediator or intermediary, an evaluator represents one party and is not truly neutral. A lawyer who investigates a third party's affairs to render an evaluation to his client, or a special prosecutor for the government, is not covered by Rule 2.3 because the investigation is not of the client's affairs for the use of third parties. And, finally, a lawyer's internal investigation for a client's use only does not come within the scope of the Rule since the results are not intended for the use or benefit of third parties and retain the confidentiality of matters related to representation of the client.

Thus, Rule 2.3 deals only with the situation where a lawyer is requested by his client to undertake an evaluation of a matter affecting the client that will be used by someone other than the client. Examples of such evaluations include: registration statements accompanying securities offered for sale; opinion letters—known to be disseminated to and relied upon by others—regarding the nature of a transaction, e.g., whether or not it is a security, or its tax consequences; a title search or opinion requested by a seller for the benefit of a buyer; and a governmental attorney's opinion for the use of private parties.

In each instance the lawyer must reasonably believe that making the evaluation is compatible with other aspects of her representation of the client, and the client must consent to the evaluation after consultation. Since the scope of the representation of the client is modified by preparation of an evaluation for use of a third-person, consultation with the client must take place on limiting the objectives of the representation and to avoid assisting any criminal, fradulent or other illegal or unethical activity. RPC 1.2. Conflict of interest [RPC 1.7] and confidentiality [RPC 1.6] concepts apply because of possible diminution of total loyalty to the client and a duty to one or more third-persons to reveal what would otherwise be confidential. Accordingly, client understanding of the evaluator's role and informed consent are essential. The duty of confidentiality remains as to all matters relating to the representation except to the extent disclosure is required in connection with a report of an evaluation. RPC 2.3(b).

A key question, of course, is the extent to which such disclosure is required. The lawyer must comply with Rule 4.1 by not making a false statement of material fact or law, and by not refusing to disclose a material fact to the third person when disclosure is necessary to avoid assisting a criminal or fraudulent act by the client. But even such limited disclosure obligation is subject to Rule 1.6 safeguarding the client's confidences, and cannot be made unless the client consents. In such circumstances, a lawyer who is prevented from making a disclosure thought necessary must decline to undertake the evaluation, and possibly withdraw from the representation if the client will otherwise commit a fraudulent or criminal act. (See Chapter 15, Terminating the Relationship).

If withholding certain information would neither be dishonest nor assisting the client in fraud, but the lawyer believes that a third party is entitled to know that information, yet the client refuses to authorize its disclosure, another possible course of action is for the lawyer to prepare the evaluation report with a statement of the material limits placed upon the scope of the evaluation review. See RPC 2.3 Comment. A red flag of this nature may cause the third party to refuse to rely upon the lawyer's evaluation and either nix the deal with the client or pursue other sources to learn information thought important to its consummation.

While the issue of the lawyer's liability for non-disclosure of information to third parties who may rely upon the evaluation to their detriment is beyond the scope of rules of ethics, it is a very real concern of the lawyer. Civil or criminal liability for aiding securities or other fraud of the client, and malpractice liability to third parties as derivative clients are among the possible consequences faced by the lawyer-evaluator. (See Chapters 6, Duty to Insure Competence—Malpractice, and 20, Lawyer as Corporate Counsel). In one leading case, a law firm was asked to prepare an opinion letter that the client could show to a potential creditor to help obtain a loan. Despite the fact that the lawyers who drafted the letter knew that several partners considered themselves as limited partners (and, thus, not individually liable for the loan), the letter stated that the client was composed of 14 general partners—which, if true, would make all of them liable for the loan. The creditor made the loan, and when the client defaulted and asserted it was a limited partnership, the creditor sued the law firm alleging that he relied upon the firm's characterization of the partnership. The law firm was found liable for negligent misrepresentation (but not fraud because there was no allegation of its intent to deceive the creditor). Roberts v. Ball, Hunt, Hart, Brown and Baerwitz (Cal.App.1976).

Thus, lawyers who make evaluations for clients which they know will be relied upon by third parties, not only have duties of loyalty and confidentiality to the client, but may well have a duty to such third parties to avoid intentionally or negligently misleading them.

Special situations arise when a lawyer is asked to respond to a financial auditor on behalf of the client. Some disclosure is at least impliedly authorized by the client's engagement of the auditor, and the ABA Statement of Policy Regarding Lawyers' Responses to Auditors Requests for Information (1975) provides useful guidance to the lawyer. The lawyer must exercise considerable judgment on many issues including what must be disclosed as "contingent liabilities".

The lawyer's role as evaluator can be useful but hazardous.

CHAPTER 22

THE LAWYER AS JUDGE: JUDICIAL ETHICS AND SELECTION

I. INTRODUCTION

> A fair trial in a fair tribunal is a basic requirement of due process. . . . To this end no man can be a judge in his own case and no man is permitted to try cases where he has an interest in the outcome.
>
> In re Murchison (U.S.1955)

Just as the attorney is bound by ethical considerations in his role as advocate, so also is he bound to act ethically in his role as judge. Naturally, because of the difference in function between the judge and the advocate, the rules pertaining to judicial conduct are different from those pertaining to the conduct of attorneys as advocates. For example, the adversary system is typified by the presence of two advocates representing clients whose interests have come into conflict. The duty of each counsel is to present her client's case in the strongest light possible, using every legitimate legal method to convince the fact-finder that her client should prevail. DR 7–101; see Comment, RPC 1.3; Chapter 16, The Adversary System. As stated in the Report of the Joint Conference on Professional Responsibility:

> An adversary presentation seems the only effective means for combatting [the] natural tendency to judge too swiftly in terms of the familiar that which is not yet fully known. The arguments of counsel hold the case, as it were, in suspension between two opposing interpretations of it. While the proper classification of the case is thus kept unresolved, there is time to explore all of its peculiarities and nuances.

The importance of an impartial and competent "referee" between the two parties is obvious: The judge must ensure that the attorneys, in their advocacy, do not step beyond what is legally or ethically permissible. Without the presence of an unbiased and competent judge performing this function, one party could gain an unfair advantage in attempting to convince the jury. Further, to the extent that the judge has cause to favor one side over the other due to personal interests or biases (rather than the merits of the case), the legitimacy of the entire adversary system is undermined.

Even when the judge is not the trier of fact, the slightest hint of bias or prejudgment on her part might unfairly affect the outcome because of the great influence she has with the jury.

The rules and principles believed to be necessary to promote proper judicial conduct are delineated in the ABA Code of Judicial Conduct [CJC] (adopted in all federal and a number of state courts) and in state and federal statutory provisions. This chapter explores those rules and principles, primarily for federal courts; local statutes and court rules should be consulted for particular modifications applicable in a given jurisdiction. With few exceptions, however, the development of judicial ethics in the CJC and in the federal system represents the modern trend.

What litigation there has been in the field of judicial ethics has virtually all occurred in the context of disqualification of judges in particular cases. In many cases where a party to a suit alleges judicial misconduct worthy of discipline, the courts have responded that the proper redress was not discipline, but appellate review of the particular case. Judicial discipline most often consists of censure when it occurs at all. Removal of judges from their positions has rarely occurred, and then only for grossly improper conduct such as criminal acts or circumstances (such as senility) tending to indicate a total inability to perform judicial duties.

State judicial commissions have been established to evaluate the performance of judges and provide procedures for discipline and removal. Greater efforts have been made in recent years to permit regulation and review of the conduct of federal judges in particular. Several senators have introduced bills which would create mechanisms for judicial censure without requiring resort to the difficult and cumbersome impeachment process, and the ABA judicial discipline standards, along with the federal circuit court rules and procedures, are evidence of the increasing concern for sanctioning incompetent judges without sacrificing judicial independence.

II. DISQUALIFICATION

A. BASIC PRINCIPLES AND RULES

Under English common law, a judge could be disqualified from sitting in a case only if he had a direct pecuniary interest in the outcome. By the twentieth century the situations in which recusal would be justified were broadened to include a "substantial" interest, even if not pecuniary.

American courts were reluctant to recognize a general right of disqualification, although some states recognized specific grounds such as pecuniary interest or relationship to a party. At the federal level, the predecessor of current disqualification statutes was Section 21 of the Judicial Code of 1911. Section 21 enabled litigants in district courts to disqualify a judge upon a showing of personal bias or prejudice for or against one of the parties.

The leading case under Section 21 was Berger v. United States (U.S.1921). The defendants in *Berger* were German–Americans convicted of violating the Espionage Act of 1917. On appeal to the Supreme Court they alleged that the bias of their trial judge prevented their receiving a fair trial. Supporting their charge were comments allegedly made by the trial judge such as: "One must have a very judicial mind, indeed, not to be prejudiced against the German–Americans in this country. Their hearts are reeking with disloyalty." The Court found that the facts alleged supported the defendants' averment; it held that a party charging a judge with personal bias must allege facts to support the charge, and that the judge may rule on the sufficiency of the affidavit, but not on the truth of the facts. The holding has been interpreted to require that the facts alleged must be assumed to be true.

B. 28 U.S.C. § 144

The successor to Section 21 is 28 U.S.C. § 144, which currently reads in part:

> Whenever a party to any proceeding in a district court makes and files a timely and sufficient affidavit that the judge before whom the matter is pending has a personal bias or prejudice either against him or in favor of any adverse party, such judge shall proceed no further therein. . . .

Although Berger v. United States was decided under Section 21, it remains an important holding because it has been consistently followed by courts in deciding cases arising under Section 144. The threshold requirement under Section 144 is that a party timely file an affidavit demonstrating the judge's personal bias or prejudice. Accompanying the affidavit must be a certificate of counsel of record stating that the averment is made in good faith. And, consistent with Section 21 as interpreted in *Berger,* the inquiry of the trial judge is limited to the sufficiency of the affidavit; the truth of the facts alleged is assumed. It is widely recognized that under Section 144 the prejudice or bias against a party must originate from an extra-judicial source rather than from the judge's participation in the litigation. Additionally, the emphasis on *personal* bias or prejudice has resulted in recusal being refused when prejudice might reasonably be perceived, such as when a judge might have a preconceived view of the merits, or bias against a party's attorney.

C. 28 U.S.C. § 455

The other federal statute that, in conjunction with Section 144, governs recusal in federal courts is 28 U.S.C. § 455. Whereas Section 144 is only applicable to district courts, Section 455 applies equally to the district courts, the courts of appeals, and the

U.S. Supreme Court; the language of Section 455 is directed at self-recusal by judges rather than at motions for disqualification by litigants as under Section 144. It is therefore self-enforcing on the part of the judge—a judge has an affirmative duty to recuse himself if he falls within its purview. However, although the statute is directed at judges, it may be asserted by litigants by way of writ of mandamus, interlocutory appeal, motion in the trial court, or assignment of error on appeal.

Recusal is specifically mandated by Section 455 when a judge: individually or as fiduciary (or a member of his immediate family) has a financial interest in the controversy that would be substantially affected by the outcome of the proceeding; has a personal bias or prejudice concerning a party; has personal knowledge of disputed evidentiary facts; has served as attorney in the matter during private practice; has previously practiced law with an attorney in the matter and such association existed while the attorney was concerned with the case. Recusal is also mandated when a judge or his spouse, or a person within the third degree of relation to either of them,* or the spouse of such a person, is a party, attorney, or material witness in the proceeding or has an interest that could be substantially affected by the outcome. When a judge's interest in a case is "direct, personal, substantial, [and] pecuniary," his failure to recuse himself constitutes a violation of the due process rights of affected litigants. Aetna Life Ins. Co. v. Lavoie (U.S.1986) (state supreme court justice cast the deciding vote and wrote an opinion establishing tort of bad faith refusal to pay a valid insurance claim, including punitive damages, while the justice was a plaintiff in pending cases seeking recovery against insurance companies for punitive damages on the same basis).

* To compute the degree of relationship, each person in the chain from the judge, to the common ancestor, to the person in question is counted as one degree. Hence, the relationship of a judge to his uncle is in the third degree: The judge's father is the first degree, his grandfather (the common ancestor) is the second degree, and his uncle is the third degree.

In addition to the above specific standards, Section 455 contains a general standard for recusal: A judge is required to "disqualify himself in any proceeding in which his impartiality might reasonably be questioned." The standard is based on circumstances as they would appear to the ubiquitous reasonable person: Once the appearance of unfairness or partiality arises, the judge should recuse himself regardless of his personal view concerning his impartiality.

Despite the apparent breadth of the standard, courts have tended to interpret it quite narrowly. In order to understand the application of the appearance of impartiality standard, it will be helpful to examine the statute in a historical perspective, looking first at the statute before its amendment in 1975, then at Canon 3C of the CJC, and finally at statements made by Justice Rehnquist when he refused to recuse himself in Laird v. Tatum (U.S.1972).

Prior to the 1975 amendment, Section 455 provided:

> Any justice or judge of the United States shall disqualify himself in any case in which he has a substantial interest, has been of counsel, is or has been a material witness, or is so related to or connected with any party or his attorney as to render it improper, *in his opinion,* for him to sit on the trial, appeal, or other proceeding therein. [Emphasis added.]

Although the subjective standard for recusal seemed to apply only to a judge's relationship with a party or his attorney, a subjective test was in fact employed whenever a judge's impartiality was questioned. Thus, despite the fact that a judge may have appeared to have a fixed view of the merits of a case or his impartiality could reasonably be questioned, he could still serve as judge in the case under the unamended statute if he was personally convinced of his impartiality.

In January of 1972 the final draft of the CJC was issued. Canon 3C(1) provided: "A judge should disqualify himself in a proceeding in which his impartiality might reasonably be questioned. . . ." According to Professor Thode, the general standard set forth included "[a]ny conduct that would lead a reasonable man knowing all the circumstances to the conclusion that the judge's impartiality might reasonably be questioned . . . [as] a basis for the judge's disqualification." Reporter's Notes to the Code of Judicial Conduct. Hence, Canon 3C(1) was intended to establish an objective standard for recusal.

In Laird v. Tatum, petitioners contended that Justice Rehnquist should disqualify himself from consideration of the case because of his statements concerning the case made prior to his appointment to the Court. The petitioners founded their motion on Section 455 (pre-amendment) and various provisions of the CJC. Despite the clear difference in language between the standards set forth in the old statute and Canon 3C(1), Justice Rehnquist, in refusing to disqualify himself under either, stated: "Since I do not read these particular provisions as being materially different from the standards enunciated in the congressional statute, there is no occasion for me to give them separate consideration."

In 1975, Section 455 was amended to incorporate the objective standard of the CJC; the amendment was a practically verbatim adoption of Canon 3C. Congress intended the change to foster public confidence in the judiciary by mandating disqualification if there was a reasonable basis for doubting a judge's impartiality; however, the comments of Justice Rehnquist in regard to Canon 3C can be read to apply directly to Section 455 (as amended), since the statute and the CJC are virtually identical. Therefore, the objectivity of the amended standard as perceived by the courts might not be of the same degree as intended by Congress. Indeed, cases decided under the amended statute have continued to hold that a judge's bias must be personal to the movant; bias against his attorney, for example, does not suffice. But cf. Hayslip v. Douglas (Fla.App.1981) (when prejudice against an attorney is of such a degree that it adversely affects the client, trial judge should disqualify himself).

The congressional intent to foster public confidence in the judiciary by incorporating an objective reasonable belief standard received substantial support in Liljeberg v. Health Services Acquisition Corp. (U.S.1988). In *Liljeberg,* John Liljeberg formed a corporation to apply for the necessary state "certificate of need" to build and operate a hospital. For two years he negotiated with Loyola University to purchase land owned by Loyola to serve as a hospital site. Federal District Court Judge Collins was a member, and regularly attended meetings, of Loyola's Board of Trustees during the negotiations. A dispute arose over the ownership of the corporation formed by Liljeberg, and suit was filed in federal court seeking a declaration of ownership of the corporation. Judge Collins, sitting without a jury, ruled in favor of Liljeberg, having not read the minutes or attended a meeting of the Loyola Board during which it was determined that the terms of the sale of Loyola land to Liljeberg would be void unless he retained control of the certificate. Judge Collins had forgotten about Loyola's interest in the property at the time of his ruling. When Health Services learned of the judge's association with Loyola, it moved to vacate the judgment on the ground that the judge was disqualified under Section 455. The Supreme Court vacated the judgment, holding that "recusal is required even when a judge lacks actual knowledge of the facts indicating his interest or bias in the case if a reasonable person, knowing all the circumstances, would expect that the judge would have actual knowledge."

In 1990, a new CJC was adopted by the ABA to replace the 1972 Code. While much of the substance remains unchanged, many of the rule numbers vary from the 1972 CJC. Since very few states have adopted the new CJC, its parallel provisions will be indicated in brackets. Significant changes and new provisions will also be noted.

D. DISQUALIFICATION IN PARTICULAR TYPES OF CASES

Disqualification is typically sought when a litigant fears that a judge has a personal bias or prejudice, or when a judge may have a preconceived view of the merits of the case. The standards involving personal bias have been discussed above.

The tentative draft of the CJC included a provision for recusal when a judge had "a fixed belief concerning the merits of the matter before him." This provision was deleted from the final draft because it could have been interpreted to require disqualification if a judge had a fixed belief concerning the law applicable to a given case. The Committee thought it both unavoidable and desirable that a judge have previously developed opinions on constitutional and other legal issues.

Courts have been reluctant to uphold allegations that a judge had predetermined the merits of a case. Those courts that have considered the issue have been more inclined to require disqualification when the judge, rather than the jury, was the trier of fact. It has been held, therefore, that a judge should have recused himself when he had obtained knowledge that a defendant had failed a lie detector test before accepting a waiver of his right to a jury trial. People v. Walker (Mich.App.1970). The court stated, however, that if the judge had possession of such knowledge in a jury trial, recusal would not be required. This statement would seem to undermine the appearance of fairness standard; for even in a jury trial, the judge uses her discretion in making evidentiary rulings, charging the jury, and determining the proper sentence. Federal judges may also comment on the weight of the evidence. The likelihood of unintended bias affecting the discharge of these duties might reasonably be questioned.

Prejudgment of the merits of a case typically occurs when a judge has been involved in prior adjudications or hearings related to the case, such as when a judge: (1) hears a case on remand after having presided at the original trial; (2) has presided at preliminary evidentiary hearings (particularly when highly prejudicial information is held to be inadmissible); (3) presides at a perjury or contempt hearing when he also served in the trial out of which the alleged violations occurred; and (4) has presided at previous trials of co-defendants. Recusal has not been widely recognized as mandatory in the above situations, except in the cases involving contempt and perjury; and even in contempt proceedings, normally a highly personal attack on the judge's integrity must be committed by the accused before recusal is mandated. See Taylor v. Hayes (U.S.1974) (judge should be recused where he was "embroiled" or "personally involved" with the defendant, and therefore unable to balance the interests of the court with the interests of the defendant). In a case of perjury, a judge usually need not recuse himself unless he has been sufficiently open and blatant in his prejudgment.

Although situations involving remand, evidentiary hearings, or prior trials of co-defendants have not normally resulted in disqualification, there are factual circumstances that might raise a reasonable question concerning prejudgment of the merits: In a remand situation, a judge may have made statements or rulings during the original trial that indicated a strong belief in guilt; in a situation involving a prior evidentiary hearing, a judge may have made an initial determination that a defendant's confession was not voluntary (although apparently reliable) and then subsequently presided at the trial; and in the case of co-defendants, a judge may have presided at two or more trials where co-defendants were convicted before hearing the third co-defendant's case. In the above circumstances, the defendant's belief in the judge's (unintended) bias would seem to be reasonable; yet courts in such cases have generally not been open to arguments for recusal.

Despite the language of Section 455 and the CJC, many judges refuse to disqualify themselves when there might seem to be a reasonable appearance of bias or prejudgment. The narrow interpretation of the standard is unfortunate: To public confidence in the administration of justice, the appearance of unfairness can be as damaging as the actual presence of unfairness. When more judges openly recognize this and realize that a motion for disqualification is not necessarily an attack on their judicial ability, a freer availability of recusal can be expected. If judges are unwilling or unable to take the lead in this area, it is incumbent upon legislators to ensure public confidence. A number of states (e.g., California) have enacted provisions that allow a litigant one peremptory disqualification *for any reason;* disqualification automatically follows. Where judicial resources so permit, peremptory challenge removes the stigma of disqualification, while ensuring public confidence in the impartiality of the judicial system.

III. APPEARANCE OF IMPROPRIETY

The general standard relevant to all facets of judicial conduct is stated in Canon 2 of the CJC: "A Judge Shall Avoid Impropriety and the Appearance of Impropriety in All of the Judge's Activities." The importance of the appearance of impropriety has already been discussed as a basis for disqualification. However, irrespective of potential disqualification, a judge should, at all times, conduct himself in a manner that promotes public confidence in the impartiality and integrity of the judiciary. Canon 2A. In fact, the Commentary to the CJC states that a judge must expect himself to be subject to public scrutiny and must, therefore, accept restrictions on his behavior that might be unduly burdensome to other citizens.

Thus, for example, the Commentary to Canon 2 provides that it is "inappropriate for a judge to hold membership in any organization that practices invidious discrimination on the basis of race, sex, religion, or national origin. Membership of a judge in an organization that practices invidious discrimination may give rise to perceptions by minorities, women, and others, that the judge's impartiality is impaired." The new CJC includes a new Canon 2(C) which provides: "A judge shall not hold membership in any organization that practices invidious discrimination on the basis of race, sex, religion or national origin." See also new Canon 3B(5) & (6). Although the new section is a welcome addition to the Code, it is unclear why, since the prohibition is only with respect to *"invidious"* discrimination, it is limited to the specified bases. It would seem that membership in an organization that practices invidious discrimination on the basis of age, handicap or sexual orientation is equally likely to give rise to the perception of impaired impartiality by members of those groups.

Section B of Canon 2 includes several specific requirements intended to avoid the appearance of impropriety: A judge should not allow her family or social relationships to influence her judicial conduct. She should not use or appear to use the prestige of her office on behalf of the private interests of others. Nor should a judge allow an impression to arise that an individual or party is in a special position of influence with her; she is, therefore, required to take action to prevent anyone from attempting to capitalize on a claim that she is in such a position. The final prohibition of Canon 2B is that a judge should not appear as a character witness unless compelled to do so in response to an official summons. This provision was adopted after the Special Committee on Standards of Judicial Conduct was informed of instances when a judge was called to exploit the prestige of her office. The specific standards of Canon 2 make certain judicial responsibilities explicit, but the avoidance of the appearance as well as the fact of impropriety remains the guiding light for *all* the activities of a judge.

IV. ADJUDICATIVE AND ADMINISTRATIVE RESPONSIBILITIES

The judge has certain adjudicative and administrative responsibilities mandated by Canon 3A & B. As mentioned in the section discussing disqualification, judges are rarely disciplined and, therefore, virtually all litigation concerning judicial ethics has occurred when a party has moved for recusal. As a result, little more can be offered regarding administrative and adjudicative duties than analysis of the CJC's principles and rules and the Committee's intent in adopting the relevant portions of Canon 3.

A. ADJUDICATIVE RESPONSIBILITIES

Canon 3A(1) [3B(2)] requires a judge to "be faithful to the law and maintain professional competence in it." The requirement that a judge be competent was new and significant at its inception, the old Canons containing no competency standard. It would be a judge's duty to be knowledgeable on all matters of law likely to come before him and to stay informed as to changes that occur in those matters. A well-informed judge can compensate for some attorney incompetence; for that reason, the duty of competence on the part of judges is of even greater importance to the administration of justice than the similar duty imposed on lawyers.

A judge is also required to maintain a courtroom atmosphere of order and decorum. Canon 3A(2) [3B(3)]. This atmosphere would appear to be fostered by the dictates of Canon 3A(3) [3B(4)]: "A judge should [shall] be patient, dignified, and courteous to litigants, jurors, witnesses, [and] lawyers . . . and should [shall] require similar conduct of lawyers, and of his staff, court officials, and others subject to his direction and control."

A further requirement of all judges is to avoid *ex parte* or other communications concerning a proceeding or pending proceeding unless authorized by law. Canon 3A(4) [3B(7) (except for "scheduling, administrative purposes or emergencies that do not deal with substantive matters or issues on the merits)]. The appearance of impropriety is great for *ex parte* communications whether or not the communication was of significance to the proceeding. The Reporter's Notes indicate that *ex parte* communications between a judge and a party (or counsel to a party) are clearly precluded; but communications among judges and between judges and court personnel fall within the provision "as authorized by law." The prohibition on *ex parte* communications has been applied to law enforcement personnel and government agencies. See, e.g., Wenger v. Commission on Judicial Performance (Cal.1981).

A related problem in the drafting of Canon 3A(4) concerned a judge's seeking the advice of disinterested experts on issues of law related to the proceeding before him. The Committee recognized the importance of such communications as well as the potential inroads to the adversary system by their use. The Commentary therefore stressed the value of a brief of *amicus curiae* for such purposes. The Committee did, however, recognize that for many proceedings the *amicus curiae* brief is too formal; therefore, a judge is authorized to obtain expert advice if notice of the identity of the expert consulted and the substance of the advice received is given to the parties and if the parties are allowed to respond. See 1990 CJC Canon 3B(7)(b).

The Committee also drafted the provision precluding communications regarding pending proceedings in order to prevent forum shopping. Without that provision, it would be possible for a party to determine how a given judge might rule on a case before it is filed. Of course, a judge who has received a communication concerning a matter that subsequently comes before him would normally be required by Canon 3C(1) [3E(1)] to disqualify himself because "his impartiality might [then] be reasonably questioned."

A judge should also refrain from public comment about a proceeding and require the same of court personnel. Canon 3A(6) [3B(9)]. However, this subsection does not prevent a judge from comment during his official duties (as from the bench) or from explaining procedures of the court for public information.

Canon 3A(5) [3B(8)] reads simply: "A judge should [shall] dispose promptly [efficiently and fairly] of the business of the court." The Committee, in adding this subsection, was apparently responding to reports of judges whose procrastination and lack of punctuality caused loss of time to jurors, attorneys, and litigants and resulted in a large backlog of pending cases. Hence, the Commentary indicates that prompt disposition of the court's business requires a judge to be punctual, to allow adequate time to dispose of matters before the court, and to require court personnel, attorneys, and parties to do the same. It has been held, however, that where a judge fails or refuses to act when circumstances require a ruling, disciplinary procedures are unavailable if there is an appropriate judicial remedy (e.g., petition for writ of mandamus). In re Charge of Judicial Misconduct (9th Cir.1982).

The final requirement of Canon 3A governs the judge's duty to regulate broadcasting, recording, or photographing in the courtroom and immediate areas. Canon 3A(7) once required generally that a judge not permit such activities. However, in 1982 this provision was amended in light of the *Chandler* case. See Chapter 17, The Lawyer and the Fair Trial/Free Press Conflict. Judges may now allow broadcasting, televising, recording, and photographing of judicial proceedings if rules prescribed by the "appropriate authority" so permit. The press activities permitted must be consistent with the parties' rights to a fair trial, and the judge should limit coverage so that it will be unobtrusive and will not distract the trial participants or otherwise interfere with the administration of justice. Canon 3A(7) was deleted from the 1990 CJC because it was believed to address a matter of court administration, rather than judicial ethics.

B. ADMINISTRATIVE RESPONSIBILITIES

A judge's administrative responsibilities include a standard of competency for efficient operation of the court. A judge is required to discharge her administrative duties diligently and to "facilitate the performance of the administrative responsibilities of other judges and court officials." Canon 3B(1) [3C(1)].

Canon 3B(2) [3C(2)] contains a provision not included in the old Canons. It places upon the judge a duty to ensure that her staff and other court officials subject to her control observe the standards of "fidelity and diligence that apply to [her]." The exact nature of standards applicable to the judge's subordinates is not clear, but presumably they would include obligations of competence, punctuality, and avoidance of public comment [and, under the new CJC, refraining from "manifesting bias or prejudice"]. Improper conduct by a judge's subordinates can result in the recusal of the judge herself, due to the resulting damage to the *judge's* appearance of impartiality. See, e.g., Hall v. Small Business Admin. (5th Cir.1983) (judge should have recused himself where his law clerk had conflict of interest).

A judge has an ethical duty to take appropriate disciplinary measures when he becomes aware of unethical conduct of lawyers and judges. Canon 3B(3) [3D(1) & (2)]. Implicit in the doctrine of separation of powers is the principle that each branch of government is master of its own house and must, therefore, regulate the conduct of its members. The requirement of Canon 3B(3) [3D(1) & (2)] reiterates the mandate of Canon 1: "A Judge Should [Shall] Uphold the Integrity and Independence of the Judiciary." Thus, a judge is obligated to participate actively in establishing, maintaining, and enforcing ethical standards so that the integrity of the judiciary is preserved. Because judges are often in the best position to observe incompetent or otherwise unethical conduct by attorneys, it is essential to the proper administration of justice that they assume a greater responsibility to report such conduct than they have in the past. Indeed, if the trial court fails to inform a criminal defendant of his lawyer's conflict of interest, the defendant's right to a fair trial may be implicated and his conviction reversed. Dunton v. City of Suffolk (2d Cir.1984) (where defendant not informed of counsel's conflict of interest and could not be expected to understand such conflict on his own, trial court had duty to inform defendant of conflict). See Wheat v. United States (U.S.1988); Cuyler v. Sullivan (U.S. 1980).

The final administrative duty of a judge concerns the manner in which he makes appointments, whether of attorneys to represent indigents or of personal staff such as clerks and secretaries. He must not make unnecessary appointments and those he does make should be based on merit rather than on politics and nepotism; otherwise, the possibility that incompetent individuals may become involved in the administration of the court's business arises.

V. QUASI-JUDICIAL ACTIVITIES

A judge's quasi-judicial activities should be those that do not cast doubt upon her dignity, integrity, and impartiality. Thus she may speak, write, or lecture on matters concerning the law or administration of justice; she may also serve as an officer of an organization devoted to improving the legal system. But, to prevent the appearance of impropriety, she may not participate in public fund raising activities for such organizations. Canon 4. The Massachusetts Supreme Court severely criticized a superior court judge for his presence at a lecture to raise funds for 24 defendants awaiting trial in Massachusetts. For this and other instances of judicial misconduct, the judge was suspended from the bench until the legislature could decide whether he might return to office. Private consultations with executive or legislative bodies or officials are proper "only on matters concerning the administration of justice" (Canon 4(B) [4C(1)]), such as court personnel, budget, housing, and procedures.

VI. EXTRA–JUDICIAL ACTIVITIES

Canon 5 reads: "A Judge Should Regulate His Extra–Judicial Activities to Minimize the Risk of Conflict with His Judicial Duties." See 1990 CJC Canon 4. Thus, avocational activities should not detract from the dignity of his office. A judge may participate in charitable or civic activities but those that would cast doubt on his impartiality should be avoided; for example, serving as a director for an organization that is likely to come before him in legal proceedings would be improper. A judge may attend a civic or charitable organization's fund raising event, but should not be a speaker or a guest of honor; nor should the judge solicit funds on behalf of the organization. A judge's business and financial dealings are limited in the same respect—they must not tend to raise the appearance of partiality, to exploit his judicial position, or to involve him in frequent transactions with persons likely to appear before him. In those few instances where a judge may accept gifts (e.g., donor is not someone whose interests have or will come before the judge and there is no appearance of impropriety), they should be reported in the same way as compensation if they are valued at over $100.

VII. JUDICIAL SELECTION

The standard anecdote is that if one wishes to become a federal judge, one should have the foresight to have as one's roommate in law school a future senator, or to be a principal participant in the election campaign of a senator or the President. Under the federal system of judicial selection, judges are appointed by the President and confirmed by the Senate. The possibility of political patronage in such a system is obvious. The concern is not that members of a particular political party will be appointed to the judiciary, but that persons unqualified for the position will be.

Although the Constitution provides for Presidential appointment of federal judges with the advice and consent of the Senate, when a vacancy occurs within a state (at least for the district courts), the real appointive power lies with the senators of the President's party for that state. By long-established custom, those senators have the prerogative of suggesting nominees; subsequent appointment by the President, practically speaking, is usually a formality. Furthermore, the Senate has the power to block an alternate candidate of the President by simply threatening to withhold endorsement. If the President does not yield, the seat simply remains vacant. The tendency of Senators to support candidates proposed by one of their number in return for similar treatment at a later date is virtually unavoidable.

For the Court of Appeals, President Carter established a United States Circuit Judges Nominating Commission consisting of a number of panels. The panels were composed of equal numbers of lawyers and laypersons who, upon the request of the President, determined if potential nominees had the necessary expertise; they then recommended to the President the five persons they considered to be most qualified. This system was an improvement over the entirely partisan appointment procedure in that it was addressed more to a potential appointee's credentials than to her connections (assuming the appointee was one of the five recommended and the recommendation procedure was untainted by politics). However, President Reagan abolished the Commission when he took office in 1981 in favor of a return to the former method of selection. When a position on the court of appeals became open, lawyers in the Department of Justice suggested various candidates, on their own initiative or on advice from other lawyers, White House staffers, and senators of the president's party representing the state for which the appointment was slated. The President would then nominate an individual and send that person's name to the Senate. Senatorial confirmation is required for appellate as well as trial court positions, but because appellate jurisdictions span several states (except for the District of Columbia), the power of any given senator is not as great.

For years, the U.S. Department of Justice has sought the advice of the ABA's Standing Committee on the Federal Judiciary regarding potential nominees for judgeships. The Committee's investigations, reports, and votes on potential nominees are kept confidential, although ratings of candidates are made public if they are in fact nominated. In Public Citizen v. U.S. Dept. of Justice (U.S. 1989), the Court held that the Committee was not an "advisory committee" as defined in the Federal Advisory Committee Act, and was therefore not required to hold open meetings and make its records and reports available to the public. The Justice Department's refusal to reveal the names of potential nominees it was considering or to provide its records and minutes of meetings was upheld.

At state and county levels, some jurisdictions use the appointment procedure and others use a combination committee-appointment procedure. The committee-appointment procedures are principally of three kinds: (1) The members of the bar association are polled and a certain number of the individuals with the highest number of votes is submitted to the appropriate official for appointment; (2) the Board of Governors of the local or state bar association is polled in the same manner; and (3) the name of a potential appointee is referred to a committee, an investigation as to his qualifications is made, and a report is submitted.

Some jurisdictions also have elections for judicial positions. This procedure has been criticized because, it is argued, the general public is not aware of a given individual's legal qualifications and ability; rather, the legal community is the only group that has observed the professional behavior of the potential judge and is, therefore, in the best position to determine his qualifications. In addition, the temptation for judicial rulings to reflect popular beliefs (even misconceptions) rather than the dictates of the law and for judges to devote inordinate time and energy to re-election efforts are cited as reasons for reducing the number of elective judgeships.

For an individual seeking an elective judicial position, the CJC has prescribed acceptable campaign behavior. See also RPC 8.2(b); DR 8–103(A) (requiring that a lawyer who is a candidate for judicial office must comply with the CJC). A candidate "should [shall] not make pledges or promises of conduct in office other than the faithful and impartial performance of the duties of the office." Canon 7B(1)(c) [5A(3)(d)(i)]. Nor should a candidate misrepresent himself in any way or announce his views on disputed legal or political issues. The Reporter's Notes indicate that the candidate is permitted to campaign on the basis of his ability, experience, and record, but the line between proper and improper statements is hazy in light of the previously stated limitations. Also, a candidate is required to attempt to stop any campaigning done on his behalf that he becomes aware of and that would be a violation of the CJC if engaged in himself.

Concerning campaign funds, a candidate should not herself solicit funds or publicly stated support. Canon 7B(2) [5C(2)]. Rather, she should establish committees to secure and manage the funds and obtain public statements for her support from lawyers and others. The requirement of committees to handle fund raising and endorsements is designed to insulate a judge, as much as possible, from an appearance of impropriety. However, the fact that public disclosure laws require the reporting of campaign contributors means that the names of contributors may eventually reach the judge; and publicly made statements, even though not solicited by a candidate, may eventually reach her ears. Allowing a candidate to receive no funds, on the other hand, would result in only affluent lawyers being able to run for office. A policy of not allowing public statements, especially by members of the legal community, could result in a lack of information on a candidate's qualifications, and would give the judge's opponent an unfair campaign advantage. These and similar problems lend support to the critics of judicial selection by election.

Canon 7A(3) [5A(2)] provides that a judge should resign his position on the bench when he becomes a candidate for elective nonjudicial office. The constitutionality of this type of provision, adopted in the vast majority of states, was upheld in Clements v. Fashing (U.S.1982). In *Clements,* several Texas officeholders—including one Justice of the Peace—challenged a Texas constitutional "resign-to-run" provision. The Supreme Court held that the state's interest was sufficient to warrant such *de minimis* interference with the officeholders' First Amendment interest in their candidacy. The state's interests lay in maintaining the integrity of its Justices of the Peace, in preventing neglect of duties, and in preventing abuses of office which Justices of the Peace might be tempted to undertake in hopes of attaining higher office.

The required comportment of judges as candidates in a campaign re-emphasizes the general standard of judicial conduct—a judge is to conduct himself in a dignified manner and to seek to minimize the appearance of impropriety in all of his conduct. The frequent reference to this standard throughout the CJC indicates it to be the overriding standard for all of a judge's activities.

CHAPTER 23

THE LAWYER AS PUBLIC LEADER AND LAW REFORMER

I. INTRODUCTION

Lawyers have the ability to exert a powerful influence on almost all facets of our society. Their training as problem solvers, relatively high income and prestige, and frequent appointment or election to positions of authority, all contribute to give attorneys significant opportunities for civic leadership and social reform. "Law is the principal instrument of power in our society, and, since it is not self-applying, the lawyer is the principal participant in its administration." Patterson & Cheatham at 63.

Although the percentages vary over time and from jurisdiction to jurisdiction, lawyers are by far the most prominent occupational group in Congress and state legislatures, in the executive branches of state and federal governments, in regulatory agencies, on the boards of directors of major corporations, and in civic organizations. In the federal government alone, studies indicate that 25 American presidents and a similar percentage of vice-presidents, cabinet members, and congresspersons have been lawyers. And these figures indicate merely the tip of the iceberg, because lawyers serve as counsel to every important decisionmaker, whether or not the decisionmaker herself is also a lawyer.

The suggested reasons for this over-representation of lawyers in positions of power are many and varied, both positive and negative. Justice Brennan has stated: ". . . [G]overnmental action that in other societies is exclusively the purview of administrators or legislators is, in America, subject also to judicial or quasi-judicial scrutiny. We have been a legalistic society from the beginning. Lawyers were conspicuous in the vanguard of the revolutionary movement and in the drafting of the Constitution, and ever since the diversity of our people, combined with their ingrained sense of justice and moral duty, has caused the society to frame urgent social, economic and political questions in legal terms—to place great problems of social order in the hands of lawyers for their definition, and in the hands of judges for their ultimate resolution. . . . The intricacy and pervasiveness of the webbing of statutes, regulations and common law rules in this country which surrounds every contemporary social endeavor of consequence give lawyers a peculiar advantage in coming to grips with our social problems." The Responsibilities of the Legal Profession at 89.

II. DUTY TO IMPROVE THE LEGAL SYSTEM

Regardless of the reasons, however, lawyers are in a unique position to effect social reform; and, at least to the extent that the legal system contributes to society's problems, the RPC and CPR make efforts to improve the legal system the ethical duty of every lawyer. Canon 8 thus provides: "A Lawyer Should Assist in Improving the Legal System." This obligation is elaborated upon in EC 8–1: "By reason of education and experience, lawyers are especially qualified to recognize deficiencies in the legal system and to initiate corrective measures therein. Thus they should participate in proposing and supporting legislation and programs to improve the system, without regard to the general interests or desires of clients or former clients." Accord RPC Preamble. See also Rule 6.4 (lawyer may serve as director, officer, or member of a legal reform organization notwithstanding that the reform may affect the interests of a client of the lawyer). Rules of law or aspects of the legal system that are outmoded, contribute to unjust results, or unfairly deny access to the system to any segment of society should be altered or eliminated. EC 8–2.

This duty of law reform is the responsibility of each individual lawyer and of the legal profession as a whole. It is not a duty that is readily susceptible of enforcement, but arises from attorneys' unique opportunity and ability to improve the operation of the law. To that extent, their law reform obligation is greater than that of other citizens. If lawyers, because of their special training, observational opportunities, experience, and privileged franchise, can more effectively perform a useful leadership function than other citizens, they are obligated to the society which provided them with such opportunities to fulfill that function.

Although the law reform duty is clear, however, the nature of that duty is much more difficult to define. Justice Powell (then-President of the ABA) once stated that the "overriding responsibility of the organized Bar is to assure the proper administration of justice." To a large degree, attorneys fulfill that duty by adhering to all of the ethical rules set out in the CPR and the RPC including, according to Justice Powell, maintaining standards for education and admission to the bar; assuring professional competency by continuing legal education; prescribing and enforcing ethical standards; preserving the quality, integrity and independence of judges; promoting improvement in substantive law; educating the public on our system of justice under law; preserving the rights of individuals guaranteed by the Bill of Rights; and assuring the broader availability of legal services. To these duties might also be added civic leadership and government service.

Because lawyers are believed by the public to be responsible for the operation (and failings) of the legal system, the price of failure to correct its defects is loss of public confidence and increased efforts to take control of the legal system and regulation of attorneys' conduct away from the legal profession. As stated in the Report of the Joint Conference, "[t]he lawyer tempted by repose should recall the heavy costs paid by his profession when needed legal reform has to be accomplished through the initiative of public-spirited laymen. Where change must be thrust from without upon an unwilling Bar, the public's least flattering picture of the lawyer seems confirmed. The lawyer concerned for the standing of his profession will, therefore, interest himself actively in improvement of the law."

Despite the Report of the Joint Conference however, the bar's failure of leadership in effecting law reform apparently continues, attracting criticism from lay commentators. For example, in his controversial history of the legal profession, Jerold Auerbach cites examples of lawyers' efforts to block reform and ameliorative legislation, and suggests that the profession has tinkered with the least significant aspects of the system while retaining laws and regulations that serve merely to protect its power, prestige and financial status. "At best, they preoccupied themselves with the most technical, professional aspects of legal issues—for example, the ethical proprieties of contingent fees rather than the social and individual costs of lives broken in industrial accidents. The result was that law reform served as 'a banner of rectitude waved in the public eye,' a shield to deflect public criticism." Unequal Justice at 64–65 (1976). See also Abel, American Lawyers (1989).

To the extent that attorneys have blocked legislation that would have eliminated unnecessary cost and delay or would have otherwise made access to legal services easier for indigents or the disadvantaged, criticism of the legal profession is undoubtedly justified. However, opposition to social "reform" may well be founded on a sincere belief that the proposed change is beneficial to neither the legal profession nor the lay public. Thus, lawyers have been condemned for opposing advertising and solicitation because it is believed that past restrictions have been advantageous to established and large law firm lawyers and disadvantageous to new attorneys and members of the public who may have been unaware of their legal rights. Attorneys who attempt to prevent lawyer advertising in order to gain financially from the ignorance of others clearly violate Canon 8 of the CPR and the spirit of the RPC Preamble. See also Rule 7.2, Comment (regarding desirability of dissemination of truthful information about legal services). On the other hand, attorneys who support advertising restrictions because they believe that all legal advertising is inherently misleading, and that it will work to the detriment of the legal profession and the public, fulfill their law reform obligations to the same extent as those who oppose such restrictions. Too often, lawyers are criticized not for failing to actively seek changes in the legal system, but for failing to seek changes that the public believes to be "right." As long as a lawyer honestly seeks to improve the legal system, she has the same right to her point of view as any other citizen.

III. TRAINING FOR POLICY-MAKING

No matter what one's view as to the extent of lawyers' law reform and public service obligations, many lawyers do serve as policy-makers. Most legal education, however, is designed to train advocates and, occasionally, advisors and negotiators. As stated by Lasswell and McDougal, "if legal education in the contemporary world is adequately to serve the needs of a free and productive commonwealth, it must be conscious, efficient, and systematic *training for policy-making.* The proper function of our law schools is, in short, to contribute to the training of policy-makers for the ever more complete achievement of the democratic values that constitute the professed ends of American polity." Legal Education and Public Policy: Professional Training in the Public Interest, 52 Yale L.J. 203, 206 (1943) (emphasis in original).

Although history has shown law faculty members to be at the forefront of social reform and public policy-making, their record in training students to assume similar roles is not as commendable. Most curricula stress interpretation and evaluation of legislation and appellate opinions, facility in trial techniques, and construction and evaluation of legal arguments in terms of logic and precedent. "[T]he curriculum offers little explicit consideration of alternative social objectives, . . . or of justifications for preference or preference priorities. Legal concepts and doctrines, which in theory are *instrumental* only, are too often presented as if they embodied the prime democratic values of society, and specific decisions are too often appraised or justified, not according to the degree to which they implement these values, but exclusively in terms of their supposed logical derivation from ambiguous definitions and doctrines." Lasswell & McDougal, supra at 206 (emphasis in original). See also Kennedy, Legal Education as Training for Heirarchy, in The Politics of Law: A Progressive Critique 40–61 (Kairys ed. 1982); Menkel–Meadow, Feminist Legal Theory, Critical Legal Studies, and Legal Education or "The Fem–Crits Go to Law School", 38 J.Leg.Educ. 61 (1988).

The 1943 assessments by Lasswell and McDougal are still true today: The social reform and civic leadership obligations of the legal profession mandate that law schools provide more courses designed to train future policy-makers in the evaluation and selection of effective and desirable social goals, legal and *non-legal* problem solving (including use of concepts and modes of analysis from other disciplines such as economics, sociology and psychology), and world problems that require policy as opposed to purely implementation analysis.

IV. CONCLUSION

The legal profession has been entrusted with the care and operation of the administration of justice, and individual attorneys have been trained and licensed to detect and remedy ineffective or discriminatory operation of our laws. The duty to assist in improving the legal system arises from this privilege and training. In addition, because Americans have come to rely on legal solutions to social ills, because lawyers have helped establish a network of statutes and regulations beyond the comprehension of most laypersons, and because lawyers are prevalent in positions of prestige, power, and financial reward, a moral obligation to work for social reform also exists—even though many of society's ills are not directly attributable to the legal system. Lawyers will only be able to fulfill this obligation effectively if law schools provide better training for policy analysis. However, the duty of attorneys to work for legal and social reform should never be understood to entail a duty to adopt any particular social or political philosophy. Attorneys are entitled to freedom of social and political thought, just as are all other citizens.

CHAPTER 24

THE LAWYER AND THE LEGISLATURE

An attorney may serve one of three primary functions in the legislature: as a legislator, as staff counsel, or as a lobbyist. Each of these roles raises specific ethical questions answered only in part by the RPC or CPR.

I. LAWYER AS LEGISLATOR

Throughout American history, lawyers have held high positions in the federal government. The legal profession has for years been the largest single occupational group in the federal and state legislatures. Forty-six percent of the members of the 100th Congress, for example, were lawyers, by far the predominant profession in both houses. Numerous reasons have been offered for the frequency with which attorneys serve as legislators:

(1) The skills of a lawyer—written, oral, legal, and interpersonal—may be easily transferred to the tasks of a legislator;

(2) Attorneys are trained to value community service as an aspect of their professional roles;

(3) The public believes that its legislators should be drawn from high status occupations, including the legal profession;

(4) The flexibility of scheduling of time in private legal practice renders attorneys somewhat more "available" than other professionals for legislative service;

(5) The visibility of legislators can be an indirect, but effective, method for engendering increased legal business;

(6) Lawyers have a "working knowledge of power" that allows them to work effectively at the tasks of a legislator; and

(7) Attorneys are accustomed to serving as "brokers of ideas as well as interests" and are therefore experienced in the types of exchanges involved in legislative work.

One empirical study of legislator-attorneys in two midwestern states indicated that they sponsored a disproportionately high number of bills and that they dominated the leadership roles of speaker and president *pro tempore* and committee chairs in technical legal areas, including the judiciary, civil and criminal procedure, and rules.

Since the lawyer-legislator is governed by the professional ethical standards for lawyers while serving in the legislature, ABA Opinion 336 (1974), she is held to a higher ethical standard than non-lawyer legislators. The RPC, CPR, and the corresponding interpretive opinions address five specific areas of concern to the lawyer-legislator and her firm.

A. HONESTY

ABA Opinion 336 (1974) makes clear that the Code prohibitions against conduct involving moral turpitude, DR 1–102(A)(3), and dishonesty, fraud, deceit, and misrepresentation, DR 1–102(A)(4), apply to a lawyer at all times, whether or not he is acting in his professional capacity as a lawyer and including when he is serving as a legislator. The committee's opinion justifies these prohibitions on the bases that all attorneys must meet certain minimum moral requirements in order to protect the public and that "[i]t would be utterly incongruous with the entire tenor of the code to find that its provisions regarding lawyers who engage in fraud, deceit, misrepresentation, or illegal conduct involving moral turpitude do not apply to them when they are acting as . . . public servants." By analogy RPC 8.4, which prohibits various forms of conduct that reflect adversely on fitness to practice law, (e.g., "engag[ing] in conduct involving dishonesty, fraud, deceit or misrepresentation"), also applies regardless of the function the lawyer is serving at the time. However, the RPC have rejected the "moral turpitude" terminology. Rule 8.4 comment.

B. CONFLICT OF INTEREST

The lawyer as legislator has a duty of loyalty to the public and to the public interest. Since many lawyer-legislators maintain some simultaneous involvement with their private law practices, particularly if they are serving in state legislatures that meet only part-time, they often are faced with conflicts of interest between their legislative loyalty to the public and their private practice loyalty to their clients. Several CPR and RPC provisions and ABA opinions consider the conflict of interest issues confronting the lawyer-legislator. See also Ch. 12.

EC 8–8, acknowledging the frequency and desirability of lawyers acting as legislators on either a full- or part-time basis, prohibits their participation in "activities in which [their] personal or professional interests are or foreseeably may be in conflict with [their] official duties." Cf. RPC Rule 1.11(c) (lawyer serving as public officer or employee shall not participate in matter in which lawyer participated personally and substantially while not in government employ). In addition, the lawyer-legislator is prohibited from any conduct which might lead a layperson to conclude that his public position is being used to further "his professional success or personal interest." ABA Opinion 192 (1939). One study of federal legislators-lawyers indicated that only one-third maintained some form of private practice while in office and that, for those with some Congressional seniority, abstention from practice was the norm.

DR 8–101(A), governing the conduct of an attorney who acts as a public official, provides:

A lawyer who holds public office shall not:

(1) Use his public position to obtain, or attempt to obtain, a special advantage in legislative matters for himself or for a client under circumstances where he knows or it is obvious that such action is not in the public interest.

(2) Use his public position to influence, or attempt to influence, a tribunal to act in favor of himself or of a client.

(3) Accept any thing of value from any person when the lawyer knows or it is obvious that the offer is for the purpose of influencing his action as a public official.

The federal Conflict of Interest Act, 18 U.S.C.A. §§ 203–205 (1982), places limits on the law practice in which a member of Congress may be engaged. Under the act, a congressperson may not receive direct or indirect compensation for representation in "any proceeding . . . in which the United States is a party or has a direct or substantial interest, before any department, agency, court-martial, officer, or any civil, military, or naval commission. . . ." More specific statutes also prevent practice by Congresspersons before the U.S. Court of Claims, Federal Circuit Court of Appeals, the Indian Claims Commission, the Securities and Exchange Commission, the Interstate Commerce Commission, the National Labor Relations Board, the Federal Trade Commission, and the Internal Revenue Service, and in all matters handled by the U.S. Department of Justice and other executive departments. Employment by beneficiaries of maritime subsidies is also forbidden by federal statute.

Acceptance of a retainer by a lawyer-legislator presents appearance of impropriety issues and has been addressed by former ABA President Ross L. Malone:

While accepting a retainer in no sense involves a surrender of independence of either thought or action on the part of the lawyer, it is not realistic to say that he has the same freedom of choice on matters affecting the client that would exist in the absence of such an arrangement. Regardless of the subjective effect upon him and his vote as a legislator, it is certain that the public would never believe—nor could it be expected to believe—that his vote would not be affected by his relationship with his client. A lawyer voting as a legislator on matters affecting the interests of a retained client invites justified criticism, if not distrust, not only of the lawyer but of the legal profession itself.

The Lawyer and His Professional Responsibilities, 17 Wash. & Lee L.Rev. 191, 206 (1960).

ABA Informal Opinion 1182 (1971) refused "[a] categorical answer" to the question of whether the Code "will necessarily and always prohibit a lawyer's representing either an individual or an organization that is likely to be affected by the passage or defeat of proposed legislation, even though the lawyer also is a legislator." The opinion interpreted the DR 8–101(A)(1) prohibitions of "special advantage" as "a direct and peculiar advantage" and of "not in the public interest" as "action (or legislation) clearly inimical to the best interests of the public as a whole," suggesting that it would be quite difficult for a lawyer-legislator to violate the Disciplinary Rule. Relying on the Code's ethical considerations, however, the committee stated that "[c]ertainly a lawyer cannot, consistently with the guidance given under Canon 9, accept a retainer where its acceptance will give the appearance of professional impropriety" or if it is given with the purpose of influencing the action of a public official in contravention of DR 8–101(A)(3).

The RPC are far more general in their treatment of the lawyer-legislator, grouping lawyer-legislators with all other government lawyers for conflict of interest purposes. See RPC 1.11 and Ch. 12 (Conflict of Interest). However, several other rules have special meaning with respect to lawyer-legislators. See, e.g., Rule 3.5(a) (lawyer shall not "seek to influence [an] official by means prohibited by law"); Rule 8.4(e) (lawyer shall not "state or imply an ability to influence improperly a government agency or official").

C. ADVERTISING

The scope of advertising that a lawyer-legislator may undertake while in office is controlled in detail by the CPR. DR 2–102(B) provides that "[a] lawyer who assumes a . . . legislative . . .

office shall not permit his name to remain in the name of a law firm or to be used in professional notices of the firm during any significant period in which he is not actively and regularly practicing law as a member of the firm." Accord, EC 2-12; RPC 7.5(c); ABA Opinion 318 (1967) (absent local law, statute, or custom to the contrary and with proper precautions to avoid misleading the public as to his degree of participation in the firm, a lawyer who temporarily holds public office may have his name retained by the firm). A lawyer-legislator who is not currently practicing law cannot hold himself out as a practicing lawyer. RPC 7.5(c); EC 2-12. Subject to the other strictures contained under Canon 2, the Code allows published or broadcasted advertising of "[p]ublic or quasi-public offices," DR 2-101(B)(6), and "limited and dignified identification of a lawyer as a lawyer as well as by name . . . [i]n political advertisements when his professional status is germane to the political campaign or to a political issue," DR 2-101(H)(1). In addition, DR 2-102(A)(2) and ABA Opinion 301 (1961) allow advertisement of the attorney's "immediate past position" even if it was in government office.

As with the lawyer-legislator herself, the lawyer-legislator's firm is prohibited by the RPC and CPR from certain forms of advertising. The name of a lawyer-legislator who either does not have the right to practice law concurrent with his legislative service or who is not actively continuing to practice law as a firm member cannot be maintained in the firm name or identified as a past or present firm member. RPC 7.5(c); EC 2-12, DR 2-102(B).

As discussed in Chapter 10, the RPC differ dramatically from the Code with respect to treatment of lawyer advertising. In general, advertisements for legal services must not be false or misleading, or "likely to create an unjustified expectation about results the lawyer can achieve." RPC Rule 7.1. These basic considerations seem especially applicable to a lawyer-legislator, whose position renders her susceptible to pressure to promise legal "favors," which she may or may not be able to achieve. Other Rules establish procedural requirements and prohibit referrals for compensation, Rule 7.2; prohibit solicitation, Rule 7.3;

limit designation of a lawyer as a "specialist" to patent and admiralty law, Rule 7.4; and describe what may and may not be printed on firm letterhead, Rule 7.5. The RPC Rules on advertising almost certainly apply to lawyer-legislators, although none of these Rules—except Rule 7.5(c) (see supra)—singles out lawyer-legislators. These Rules are dealt with more fully in Chapter 10.

D. LIMITATIONS ON THE LAWYER–LEGISLATOR'S FIRM

Obviously the reduced time and income brought to a firm by a partner's term as a legislator are practical disadvantages to her service, as are the unavailability and divided attention of the lawyer-legislator to her clients and her firm during that time. Of more significant potential harm to the lawyer-legislator's firm, however, is the rule of vicarious disqualification, DR 5–105(D), RPC 1.10(a), which provides that when a lawyer is required to decline or withdraw from employment under a disciplinary rule or RPC involving conflict of interest, no lawyer affiliated with her or her firm may accept or continue such employment. Considering, for instance, the representation which is forbidden to a lawyer-congressperson under the various federal statutes, see discussion supra, such vicarious disqualification of the firm can restrict significantly its practice. One response to such statutes is a "dual partnership" or "double door" arrangement in which the legislator's name appears only in the one of two firms handling non-federal matters. Alternatively, in response to a 1943 ruling by the Attorney General, bookkeeping arrangements under which the legislator-partner is precluded from participating in the income from the prohibited federal practice have been employed to circumvent the federal Conflict of Interest Act. The legislator and his firm must decline federal business and refer clients to other attorneys in the absence of such arrangements. The violation of these conflict of interest statutes by the lawyer-legislator's firm, however, has not resulted in discipline by the profession, but a special committee of the Association of the Bar of the City of New York, emphasizing the dilution of loyalty principle underlying the vicarious disqualification rule, recommended that proper ethical conduct would involve termination of all dual arrangements and refusal by the firm of any employment forbidden to the congressperson. See also ABA Informal Opinion 1182 (1971) (although not a question free from doubt, the same rules should apply to the partner as to the lawyer-legislator). See Ch. 12 including discussion of RPC 1.11.

Acceptance by one firm member of employment to appear before a legislative committee on which another firm member is serving is prohibited even if there is full disclosure and the legislator is not sharing in the fee, ABA Opinion 296 (1959), unless specifically allowed by state constitutional, statutory, or legislative provisions, ABA Opinion 306 (1962).

E. LIMITATIONS AFTER LEAVING LEGISLATIVE OFFICE

The Canon 9 prohibition against the appearance of impropriety requires a lawyer who has left his legislative position to refuse employment connected with any matter for which he had substantial responsibility as a legislator. DR 9–101(B); EC 9–3. Accord RPC 1.11(a). Whereas DR 9–101(B) states the basic rule, RPC 1.11(a) provides the exception that the lawyer's colleagues in the firm may participate in the representation if the disqualified lawyer is screened from participation, is not apportioned any of the fees, and written notice is promptly given to the appropriate agency official to determine conformity with the rule. Presumably the DR 9–101(C) prohibition against an attorney's statement or implication that he is able to influence improperly or on irrelevant grounds the legislative body applies to the former legislator-lawyer. Accord, RPC 8.4(e). An attorney may advertise only his "immediate past position," DR 2–102(A)(2); ABA Opinion 301 (1961), and consequently can employ a past legislative position for advertising purposes only if it was his most recent previous position. As discussed supra, the RPC are far less restrictive of lawyer advertising. Thus, the former lawyer-legislator is prohibited from revealing his past employment only if such a revelation would be false or misleading, or if it would give the impression of improper influence on his former colleagues or unjustified expectations of success. Rule 7.1; Rule 8.4(e).

II. LAWYER AS STAFF COUNSEL TO THE LEGISLATURE

Very little has been written on the particular role of staff counsel to the legislature. Of first importance to legislative staff counsel must be the identification of his client, either as a particular legislator, or more frequently as the legislative body as a whole.

Due to the unseen nature of their work, legislative staff counsel are in an unusually powerful position to influence the course of legislation. Because he is not elected or subject to removal by the public, however, legislative counsel should have a higher set of ethical standards, both to avoid making policy and to act as a legal technician. Presumably, the prohibitions against statements or implications of ability to influence improperly or on irrelevant grounds a legislative decision apply to legislative staff counsel. RPC 8.4(e); DR 9–101(C). See also ABA Opinion 184 (1938) (endorsement of former administrative agency attorney on his resignation implies that he has an advantageous position before such an agency and is "highly reprehensible").

One commentator has noted two kinds of actions by legislative counsel that can border on the unethical. The first, the "art of deliberate ambiguity" in drafting legislation, can serve either as a "pernicious" tool for impairing the intended impact of the legislation or as a realistic tool for delegating interpretive authority to judges and administrators. The second, the "manufacture of legislative intent," involves insertion of statements that would likely not have been accepted if clearly expressed in the statute into a connected committee report, provoking a certain interpretation of ambiguous statutory language.

III. LAWYER AS LOBBYIST

The role of the legislative lobbyist involves keeping up-to-date on bills of interest to his clients and being available to testify before legislative committees or for formal lobbying. Informal lobbying, or efforts directed toward individual legislators, can frequently be more effective than formal lobbying. Legislators rely on lobbyists to suggest issues related to bills being considered, to present those issues concisely, and to represent the views of a coherent interest group before the legislature. Frequently the background of lawyer-lobbyists includes a term of service as a legislator, so that they are quite knowledgeable about the operation and informal power structure of the legislature.

The unusual situation of the lobbyist, who is often quite skilled at his special advocacy role and who is not often met by an adversary, results in the likely possibility that conflicting positions and interests will not be equally well-represented before the legislature. It has also been observed that the influence of a lawyer-lobbyist is negatively correlated with the number of lawyer-legislators available to speak to the legal advantages on the other side of the issue. One commentator has urged that the availability of attorney-lobbyists only to those who can financially afford them should require the lobbyist to consider the merits, rather than the interests of his fee-paying client, as the most significant determinant of his position. Mikva, Interest Representation in Congress: The Social Responsibilities of the Washington Lawyer (1970). This suggestion has not been adopted anywhere as a formal rule, however.

Lobbying activity is usually controlled by statute. These statutes typically require registration to show the interests represented or contributions received. Corrupt practices acts and court rules rendering contingent fees for lobbying illegal also serve to regulate lobbying activity. Since the statutes and rules regulating lobbying typically prohibit only the most flagrant abuses and since much lobbying activity occurs covertly, it has acquired a reputation for being a less-than-ethical activity. The importance of lobbying in allowing interest groups to be heard prior to the enactment of new law, however, does render the lobbyist's role an important one.

Recognition of the unique role of the lawyer-lobbyist may be the reason why the Code addresses the role specifically in its ethical considerations but not its disciplinary rules. The Code requires the lawyer-lobbyist to identify the capacity in which he appears before the legislature. EC 8–4; EC 7–16. See RPC 3.9. If he is lobbying on behalf of a client, the lawyer-lobbyist may advocate legislative changes with which he does not agree. EC 8–4; comments to RPC 1.2, 3.3. If purporting to act on behalf of the public, however, a lawyer-lobbyist should advocate only those legislative changes which he believes conscientiously to be in the public interest. EC 8–4. In addition, "[f]raudulent, deceptive, or otherwise illegal conduct by a participant in a proceeding before a . . . legislative body is inconsistent with fair administration of justice, and it should never be participated in or condoned by lawyers." EC 8–5. Accord, RPC 3.3(a), 8.4. A lawyer having unprivileged knowledge of such conduct before a legislative body should, under EC 8–5, reveal that knowledge to the appropriate authorities. Even if the information is otherwise privileged, disclosure is permitted if necessary to avoid assisting a criminal or fraudulent act by the client. RPC 3.3(a)(2), (b).

A lawyer-lobbyist who has a partner serving as a lawyer-legislator is controlled by ABA Opinions 296 (1959) and 306 (1962). Taken together, these opinions require that, absent state statutory, constitutional, or legislative provisions to the contrary, a lawyer-lobbyist may not lobby before the legislature in which a partner or associate is serving even if disclosure of potential conflicts of interest, voluntary disqualification of the lawyer-legislator, and lobbyist registration compliance have been made.

As with the lawyer-legislator and legislative staff counsel, a lawyer-lobbyist is prohibited from stating or implying that he is able to influence a legislative body improperly or on irrelevant grounds, RPC 8.4(e); DR 9–101(C), and is bound by the prohibitions against dishonesty and misrepresentation, RPC 3.3(a)(1), (2), (4), 3.4(b), 4.1, 8.4(c); DR 1–102(A)(4).

CHAPTER 25

PROFESSIONAL VS. PERSONAL RESPONSIBILITIES: CAN A GOOD LAWYER BE A GOOD PERSON?

A lawyer, as a professional, is expected to give primacy to a client's interests over those of other persons or the lawyer's own interests. This requires role-differentiated behavior. That is, when a person acts as a lawyer, his behavior and responsibilities may be different than when the lawyer acts in a personal capacity. The behavior required by the professional role may be considered either more ethical or less ethical than that expected of non-lawyers acting in similar circumstances.

Thus, misrepresentations of a material fact by a lawyer-negotiator would be unethical whether or not similar statements by a non-lawyer would make a transaction voidable because of fraud. Similarly, personal solicitation of business for pecuniary gain by a lawyer is considered unethical even though it is not improper for most non-lawyer businesses to seek customers in this manner. Even when a lawyer is playing another role, whether it be real estate dealer, car salesman, or politician, the lawyer is expected to rise above the morals of the market place if they are not as high as the standards required of attorneys. One of the great disappointments of the Watergate scandal, as noted by former White House counsel John Dean, was that so many lawyers were involved in deception and obstruction of justice and behaved no better than the non-lawyer politicians involved.

By contrast, a lawyer's professional obligations may permit, and, in some cases, require behavior that would be considered less virtuous than that expected of a non-lawyer, or even contrary to the lawyer's own moral convictions. The duty to keep a client's confidences justifies a lawyer not revealing a client's private confession to murder or to where a missing person's body was buried, even to an anguished father who pleads to learn whether his missing daughter was dead or alive. (See Chapter 11, Confidentiality). Likewise, the duty of loyal advocacy permits a lawyer to attempt to impeach an adverse witness who the lawyer believes has testified truthfully. (See Chapter 16, Lawyer as an Advocate).

The public's puzzled reaction to such examples gives rise to accusations that lawyers are simply hired guns or mouthpieces who seem to have no personal or moral responsibility for the consequences of their actions. Thus, the suggestion has been made that the lawyer's role is an amoral one.

While we have attempted to explain the nature of the lawyers' role in the adversary system and the importance of preserving a client's confidential communications, the fact is that many lawyers are also uncomfortable in these situations. Increasing numbers of lawyers also express feelings of discomfort with a schizophrenic existence that requires different behavior when representing clients than when acting on one's own as a moral being and concerned citizen. This has led a number of philosphers and legal scholars to consider whether a good lawyer can be a good person.

Those who defend the lawyer's traditional professional role emphasize the distinction between the function of a lawyer as a loyal confidant and advocate and that of a judge who impartially, after hearing adversary presentations from each side, dispenses justice. To limit the lawyer's loyalty to the client due to equitable concerns for others would deprive the judge of a presentation of law and evidence most favorable to the client, distort the assumptions of the system, and confuse the roles of the players. (See Chapter 16). Without the undiluted aid of a lawyer as advocate, or as a special purpose friend [see C. Fried, 1976], the client would be deprived of the full benefits of the law, and of human dignity which our legal system purports to safeguard.

Professor Stephen Pepper has gone beyond the adversary justification in concluding that lawyers are good persons. He postulates that law provides the desirable qualities of individual autonomy, equality of treatment, and diversity or individuality. As such, law is a public good which should be available to all. But access to the law realistically depends upon access to and the aid of a lawyer. Clients depend upon lawyers' knowledge and ability in matters of utmost concern, and without which, they would be deprived of the benefits of the law, and of their human dignity. Meaningful access to the law therefore requires a lawyer who will serve the client's interests without moral screening based upon the lawyer's own values. The lawyer who provides such unfiltered access empowers the client with first-class citizenship and performs a social good. Pepper, 1986.

Critics of the lawyer's "amoral" role seek to bring about greater moral accountability for a lawyer's actions on behalf of a client. As discussed in Chapter 16, the lawyer's duty of zealous advocacy must be exercised within the limits of the law. But are those the only limits? And should the standards for the advocate (especially, as is often the case, the criminal defense advocate) determine the measure of accountability of a lawyer as adviser, negotiator, or in other roles when the checks and balances of an impartial judge and counter-adversary presentation of other parties' lawyers are not available? These critics, relying on analyses ranging from legal and socioeconomic concerns to religious and moral philosopy, answer such questions in the negative. They call, among other things, for a greater recognition of the values of truth, morality as a human being and creature of God, concern for others and for the interests of the public, and for less priority to be given to the confidences and short-range selfish interests of clients, especially when lawyers are performing functions other than that of defending a person accused of a serious crime.

With apologies to traditional moral philosophers, the response to these calls for reformation is: "It depends". Few would debate the moral or legal justification for a different set of obligations for prosecutor and criminal defense counsel regarding, for example, disclosure of adverse facts. The role being played in law (as in life) clearly influences the choice of morally justified behavior in that role. The more difficult question is whether we have selected the appropriate balance among the relative goods (and evils) involved in each lawyering role. For example, the protection of client confidences balanced against the need to protect the public from harm; the search for the truth balanced against legitimate privacy expectations based on protection of human dignity and fostering socially desirable relationships. Any attempt to resolve these issues requires consideration of several factors, including: (1) the extent of freedom a lawyer has in selecting clientele; (2) the extent to which the client or the lawyer is responsible for determining particular professional behavior; and (3) whether the lawyer is acting as an advocate in criminal or civil proceedings or in some non-litigative capacity.

(1). Many lawyers want to pick and choose the clients they represent. In the words of William Kunstler, they want to defend only those they love. This has led to the formation of "cause" rather than "client" oriented law firms. This is not an unwelcome, nor indeed a particularly new, development. For a long time there has been an imbalance of too many law firms dedicated to the causes of the affluent and better organized clients and not enough lawyers to help the poor and unorganized. Less privileged persons need legal representation and efforts to reform the law and its administration so that it protects rather than discriminates against them.

Environmentalists, tenants, consumers and minorities are as much entitled to zealous, loyal, and dedicated representation as are developers, landlords, businesses, and South African investors, but a lawyer for the latter type of clients should no more be criticized for guilt by association than a lawyer for the former type of clientele or an attorney who chooses to represent criminal defendants or other unpopular persons.

While a lawyer is under no obligation to act on behalf of every person who seeks his services, the professional obligation to make legal services fully available to all who may need them requires that there be at least one competent lawyer willing to represent every potential client. Consequently, lawyers are admonished not to refuse to represent a poor or unpopular client, except for compelling reasons. Otherwise such individuals would be unable to secure adequate legal representation and, consequently, a fair trial or equal protection of the law. For this reason, it is a professional axiom that representation by a lawyer does not constitute an endorsement of, nor necessary personal agreement with, the client's cause. RPC 1.2(b); see RPC 6.3, 6.4.

Nevertheless, as long as all elements of society can be served, it is probably desirable that lawyers are able to serve causes in which they believe and clients with whom they are comfortable. Thus, in most instances, lawyers are free to choose for which law firm or business they will work, what clients they will represent or decline, and what form of law practice—private, government, commercial, poverty, estates, environmental, etc.—they will engage in. Shared values and comfort with one's clientele, without sacrificing independent judgment, minimizes the role differentiation and strain of the lawyer's function.

(2). Once, however, legal representation of a client is undertaken, the lawyer's options are more narrowly defined. It has been stated that it is a lawyer's obligation to do for the client whatever the client would do for himself if the client possessed the lawyer's legal knowledge and skills. While a principal purpose of legal representation is to enable a lay person to exercise personal autonomy within the legal system, this does not require a lawyer to assume the identity of an amoral law book. Professionalism does not negate all exercise of personal moral judgment. To the contrary, the CPR admonishes lawyers to exert their best efforts to ensure that decisions of their clients are made only after the client has been informed of all relevant considerations. These are not confined to purely legal considerations, but include "those factors which may lead to a decision that is morally just as well as legally permissible. He may emphasize the possibility of harsh consequences that might result from assertion of legally permissible positions." EC 7–8; see RPC 2.1.

A lawyer who represents a developer may be in a very good position to influence the client's actions so that they make environmental as well as business sense. Or a lawyer may persuade a manufacturer-client that a more expensive but pollution-free method of production, in the long run, will be of benefit to the goodwill of the business, its freedom from government control and "do-gooder" harassment, as well as the healthier survival of the client's children and grandchildren, and other inhabitants of the earth.

A lawyer should not assume that a client always desires to maximize self interest. A number of writers have suggested that it is the client's conscience that should guide the lawyer's behavior and not the lawyer's conscience or the lawyer's speculation as to what the client desires or is in the client's best interest. While the CPR urges a lawyer to "always act in a manner consistent with the best interests of his client", it adds that when such action seems unjust, the lawyer may ask the client for permission to forego the action. EC 7–9. The Model Rules require that a lawyer consult with the client before courses of action are chosen, whether they involve objectives of the representation (which are generally for the client to determine) or the means to pursue those objectives (for which lawyers generally have responsibility). RPC 1.2, 1.4. Thus, a client should be consulted before a lawyer seeks to take advantage of an unprepared adversary in court, or an unrepresented or relatively weak bargaining opponent in a negotiation. The client may be quite willing to do that which is fair and just whether to protect his reputation, make points for future dealings with the same adversary, or simply because the client may be a decent human being.

While a lawyer, after consultation with the client, may decide certain strategic and tactical matters not affecting the merits of a cause or substantially prejudicing the rights of a client, the lawyer must, otherwise, accept the client's judgment so long as it does not call for conduct which is unlawful or will violate a disciplinary standard. In the event that the client insists upon a legal but morally questionable course of action, the lawyer may have an option to withdraw. (See Chapter 15, Terminating the Relationship). Withdrawal, however, should not be a lightly selected alternative. Aside from the disruption to the representation, and loss of revenue, the lawyer, who is a good person as well, loses the opportunity to exert beneficial leverage on the client in future transactions. In any event, the ability to withdraw from representation of a client, as well as the degree of professional discretion in other regards, depends upon whether the lawyer is serving as an advocate before a tribunal or in some other non-litigative capacity.

(3). An advocate represents a client in court, before administrative agencies, before an arbitrator or whenever there is a presiding, impartial decision-maker, an equal opportunity for other parties to present their case and challenge that of their opposition, some orderly rules of procedure, and a rational basis for determining the outcome. Non-advocacy roles include advisor, counselor, negotiator, planner, mediator and evaluator. (See Chapters 19, 21).

For the most part, an advocate deals with past conduct and must take the facts as he finds them, while non-advocates primarily assist a client in determining the course of future conduct and relationships. A lawyer who agrees to serve as an advocate, must loyally safeguard his client's interests, urge any permissible construction of the law favorable to the client—without regard to the lawyer's personal opinion as to what construction will ultimately prevail—and, in general, must resolve any doubts as to the law and facts in his client's favor. An advisor, however, should candidly inform the client of his professional independent opinion of the law and the likely legal resolution of the client's case as well as the practical effects of such decision, and may refer to moral, economic, social and political factors relevent to the client's proposed course of action. RPC 2.1; CPR EC 7–3, 7–5, 7–8. For example, a lawyer acting as a tax advisor should warn the client of possible non-deductibility of certain expenses, but if the client insists on taking them, and the lawyer continues to represent him as an advocate, the client is entitled to the lawyer's best efforts in overturning the tax assessment and minimizing the client's liability.

A lawyer who is not acting as an advocate is free to withdraw from representation whenever a client rejects her advice, whether of a legal, moral, or practical nature. Whereas an advocate can normally withdraw only with permission of the tribunal before which the matter is pending. The advocate must subordinate her own concepts of morality and public interest and accept the judgment of the client made within the framework of the law.

Professor Murray Schwartz has capsulized three standards which might apply to the various lawyer-client relationships:

(1) The total client-commitment model, applicable to the advocate, that a lawyer should do everything for his client that is lawful and which the client would do for himself if he had the lawyer's skill and knowledge;

(2) The individual preference model which, according to the CPR, applies to the non-advocate, that a lawyer *need not* do for his client that which the lawyer thinks is unfair, unconscionable or unjust, even if lawful;

(3) An alternate standard for the non-advocate which Professor Schwartz believes may have merit, that the lawyer *must not* do for his client that which the lawyer thinks is unfair, unconscionable or unjust.

Thus, faced with a disagreement with a client over a legal but, in the lawyer's opinion, unfair, unconscionable, or unjust course of action, the lawyer acting as an advocate must accept the client's judgment and continue to represent him, whereas a non-advocate attorney *may,* under the CPR Standard, withdraw from representation, and *must,* under the alternate standard, withdraw from representation if the client persists in the questioned course of action.

Professor Schwartz suggests that while the effective working of the adversary system requires a lawyer to maximize the likelihood that the client will prevail and relieves the advocate of legal, professional, and moral accountability for seeking this end, different principles apply to the lawyer acting as non-advocate because of the absence of an impartial decision-maker to control the proceeding and adjudicate the controversy. Specifically, he recommends that the non-advocate lawyer refrain from assisting the client by "unconscionable" means or to achieve "unconscionable" ends. "Unconscionability" is to be measured by substantive law standards applicable to the law of recission, reformation and torts, and roughly equates to "unenforceable if challenged." Schwartz concludes that a non-advocate should be held *morally* accountable for means employed or ends sought for a client which the lawyer believes are immoral or unjust, even if the lawyer is neither legally nor professionally accountable. See M. Schwartz (1978).

While not prescribed by the Code or Rules, this method of analysis could prove useful to a lawyer faced with an apparent conflict between personal convictions and professional obligations.

Professor Schwartz further explores this type of dilemma in an article suggesting that a civil litigator, unlike a criminal defense attorney, cannot avoid moral accountability for her actions in aiding a client's immoral but lawful objectives. As noted in Chapter 16, on the role of the advocate, there are persuasive reasons for placing a greater value on the lawyer's duty to aid ascertainment of the truth in civil litigation than can be expected of defense counsel in criminal trials. Accepting this premise, Schwartz would limit the ability of a client to pursue an immoral—but not unlawful—course of action with the aid of a lawyer of his choice. The lawyer, unless perhaps "the last lawyer in town" or appointed by a court to assure minimum access to legal services, would be accountable to her own values, societal and philosophical moral standards, but not, apparently, professional discipline. The desire to avoid personal and social censure, however, provides a basis for reconciling a lawyer's professional role and personal values and may deter immoral activity by potential clients. M. Schwartz, 1983.

The reconciliation of one's personal and moral obligations with one's professional duties is, in fact, part of the exercise of professionalism. This does not mean professional functions must always be subordinated to personal responsibilities, or vice versa. Rather it proposes a balancing of the two. As too many a law-trained person has learned from family and friends, one cannot turn off their professional self at 5 p.m., and back on again at 8 a.m.

Professional roles influence personal life, and personal values and attitudes influence professional performance. Lawyers, in their professional role, do not simply deal with legal issues, but with human beings whose transactions, relations, and other activities give rise to actual or potential problems with legal aspects. How the lawyer reacts to that human client (even corporations must communicate and transact business through human beings) is bound to be influenced by both the lawyer's personal and professional self.

Thus, it may be useful to recognize both that: (1) moral and public interest considerations should influence performance of professional functions; (2) personal responsibilities may be modified, with moral justification, by the specific role that a lawyer is performing. The relative influence of personal considerations and of professional precepts will vary with the particular role being executed, whether prosecutor, criminal defense counsel, civil litigator, business advisor, consumer lobbyist or public official.

The function of a lawyer does involve role differentiation, but there is significant social utility in having lawyers serve these various roles in different ways with different moral responsibilities. Moreover, the fact that the moral adjustment may vary with changing roles and circumstances is both desirable and no more reprehensible than the fact that a good person performs differently, but with equal morality, the roles of mother, daughter, lover, and friend, as well as legal advisor or advocate.

INDEX

References are to Pages

ACCEPTING EMPLOYMENT, 317, 323–324

ACCREDITATION OF LAW SCHOOLS, 44–45

ADMISSION PROCESS, 62–64

ADMISSION REQUIREMENTS, 39–50
Character requirements, 50–55
Citizenship, residency, and age, 47–50
Competence qualifications, 42–45

ADVERTISING, 178–185, 190–194
Antitrust, 179–180
By arbitrators and mediators, 448–450
Class action plaintiffs, 193
Client testimonials, 194
Commercial speech, 180–182
"Dignified", 183
False or misleading, 183–184
Fees, 286–287
Fields of practice, 184–185
Firm names, 185–186
Targeted mail and newspaper ads, 190–193
Television, 184, 193–194
Trade names, 186
Unjustified expectations, 186

ADVERSARY SYSTEM, 304–361
Compensating witnesses, 358–360
Conduct at trial, 343–358
  Appeals to emotion, 352–353
    Closing argument, 353
  Disclosure of adverse evidence, 343–347

ADVERSARY SYSTEM—Cont'd
Disclosure of adverse legal authority, 347–349
Impeaching the truthful witness, 349–351
Role of the prosecutor, 318, 350, 377–378, 384–390
Rules of evidence, 351–353
Trial disruption, 354–357
"Political trials," 354–356
Defense of the "guilty" client, 320–324
Delay tactics, 325–326
Duty of loyalty, 310–311
Duty of zealous advocacy, 311–314
Within the bounds of the law, 311–314
Lying client or witness, 326–343
Overzealousness, 314–317
Preparation for trial, 314–317
Witnesses, 315, 317–320
"Anatomy of a Murder" approach, 315–317
Purpose of, 304–309
Student pro bono requirements, 176–177

ADVICE ON NON-LEGAL MATTERS/ISSUES, 501–502

ADVOCATE VS. COUNSELOR, 501–503

ALCOHOL ABUSE, 59–60, 77–78, 59–60

ALTERNATIVE DISPUTE RESOLUTION (includes arbitration and mediation), 419–456
Advertising, 448–450
Appearance of impropriety, 433–434
"Rigged awards," 433
Competence, 422–424
Conflicts of interest, 435–437
Former client, 435–437
Withdrawal, 435
Confidentiality, 437–443
Waiver, 441
Consultation, 424–428
Duty to use, 451–454
Fees, 443–445
Impartiality, 429–433
Intermediation, 420
Lawyer as evaluator, 454–456
Disclosure requirements, 455–456

ALTERNATIVE DISPUTE RESOLUTION (includes arbitration and mediation)—Cont'd
Pro bono, 450–451
Role of independent counsel, 425
Sources of guidance, 420–422
Unauthorized practice, 445–448

AMERICAN BAR ASSOCIATION, HISTORY OF, 28–32
Canons of Professional Ethics, 20
Code of Professional Responsibility,
Canons, definition of, 21
Criticism of, 22
Disciplinary rules, definition of, 21
Ethical considerations, definition of, 21
History of, 20–23
Scope of, 20–21
Rules of Professional Conduct, 22–26
Adoption by state bars, 23–25
History of, 22–23

APPEARANCE OF IMPROPRIETY, 59, 226–228, 236, 254–256, 434, 491
Judges, 467–468

ATTORNEYS' LIENS, 287–289
Charging, 289
Retaining, 287–289

BAR ASSOCIATIONS, HISTORY OF, 27–30
Mandatory membership, 33–37

BARRISTERS, 27–28

CHAMPERTY, 271–272, 285

CLIENTS' SECURITY FUNDS, 259–260

CODES OF ETHICS, 19–26

COMMITTEES ON PROFESSIONAL ETHICS, 37–38

COMPETENCE, 72–81
Discipline, 59, 74–79
Duty to report lack of, 66–67, 77, 79–80
Ethical aspects, 59, 74–77
Importance of, 73–74

COMPETENCE—Cont'd
In Alternative Dispute Resolution, 422–424
Neglect vs. negligence, 75–76
Qualifications for admission, 42–47

CONFIDENTIAL PRIVILEGES AND SECRETS, 195–221
Basis for privilege, 196–197
Confidences vs. secrets, 198, 200
Consent to disclosure, 202
Disclosure necessary to defend attorney, 207–209
Disclosure of client fraud or criminal activity, 211–221, 328–330, 333–334
Disclosure to associates and employees, 199
Disclosure to third persons, 209–210
General rule, 197
Identity of client and fact of retainer, 203–206
In Alternative Dispute Resolution, 437–443
Nonlegal advice, 206
Procedural aspects, 201

CONFLICT OF INTEREST, 222–253, 435–437, 486–488
Advancing costs and expenses, 230–231
Contingent fees, 271–276
Defined, 222
Disqualification, 248–252
In alternative dispute resolution, 435–437
Lawyer as witness, 231–232
Lawyer's personal interest, 228–232
Representing adverse interests, 233–240
    Borrower-lender, 235
    Buyer-seller, 235
    Corporations and labor unions, 245–248
    Former government attorneys, 241–244
    Former vs. present clients, 239–240
    Husband-wife, 236
    Insurer-insured, 233–235
    Intermediary, 420, 435
    Multiple criminal defendants, 237–239
    Multiple plaintiffs, 236–237
Settlement, 272–273

CONTINUING LEGAL EDUCATION, 100–104
Mandatory, 100–101
Voluntary, 101

CORPORATE LAWYERS, 406–414
Advisory role, 412–414
Advocacy role, 406–412
Failure to correct misleading statements, 411–414
Identifying "the client," 406–407
Identifying the client's interests, 408

CORPORATIONS
Practicing law, 137–138
Self-representation, 137–138

COUNSEL OF CHOICE, 93

DECISIONS MADE BY CLIENT VS. THOSE BY ATTORNEY, 313

DEFENDING CLIENTS KNOWN TO BE GUILTY, 320–325

DISCIPLINARY PROCEEDINGS, 55–61, 64–71
Criminal proceedings compared, 58–59, 68–70
Disciplinary process, 55–61, 64
Lay involvement, 61, 81
Mental or physical disability, 59–60, 69
Misconduct, 56
Moral turpitude, 57–58
Procedural standards, 57–58, 61, 68–70
Purpose of, 56, 58–59
Reform of, 65–66

DIVISION OF FEES
See Fees and Liens

DUTY TO MAKE LEGAL SERVICES AVAILABLE, 146–156

DUTY TO REPORT MISCONDUCT, 77, 79–80

DUTY TO REPRESENT THE POOR, 147–151
Civil matters, 150–151
Criminal cases, 148–149

DUTY TO REPRESENT THE UNPOPULAR, 151–155
Civil matters, 154–155
Criminal cases, 152–154

ETHICS OPINIONS, 37–38

FAIR TRIAL VS. FREE PRESS, 362–376
Prejudicial nature of unlimited publicity, 363–368
Procedures designed to limit prejudice, 368–376
  Closure of trials and pretrial hearings, 370–371
  Discovery, 371–372
  "Gag Orders,"
    Attorneys, 372–373
    Press, 368–369
Television in the courtroom, 373–376

FEES AND LIENS, 262–292
Fees, 262–287, 443–445
  Advertising of, 283–284
    Information permitted, 283–284
  Collection of, 284–287
  Contingent, 271–277
    Criminal cases, 274
    Divorce cases, 275
  Division of, 278–282
    With lawyers, 278–280
    With non-lawyers, 280–282
  Of Arbitrators and Mediators, 443–445
  Reasonableness of, 265–271
  Schedules, 267–269

FIDUCIARY RESPONSIBILITIES, 254–261
Commingling, 255–257
Misappropriation, 258–259
  Sanctions, 258–259

GOVERNMENT LAWYERS, 415–418
Duty to disclose wrongdoing, 416–417
Duty to resign, 417–418
Identifying "the client," 415

GROUP AND PREPAID LEGAL SERVICES, 126, 166–171
Antitrust aspects, 143–144, 170–171
Ethical problems, 168–170
Insurance aspects, 167–168
Unauthorized practice, 138–139

IMPLEMENTING THE DUTY TO MAKE LEGAL SERVICES AVAILABLE, 157–178, 498–499
Ethical problems, 158, 163–164

IMPLEMENTING THE DUTY TO MAKE LEGAL SERVICES AVAILABLE—Cont'd
Lay intermediaries, 163
Legal aid and public defender services, 158–159
Legal Services Corporation, 160–163
Mandatory pro bono representation, 158–159
O.E.O. Legal Services Program, 160

INEFFECTIVE ASSISTANCE OF COUNSEL, 90–96
Attorney's conflict of interest, 239, 295
Habeas corpus, 96–98
Prejudice, 95
Procedural limitations, 96–98
Retained vs. appointed counsel, 93, 96
Standards for determining, 94–96

INNS OF COURT, 28, 102

INTEGRATED BAR ASSOCIATIONS, 32–37

IOLTA, 162, 257–258

JUDGES, 457–477
Adjudicative responsibilities, 468–471
Administrative responsibilities, 471–472
Appearance of impropriety, 467–468
Clerks and staff, 471–472
Discipline, 458
Disqualification, 459–467
Ex parte communications, 469
Extra-judicial activities, 467–468, 473
Peremptory challenge, 466–467
Quasi-judicial activities, 472
Selection, 473–477
Elective campaign, 475–477

JUDICARE, 164–166

LAW STUDENT CLINICAL PROGRAMS, 121–122, 175–176

LAWYER AS ADVISOR AND NEGOTIATOR, 395–405
Advisor, 395–399, 412–414, 501–503
Negotiator, 399–405
Communicating with adverse parties, 402–404

LAWYER AS ADVISOR AND NEGOTIATOR—Cont'd
Honesty, 400–401
Settlement, 402–405
Threatening criminal charges, 401–402

LAWYER AS EVALUATOR, 454–456

LAWYER AS "HIRED GUN," 496

LAWYER AS LEGISLATIVE STAFF COUNSEL, 492

LAWYER AS LEGISLATOR, 484–494
Advertising, 488–490
Conflict of interest, 486–488
Disqualification of law firm, 490–492
Honesty, 485–486

LAWYER AS LOBBYIST, 275, 493–494

LAWYER AS NEUTRAL, 419–451

LAWYER AS PUBLIC LEADER AND LAW REFORMER, 478–504
Civic duties, 482–483
Duty to improve the legal system, 479–482

LAWYER REFERRAL, 174

LEGAL CLINICS, 171–173

LEGAL PROFESSION, 1–6
Organization of the bar, 27–37, 40–42
Scope, 1–6, 30, 32–33
Structure, 29–30, 32–33
Supervision, 19, 40–42

MALPRACTICE, 81–90
Actions for, 83
Causes of increasing number of suits, 82–83
Defenses, 87–88
Frivolous suits, 98–99, 324–326
Liability to third parties, 88–89
Limiting liability, 89–90
Office management, 84–85
Poor "customer relations," 84–85
Relation to ethical standards, 25–26, 59, 74–78, 87

MALPRACTICE—Cont'd
Standard of care, 85–87

MEANING OF PROFESSIONAL RESPONSIBILITY, 1–6

MODEL RULES OF PROFESSIONAL CONDUCT, 23–26

MORAL CHARACTER
See Admission Requirements; Disciplinary Proceedings

PROFESSIONAL VS. PERSONAL RESPONSIBILITY, 9–10, 495–504

PROFESSIONALISM, 7–11

PROSECUTOR'S ETHICAL RESPONSIBILITIES, 377–394
Conflicts of interest, 383–384
Discipline, 392–394
Discretion to charge, 378–381
Duty to ensure fair trials, 384–390
  Comment on defendant's silence, 387–388
  Disclosure of exculpatory evidence, 389–390
  Expression of personal opinion, 385, 386–387
  Improper argument, 385, 386–387
  Presentation of false, misleading, or inadmissible evidence, 388–389
Interference with client-attorney relationship, 318, 391–392
Plea bargaining, 381–382
Supervising the police, 390–391

PUBLIC IMAGE OF LAWYERS, 12–18

PUBLIC INTEREST LAW, 173–174
Solicitation, 174

RE–CERTIFICATION EXAMINATIONS, 103–104

RIGHT TO COUNSEL, 90–94

RULE 11, 98–100

SOLICITATION, 186–194
Financial gain, 189–193
Group legal services, 187–189
In person, 189–193
Political issues, 187–189

SOLICITORS, 28

SPECIALIZATION, 104
Advertising of, 105, 184–185
Certification, 108
Ethical aspects, 105–107
ABA Model Plan, 110
Self-designation, 108–109
Trial advocacy, *Peel* Case

SUBSTANCE ABUSE, 59–60, 77–78

TAX ADVICE, 13

UNAUTHORIZED PRACTICE OF LAW, 112–145, 445–448
Antitrust aspects, 142–144
Definition of, 117–121
Enforcement, 123–124
Goals of rules against, 114–116
In alternative dispute resolution, 445–448
Non-resident attorneys, 131
  Pro hac vice, 132–133
  Reciprocity, 133–135
Practice before administrative tribunals, 128–130
Public interest test, 121–122
Self-representation, 135–142
  Corporations, 126–128, 137–138
  Jailhouse lawyers, 139, 177

WITHDRAWAL, 293–303
Fees upon, 289–292
Good cause, 299–301
Mandatory, 296–298, 320, 328–330
Permissive, 287, 298–299, 322–323, 328–333
Procedure, 301–303

†